Frommer's®

Egypt

2nd Edition

by Mohamed El Hebeishy

WILEY

Wiley Publishing, Inc.

ABOUT THE AUTHOR

There is nothing like an insider's perspective, and when it comes to Egypt, **Mohamed El Hebeishy** knows what he's talking about. In 2004, Mohamed left a fruitful career as a financial analyst for his passion—travel writing. Since then he has been intensely traveling in his homeland (Egypt) and throughout the region, bringing an insightful dimension of the Middle East into perspective. His work is periodically published in several newspapers and magazines, and he is also author and photographer of the widely acclaimed coffee-table book *Egypt Rediscovered.*

Published by:

WILEY PUBLISHING, INC.

111 River St.
Hoboken, NJ 07030-5774

ISBN 978-0-470-59156-7

Editor: Anuja Madar
Production Editor: Eric T. Schroeder
Cartographer: Liz Puhl
Photo Editor: Richard Fox
Production by Wiley Indianapolis Composition Services

Front cover photo: Montana: Giza: Camel in foreground, pyramids in background ©Doug Pearson/Corbis
Back cover photo: Egypt, Aswan: *feluca* sailing on the Nile, Mausoleum of Aga Khan in background ©Hugh Sitton / Getty Images

For information on our other products and services or to obtain technical support, please contact our Customer Care Department within the U.S. at 877/762-2974, outside the U.S. at 317/572-3993 or fax 317/572-4002.

Wiley also publishes its books in a variety of electronic formats. Some content that appears in print may not be available in electronic formats.

Manufactured in the United States of America

5 4 3 2 1

CONTENTS

4 SUGGESTED EGYPT ITINERARIES 69

5 ACTIVE VACATION PLANNER 81

6 CAIRO 92

7 ALEXANDRIA & THE NORTH COAST 160

8 THE SINAI PENINSULA 186

9 THE RED SEA COAST 221

10 UPPER EGYPT 262

11 THE WESTERN DESERT 303

12 FAST FACTS 341

13 USEFUL TERMS & PHRASES 346

INDEX 357

LIST OF MAPS

ACKNOWLEDGMENTS

It is impossible to remember how many times I decided to hit the road and discover my own country, and it is equally impossible to remember each and every person who I met along the way and who deserves a wholehearted and sincere thank you. However, there are a couple of people I must thank. The eloquent Ahmed El Mestekawy of Zarzora Expedition, with whom cruising the endless Great Sand Sea is as relaxed as crossing a side street back home. The restless traveler Rosemarie Parks; now I am sure age will never keep me away from the road. Super supportive Ahmed Shitawey, whose out-of-the-box ideas leave me thinking how creatively impotent I can be. The editor of this edition, Anuja Madar; I really enjoyed working on this assignment with her. My sons, Aman Allah and Taymour; going home and hugging both of them wipes away all the hardship of life in just a fraction of a second. Last, first, and always, the only human being, out of a 6.7-billion world population, with whom I want to grow old, my wife Heba Osman.

HOW TO CONTACT US

In researching this book, we discovered many wonderful places—hotels, restaurants, shops, and more. We're sure you'll find others. Please tell us about them, so we can share the information with your fellow travelers in upcoming editions. If you were disappointed with a recommendation, we'd love to know that, too. Please write to:

Frommer's Egypt, 2nd Edition
Wiley Publishing, Inc. • 111 River St. • Hoboken, NJ 07030-5774

AN ADDITIONAL NOTE

Please be advised that travel information is subject to change at any time—and this is especially true of prices. We therefore suggest that you write or call ahead for confirmation when making your travel plans. The authors, editors, and publisher cannot be held responsible for the experiences of readers while traveling. Your safety is important to us, however, so we encourage you to stay alert and be aware of your surroundings. Keep a close eye on cameras, purses, and wallets, all favorite targets of thieves and pickpockets.

FROMMER'S STAR RATINGS, ICONS & ABBREVIATIONS

Every hotel, restaurant, and attraction listing in this guide has been ranked for quality, value, service, amenities, and special features using a star-rating system. In country, state, and regional guides, we also rate towns and regions to help you narrow down your choices and budget your time accordingly. Hotels and restaurants are rated on a scale of zero (recommended) to three stars (exceptional). Attractions, shopping, nightlife, towns, and regions are rated according to the following scale: zero stars (recommended), one star (highly recommended), two stars (very highly recommended), and three stars (must-see).

In addition to the star-rating system, we also use seven feature icons that point you to the great deals, in-the-know advice, and unique experiences that separate travelers from tourists. Throughout the book, look for:

Finds	Special finds—those places only insiders know about
Fun Facts	Fun facts—details that make travelers more informed and their trips more fun
Kids	Best bets for kids, and advice for the whole family
Moments	Special moments—those experiences that memories are made of
Overrated	Places or experiences not worth your time or money
Tips	Insider tips—great ways to save time and money
Value	Great values—where to get the best deals

The following **abbreviations** are used for credit cards:

AE American Express
DC Diners Club
DISC Discover
MC MasterCard
V Visa

TRAVEL RESOURCES AT FROMMERS.COM

Frommer's travel resources don't end with this guide. **Frommers.com** has travel information on more than 4,000 destinations. We update features regularly, giving you access to the most current trip-planning information and the best airfare, lodging, and car-rental bargains. You can also listen to podcasts, connect with other Frommers.com members through our active-reader forums, share your travel photos, read blogs from guidebook editors and fellow travelers, and much more.

The Best of Egypt

There is no one thing, or even a group of things, that can wrap up the best of Egypt. The country is so diverse and full of surprises, that even after more than 30 years of calling it home, it still manages to surprise me. Go monument-hopping in Luxor; enjoy a tranquil sunset *feluca* sail down the great river Nile in Aswan; get lost in the labyrinth of historical Islamic Cairo; or go on an urban adventure to the capital's City of the Dead. The pyramids might be a tourism cliché, but you'll no doubt be stunned and wonder how could they could have been built 5,000 years ago. You can't be in Egypt and miss out on the Red Sea; it offers some of the world's most remarkable diving spots and a great opportunity if you are into kitesurfing or freediving. A night camping in the White Desert should be mandatory for any visitor to the country simply for its naturally carved rock formations. Partygoers can watch the sun come up in Hurghada or Sharm El Sheikh, while relaxation seekers can spend quality time lazing the day away on the tranquil beaches of the Red Sea coast. Egypt doesn't fall short when it comes to one-of-a-kind accommodation options, either. Enjoy a boutique stay while on tour in the capital, get back to basics at the ecofriendly Adrére Amellal in the Siwa oasis, be pampered at Oberoi Sahl Hashish, or relish the originality of Nubian Anakato. Egypt's culinary adventures are just as diverse; savor camel meat with chili chocolate at Bordiehn's, or taste local delicacies at Sofra or Abou El Sid. Shopping might not be Egypt's prime attraction, but an evening spent browsing the stalls in Khan Al Khalili is a night worth planning for.

1 THE BEST UNIQUELY EGYPTIAN EXPERIENCES

- **Sound and Light Show at Karnak Temple** (Luxor): Justly famous for its massive hypostyle hall, this vast temple complex reveals a whole new side of itself at night. Follow the narration through the ancient courtyards, and try to snap a picture of the dramatic lighting effects. See p. 271.
- **Palm Sunday in Coptic Cairo** (Cairo): Celebrate the first day of Holy Week with one of the oldest Christian communities in the world. Children and families crowd the ancient church-lined street giving out crosses and little figures made of local palm leaves. See p. 123.
- **Sunrise atop Mount Sinai** (St. Catherine): This is where Moses is said to have received the tablets containing the Ten Commandments. The view across the rugged mountains of Sinai as the sun rises is unforgettable; a night hike will get you there in time. See p. 214.
- **A stroll down Al Mu'izz le-din Allah Street** (Cairo): A mosque after a mosque after a *sabil* after a *khan*—this recently turned pedestrian street is living testimony to the Islamic civilization's wonders and a reference to its different cultures. See p. 96
- **Camel diving safari to Ras Abu Galum** (Dahab): Reaching your diving site with a jeep or boat is classic, but via camel it's avant-garde. Straddle slowly on camelback between the Red Sea and the majestic mountains of Sinai to

eventually reach Egypt's hidden Eden—Ras Abu Galum. Here, diving is simply unparalleled. See p. 204.

- **Meditate in the Great Pyramid** (Cairo): Bend and squeeze yourself all the way through to the burial chamber. The nucleus of the ancient world's sole surviving wonder may be missing impressive paintings and stunning reliefs, but it retains a high spiritual status. Take a moment to meditate; similar places throughout the world can be counted on one hand. See p. 110.
- **Camping in the White Desert** (Western Desert): The surrealistic creativity of Mother Nature blooms in the White Desert, with its wind-carved chalk statues; here is a mushroom, while over there a chicken under a tree. As far as you can see, oddly shaped white rock formations dot the horizon. See p. 324.
- **Sailing the Nile** (Cairo or Aswan): This is my favorite Egyptian experience, a slow unwinding sail on the waters of the Nile in a *feluca.* Go for one amidst the exotic boulders and river islets in Aswan, or in Cairo where you can enjoy a backseat view of the hustle and bustle of the capital's frenzied streets. See p. 282 and p. 301.
- **Tea at Fishawy's** (Cairo): What could be more Egyptian than drinking sweet tea among the spices, gewgaws, and crowds of a densely packed souk? Watch the masses of people from all over the world, and haggle with merchants who will stop by with everything from saffron to sun hats. See p. 152.

2 THE BEST ACCOMMODATIONS

- **Adrére Amellal** (Siwa; ✆ **02/27367879;** www.adrereamellal.net): Gorgeous local scenery meets gorgeous local architecture in this high-end, high-concept, all-inclusive ecolodge. Bask by the pool, eat local foods, and pamper yourself in the palatial bathroom, all with an ecofriendly peace of mind.
- **Alf Leila** (Dahab; ✆ **069/3640595;** www.alfleila.com): The creativity of Alf Leila's former fashion designer owner is apparent in every corner; Eva Hoffman has turned an ordinary two-floor house into a *1,000 Nights* fairy-tale-like boutique hotel.
- **Al Tarfa Desert Sanctuary** (Dakhla; ✆ **092/9105007** or -9; www.altarfa.travel): The harshness of the desert is wiped away with Al Tarfa's classy and authentic style, relaxing ambience, and pampering spa—all available in the heart of the Western Desert.
- **Anakato** (Aswan; ✆ **097/3451744;** www.anakato.com): Truly authentic, this traditional house-turned-hotel offers a rare opportunity to get up-close-and-personal with the Nubian culture. Located in the middle of a Nubian village, Anakato is a different lodging experience wrapped in a relaxing ambience, artistic decorations, and stunning Nile vistas.
- **Belle Epoque *dahabeeyas*** (Luxor and Aswan; ✆ **02/25169649;** www.dahabiya.com): This is how aristocratic ladies and noble gentlemen of the 19th century sailed down the Nile. Evoke the classic experience with one of the last remaining original *dahabeeyas.*
- **El Karm** (St. Catherine; ✆ **010/1324693**): A lodging facility that qualifies as a destination as well. Classic Nabatean-style rock work combines gracefully with simple architecture here in the middle of the Sinai High Mountains region. This is a clean, quiet getaway for those willing to rough it just a little bit.

- **Kempinski Nile Hotel** (Cairo; ✆ **02/27980000;** www.kempinski-cairo.com): The capital's latest hotel addition is in a league of its own. Enjoy personalized butler service or a private party on top of the glass-covered pool, while kids are pampered with bedtime milk. Here all guests are given the star treatment.
- **Hotel Al Moudira** (Luxor; ✆ **095/2551440;** www.moudira.com): This is a lovingly put together boutique hotel on the edge of the desert. The individually designed and decorated rooms are spread through a splendidly understated garden, and the pool is a tranquil work of art.
- **Le Riad Hotel de Charme** (Cairo; ✆ **02/27876074** or -5; www.leriad-hoteldecharme.com): Open the door and step into a world of vibrant colors. Themed individually, Le Riad's 17 suites bring a modern artistic touch to the monument-infested Al Mu'izz le-din Allah Street; my favorite suite is Calligraphy.
- **Mövenpick El Quseir** (El Quseir; ✆ **065/3332100;** www.moevenpick-hotels.com): This low-key, family-friendly resort hugs the coastline, blending with the local scenery and making a perfect setting for a romantic getaway—even if you have to take the kids along.
- **Oberoi Sahl Hashish** (Hurghada; ✆ **065/3440777;** www.oberoihotels.com): There are no rooms here, but about 100 suites that take you on a luxury roller coaster. Enjoy a royal spa treatment or jump into your own private pool.

3 THE BEST EATING EXPERIENCES

- **Abou El Sid** (Cairo, Alexandria, and Sharm El Sheikh; ✆ **02/27359640,** 03/3929609, and 069/3603910; www.abouelsid.com): Here you can savor traditional Egyptian plates in an intimate atmosphere decorated with icons of Egyptian culture from the golden days of music and film. Local delicacies *wara ainab* and *mombar* taste better here than anywhere else.
- **Abu Ashraf** (Alexandria; ✆ **03/4816597**): Seafood in Egypt doesn't get better than this; pick and choose your meal from a collection of freshly caught fish displayed on an icebox by the entrance, and enjoy an assortment of local salads and appetizers while your meal is being prepared.
- **Bordiehn's** (Hurghada; ✆ **065/3451292;** www.bordiehn.com): Bordiehn's fuses Egyptian and neo-German cuisine, resulting in dishes such as the signature Local Hero; enjoy your camel meat.
- **Blue House** (Dahab; ✆ **016/7971416**): Homemade recipes are the real edge of this small family business. Blue House serves exotic Thai dishes that beat Bangkok's famous street food. Savor your Panang curry while enjoying the seaside view of Dahab's promenade.
- **El Sheikh Wafik** (Alexandria; ✆ **012/3249623**): Dessert in Alexandria is synonymous with El Sheikh Wafik, located at the very end of Bahri. The seating area lacks character and the menu is limited to four items, but the sweet couscous they serve could easily rival anything in Morocco.
- **Kosheri El Tahrir** (Cairo; ✆ **02/21234567**): There is simply no better place in Egypt to savor *kosheri.* You won't find ambience and character here, but you will find authentic taste and originality.
- **Leila's Bakery** (Dahab; ✆ **069/3640594**): From cheese *laugen* and nut rolls to *zwetschgen-nudein* and

applestrudel, Leila's Bakery brings you German baked goods at their finest. And if rolls are not your thing, you can always go for any of the sandwiches in freshly baked baguettes.

- **Mogul Room** (Cairo; ✆ **02/33773222;** www.oberoimenahouse.com): It's a long drive from Downtown Cairo, but the Mogul Room would be worth it even if it was another hour. The food is the best Indian meal in town, and the location—the lush, 19th-century Mena House Oberoi at the pyramids—adds a different spice to your meal.
- **Pier 88** (El Gouna; ✆ **018/4108820**): Fancy a candlelit dinner on a tiny floating pier where you can indulge in a sophisticated swordfish carpaccio or a mouthwatering Wagyu beef sirloin? Dinner at Pier 88 certainly qualifies for a memorable dining experience difficult to match elsewhere in Egypt.
- **Said Alam** (El Quseir): Technically speaking, there is no restaurant to start with; just a couple of tables and chairs set up on a sidewalk in the sleepy town of El Quseir. But when it comes to *fuul,* it's hard to imagine this version can be rivaled anywhere else in Egypt. Skip the Mövenpick and come here for breakfast.
- **Sofra** (Luxor; ✆ **095/2359752;** www.sofra.com.eg): Typical Egyptian rural ambience sets the mood for this exquisite restaurant tucked away in a Luxor back street. As for the food, Sofra, "dining table" in Arabic, serves a collection of Egyptian delicacies that includes *sayadeyet gambary, kamonia,* and the restaurant's signature *kebdet* Sofra.

4 THE MOST POPULAR EGYPTIAN SITES

- **Coptic Cairo** (Cairo): A token to the period when Christianity was the dominating religion, Coptic Cairo is tucked away in a small part of the much larger modern city. The Coptic Museum is the highlight of your visit with its priceless relics, icons, and the manuscript collection of the Gnostic Gospels. See p. 123.
- **Egyptian Museum** (Cairo): The country's largest collection of artifacts all in one place; from gripping mummies and giant statues to the finely painted Fayum portraits and Tutankhamen's stunning golden mask. See p. 104.
- **Islamic Cairo** (Cairo): A labyrinth of zigzagging alleyways and side streets that conceals a historical surprise around every corner, the majestic Islamic Cairo plays host to an incredibly vast collection of architecture wonders. From mosques and *madrasas* to *khans* and palaces, the sites here are uncountable. See p. 114.
- **Karnak Temple** (Luxor): A dozen or so temples in one, this cluster of Ancient Egyptian wonders is highlighted by the grand temple's hypostyle hall. The awe-inspiring hall has 134 columns with some reaching as high as 21m (69 ft.); anything of human scale is instantly dwarfed. See p. 268.
- **Luxor Museum:** It may be smaller than the Egyptian Museum in Cairo, but the Luxor Museum is better lit, better organized, and better documented. It houses an impressive display of Ancient Egyptian artifacts that includes the famous Luxor Cache. See p. 268.
- **Nubian Museum** (Aswan): This is a long-overdue monument to the land of Nubia, which was flooded by the construction of the Aswan High Dam in the early 1970s. The museum is an attempt to re-create the lost culture, as it leads the visitor through the history of the land, from its heyday when Nubian kings ruled Egypt all the way to

its rather abrupt modern truncation. See p. 293.

- **The Pyramids** (Cairo): Egypt's number-one site is as vast and imposing as when it was built more than 4 millennia ago, and the impact is not dimmed by the crowds of tourists and touts. See p. 108.
- **St. Catherine's Monastery** (Sinai): One of the oldest continually working Christian monasteries in the world, St. Catherine's is uniquely steeped in tradition. In addition to its historical and religious importance, the monastery doesn't fall short on the religious art front with its rare collection of 8th- and 9th-century icons. See p. 214.
- **Valley of the Kings** (Luxor): Since it was first excavated at the beginning of the 20th century, this steep-sided valley on the West Bank in Luxor has long been drawing tourists to its underground complex of richly decorated tombs. See p. 274.

5 THE BEST LEAST-VISITED EGYPTIAN SITES

- **Bagawat Necropolis** (Kharga): One of the largest ancient Christian cemeteries in the world, the Bagawat Necropolis in the Western Desert still comprises more than 260 domed mausoleums, some of which contain exceptional wall paintings depicting Biblical scenes. See p. 335.
- **City of the Dead** (Cairo): This huge Islamic necropolis is awash with historical mausoleums, mosques, and other buildings, such as *tekiyyas* and *khanqahs*, that bring important insight into the late periods of Islamic rule. The City of the Dead is used today as a functional cemetery as well as a home for grave squatters. See p. 118.
- **Imhotep Museum** (Cairo): Dedicated to the Ancient Egyptian polymath Imhotep, to whom the design of the very first Egyptian pyramid is credited, this museum will certainly surprise you with its collection of artifacts, neat displays, and excellent documentation. See p. 155.
- **Monastery of St. Anthony** (Red Sea): Set in the middle of the magnificently stark scenery of the remote Red Sea coast, this ancient monastery was built on the site near Anthony's cave where his followers established a camp. St. Anthony's burial site is decorated with some of the richest Coptic art in the world, while the ascent to his cave makes a lovely spiritual trek. See p. 229.
- ***Sama Khana*** (Cairo): A remarkably different site than any of Egypt's attractions, the *sama khana* was once a venue where whirling dervishes performed their Sufi rituals. Now brilliantly restored, it warrants a visit for its distinctive architecture and decorative style. See p. 122.
- **Temple of Horus at Edfu** (Upper Egypt): Its location away from the Nile inundation and its relatively recent completion date (during the Roman period) has contributed to the very good state of preservation this temple enjoys. If you make it to Upper Egypt, the Temple of Horus at Edfu shouldn't slip off your must-see list. See p. 279.
- **Wadi El Hitan** (Fayum): This UNESCO World Heritage Site is like an open-air museum of natural history with its rare collection of fossilized whale skeletons. Yes, the barren desert where you stand was once upon a time a vast sea. See p. 158.

6 THE BEST NIGHTLIFE

- **Al Fanar** (Sharm El Sheikh; © **069/3662218;** www.elfanarsharm.com): One of Sharm El Sheikh's best private beaches during the day, Al Fanar turns into a nightlife hot spot with its cliff-edge open-air dance floor. The vistas are stunning and the atmosphere is electrical.
- **Hed Kandi** (Hurghada; © **016/8833556;** www.hedkandibeachbar.com): This is where party animals fulfill their hedonist pilgrimage to the party capital of the Red Sea. Dress to impress, and get ready for dusk-till-dawn dancing with top DJs on the decks.
- **L'Aubergine** (Cairo; © **02/27380080**): My favorite Egyptian nightspot, L'Aubergine's ground floor is the perfect place for a catch-up conversation with your friends along with some good quality food and a lot of drinks. The upper floor is reserved for danceaholics.
- **Little Buddha** (Sharm El Sheikh and Hurghada; © **069/3601030** and 065/3450120; www.littlebuddha-sharm.com and www.littlebuddha-hurghada.com): This swanky nightspot is Buddha Bar's little sister. Put on your sexiest dress, and head here for a fine-dining experience, a chill lounge, or an intense night of dancing to the rhythms of Buddha Bar's signature music.
- **Pacha** (Sharm El Sheikh; © **069/3600197** or -8, ext 300, or 012/2180873 for VIP area; www.pachasharm.com): This place has got it all, from a huge jam-packed dance floor and go-go dancers to foam parties and after hours at the VIP lounge. Pacha is your ultimate nightlife experience in Egypt.
- **Tamarai** (Cairo; © **02/24619910;** www.tamarai-egypt.com): This glitzy open-air restaurant and lounge is where the crème de la crème of Cairo's beautiful people hang out. Even if you don't care to see and be seen, the relaxing ambience of the place, its stunning interiors, and super scenic Nile views make it worth going.

7 THE BEST OUTDOOR ACTIVITIES

- **Bird-watching** (Aswan): Located on the Europe–Africa bird migration route, Egypt is any bird-watcher's heaven. Hundreds of different bird species are possible to sight in destinations throughout the country; the easiest, most guaranteed, and most rewarding is certainly Aswan. Herons, ibises, cormorants, and moorhens are just a sample of what you could see. See p. 292.
- **Freediving** (Dahab): Take your snorkeling experience to new depths or test your own physical limits as you challenge deeper sea levels without diving equipment. Dahab is about the best location in Egypt to embark on this thrilling activity. See p. 204.
- **Kitesurfing** (Red Sea): Knee- to waist-deep reefless lagoons with favorable wind conditions sound like an ideal place for kitesurfers, and Egypt has a couple of these perfect lagoons. Head for El Gouna if you want to have a culinary or nightlife scene on the side, or go to Hamata if you are only interested in the sport. See p. 91 and p. 224.
- **Rock climbing** (Dahab): The latest addition to Egypt's outdoor activities, rock climbing is gaining new fans by the minute. If you are an experienced climber or want to try it out for the first time, head to Dahab, where the country's best boulders are. See p. 89.

- **Sandboarding** (Siwa): Ever fancied a speedy glide on soft sand instead of snow? Some of the great Sahara's best dunes are right here in Siwa, ready to take you on a hair-raising ride down 100m-high (328-ft.) sand dunes. See p. 308.
- **Trekking** (St. Catherine): The Sinai Peninsula, with its High Mountains region, is home to St. Catherine and is the perfect trekking opportunity in Egypt. Go for a leisurely walk, or gear up for more challenging treks to mountain peaks and natural pools. See p. 215.

8 THE BEST DIVING SPOTS

- **Abu Dabab** (Marsa Alam): There are no reefs here, making it a different dive than your usual Red Sea one, but you have an opportunity to encounter one of the few remaining dugongs. See p. 251.
- **Elphinstone** (Marsa Alam): This huge table mountain rising from the abyss offers an almost guaranteed opportunity to sight more than one kind of shark, including hammerhead. See p. 252.
- **Fury Shoal** (Hamata): An immense reef system that, in addition to big fish and sharks, offers cave dives, a coral-crusted shipwreck, and a possibility (if you come at the right time of the year) to dive with whale sharks. See p. 258.
- **Jars** (Alexandria): Diving the Mediterranean is completely different from the Red Sea; it misses on underwater colors and exotic fish but scores high on historical artifacts. At Jars the seabed is littered with historical relics and dozens of Greco-Roman amphorae. See p. 166.
- **Pharos Lighthouse** (Alexandria): Pharos offers a historical dive with hieroglyph-bearing stones, broken statuaries, and the remains of the famous Alexandrian lighthouse. See p. 166.
- **Ras Abu Galum** (Sinai): Here you can experience the best of a Red Sea dive all at once: coral gardens, vibrantly colored fish, and, if you are lucky, an encounter with a manatee. See p. 204.
- **Ras Mohamed National Park** (Sinai): This thin finger of a reef, where the deep waters of the Gulf of Aqaba meet the warm shallow waters of the Gulf of Suez at the southern tip of the Sinai Peninsula, offers some fantastic dive sites that include stingray-rich Jackfish Alley and the rather unusual Yolanda Reef; don't forget to pose for a picture next to the sunken BMW. See p. 193.
- **Sataya** (Hamata): You are not here for the corals or the sharks—you are here for the dolphins. Enjoy a close encounter with the lovable creatures in their own turf. See p. 259.
- **Seven Pillars** (Safaga): As easy for beginners as it is rewarding for experts, the Seven Pillars site off the Sheraton Soma Bay beach has a resident Napoleon fish. It's named for the coral pillars that rise (almost) to the surface from a depth of between 10 and 12m (33–39 ft.) and plays host to scores of puffer, lizard, and lion fish. See p. 240.
- **St. John's** (Red Sea): In addition to mind-boggling wall dives and gigantic shoals of barracuda, tuna, batfish, and snappers, Egypt's southernmost dive site is a shark zone. St. John's is one of the best locations in the Red Sea to dive with the lovely aquatic beasts. See p. 260.
- **Strait of Tiran** (Sharm El Sheikh): A treacherous waterway to navigate, the Strait of Tiran is a diving hot spot with its famous quartet of sites: Gordon,

Jackson, Woodhouse, and Thomas. See p. 193.

- **The Wreck of the *Thistlegorm*** (Red Sea): Thirty meters (98 ft.) below the surface, between the red resort city of Hurghada and the Ras Mohamed National Park, lies this World War II cargo vessel. Check out the vintage motorbikes as well as a pair of locomotives that were flung from the wreck by the force of the explosions that sank it. See p. 233.

9 THE BEST SHOPPING EXPERIENCES

- **Azza Fahmy Boutique** (Cairo; © **02/27358354**): World-renowned Egyptian jewelry designer Azza Fahmy displays her most recent collection here. Using traditional motifs and Arabic calligraphy, her designs are one-of-a-kind pieces of art that deserve every penny of the hefty price tags they come with. See p. 146.
- **Aswan Souk:** Even though it is rapidly becoming more touristy, Aswan's souk still retains the essence of its trading heyday. In addition to the typical fare of T-shirts, bottles of colored sand, and machine-made Pharaonic statuettes, you can find genuine wooden artifacts and African masks. See p. 302.
- **Fair Trade Egypt** (Cairo; © **02/27365123**): Here you have low-hassle access to a range of folk crafts from around Egypt. This is a particularly good place to pick up pottery from Fayum or handmade scarves from Upper Egypt. Proceeds go to support community development NGOs.
- **Khan Al Khalili** (Cairo): This centuries-old souk in the heart of old Cairo is a must for anyone who has the shopping bug or just wants to experience the real hustle and bustle of a Cairene shopping experience. Take cash, and be prepared to haggle. This is the best place in town to buy novelty T-shirts, souvenirs with your name printed in hieroglyphics, and those little bottles of colored sand that have pictures of camels in them. See p. 119.
- **Khan Misr Touloun** (Cairo; © **02/33652227**): Across the street from Ibn Tulun Mosque, this place feels like Ali Baba's cave, with hundreds of souvenirs, trinkets, and knickknacks from glassware to pieces of furniture. See p. 147.

Egypt in Depth

It's not easy to find a country whose recorded history spans 5,000 years and has its own branch of science (Egyptology). Egypt is a history overdose, from dynastic Pharaohs to ambitious Greeks, exploiting Romans to conquering Arabs, and commercial Brits to patriotic Free Officers. This end-to-end, yet dissimilar, "Veni, vidi, vici" has left a heavy footprint on Egyptian culture.

The Pharaohs built one of the most advanced civilizations known to history; they were entrepreneurial inventors and excellent polymaths who created colossal temples and the oldest surviving wonder of the world—the pyramids. Their civilization has an aura of magnetic mysticism that attracts people to visit the country; from perplexing paintings on ancient tombs and unresolved mummification mysteries to one-of-a-kind statues and sophisticated rituals. To get the full picture, head to the world's largest open-air museum, as Luxor is known, or spend (at least) half a day exploring the Egyptian Museum.

But Egypt's history is not all about dynastic Pharaohs and their remarkable achievements. Greco-Roman Egypt left us with ancient wonders as well as gossipy thrills. Alexandria's treasures might have sunk, but the romance of Antony and Cleopatra still lives in our memories. Islamic Egypt can be equally attractive. More than a millennium of Islamic dominance has left its mark on Egypt's identity; from horizon-breaking minarets and fascinating architecture to flawless calligraphy and time-honored traditions. Islamic Cairo is Egypt's finest example of different sultanates' influences melting together in the bigger pot of Islam; a Fatimid gate leads to a Mamluk *madrasa*, while the Ayyubid-in-origin Citadel is most famous for its grandiose Ottoman mosque.

By the middle of the 19th century, national sentiments dominated the stage, and soon the last occupying British soldier was on his way out. Post-colonial Egypt was a phase of remarkable events that shaped the country's history—and continues to shape its present. First came the Arab-Israeli conflict and Sadat's blunt peace initiative, then came the rise of the Islamic Movement and the changes it still inflicts on Egypt's society.

With independence came an opportunity for Egyptian talents to thrive; their works have been recognized with awards from the Nobel Prize to Cannes Film Festival. However, with independence also came military rule. Though medal-adorned military suits might have been traded for formal ones, the firm grip on power still prevails. The lack of effective democracy, the global economic crisis going local, and the imbalanced social structure with a wave of fundamentalists preaching an ill-interpreted version of Islam are all elements pressing on Egypt today. In such draconian times, we are left dismayed with one question: Will the wind of change finally blow eastward, or will it simple pass over Egypt and leave the country in wait for a better tomorrow?

1 EGYPT TODAY

There are no volcanoes in Egypt, but there's a virtual one on the verge of eruption.

The global downturn is a triple threat to Egypt's economy: Profits brought into the Suez Canal have fallen 10% in the last

2 years due to the threat of Somali pirates; tourism is slowing down, reporting a 2% decline in 2009; and remittances sent by Egyptians working abroad spiraled 6% in the latter half of 2009.

While the state of Egypt's economic climate has only recently taken a turn for the worse (the economic growth rate slowed from 7% in 2007 to 4.5% in 2009), its social one has been, and still is, tumbling into turmoil.

The country's economy is controlled by a small group of elites, while more than 40% of the population lives under the poverty line on $2 a day—and this gap is growing by the day.

The mismanaged education system is adding to the dilemma, with more than a quarter-million university students and one million high school students graduating every year, which is more than the local labor market can absorb. At the same time, corruption has gravely institutionalized, whether on the micro level of getting one's car registered or the macro level of infrastructure and mega projects. Not being able to find employment, the workforce, represented by Egyptian youth, ends up in one of three scenarios: "One is better than zero," which is when energetic, young Egyptians settle for disgracefully underpaying jobs. For example, a junior accountant in a local firm is paid the equivalent of $150 a month, by no means enough to sustain an independent life. Second, "finding a new land," when the better qualified youth seek jobs in Gulf States, register for the U.S. annual lottery, or apply for immigration to Canada. This brain drain is gradually leading to a socioeconomic vacuum, as most of those leaving are middle-class Egyptians, a class vanishing as you read this. The lesser qualified fail to find a legitimate working opportunity abroad and, determined to leave the country, turn to Libya from which they board small, overfilled boats heading to Europe. Some end up in Italian jails, others die at sea. The last, and most devastating, is "giving up," which finds youth wasting their days at a traditional coffee shop smoking *shisha* and playing backgammon. They are consumed by frustration and start falling, one by one, to depression, drug addiction, or fanatical fundamentalism.

On the political front, the grass doesn't look any greener.

Since the assassination of late President Anwar El Sadat in 1981, a State of Emergency has been declared, giving police the right to detain, without charges, any Egyptian national anywhere in the country at any time. Freedom of speech is nominally tolerated, yet within limits, and objections can only be made peacefully, without crossing any red lines, lest you want to be a bad Egyptian. If revolutionary urges arise and you organize or lead demonstrations, the State of Emergency will be enforced. State-sanctioned torture is systematic rather than ad hoc, and the government is growing a disgraceful reputation for atrocious human rights violations. For the past 29 years, the ailing president has been unanimously voted for, first in presidential referendums and most recently in a puppet election that can be best described as a farce. The National Democratic Party (NDP) dominates the political stage, while the opposition is chiefly represented in the Muslim Brotherhood. Though it is unconstitutional to formulate a political party based on religious views, the longstanding Muslim Brotherhood, which was founded in 1928, is awkwardly tolerated. Raiding arrests frequently shake, but never topple, the hard-liners' party. Middle- and upper-middle-class Egyptians skeptically perceive the Muslim Brotherhood as lightweight Taliban in formal suits. As for the masses, whose daily lives are a burgeoning struggle, their perception and support to the Muslim Brotherhood varies considerably; from frantically in favor to subtly neutral.

The million-dollar question is whether the incumbent president, Hosni Mubarak, will run for his sixth term in office in the upcoming 2011 elections or dynastically groom his son, Gamal, to succeed him.

2 RELIGION

Egypt is predominately a Sunni Muslim country, but a few other religions and sects exist. Egyptian Christians, known as Copts (conquering Arabs back in A.D. 640 gave this name to Egyptians in general, but it later became associated with Christian Egyptians only), are the biggest religious minority, representing 10% of Egypt's 83 million people. For as long as Muslims and Christians have lived side by side in Egypt, they have managed to coexist peacefully; however, sectarian violence sporadically flares. The worst recent episode took place in 2000, when a row between a Muslim and a Copt in the small village of Al Kosheh in Upper Egypt escalated. The death toll topped 20 villagers.

In addition to Copts, there are Jews, Shiite Muslims, and Bahais. Jews are the smallest group with only a handful still calling Egypt home; they are mostly elders. Shiite Muslims and Bahais are (unofficially) estimated to total 2,000 each. While Shiite Muslims shy away from the spotlight, Bahais have recently grabbed media attention. In Egypt, identification cards note a citizen's religion; Islam, Christianity, and Judaism are the options one can choose from. After a very long legal battle, a debated win was claimed in April 2009; Bahais were allowed to put a dash instead of a specific religion. This might be a compromise rather than a hands-down win, since the government's decree gave this "dash right" only to the Bahais; neither atheism nor agnosticism are tolerated in Egypt.

Egypt's apparent conservatism is more show than substance, influenced by foreign radical schools of thought rather than deeply rooted traditions. Back in the '70s, women walked freely wearing sleeveless minidresses, but today the majority of women on Cairo's streets are veiled; step into rural Egypt, and you can start counting unveiled women. The veil, or *hijab,* as it is called in Arabic, is not part of Egypt's tradition, but a Wahhabi trend imported from Saudi Arabia. It flourished in the '80s and with the Islamic movement, and has passed through a number of stages over the last 2 decades. Today it has prevalence in Egyptian society in various forms, from the simple headscarf covering a woman's hair to the all-black, loose robelike *abaya,*

The Rise of Islam

During the 7th century, a young modest man by the name of Mohammad Ibn Abd Allah called people to refrain from paganism and wrongdoing and, instead, embrace the worship of one god, Allah, and treat all people equally and respectfully. His calls fell on deaf ears, and Islam-resisting tribe heads, fearing loss of power, embarked on persecuting Mohammad's followers. Despite this, Islam attracted more and more people, and its power base grew immensely. Soon, Islam dominated the Arabian Peninsula, with its base in the holy cities of Mecca and Medina. The once-scattered and fragmented tribes were now united under one banner. A power-sweeping religious force was on the march with one purpose in mind—the call for prayer to be heard in all four corners of the globe.

Ramadan

Ramadan is Islam's holy month, marking the time when the holy Quran was first bestowed upon Mohammad. It is observed with dawn-to-dusk fasting and extra evening prayers, and requires Muslims to abstain, not only from food and water, but from pleasures in general, including sex (a Muslim man can't have sex with his wife during this month, and some scholars abstain from any sign of affection). Families use this time to get together and strengthen ties that have been neglected throughout the year, and homes' balconies are decorated with lights and *fanoos* (a special lantern). Ramadan also marks a time for charity, which can be found in the numerous eateries across the country where the poor can get a free hot meal.

Surprisingly, Ramadan is a good time for the local economy, as television channels charge double the amount to advertise to captive audiences, and the number of soap operas (p. 41) produced for this time triples. Saudi Arabia also sees a boost in its economy, as some devoted Muslims perform the lesser pilgrimage, *umra,* during this time. Unfortunately, Ramadan also sees shorter working hours, and the struggle to be without food and water (particularly on hot summer days) leads to slower and, perhaps, less friendly interactions.

For tourists, Ramadan can be an interesting time to visit Egypt, especially if you are targeting Cairo; those who head to Sharm El Sheikh or Hurghada won't feel the impact as much. Hours for attractions can be affected, so it's best to check prior to your visit, but you should be safe if you visit between 10am and 2pm. Female travelers should take care to dress modestly, particularly during Ramadan. Locals are accustomed to being around non-Muslims, as more than 10% of Egyptians are Christians, but should you want to eat or drink during the day, it's best to be discreet. Most eateries, especially fast food ones, are open as usual, but expect tortoise-paced service, and hours at high-end restaurants are adjusted to accommodate Ramadan's main meals, *iftar* (the one after sunset) and *sohour* (the one before sunrise). Reservations are essential. Consuming alcohol during Ramadan is permitted as long as you are not Egyptian, regardless of your religion; Egyptians, Muslims or not, won't be served. Liquor stores close for the month (though some clandestinely home-deliver), as do *kosheri* eateries and nightclubs, especially those featuring belly dance shows.

Ramadan follows the lunar Islamic calendar, and year after year, it roughly advances by 11 days in the Gregorian calendar. The table below reflects Ramadan start and end dates over the next 3 years.

Year	Start	End
2010	Aug 11	Sept 9
2011	Aug 1	Aug 29
2012	July 20	Aug 18

to the hotly debated *niqab,* which covers the entire face and body except the eyes.

Of course, not all Egyptians grow beards and cover up from head to toe. Liberal Muslims make up a substantial part of society; however, the tolerance between the two camps is thinning by the day, signaling a great rift that may soon wreck Egyptian society.

3 LOOKING BACK AT EGYPT

THE PHARAOHS The traditional starting point for Ancient Egyptian history is around 3000 B.C. Documentary evidence isn't very good this far back, and what there is tends to be subject to periodic academic reinterpretation. What we do have, however, is a tablet known as the Narmer Palette (on display in room no. 43 on the ground floor of the Egyptian Museum; p. 104), which shows Narmer wearing the crowns of Upper and Lower Egypt and pondering a stack of headless prisoners. Discovered by British archaeologist James E. Quibell in 1897–98 and dated around 3000 B.C., this palette was long thought to represent the moment at which the two kingdoms were united under a single ruler, whose capital was Memphis (p. 154). Founded in 3100 B.C. as the city of Menes, Memphis was a splendid city that promoted art and fostered architecture. It is believed that in its heyday, Memphis was a cosmopolitan magnet harboring a large population of Egyptians as well as foreign residents.

The Pharaohs ruled Egypt for more than 2,700 years and devised precise theories for predicting the motion of the stars and planets, built sophisticated irrigation schemes, and developed systems of taxation and government that gave them the power to construct enormous temples, complexes, and monuments that have survived until modern times. Their years are divided, according to their own system, into the regnal years of their rulers, and these in turn are grouped into 31 dynasties, which are divided into three kingdoms—Old, Middle, and New—interrupted by three intermediate periods.

The **Old Kingdom** (2686–2181 B.C.) saw the construction of some of the most enduring and best-known symbols of Ancient Egypt—the Pyramids. Zoser (Djoser) sowed the seeds by building Egypt's first pyramid in 2650 B.C. The Step Pyramid (p. 154) at Saqqara was a monumental achievement not to be overshadowed until the Great Pyramid of Khufu (p. 110) was built. Khufu (Cheops) was only the second ruler of the 4th Dynasty, but building pyramids ran in the family; his father, Sneferu, built the Bent and Red pyramids (p. 154) in Saqqara, while Khufu's son Khafre (Chephren) built the second-largest pyramid at Giza.

DATELINE

- **3100–2686 B.C. Early Dynastic Period.** Narmer unites Egypt for the first time, with his capital in Memphis.
- **3000 B.C.** Narmer depicted in the Narmer Palette wearing the crowns of Upper and Lower Egypt.
- **2686–2181 B.C. Old Kingdom Period.** The Giza Pyramids and the necropolis in Saqqara are built.
- **2650 B.C.** Zoser of the 3rd Dynasty builds Egypt's very first pyramid—the Step Pyramid.
- **2613–2589 B.C.** Reign of Sneferu; he builds the Bent and Red pyramids at Dahshur.
- **2589–2566 B.C.** Reign of Khufu; the Great Pyramid is built.
- **2181–2133 B.C. First Intermediate Period.** The country is fragmented; the power of the rulers in Memphis barely extends beyond the city.
- **2040–1786 B.C. Middle Kingdom Period.** Upper and Lower Egypt are reunited under 11th Dynasty Mentuhotep II.
- **1786–1552 B.C. Second Intermediate Period.** Asiatic tribes from Palestine, known as Hyksos, ascend to power.
- **1552–1527 B.C.** Ahmose I rids Egypt of the Hyksos.

continues

Fun Facts **Misr**

The most widely accepted theory tracks the origin of the word Misr (Arabic for Egypt) to Misraim, son of Ham and grandson of Noah. However, a group of scholars assume Misr is taken from the hieroglyphic word Memphis.

Khafre is also reputed for building a massive human-headed lion statue that Ancient Egyptians called Harakhte (Horus of the Horizon); we call it the Sphinx. The Giza Pyramids trio finally came to completion by another 4th Dynasty king, Menkaure (Mycerinus). The Old Kingdom was aptly named the Age of Pyramids.

In a span of 70 days, during the 7th Dynasty (2181–2173 B.C.), Egypt changed kings 70 times. Centralized control broke down, several communities splintered, and independent principalities were created, thus establishing Egypt's First Intermediate Period (2181–2133 B.C.). Anarchy finally came to an end when Mentuhotep II led the Thebans to victory over the rival capital of Heracleopolis. Order was established once again, giving birth to the **Middle Kingdom** (2040–1786 B.C.).

The peace brought by the Middle Kingdom sparked a revival in monument building, as reigning kings were competing in building pyramids at Dahshur and Fayum (p. 154). But the Middle Kingdom was not all about colossal tombs; it was an era characterized by the expansion of Egyptian territory campaigning in Nubia, Libya, and Palestine. Middle Kingdom dynasties were skillful crafters of bureaucracy, the same bureaucracy that led to their demise. Asiatics from Palestine, known as Hyksos, settled in Egypt and gradually infiltrated the bureaucratic government. Soon power started to decline, and disintegrated Egypt entered the Second Intermediate Period (1786–1552 B.C.). By 1674 B.C., Hyksos firmed their grip on Lower Egypt, established the 15th Dynasty, and moved the capital to the eastern Delta town of Avaris.

Soon after he ascended to the throne, Ahmose I (Amosis) completed the expulsion of Hyksos from Egypt. He is credited for establishing the **New Kingdom** (1552–1069 B.C.), an era that can easily be described as Ancient (if not Ancient and modern) Egypt's golden age. While Memphis was still the capital, Thebes was adorned with gigantic temples and prolific tombs. Most of Luxor's main attractions, such as Luxor Temple, Karnak Temple,

- **1552–1069 B.C. New Kingdom Period.** Ancient Egypt's "golden age," in which many of the most spectacular monuments, such as Luxor Temple, Karnak Temple, and the Valley of the Kings, are built.
- **1506–1494 B.C.** Reign of Tuthmosis I, who annexes Upper Nubia, campaigns in Syria, and reaches the Euphrates.
- **1490–1468 B.C.** Hatshepsut reigns as regent queen; she is one of Ancient Egypt's most successful rulers.
- **1468–1436 B.C.** The title Pharaoh is claimed for the first time in history by Tuthmosis III.
- **1364–1347 B.C.** Akhenaten starts a new religion in the new-found city of Akhetaten at Tell al Amarna near Minya.
- **1347–1337 B.C.** Egypt's celebrity Pharaoh, Tutankhamun, ascends to the throne as a boy of about 9 years old.
- **1289–1224 B.C.** Ramses II's longevity allows him to leave several monuments, including the world-famous temple in Abu Simbel.
- **1069–715 B.C. Third Intermediate Period,** characterized by overlapping family lines and regional disputes.
- **945 B.C.** Libyan prince Shoshenq I firms his grip on power; the 22nd (Bubasite) Dynasty is established.

and Valley of the Kings (p. 274), date back to the New Kingdom. Thebes also witnessed the birth of a new deity—Amun-Ra. The new state divinity was a combination of the Theban god Amun and Heliopolis god Ra.

A cadre of ambitious rulers took Egypt's borders to the next level. Tuthmosis I (Tuthmose) swept through the southern territories, annexing Upper Nubia (now part of Sudan) to his throne. He also led military campaigns into Syria and reached as far as the Euphrates. His grandson followed suit; Tuthmosis III was a leading conqueror and expanded Egypt's borders into Palestine and Syria. He was the first Ancient Egyptian king to claim the title Pharaoh (Great House), previously used in reference to the royal palace rather than the king himself.

Hatshepsut ruled as the regent queen when her dead husband's son by a concubine, Tuthmosis III, was young. She was one of the most successful rulers of the New Kingdom, and doubly notable for having been a woman. An entrepreneur, she oversaw the famous maritime expedition to the faraway Land of Punt (now part of Somalia). Details of the expedition can today be seen in the spectacular Mortuary Temple of Hatshepsut (p. 272) on Luxor's West Bank.

Akhenaten is a controversial Pharaoh famous for his radical decisions and new religion. Born Amenhotep IV (Amenophis), Akhenaten, after only 5 years on the throne, abruptly abandoned Thebes and its gods and attempted to found a new capital at Tell Al Amarna in Middle Egypt. He called it Akhetaten, as it was dedicated to the worship of a new deity—Aten, the life-giving force of light represented in the sun disc. This new religion was doubly controversial for the fact that this, unlike the polytheism that was practiced, was monotheistic. Room no. 3 in the Egyptian Museum has some of the most extraordinary, stylized depictions of this unusual man. Akhenaten's capital was short-lived, and soon Memphis regained its national status as the country's capital. In fear of the mighty power of Amun-Ra's priests, Akhetaten was abandoned, and the 9-year-old Pharaoh Tutankhaten ("living image of Aten") was renamed Tutankhamun ("living image of Amun"). Egypt's celebrity Pharaoh is well known for his treasure-filled tomb (p. 276) discovered by Howard Carter in 1922.

Fun Facts **Arab Proverb**

"Man fears Time, yet Time fears the Pyramids."

- **747–332 B.C. Late Period.** Egypt struggles to regain unity, while successive invasions dominate the horizon.
- **747–656 B.C.** King Piankhy of the Kushites conquers Egypt, establishing the reign of the 25th Dynasty, dubbed the Black Pharaohs.
- **664–525 B.C.** Assyrians defeat the Kushites and establish the 26th (Saite) Dynasty, installing Psammetichus on the throne.
- **525–404 B.C.** Cambyses concludes the conquest of Egypt; the 27th (first Persian) Dynasty is established.
- **343–332 B.C.** Artaxerxes III reduces Egypt to a satrapy; the 31st (second Persian) and the last Ancient Egyptian dynasty.
- **332 B.C.** Alexander the Great arrives, orders the building of Alexandria, is crowned Pharaoh in Memphis, and leaves.
- **332 B.C.–A.D. 30 Ptolemaic Period.** Egypt is under the control of a Macedonian dynasty, with its capital in the city of Alexandria.
- **304–283 B.C.** Ptolemy Soter is left to run Egypt in Alexander's absence, makes himself ruler, and establishes a dynasty after Alexander's death.

continues

Fun Facts The Battle of Megiddo

In 1468 B.C., Tuthmosis III heroically led the Egyptian army in the first battle of Megiddo against the allied forces of Kadesh. According to the Bible's Book of Revelations, the ultimate battle of Armageddon shall take place on the very same hilly site of Megiddo.

The most famous of the New Kingdom's Pharaohs is certainly Ramses II, who reigned an incredible 66 years. Ramses II, known as Ramses the Great, built some well-known monuments including the temple at Abu Simbel, the Hypostyle Hall at Karnak Temple, additions at Luxor Temple, and the Ramesseum (p. 273). Soon after he died, Egypt's golden age started fading to black. The Third Intermediate Period (1069–715 B.C.) and the subsequent epoch known as the Late Period (747–332 B.C.) were both marked with successive invasions and rebellious revolts. In 945 B.C., Libyan prince Shoshenq I gained control of Lower Egypt and established the 22nd Dynasty. During this time, known as the Bubasite Dynasty, the Libyans ruled for more than 200 years. Noticing an opportunity in the ongoing turmoil, the Kushite King Kashta invaded from the south. His successor, Piankhy, conquered the whole of Egypt and established the 25th Dynasty (747–656 B.C.), better known in history as the Black Pharaohs. Kushites finally retreated in the face of the marauding Assyrians, who in turn established the 26th (Saite) Dynasty. Persians came next, with Cyrus the Great entrusting the conquest of Egypt to his son Cambyses. The job was completed in 525 B.C. after Egyptian forces were defeated in the Battle of Pelusium. The 27th (first Persian) Dynasty was established. A respite of independence took place for a brief period before Persians took over once more in 343 B.C., establishing the 31st, and last, of Ancient Egypt's dynasties.

WHO IS NEXT TO CONQUER History's timeline has it that the Pharaonic Period ended in 332 B.C. with the successful invasion of Egypt by Alexander the Great, a Macedonian with a brilliant, but rather short, career. The Egypt that Alexander invaded was already under occupation by the Persians, and Alexander, rather than defeating any kind of Egyptian resistance, was welcomed as a liberator. At the same time, he made an obeisance to Egyptian deities and left local administrative

- **A.D. 30–640** During the **Roman Period,** Egypt is the breadbasket of Rome; Christianity flourishes.
- **451** Council of Chalcedon expels Egyptian Christians out of the Christian World. Eastern Christianity splinters.
- **639–642** The Arab conquest of Egypt; the Byzantine army is destroyed at Babylon; Alexandria surrenders in September 642.
- **642–661** Egypt is governed as part of the Islamic Empire under the Al Khulafa al Rashidun, the First Islamic Caliphate.
- **661–749** The second Islamic Caliphate, **Umayyad,** is established with Damascus as the empire's capital. Egypt is a province.
- **749–1285** The third Islamic Caliphate, **Abbasid,** is established with Baghdad as the empire's capital. Egypt becomes a province.
- **868–905** Ahmed ibn Tulun breaks away from the Abbasid court establishing the **Tulunid Dynasty.**
- **905–935** **Abbasid Caliphate** restores its grip over Egypt.
- **935–969** Muhammad bin Tughj establishes the short-lived **Ikhshidid Dynasty.**
- **969–1171** Shiite Muslims from North Africa invade the country establishing the

Fun Facts KV62

Tomb no. 62 in the Valley of the Kings belongs to Tutankhamun. Discovered intact in 1922, the tomb was believed to be guarded by the "Curse of the Pharaohs." Several unfortunate events took place after the tomb's discovery; none made the curse more plausible, but rather more enigmatic. As Howard Carter broke into the Pharaoh's tomb, a cobra broke into Carter's bird cage and ate his canary. In Ancient Egyptian beliefs, the royal cobra, often adorning Pharaohs' heads, protects them against their enemies. Lord Carnarvon, who financed the excavation and accompanied Carter, died 6 weeks after the historic discovery as a result of a mosquito bite. It is believed that at the exact moment of his death, lights went out in Cairo, and at his palace in the U.K. his dog gave a distressful howl and fell dead. Could it be the curse of the Pharaohs?

structures intact. On November 14, 332 B.C., in Memphis, he was crowned Pharaoh. He founded the coastal city of Alexandria but never lived to see it prosper into the Old World's leading metropolis; he abruptly left Egypt, entrusting the country's affairs to one of his generals, Ptolemy.

After Alexander's death in 323 B.C., there was a dispute over his body, which Ptolemy won. This was a vital battle, because the burial of a predecessor was a crucial rite of succession in Macedonian tradition. By burying Alexander's body in Egypt (the exact whereabouts remain a mystery, though rumored to be in Alexandria), Ptolemy was able to lay claim to legitimacy, name himself Ptolemy Soter (savior), and found a dynasty that would rule Egypt for the next 3 centuries until A.D. 30, when Gaius Octavius Thurinus (later known as Gaius Julius Caesar), recently crowned Emperor Augustus of Rome, effectively took over control and Egypt became a province of the Roman Empire.

HAIL CAESAR The transition from Ptolemaic to Roman rule was similarly a matter of a slow fade rather than a dramatic change. The Ptolemies had gone to some lengths to publicly integrate their regime into Egyptian society, adapting Greek religious figures to match local mores, building or rebuilding temples in the southern parts of the country, and even going so far as to follow the Pharaonic practice of marrying their siblings. As the

Fatimid Caliphate. Al Mu'izz le-din Allah orders the building of Egypt's capital, Al Qahira (The Victorious).

- **1171–1174** Egypt reverts to the Abbasid court briefly.
- **1174–1250** Salah al Din Yusuf ibn Ayyub establishes the **Ayyubid Dynasty,** seeing off the European Crusaders.
- **1250–1382** Turkic Mamluks establish the first Mamluk Sultanate, known as the **Bahri Dynasty.**
- **1382–1517** Circassian Mamluks revolt, ascend to power, and establish the **Burji Dynasty.**
- **1517–1798 Ottoman Rule.** Egypt is a province once again, heavily exploited by Istanbul.
- **1798–1802 Napoleonic Interlude.** Bonaparte's occupation is thwarted by the combined efforts of the Ottomans and the British.
- **1805–1848** Mohamed Ali reasserts Ottoman rule, establishes hereditary rule as an Ottoman viceroy, and undertakes modernization of the country.
- **1805-1867** Egypt is an Ottoman province ruled by Mohamed Ali's bloodline.
- **1867-1914** Egypt enjoys a higher level of sovereignty, declared the **Khedivate of Egypt.**

continues

Fun Facts The Oldest Pharaoh

The average life expectancy in Ancient Egypt was as low as 40. Ramses II died at 96. He had 200 wives and concubines, and fathered 96 sons and 60 daughters. Ramses II outlived 13 of his heirs.

Roman pressure mounted on the militarily and politically weaker Ptolemaic dynasty, it was inevitable that their politics become intertwined. Cleopatra VII played Roman politics with verve but lost in the end. She bore a son for Gaius Julius Caesar before he was knifed by his opposition. She then shifted her allegiance, and favors, to Mark Antony. When he, too, was defeated, she killed herself, allegedly by allowing a pet asp (snake) to bite her. Her son, and Caesar's, ruled, briefly and nominally, before being executed by the victorious Roman Emperor Augustus, inaugurating Roman rule over Egypt.

The centuries of Roman rule in Egypt were characterized by gradually stricter and heavier military control of the country, combined with an ever more efficient bureaucracy (at least until the 3rd century A.D.). Other than building trading posts, the Romans didn't do much to develop Egypt, a country that was regarded as the breadbasket of the vast Roman Empire. The main highlight of the Roman era is of course Christianity. With the preaching of St. Mark, Christianity was introduced to Egypt. Though persecuted, at first, by the Romans, it flourished among the Egyptians. Undoubtedly, the situation eased up significantly once the Christian Constantine (known as Constantine the Great or St. Constantine) was declared emperor in A.D. 306, and the Edict of Milan (which made Christianity legal) was circulated in A.D. 313. By the 5th century A.D., Egypt had not only largely made the transition from 4,000-year-old deities of Pharaonic Egypt to a relatively new monotheistic cosmology, but also from a country ruled by native Egyptians to a province of empires.

There were flies in the religious ointment, and the chief one was that the church in Egypt was on the wrong side of the Council of Chalcedon, which in A.D. 451 ruled on what now seems a rather abstruse religious question concerning the physical and spiritual nature of Christ. Suffice it to say that the Egyptian Church professed a belief in the Monophysite nature of Christ, rather than the belief that his essential being was both divine and

- **1859–1869** Lavish ceremony marks the inauguration of the Suez Canal.
- **1871** Opening of the Khedival Opera House.
- **1881–1882** **Urabi Movement** ends with Egyptian forces defeated in the Battle of El Tell el Kebir; British forces occupy Egypt.
- **1902** Construction of the first Aswan Dam.
- **1914-1922** All ties with the Ottoman Empire are severed; the **Sultanate of Egypt** is declared, yet as a British protectorate.
- **1919** Deporting Egyptian nationalists to Malta sparks civil disobedience known as the **Egyptian Revolution of 1919.**
- **1922** Howard Carter discovers the Tomb of Tutankhamun.
- **1922-1953** Nominal independence granted; the **Kingdom of Egypt** is declared.
- **1928** Schoolteacher Hassan al Banna founds the Muslim Brotherhood.
- **1936** The Anglo-Egyptian Treaty of 1936 is signed; an emasculated independence is granted.
- **1948** The coalition of Arab armies (Egypt, Syria, Lebanon, and Jordan) suffers a heavy defeat by the hands of the newly created Israel.
- **1951** Guerrilla warfare ravages the Canal Zone.

human, and refused to alter its view despite having been ruled out of bounds by a Byzantine council that had declared itself infallible. Egyptian Christians, Copts, were deemed heretic and expelled out of the Christian World. Romans continued to exploit the country, and Egyptians were longing for another liberator. This time it was a small army of horsemen riding from the Arabian Peninsula under the banner of a new prophet: Mohammad.

THE ARAB CONQUEST Babylon (now in Coptic Cairo, p. 123) was a strategic and well-fortified, but provincial, town on the Nile. The fortress there guarded important port facilities and the entrance to an ancient system of waterways that, at its height, enabled navigation between Cairo and the Red Sea. In late 639, a small army crossed the Sinai Peninsula. Commanded by the energetic general Amr Ibn Al A'as, they headed straight to Babylon. Fresh from victories in Palestine and Syria, the men had little difficulty wrapping up the whole conquest of Egypt in about 3 years. There are different perspectives on the ease with which this band of 4,000 men, which even with reinforcements only reached about 15,000 by the end of the campaign, managed to conquer one of the richest provinces of the Byzantine Empire. But a population that was not inimical to the invaders, who seemed to offer the Monophysite Copts a greater degree of religious tolerance than their nominal coreligionists had, combined with general fatigue on the part of the Byzantines after centuries of conflict frames the most likely explanation. Following the footsteps of preceding Greeks, the Arabs opted for a new capital (Fustat [The Tent]), founded by the banks of the Nile near the ancient capital of Memphis, not far from the pyramids at Giza.

When Mohammad died in A.D. 632, leadership of his rapidly expanding religion passed first to one of his most entrusted aides, Abu Bakr, and subsequently to three more caliphs (Omar, Osman, and finally Ali). These four became known as the Al Khulafa Al Rashidun, or the Rightly Guided Caliphs. The last of these men, Ali Ibn Abi Talib, was not only the prophet's cousin, but married to his daughter, Fatima. Ali lost a power struggle to a man

Fun Facts **Time Flies!**

It may seem that Cleopatra and Khufu were part of the same Ancient Egyptian era, but the time between them is half a millennium more than that between Cleopatra and today, making Khufu more ancient to her than she is to us.

- **1952** Black Saturday; anti-colonial riots devastate the capital.
- **1952** Free Officers Movement seizes power; King Farouk abdicates.
- **1953** The constitution is abrogated, all political parties dissolved; the **Republic of Egypt** is declared.
- **1953–1954** Mohamed Naguib's nominal presidency.
- **1954–1970** Charismatic Gamal Abdel Nasser takes office.
- **1956** Great Britain completes its withdrawal.
- **1956** The Suez Crisis is prompted by Nasser's nationalization of the Suez Canal; Great Britain, France, and Israel invade the Canal Zone.
- **1958-1961** Egypt and Syria merge, forming the United Arab Republic. Egypt retains the name even after Syria secedes.
- **1965** King Farouk dies in Rome.
- **1967** The Six-Day War. Israel takes over the Sinai Peninsula, Golan Heights, West Bank, and East Jerusalem.
- **1967-1975** The Suez Canal is closed; international maritime goes back to the Cape of Good Hope route.

continues

Islam's Most Respected Martyr and the Day of Ashura

Saints are prohibited in Islam, but there is martyrdom. To Muslims, especially Shiites, Al Hussein is Islam's most respected martyr, and his death is commemorated on Ashura, the tenth day of the first month of the Islamic calendar. When Mohammad immigrated to Medina in Saudi Arabia, he found Jews observing the same day, which at the time coincided with Yom Kippur, by fasting. As Islam recognizes Moses as a prophet, Mohammad fasted on that day and recommended his followers do so, too. Ashura is observed for two different reasons, which chiefly depends on the sect. Shiites mainly observe it as a day of mourning for the death of Al Hussein, while Sunnis observe it as day of fasting following Mohammad's example. However, it is not clear-cut, and overlapping between sects occurs.

named Mu'awiya Ibn Abi Sufyan, who had been appointed governor of Syria by Ali's predecessor, Osman. This was the moment when a schism fractured the unity of Muslims. A group of Ali followers would not accept this new succession. They called themselves the supporters of Ali, or *shia'at* Ali, to differentiate themselves from the supporters of the new Damascus-based Umayyad dynasty founded by Mu'awiya, who associated themselves with the *sunna,* or way of the Prophet. Supporters of Ali believed the caliphate to remain in the lineage of Mohammad and nominated Al Hussein, Ali's son and Mohammad's favorite grandson, to assume the caliph's position. To lobby for support, Al Hussein decided to head to Kufa, the caliphate's capital at the time, now located in Iraq. On his march, Al Hussein's small entourage was massacred by the heavily armed Umayyad forces. October 9, 680, marks the Battle of Karbala and the day Muslims split into Sunni and Shiite.

Dominance over the fast expanding Islamic Empire went first to Damascus during the Umayyad Caliphate (661–749) and later to Baghdad during the Abbasid Caliphate (749–1285). Egypt under Umayyad rule witnessed an influx of Arab immigrants and enjoyed a period of political stability, while during the Abbasid rule it flourished intellectually. When the Abbasid first ascended to power, they gave Egypt a new capital and called it Al Askar (The Soldiers). Little more than a century later, during the Tulunid

- **1970–1981** Anwar El Sadat's presidency.
- **1971** The country is once again renamed, now the Arab Republic of Egypt, which still holds today.
- **1971** Aswan High Dam completed.
- **1973** October War breaks out.
- **1977** Sadat visits Tel Aviv, revitalizing the peace process.
- **1978** Camp David Accords lay out terms under which Israeli forces return the Sinai Peninsula to Egypt.
- **1978** Sadat and Israeli Prime Minister Menachem Begin are jointly awarded the Nobel Peace Prize.
- **1979** Israel-Egypt Peace Treaty is finally signed.
- **1979-1989** Egypt is expelled from the Arab League.
- **1981** Sadat is assassinated during a military parade.
- **1981–present** Hosni Mubarak's presidency.
- **1991** In exchange for a reported $20 billion, Egypt takes part in the operation to drive Iraqi forces from Kuwait.
- **1995** Mubarak narrowly escapes an assassination attempt in Ethiopia.
- **1997** Fifty-eight people are killed in an attack by terrorists in Luxor.

The Eccentric Caliph

Al Hakim be-amr Allah was the third Fatimid caliph to rule Egypt. A competent administrator in many regards, he was also palpably crazy. Amongst his better-known edicts were bans on *molokheya,* a staple dish in Egypt; restrictions on women going out at night or to public baths; and ordering shoemakers not to manufacture any women's shoes. In contrast to other Fatimid rulers, Al Hakim decreed a number of edicts that persecuted Christians, Jews, and Sunnis, including the prohibition of celebrating Epiphany and the destruction of some churches (such as Church of the Holy Sepulcher) and convents. He was in the habit of taking long walks during the night with little or no guard, and on one of these walks he disappeared and was murdered. Accusations point to his sister Sitt Al Mulk.

Dynasty, Egypt's capital changed again to the newly built Al Qatai (The Wards). Abbasid-appointed Turkic governor of Egypt, Ahmad Ibn Tulun, broke away from the Abbasid court and established the Tulunid Dynasty (868–905). He later annexed Syria and Palestine. After a brief Abbasid power restoration, another Turkic governor followed Ibn Tulun's footsteps. This time it was Muhammad Ibn Tughj establishing the short-lived Ikhshidid Dynasty (935–969). The only thing that remains from Al Askar or Al Qatai is the Ibn Tulun Mosque (p. 34), with its famous (and the country's only) semi-spiral minaret.

THE FATIMIDS For Egypt, the Shiite versus Sunni sectarian struggle might have all been irrelevant, except that as the Islamic Empire expanded across North Africa and ultimately into Spain, the neighboring territory of Tunisia was taken over by a Shiite group who were originally supporters of Ismail Bin Ja'far and were known, as a result, as Ismailis. Because they traced their parentage back to Fatima, daughter of Mohammad and wife of Ali, they also came to be known as the Fatimids. By the time the Fatimids were established in North Africa, about 3 centuries had passed since the original dispute, and the capital of the Islamic Empire had moved from Kufa to Damascus, and later to Baghdad. No matter—the first obstacle on their march remained the same: Egypt.

After a number of failed invasions, a 100,000-man Fatimid army commanded

- **2003** Riots erupt in Cairo in protest of the U.S. invasion of Iraq, despite Egypt's non-participation.
- **Sept 2005** Mubarak wins first multiple-party elections; begins his fifth consecutive term in office.
- **Mar 2007** Amendments to the constitution are designed to preserve security forces' power and restrain the Muslim Brotherhood's political advances.
- **Apr 2007** Amnesty International criticizes Egypt over its human rights record.
- **Oct 2007** Journalist imprisoned; opposition and independent newspapers protest.
- **Apr 2008** Civil disobedience planned for April 6; heavy police presence hampers it from gaining momentum.
- **May 2009** In fear of swine flu, Egypt authorizes a pig cull, angering Coptic pig farmers.
- **June 2009** U.S. President Barack Obama addresses the Muslim world in a galvanizing, yet fruitless, speech from Cairo University.

continues

In the Beginning: The Story of Egyptian Cosmology

A lot can change over 2,500 years, and the story of Egyptian cosmology is mind-bendingly complex. At its root, however, there is a story of creation that is as elegantly simple as it is intriguingly evocative.

In the beginning, there was chaos, and all was filled with the primordial, unformed, and unconscious waters known as Nun. From these waters, a god, Ra, willed himself into physical existence. This god was alone and contained both male and female principles. Ra spat from his mouth two children: Shu, who became God of Air and was shown in paintings wearing an ostrich feather on his head, and Tefnut, who was the Goddess of Mist and depicted as a woman with the head of a lioness. As a result, the world was ordered, and the chaos abated.

You will often see Ra in a solar bark, which he used to traverse the sky each day. On his head, he has a rearing cobra. It seems that early in the story he had to send out his eye—at that moment he was still incompletely formed and had only the one—in search of his children. When the eye returned, it found that, while it had been gone, Ra had grown a second one, which angered it. In order to calm the situation, Ra gave his first eye, the sun, greater power than his second, the moon. The first he expressed as the rearing cobra that you will see on his head and which you will also see as a protective headdress worn subsequently by the Pharaohs.

Once he had eyes and children, Ra wept, and his tears became humans. Meanwhile, Shu and Tefnut had been busy procreating, and the results of their

by the Sicilian general Jawhar Al Siqilli finally succeeded in taking the country from the local allies of Baghdad, the Ikhshidid Dynasty, in A.D. 969. Al Mu'izz ledin Allah was the Fatimid caliph at the time, and his very first order concerning Egypt was to build a new capital; it was named Al Qahira (The Victorious). Four years later, Al Mu'izz transferred the Fatimid caliphate capital from Mahdia in Tunisia to his newly built Al Qahira; the massive walls of the city define much of what we now know as Islamic Cairo.

As outsiders, the Fatimids trod lightly when it came to religion. Though they were prodigious in their construction of monuments (which include Al Azhar Mosque and Bab Zuweila, p. 116), there was little pressure on the mass of Sunnis to conform to Shiite practice (though there was at times heavy promotion of Shiite festivals), and Christians and Jews alike (despite a few notable and violent exceptions) were allowed to go about their lives. On the whole, the Fatimids presided over a period of stability and relative prosperity in which education and the spread of knowledge (they endowed several large public libraries and countless schools) were high priorities. Moreover, they inherited holdings built up by two strong and capable short-lived dynasties, the Tulunid and the Ikhshidid, and had the resources not only of North Africa to draw upon, but Syria and Sicily as well.

The first three Fatimid rulers were strong and competent (though the third was more eccentric), but the government began to crack soon after with a series of young and incompetent caliphs who union were Geb, the God of the Earth, and Nut, the Goddess of the Sky. Geb was depicted with a goose on his head, and is often referenced with a picture of a goose alone. Nut, on the other hand, was frequently depicted as a naked woman arched over the world. It is in this capacity that she was thought to give birth to the sun each morning and then eat it in evening.

It was Geb and Nut who ultimately gave birth to most of the rest of the gods who figure in Ancient Egyptian cosmology, but first there was a problem that had to be overcome. It seems that Ra himself, the most powerful god, was in love with Nut, and when he found out that she and Geb were involved (so to speak), he cursed her, saying that she would not be able to give birth on any day of the month. The cosmos were evolving, however, and soon enough a loophole opened up. Thoth, the God of Wisdom, who was also associated with the moon, somehow wrested from the moon 5 extra days.

The connection to the mundane world is clear: The Ancient Egyptian calendar added 5 days to the end of the year to make up for the shortcomings of the lunar year. The cosmological significance, however, was even more profound. During these days—which belonged to no month—Nut rapidly began to have children. In short succession, she gave birth to Osiris, Horus, Set, Isis, and Nephthys. With these, the basic cosmological population of Ancient Egypt was complete, and the long drama of their conflicts and loves could begin in earnest.

allowed the government to slip into the hands of military commanders and the economy into shambles. Amidst the turmoil, a Sunni Kurd by the name of Salah Al Din Yusuf Ayyub gradually ascended to power; first by taking the post of vizier (chief minister) of Egypt in 1169. By this point, the Fatimid caliphate was in the hands of a scattering of querulous, epigenous siblings who were not up to the challenge of running Cairo, let alone a whole country under attack from a wearying succession of heavily armed invaders from the still undeveloped northern regions of Europe. After briefly reverting to the Abbasid court, Salah Al Din declared himself Sultan of Egypt and established the Ayyubid Dynasty (1174–1250).

Salah Al Din immediately set about modernizing the defenses of Cairo, which included the construction of the Citadel (p. 118) that now overlooks the old Fatimid city and the completion of expanded walls. He then set about using his rule of both Syria and Egypt to stop the crusaders and shove the plundering hordes of Christian Europeans back to their miserable chilly climes. The Ayyubid Dynasty sowed the seeds of its own destruction with one of the keystones of their military successes against the Europeans—Mamluks.

THE SLAVE KINGS Mamluk literally means "the owned," and though the practice of conscripting imported slaves into the army was first practiced by the Abbasids, the Ayyubids heavily relied on it. Forming ruthless and highly effective corps of soldiers without particular ties to soil or family, Mamluks quickly seized

Gods & Goddesses of Ancient Egypt

At a time when man worshiped powers of nature, out of fear rather than belief, the Ancient Egyptian mythology tackled heaven and hell, and the afterlife. Ancient Egyptians worshiped a wide array of deities, though at the end they all traced back to one—Ra. Polytheistic or monotheistic, opinions vary; all agree, however, that it is rather mystical.

Amun (Amun-Ra): Though worshiped as early as the 5th Dynasty, it wasn't until the 11th Dynasty that this god had temples dedicated to him. His importance was linked with the shift of power from the north to the Upper Egyptian city of Thebes, where he became the King of Gods. His temple at Karnak is one of the most impressive monuments in Egypt. He was usually shown as a human with a double crown, holding a staff in one hand and an ankh in the other.

Anubis: The God of Mummification and the dead is usually shown as a human figure with a black head of a jackal; his black color associates him with decaying bodies (death), and he is mostly depicted on tombs. Anubis's list of duties included overseeing the mummification process and placing the heart on the Scales of Justice during the Judging of the Heart. Those who fail the test suffer a second death, as they would be fed to Ammit. A personification of divine retribution, Ammit is often portrayed as a hybrid of three creatures: a crocodile's head, a lion's upper torso, and a hippo's lower one.

Geb: The God of Earth was often portrayed as a crowned man. Vegetation sprung from his body, and earthquakes were his laughter.

Hathor: The Goddess of Joy, Music, and Love is depicted as either a cow with a sun disc between her horns or a woman in queenly raiment with a tiara of a sun disc embedded between cow horns. With artisans, musicians, and dancers as her priests, rituals involved in the cult of Hathor were nothing less than works of art. Stories have it that Ra was once depressed, and in order to cheer him up, Hathor danced for him. Since then, she has been seen as an incarnation of dance.

Horus: The King of Gods on earth was a multifaceted and almost ubiquitous god, of whom there were more than a dozen manifestations. One of these is the winged sun disc that you will see over the doorways of many temples. It signifies that you are under the protection of the gods. Horus was also the falcon, and in this form you will see him all over the place, including on the EgyptAir logo. Horus is the happy ending to Osiris's legend.

Isis: Depicted as a beautiful woman in a long sheath dress, the major goddess of the Egyptian pantheon was often begged for guidance, pleaded with for peace, and regarded as a foremost protector. Isis held the title Queen of Gods, and she played the leading heroine in the mythical Osiris legend. Worshiping Isis was rather universal, extending to the Greco-Roman World as soon as Alexander the Great conquered Egypt.

Maat: The whole universe would have succumbed to disorder if it wasn't for Maat, Lady of Truth and Order. During the Judging of the Heart, one's heart would be put on the Scales of Justice and weighed against the feather of Maat. Ancient Egyptians believed the heart was where the soul resided. Those whose souls were pure of sin would have hearts that wouldn't outweigh Maat's feather, leaving the scale balanced, and would be permitted to Aaru, the Pharaoh's version of heaven.

Nephthys: Lady of the Wings, she casts her protection upon household women. She is Isis and Osiris's sister and Set's sister-wife.

Nun: Nun was the God of the Primeval Waters, which were Ra's precreation dwelling. After order was imposed by Ra's act of spitting out Shu and Tefnut, Nun did not vanish but receded to the edge of being and became the abode of luminal beings. If you can spot the wavy-patterned paving at the edges of Karnak Temple, you will have found the realm of Nun surrounding the well-ordered and safe home of the gods. If you see Nun depicted as a man bearing a solar boat laden with human figures, he is representing the underworld.

Nut: The Goddess of the Sky is seen arched over other figures, depicted as a naked woman. She was the protector of the gods and the mother of Osiris, Set, Isis, and Nephthys.

Osiris: A god of wide-ranging powers over death and resurrection, as well as the underworld, Lord of the Dead, Osiris, was also the first king of humans. He is often shown as a mummy, whose hands stick out through the white cloth wrapping his body, and wearing a distinctive crown with twin plumes.

Ra: The god of all gods, Ra is the one who gave birth to the first two other gods, Shu and Tefnut, and brought order to the original chaos. One of his main functions was to pilot the solar boat across the sky each day, and you will often see him seated in a boat with the rearing cobra of the sun on his head.

Set: One of the children of Geb and Nut, Set was the God of Violence, Darkness, and Chaos. He was driven to the desert by Horus, his nephew, after he murdered Osiris.

Shu: The God of Air was one of the first gods, along with his sister Tefnut, to be born to Ra. Like Atlas to the Greeks, Shu carried the heavens, stopping it from falling on earth.

Tefnut: The Goddess of Mist once argued with her brother and left for Nubia. Disguised as a cat, she destroyed any human or god who approached her. Only Thoth managed to convince her to return.

Thoth: Depicted with the head of an ibis, Thoth was the God of Wisdom and Science. It was Thoth who helped Osiris to bring civilization to mankind and who helped Anubis with the first rites of mummification that led to Osiris's resurrection.

The Cruelest Cut: The Tale of Two Brothers

One of the most dramatic conflicts of Egyptian mythology took place between Osiris, the God of the Underworld, and his brother Set, the red-headed God of Violence and Darkness. The story developed over centuries, adding some aspects and altering others, but one of the more complete versions goes like this:

Osiris, in his human form, was a good and wise king of the humans, bringing them civilization, agriculture, and wine with the assistance of Thoth, God of Wisdom. He was so popular and successful, in fact, that he aroused the jealousy of his brother Set, who one day tricked him into laying down in an elaborately decorated coffin. Set then sealed the coffin with hot lead so that his brother would asphyxiate, and threw it into the Nile. When Osiris's wife Isis found out about the murder, she set out to find the coffin. The first thing she found, however, was that her husband had had a brief affair with her sister, Set's wife, and that a child had been born as a result. Fearing Set's anger, Isis's sister had abandoned the child in the forest. Isis immediately went out and found the boy, who had (in a manner typical of the abandoned progeny of gods) been protected by wild dogs and took him in, naming him Anubis.

Eventually the coffin was found on the shores of a distant land (one account has this as the coast of Syria) and brought back to Egypt. The unremittingly vengeful Set, however, tracked it down, and this time tore Osiris's corpse into between 14 and 42 pieces (sources vary on this point). He threw the pieces, once again, into the river.

Isis set out untiringly once again to find the body, this time traveling the length of Egypt to retrieve the pieces. Whenever she found a piece, she engaged in an elaborate ruse to conceal from Set what she was up to. She pretended to bury the body part on the spot, but actually concealed it on her person and transported it to her home, where Anubis, with the help of Thoth, was gradually putting his uncle back together again. In the end, she found almost all the pieces—unfortunately Osiris's phallus had been eaten by a Nile carp and a fake one had to be substituted. Even so, the story had a happy ending: The reassembled Osiris was revived and was able to father Horus before ascending to heaven. Horus subsequently vanquished Set in a series of trials and banished him to the desert.

control, marrying into the royal lineage. In 1249, Al Malik Al Salih, the last Ayyubid Sultan, died. His widow and de facto ruler of Egypt, Shagaret Al Durr (for whom a street in Zamalek is still named), wanted to ensure her grip on power; she married Izz Al Din Aybak, a top-ranking Turkic Mamluk. This marked the birth of the first Mamluk sultanate, known as the Bahri Dynasty (1250–1382). Though they repeatedly defeated several Mongol invasions and fought the remnant Crusader States in Palestine, treachery was deeply imbedded in the system. Over a span of 132 years, the Bahri Dynasty had 31 different sultans. The succeeding Burji Dynasty (1382–1517) was even more turbulent; conspiracies, murders, and treason in the royal palace were common. Nevertheless, during breaks from the bloody race to power, several remarkable monuments were erected; Islamic Cairo

(p. 114) is awash with Mamluki heritage. The Burji Dynasty was established after a revolt in Syria broke out, and later spread to Egypt, when the Circassian Mamluk Al Zahir Barkuk took over. After 134 years, the days of power for the Mamluk were numbered, as Janissaries from the Anatolian highlands were on the march. The Ottomans were coming.

THE OTTOMANS On August 24, 1516, before the second-to-last Mamluk Sultan, Qansuh Al Ghuri, could properly engage with the Ottoman forces in the Battle of Marj Dabiq, near Aleppo, Syria, Ottoman artillery devastated his forces. In January 1517, Selim I, often known as Selim the Grim, entered Cairo after the 1-day Battle of Raydaniyah took place outside the capital. The Ottomans dealt with Egypt just as the Romans had; they milked the cash cow through exploitation and heavy taxation. The heydays of art and architecture that flourished during the preceding Mamluks came to an end, and the country was left in neglect. Though the Mamluk sultanate was now part of history books, the Mamluks themselves lingered on, remaining as the lords of the society after changing their title to *bey.* In fact, their power grew once more and started rivaling that of the pasha (at the time, it was the title for the Ottoman governor; now, etymologic *basha* is a colloquial word that substitutes for Mr.). Nonetheless, enmity retained its former position among the *beys,* as it once did among the Mamluks. By the end of the 18th century, Egypt was on the brink of disintegration. This ostensibly paved the way for another European military campaign. No crusaders this time, but rather a restless erratic leader by the name of Napoleon Bonaparte.

THE FRENCH INTERLUDE Though brief, Napoleon's occupation marks a key moment in European relations with Egypt. Previous invasions from Europe had been beaten back, if not easily then at least effectively. Not so this time. At the Battle of the Pyramids in July 1798, Napoleon's musket-armed infantry thrashed the cavalry-based Mamluk army. Despite this crushing tactical triumph, the strategic situation was about to get dramatically worse. Unfortunately for Napoleon, a British fleet under Horatio Nelson was already stalking Napoleon's naval forces off Alexandria. The French fleet was totally destroyed.

Along with his army, Napoleon imported a team of more than 150 civilian scholars, as well as around 2,000 engravers and artists. They spent their time cataloging everything they could get their hands on. Eventually they were able to produce the *Description of Egypt,* a mammoth (some of the volumes are nearly 1m/3⅓-ft. squares) 20- or 37-volume (depending on the edition) set of plates and texts on just about everything in Egypt. This included some

Trading Up

To finance all the campaigns and coups that marked their age, the Mamluks needed a lucrative monetary source—trade. Playing the role of middlemen, they controlled land and sea trade routes connecting South and Southeast Asia to Europe. As international trade grew and commercial exchange intensified, several trade deals were signed primarily with Venice, which in turn became their favorite trading partner. It is believed that Venetians had permanent diplomatic representatives in major cities across the Mamluk sultanate. Francesco Foscari, the famous Doge of Venice, was born in Mamluk Egypt.

Fun Facts **The Last of the Mamluks**

Dutch painter Willem De Famars Testas's *The Last of the Mamluks* is inspired by the myth of Hassan, who escaped from the Citadel when he apparently cut his way through the Turks and jumped, while on his horse, off the Citadel's walls.

dramatically large monuments and a good number of Pharaonic artifacts, decorated with a mixture of pictorial symbols, that remained undecipherable until the Rosetta Stone—also unearthed by the French—was translated 30 years later. Apart from their academic value, the illustrations of massive ruined temples would define Egypt for many decades in the European mind as the seat of a mysterious and powerful lost civilization.

Sensing the inevitability of embarrassing failure, Napoleon got out of Egypt in 1799, leaving his army to struggle against a combination of Ottoman and British forces. Decimated by disease and conflict, the remnants of the army he left behind were shipped back to France by 1802.

MODERNIZATION OF EGYPT In the wake of the French retreat from Egypt, the Ottoman administration in Istanbul appointed an Albanian, Mohamed Ali, viceroy of the reclaimed province. The new ruler took power in 1805, and 6 years later liquidated what remained of the Mamluks in a classic piece of ruthless treachery. Having invited them to dine at the Citadel, he allowed them to leave together through Bab Al Azab, the gate that now lets out onto Midan Al Qala'a, below the Citadel and in front of the Madrasa of Sultan Hassan. Though the gate is unfortunately now sealed, you can see from the walls above that between the top and the lower gates there is a narrow defile enclosed by high walls. Once his guests were in this chute, Mohamed Ali simply had both gates closed, and from there it was a simple enough matter to have his loyalists shoot the well-fed and probably tipsy Mamluks. Having thus eliminated the possibility of serious opposition, Mohamed Ali could set about pursuing a remarkably energetic policy of reform and modernization aimed at bringing Egypt up to military and economic parity with Europe. He succeeded to a great extent, building a navy and an army that was the most effective in the region and forcing the Ottoman sultan to establish his family as the hereditary rulers of Egypt. To finance his ambitious reforms, Mohamed Ali converted much of Egyptian agriculture to the production of cotton for sale in Europe.

Mohamed Ali died in 1849, and his successors, primarily his grandson Ismail Pasha, continued the path of modernization. Once he clinched an Ottoman decree granting more sovereignty and declaring the Khedivate of Egypt, Ismail Pasha went on a reform spree. Old canals were repaired and new ones dug, a postal service was founded, bridges were erected across the Nile, and a magnificent opera house was built. One particular reform, however, was to have unforeseen consequences: opening Egypt to Western expertise and investment also made it possible to start borrowing money in large quantities. Initially, harsh taxation and manipulating the cotton market had been sufficient to balance out the budget, but soon enough the practice of borrowing money to make up for domestic shortfalls became commonplace. By 1875, debts driven by the expense of modernization and a profligate elite brought Egypt's financial situation to a precarious status, and the country's share of the Suez Canal was sold to the British.

THE BRITISH OCCUPATION By the 1870s, Egypt's financial position had gotten worse. While the masses were squeezed to make ends meet, the elite enjoyed a relaxed life. European involvement infiltrated the country in all aspects: the civil service, the army, and business. The situation was aggravating. Egyptian army general Ahmed Urabi led a nationalist movement that became known as the Urabi Movement. Chanting the slogan "Egypt for the Egyptians," anti-European riots erupted in Alexandria on June 11, 1882. Fearing Urabi would depose the Ottoman khedive and nationalize the Suez Canal, the British fleet intervened, bombarding the coastal city of Alexandria with inappropriate force. By September the same year, British ground troops landed in Ismailia and engaged with the Egyptian forces at the Battle of El Tell El Kebir. Superior military proved successful for the British; Ahmed Urabi Pasha was defeated and later exiled in Ceylon, and Egypt was effectively occupied.

The sole development in Egypt under British occupation was commercialized tourism. Fueled by images of Ancient ruins brought back by the French expedition, Egypt quickly became a required stop on any grand tour. At first it was the reserve of a wealthy few, but by the end of the 19th century, with British troops on the ground in Cairo to guarantee the safety of Her Majesty's middle classes, Egypt was open to anybody with time for a vacation and the money for passage on one of the regular liners.

Parallel to the opening of the tourist market ran the development of archaeology. This, too, began as a pastime for those wealthy enough to winter at the aptly named **Winter Palace** (p. 281) in Luxor and fund a crew of locals to dig about in what became known as the **Valley of the Kings** (p. 274). The British attempted to control the process by forming a professional antiquities service that supervised the digging and tried to ensure that the most significant pieces stayed in Egypt, but local dealers and diggers, delighted at this sudden cash market for buried leftovers, went to work, and soon enough, between local supply and foreign demand, a roaring export trade in everything from pottery to mummies had developed. It was after World War I before the professionals started to get a grip on the situation and qualified, institutional projects began to be favored over the efforts of financially gifted amateurs.

THE ROAD TO INDEPENDENCE As World War I broke out, the British and Ottomans stood on opposite sides of the frontier. Egypt severed all ties with Istanbul, and the sultanate of Egypt was declared as a British protectorate. By the end of the war, nationalistic sentiments

Fun Facts Money Well Spent

One-time viceroy of Egypt, Khedive Ismail, appreciated the arts. He commissioned Italian opera composer Giuseppe Verdi for 150,000 francs to write *Aida,* which premiered at the Khedival Opera House in Cairo on Christmas Eve, 1871. To commemorate the inauguration of the Suez Canal, he commissioned Frenchman Frédéric Auguste Bartholdi to sculpt a huge statue of a woman bearing a torch. Because the canal drained Egypt's budget, the *Light of Asia* statue was remodeled into what eventually became the Statue of Liberty.

grew stronger, materializing into a political party known as Al Wafd (The Delegate). A group of Al Wafd, led by patriotic Saad Zaghloul, requested to attend the Paris Peace Conference in an attempt to lobby for independence. As their plea fell on deaf ears, Saad Zaghloul distributed thousands of "power of attorney" papers to be signed by Egyptian citizens. The campaign proved successful and posed a threat to the British occupiers. On March 8, 1919, Saad Zaghloul and two other Al Wafd leaders were deported to Malta. This sparked the nonviolent civil disobedience movement known as the Egyptian Revolution of 1919. Three years down the line, Egypt was declared independent, and a new constitution was implemented the following year. However, the independence was rather nominal, as the British retained their power over the country's foreign affairs, Sudan (part of the Anglo-Egyptian Condominium since 1899), and most importantly the Suez Canal. Puppet Sultan Fuad I issued a decree adopting the title King of Egypt.

In 1936, King Farouk succeeded his father King Fuad I. Claiming the title King of Egypt and Sudan, once in office, he immediately signed the Anglo-Egyptian Treaty of 1936. Egypt's independence was once again crippled by the treaty's own articles. It dictated, among other conditions, that as part of a military alliance all British troops be withdrawn from Egypt, other than a 10,000-men force and 400 Royal Air Force stationed in the Suez Canal Zone. The treaty was largely overlooked once World War II broke out. Though Egypt retained a neutral position, it played a strategic pivotal role with the Allies in a bid to halt the Axis drive across North Africa. The struggle came to a head in 1942 at El Alamein, a virtually empty stretch of desert on the north coast some 80km (50 miles) west of Alexandria. German and Italian tank and infantry had been making rapid eastward progress that, had it not been halted, would have resulted in them capturing strategically vital supply routes and oil supplies, dealing the Allied war effort in Europe a serious blow. Ultimately victorious at El Alamein, however, the Allies were then able to reverse the defeats of the previous months and put an end to German and Italian ambitions in the Middle East.

By the end of World War II, it was clear that the era of direct colonial rule in the region was over. Anti-colonial sentiments grew, and were rather augmented after the Arab armies' (Egypt included) defeat in 1948, the first of the Arab-Israeli ongoing conflict series. By October 1951, patriotic Egyptians turned to guerrilla warfare in the Canal Zone. And on January 25, 1952, British troops stationed in Ismailia attacked an Egyptian police barrack resulting in the deaths of 50 Egyptian policemen. The very next day, violent riots broke out in Cairo, torching and burning anything and everything foreign-related. At

The Mummy Parties

Fueled by a fervent craze for anything Ancient Egyptian, a dreadful trend came into fashion during the 19th century—mummy parties. During the so-called social gatherings, smuggled mummies were unwrapped to fulfill the host's ego and then disposed of. Amulets were often given as gifts for high profile guests; mummies' linen wrappings were used to make thick, dark paper for butchers' use; and mummy bodies were used as material for oil paint dubbed "mummy brown."

Fun Facts Ladies First

The Egyptian Revolution in 1919 marked the first time local women participated in protests. Chanting the slogan "Long live the crescent with the cross," they used civil disobedience to pressure the oppressing regimes.

the end of "Black Saturday," 750 establishments had been burned to the ground, 30 people lost their lives, and hundreds were injured. Six months later, on July 23 (now observed as Egypt's National Day), a group of officers known as the Free Officers Movement, led by Lieutenant General Mohamed Naguib, overthrew the British-protected government and forced King Farouk to abdicate. The following day, King Farouk boarded his royal yacht and sailed into exile. He was accompanied by his 6-month-old son, Fuad II, who, at that point in time, was the last king of Egypt.

HEROIC YEARS—TROUBLED YEARS Though the revolution was led by Mohamed Naguib, who the Free Officers initially installed as president in January 1953, after dissolving all political parties, abrogating the constitution, and establishing the republic, his role was rather symbolic. The one who held all the marionette threads was the charismatic army officer Gamal Abdel Nasser. In 1954, after Mohamed Naguib was forced to resign, Nasser assumed the responsibility of Egypt's Head of State. Negotiations with the British were underway, and a withdrawal agreement was formulated. The last British soldier left the Suez Canal on June 18, 1956. Nasser's group of officers arrived under the banner of reform; however, they didn't have any specific program in mind. Most of their initial moves were aimed at consolidating control, and over the next 4 years political parties were banned; foreign companies were nationalized; the main representative of the Islamic Movement, Muslim Brotherhood, was made illegal; and a new constitution was promulgated to give President Nasser broad powers over the government.

One of Nasser's first moves on the international stage marked a significant turning point in Egypt's relationship with the West. When the World Bank backed out of a tentative agreement to fund the building of the Aswan High Dam, Nasser announced that he would nationalize the Suez Canal and use the revenue to pay for the dam. The canal was still jointly owned by the British (who had purchased Egypt's share of the waterway 80 years before) and the French, who had acquired the original concession to build it. At the same time, Egypt closed the Strait of Tiran (now a prime diving spot off the coastal resort city of Sharm El Sheikh) to Israeli shipping, choking off a key supply route of oil, largely provided by Iran at the time.

The announcement and the closure of a vital shipping lane prompted a joint British, French, and Israeli operation to attack Egyptian forces in the Canal Zone in the fall of 1956. They were quickly forced to withdraw by the United States, which had initially acquiesced to the plan. Once the forces had withdrawn, Egypt seized not only the canal but other British- and French-held businesses in the rest of the country. The U.S.S.R. subsequently funded the construction of the Aswan High Dam.

Nasser's apparent victory over the former colonial powers made him enormously popular in Egypt and throughout the Middle East; it turned him into a major force in regional politics and a

Fun Facts **Sixth of October: The Landmarks**

Egypt's victory on the 6th of October is commemorated throughout the city: The notoriously jampacked bridge you are destined to use during your visit to the capital, a newly built university, and a Cairene suburb are all named after it.

leader of the pan-Arab movement. Nasser endorsed anti-colonial revolutions and inspired other Arab nationalist leaders, namely Muammar Al-Gaddafi of Libya and Ahmed Ben Bella of Algeria. In 1958, in a bid to promote Arab Nationalism, Egypt and Syria merged. Short-lived, the United Arab Republic, headed by Nasser, dissolved 3 years later after Syria seceded. Nasser's fast-growing reputation took a heavy blow in 1967 when Israel launched a military offense known as the Six-Day War. Defeating another Arab coalition, it succeeded in annexing the Sinai Peninsula from Egypt, the Golan Heights from Syria, and Palestine's West Bank and East Jerusalem from Jordan. In the wake of the loss, Nasser tendered his resignation but stayed on after massive demonstrations of support. He died in 1970 of a heart attack.

Nasser was succeeded by his vice president, Colonel Anwar El Sadat. Sadat, though expected initially to be a transitional figure, maintained his control, consolidated his position against his rivals, and became a power in his own right. He reversed a number of Nasser's positions, reopening Egypt to the West and ultimately making peace with Israel. The high point of his presidency came on October 6, 1973, when Egyptian forces launched a surprise and boldly executed attack on the well-fortified Israeli defenses on the Suez Canal's east bank. The attack, orchestrated with a massive Syrian attack on the Golan Heights, commenced what came to be known as the October War, or the Yom Kippur War, as it coincided with Jews' holiest day of the year. On October 22, the U.N. Security Council passed Resolution 338, calling for a cease-fire. Most heavy fighting came to a halt 2 days later.

The years that followed witnessed several peace processes that were more show than substance. Frustrated by this, Sadat took matters in his own hands. In 1977, while delivering a speech in Egypt, he stated that he would go anywhere, even Jerusalem, to discuss peace. Israel responded positively, and Sadat was the first Arab leader to visit the state. On one hand, it boosted the peace process, eventually leading to full normalization of diplomatic relations, but on the other, Egypt's relations with other Arab states deteriorated excessively, leading to Egypt's suspension from the Arab League in 1979. Egypt's position as a regional pro-Arabism sponsor was lost overnight. U.S. President Jimmy Carter brokered the renowned Camp David Accords, which were finally signed on September 18, 1978. The Israel-Egypt Peace Treaty followed suit 1 year later. Under both agreements, Egypt restored its sovereignty over Sinai, though the peninsula would remain largely demilitarized. Egypt was also handed an annual aid package second in size only to Israel's. In return, Israel was guaranteed freedom of passage through the Suez Canal and other nearby waterways (primarily the Strait of Tiran), state recognition, and formal establishment of diplomatic ties. Sadat and Israeli Prime Minister Menachem Begin were jointly awarded the Nobel Peace Prize in 1978. Evoking Islamists' scorn back home, Sadat's presidency was abruptly cut short in 1981. He was

Fun Facts **Death to the Pharaoh**

It is said that while lead assassin Khalid El Islambouli shot at Sadat he cried, "Death to the Pharaoh!" In colloquial Egyptian Arabic, *fara'aon* (Pharaoh), is a word often used to refer to someone as a tyrant. This is mainly driven by the portrayal in the Quran of the Old Testament Pharaoh of Egypt as an outright autocrat.

assassinated by members of an Islamic organization while reviewing troops at the annual 6th of October military parade. Air Force General and Vice President Hosni Mubarak took over as Egypt's fourth, and current, president.

4 ART & ARCHITECTURE

ARCHITECTURE

Ever since the birth of Egyptian civilization, architecture has played a key role in the lives of Egyptians, if not for ordinary men, then certainly for glory-seeker rulers; from grandiose Pharaonic pyramids and temples to Mamluki mosques with finely carved minarets and later the Belle Epoque of Cairo's Downtown with its exquisite Art Deco.

DAYS OF THE TEMPLES Any architectural tour of Egypt should start with the Great Pyramid of Khufu at Giza. Pause for a moment to consider it not as simply a gigantic heap of rock or a historical monument so photographed it has been familiar to you since childhood, but as a very large public work of art. The symmetry and proportions are a stunning combination of grandiosity and simplicity and make much that followed seem somewhat overweening by comparison.

Some of the most impressive artifacts of later Pharaonic periods are the temples. You'll notice after visiting a few that they tend to follow a standard pattern. Remember as you enter that you are being led on a symbolic journey from the mundane world of the living, a world of space and light, to the realm of the gods. Notice how spaces become more cramped, with ceilings lowering and sometimes the floor coming up as well, and the light is more restricted as you penetrate toward the core of the temple. The main entrance is through the middle of a massive wall, called a pylon. When the temple was in use, the pylon would have been topped by a row of colorful flags that snapped and waved in the breeze. Inside, you'll find yourself in a courtyard. Beyond the courtyard is a densely columned hypostyle (a Greek term that simply means "supported by pillars") hall that was originally roofed and only dimly lit by small, high windows. At the back of the hall there is the bark of the god, the place his or her representation was set for ceremonies. Beyond the bark is the *naos,* an enclosed cabinet—the smallest and darkest place in the whole temple—where the representation of the god was kept.

You will find these patterns played out over and over again, at temples such as Luxor, Karnak (though keep in mind here that it was built and enlarged by successive rulers), and Edfu.

The people who built the temples, meanwhile, weren't living in them, of course. It should come as no surprise, however, that a society as sophisticated as the Egyptians, and with as much engineering knowledge and architectural finesse, developed very comfortable domestic housing. By the Middle Kingdom, three- and even four-story urban houses were common, with amenities that would not be developed in Europe for more than 3,000 years. Ruins show that a central courtyard, or a large room with a high, column-supported ceiling, was common, as well as stairwells to contain internal staircases, comfortable bedrooms, and tiled bathrooms with running water.

MINARETS Cairo has one of the richest collections of Islamic architecture in the world, densely congregated in Islamic Cairo. It offers a wide array of architecture and styles from the different epochs and eras of the Islamic Empire. As you wander through their courtyards and admire the arches, towers, and decorations that make these magnificent structures some of the greatest religious monuments in the world, noticing a few simple aspects will help you locate yourself in a sometimes-confusing mass of historical details.

The single easiest feature to pick out when you look at a mosque is its minarets—the towers from which the call to prayer is issued five times a day. Almost every mosque has at least one. Interestingly, the first mosque in Egypt (in Africa, for that matter), the mosque of Amr Ibn Al A'as (named for the leader of the army that successfully defeated the Byzantine defenders of Egypt in 640), was built without minarets. They were added some 30 years after the mosque was first built and have been rebuilt several times since. The design of the minarets that you will see, however, changes quite clearly over time. They start with the simple, square Ayyubid tower with a veranda, on top of which there is a second, slightly more elaborate stage with a simple dome on top. The Mamluks elaborated on this with two, or even three, separate stages above the first veranda. The pencil-shaped Ottoman minarets, meanwhile, represent a visually striking contrast with their predecessors. Know your minarets, then, and you'll know the period of the mosque you're looking at.

The other fairly easy and reliable clues can be had by looking at the shape of the door and window arches. Pointed arches, which you will see in many periods, came into use early, but the keel arch, which you see in the porticos at Al Azhar, was a distinctly Fatimid innovation. With Mamluk designs, however, you begin to see square-shaped windows and windows with bands of different-colored stones.

One of my favorite mosques anywhere is the Ibn Tulun Mosque in Cairo. This is pretty much all that remains of Al Qatai, the capital that was built by the short-lived Tulunid Dynasty (868–905). Ahmed Ibn Tulun, to whom the Ibn Tulun Mosque is attributed, was raised at the Abbasid court in Iraq. It is apparent how he was influenced by Samarra's Great Mosque of Al Mutawakil and its renowned Spiral Minaret. Three main similarities to notice as you enter: First is the *ziyada*. This literally means "extra," and refers to the extra land that lies like a moat around the mosque. This separates the mosque, as a holy place, from the marketplace, and gives the whole building a tranquil quietness. Second is the plaster decoration—the arches are crusted with carved stucco. These touches are directly imported from Samarra in Mesopotamia. Third is the minaret, with its semi-spiral design. It is said that there are a thousand minarets that loom in Cairo's horizon; this is the only spiral one.

Though the mosque of Ibn Tulun has distinct features, it also has similarities with other mosques, such as the *mihrab*, the niche in the wall that indicates the direction of Mecca. Originally there was a single *mihrab*, above which is written the standard Muslim opening to prayer, "There is no god but Allah, and Mohammad is the messenger of Allah," but over the years several more have been added. Note also the *minbar*, or the often-wooden pulpit, reached by a set of stairs, from which the Friday sermon is delivered. *Sahn,* the central courtyard, is also a feature of some later mosques, such as Al Hakim, Barkuk, and Al Azhar.

Al Azhar is probably the most famous of Cairo's Fatimid mosques, though it has been added to and reworked so much that it's unfair to credit any particular dynasty now with the whole. The entrance is typically Mamluk, but the central courtyard is all Fatimid. Note particularly how the keel arch of the porticos contrast with the pointed Mamluk arches.

When it comes to Mamluk- and Ottoman-style architecture, Cairo provides a lovely juxtaposition in the Madrasa of Sultan Hassan and the Mosque of Mohamed Ali. The massive *madrasa* is located immediately below the Citadel where, almost 5 centuries later, Mohamed Ali would build his mosque.

The *madrasa* is a great example of Mamluk architecture. Not only does it have typical minarets, with multiple upper stages, but the sheer mass of it shows the Mamluk tendency to overawe with size. Inside, the big difference from the earlier buildings is that the congregational layout had been left far behind in favor of a cruciform plan in which the central courtyard opens into four enormous *liwans* (covered spaces that are enclosed on three sides). Each *liwan* was devoted to one of the four *madrasas* that existed here, and the doors on the back walls lead to student accommodations. Decorative glass lamps would have hung for light, and the stone paneling is also fairly typical of Mamluk buildings.

The Mosque of Mohamed Ali, meanwhile, is immediately identifiable from any angle as an Ottoman mosque and will look familiar to anyone who has visited Istanbul. Even from below you can see its large dome and tall, thin minarets. If you do visit the Citadel and go inside the mosque, check out the ablution area in the middle of the courtyard, as it is distinctively Turkish.

ART DECO A revival in Egypt's architecture was sparked by one of Khedive Ismail's visits to Paris. Struck by the layout of the city, he came back with a Cairo makeover plan. Tree-lined streets, statues-adorned roundabouts, and finely decorated Parisian-inspired buildings; this is how Downtown, then called Ismailia, looked at the height of Egypt's Belle Epoque. Another wave of architecture splendors came in the early 20th century, when Belgian industrialist Baron Empain arrived in Egypt. Eyeing a railway tender, he lost the bid to a British competitor but ended up building the new town of Heliopolis. Targeting luxury seekers, Heliopolis, known also as Misr El Gedida, was made up of large avenues, huge gardens, terraced villas, and residence blocks with spacious balconies. A stroll on Korba (the most well-preserved remaining avenue) is a must for architecture enthusiasts as is a stop at Empain's Indian-inspired **Baron Palace** (p. 114). Sadly, after the 1952 revolution, most of the nouveau riche, aristocrats, and foreign residents fled the country, and their property fell in disrepair; deterioration was inevitable. Downtown, however, was luckier than Heliopolis, as the latter fell victim to cash-hungry property developers and an exploding population, resulting in cement high-rises that mark the disappearance of a once beautiful Heliopolis.

ART

Art is a cultural milestone that goes hand in hand with civilization, and at times even precedes it. In a country with a 5,000-year-old civilization, art is an ever-changing world of schools, techniques, shapes, and concepts.

ART FOR THE DEAD It is fairly conclusive to assume Ancient Egyptian art to be of a religious nature. Whether Pharaohs or commoners, Ancient Egyptians highly valued religion, death, and the life after it; no wonder temples and tombs constitute the majority of monuments they left behind. From crafting papyrus and clay pottery to carving gigantic statues and painting tomb walls in lively colors, art in Ancient Egypt took different shapes and forms. Ancient Egyptians excelled in papyrus crafting, using it for both writing as well as painting. Among the most famous is the papyrus known as the *Book of the Dead,* an illustrated funerary text that accompanies the deceased in his journey to the afterlife. The use of vases and amulets weren't restricted to decorative purposes; they were also important objects placed in tombs and were used as containers for the deceased's body parts, which were removed during mummification. Ancient Egyptians were excellent sculptors, meticulously carving small statues as well as gargantuan ones; head to Abu Simbel for the four 20m-high (67-ft.) seated statues of Ramses II, or to Luxor for the 18m-high (60-ft.) twin statues making up the Colossi of Memnon. Mineral-based paints, through the work of talented artisans, tell stories more than 3,000 years old, from day-to-day scenes and portraits of Pharaohs to heroic war epics and the journey to the afterlife. Through the different Egyptian kingdoms, art portrayed the human figure with perfectly chiseled body lines, but this was temporarily forsaken for a more creative and kinetic school, known as Amarna Art. Associated with Akhetaten, the newly established capital at Tell El Amarna, Amarna Art brought more life into the depicted scenes, ditched the classic perfect lines and adapted more realistic curvy ones, and started portraying human figures as individuals: Some enjoyed a slimmer body, while others were depicted with big thighs and prominent breasts. In a way, Amarna Art was Ancient Egypt's Renaissance, but, like the new capital, it, too, was short-lived.

ICONOGRAPHY Funerary masks existed since the time of the Pharaohs, but by the 1st century B.C. they took a different twist. A self portrait was painted on a wooden panel that covered the face, and at times the face and the upper chest. This was often attached to the deceased's coffin. Since most of the recovered ones were from the Fayum area, they were dubbed the Fayum Portraits (on display at the Egyptian Museum, p. 104, as well as the Metropolitan, the Louvre, and the British Museum). The practice of Fayum Portraits continued all through the 3rd century A.D.

Coptic Christianity in its early days relied heavily on iconography; a graphic Bible was essential for the illiterate disciples to stay in touch with their new religion. Iconography started off crudely and was later refined, yet retained a simplified, less decorated line, especially when compared to its preceding Ancient Egyptian one. By the 4th century iconography spread, with icons painted on church walls all over the country. Samples of talented Coptic artisans' work can be seen in the recently restored pieces at the **Church of St. Anthony** (p. 229), and the series of 18th-century icons showing the martyrdom of St. George found in the **Hanging Church** (p. 126) and at the **Coptic Museum** (p. 124). In Islam, however, portraying Mohammad, along with other historically important religious figures, is forbidden. In fear of idolatry, artisans, especially during the early centuries of the Islamic Empire, refrained from depicting human figures in general.

ISLAMIC ART Artisans during the Islamic Empire concentrated their creative talents into geometrical motifs (later to be known as arabesque) and calligraphy. Vegetals (the use of plants, in total or in part, as a motif for decorative purposes) and symmetrical patterns infiltrated various forms of art, from carpets and metalwork to ceramics and *mashrabeya,* a screen of finely carved wood in repeated, abstract, geometric forms. The screens, which allow air to sweep through the room, were later adapted into homes for ventilation.

Calligraphy is the most highly regarded form of Islamic art, used in depicting verses from the Quran on walls and ceilings of mosques, *madrasas,* and mausoleums. For illiterate Muslim Egyptians, calligraphy had a talismanic nature to it. Over time, calligraphy's letters and words evolved into decorative shapes and animal figures. Most of Islamic Cairo's mosques are awash with eye-grabbing scripts, and once it reopens, the **Museum of Islamic Art** (p. 121) will be a good place to take a closer look at examples.

Islamic art in Egypt witnessed its "golden age" during the Mamluk sultanate (both dynasties). Existing arts prospered through the mega projects commissioned by successive sultans, royal patronage, and the opening of European markets through Venetian trade, and new art forms, such as enameled and gilded glass, started to emerge and rapidly develop. The best examples can be found in **Barkuk Mosque**'s (p. 118) colored-glass windows, or in **Taz Palace**'s (p. 122) bathroom with colored-glass ceiling.

CONTEMPORARY ART As the modernization of Egypt progressed, a revival in the art scene started to emerge; figurative sculpture was once again reawakened after a long period of hibernation during the different Islamic epochs, photography and painting were being embraced by emerging artists, and, finally, art was introduced to the educational system. In search of identity, Egyptian artists adapted a neo-Pharaonic school of art, with Mahmoud Mokhtar's pioneering masterpiece *Egypt Awakening,* which today stands in front of Cairo University. The granite statue depicts a firm-looking sphinx next to a female peasant lifting, if not throwing off, her veil; Mokhtar was a strong believer in the emancipation of women.

The modern art scene in Egypt took different evolutionary turns; from influential strokes of surrealism, cubism, and dadaism schools to national identity seekers exploring symbolism and abstract expressionism. A rather interesting school of artistic thought materialized with the magnum opus of avant-garde innovator Hassan Fathy. A theorist, architect, and artist, Fathy believed in revitalizing traditional art concepts through modern techniques; his architectural project New Gourna (p. 274), a whole village model, is a living testament to his success, at least artistically.

The new wave of today's contemporary artists has trundled unconventional lanes reaching national and international podiums. The growing-by-the-minute list includes Nubian painter Fathi Hassan (not to be confused with Hassan Fathy), with his enigmatic portraits documenting the heritage of his homeland; New York–based Ghada Amer, with her inspirational work on canvas, textiles, and paper; Venice Biennale award-winner Medhat Shafik, with his exquisite print-making and set designs; and video artist Moataz Nasr, with his remarkably creative installations.

5 EGYPT IN POPULAR CULTURE

BOOKS

Without a doubt, the late Naguib Mahfouz is Egypt's most well-known novelist, but the 1998 Nobel Prize winner, along with other prominent names such as Taha Hussein and Youssef Idris, belongs to a rather classic school of literature that has substantially evolved through the years. Today, the Egyptian literature scene is getting more dynamic with new authors, columnists, photographers, and even bloggers making their way to the bookshelves. Indeed there is a new book being published every other week; however, the quantity is surpassing the quality, and one needs to be selective. Young bloggers and journalists are becoming trendsetters with their open criticism of the political and social situation in Egypt. The regime, with its facade of prodemocracy, allows some room for self expression and freedom of speech; that's, of course, as long as the "red lines" are not crossed. Unfortunately, the majority of blogs and column collections that are published as books are available only in Arabic. If you speak the language, look for Rehab Bassam's *Rice Pudding for Two* or Osama Gharib's *Egypt is My Stepmother.*

Most of the books listed in this section are available in English and can be purchased online. However, serious readers will find a morning browsing the shelves of any of Cairo's main bookstores (p. 145) time well spent.

CLASSICS The picture is incomplete until you read a couple of Egyptian classics.

- Naguib Mahfouz, *The Cairo Trilogy: Palace Walk, Palace of Desire, and Sugar Street* (AUC Press, 2001): Mahfouz traces the lives of three generations of an early-20th-century family. A classic, and indispensable, read for anyone seriously interested in Cairo.
- Naguib Mahfouz, *Adrift on the Nile* (AUC Press, 1999): If you don't have the time to get through a thick tome, this is one of the slimmest and most readable of Mahfouz's *oeuvre* and tells the tale of a group of louche Bohemian wannabes and their drug-addled evenings on a Nile houseboat.
- Taha Hussein, *The Days* (AUC Press, 2001): An autobiography in three parts that tackles the ins and outs of one of Egypt's most influential writers, hailed "the dean of Arabic literature."
- Youssef Idris, *City of Love and Ashes* (AUC Press, 1998): It is 1952, and the heat for the revolution is building up. The mood of an apprehensive Cairo is finely crafted by the pen of the "Arabic short story guru."

MODERN & CONTEMPORARY For an insider's perspective of recent events and developments shaping the country's present, and perhaps future, the below titles are excellent choices.

- Alaa Al Aswany, *Yacoubian Building* (AUC Press, 2006): This book, and the film that followed, kicked up some dust in Egypt for its frank look at the lives of a cross-section of contemporary Cairene society.
- Galal Amin, *Whatever Happened to the Egyptians?* (AUC Press, 2000): Academic research and personal opinion make up this insightful analysis on the changes that shaped Egyptian society from the 1950s to present. The sequel: *Whatever Else Happened to the Egyptians?* was published 4 years later.
- Ibrahim Abdel Meguid, *No One Sleeps in Alexandria* (AUC Press, 2006): Tackles Muslim-Coptic relations and how they entangle in light of the World War II danger looming on the Alexandrian horizon.
- Khaled Al Khamissi, *Taxi* (Aflame Books, 2008): Anecdotes from Egyptian society

An Excerpt

"All the men I did get to know, every single man of them, has filled me with but one desire: to lift my hand and bring it smashing down on his face. But because I am a woman I have never had the courage to lift my hand. And because I am a prostitute, I hid my fear under layers of make-up."—Nawal El Saadawi, *Woman at Point Zero*

Arab Booker Prize

In April 2007, the Emirates Foundation, in association with the Booker Prize Foundation, launched the International Prize for Arab Fiction (IPAF), dubbed the Arab Booker Prize. The prestigious award aims to reward exceptional Arabic-writing novelists and promote Arab literature worldwide. In addition to a $60,000 grand prize, the winning novel is guaranteed an English translation. In its first year in 2008, the prize went to the Egyptian novelist Bahaa Taher for his outstanding *Sunset Oasis* (McClelland & Stewart, 2009). Taking place in the remote oasis of Siwa in the late 19th century, it tells the memoirs of a disgraced Egyptian military officer and his history-enthusiast Irish wife. In 2009, the breathtaking *Azazel* (Beelzebub), by Egyptian scholar and researcher Youssef Ziedan, won the grand prize. Set in the 5th century, the historical novel tackles the doctrinal differences that smudged the early days of Christianity. The novel took some heat when first published, and was described by the Egyptian Coptic Church as "the Arabic version of *The Da Vinci Code*."

as told to the author by the different taxi drivers he encounters while in Cairo.

- Nabil Shawkat, *Breakfast with the Infidels* (Dar Merit, 2006): The lightly off-the-wall observations of an ex-national columnist, screenwriter, and bon vivant offer a new perspective on the Egyptian experience.
- Nawal El Saadawi, *The Hidden Face of Eve* (Zed Books, 2007): Saadawi, a medical doctor from a large, rural, Egyptian family, is uniquely positioned to offer not-always-cheerful insights into the position of women in Egypt.
- Nawal El Saadawi, *Woman at Point Zero* (Zed Books, 2007): Undoubtedly Saadawi's best novel. It tells of the trials and tribulations of a female sex worker who killed a pimp and now faces capital punishment.
- Salwa Bakr, *The Golden Chariot* (AUC Press, 2008): Shattered dreams and life stories from different social levels are told by female inmates passing another long prison night. Funny, witty, and at times blunt.
- Sonallah Ibrahim, *Zaat* (AUC Press, 2004): Deliciously biting satire from one of Egypt's most controversial novelists. Not only is it more readable than most of its competitors, it will give you a distinct sense of the ironies and perplexities of life in Egypt.

GENERAL INTEREST Every once in a while, an Egyptian enthusiast surprises us with a groundbreaking book. Here are some of the selected few.

- Ahmed Fakhry, *Bahariyah and Farafra* (AUC Press, 2003): An insightful peek into the distant world of the desert oases.
- Fathi Malim, *Siwa: From the Inside* (Katan Books, 2001): This is a short-but-fascinating look at Siwa by a resident. You're not going to read this stuff anywhere else.
- Haggag Hassan Oddoul, *Nights of Musk: Stories from Old Nubia* (AUC Press, 2008): A much-needed documentation of Nubian history and their diaspora after the building of the Aswan High Dam.
- Mohamed El Hebeishy, *Egypt Rediscovered* (Manuscript, 2007): This is my own coffee-table book with extended essays; it sheds some light on Egypt's most hidden treasures.
- Rafik Khalil & Dina Aly, *The Natural Heritage of Egypt* (self-published, 2003):

A stunning pictorial journey through the landscape, flora, and fauna of Egypt.

- Salima Ikram, *Divine Creatures* (AUC Press, 2005): Everything you ever wanted to know about mummies, as well as mummified animals buried with their owners or just on their own.
- Samir Raafat, *Cairo, the Glory Years* (Harpocrates, 2003): Really the only book on the villas of 19th-century Cairo.

FILM

Regionally speaking, it should have been called Cairowood. While Saudi Arabia launched its first film *Keif El Hal* (How Are You?) in 2006, the first full-length Egyptian movie *Kobla fil Sahara* (A Kiss in the Sahara) beat it by a good 79 years. The 1940s and 1950s were dubbed the Golden Age of Egyptian Cinema, with more than 100 fairy-tale-ending movies produced annually. During the 1960s and 1970s, things took a different turn, with more reality-based movies gaining ground. Hailed among the best Egyptian movies ever made, 1959's *Doa'a Al Karawan* (Nightingale's Prayer) and 1971's *Thartharа Fawk Al Neal* (Adrift on the Nile) are both must-sees. If a copy with English subtitles proves difficult to find, you can always read the original novels (p. 145). Though the 1980s and 1990s witnessed the worst decline in both number of produced films and their respective quality, the era saw Egypt's legendary director Youssef Chahine entering his golden age. Known for his controversial points of view, daring ideas, and atypical directing style, Chahine was honored in 1997 during the Cannes Film Festival with the Lifetime Achievement Award. His curriculum vitae of widely acclaimed films includes *Awdet Al Ibn Al Dal* (The Return of the Prodigal Son), *Wada'an Bonaparte* (Adieu Bonaparte), and *Al Youm Al Saddes* (The Sixth Day). Chahine's debut, *Al Mohagir* (The Migrant), was nationally criticized by conservatives and religious groups for its depictions of religious characters; something widely proscribed by Islam.

Today's Egyptian cinema is witnessing a revival with more than 40 films being produced annually; however, the lack of creativity is an issue. In 2008, Chahine's protégé Khaled Youssef directed his first blockbuster *Hiina Maysara* (Until Better Days), a traumatizing wake-up call depicting the inhumane daily struggles Cairo slum dwellers endure. The movie hit it big in the box office, but half a dozen films plying the same line followed suit. In 2009, the long awaited *Hassan wa Morcos* (Hassan & Marcus) was released. Starring Egypt's longstanding superstar Adel Imam and Golden Globe–winner Omar Sharif, the film tackles the relationship between a Muslim sheikh and a Christian theologian in light of the religious extremism and the sectarian violence that flares every now and then.

I Want My MTV!

MTV-like satellite channels dominate Egyptian and Arab television screens. From Rotana and Mazzika to Nogoom and Melody, they all play the same bouquet of smoldering, and at times bawdy, singers surrounded by scantily clad dancing girls; a picture far from what an Islamic MTV might look like. The recently launched 4Shbab is on the other end of the spectrum, with MCs and rappers preaching religious and moral values without a single female in sight.

TV

Because of television, Egypt's Arabic dialect is understood throughout the Arab world. Egypt pioneered the regional entertainment scene with soap operas playing the leading role. The all-time classic, which ran for five seasons, is *Layali El Helmia* (El Helmia Nights), which tells the story of two Egyptian families who belong to different social classes but share the same quarter. Recently, *El Haj Metwalli* (Hajji Metwally), a rags-to-riches comedy that depicts the relationship between an Egyptian merchant and his four wives, yielded a huge success. At the same time, it sparked a debate about polygamy and its social consequences. In Egypt, Muslims are permitted by law and Islamic doctrine to have up to four wives.

Ramadan (p. 12) is time for abstaining and self discipline, but for some, it is the hive of soap operas. Through the spreading of satellite television across the Arab world, Egypt has a good business opportunity, but recently Syria is competing for a share of the pie. There are about 70 soap operas produced annually to be aired during Ramadan. Before, the majority of the 70 were produced in Egypt, but today about 30% are coming from Syria.

MUSIC

Lebanese singers have dominated the center stage of the Arab pop scene, but Egyptian superstar Amr Diab still reigns, at least locally. The phenomenal singer kick-started his career in 1983, but it wasn't until 5 years later that his studio album *Mayyal* (I Like You) stormed the charts. He has faced little competition until recently with the (in my opinion) mediocre Tamer Hosny.

Sha'abi music has its own audience among the alleys and back doors of poor Cairo. Music for the masses, as the name *sha'abi* aptly translates to, took off as a traditional reflection of the Egyptian culture. It is chiefly characterized by the use of local musical instruments such as the *tabla* drum and flutelike *mozmar*. At the hive of *sha'abi* music is El Rayess Metkal. Today, *sha'abi* has taken a dramatic detour into farcical lyrics and monotonous tunes. Still, so-called artists such as Saad El Soghier and Shabban Abdel Rahim have their fans.

Fifty years ago, the music scene was dominated by Om Kolthoum, hailed as "the lady of Arabic singing." Her live concerts played on the first Thursday of every month, and were as sacred as prayer time to pious devotees. The charismatic *El Set* (the lady), as she was often nicknamed, passed on, but you can see her today at her small museum or find her records being played in a traditional coffee shop concealed in the narrow alleyways of Downtown.

Independent bands and solo performers are making their mark on today's music scene. Grammy award–winner Fathy Salama mixes jazz with Arab elements, and periodically gigs in Cairo with his Sharkiat band. The band Wust El Balad, meaning "downtown" in Arabic, fuses local lyrics and Arabic music in a mold of lively soft rock. They are aptly dubbed the "voice of the youth."

Tips For the Vegetarian

In the Egyptian phrasebook of gastronomy, meat *(lahhma)* refers to beef, lamb, and mutton, and minced meat is not considered meat. Be very specific when ordering food, making sure that your dish does not have meat or minced meat.

6 EATING & DRINKING IN EGYPT

FOOD

Egyptian cuisine revolves around two main ingredients: fava beans and meat. *Fuul,* a heavy stew of beans spiced with black pepper and cumin, is the nation's standard dish for breakfast and can easily keep you full for the day. A couple of *fuul* variants are common. *Fuul eskendrani,* courtesy of Alexandria, gets a good fare of tomato sauce, while *fuul bel bayd* mixes in scrambled eggs. Beans are also the base for other Egyptian dishes, mainly *tameya* and *besara.* The former is an Egyptian version of falafel, with fava beans mashed, shaped into balls, and deep-fried, while the latter is a cooked beans-based pesto often garnished with fried onion. In Egypt, meat is food for the wealthy, with poorer families serving it once or twice a year. Ironically, many Egyptian dishes are either meat-based or have meat as part of the recipe. The most famous meat dish is the Turkish kebab, while *kofta* is ground meat shaped around a skewer and grilled. *Shish tawook* is a local kebab that grills chicken instead of meat.

There are a few local dishes that you shouldn't miss. Sautéed eggplant, mixed with bell pepper, tomato, and minced meat, is baked into Egyptian moussaka. If you are a vegetarian, L'Aubergine (p. 150) serves the best vegetarian moussaka in town. *Molokheya* is another vegetarian dish. It is a gluey, green, souplike mush made from Jew's Mallow. Traditionally it is served with roasted rabbit on the side. *Mahshi,* or *dolma,* is another Turkish-inherited dish (note the Ottoman footprint on Egyptian cuisine), where bell pepper, eggplant, tomato, and zucchini are stuffed with a mixture of rice, herbs, and often minced meat. One very tasty *mahshi* variant is *wara ainab,* where vine leaves are wrapped around the same rice-based mixture. For a good taste of Egyptian delicacies, head for Abou El Sid (p. 139). *Kosheri* is food for the masses. The typical Cairene dish is a mix of lentils, macaroni, rice, and chickpeas garnished with slices of fried onions and hot tomato sauce on top. Kosheri El Tahrir (p. 141) is a clean, air-conditioned, inexpensive place to try it out.

DRINKS

The country's national drink is tea, or *shai.* Egyptians drink it in the morning, after meals, in the afternoon, in the evening,

Something Smells Fishy

Sham El Nessim was first celebrated more than 4,500 years ago. Back then it was called Shamo. Ancient Egyptians celebrated the arrival of the spring season by offering salted fish, lettuce, and scallions to their deities, while colored eggs dangling from temples' ceilings were used as decoration to greet the visiting Pharaoh. Much has changed through the ages, but somehow Shamo survived, with some modifications. Translated to "breathe the air," Sham El Nessim has been incorporated into the Egyptian almanac, marking the Monday following Coptic Easter and celebrated by Muslims and Christians alike. It is the time when Egyptians head to the countryside, city parks, or at least a patch of green grass, where they partake in the traditional meal of *fessikh.* The Egyptian delicacy is a salted grey mullet renowned for its overly pungent smell. Eaters should be cautious, as botulism contracted from the smelly culprits can prove poisonous.

The Dying Creed

To the rest of the world, licorice is candy, but in Egypt, it's consumed as a juice called *erk sous.* Hawkers in baggy, Turkish-style pants rove the streets clapping their cymbals and screaming their lungs out for the cold drink. Sellers pour the brownish liquid from a giant container, adorned with long plastic flowers, that they hold some distance from the glass to foam the drink. This age old "moving juice bar" is, unfortunately, coming to an end, as fewer people are willing to move around with such a weight to carry, and it is much easier to grab a soda from the grocery around the corner.

and, if they could, while sleeping. As a visitor and a guest, you will generally be treated to *shai fetla,* which literally means "thread tea" but refers to the tea bag, which hangs from a thread. *Shai kosheri* is a rougher variant with a spoonful of loose tea at the bottom of the glass. Tea with mint, *shai bi-na'ana'a,* is popular, or you can have just straight mint in hot water, *na'ana'a.* Youth are abandoning the traditional drink for coffee, from black American coffee to sophisticated *espresso con panna.* The traditional Turkish coffee, *ahwa torky,* is thick, black, and strong, and comes in three sweetness levels. No sugar at all is *sada; mazbut,* which means "medium," will get you something moderately sweet; and *ziyada,* which simply means "extra," will result in something that, for most people, is unbearably syrupy.

Egypt enjoys a wide range of fresh and traditional juices, including orange, lemon with mint, watermelon, mango, banana with milk, guava, and, though harder to find, mandarin, all fresh and served in season. The traditional menu contains more unfamiliar drinks. Hibiscus, *karkade,* is a refreshing summer drink that helps lower blood pressure and can be drunk as a hot tea in winter, when cinnamon with milk *(kerfa bel laben)* is also good. Carob *(kharoub)* and tamarind *(tamr hindi)* are also known for their health benefits, but are more common during Ramadan. During summer, look for *sobia,* a sweet drink made of coconut, fermented rice, and milk.

The alcohol scene has dramatically changed over the last few years. The new era was marked with the acquiring of Al Ahram Beverages Company (ABC), Egypt's main brewery and wine producer, by Heineken back in 2002. Locally brewed Heineken is widely available, but if you are up to trying a hard-core local brew, then go for Stella. Locally brewed since the 19th century, it aptly holds the "oldest Egyptian beer" title. Local wines are far from competing with their Italian counterparts, but some can be tried out: Caspar for white wine and Chateau des Reves, Scheherazade, and Cape Bay when it comes to red. It is important to note that inconsistent temperatures at which Egyptian wine is stored may lead to different bottles of the same brand tasting differently. ID Edge is Egypt's version of Bacardi Breather. The fizzy drink comes in with three flavors, watermelon, lime, and green apple, each with two different alcohol concentrations (5% and 10%).

Egypt is a predominantly Muslim country and only a handful of supermarkets sell alcohol. However, local liquor chain Drinkies has stores all over the capital and in some other cities as well.

3

Planning Your Trip to Egypt

Egypt is a big, diverse country that encompasses some of the most verdant and fertile farmland in the world, stretching across thousands of miles of the most forbidding and remote desert on Earth and bordering on two seas. As culturally diverse and exciting as it is topographically varied, Egypt offers visitors a chance to explore 5,000 years of history, while a burgeoning outdoor-adventure industry gives you a chance to explore the empty expanse of the desert on camel, sandboard down mountainous dunes, sailboard, or just lie on the beach and enjoy the pristine azure of the Red Sea.

Egypt sits on the northeast corner of Africa, and though it is generally lumped in with the Middle East, it remains, technically at least, an African country. To the west, it shares a long desert border with Libya, and to the south it borders on Sudan. To the east there is a short land border with the Gaza Strip, controlled by the Palestinian Authority, and a much longer one with Israel. With a total area of around 1 million sq. km (386,000 sq. miles), it is about three times the size of New Mexico, but the vast majority of the 80 million people who live in Egypt are squeezed into a narrow, densely populated strip of fertile land that runs along the Nile Valley and Delta.

Tourism is one of the Egyptian economy's top three earners, with new destinations constantly being explored; keep an eye on Taba, Marsa Matruh, and Hamata. Recent years have also witnessed a tourism development revival, particularly along the Red Sea coast, Sinai, and Luxor. Generally speaking, Egypt is an easy country to get around, and services are economically priced, so spur-of-the-moment travel is quite practical. However, this is a developing country at the end of the day, and some basics are simply not there; not everybody speaks English, even in positions where you expect them to (the ticket officer in the train station, the bus conductor); time is a matter of no importance (a 5- to 30-minute delay is not considered a delay); and bureaucracy is the name of the game (something that should take an hour to finish can easily take two). If you don't wish to lose time buying bus and plane tickets, or making hotel reservations, you might want to travel with a tour group. In addition to Cairo International Airport, most of the country's airports are well serviced by the national carrier, EgyptAir, some major international airlines, as well as a plethora of budget airlines, making Egypt accessible, especially if you are coming from Europe. There are almost no medical requirements to enter the country unless you are coming from sub-Saharan Africa, and getting your visa upon arrival is a straightforward 10-minute process.

Egypt is a lovely year-round destination; just plan your itinerary carefully. Upper Egypt's strong sun can easily ruin your vacation in Luxor or Aswan if you opt to go there in summer, while the winter season rain showers on the Mediterranean coast can easily leave you soaked in Alexandria. Egypt is considered one of the safest places for travelers, but harassment is a growing concern, with single female travelers getting the worst of it. That said, some precautions, when taken into consideration, can significantly reduce your chances of being harassed. Specialized travel and dedicated trips are still in their infancy in Egypt, but if you look deep enough, you can find some rewarding trips.

1 WHEN TO GO

WEATHER

Egypt is a year-round destination, with fall (Sept–Nov) and spring (Feb–Apr) being the best seasons to go anywhere in the country. Cairo is hot and muggy during summer (May–Sept), and most residents take their vacations during this period, if possible. Upper Egypt and the Western Desert can also be uncomfortably hot, and are best avoided until the summer season is over. The Red Sea coast and the Sinai Peninsula see temperatures crossing 90°F (32°C), but the sea breeze dilutes the effect and the weather turns lovely, especially at night. If you are visiting Egypt during summer and don't want the heat to put you off, then head to the Mediterranean coast, but note that Alexandria and Marsa Matruh are popular with locals, and you'll end up vacationing with millions of locals who swarm the lovely beaches. Female sunbathers will probably feel uncomfortable, especially if unaccompanied.

Winter (Dec–Jan) is a pleasant time to go to Upper Egypt and visit its renowned monuments. Cairo can get a bit chilly, while wind makes it a bit cold on the Red Sea coast and Sinai's two coasts. The Western Desert and the Sinai High Mountains region are pleasantly sunny during daytime, but once night descends temperatures plunge; be well prepared for very cold nights, especially if you are sleeping outdoors. In Sinai, Mount Sinai is capped with snow during these two months. The Mediterranean coast should be avoided during this time of the year unless you are fine with rain showers.

High and low seasons follow a combination of weather patterns and holidays. The summer's heat puts off foreign travelers from visiting Egypt, but the local market makes up for it, as Egyptian families opt to spend their summer vacation on the Mediterranean coast. The Red Sea coast has a short high season in August, when Italian tourists swarm the resorts during their annual vacation time. Winter, in general, is regarded as high season with the exception of Alexandria and Marsa Matruh, where rain brings very low accommodation prices. Throughout the country, prices skyrocket during Christmas, New Year's, and Easter.

To avoid the crowds, go against the seasons, but be prepared for some serious heat if you're headed for Upper Egypt during summer. Luxor in August is not for the faint of heart, and venturing out to the sights without a fairly serious sunblock, an extravagantly brimmed sun hat, and a couple of liters of water is simply unwise. Personally, I would try to stay at the margins of the high season and visit around the first 2 weeks of November or June. The same goes for Cairo, the Red Sea coast, and Sinai.

The main thing to watch on the north coast is the Egyptian school schedules. Once the Egyptian schools and universities let out, cities and beaches on the Mediterranean become very noisy and crowded, and Western tourists, women in particular, will find themselves subject to substantial unwelcome attention. For this reason I would advise visiting Alexandria in March and April or October and November.

Note: Attractions extend their hours by 1 hour in summer; hours for attractions in this book are listed for winter.

Average Monthly High/Low Temperatures

		Jan	Feb	Mar	Apr	May	June	July	Aug	Sept	Oct	Nov	Dec
Alexandria	Temp. (°F)	64/50	65/50	68/53	75/58	79/63	83/69	84/73	86/74	84/72	81/66	74/59	67/52
	Temp. (°C)	17/10	18/10	20/11	23/14	26/17	28/20	28/22	30/23	28/22	27/18	23/15	19/11
		Jan	Feb	Mar	Apr	May	June	July	Aug	Sept	Oct	Nov	Dec
Cairo	Temp. (°F)	65/49	68/50	73/54	82/59	89/64	93/70	93/72	92/72	90/69	85/65	75/58	67/51
	Temp. (°C)	18/9	20/10	22/12	27/15	31/17	33/21	33/22	33/22	32/20	29/18	23/14	19/10
		Jan	Feb	Mar	Apr	May	June	July	Aug	Sept	Oct	Nov	Dec
Hurghada	Temp. (°F)	68/55	70/57	74/62	81/69	86/75	90/80	91/82	92/83	89/79	85/74	78/66	71/58
	Temp. (°C)	20/12	21/13	23/16	27/20	30/23	32/26	32/27	33/28	31/26	29/23	25/18	21/14
		Jan	Feb	Mar	Apr	May	June	July	Aug	Sept	Oct	Nov	Dec
Luxor	Temp. (°F)	70/45	74/49	83/56	93/65	100/71	104/76	104/78	102/77	99/74	93/68	81/56	73/48
	Temp. (°C)	21/7	23/9	28/13	33/18	37/21	40/24	40/25	38/25	37/23	33/20	27/13	22/8
		Jan	Feb	Mar	Apr	May	June	July	Aug	Sept	Oct	Nov	Dec
Siwa	Temp. (°F)	67/39	71/41	77/46	86/53	94/61	100/66	101/69	100/68	95/64	90/58	80/50	70/41
	Temp. (°C)	19/3	21/5	25/7	30/11	34/16	37/18	38/20	37/20	35/17	32/14	26/10	21/5

HOLIDAYS

Public holidays in Egypt are a mix of secular celebrations of the achievements of the post-1952 state and religious holidays. Islamic religious holidays can be a little hard to pin down sometimes, because they occur according to the Islamic lunar calendar; the dates, according to the more common Gregorian calendar, move about 11 days earlier every year. The dates provided for any Islamic holiday throughout this book are based on astronomical calculations of when each lunar month begins; however, in real life, it depends on an actual spotting of the new moon.

Government offices (including visa extensions) and many public services (such as banks) are closed for secular holidays such as July 23 or October 6. Most general services, including money-change offices and major tourist sights, operate as normal, however.

Religious holidays carry more social significance and provide you with fascinating opportunities as well as potentially insurmountable obstacles. Ramadan, the month of fasting that precedes Eid El Fitr, is a great example. On the one hand, it's a fascinating time to be in Egypt: The streets are decorated and, once the sun goes down, the streets of poorer neighborhoods are filled with parties and celebrations that go on most of the night. On the other hand, the already brief Egyptian working day is substantially shortened during Ramadan, which means that getting the most minor arrangements made or changed can quickly become a frustrating exercise. For more on Ramadan, see. p. 12.

For an exhaustive list of events beyond those listed here, check http://events.frommers.com, where you'll find a searchable, up-to-the-minute roster of what's happening in cities all over the world.

Here are the high points of the annual holiday schedule in Egypt:

- **Coptic Christmas,** January 7: This is when Orthodox Christians celebrate the birth of Christ. It has been made a national holiday only recently.
- **Police Day,** January 25: In 2010, the Egyptian government decided to declare Police Day a national holiday. Taking into consideration the lack of real political freedom in Egypt and the notorious reputation of the Egyptian Police, I fail to even comment.
- **Moulid an-Nabi,** approximately February 15, 2011; February 4, 2012; and January 24, 2013: Muslims celebrate

the birth of Prophet Muhammad much differently than Christians celebrate the birth of Jesus; there are no Christmas carols, special prayers, or big family gatherings—just the state television airing a couple of Islam-oriented movies and people buying some special sweets (such as the sesame seed–based *sensemeya*), which are more traditional than religious.

- **Sham El Nessim/Easter,** April 25, 2011; April 16, 2012; and May 6, 2013: This celebration of spring cuts across social and religious lines in Egypt, and on this day everybody who can collect a meal in a basket and get out of the house goes for a picnic. See p. 42.
- **Sinai Liberation Day,** April 25: This commemorates the completion of the Israeli withdrawal from Sinai on April 25, 1982.
- **Labor Day,** May 1: Paying lip service to the socialist propaganda of yesteryear, the Egyptian government still celebrates May Day.
- **Revolution Day,** July 23: This commemorates the 1952 Free Officers revolution that saw the end of the Egyptian monarchy and the birth of the new republic.
- **Eid El Fitr,** approximately September 10, 2010; August 30, 2011; and August 19, 2012: Celebrated over 3 days, it marks the end of the fasting month of Ramadan. It is a time of big family gatherings where traditional *kahk* and *ghouraiyyeba* sweets are baked and shared. Eid El Fitr translates to The Feast of Breaking the Fast.
- **Armed Forces Day,** October 6: This commemorates October War, or the Yom Kippur War, and the crossing of the Suez Canal by Egyptian forces in 1973.
- **Eid El Adha,** approximately November 15, 2010; November 6, 2011; and October 26, 2012: The Feast of Sacrificing, as the name translates, commemorates the completion of the Hajj to Mecca as well as Ibrahim's willingness to sacrifice his only son. It is celebrated over a 4-day period and marked with sacrificing livestock and handing out much of the meat to the needy.
- **Islamic New Year's Day,** approximately December 7, 2010; November 26, 2011; and November 15, 2012: This marks the first day of the new Islamic year. Compared to New Year's Eve, it is poorly celebrated. A Good Day to Stay In and Read.

The killing of livestock during Eid El Adha is allowed outside official slaughterhouses, and there will likely be a great number of cattle being slaughtered in basements or on rooftops throughout the country. If you can't cope with the blood, it would be better if you stayed in and read. Most of the slaughtering takes place during the first day of Eid El Adha right after the special Eid prayers end, roughly 1 hour after dawn breaks.

. . . And the Pharaohs Play Football

Egyptians take football (soccer) seriously, and their national team has deservedly won the African Cup of Nations seven times, including the last three in 2006, 2008, and 2010. If you happen to be in the country, specifically Cairo, during the next continental championship, a FIFA world cup qualifier, or an important match of any sort, be aware that 2 hours before the match starts, streets will turn into a deadlock, and once the referee blows his final whistle, Egyptians go parading in the streets bringing traffic to a complete standstill; that is, of course, if Egypt wins.

2 ENTRY REQUIREMENTS

PASSPORTS

Your passport must have a minimum of 6 months' validity beyond the day you enter Egypt.

VISAS

Please see "Visa Information" in chapter 12.

CUSTOMS

What You Can Bring into Egypt: Egypt imposes large import duties on electronics, including cameras, stereos, and laptop computers, but as long as you are bringing in items for personal use, there should be no issue.

You are allowed to bring in (or take out) up to LE5,000; given the ease with which you can exchange money inside the country and the bad rate of exchange outside of Egypt, this should not cause a problem. Foreign currencies to a value of $10,000 can be brought in.

Duty-free allowance on arrival is: 200 cigarettes, 25 cigars, or 200 grams of tobacco; 1 liter of alcoholic beverages; a reasonable quantity of perfume and 1 liter of eau de cologne; noncommercial articles up to a value of LE100; personal items such as hair dryers and razors. Interestingly, these allowances are made "irrespective of age." Prohibited items include birds (live, stuffed, or frozen), Viagra, antiques, narcotics, cotton, and "items offensive to Islam."

What You Can Take Home from Egypt: You cannot export more than LE5,000 or an equivalent of more than $10,000 in any foreign currency. You are also not allowed to take out drugs, food, silver, or gold bought on the local market (these last two have an exception for "very small quantities for personal use"). ***Note:*** At press time, the ban on bringing any kind of bird back from Egypt to the United States was still in effect.

U.S. Citizens: For specifics on what you can bring back and the corresponding fees, download the invaluable free pamphlet *Know Before You Go* online at www.cbp.gov. (Click on "Travel," and then click on "Know Before You Go! Online Brochure.") Or, contact the U.S. Customs & Border Protection (CBP), 1300 Pennsylvania Ave. NW, Washington, DC 20229 (✆ **877/287-8667**) and request the pamphlet.

Canadian Citizens: For a clear summary of Canadian rules, check out the *I Declare* brochure issued by the Canada Border Services Agency (✆ **800/461-9999** in Canada, or 204/983-3500; www.cbsa-asfc.gc.ca). Go to their website, click on "Publications and Forms," and then on "Guides and Brochures."

U.K. Citizens: For information, contact HM Customs & Excise at ✆ **0845/010-9000** (from outside the U.K., 020/8929-0152), or consult its website at www.hmce.gov.uk.

Australian Citizens: A helpful brochure available from Australian consulates or Customs offices is *Know Before You Go.* For more information, call the Australian Customs Service at ✆ **1300/363-263,** or log on to www.customs.gov.au.

New Zealand Citizens: Most questions are answered in a free pamphlet available at New Zealand consulates and Customs offices: *New Zealand Customs Guide for Travellers, Notice no. 4.* For more information, contact New Zealand Customs, The Customhouse, 17–21 Whitmore St., Box 2218, Wellington (✆ **04/473-6099** or 0800/428-786; www.customs.govt.nz).

MEDICAL REQUIREMENTS

There are no medical requirements for entering Egypt unless you are coming from sub-Saharan Africa, in which case a valid yellow fever vaccination certificate is required.

GETTING TO EGYPT

By Air

Egypt has a dozen functioning airports spread out across the length and breadth of the country, 10 of which receive international flights. Abu Simbel airport is virtually EgyptAir exclusive, and Kharga airport is temporarily not receiving any commercial flights. Egypt is well served by major airlines with many flying to Cairo on a daily basis. Most of the major airlines have their main offices in the capital.

- **Air France** (2 Tala'at Harb St., Downtown; © 02/27706250)
- **Alitalia** (inside the Nile Hotel, Corniche El Nil; © 02/24584867)
- **BMI** (19 El Bostan St., Downtown; © 02/ 23962121)
- **British Airways** (inside the Intercontinental Residence Suites, Heliopolis; © 02/24800380)
- **Delta Air Lines** (15 Ismail Mohamed St., Zamalek; © 02/27362030)
- **Emirates Airlines** (18 Batal Ahmed Ibn Abdulaziz St., Mohandiseen; © 02/19899)
- **Iberia Airlines** (15 El Tahrir Sq., Downtown; © 02/25795700)
- **KLM** (2 Tala'at Harb St., Downtown; © 02/27706251)
- **Lufthansa** (6 El Sheikh El Marsafy St., Zamalek; © 02/19380)
- **Olympic Airlines** (23 Kasr El Nil St., Downtown; © 02/23931318)
- **Swiss Air** (6 El Sheikh El Marsafy St., Zamalek; © 02/19380)
- **Turkish Airlines** (26 Mahmoud Bassyouni St., Downtown; © 02/25784634)
- **United Airlines** (16 Adly St., Downtown; © 02/23911950)

Egyptian Airports

CAIRO (CAI) Cairo International Airport is the main international hub for Egypt. It is the country's biggest and busiest airport, and it is well serviced by major airlines. The airport lives up to international standards, and offers a wide range of facilities that includes restaurants, cafes, and bars. Recent expansions include an additional state-of-the-art terminal, T3, which was inaugurated in April 2009. EgyptAir, which has a virtual domestic monopoly, uses Cairo International Airport as its hub for internal flights.

SHARM EL SHEIKH (SSH) Sharm El Sheikh International Airport now receives international flights directly from all over the world from major airlines including Alitalia, Austrian Air, British Airways, LOT Polish Airlines, Royal Jordanian, as well as many low-cost operators such as Air Berlin, Condor, easyJet, Thomas Cook, and Transavia. This is a good port of entry to the Sinai, as Dahab, St. Catherine, and Taba are just a few hours' drive from Sharm El Sheikh.

ALEXANDRIA BORG AL ARAB (HBE) Farther outside Alexandria than Al Nozha airport, but with more modern facilities and a longer runway, this airport is serviced by EgyptAir, Emirates, United Airlines, and the Middle Eastern budget airline Fly Dubai. There is a shuttle bus service that takes you from the airport into the middle of Alexandria.

ALEXANDRIA AL NOZHA (ALY) This airport is much closer to the city than the newer Borg Al Arab facility, but it has an unnervingly short runway. National airline EgyptAir and regional budget airline Air Arabia both use this airport.

LUXOR (LXR) This airport is serviced by internal EgyptAir flights as well as major and budget airlines such as Air Berlin, Thomson, Iberworld, and Transavia. This airport is small, modern, and conveniently located close to town.

ASWAN (ASW) Though an international airport, it is mainly serviced by internal EgyptAir flights and international Iberworld ones. This airport is small, clean, and well organized, but a bit far from Aswan proper.

ABU SIMBEL (ABS) This airport is exclusively for EgyptAir tourist flights. Some of the flights coming from Cairo layover in Aswan; check before you purchase your ticket.

HURGHADA (HRG) This modern airport effectively serves El Gouna, Hurghada, Safaga, and El Quseir. It is served internationally by budget airlines such as Condor, Air Berlin, Thomas Cook, Thomson, and Transavia, as well as internally by EgyptAir.

MARSA ALAM (RMF) Egypt's only privately owned airport (www.marsa-alam-airport.com) is among its best. It has a rapidly growing list of airlines that includes EgyptAir, Condor, Air Berlin, Thomson, and Transavia. It boosts tourism along the southern part of the Red Sea coast, providing easy access to El Quseir, Port Ghalib, Marsa Alam, and even Hamata.

MARSA MATRUH (MUH) Functioning only during summer, this airport is serviced by internal EgyptAir flights and, as of summer 2010, Thomson.

TABA (TCP) One of Egypt's small airports, it is served internationally by Thomson and Transavia. Recently, EgyptAir has resumed its twice weekly internal flight to Taba.

KHARGA (UVL) At press time, there were rumors about EgyptAir resuming its weekly internal flight to Kharga.

By Land

Egypt shares land borders with four countries: Libya, Sudan, the Palestinian Territories, and Israel. The border crossing at Rafah often makes headline news, with frequent closures and the hostilities that continuously ravage the Gaza Strip. Crossing to Sudan is currently restricted to the Lake Nasser ferry, but a highway connecting the two countries is entering its final stages. Though the Red Sea Coastal Highway runs south of the border and into Sudan, it crosses the politically disputed Hala'ib Triangle, currently a tourism no-go zone. The border crossing at Salloum–Amsaad is the main Egypt–Libya overland gateway; however, it is often very crowded with Egyptian laborers crossing the border for an extra buck. Despite the official website (www.mfa.gov.eg) confirming that the tourist visa can be obtained upon arrival at the Salloum–Amsaad border crossing, travelers' reports say otherwise; if you are coming overland from Libya, play it safe and apply for an Egyptian visa before you take off. The most tourist-friendly border crossing to Egypt is the Taba–Eilat crossing from Israel, where you can get a normal 30-day visa or a 14-day Sinai-only one (for more on visas, see p. 343). As of January, 2010, Israel levied an NIS94 border-crossing fee on all travelers heading to Egypt. You can pay it with a credit card if you are short on Israeli shekels.

By Boat

With lengthy coasts overlooking the Mediterranean and Red seas, Egypt has a number of harbors and ports, of which 10 are international points of entry. Three ports mark the Mediterranean coast (Alexandria, Port Said, and Damietta), while seven mark the Red Sea (Taba, Nuweiba, Sharm El Sheikh, Suez, Hurghada, Safaga, and Port Ghalib). A 30-day tourist visa can be obtained upon arrival at any of the 10 harbors.

GETTING AROUND

Booking tickets for transport inside Egypt is very straightforward. Plane tickets can be booked online, and bus and train tickets can be purchased at the appropriate stations. If you want to save an extra hour or two, avoiding traffic to and from the stations, you can more comfortably book through a travel agency or a tour operator. Expect to pay a premium, of course, for this service. In the case of train tickets (which pay no commissions to agents), it will help if you have other business to do with that agent—book your pyramid tour and your car rental at the same time as you ask for your train tickets.

There are literally thousands of travel agents in Egypt, and the main squares in tourist destinations are crowded with musty offices where papers are piled on top of broken computers. It is very much a caveat emptor market.

Travco (✆ **02/27362042** or 02/27354493; www.travco.com) has a comprehensive network of branches throughout Cairo and extending beyond the borders of Egypt to other countries in the Middle East and Europe. Other well-reputed local tour operators include **Guardian Travel** (5a Mariutiya Rd., Giza; ✆ **02/37404747;** www.guardiantravel.com) and **Garden City Travel** (20 Maamal Al-Sokar, Garden City; ✆ **02/27940663** or 02/27954636; www.gardencitytravel.net). International names include the well-reputed **Thomas Cook** (✆ **02/26962139** or -40; www.thomascookegypt.com) and the locally franchised **American Express** (✆ **02/24130293** or -5; www.amexfranchise.com), with its widespread network of branches yet inconsistent level of service.

By Plane

Getting around Egypt means covering substantial distances from one tourist destination to the next. Though there is reliable bus service between most places and excellent train service to a few, the best way to get around is by air.

EgyptAir (✆ **090070000** within Egypt; www.egyptair.com) has a virtual monopoly on internal flights. The service they provide has recently witnessed substantial improvements, so you no longer have to suffer (at least not as frequently) from uncomfortable seats, lost luggage, or frustrating delays. Tickets can be booked with any travel agent or at an EgyptAir travel office (where service is friendly but kind of slow), but booking online beats both these options hands down. It's quick, easy, and cheap.

By Train

There is a functional north–south railway backbone in Egypt, so travel by train between Aswan in the south and Alexandria in the north is a pleasant and practical way of seeing the country and getting to where you're going. With the exception of the seasonal (June–Sept) express train service to Marsa Matruh, there is no useful service outside this corridor.

Cairo has two main train stations (Ramses and Giza) from which most trains arrive and depart. Not all trains, especially those heading south to Upper Egypt, allow tourists on board (government claims security concerns). Tourists are allowed to use all trains mentioned in this guide.

The big difference in comfort level and the small difference in price make it worth traveling first class. Note, however, that the air-conditioning is usually cranked to maximum in both first and second class, so bring a sweater or a scarf for train travel, even in the summer.

By Car

There are two ways to see Egypt by car: hiring a car with a driver or hiring one that you drive yourself. I recommend the former, simply because it's the low-hassle option, with the driver taking care of most of the problems associated with driving yourself.

Driving yourself is a viable option if you have quick reflexes and nerves of steel, and it will probably work out to be cheaper and more flexible if you're driving from town to town. On the other hand, for getting around Cairo, I recommend taking taxis or hiring a car with a driver. Between congestion and lack of parking, your own car is more of a burden than anything else.

The most important thing to consider is that the standard of driving in Egypt, particularly on highways, is appallingly bad. Locals think nothing of passing on blind corners or coming up on the crest of a hill. Opposing traffic is simply expected to make room by pulling off the road. Signaling follows a different protocol; for example, a driver on the highway with the left turn signal flashing may be indicating to you that it's not safe to pass, or that he plans to turn left, or that he forgot to turn off his indicator in the first place. Note that Egyptians drive on the right, in theory at least.

Speed limits vary between 60kmph (37 mph) inside towns to between 90 and 100kmph (56–62 mph) on highways; with the only exception being the Cairo–Ain Sokhna Highway enjoying a 120kmph (74 mph) speed limit. Congestion means that you'll rarely get over 20kmph (12 mph) in the city (mainly Cairo year-round and Alexandria during summer), but highway limits are routinely ignored. Main highways, especially the Cairo–Alexandria Desert one, are monitored by radar at least during the daytime. It is quite different from Europe and the U.S.; here a police officer will hide with the radar device somewhere off the road, and if your car is detected, he calls the security checkpoint ahead, where you will be stopped and have your driving license confiscated (you can get it after paying a fine at the Traffic Police Headquarters in Darasah, Cairo). Cars coming from the opposite direction have probably spotted the security checkpoint on your side of the road, so if you see them repeatedly flashing their lights, slow down immediately; drivers demonstrate solidarity, at least toward fellow civilians.

Petrol, though getting to be more expensive, is still extremely cheap by Western standards—between LE1.75 and LE1.85 per liter (LE6.62–LE7 per gallon) for regular and premium petrol. Diesel costs L1.10 a liter (LE4.16 a gallon). Expect to tip the attendant LE1 for a fill up and the person who cleans your windshield another LE1.

Gas stations are not hard to find, though they tend to be widely spaced out in the desert and on the Red Sea Coastal Highway, so it's wise to fill up the tank at every opportunity—you never know when any particular station is going to run out and leave you wondering whether you can make it to the next one.

There are a few toll roads in Egypt, mainly implemented on the roads running out of Cairo (such as Cairo–Ain Sokhna and Cairo–Alexandria); expect to pay between LE2 and LE5. More of a hassle are the security checkpoints, where you may be asked to disclose your documents (driving license, car registration, car-rental contract if applicable, and sometimes your passport), and answer a few questions (where are you from, where are you heading, and, more frustratingly, why are going there?). Keep a smile on your face and stick to the point; losing your temper (if the questions get provocative) or being too casual (by giving detailed answers) will result in unneeded delays. ***Note:*** Coming from the Sinai Peninsula to Egypt mainland, the very last security checkpoint before you take the Ahmed Hamdy Tunnel will almost certainly stop you to search your vehicle. Weapons and drugs are what they are looking for, and even a small quantity of marijuana can get you in big trouble.

Note: At press time, foreigners were not allowed on the Western Desert roads between 6pm and 6am.

Road maps can be found at major bookstores in Cairo (p. 145).

For renting a car, most of the well-reputed international agencies operate in Egypt such as **Hertz** (© **02/35391380** or -3; www.hertzegypt.com), **Avis** (© **02/27947081;** www.avisegypt.com), and **Sixt** (© **02/27031018;** www.sixt.com). Renting a car from a local agency is a hit and miss affair; check out CRC (p. 101 and p. 191) or Shahd (p. 232).

By Bus

Buses are how the majority of Egyptians get around the country. You can get almost anywhere on the bus, and the service is reliable and relatively safe.

There are a number of bus companies that run the length and breadth of the country (contact information for the following differs per destination and is listed in coordinating chapters). **Go Bus** heads the league, while **Super Jet** was one of the first to operate in the country (though it has lost most of its heyday charm, it still provides okay service). **East Delta Bus Company** has an acceptable level of service and a very comprehensive network, so you might end up using it if you are going to less frequented destinations. **Upper Egypt Bus Company** should always remain your last resort; buses are not in the best condition, and the service they provide doesn't even meet the acceptable level. Like trains, all buses tend to turn the air-conditioning to arctic levels; grab a sweater or a shawl. Most buses play an Arabic movie or two, depending on the trip duration, with the volume often turned to the max; don't forget to pack a pair of earplugs, update your iPod, or have an interesting book or two.

In Cairo, there are two main bus stations: the centrally located main bus station, Turgoman, and the much smaller Almaza Bus Station in Heliopolis. Between the two, all Egyptian destinations are covered.

4 MONEY & COSTS

The Value of Egyptian Pound vs. Other Popular Currencies

LE	US$	Can$	UK£	Euro (€)	Aus$	NZ$
1	$0.18	C$0.19	£0.11	€0.13	A$0.20	NZ$0.25

It's always advisable to bring money in a variety of forms on a vacation: a mix of cash, credit cards, and perhaps traveler's checks. American dollars, pounds sterling, and euros are all easily exchanged in Egypt, and Cairo International Airport has a number of 24-hour banks that give the same rates as in town. It's easy to exchange enough on arrival to cover tips and the cost of transport into town.

Unlike exchange bureaus in many countries, most of the exchange offices *(maktab sarafa)* in Egypt offer competitive rates. They also offer longer hours and quicker service. Hotels, however, offer bad rates of exchange and should be avoided except in emergencies.

Since the Egyptian pound stabilized, after a sharp fall in 2003, there has been no black market for hard currencies. There is no real advantage to changing on the street.

CURRENCY

You will find Egypt cheap compared to the U.S. and most European countries. Like most third-world countries, however, Western goods are available in major centers, but usually at prices that are well beyond the reach of most of the working population. In fact, you will find various services, including midrange and upper-range accommodations, priced in "hard currency" (U.S. dollars or euros, generally) rather than Egyptian pounds (LE); it is a protection technique in case of any sudden local currency fluctuation. To get a feel of how much things cost in Egypt, the table below is a good indicator; prices are average and may be subject to taxes and service charges.

What Things Cost in Egypt	LE
Taxi from Cairo airport to Downtown	70.00
Round-trip airfare from Cairo to Sharm El Sheikh	600.00
Double room (very expensive)	2,500.00
Double room (expensive)	1,500.00
Double room (moderate)	400.00
Double room (inexpensive)	100.00
Dinner for one, without wine (very expensive)	200.00
Dinner for one, without wine (expensive)	120.00
Dinner for one, without wine (moderate)	60.00
Dinner for one, without wine (inexpensive)	10.00
Local taxi ride (short/medium/long)	5.00/20.00/80.00
Bottled water 1L (grocery shop–hotel)	2.00–12.00
Can of soda 330mL (grocery shop–hotel)	2.50–15.00
Cup of coffee (traditional coffee house–modern cafe)	2.00–15.00
Can of local beer 330mL (liquor store–hotel)	6.00–30.00
Bottle of local wine (liquor store–hotel)	45.00–300.00
Admission to sites/museums	10.00–100.00

ATMS

The easiest and best way to get cash away from home is from an ATM (automated teller machine), sometimes referred to as a "cash machine" or a "cashpoint." The **Cirrus** (© **800/424-7787;** www.mastercard.com) and **PLUS** (© **800/843-7587;** www.visa.com) networks span the globe and are easy to access in all major tourist spots in Egypt. Go to your bank card's website to find ATM locations in your destination. Be sure you know your daily withdrawal limit before you depart. ***Note:*** Many banks impose a fee every time you use a card at another bank's ATM, and that fee can be higher for international transactions (up to $5 or more) than for domestic ones (where they're rarely more than $2). In addition, the bank from which you withdraw cash may charge its own fee. For international withdrawal fees, ask your bank.

ATMs can be found around every corner in Cairo and other major Egyptian cities. The general rule is the smaller the city is, the fewer ATMs you'll find, if any. And once you reach the far and away places, ATMs become a distant dream. Expect a handful of ATMs in Aswan, one in Siwa, and none in Hamata.

CREDIT CARDS

Credit cards are another safe way to carry money. They also provide a convenient record of all your expenses, and they generally offer relatively good exchange rates. Paying with a credit card in Egypt is an option widely available mainly in mid- and high-end tourist facilities. Though it is rare, sometimes the merchant will increase the price by 1.5% to 3% to cover the bank's commission; outside your five-star hotel premises and glossy shopping malls, it is best to pay in cash. Networkwise, Visa and MasterCard are the most widely available and accepted, followed,

Rack Rate vs. Real Rate

The dilemma of rack versus real rate is faced by any independent traveler headed to a package holiday destination (such as Marsa Alam). The rack rate is basically the walk-in rate, but it is often exaggerated to justify why vacationers are better off booking through tour operators. Few well-reputed accommodation facilities keep the difference between the two prices at a minimum.

by a good distance, by American Express. "Can I pay with Diner's Club?" will get you a disoriented face for a reply.

TRAVELER'S CHECKS

Most banks and many exchange offices will cash traveler's checks, albeit at a less advantageous rate than cash. Upper-range tourist hotels also generally provide facilities for cashing traveler's checks and make it possible to settle your bill with them, though it is their least favorite option.

5 HEALTH

STAYING HEALTHY

Public health standards in Egypt are not really a role model and can easily give you unneeded trouble that could range from diarrhea to hepatitis. To play it safe, refrain from eating street food (very budget eateries or food stalls and carts, especially in poor districts), and stick to drinking bottled water (make sure it is well-sealed before you buy it; some counterfeit bottles are often leaked to the market).

General Availability of Health Care

Contact the **International Association for Medical Assistance to Travelers** (IAMAT) (✆ **716/754-4883** or, in Canada, 416/652-0137; www.iamat.org) for tips on travel and health concerns in the countries you're visiting, and for lists of local, English-speaking doctors. The U.S. **Centers for Disease Control and Prevention** (✆ **800/311-3435;** www.cdc.gov) provides up-to-date information on health hazards by region or country and offers tips on food safety. **Travel Health Online** (www.tripprep.com), sponsored by a consortium of travel medicine practitioners, may also offer helpful advice on traveling abroad. You can find listings of reliable medical clinics overseas at the **International Society of Travel Medicine** (www.istm.org).

COMMON AILMENTS

TROPICAL ILLNESSES There is a very limited risk of *Plasmodium falciparum* and *Plasmodium vivax* malaria in the oasis of Fayum during the summer months (June–Oct). It has been a decade since any indigenous case was reported, but you should still use a good insect repellant and a mosquito net at night if you are visiting the oasis during these months.

Egypt's first confirmed case of the H5N1 strain of avian flu was back in March 2006. By July 2007, there had been 37 more cases and 15 fatalities. H1N1 dealt a much harder blow; the first case was discovered in June 2009, but 8 months down the line, the number went up to 16,000. According to the Ministry of Tourism, the number of fatalities totaled 268 by February 2010. With Egypt's virtually nonexistent standard of public hygiene, outbreaks of both H5N1 and H1N1 remain a possibility. Travelers should check the news and the websites of the **World Health Organization** (www.who.int/countries/egy/en) and the **Centers for Disease Control and Prevention** (wwwn.cdc.gov/travel/destinationEgypt.aspx) for updates before traveling. ***Note:*** In the event of a serious outbreak, acquiring Western medical supplies in Egypt would be extremely difficult.

DIETARY RED FLAGS Tap water in Egypt is not potable and should be avoided. Only drink bottled water from a sealed bottle, and if you have doubts about the contents, get another one. This is not usually a problem, as upmarket and tourist restaurants will automatically provide bottled water. In private homes, particularly in poorer districts and outside big cities, you may be offered a glass of tap water. Politely refuse but don't ask for a bottled one, as your host may take it as an insult.

Fresh fruit juice from the street-side juice shops is a judgment call as they contain tap water.

BUGS, BITES & OTHER WILDLIFE CONCERNS There is rabies in Egypt, and care should be exercised not only with wildlife, but with semi-domestic animals such as feral cats and dogs as well.

The deserts of Egypt contain a variety of poisonous insects and snakes. Take care when hiking, especially in summer; wear closed-toe shoes, and don't go reaching into nooks and crannies. Turn over rocks with a stick and watch where you're putting your feet. A guide with first-aid training is a plus, but quite difficult to find.

Mosquitoes and a variety of other biting insects may not be life-threatening, but they can certainly spoil the fun. Five-star resorts spray heavily for insects and keep rooms pristine. If you are staying in mid-range or budget-range accommodations, I recommend having some good bug repellent handy, as well as a can of insecticide. It's best to bring the repellent with you, but there are a variety of lethal sprays available on the local market, including Raid.

RESPIRATORY ILLNESSES Air quality is a serious problem in Egypt—in Cairo especially. Some government sources say that the situation has improved in recent years, but levels of lead and particulates in the capital still often exceed even relatively lax domestic standards and are frequently several times the amounts considered safe under international standards. Tourists with asthma or other respiratory problems should limit the amount of time they spend in Cairo.

SUN/ELEMENTS/EXTREME WEATHER EXPOSURE Heat stroke and excessive sun are both potential problems in Egypt, particularly during the summer months. You should be prepared with sunblock, a good sun hat, and a way to replace electrolytes lost to sweating, such as oral rehydration salts, which are available over the counter at almost any Egyptian pharmacy for around LE2 a dose.

WHAT TO DO IF YOU GET SICK AWAY FROM HOME

At any hospital in Egypt, you will be expected to pay upfront, with the majority accepting cash only, for any treatment. Keep this in mind in the event of an emergency—arriving at the clinic with your wallet is very important.

Medicare and Medicaid do not provide coverage for medical costs outside the U.S. Before leaving home, find out what medical services your health insurance covers. To protect yourself, consider buying medical travel insurance.

Very few health insurance plans pay for medical evacuation back to the U.S. (which can cost $10,000 and up). A number of companies offer medical evacuation services anywhere in the world. If you're ever hospitalized more than 150 miles from home, **MedjetAssist** (✆ **800/527-7478;** www.medjetassistance.com) will pick you up and fly you to the hospital of your choice virtually anywhere in the world in a medically equipped and staffed aircraft 24 hours day, 7 days a week. Annual memberships are $225 individual, $350 family; you can also purchase short-term memberships.

If you suffer from a chronic illness, consult your doctor before your departure. Pack **prescription medications** in your carry-on luggage, and carry them in their original containers with pharmacy labels—otherwise they won't make it through airport security. Carry the generic name of prescription medicines in case a local pharmacist is unfamiliar with the brand name. There is no shortage of **drugstores** in Egypt, and they're found in every neighborhood selling everything from shampoo to antibiotics. Most of their products are available over the counter. Pharmacists are also relatively well trained in Egypt and are commonly used for a wide range of medical advice. The list of well-stocked pharmacies that have multiple branches (mainly in the capital with one or two in other major cities), accept credit card payments, are open 24 hours, and do deliveries is headed by **El Ezaby** (✆ **19600**) and includes **Seif** (✆ **19199**), **Ali's Image** (✆ **19770**), and **Delmar & Atallah** (✆ **19955**).

The government-owned-and-operated **hospitals** should not be considered due to their deteriorating conditions; it is better to stick to private ones. Find a list of recommended hospitals throughout the country on p. 342.

Reputed medical clinics in the capital include **Shaalan Surgicenter,** 10 Abd El Hamid Lotfi St., Mohandiseen (✆ **02/37605180**); the outpatient clinic is around the corner at 11 Al Anaab St., open 9am to 10pm daily except Friday. **Degla Medical Center,** 4 St. 2003, Degla, Maadi (✆ **02/5213156** or 02/2523157), is open 9am to 10pm daily except Friday. Laboratories in Cairo include **Alpha Scan,** 35 Adan St., Mohandiseen (✆ **02/33363310**); **Cairo Radiology Center,** 35 Soliman Abaza St., Mohandiseen (✆ **19144**); and **El Borg Lab,** 49 Noubar St., Downtown (✆ **19911**).

6 SAFETY

Generally speaking, Egypt is a very safe place to be and travel around. Independent travelers and groups alike can wander at will, exploring deserted temples and crowded tourist sites without worrying about anything other than being overcharged for souvenirs and taxi rides. However, this is not utopia, and some safety measures and common sense should be employed.

Petty crimes are uncommon, but they do exist, especially in crowded non-touristy areas; no need to worry about your wallet while in the Egyptian Museum, but pay extra attention when in Ramses Train Station. Egyptians in general are not aggressive people, but they are short tempered; street violence sometimes flares. It takes a lot of provocation and occurs in areas and situations that tourists are unlikely to encounter. Venturing into less touristy, low-class, poor areas, especially after dark, might increase the probability of armed robbery; keep it to daylight hours or skip it all together.

The threat to personal safety from political instability is low. Cairo has seen sporadic, usually low-key, demonstrations by various pro-democracy and reform groups in recent years, and these are best avoided. The crackdown by security forces is usually harsh and indiscriminant.

Harassment is a real threat in Egypt. While males often find themselves subject to overcharging and a never-ending flow of insisting touts, women get the much darker side of harassment. In public areas, verbal harassment is very common, while in more crowded ones, it may escalate to groping. For more information, see "Harassment" p. 96.

Tips To Wear or Not to Wear; That Is the Question

What to put on can be quite perplexing, especially for female travelers. To maintain a fine balance between respecting the rather conservative Middle Eastern culture of Egypt without curbing your own personal freedom and minimizing unwanted attention, there is one golden rule to follow—"When in Rome, do as the Romans do." Egyptians adhere to a rather conservative dress code that is usually casual in nature. That said, if you are in Cairo during summer, a short-sleeve shirt and a long skirt or loose pants are normal; going to the pyramids, the museum, or downtown in a cropped top and low-slung jeans is asking for trouble. If in Hurghada or Sharm El Sheikh, a two-piece swim suit is normal, but please keep your bikini top on and don't forget your cover-up when crossing the street to buy the sunscreen you forgot back home. Going clubbing in a sexy little dress goes without saying, but put on a shawl until you make it to the club.

Drugs of all sorts (from hashish and *bango* [locally grown marijuana] to black sugar and crack) are officially illegal. Possession of a small quantity for personal consumption leaves you open to blackmail and a host of other best-avoided entanglements, while trafficking leaves you in need of a very good lawyer.

Prostitution is illegal in Egypt, and if you're caught red-handed, you might end up in another blackmailing situation. Sex outside wedlock could be considered a felony in Egypt, but it is largely overlooked. Sharing the same hotel room with your partner is quite normal as long as both parties are non-Egyptian passport holders and of different genders. Gay men can find themselves in discriminatory situations, especially in lower than mid-range tourist facilities. For more information, see "The Gay & Lesbian Scene," p. 153, and "Gay & Lesbian Travelers," p. 59.

Traffic is perhaps the greatest routine threat to personal safety in Egypt. Extreme care should be exercised in crossing the road and in driving. Highways can be hazardous, not because of any banditry threat but because of the way locals drive; play it safe when renting a car, and hire a driver as well. For more information, see p. 51.

Many governments maintain advisory pages online that provide useful, up-to-date information on everything from the potential for political instability to the latest outbreaks of avian flu. Registration with your country's embassy in Cairo can also help consular officials warn you of problems and contact you in the event of a situation back home.

7 SPECIALIZED TRAVEL RESOURCES

Egypt has some great pros for certain travelers as well as dreadful cons for others; while students enjoy a good 50% discount on admission to sites, gays and lesbians have to be very discreet about something as personal as their own sexuality.

In addition to the Egypt-specific resources listed below, please visit Frommers.com for other specialized travel resources.

Rules of Engagement

- Only liberal Egyptians kiss the opposite sex when they greet. Don't even reach out a hand for a handshake if the opposite sex is a veiled woman or a beard-growing man.
- When cheek kissing, it is twice; thrice is more Lebanese than Egyptian.
- Two girls holding hands while walking is common, and men cheek kissing is customary.
- If invited to an Egyptian house for dinner, grab a bottle of wine only if you are sure your host drinks. Play it safe and opt for some pastries, flowers, or chocolate.
- For the female traveler, pat an Egyptian male on the shoulder only if he is a dear friend, otherwise you risk being misunderstood.
- If you fall for an Egyptian girl, rest assured no hotel will allow you to check in without a marriage certificate.
- "How much money do you make?" is a question to avoid asking as well as answering. Those who ask it will probably have a hidden agenda.
- In Egypt, everybody smokes. In the streets, only men do. However, women smoking *shisha* (water pipe) is tolerated.
- The pavement is for pedestrians, but this is not always the case, and at times you'll share the pavement with motorbikes and other traffic.
- Be careful when crossing the street, as cars don't stop for pedestrians.

GAY & LESBIAN TRAVELERS

Egyptian tradition doesn't tolerate homosexuality; the major religion frowns upon it, and though it's not a crime here, men arrested for their sexual orientation are usually tried and convicted of debauchery. As a foreigner, you won't be hunted down in the streets, but you can easily find yourself in discriminatory situations with lots of doors being slammed in your face and can be mocked, bullied, and, perhaps, thrown out. However, this is unlikely to happen in upmarket tourist facilities. In any event, you are kindly requested to refrain from displaying affection in public. The local gay scene is totally underground, with the security services actively working against it. Cases of entrapment followed by detention and claimed torture are regularly documented by human rights groups such as Human Rights Watch. Websites such as www.gayegypt.com are routinely monitored by the security services, and chat groups are used to set up fake meetings.

Lesbians, meanwhile, have no public profile as a group, and there is no "scene" as such. Because of this, couples can hold hands in public—this is what friends do in Egypt—but any further display of affection is not recommended; keep it to the privacy of your hotel room.

Gay Egypt (www.gayegypt.com) details cruising locations in many of Egypt's main cities. Much of the information appears to be outdated, but it should still provide some useful leads as well as still-relevant warnings of dangers.

TRAVELERS WITH DISABILITIES

Most disabilities shouldn't stop anyone from traveling. There are more options and resources out there than ever before, but Egypt poses a number of challenges. Cairo is emblematic of the difficulties that you will face: high curbs, a complete absence of ramps, and broken pavement. The situation is best in the high-traffic tourist areas. A couple of high-end hotels and resorts along the Red Sea coast and in Luxor and Sharm El Sheikh now offer a few wheelchair-accessible rooms, while dive centers such as Camel Dive Club (p. 84) in Sharm El Sheikh and Ilios (p. 85) in Hurghada have special diving programs tailored for less mobile customers.

FAMILY TRAVEL

Egyptian society is very family-oriented. Children of all ages are gladly accepted in virtually every context. However, Egypt has less specifically child-oriented activities than other countries, and other than public parks with a kids' area, such as Al Azhar Park (p. 116) in Cairo, and high-end hotels, such as the Fairmont and Kempinski, which offer babysitting, kid-oriented outings or dedicated facilities are a rarity.

Most upmarket hotels in Egypt share a standard policy where one child under 12 enjoys a free stay in his parent's room. In the case of a family traveling with two children and all family members sharing the same double room, one child, if under 6, stays free, while the second, if between 6 and 12, enjoys a 50% discount.

To locate accommodations, restaurants, and attractions that are particularly kid-friendly, refer to the "Kids" icon throughout this guide.

WOMEN TRAVELERS

Single female travelers in Egypt face some challenges, and it's important to get the cultural cues correct in order to minimize hassle and harassment.

First, recognize that simply by being an unaccompanied woman, you are perceived as potentially available. Second, realize that though Egypt is largely a conservative society, its counterparts in Europe and the U.S. are often perceived as free and easy, particularly with regard to matters of sexual relations. Western women figure large in the Egyptian-male imagination as a potential one-night stand. The result is that you will be on the receiving end of a range of comments and invitations in the street, and you may find yourself being crowded and groped in markets and other tight spots. For more on harassment and tips to avoid it, see p. 96.

For general travel resources for women, go to www.frommers.com/planning.

AFRICAN AMERICAN TRAVELERS

Unfortunately, Egyptians tend to generalize and often judge by people's appearances. African-American travelers have experienced difficulties while traveling in the country, but recent second-hand travelers' accounts project a light at the end of the tunnel with much less verbal harassment reported.

JEWISH TRAVELERS

By the 1940s, and prior to the creation of Israel in 1948, the Jewish population of Egypt mounted up to 75,000, almost .5% of the country's total population at the time. But half a century down the road, it has dwindled significantly, and now only a handful of Jews, mostly elders, still cling to their Egyptian nationality. Israel maintains full diplomatic relations with Egypt since the signing of the Camp David Accords and the peace treaty that followed; however, not all Egyptians are for diplomatic ties and the bilateral agreement that seems to strengthen the countries' relations. Resentment against Zionism often surfaces when violence erupts east of the borders, especially when fellow Arab Palestinians, Lebanese, or Syrians are involved. Zionism and Judaism are often mixed up, so even if you are not an Israeli passport holder but believe in the Judaic faith, it is not advisable to roam Cairo's street wearing a kippot.

SENIOR TRAVELERS

The idea of student discounts is now well rooted in Egypt, but the idea of similar discounts for seniors is unfortunately not. Egyptians are, however, on the whole more respectful to their elders, but expect respect rather than discounts.

STUDENT TRAVEL

Students traveling in Egypt are offered a 50% discount when it comes to admission fees for sites. Deviation from the rule of thumb occurs when the adult's admission is LE35, LE25, and LE15, and the student's reduced admission becomes LE20, LE15, and LE8, respectively. Another exception is the Royal Mummies Exhibit at the Egyptian Museum, where students pay LE60. Sites charging admission of LE10 and below offer no discount. Throughout this guide, all the admission prices mentioned are for adults.

SINGLE TRAVELERS

Generally speaking, Egypt is an easy country to travel around, and a single backpacker won't draw too much attention. However, if you are a single female traveler, things will get complicated. See "Women Travelers," p. 60, for more information. Package holiday destinations (such as Marsa Alam) are groups-oriented, and independent travelers, whether single or not, will find it difficult to find value for money accommodation. See "Rack Rate vs. Real Rate," p. 55, for information. All accommodation prices listed in this guide are on a double-occupancy basis; single travelers should expect a discount, but not a hefty one.

Many tour companies offer singles-only trips. **Singles Travel Company** (✆ **888/286-8687;** www.singlestravelcompany.com) offers budget-oriented singles-only escorted tours to places such as Italy, Belize, and Egypt. **All Singles Travel** (✆ **800/717-3231;** www.allsinglestravel.com) arranges Egypt tours with good hotels and possible extensions to see Israel as well. **Backroads** (✆ **800/462-2848;** www.backroads.com) offers "Singles + Solos" active-travel trips to destinations worldwide.

For more information, check out Eleanor Berman's classic ***Traveling Solo: Advice and Ideas for More Than 250 Great Vacations,* 5th Edition** (Globe Pequot), updated in 2005.

For more information on traveling single, go to www.frommers.com/planning.

VEGETARIAN TRAVEL

Vegetarian options are not that common in Egyptian restaurants. The best bet remains ordering a variety of appetizers. Between stuffed vine leaves and hummus, yogurts and cheeses, and fresh bread, a good restaurant can provide a well-balanced and filling meal. Make sure you ask before ordering the stuffed vine leaves—these are sometimes cooked with a small amount of minced meat inside. Note that in Egypt meat refers to beef, lamb, and mutton.

One potential boon to vegetarian travelers is that the Christian community in Egypt maintains a rigorous fasting calendar. Unlike the Muslims, who abstain from food or drink during daylight hours, the Coptic community eschews meat and dairy products during their fasts. Inquire about "fasting foods" at restaurants and bakeries.

8 SUSTAINABLE TOURISM

About 10% of Egypt's land has been declared natural protectorates and national parks; however, don't get your hopes up, this is nothing compared to the parks of Kenya or Tanzania. Between the natural lack of game and the lenient enforcement of nature laws, most of Egypt's already small wildlife has been wiped out. Marine life and avifauna still have a chance, but little is being done to protect and conserve, at least by the official governing body, the **Egyptian Environmental Affairs Agency** (EEAA; www.eeaa.gov.eg). The EEAA manages all of Egypt's 24 natural protectorates and national parks, but they are short on funds, well-trained staff, and equipment. They depend heavily on funds that, if and when they materialize, are often spent on glossy brochures, nicely crafted signage, and, in some cases, rarely open visitor centers. Not all protectorates and parks are frequented by tourists or even have the infrastructure to accommodate any. For example, Lake Burullus Natural Park is one of Egypt's important wetlands and is a great place for bird-watching; however, other than a rusty sign that tells you where you are, there is absolutely nothing. Those protectorates and parks exploited by tourism are usually sold as half- or full-day excursions with little, if any, emphasis on their ecological importance or the rules that should be followed to minimize the impact on their fragile environments. Among the most visited national parks and natural protectorates in Egypt are **Ras Mohamed National Park** (p. 193), where you can dive or snorkel spectacular reefs; **Nabq Natural Protectorate** (p. 195), with its mangrove thickets and awe-striking landscapes; **Wadi El Gemal Natural Protectorate** (p. 255), where Egypt's last remaining gazelle herd still clings to survival; **Saluga and Ghazal** (p. 292), offering a world-class bird-watching opportunity; **Samadi Reef**, for an up-close-and-personal encounter with dolphins in the wild; and **Wadi El Rayan** (p. 158), with its small waterfalls, great desertscapes, and the millennia-old whale skeletons fossils in **Wadi El Hitan** (p. 158).

Sustainable tourism in its broader sense is still in its infancy, and up to a few years back, scant attention was paid in Egypt to the environmental impact of the millions of tourists who visit every year. Today things are seeing a small change with a number of resorts on the Sinai Peninsula, down the Red Sea coast between El Gouna and Marsa Alam, and even in Cairo beginning to participate in environmental certification programs designed to assess their environmental footprint and maximize their sustainability. One of the most common ones is **Green Globe 21** (www.ec3global.com/products-programs/green-globe); the program is named for the U.N. environmental **Agenda 21** program (www.un.org/esa/sustdev/documents/agenda21/index.htm). You can contribute to making tourism greener by learning about the program and asking about it when you make your booking: Make it clear that your tourist dollars prefer to flow to sustainable enterprises.

Additionally, a number of local Egyptian NGOs have emerged that work on raising awareness of environmental issues and train tourism workers in ways that they can preserve the natural capital on which their jobs depend. Leading the pack is the **Hurghada Environmental Protection and Conservation Association (HEPCA)** (© **065/3445035**), which is focused on marine issues along the Red Sea coast. For more about their efforts to protect marine life, coral, and wrecks, see p. 82, or check www.hepca.com. **Environmental Quality International** (www.eqi.com.eg) is a private consulting firm that has done an enormous amount in the isolated desert oasis of Siwa, including the development of Adrére Amellal ecolodge (p. 310).

9 SPECIAL-INTEREST TRIPS & ESCORTED TOURS

SPECIAL-INTEREST TRIPS

While most visitors to Egypt are looking for some sun and fun or a dose of culture with their history, some have more specific interests, which can vary from nature aficionados straddling Egypt's last wildlife frontier in search of a fleeing gazelle to belly dancing fans who want to absorb the traditional art to the fullest. Though Egypt's diversity warrants a long list of enticing special-interest trips, the promising list is currently limited. Here is an overview of what's on offer.

General Resources for Green Travel

In addition to the resources for **Egypt** listed above, the following websites provide valuable wide-ranging information on sustainable travel. For a list of even more sustainable resources, as well as tips and explanations on how to travel greener, visit www.frommers.com/planning.

- **Responsible Travel** (www.responsibletravel.com) is a great source of sustainable travel ideas; the site is run by a spokesperson for ethical tourism in the travel industry. **Sustainable Travel International** (www.sustainable travelinternational.org) promotes ethical tourism practices, and manages an extensive directory of sustainable properties and tour operators around the world.
- In the U.K., **Tourism Concern** (www.tourismconcern.org.uk) works to reduce social and environmental problems connected to tourism. The **Association of Independent Tour Operators (AITO)** (www.aito.co.uk) is a group of specialist operators leading the field in making holidays sustainable.
- In Canada, **www.greenlivingonline.com** offers extensive content on how to travel sustainably, including a travel and transport section.
- In Australia, the national body which sets guidelines and standards for ecotourism is **Ecotourism Australia** (www.ecotourism.org.au). **The Green Directory** (www.thegreendirectory.com.au), **Green Pages** (www.thegreen pages.com.au), and **Eco Directory** (www.ecodirectory.com.au) offer sustainable travel tips and directories of green businesses.
- **Carbonfund** (www.carbonfund.org), **TerraPass** (www.terrapass.org), and **Carbon Neutral** (www.carbonneutral.org) provide info on "carbon offsetting," or offsetting the greenhouse gas emitted during flights.
- **Greenhotels** (www.greenhotels.com) recommends green-rated member hotels around the world that fulfill the company's stringent environmental requirements. **Environmentally Friendly Hotels** (www.environmentally friendlyhotels.com) offers more green accommodation ratings.
- For information on animal-friendly issues throughout the world, visit **Tread Lightly** (www.treadlightly.org). For information about the ethics of swimming with dolphins, visit the **Whale and Dolphin Conservation Society** (www.wdcs.org).
- **Volunteer International** (www.volunteerinternational.org) has a list of questions to help you determine the intentions and the nature of a volunteer program. For general info on volunteer travel, visit **www.volunteer abroad.org** and **www.idealist.org**.

Academic Trips & Language Classes

Available through educational centers and colleges rather than tour operators and travel agencies, academic trips to Egypt are not commercially exploited. Check the **Francis and Louise Hutchins Center for International Education** (www.berea.edu/cie); from time to time it offers its students an academic trip to Egypt fostering cross-cultural understanding.

The **American University** in Cairo's Arabic Language Institute (www.aucegypt.edu) has a very comprehensive Arabic language program. The program includes day trips in Cairo and possible overnights to Luxor, Aswan, and Alexandria. The **American Research Centre** in Egypt (www.arce.org) offers a "Beginning Arabic" summer language program in Cairo. It also includes cultural tours in the capital as well as weekend excursions to the Red Sea.

Adventure & Wellness Trips

Diving is Egypt's number-one outdoor activity, and literally every diving center in the country can offer you a diving package holiday of some sort; if not including accommodation then at least recommending one. Among the best diving centers that offer a full diving package holiday in Egypt are **Camel Dive Club** (www.cameldive.com) and **Red Sea Diving Safari** (www.redsea-divingsafari.com). If you are a hard-core diving addict, consider a 1- to 2-week safari on a liveaboard going where 1-day boat trips don't; check out **Emperor Divers** (✆ **012/2340995;** www.emperordivers.com) or **Blue Planet Liveaboards** (✆ **065/3559124;** www.blueplanet-liveaboards.com).

For adventure trips away from the Red Sea reefs and corals, **Sheikh Sina Bedouin Treks** (www.sheikhsina.com) offers adventure trips that focus on trekking in the Sinai High Mountains region, and **Badawiya Expedition Travel** (www.badawiya.com) has a long list of desert-based adventure trips all over the Western Desert.

Lake Nasser Adventure (www.lakenasseradventure.com) offers safari trips, in addition to their standard fishing ones, where you can get a glimpse of Egypt's wildlife.

La Résidence des Cascades (www.residencedescascades.com) offers golf-oriented holiday packages, and **Egypt Golf Tours** (www.golfegypt.nl) has a number of different golfing trips on offer.

Wellness trips to Egypt vary from spa and yoga vacations to country tours in search of the ultimate meditation spots. The **Algotherm Red Sea Thalasso & Spa** at La Résidence des Cascades (www.residencedescascades.com) has a full program of spa therapies available. **Rock Sea** (www.rocksea.net) often organizes yoga seminars and workshops in its huge white tent, dubbed the Dome, and **Science of Life** (www.scienceoflife.co.uk) has some interesting 1-week yoga retreats in Sinai. For a precious spiritual experience that includes meditation sessions in several Ancient Egyptian sites (including a private one insidethe Great Pyramid burial chamber), check out **Sacred Earth Journeys** (✆ **877/874-7922;** www.sacredearthjourneys.ca) and **Heartslight** (✆ **319/365-3398;** www.heartlights.net).

Belly Dancing Trips

The traditional Egyptian art of belly dancing is hitting it big in the U.S. and Latin America with dozens of workshops, seminars, and festivals springing up. In Egypt, escorted by professional belly dancing instructors, trips focus on attending shows, participating in classes and workshops, as well as having the option of performing publicly. **Yalla Tours** (www.yallatoursegypt.com) has a 1-week standard belly dancing trip on offer, while **World Belly Dance** (www.worldbellydance.com) has less frequent, but super, 11-day tours; keep an open eye for new announcements.

Volunteer & Working Trips

Traveling with the purpose of volunteering is a double win. Though Egypt misses big time on volunteering for environmental purposes, it has a wide range of choices when it comes to social issues and community development. Volunteer opportunities vary from teaching English and participating in awareness-raising campaigns to helping local Bedouins in Sinai build small dams to providing medical consultancy to impoverished Egyptians living in rural Upper Egypt. For comprehensive lists of what's available, check **Idea List** (www.idealist.org), **World Volunteer Web** (www.worldvolunteerweb.org), and **Responsible Travel** (www.responsibletravel.com).

ESCORTED GENERAL-INTEREST TRIPS

Escorted tours are structured group tours with a group leader. The price usually includes everything from airfare, hotels, and meals to tours, admission costs, and local transportation.

Despite the fact that escorted tours require big deposits and predetermine hotels, restaurants, and itineraries, many people derive security and peace of mind from the structure they offer. Escorted tours—whether they're navigated by bus, motor coach, train, or boat—let travelers sit back and enjoy the trip without having to drive or worry about details. They take you to the maximum number of sights in the minimum amount of time with the least amount of hassle. They're particularly convenient for people with limited mobility, and they can be a great way to make new friends.

On the downside, you'll have little opportunity for serendipitous interactions with locals. The tours can be jampacked with activities, leaving little room for individual sightseeing, whim, or adventure—plus they often focus on the heavily touristed sites, so you miss out on many a lesser-known gem.

There are hundreds, if not thousands, of tour operators who feature Egypt in their brochures. At the high end of the scale is American luxury travel company **Abercrombie & Kent** (**© 800/554-7016**; www.abercrombiekent.com). More on the economical front is British-based **Insight Vacations** (www.insightvacations.com), which has economically priced tours that hit all of Egypt's must-see sites. The young and energetic Aussie **Gecko's Adventure** (www.geckosadventures.com) is a cross between an escorted trip in its classic sense and independent travel; groups average nine travelers who stay in small, clean, locally owned guesthouses and are often led by local guides. The structure of the trips' itineraries allows you the luxury of free time to stop at that stall in the market or take off on a culinary adventure later in the evening.

10 STAYING CONNECTED

TELEPHONES

To call Egypt:

1. Dial the international access code: 011 from the U.S. or Canada; or 0011 from Australia; 00 from the U.K., Ireland, New Zealand, and the rest of the world.
2. Dial the country code, 2.
3. Dial the area/mobile operator code and then the number.

To make international calls: To make international calls from Egypt, first dial 00 and then the country code (U.S. or Canada 1, U.K. 44, Ireland 353, Australia 61, New Zealand 64). Next, dial the area code and number. For example, if you wanted to call the British Embassy in Washington, D.C., you would dial 00-1-202-588-7800.

For directory assistance: The once-disastrous state of directory assistance in Egypt has undergone a miraculous transformation in recent years. Now you can dial 140 and get English-speaking directory assistance for inside Egypt that is accurate and up to date. The same service exists online at www.140online.com, but the numbers are less likely to be up to date and it is only in Arabic. For business phone numbers and addresses, try www.yellowpages.com.eg. For international directory assistance, dial 144.

For operator assistance: If you need operator assistance in making a call, dial 120 if you're trying to make an international call and 140 if you want to call a number in Egypt.

Toll-free numbers: Toll free numbers start with 0800 in Egypt. Calling an 800 number in the States from Egypt is not toll-free; in fact, it costs the same as an overseas call.

Hot lines: These are 5-digit numbers that often start with 1. They require no area code to dial.

All telephone numbers in Egypt, including mobile ones, are 7 digits except for landlines in Cairo. In 2007, Cairo phone numbers (area code 02) were changed from 7 to 8 digits. The rule of thumb is on the west side of the Nile (Giza, Harem, Mohandiseen, Agouza, Dokki), add a 3 to the beginning of the number. On the east side of the river, and in the middle of the river (Downtown, Heliopolis, Maadi, Garden City, Zamalek, and Manial), add a 2.

CELLPHONES

Three GSM mobile operators dominate the scene in Egypt: **Etisalat** (www.etisalat.com.eg; code 011 and 014), **Mobinil** (www.mobinil.com; code 012, 017, and 018), and **Vodafone** (www.vodafone.com.eg; code 010, 016, and 019). They are quite competitive, with an endless stream of new offers and attractive packages. Coverage-wise, nothing distinguishes one from the other, as they all cover most of Egypt's urban centers but don't extend to cover less inhabited ones; St. Catherine is well covered, but El Karm is not.

Having a mobile phone while in Egypt is a good idea—and easy; you will buy a phone number and a prepaid phone credit, which can be used with your own unlocked phone. If you don't have your own phone, less than LE200 covers the phone, SIM card, and credit. Tariff plans can get complicated and confusing, but as a general guideline expect to pay LE0.50 per minute for calling another mobile line in Egypt, and LE2.25 to LE4.50 per minute if you are calling overseas. Sending a local SMS costs LE0.50, while an international one costs LE0.80. Incoming calls are free of charge.

North Americans can rent a phone before leaving home from **InTouch USA** (✆ **800/872-7626;** www.intouchglobal.com) or **RoadPost** (✆ **888/290-1606** or 905/272-5665; www.roadpost.com). InTouch will also, for free, advise you on whether your existing phone will work overseas; simply call ✆ **703/222-7161** between 9am and 4pm EST, or go to **http://intouchglobal.com/travel.htm**.

INTERNET/E-MAIL

Without Your Own Laptop

Internet access in most of Egypt is cheap and easy, with even the smallest and most out-of-the-way villages sporting at least rudimentary Internet capacity. You may have to elbow game-playing kids out of the way, but you'll be able to check the news and collect your messages.

For specific recommendations, see "Fast Facts" and/or "Tourist Information" in the appropriate destination chapter.

With Your Own Laptop

For travelers with Wi-Fi–equipped laptops, life is good in Egypt. In Cairo, almost every cafe features free wireless, and those that don't are usually within range of one that does. Additionally, all three mobile operators provide Internet access through a small 3G USB modem that is connected to your laptop. The modem itself costs LE100, and the Internet line can be recharged with scratch cards (the same concept as telephone lines). Going prepaid, the first 17 to 20MBs, depending on the mobile operator, are free of charge, and each additional MB costs about LE0.30.

The big hotel chains in Egypt have also jumped on the Wi-Fi bandwagon, but for the time being they are not offering it for free. The irony of charging an average of LE150 a day for Internet access when it's available for free just across the street in a cafe or at their three-star competition is lost on them.

If your laptop is not Wi-Fi equipped, there is cheap and good dial-up access throughout the country that you can access from your hotel room. Most hotels and Internet cafes will also let you plug into their network through the Ethernet port on your laptop.

Cairo International Airport (all three terminals) provides free Wi-Fi.

Ethernet patch cables are easy to find (and are generally supplied by hotels with in-room high-speed Internet), but replacement power cords, even for very common laptop models, are not.

Censorship

The Internet is not widely censored in Egypt, though access to some sites that are critical of the government have been blocked. A greater concern for some will be the monitoring of certain sites (such as www.gayegypt.com) and the use of chat rooms to set up gay men for unpleasant encounters with the police.

11 TIPS ON ACCOMMODATIONS

Accommodations in Egypt run the gamut from flea-pit to palatial, and an enormous number of choices exist throughout the country. Despite the numbers, however, both value for money and style can be a little hard to find.

At the palatial end of the market, there has been a huge, and often slapdash, investment in holiday resort–style facilities—big, glitzy hotels designed to live up to a not-always-realistic idea of what luxury truly is. At the low end, the emphasis has been on delivering the cheapest beds to backpackers, with little thought to cleanliness, let alone quality. However, exceptions to both ends do exist, as well as a handful of stylish accommodations that you don't want to miss out on. Most of these fabulous options dominate the best of Egypt's accommodations (p. 2).

That said, every city has its gems, and with careful perusal of this guide, you can now visit most parts of the country and be well accommodated on a variety of budgets.

Egyptian hotels are rated by the Ministry of Tourism on the basis of a star system. The rankings are complicated and obscure, and they're based on size, facilities, and service. However, in reality, some five-star tourism establishments provide the worst service you could imagine and a two-star one can be all about professionalism. My advice? Ignore the Ministry of Tourism's star rating system, as it can be quite confusing, if not misleading, when it comes to deciding which hotel to stay at.

At the higher end of the market, foreign-run chains dominate and offer substantially better service than their scarce domestic competition. Prices in these hotels are quoted and charged in U.S. dollars or euros. You can still pay the equivalent in Egyptian pounds, but you will likely be charged a disgracefully low exchange rate. Here are the key players in this segment of the hotelier market:

- **Accor/Sofitel** specializes in blandly renovated heritage properties such as the Old Winter Palace in Luxor, the Cataract in Aswan (closed for renovation till 2011), and the Cecil in Alexandria. They certainly add a touch of style to your stay, but they are generally overpriced for the level of service they provide.
- **Four Seasons** is among the best hotel chains in Egypt. Its hotels are well designed and well run by a very

professional staff, but they miss on individualized service and personalized luxury.

- **Hyatt**'s Cairo property goes all out to impress with its cavernous, glitzy lobby, but follows up with characterless, overpriced rooms. The chain's Sinai resorts, however, are top-notch.
- **Kempinski,** whether in Soma Bay, Safaga, or Cairo, is cut from a completely different cloth. These guys know what luxury is, what their high-end customer is looking for, and they deliver with excellence and style. If you want to treat yourself, don't miss out on Kempinski.
- **Marriott**'s Egypt hotels are generic, cookie-cutter properties for the most part, but they make up for lack of character with professional service and above-average food. The exception is the Cairo Marriott, which has some character but below-average food.
- The **Méridien** hotels in Egypt rise considerably above their Accor siblings, and feature some of the most stylish decor in the country. If snappy color schemes matter to you, forget the Four Seasons and head to the Méridien.
- **Mövenpick**'s properties in Egypt either make it to the "don't miss" list or the "best avoid" one. Its resort in El Quseir is among the most recommended accommodation facilities in the country, while the one in Aswan is completely out of place.
- **Oberoi** competes with the Four Seasons in terms of price, and wins hands-down on location with a hotel next to the pyramids in Giza, one on a long, lovely sweep of beach south of Hurghada, and even a cruiser that sails down the Nile.
- **Pyramisa** is a chain to avoid unless you run out of choices. Some of the facilities look great on paper, and some (such as the Isis Island resort in Aswan) are fun, but facilities are second rate, and the food can be truly bad.

4

Suggested Egypt Itineraries

The large and diverse country of Egypt has a lot to offer visitors, from amazing Ancient Egyptian pyramids, temples, and tombs to religiously significant and artistically beautiful Coptic iconographies and grandiose mosques. The outdoor scene is no less enticing than its cultural and historical counterpart, with everything from diving with sharks in the Red Sea to kitesurfing. And if you're keeping up with the latest trends in the thrilling outdoor sports scene, perhaps you want to try freediving or rock climbing. If you want to sample it all—and you can—you can spend a week hitting the classic Egypt sites or an intense 2 weeks on what I call the King's Circuit (p. 78).

1 REGIONS IN BRIEF

CAIRO & ENVIRONS The capital of Egypt is a massive, densely populated city of around 17 million people. It is crammed with a diverse array of must-see sights, which range from great works of Ancient Egyptian architecture and an Art Deco–rich downtown to an eccentric Hindu-styled palace and a rarely visited dancing hall. However, Cairo is, by the same token, probably not a place that you want to spend more than a couple of days; the air is polluted, and the roads edge closer to gridlock with every week.

The pyramids of the Giza Plateau, maybe the most famous works of public architecture on Earth and the only one of the original Seven Wonders of the World still extant, lie on the western outskirts of the city. A short drive into the countryside to the south lie the remnants of the ancient capital of Memphis, as well as the sites of Dahshur and Saqqara.

THE MEDITERRANEAN COAST Egypt's Mediterranean coast has long been a world apart from the interior of Egypt, and did not become important until it was invaded by Alexander the Great (for whom Alexandria is named) in 331 B.C. and the city flourished during the Greco-Roman period. Evidence of this past can still be seen in the stunning Roman mosaics that have been unearthed at the Villa of the Birds, the densely interwoven cosmogony of the Catacombs of Kom El Shoqafa, and even the gleaming wood and brass of the old coffee shops around Saad Zagloul Square.

Recently the coast to the east and west of Alexandria has experienced something of a resurgence as a summer getaway for upper-class Cairenes escaping the muggy July and August heat of the capital. Holiday villas now blight miles of once-pristine white beach. Most foreigners, however, keep to Alexandria or Marsa Matruh when visiting the Mediterranean coast. Marsa Matruh is a small coastal town located about 300km (186 miles) west of Alexandria. It enjoys some of the best Mediterranean beaches out here, but it is marketed as a summer vacation destination for locals rather foreigners. A direct flight

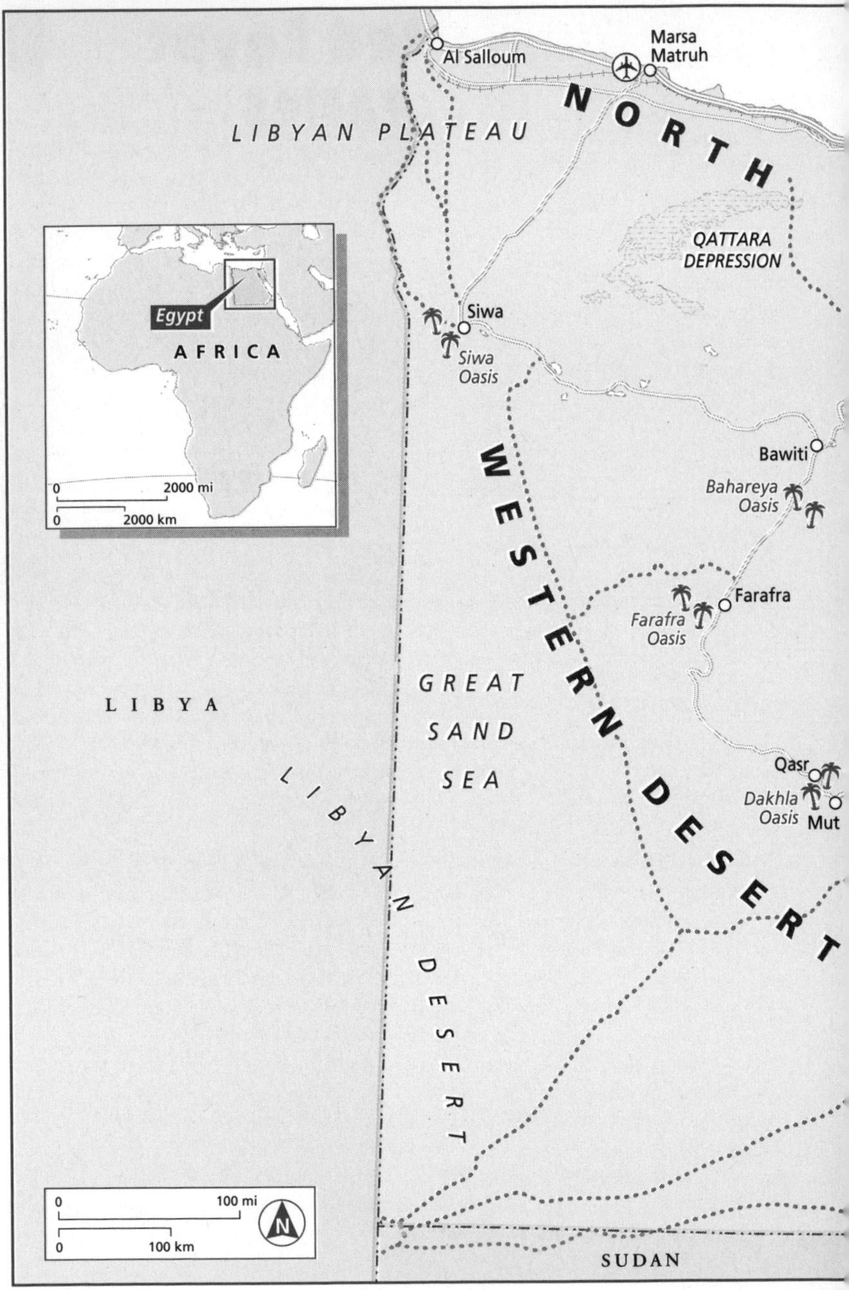
Al Salloum
Marsa Matruh
NORTH
LIBYAN PLATEAU
QATTARA DEPRESSION
Egypt
AFRICA
0
2000 mi
0
2000 km
Siwa
Siwa Oasis
Bawiti
Bahareya Oasis
WESTERN DESERT
Farafra
Farafra Oasis
GREAT SAND SEA
LIBYA
Qasr
Dakhla Oasis
Mut
LIBYAN DESERT
0
100 mi
0
100 km
N
SUDAN

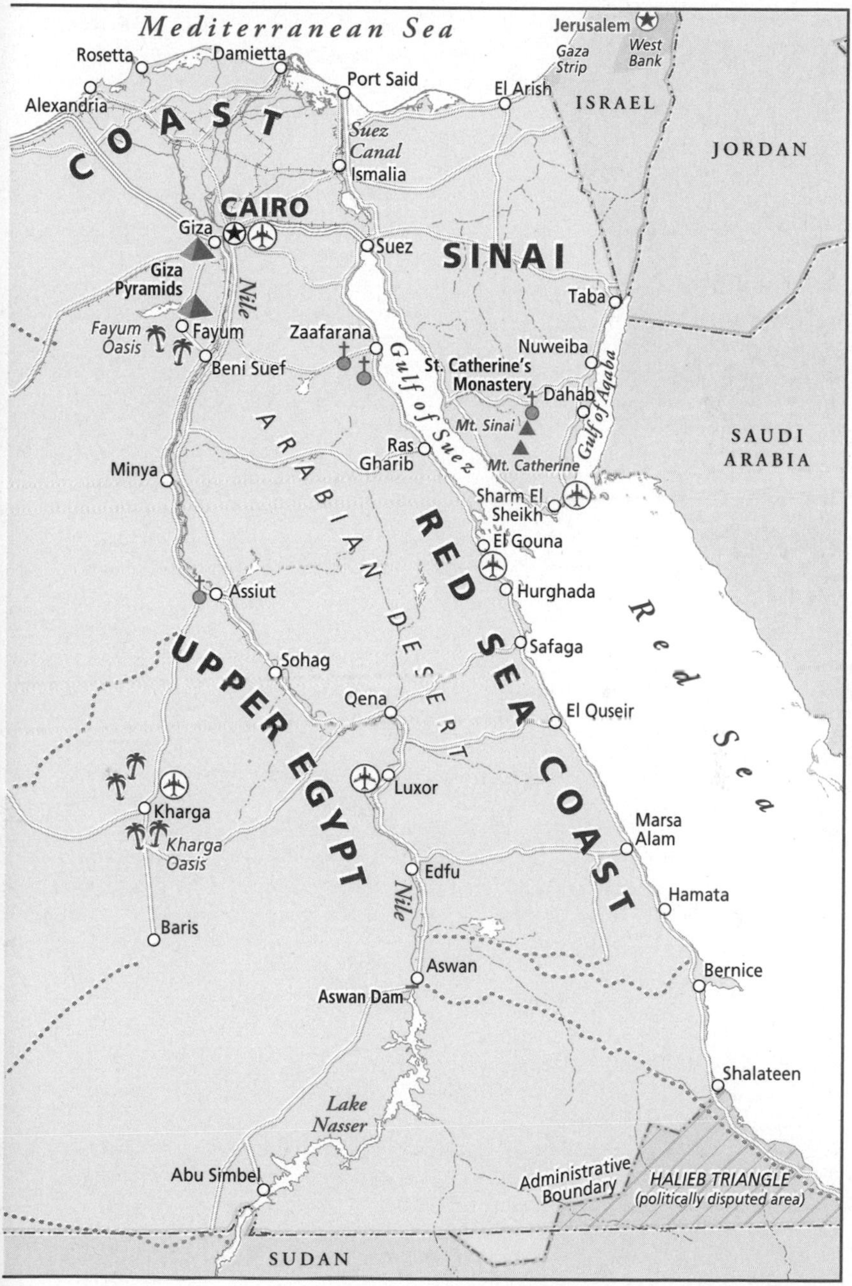
Mediterranean Sea
Rosetta
Damietta
Port Said
Alexandria
El Arish
Jerusalem
Gaza Strip
West Bank
ISRAEL
JORDAN
COAST
Suez Canal
Ismalia
CAIRO
Giza
Suez
SINAI
Giza Pyramids
Nile
Taba
Fayum Oasis
Fayum
Zaafarana
Nuweiba
Beni Suef
Gulf of Suez
St. Catherine's Monastery
Dahab
Gulf of Aqaba
Mt. Sinai
ARABIAN DESERT
Ras Gharib
Mt. Catherine
SAUDI ARABIA
Minya
Sharm El Sheikh
RED SEA COAST
El Gouna
Assiut
Hurghada
Red Sea
Safaga
UPPER EGYPT
Sohag
Qena
El Quseir
Luxor
Kharga
Kharga Oasis
Marsa Alam
Edfu
Hamata
Baris
Aswan
Bernice
Aswan Dam
Shalateen
Lake Nasser
Abu Simbel
Administrative Boundary
HALIEB TRIANGLE
(politically disputed area)
SUDAN

connecting Marsa Matruh to a couple of British cities took off in summer 2010; a change in Marsa Matruh's tourism scene is on its the way.

UPPER EGYPT From the Valley of the Kings and Tutankhamun tomb to Karnak Temple and the Colossi of Memnon, Luxor hosts the largest concentration of Ancient Egyptian monuments anywhere in the country. Upper Egypt is also home to Nubia, which has a culture, history, and way of life all its own. Coming from Cairo to Aswan, you will immediately notice the change in atmosphere. Gone is the hustle and bustle of the big city, replaced by a laid-back attitude that takes the days as they come and seems to match the monuments themselves for timeless tranquillity. With fewer must-see sights than its neighboring monument-infested Luxor, Aswan is the place to unwind—go for a sunset sail on the Nile and wander the souk in search of local handicrafts.

SINAI PENINSULA A mining ground during Ancient Egyptian dynastic rule and a fighting ground during the 1960s and 1970s, the Sinai did not come into its own as a tourist destination until the 1980s, when Egyptians and foreigners began to flock to the deserted, palm-lined beaches and miles of pristine coral on the Sinai's Eastern Coast. Twenty-five years later, the main center of Sharm El Sheikh is a thriving, and still growing, city.

The Sinai Peninsula is not all about luxurious resorts or diving; the Sinai High Mountains region offers some of the best hiking and trekking opportunities in the country, in addition to breathtaking landscapes and a must-see 6th-century monastery. Laid-back Dahab offers a great opportunity to just sit back and relax or go for a heavy dose of outdoor activities that includes freediving, rock climbing, and the latest craze in town—camel diving safaris.

RED SEA COAST The stretch of coastline from El Gouna to Hamata is the new boomtown of Egyptian tourism, a spectacular desert coastline that's marked with great tourist destinations. While Hurghada is the sun-and-fun capital of the Red Sea, it was the first Red Sea destination to welcome tourists, and first-time mistakes are evident, especially when it comes to urban planning. El Gouna is a role model, with its beautiful landscaping and well-executed designs, while Safaga still retains an adventurous diving spirit that goes back to the early days when divers stayed in ramshackle huts, used wrecked 4×4s, and drove on dirt roads just to go for a dive. El Quseir offers a dash of history in to your Red Sea visit, while Marsa Alam is the new diving mecca, with its mind-boggling diving sites. Hamata is tourism's last frontier on the Red Sea coast. Enjoy pristine beaches, virgin diving spots, and great kitesurfing.

WESTERN DESERT OASES The vast stretch of desert to the west of Cairo, Luxor, and Aswan is a rough oblong bordered by Libya to the west and the Nile Valley to the east, with the top and bottom defined by the Mediterranean and Sudan, respectively. In prehistoric times, this desert was alternately savanna and vast areas submerged in water, and the fossilized traces of whales in Wadi El Hitan prove it. At the same time, rock paintings showing life of early hunter-gatherers is the highlight of your visit to the gigantic plateau of El Gilf El Kebir.

There are five main oases in the desert—Siwa in the north and, heading south, Bahareya, Farafra, Dakhla, and Kharga. Each of these communities has its own character and is the stepping-off point for expeditions into the surrounding desert. Spend a night in the White Desert amongst the outlandish white outcroppings, explore the ancient mud-brick town of Qasr in Dakhla, visit the ancient Christian Bagawat Necropolis in Kharga, or sandboard the goliath dunes around Siwa.

2 MY NAME IS TUT

Ancient Egyptian heritage is a magnet that draws hundreds of thousands of tourists from all four corners of the globe. If you're a history buff—or just want a heavy dose of the country's famous sites—this 1-week itinerary is guaranteed to satisfy your hunger for Ancient Egyptian history and culture.

Day 1: The Giza Pyramids

If you are here for the Pharaohs, then there is no better start than the **pyramids** (p. 108). Get to the site very early in the morning, as tickets to the Great Pyramid of Khufu sell out quickly. Enjoy your adventure into the heart of this spiritually inspiring place before checking out the amazing **Solar Boat Museum.** The museum and the pyramids trio will keep you busy until about noon, when you can wave a taxi down and head to the **Egyptian Museum** (p. 104). The two-story museum is one of Egypt's most comprehensive, with a plethora of statues, coffins, funerary items, and artifacts that belong to the great Ancient Egyptian civilization. However, there are two exhibits you can't afford to miss; the Tutankhamun Collection and the Royal Mummies Exhibit. You'll likely be too busy to stop for lunch, so be sure to pack snacks and plenty of water (at least two large bottles in summer).

Day 2: The First Capital

Depending on your interest in Ancient Egypt, you don't want to leave today's capital, Cairo, before checking out the country's very first, **Memphis** (p. 154). Nothing much remains but a handful of statues (including a giant 13m/43 ft. one of Ramses II), but combining Memphis with the nearby **Dahshur** (p. 154) and **Saqqara** (p. 154) makes a good Ancient Egyptian excursion out of Cairo. Dahshur plays host to the rather unusual **Bent Pyramid** (p. 154), while Saqqara is where Egypt's oldest pyramid, the **Step Pyramid** (p. 154), is located. Saqqara also encompasses one of the country's most amazing museums, the **Imhotep Museum** (p. 155). Your excursion will come to an end around sunset, giving you enough time for a short rest before catching the sleeper train to Luxor.

Days 3, 4 & 5: A Heavy Dose of Ancient Egypt

Luxor has the largest concentration of Ancient Egyptian monuments anywhere in the country, and with so much to see, finishing it in 1 day is simply impossible; plan 3 days if you want to cover most of the attractions without being stressed on time. During the first day you'll be able to visit the **East Bank** (p. 268) monuments, which include Luxor Temple, Karnak Temple, Luxor Museum, and the Mummification Museum, while the second and third days should be entirely dedicated to the **West Bank** (p. 270) sites, which include the Mortuary Temple of Hatshepsut, Valley of the Kings, Valley of the Queens, the necropolis Deir El Medina, and the Colossi of Memnon. While the different temples and tombs are within proximity to each other, you'll want to spend ample time at each.

While in Luxor, don't skip the chance for a hot-air balloon or small Cessna plane ride, which can provide a different perspective—literally—to your sightseeing experience here.

Day 6: In Transit

After the heavy dose of Ancient Egypt you've just had in Luxor, it's a good idea to sit back and relax for a day. Enjoy laidback Aswan before continuing the next day to the grand finale at the Temple of

Abu Simbel. While in Aswan, head to the **Nubian Museum** (p. 293), which sheds some light on the distinctive Nubian culture from Ancient Egyptian times and through the ages; hop to Aswan's west bank for a quick visit to the **Tombs of the Nobles** (p. 293), or head to **Elephantine Island** (p. 291) to visit the remains of the island's once-famous three temples.

The train is the easiest way to leave Luxor or Aswan, but this means you'd miss one of Ancient Egypt's most stunning and well preserved temples, the **Temple of Horus at Edfu** (p. 279). Edfu is a small town that lies on the way between Luxor and Aswan, and it's worth paying a bit extra to hire a car with a driver for the day so you can visit the temple.

Day 7: I Am a God

There is simply no better way to wrap up your Ancient Egyptian tour of the country than the **Temple of Abu Simbel** (p. 298). It was built by the longest ruling Pharaoh, Ramses II, and is where the self glorified Pharaoh was deified. In more recent times, the Temple of Abu Simbel was the center of the world's attention as archaeologists were racing against time to save it from drowning under the rising water of Lake Nasser.

Twice a year, the sun shines on Ramses II's face in the temple's sanctuary; if you want to plan your visit around this, the dates are February 22 and October 22.

3 THE CROSS & THE CRESCENT

Both Christianity and Islam have played major roles in Egypt's history and continue to strongly impact the country's present. From the strongly religious Christian Roman period to a succession of Islamic caliphates, dynasties, and sultanates, each has left a heavy mark on the country's culture and heritage.

Day 1: Coptic Cairo

Coptic Cairo (p. 123) is home to a number of sites, and the easiest way to get here is by using the Metro; the Mar Girgis station directly faces Coptic Cairo's main entrance.

The **Fortress of Babylon** (p. 126), once a defensive structure, takes a more religious role today, and plays host to the **Hanging Church** (p. 126) nestled on the fortress's Iron Gate. Coptic Cairo is also home to the atmospheric **Church of St. George** (p. 124), the splendid **Coptic Museum** (p. 124), and **Ben Ezra Synagogue** (p. 123). A stone's throw from Coptic Cairo is Egypt's, as well as Africa's, very first mosque—Amr Ibn El A'as Mosque. Though what you see today is an assortment of additions done by different Islamic rulers, it's a good introduction to Islamic Cairo, where you'll head on Day 2.

Day 2: Islamic Cairo

Islamic Cairo (p. 114) is spread over a relatively large area, so expect a day full of walking. Start your tour from Bab El Futuh and down Al Mu'izz le-din Allah Street, named after the Fatimid caliph who ordered the building of Cairo. Today the street is dotted with different mosques, *sabils,* and all types of historical buildings that belong to different Islamic periods; these all shed light on some important aspects of history. Al Mu'izz le-din Allah Street eventually cuts Al Azhar Street and ends at **Bab Zuweila** (p. 116), one of Fatimid Cairo's last remaining city gates that today hosts a tiny museum. Take a detour back to the Al Azhar Street and visit **Wekalet El Ghuri** (p. 123) before crossing the street toward **Khan Al Khalili** (p. 119). Khan Al Khalili's main street, an

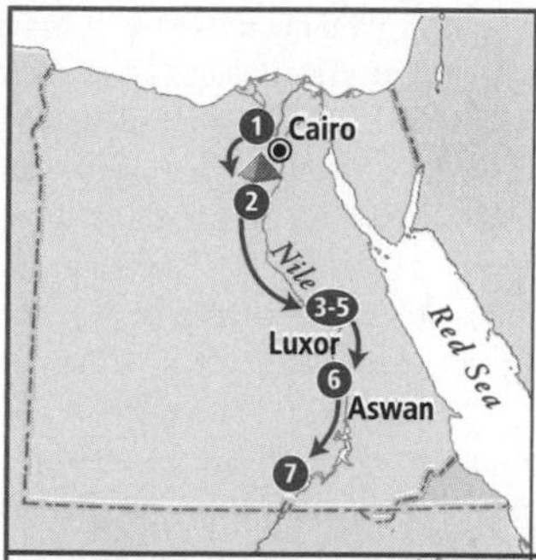

My Name is Tut

Day 1: The Giza Pyramids

Day 2: The First Capital

Days 3, 4 & 5: A Heavy Dose of Ancient Egypt

Day 6: In Transit

Day 7: I Am a God

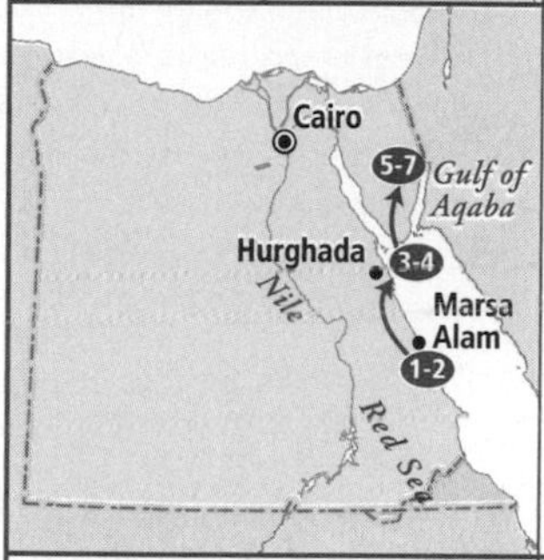

Pump Up the Adrenaline

Days 1 & 2: Diving with Sharks

Days 3 & 4: The Perfect Lagoon

Days 5, 6 & 7: Freediving or Rock Climbing?

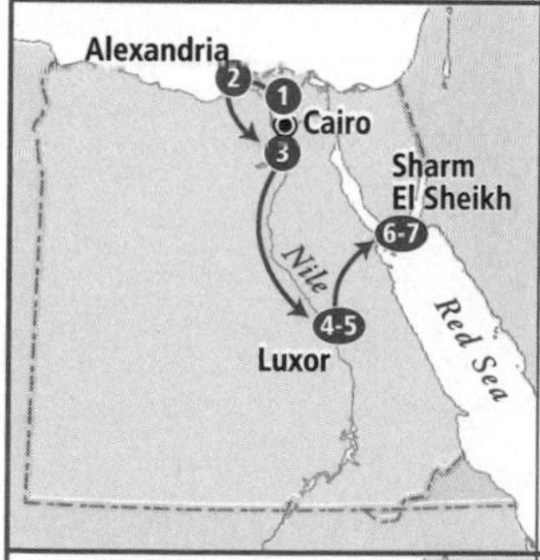

Classic Egypt

Day 1: Cairo

Day 2: A Day in Alex

Day 3: Back in Cairo

Days 4 & 5: Luxor

Days 6 & 7: Sharm El Sheikh

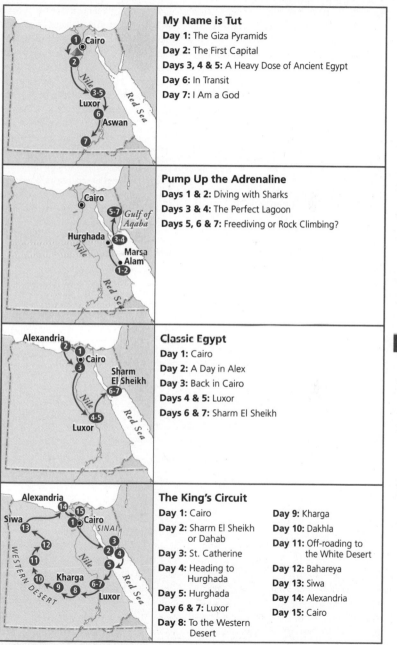

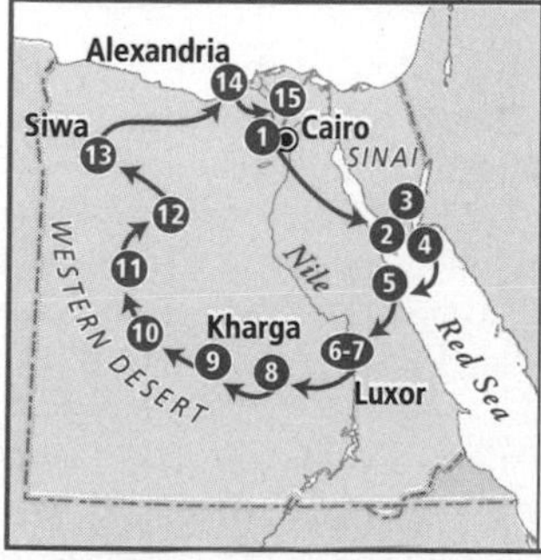

The King's Circuit

Day 1: Cairo

Day 2: Sharm El Sheikh or Dahab

Day 3: St. Catherine

Day 4: Heading to Hurghada

Day 5: Hurghada

Day 6 & 7: Luxor

Day 8: To the Western Desert

Day 9: Kharga

Day 10: Dakhla

Day 11: Off-roading to the White Desert

Day 12: Bahareya

Day 13: Siwa

Day 14: Alexandria

Day 15: Cairo

alley to be more precise, is lined with stalls and shops that sell a wide array of Egyptian souvenirs, from typical cotton shirts with "Egypt" printed in bold lettering to a golden medallion with your name engraved in hieroglyphics.

No matter where you go for dinner (probably Naguib Mahfouz Café or Taj Al Sultan), make sure you have tea at **El Fishawy** (p. 152). This place is an institution and one of the most uniquely Egyptian experiences you can have.

Day ❸: More Islamic Treasures

Islamic Cairo needs a second day. Start your day with an early-morning visit to the **Mosque of Ibn Tulun** (p. 121), which shares more similarities with the Great Mosque of Al Mutawakil in Samarra, Iraq, than to any of its fellow Cairene mosques. Right next door is **Bait al Kritliya** (p. 117) and its great collection of antiques, while down Saliba Street (in the direction of the Citadel), you will come to the unique **Taz Palace** (p. 122) and the equally enticing **Sama Khana** (p. 122). Before reaching the Citadel, you will come to three more sites: **Madrasa of Sultan Hassan** (p. 120), **Mosque of Al Rifa'ai** (p. 120), and the **Blue Mosque** (p. 117). The **Citadel** (p. 118), with its Ottoman-styled Mohamed Ali Mosque, marks the end of your tour of Islamic Cairo. Once you've done the sites, head back toward the Mosque of Ibn Tulun, where you'll find the **Khan Misr Touloun** (p. 147) souvenir shop right in front; it's a shopping experience you don't want to miss. Contrary to the rest of the Egyptian souvenir shopping scene, Khan Misr Touloun keeps fixed prices and fixed opening hours.

4 PUMP UP THE ADRENALINE

This 1-week itinerary is for thrill seekers who feed on outdoor activities and adrenaline-pumping experiences.

Days ❶ & ❷: Diving with Sharks

The Red Sea is an underwater dreamland, but if sharks are what you're looking for, then go south. **Marsa Alam** (p. 250) is a new and emerging destination that features some pristine beaches and downright thrilling diving spots. Dive **Abu Dabab** (p. 251) for a close encounter with the last of the remaining dugongs, or **Elephantine** (p. 291) for a thrilling dive with hammerhead sharks. Marsa Alam is a package holiday destination with some packages tailored to divers; see "Adventure & Wellness Trips," p. 64, for recommendations.

Days ❸ & ❹: The Perfect Lagoon

If Marsa Alam is a diver's heaven, then **El Gouna** (p. 222) is certainly a kitesurfer's fantasyland. From Mangroovy to Buzzha beaches, reefless, knee- to waist-deep lagoons with favorably blowing winds create the perfect conditions for kitesurfing. Though there are other places along the Red Sea coast (Hamata, for example) that can be as thrilling as El Gouna, when it comes to kitesurfing, El Gouna is the only place you have the option of downing a cold one or going out and partying after a day of intense kitesurfing.

Days ❺, ❻ & ❼: Freediving or Rock Climbing?

From the coastal city of Hurghada, take the ferry (three times a week) to glamorous Sharm El Sheikh, from where you can easily pick up a bus or a taxi to Dahab. The laid-back coastal town has some of the most thrilling outdoor activities you won't find elsewhere in the country; put your physical capabilities to the test as you go

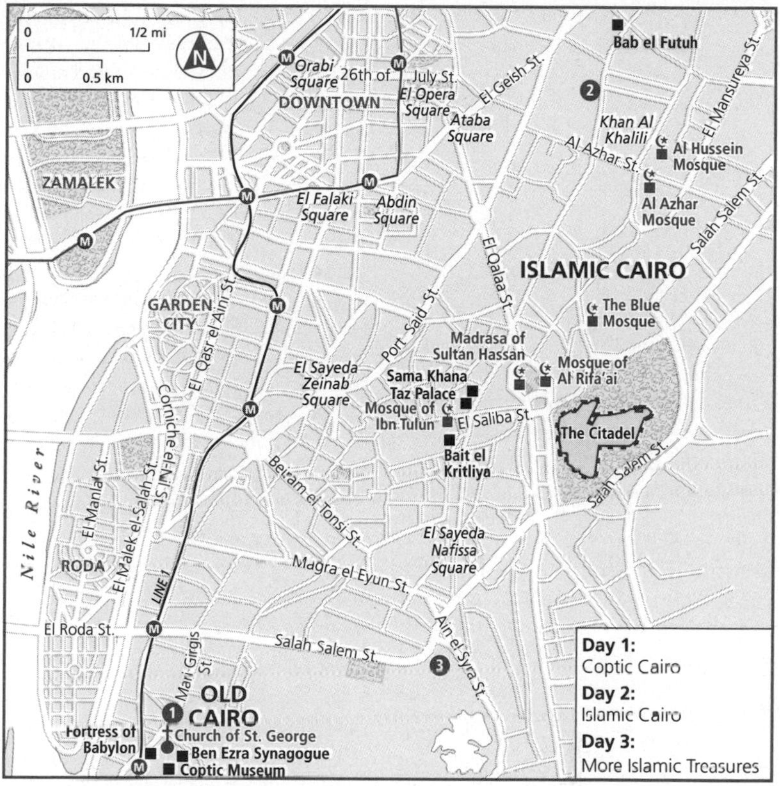

freediving, or challenge Sinai's most beautiful boulders as you go rock climbing.

Dahab's famous promenade is dotted with fantastic restaurants, where you can stock up on additional calories to be burned the morning after.

5 CLASSIC EGYPT

If you don't wish to go off the beaten track and want to hit the biggest sites, this 1-week itinerary will allow you to sample a bit of everything.

Day 1: Cairo

Have a typical *fuul* and *tameya* breakfast before you hit the road on your packed 1-day tour of the Egyptian capital. First, head to the millenniums-old **pyramids** (p. 108) before going to the **Egyptian Museum** (p. 104). By the time you finish it will be around sunset, and a stroll in

downtown (p. 101), with its amazing Art Deco and never-ending stream of local shoppers, will add to your local experience. When you've had enough, wave a taxi down and go souvenir shopping at **Khan Al Khalili** (p. 119); don't forget bargaining is the name of the game here.

Day ❷: A Day in Alex

With the frequency of trains and buses (almost hourly) that run between Cairo and Egypt's second-largest city, Alexandria, a day trip couldn't be easier. A lovely cappuccino with a croissant at the **Brazilian Coffee Store** (p. 176) is an ideal start to the day. Follow it by a typical Egyptian breakfast at **Mohamed Ahmed** (p. 178), and then head for a day of sightseeing that includes **Kom El Dikka** (p. 169), with its Roman theater and amazing Villa of the Birds; the underground **Catacombs of Kom El Shoqafa** (p. 168); Alexandria's answer to Cairo's Citadel, yet on a much smaller scale, **Qaitbey Fort** (p. 171); and the **Bibliotheca Alexandrina** (p. 167), with its cutting-edge design. A typical Alexandrian seafood lunch, perhaps at **Abu Ashraf** (p. 176), is not to be missed, and dessert at **El Sheikh Wafik** (p. 177) goes without saying. Have one final stroll on the city's lovely Corniche before catching the train back to Cairo.

Day ❸: Back in Cairo

The goliath capital needs more than a day to just get a feel for it. There is no way to cover it all in a day or two, but if you're into Islamic monuments, start with a stroll down Al Mu'izz le-din Allah Street, followed by a visit to the architecturally distinctive **Mosque of Ibn Tulun** (p. 121), the lovely **Bait al Kritliya** (p. 117), the beautiful **Taz Palace** (p. 122), and the peculiar **Sama Khana** (p. 122) before you wrap up your visit with the **Citadel** (p. 118) and its Ottoman-styled famous Mohamed Ali Mosque. If you prefer to discover the Coptic side of the city, head to Coptic Cairo for the peculiar **Hanging Church** (p. 126), the **Church of St. George** (p. 124), and the **Ben Ezra Synagogue** (p. 123).

Take the sleeper train tonight so that you can start Day 4 in:

Days ❹ & ❺: Luxor

Luxor has the largest concentration of Ancient Egyptian temples and tombs in one place. Dedicate Day 4 to the **East Bank** sites (p. 268) and Day 5 to the **West Bank** ones (p. 270).

Days ❻ & ❼: Sharm El Sheikh

After a heavy menu of Ancient Egyptian monuments in Luxor and a condensed itinerary in Cairo, now is a good time to sit back and relax. Head to Sharm El Sheikh to work on your tan and nonstop partying from dusk till dawn.

EgyptAir has five weekly flights that connect Luxor directly to Sharm El Sheikh without stopping over in Cairo.

6 THE KING'S CIRCUIT

This comprehensive itinerary is for the hard-core globetrotter who doesn't mind roughing it a bit and spending considerably long periods of time in buses, ferries, and various forms of public transport. This 15-day itinerary covers most of Egypt, which isn't easy, but it's certainly rewarding.

Day ❶: Cairo

Kick off your tour in Cairo. Visit the **pyramids** (p. 108), the **Egyptian Museum** (p. 104), and **Coptic** (or **Islamic**) **Cairo** (p. 123/p. 114). Go for a stroll in **downtown** (p. 101) to get a true feel of the city, and sample some Egyptian delicacies. Wrap up your day with souvenir shopping in **Khan Al Khalili** (p. 119) and a typical Egyptian tea at **El Fishawy** (p. 152).

Later that night, catch a bus heading to either Sharm El Sheikh or Dahab.

Day ❷: Sharm El Sheikh or Dahab

The choice is yours: If you want to spice up your itinerary with a hot beach party or European-worthy nightlife, then head to Sharm El Sheikh. If you prefer a more laid-back place with some enticing outdoor activities, then head to Dahab; the slow rhythm will help you relax after the long bus drive. Once your energy level is fully recharged, go **rock climbing** (p. 205) or **freediving** (p. 204).

Arrange an organized tour (public transport from either Sharm El Sheikh or Dahab was unreliable at press time) for the next day, when you'll head to:

Day ❸: St. Catherine

You can't leave Egypt without visiting one of the oldest functioning monasteries in the world, **St. Catherine's Monastery** (p. 214), set in the middle of a mountainous village amidst the Sinai High Mountain region. The monastery and its museum host some of the rarest icons in the history of Christianity, as well as the burning bush, from which God spoke to Moses. If you plan to complement your visit to the monastery with a night ascent to **Mount Sinai** (where Moses received the Ten Commandments), it's recommended that you check into the monastery's guesthouse; it's conveniently located and builds on the spirituality of the trip.

Day ❹: Heading to Hurghada

The easiest way from the Sinai Peninsula to the Red Sea coast is to pick up the ferry from Sharm El Sheikh to Hurghada. It runs three times a week, leaving Sharm El Sheikh at either 5 or 6pm. This leaves you with most of the day to relax on the beach and work on your tan. By the time the ferry reaches Hurghada, it's going to be somewhere between 8 and 9pm; about time to check into your hotel, put on your clubbing clothes, and go party.

Day ❺: Hurghada

The Red Sea tourism epicenter accommodates all types of tourists; sun worshipers, thrill seekers, hard-core divers, and partygoers. See which group suits you best, and join in—just don't forget to book your bus ticket leaving to Luxor at 8am tomorrow.

Days ❻ & ❼: Luxor

Hosting the largest collection of Ancient Egyptian temples and tombs all in one place, you won't be able to finish Luxor in 1 day, even if you're not that into Ancient Egypt; reserve Day 6 for the **East Bank** (p. 268) and Day 7 for the **West Bank** (p. 270).

Day ❽: To the Western Desert

This is the toughest part of the whole itinerary, as going from Luxor to the Western Desert oases is not that common. Head to Luxor's train station very early in the morning to pick up the train going north to Assiut; from there you need to pick up the bus, or alternatively a minibus, heading to Kharga. By the time you reach the oasis, it will be sunset; check into your hotel, have a stroll, go for dinner (probably back at your hotel, as Kharga's culinary scene is downright poor), and call it a night relatively early.

Day ❾: Kharga

Kharga is more of a stop rather than a destination, but since you're here, make time to see the **Bagawat Necropolis** (p. 335), an ancient Christian necropolis that hosts more than 260 mausoleums and a handful of chapels; the rarely visited **Kharga Museum** (p. 336), and, if you're lucky, the **Temple of Hibis** (p. 336). Once you're done, head straight to the bus station to catch the bus leaving to Dakhla. If you're tired of hopping from one bus to another and want to pamper yourself a bit, stay at Al Tarfa Desert Sanctuary in Dakhla and arrange for them to pick you up from Kharga. However, be financially prepared; between this special arrangement and the accommodation, you will end up with a hefty bill.

Day ⑩: Dakhla

The largest of all the Western Desert oases, Dakhla has a lot to offer, from the abandoned towns of **Balat** (p. 328) and **Qasr** (p. 329) and the beautifully decorated Roman tombs of **Muzwaka** (p. 329) to prehistoric **rock engravings** (p. 330) and a midnight bath in a natural **hot spring** (p. 329).

Day ⑪: Off-roading to the White Desert

You're in the desert, and sticking to the tarmac road defies the whole purpose. Arrange with your travel agency a 2-day, 1-night desert excursion. Plan it in such a way so that they pick you up from Dakhla and go off-road all the way to the mesmerizingly beautiful **White Desert** (p. 324), where you will camp for the night. The next morning should include visiting the **Black Desert** (p. 316) and **Crystal Mountain** (p. 318) before finishing the tour at Bahareya oasis. This is more of a tailor-made trip rather than a standard one, and thinking of who can execute it with excellence, only two names spring to my mind: **White Desert Tours** (p. 88) and **Badawiya Expedition Travel** (p. 88).

Day ⑫: Bahareya

Stay here for half a day to check out the oasis's different sites, including the stunningly beautiful **Golden Mummies** (p. 319) and the Ancient Egyptian **Tomb of Banentiu** (p. 319) and **Tomb of Zed-Amunerankh** (p. 320) before taking off in a rented 4×4 heading to Siwa oasis. For more on specially arranged vehicles making the desert run between Bahareya and Siwa, see p. 318.

Day ⑬: Siwa

This is like no other place in Egypt, and if you think you have paid a lot for the 4×4 that brought you here, Siwa's distinctive Berber culture and beautiful sites will generously reward you for every penny you've paid. Enjoy the one-of-a-kind ruins in the old town of **Shali** (p. 308), the Ancient Egyptian tombs of **Gebel Al Mawta** (p. 307), and the ruins of Siwa's enigmatic **Temple of the Oracle** (p. 309). While in town, make sure you have enough time to go for at least a half-day **sandboarding** (p. 308) excursion; gliding across the dunes here is an unforgettable experience.

Day ⑭: Alexandria

Picking up the first bus out of Siwa, you should be in Alexandria later in the afternoon. Leave your luggage in the room and go out for dinner, perhaps for typical Alexandrian seafood at **Abu Ashraf** (p. 176) or a lighter meal at **Chez Gaby au Ritrovo** (p. 178), followed by dessert at **El Sheikh Wafik** (p. 177) and a stroll along Alexandria's lengthy Corniche. On your way back to the hotel, stop by **Spitfire** (p. 179) for a typical Alexandrian drinking experience.

Day ⑮: Cairo

Spend most of the day visiting Alexandria's numerous sites (see Day 2 under "Classic Egypt") before catching the train back to the capital. By the time you reach Cairo, you'll be exhausted, but happy, so rest up for your return home tomorrow.

5

Active Vacation Planner

If you think Egypt is all about historical sightseeing, and that relaxing by the beach or diving is as far as outdoor activities go, then you're only seeing part of the picture. Watersports, kitesurfing in particular, are hitting it big along the Red Sea coast, from El Gouna in the north and all the way south to Hamata. In Dahab, adrenaline junkies can try their hand at freediving, while rock climbers can tackle some of the best boulders. If you're into trekking, head to St. Catherine; the area is characterized by high mountains that give your hike a photogenic edge. Out in the Western Desert, safari trips are picking up. Go for the classic jeep safari or the slow-paced camel one; just make sure you go sandboarding on the colossal dunes around Siwa and visit the White Desert with its alien-like terrain and scenic desertscapes. If you want to mix things up, a camel diving safari combines a camel ride with Red Sea diving.

1 THE LAY OF THE LAND

Egypt may not offer the wildlife encounters found on game drives throughout Africa, but here you can straddle camels to see a rare gazelle or speedboat the gigantic Lake Nasser in search of Nile crocodiles.

WILDLIFE Wadi El Gemal Natural Protectorate, Lake Nasser, and the Sinai High Mountains region are the best places to view wildlife in Egypt. Wadi El Gemal Natural Protectorate offers the last dorcas gazelle (p. 255) stronghold. In addition, around Hamata Mountain, located within the protectorate premises, cameras have successfully recorded several Nubian ibex individuals. The remote Wadi El Allaqi is one of Lake Nasser's widest valleys, which acts as a natural drainage for the lake. A visit will be rewarded with a plethora of birds, in addition to gazelles, foxes, jackals, and Nile crocodiles. In the past, crocodiles plied the full length of the river, but since the building of the Aswan High Dam, they have been confined to Lake Nasser. Though unofficial statistics estimate their local population to exceed 70,000, the labyrinth-like Lake Nasser is huge, and spotting one is not an easy job. The Sinai High Mountain region plays hosts to a number of elusive species, among which are Nubian ibex, rock hyrax, and striped hyena. It was once home to the critically endangered Sinai leopard, which is likely extinct locally.

BIRDS Being on the migration route of many species, Egypt is a world-class birdwatching destination. Lake Nasser tops the local list with a diverse variety of bird species: flamingos, herons, Egyptian geese, spoonbills, kites, cranes, storks, and pelicans. The Red Sea, specifically offshore islands such as the Hamata Archipelago, is an excellent spot for sighting terns, gulls, brown boobies, sooty falcons, and ospreys. Qarun Lake in Fayum,

Going . . . going . . . gone!

Little more than 10% of Egypt's land is dedicated to national parks and natural protectorates, but other than donated signs and glossy brochures, not much is being done in terms of preservation and awareness. Protectorates, managed by the **Egyptian Environmental Affairs Agency** (✆ **02/25256452;** www.eeaa.gov.eg), are often ill-equipped and short on staff, resulting in no tangible protection being enforced. The land protectorates are serving as a playground for four-wheel drivers, whether so-called sports hunters or hard-core poachers. As recently as the 20th century, gazelle herds numbered in the hundreds, addax and scimitar-horned oryx roved the sandy dunes of the Western Desert, and cheetahs survived in the oil-rich Qattara Depression—but now they are all gone. Unfortunately, wildlife is facing their bleak destiny on their own. Marine protectorates face different kinds of dangers with divers' irresponsible behavior and operators' unprofessional attitudes posing as the main threats (see box "Shark Feeding" on p. 258).

Fortunately, activists are stepping in. The **Hurghada Environmental Protection and Conservation Association** (HEPCA; ✆ **065/3445035;** www.hepca.com) is a local NGO established by members of the Red Sea diving community. Through lobbying and several awareness-raising campaigns, they have managed to enact and enforce protective measures aimed at saving the precious Red Sea corals. One of their most recent campaigns succeeded in safeguarding the dugongs' natural habitat at Abu Dabab (p. 251).

along with Burullus, Manzala, and Bardawill lakes farther north, offers a good opportunity for plovers, egrets, coots, avocets, ducks, and kingfishers. The border town of Shalateen (p. 257) is your ultimate destination if you are looking for Egyptian or lappet-faced vultures.

MARINE LIFE Enjoying two stretching coasts, the world's longest river, and a number of water bodies and wetlands, Egypt flourishes with marine life. For tourists, the Red Sea is the main underwater destination. In addition to numerous species of coral, the Red Sea is bountiful with different species, from colorful parrotfish and vibrant Spanish dancers to enigmatic sharks and ferocious barracudas. And if you come at the right time of year, you might enjoy the ethereal experience of diving next to a whale shark. The Red Sea's distinct ecology provides habitats to several endangered species such as the green turtle and the dugong. Different species of dolphins call both the Mediterranean and the Red seas home, though the latter provides a better opportunity for viewing.

BOTANY More than 90% of Egypt is desert, but plant life still flourishes. Aswan features the country's hidden botanical gem, Kitchener's Island, while the capital is home to the historical Al Orman Botanical Garden. The former features local as well as tropical plants and trees, while the latter features a rocky garden with more than 200 species of cactus and succulents. If you are a dedicated gardener, try to schedule your visit to the capital around May, when the **Tree Lovers Association** (TLA; ✆ **02/25195240**), an environmental NGO, (non-governmental organization) has its annual Tree Walk. Lotfy Boulos, the country's lead botanist, leads the walk through Maadi, the capital's greenest suburb.

2 ACTIVITIES A TO Z

DIVING

Diving is still Egypt's number-one outdoor activity, and whether you're an expert or a beginner, Egypt offers some of the best diving in the world. Not only is there unparalleled sea life in the Red Sea, including some of the most spectacular corals anywhere and sea life that ranges from massive schools of fish to sharks, but also coral-crusted wrecks and sunken World War II ships with their military equipment still on board. The Red Sea is not your sole diving spot in Egypt; diving in the Mediterranean is starting to take its first baby steps. Off Alexandria the waters conceal the treasures of Ancient Egypt, Greco-Roman archaeological remains, as well as 18th-century naval wrecks that once sailed under the Napoleonic flag.

Prices for 1-day boat trips vary depending on the number in your group and the method of transportation (a speedboat or a normal one), but you can expect to pay as low as 25€ or as high as 105€. Prices include lunch, drinks, and snorkeling, but not diving, equipment.

Note: The 25€-trips are more dedicated to snorkelers; the price quoted doesn't include the cost of the dive guide, without whom you are not allowed to dive. Expect the price to at least double if you are going deep underwater.

Alexandria

Alexandra Dive, Corniche, next to Fish Market restaurant (© **03/4832045;** www.alexandra-dive.com), is about the only recommendable diving center as far as the entire

Tips Taking a Dive

Egypt is a great place to start your diving classes, and most diving centers can accommodate you for the first two courses (Open Water and Advanced Open Water), which are basically what you need to enjoy the underwater world of the Red Sea. Choose your diving center carefully, and make sure that they are registered and certified by the American-based **Professional Association of Diving Instructors (PADI)**—all the companies listed in this guide are PADI certified. A good way to find more centers near your destination is to visit the PADI website (**www.padi.com**).

You can also do a few simple checks on your own at the dive center if you have doubts. Ask to have a look around. A dive center with nothing to hide will have no problem giving you a tour of its equipment and compressor room. Everything should look neat and well organized. Equipment should be clean and well cared for. The compressor used to fill the bottles is vital and should not be close to any source of potential contamination. If you have any doubts, hold a clean white T-shirt over the air outlet while the compressor is running; if there's any residue left on the shirt, think twice about breathing from tanks that have been filled there.

Prices for an Open Water course average 285€ to 395€ each; however, combining it with the Advanced Open Water gets you a discount.

Mediterranean coast is concerned. They offer diving trips to sites around the city of Alexandria, including Jars (littered with Greco-Roman amphorae), Pharos (what remains of Alexandria's famous lighthouse), and wrecks (sunken boats that belonged to Napoleon's fleet).

Sinai

Sharm El Sheikh

Sharm El Sheikh started as a divers' destination, and there's no shortage here of highly competent centers. The short list below provides a starting point, but it's definitely not exclusive. Prices are not affected by the abundance of diving centers in Sharm El Sheikh; to the contrary, the high tourist demand results in relatively higher prices when compared to other diving destinations, such as neighboring Dahab.

The **Camel Dive Club,** Camel Hotel, Ne'ama Bay (✆ **069/3600700;** fax 069/3600601; www.cameldive.com), is a Ne'ama Bay landmark that offers some great diving programs, is the best value for money in a midrange hotel, and has a great bar and some of the best food in the city. They also offer special diving courses for people with special mobility.

Diving World Red Sea, Travco Marina, Sharm El Maya Bay (✆ **069/3660065;** www.divingworldredsea.com), is one of the bigger Egyptian dive businesses. It started in Hurghada and now has centers up and down the coast. It's not the most intimate of outfits, but prices are good and service should be reasonable.

Oonas Dive Club, Ne'ama Bay (✆ **069/3600581;** fax 069/3600582; www.oonasdiveclub.com), is another veteran Sharm El Sheikh diving center. It is one of the best and certainly one of the most expensive.

Sinai Divers, Ghazala Hotel, Ne'ama Bay (✆ **069/3600697;** www.sinaidivers.com), is the best service you can expect from a well-reputed diving center that has been around since Ne'ama Bay was made up of only a few hotels and a couple of shopping bazaars. However, the best service in town comes with a premium; expect higher than average prices.

Dahab

Good diving and a great laid-back attitude characterize this funky alternative to the glitz and gloss of neighboring Sharm El Sheikh. Despite its mellow style, however, Dahab is serious about its diving and its professional standards. There are lots of PADI-certified, high-quality dive businesses to choose from.

Desert Divers, Masbat (✆ **069/3640500;** www.desert-divers.com), is a diving center with a mission; it trains local Bedouins to become dive guides. It pioneered the idea of camel dive safaris, where you trek up the coast with camels to do the shore dive. In addition to great diving programs and excursions, they also offer freediving (p. 204) and rock climbing (p. 205) courses.

Freediving

Whether you want to discover new depths without having to put on full diving gear or just want to push yourself through another challenge, freediving is worth a try. **Desert Divers** (✆ **069/3640500;** www.desert-divers.com) has a 1-day intro course (75€) that offers a good teaser.

Catch Your Breath

As the name implies, a rebreather is a breathing set that recycles exhaled gas. It is much lighter to carry and gives you much more time underwater than the more common breathing sets. Since the gas you are exhaling is going back into the rebreather, there are no bubbles that may scare surrounding marine life. All these benefits come with a premium, though; expect higher equipment prices if you are going for a rebreather. In Egypt, **Orca Dive Club,** with its multiple branches, is among the very few diving centers in the country that has rebreathers on offer.

Big Blue's (✆ **069/3640045** or 010/1945466; www.bigbluedahab.com) logo says it all: It's time to chill out and dive. Big Blue is a brand-new dive center right next to the water, which means a great combination of uptight standards and chilled-out diving.

The dive center at the **Nesima Resort,** Mashraba (✆ **069/3640320;** fax 069/3640321; www.nesima-resort.com), not only has a first-class reputation, but is conveniently located in one of the nicest places to stay and eat in the middle of Dahab. It's not the budget option, but it's certainly comfy.

The Red Sea

El Gouna

With better facilities, better food, and an all-around friendlier atmosphere than Hurghada, all within range of the same dive sites, I don't know why anyone goes anywhere other than El Gouna. Come here, or spend your holiday in Hurghada wishing you had. If Orca's all booked up, try the Dive Center at the Sheraton Miramar.

Orca Dive Club El Gouna, Abu Tig Marina (✆ **012/2480460;** fax 065/3580171; www.orca-diveclub-elgouna.com), is a branch of the well-established Orca Dive Club, whose many branches dot the Red Sea coast. The golden rule says that if you are in a town where Orca Dive Club is, don't hesitate; dive with them.

If your accommodation tastes are a little more upmarket than the Abu Tig Marina, **TGI Diving** (✆ **065/3545606,** ext 19; www.tgidiving.com) is located on its own little island right in front of the Sheraton Miramar.

Hurghada

Hurghada may rank last when it comes to urban planning, but it is one of the best-established centers for diving along the Red Sea Coast. It abounds with good-quality, professional dive centers, both in the hotels and operating independently. Here is a sample list.

Dive Buddy, Sakala (✆ **012/3214820;** fax 065/3442233; www.divebuddyredsea.com), is a lot smaller than the big hotel-based centers and has a cozier, more casual atmosphere.

Ilios, Steigenberger Al Dau (✆ **065/3465442;** fax 065/3465410; www.iliosdiveclub.de), is a real five-star operation, with the plush comforts of the Steigenberger at its disposal. If you have to be right in Hurghada, you may as well splurge. Ilios offers diving courses designed for people with special mobility; please check their website for requirements and conditions.

The Hurghada branch of **Subex,** Dahar (✆ **06/53547593;** fax 065/3547651; www.subex.org), is well known on the coast. It's not the cheapest, but you're in good hands.

Safaga

Safaga might be one of the long sought-after diving destinations on the Red Sea coast, but it certainly lacks the tourism development its northern neighbor, Hurghada, enjoys. Be prepared for some roughness around the edges and a limited number of diving centers to choose from.

The **Dune Diving Center** (✆ **065/3253075;** www.duneredsea.com) is a well-established dive center in the older part of town that's popular with French divers. Unlike most centers on the coast, Dune is a freestanding business away from any hotel, but they can recommend local accommodations, and daily prices include hotel transfer. Dune is an easy walk to El Yasmin (p. 242) and the Nemo Hotel (which runs its own, competing, dive outfit), and a short drive from the Menaville. The Soma Bay cluster of resorts is a little farther, but no more than a 15-minute drive.

The **Nemo Diving Center** (✆ **010/3648708** or 010/1137707; www.nemodive.com) is run by a Belgian-Dutch partnership and has long been in operation. In addition to the diving center, they also run the **Nemo Hotel** (p. 242), which makes the arrangements for accommodations quick and easy.

El Quseir

While El Quseir doesn't hit it big when it comes to shore dives, Safaga's dive sites up north, as well as marvelous diving sites of Marsa Alam farther south, are all within an hour's reach.

Subex, Sirena Beach (✆ **065/3332100;** fax 065/3332124; www.subex.org), is one of the nicest facilities on the coast. Tucked into one end of a small bay with the Mövenpick (p. 246), it has a lovely veranda bar and lunch spot, and the reef is an easy beach dive. Though it's not the budget option when it comes to diving the Red Sea, it's good quality and value for money.

Port Ghalib

The new kid on the block, Port Ghalib is rapidly growing a reputation for an all-in-one tourist destination where you can enjoy the sea and the desert, diving and a safari. As far as diving is concerned, there is currently one diving center in town; the well-reputed **Emperor Divers,** Marina Lodge (✆ **012/7372126;** fax 065/3700432; www.emperordivers.com), is a big, well-established company with several centers on the Red Sea coast as well as in Sharm El Sheikh. The comprehensive website allows you to pick up last-minute deals.

Marsa Alam

The Red Sea's new diving prima donna, Marsa Alam, offers some world-class diving spots and diving centers.

Oasis Diving Center (✆ **010/5052855;** www.oasis-marsaalam.com) is right on top of a prime reef-side dive spot and an easy ride to the highlights Elphinstone, Abu Dabab, Dolphin House, and more than two dozen others. Equipment is in mint condition and service will probably exceed your expectations. It is recommended to stay on-site at the divers-oriented Oasis Resort (p. 254).

The **Orca Dive Club,** Abu Dabab (✆ **010/1415059** or 017/4377301; fax 065/3555851; www.orca-diveclub-abudabab.com), is one of a string of Orca centers up and down the coast. This one is located right on the beach at Abu Dabab, across the road from the Abu Dabab Diving Lodge (p. 255).

Liveaboards

Some sites, such as Zabargad Island, Brothers Island, Daedalus Reef, and St. John's Reef, are not doable on a 1-day trip, so a couple of dive centers operate 1- to 2-week safaris on liveaboards, where diving is the name of the game (three to four dives a day). Prices on a full-board basis vary from 650€ to 1,000€ depending on the trip duration. Check **Emperor Divers** (✆ **012/2340995;** www.emperordivers.com) or **Blue Planet Liveaboards** (✆ **065/3559124;** www.blueplanet-liveaboards.com) for trip schedule and itineraries.

Pioneer Divers has four centers in the Marsa Alam area, all within an hour of 15 to 20 dive sites and each close to accommodations. The center on the grounds of the Kahramana Resort (p. 253), for example, is within 15 to 30 minutes by speedboat of both Elphinstone and Abu Dabab. The center close to Shagra Ecolodge Village, meanwhile, has reasonably priced all-inclusive accommodations. Visit the website (www.redsea-divingsafari.com), or call its Cairo office, 53 El Hussein St., Dokki (✆ **02/33379942** or 02/33371833; fax 02/37494219), to decide which works best for you.

Hamata

There are no diving centers southward of Hamata, the last diving frontier, and even here, there are only a few. **Orca Dive Club,** Zabargad Dive Resort (✆ **012/7468823;** fax 065/3555851; www.orca-diveclub-hamata.com), is the best recommendation here. Similar to any other Orca Dive Club branch along the Red Sea coast, staff are affable, service is professional, and equipment is more than perfect.

SAFARIS & TREKKING

The romance of the open desert, combined with spectacular and varied scenery, is turning the Western Desert of Egypt, virtually unknown 30 years ago outside a small circle of explorers, into a major tourist destination. The Sinai Peninsula, which offers a different environment with a more mountainous terrain, is catching up with the Western Desert, while the Eastern Desert, sandwiched between the Nile River and the Red Sea, is lagging behind with popular activities more in the vein of short quad and mountain bikes excursions than proper safaris.

With the tourists have come two developments. First, the inevitable expansion of outfits offering guiding and safaris is swamping the market with inexperienced guides looking to cash in on the rush. Second, well-organized efforts are being made to train guides and to clean up and maintain the natural beauty on which the industry is based.

If you've never been in the desert, it's hard to imagine how easily you can get lost or stuck. And with temperatures that can run to 120°F (50°C), you can get into serious trouble. Remember when you book a guide that you're trusting him—his driving, his navigation, his judgment, and his equipment—with your life. Apart from this, you're also trusting him to cook decent meals, respect your privacy, and not cut his costs by jamming you in with another group or by neglecting his equipment.

If you have a good company or guide, pricing is going to be pretty much "you get what you pay for." The daily rental of a good 4×4 with a guide/driver can vary between LE350 and LE900, while a 1-night camp in the desert averages LE200 to LE400 per person in a group. In addition to the 4×4 transport, price includes a simple dinner (usually *kofta,* rice or pasta, and salad) and some sort of bedding (usually a tent). Prices vary depending on the group count and the vehicle type; these are two important things you need to check before paying any deposit.

The recommendations below may be divided by oasis, but by definition these guides all have a scope of expertise that runs well beyond the narrow boundaries of their town or immediate home area. You'll be able to find cheaper guides, but not necessarily better.

Western Desert

Cairo-Based Companies

The **Shannon Desert Tribe,** Maadi (✆ **010/1778188;** ashannon@internetegypt.com), is run by the legendary Amr Shannon, who seems to be laying off desert guiding and heading into early retirement. If you can get him to take you into the desert, however, it's your lucky day. If he's too busy, follow his recommendations on alternatives.

Badawiya Expedition Travel, Maadi (✆ **02/25260994;** fax 02/25287273; www.badawiya.com), was originally based in Farafra, where it remains heavily involved in training and development, but it now runs safaris through the Western Desert. Badawiya offers pretty complete packages and can even arrange your visa and pick you up at the airport if you need. Their comprehensive list of excursions includes camel safaris with prices starting at 192€ (per person, minimum six people) for a 3-day trek.

Siwa

Abd Allah Baghi (✆ **011/1180680;** shali55@hotmail.com) is the doyen of Siwa guides and an all-around pleasant and helpful guy who speaks great English. Like Amr Shannon in Cairo, Abd Allah is well established with an A-list clientele, so he may not be able help you directly, but his judgment on who can take his place is to be trusted.

Abu Zahra Family (✆ **010/6118139;** www.bedouinsafari.org) is a local Bedouin family business with a good reputation for being attentive to their customers' needs. Their website features only three different safari programs, but they can accommodate tailor-made ones.

Bahareya

White Desert Tours (✆ **02/38473014;** fax 02/38472322; www.whitedeserttours.com) is run by an Arabic-speaking German transplant to the oasis, Peter Wirth, who also runs the International Health Center (known locally as Peter's Hotel, see p. 320). Peter uses the best local guides to put together excellent safaris that range from simple tours of local sites to more elaborate trips out to Dakhla and beyond. He can also arrange pickup in Cairo.

The diminutive and rather gruff **Badri Khozam,** Bawiti (✆ **012/7313908;** desertsafarihome@hotmail.com), has been running tours and safaris around Bahareya for about as long as anyone can remember. He can be found at his Desert Safari Home (p. 320). His English is very good.

Tour de Gilf

Touring El Gilf El Kebir is not a job for rookies. **Zarzora Expeditions,** Mut (✆ **010/1188221;** www.zarzora.com), runs 2-week safari trips with a price tag of 1,500€ per person on an all-inclusive basis. They are meticulous about their business, nailing down the smallest details, and are always ready with an extra whatever; don't worry if your sleeping bag got lost by your airline.

Rock Climbing

The boulders in Wadi Ginay—a 10-minute drive from Dahab—make for one of the best rock-climbing sites in Egypt. It comes as no surprise that it draws the sport's addicts from all over the world. **Desert Divers** (✆ **069/3640500;** www.desert-divers.com) is a reliable and professional rock-climbing operator that offers beginning and advanced courses (2-day courses range 175€–195€), as well as 1-day rock-climbing excursions (55€ per person including gear and guide).

Mohamed Kosa (✆ **012/2248570**) is tall and a little forbidding when you first meet him, but his face splits with one of the widest smiles in the oasis. He is one of the best known and most competent deep-desert guides around, and his basic English is sufficient.

Farafra

If you're in Farafra, you're probably already hooked up with **Badawiya Expedition Travel.** If you're not but want to be, just head over to the Badawiya Hotel (p. 324), and they'll fix you up.

Rahala Safari is owned and operated by Ahmed Abed (✆ **010/3064733;** www.rahala-safari.com), a third-generation guide who moonlights as an English teacher, so his ability to communicate information about the places, the history, and the Bedouin culture is unparalleled. In addition to the usual fare of jeep and camel safaris, Rahala Safari offers guided walking tours (average 55€ per person per day) as well as jeep driving courses should you feel like off-roading on your own.

Dakhla

The heart of the Western Desert, Dakhla is a big oasis with lots to offer both within its vicinity and beyond.

Abdel Hamid runs the **Dohous Bedouin Camp** (✆ **010/6221359;** www.dakhlabedouins.com) as a base for desert excursions by jeep or camel. The camels live just behind the camp, so you can even check them out and choose your favorite.

Hatem Mohamed Shafik, who runs the **Bir Gebel Hotel and Camp** (✆ **012/1068227;** fax 092/7727122; elgabalcamp@hotmail.com), also organizes local safaris. There's not going to be anything elaborate about the affair, but for a few nights in the desert close to the oasis at a decent price, you'll be in good hands.

Sinai

Sparsely populated but impressive and ruggedly beautiful, the Sinai Peninsula used to be pretty inaccessible without your own 4×4 and a thick Rolodex of contacts. Fortunately, things are taking a different turn with more responsible tour operators stepping in.

Sheikh Sina Bedouin Treks, St. Catherine (✆ **011/2551150;** www.sheikhsina.com), is a task force of different Bedouin tribe members who own and operate this trekking business. Knowing their region inside out, they can literally take you anywhere you want to go. Their holistic list of hikes ranges from a few hours' leisurely walk to the arduous 14-day Sinai coast to coast hike.

Desert Divers, Dahab (✆ **069/3640500;** www.desert-divers.com), arranges trips that run the gamut from overnights between Dahab and St. Catherine with jeeps to a 2-week trans-Sinai camel trek. A partnership between a local Bedouin and a Canadian, Desert

Divers is a company that can access the best of local knowledge while providing excellent service.

Eastern Desert (Red Sea)

The least developed of the desert trio, the only tour operator that can provide a real desert experience is **Wadi El Gemal Safari,** Marsa Alam (✆ **012/1027161**), which offers a handful of jeep and camel safaris.

SANDBOARDS, DIRT BIKES & QUADS

There is one thought that goes through the head of a skier or a boarder when they first see a really big sand dune, but all too often there's nothing they can do about it. Packing your board along for your desert safari just isn't something that most people think about. Fortunately, there are now an abundance of boards to be rented in Egypt, mainly concentrated around the Western Desert oases, specifically Siwa. Literally any business, even a bazaar shop, can rent you a board. For a good quality sandboard and a professional tour operator, check out **Somewhere Different** (✆ **016/5840018;** www.somewheredifferent.com). They rent mint-condition equipment for LE50 a day and offer full-day sandboarding excursions for LE700 (including equipment rental).

Quad safaris, on the other hand, are a dime a dozen. On the whole, they offer a low-value combination of nonexistent safety standards and boring drive-in-a-line driving. Sinai Safari Adventures, Sharm El Sheikh (✆ **019/7276163**), has a diverse collection of quads, rhino quads, and the more thrilling Argocats. The excursions won't take you out to a real desert, but rather to the dirt tracks not far from Sharm El Sheikh proper. Prices for a 2-hour excursion vary from LE120 for single quads to LE350 (fits two) for rhino quads or Argocats.

KTM Egypt, Ne'ama Bay (✆ **010/1794907;** fax 02/22599446; www.ktmegypt.com), is on a different level. It's a little pricier than most places, but it also offers top-flight KTM bikes (ranging from little 50cc kiddy bikes to full-on 600cc desert-eating monsters), quads, buggies, and even 4×4s. It has well-trained instructors and offers full-on European spec safety equipment. The practice track at its elaborate facilities, on the edge of the desert outside Ne'ama Bay in Sharm El Sheikh, is long and twisty and features one very imposing jump. You'll pay LE900 for a 2-hour bike excursion, LE200 for the same excursion but with a single quad, and LE300 if you go for a double quad.

For biking the Western Desert, try Franco Picco's (if you don't know the name, do an Internet search for this well-known Italian rally biker before you get on one of his bikes) outfit based at the **International Hot Spring Hotel** (✆ **02/38472322** or 012/3212179;

Sailing the Desert

Desert sailing might not sound logical at first, but **Red Sea Desert Adventures,** Hamata (✆ **012/3993860;** www.redseadesertadventures.com), makes it possible. The whole idea revolves around a three-wheel metal cart, equipped with mast and sail, that glides on the flat desert terrain. The 2-hour excursion comes with a 50€ per person price tag. In addition, Red Sea Desert Adventures also offers a couple of classic jeep safaris that average 45€ per person for a half-day tour.

www.whitedeserttours.com) in Bahareya. At around $250 per person, per day (all inclusive), it's not cheap, but there is no better thrill than a few days of blasting over sand dunes on long-range 600cc Yamahas. Tailor-made tours are always an option.

WIND- & KITESURFING

In Egypt, while windsurfing is well-established, kitesurfing is relatively new. Both sports fit naturally with the long, windy coastlines of both the Red Sea coast and Sinai Peninsula. You'll find the well-developed and better-equipped centers on the Red Sea coast rather than in Sinai. A beginner's course averages 260€, while an instructor's one costs 565€. Equipment rental varies from one center to the other, but hovers around the 90€ mark.

Sinai

Dahab

Dahab is the surfing capital of the peninsula, but a couple of Russian tourists–dedicated centers located on the lagoon are dedicated to kitesurfing. They don't offer much if you are here to learn technique, but if you are already a certified kitesurfer and just want to rent equipment (45€/65€ for half/full day), then stop at either **Soul Kiter** (✆ **016/2495508;** www.soul-kiter.com) or **Happy Kite** (✆ **019/2244822;** www.happy-kite.com). ***Note:*** Have a thorough look before renting; not all the items are in perfect condition.

Red Sea

El Gouna

This is surfers' dreamland, with Mangroovy Beach, a little north of town, offering first-class facilities on a beach that combines a long, shallow walkout for beginners and some big waves farther out for experts, all within a 5 minute *tok-tok* ride of Gouna's great hotels, bars, and restaurants. A number of companies here teach and rent equipment, including **Kitepower** (www.kitepower-elgouna.com) and **Red Sea Zone** (✆ **010/2955209;** www.redseazone.com). Buzzha Beach is a new emerging sports beach, unofficially dedicated to restless kitesurfers. **Kite Boarding Club El Gouna** (✆ **014/2635528** or 012/6610878; www.kiteboarding-club.de) has a big station here with excellent-condition equipment and an on-site equipment repair facility.

Safaga (Soma Bay)

A combination of friendly staff, excellent up-to-date equipment, and great wind and sea conditions make the **7BFT Kite House** (✆ **010/1701685;** www.7bft-kitehouse.com) one of the best kitesurfing centers in Egypt. Following suit is the **watersports center** at Kempinski (p. 240), with its wide variety of courses that cover wind- and kitesurfing as well as catamaran sailing.

Hamata

Hamata is a new surfing hot spot on the Red Sea coast and certainly El Gouna's only competition, with its prevailing wind and reefless, knee-deep lagoon. **Kite-Village** (✆ **016/1825751;** www.kite-village.com) might at first appear basic, but they have brand-new equipment and some of the most skillful, professional, and easygoing instructors along the coast.

6

Cairo

When Al Mu'izz le-din Allah ordered the building of his new Fatimid capital in A.D. 969, he would have never thought that this small city by the Nile would one day sprawl almost 13km (8 miles) wide and host more than 20 million souls. It would have needed a real fertile imagination to foresee today's intense atmosphere, dynamic rhythm, and constantly shining city lights.

Some say that Al Qahira—The Victorious—lives up to its name; though numerous conquerors came and went, none managed to vanquish Cairo's soul. Arabs, Mamluks, Turks, the French, and, recently, the Brits have all left their imprints on the city's walls that, when infused with the local tradition, give the place its distinct flavor and identity. Cairo is one of the few places in the world that fails to be described in just one word: It's neither religious nor secular, Islamic nor Coptic, Sunni nor Shiite, Arabic nor African; rather it is all the elements fused into one goliath Egyptian Cairo.

But beyond entwining heritage, cultural richness, and historical diversity, the megalopolis Cairo retains an unfathomable way of striking you, either as the destination of your dreams or as an unlivable place right out of Dante's *Inferno.* Some consider its chaotic streets, battlefield veterans in driver's seats, and the suicidal way its inhabitants cross the streets part of the vibrancy of the place, while others are left stunned and deterred. Downtown is Cairo's pulsating heart, a heaving district constantly in motion; some love the fact that they can stroll its streets at midnight, while others can't do with the level of noise. Cairene streets are infested with all types of monuments; some are clustered in one district such as Islamic or Coptic Cairo, while the vanishing Belle Epoque, with its Art Deco buildings, are more difficult to find, concealed amidst an ocean of ugly-looking cement buildings. Some enjoy the search while others are put off by the logistical hassle of negotiating traffic-jammed streets. Bargaining is part of this city's dwellers' genes, and though they will engage in cutthroat haggling over an extra pound or two, they can wholeheartedly insist on paying for your drinks or having you over for dinner. Those same warm and cordial people will fervently cheer their national football team as if Egypt is their sole beloved, and yet throw garbage on the street as if they couldn't care less.

Cairo is a huge question mark that extends beyond the physical dimension of the place and into a perplexing sea of contradictions. It all depends on how you are willing to embrace quintessential Cairo—with open arms or a frowning face.

1 ESSENTIALS

GETTING THERE

BY PLANE Egypt's main airport, **Cairo International Airport** (www.cairo-airport.com; airport code CAI), is undergoing a complete makeover. The renovation of Terminal One (mostly used by foreign carriers), the inauguration of the state-of-the-art Terminal

Three (predominantly used by EgyptAir and Star Alliance members), and the opening of Air Mall, where you can go for last-minute souvenir shopping or grab a quick bite, are already complete. Still in the pipeline are the equally ambitious renovation plans for Terminal Two, the development of a 350-room five-star hotel, and the launching of a high-tech electrical train connecting all three terminals. Cairo's airport shuttle bus is free and connects all three terminals but doesn't go beyond the airport limits.

There are several options for getting to your hotel from the airport. The misleadingly named **Cairo Shuttle Bus** (✆ **19970;** www.cairoshuttlebus.com) is actually a limousine service, not a shuttle bus. An actual limo ride is the easiest way into town, and there are several companies that offer this service at fixed prices (per district and type of vehicle); checking around with some negotiation can get you a very slim discount. After you are done with Customs and have your luggage, leave the arrivals hall through the very first door to your left (or ask the information desk where you can pick up a limo, and they will direct you), where you will find an organized line of limos (something not that common in Egypt). Fares are fixed and posted next to the pickup area; the table below reflects the per vehicle prices valid at the time of researching this edition.

Transport from Cairo International Airport

	Mercedes	van	sedan
Heliopolis	LE110	LE70	LE60
Downtown	LE155	LE100	LE80
Zamalek	LE165	LE110	LE90
Maadi	LE200	LE120	LE100
Giza	LE230	LE150	LE120

Going for the cheaper black-and-white taxi option comes with a lot of hassle. A committee of touts will be waiting for you once you step out of the arrival hall, offering their old wrecked affairs for a ride into town. Haggle, negotiate, and bargain, and don't pay more than LE40 if you are heading to a place as close as Heliopolis and LE150 if you are heading to one of the hotels close to the pyramids at the far end of Cairo. Travelers on a budget can consider taking the airport shuttle bus to the airport bus station from where they can pick up the local bus. The local bus service supposedly runs 24 hours, but things slow down after midnight, reaching a near standstill by 2am. There are also buses leaving to Alexandria, departing on an hourly basis between 4am and 7pm and every 1½ hours between 7pm and midnight. Bus tickets to Alex range from LE35 to LE40.

BY BUS Arriving in Cairo by commercial bus is a lot easier than it used to be, and is very likely to be presented to you as an option if you are in Sharm el Sheikh, Hurghada, or Marsa Alam (having arrived by charter flight direct to one of these coastal resort towns) and want to visit the capital. Buses run the length and breadth of the country frequently and fairly reliably, and, despite Egypt's notorious road accidents record (due to reckless driving, poor road maintenance, and outdated trucks that somehow have managed to escape the graveyard), they may offer an appealing way of seeing the countryside and meeting people. Bus rides in Egypt often come with a movie, usually an Arabic one with the volume turned to the max, and freezing cold air-conditioning, so pack a blanket (or at least an extra sweater) and have earplugs on hand.

Coming into Cairo by bus, you're likely to stop at a number of places as you enter the city. Unless you have a firm grip on the city's layout—which can be pretty tricky after dark—stay on the bus until the final stop at the **Turgoman Bus Station,** the capital's

Tips: Buying Train Tickets

There are three different places to buy tickets in Ramses Train Station, depending on where you're headed. Two things remain the same: They are all open 24 hours, and not all the employees speak good English. To avoid any possible misunderstanding, double-check the prices with the tourist information office by the main entrance before you head to the wickets.

If you're headed north to Alexandria, the ticket office is in the back-right corner of the main hall of Ramses Train Station. (Put your back to the trains and look a little to your right—over in the corner, there is a line of ticket windows.)

If you're taking a sleeper train south to Luxor or Aswan, the office is directly ahead of you if you're in the main hall with your back to the trains.

Finally, if you're headed south to Luxor or Aswan in a seat, you have to head through the main hall (leaving the trains to your right) and through to a second set of platforms that are outside and behind the main hall. Turn sharply left when you get there, and you'll see a tunnel underneath the tracks. Go through the tunnel, turning right at the end. The ticket offices for Upper Egypt are about 20m (65 ft.) ahead of you on the left.

Tickets can also be purchased from other locations around the capital, namely Kobri El Koba and Maadi Metro stations, as well as Egypt Telecom branches in Heliopolis and Almaza. You can log onto **www.egypt.gov.eg** to buy train tickets online, but you must know Arabic.

main station. It is quite centrally located, so both downtown and Zamalek are about an LE10 taxi ride away. Note that the street signs leading to Turgoman Bus Station actually read CAIRO GATEWAY (an unpopular name among the locals).

BY TRAIN Trains are a delightful way to travel in Egypt; if not for the ride, then at least for the fascinating views of village life. Contrary to the loose Egyptian interpretation of punctuality, trains usually leave (if not arrive) right on time, making train travel to nearby destinations such as Alexandria just as convenient and quick as flying; and it's cheaper and more environmentally friendly. Nonetheless, depending on how much time you have, they may not be the best way to get to your destination. If you're headed to Upper Egypt on a tight schedule, you're probably better off flying.

Cairo's main station is the centrally located **Ramses Train Station,** a stone's throw away from downtown and Zamalek, which adds a convenient advantage if you opt to stay in either of the two districts. Ramses Train Station is another historic Cairene building that dates back to the late 20th century and plays host to the Railway Museum (p. 107). Second in line is the **Giza Train Station,** a modern and, consequently, less interesting train station that is oddly located away from most of the hotels and sites. Each of the two train stations (✆ **02/25753555** or 19468) is connected to at least one Metro line (p. 99).

BY CAR Arriving in Cairo by car is exciting—probably too exciting for most travelers. Unless you are already experienced at driving in Africa and, more specifically, Egypt, I suggest you hire a car with a good driver. It is also strongly recommended that you be off the highways by dark; they are not for the fainthearted during the day, and they're downright dangerous at night.

The excellent *Cairo: The Practical Guide* (AUC Press, revised edition 2008), available at branches of the American University in Cairo Bookstore and Diwan (p. 145), will help once you've penetrated the confusing sprawl of highways and sideways that surround the perimeter districts of Heliopolis, Maadi, and Shobra al Kheima.

TOURIST INFORMATION

Ministry of Tourism information offices in Cairo are a hit-or-miss affair. Some are quite helpful, while others are a waste of time. (By contrast, these offices are generally excellent in the smaller towns and cities.) I find the office in Ramses Train Station's main hall, next to the sleeping-car office (© **02/25790767**), to be the most useful office in Cairo, but the office at 5 Adly St. (© **02/23913454**) may be helpful as well. I wouldn't recommend you go out of your way to get to either, though. Your time in Cairo is better spent with a trip to one of the bookstores listed in the "Shopping A to Z" section (p. 144) to buy a few maps and a book or two.

ORIENTATION

Standard rules of urban planning have miserably failed when it comes to Cairo; this city has haphazardly expanded over and over again. The result is a mammoth-size megalopolis the defies logical thinking, proves difficult to navigate on all levels, has grown a notorious reputation for traffic congestion, misses on green patches, and has slums right next door to posh districts. For the visiting tourist, the easiest way to manage Cairo's geography is to deal with it broken down into four main blocks.

BLOCK A: AIRPORT, HELIOPOLIS & NASR CITY Though the Heliopolis project kicked off during the early years of the 20th century, most of what is here today are cement high-rises that were built during the property boom of the 1980s. Other than the Baron Palace, there is not much to do or see here; however, it is close to the airport. If you don't have any business to attend to in Misr El Gedida, as Heliopolis is often referred to in Arabic, you can eliminate this option when it comes to deciding on where to stay in Cairo.

BLOCK B: CAIRO EAST OF THE NILE This is the area squeezed between the Nile and Block A; it includes downtown, Zamalek, Garden City, and Islamic and Old Cairo. This is Cairo's nonstop beating heart. Downtown is one of the Egyptians' main shopping areas, and other than Sundays, it thrives with endless waves of shoppers. Heads up, though; the downtown area can get uncomfortably crowded a few days before festivities (especially Islamic ones). Once upon a time, Cairo's downtown was home to aristocrats

Renewing Your Visa

If you think that you're going to need more than the 30 days in the country that the airport visa gives you, it's best to get it extended before you leave Cairo. The office is in Tahrir Square, across from the Egyptian Museum, in the gigantic Soviet-inspired monolith known as the Mugama'a. Visa renewal is a same-day service if you show up early in the morning and are ready with your passport (original and photocopy) and a passport photo. It costs LE68 and you should, in theory, be given a 6-month extension; however, arbitrary judgments have been reported, especially for those who are not U.S., Europe, or Gulf State nationals.

Tips Harassment

By international standards, Cairo is astonishingly safe, especially when it comes to crimes of a violent nature. Nevertheless, one should not abuse such safety, and it would be best to refrain from venturing into tourist-unfriendly areas and sprawling slums on the outskirts, especially after dark. One growing issue remains lurking in the shadows, and most recently in broad daylight—harassment. Due to sexual frustration, undervaluing of ethics and morals, as well as the wrong perception of Western nations, sexual harassment targeting women is on the rise. Though no rape instance has been recorded, the threat is far from simple catcalls. In a recent study by the Egyptian Centre for Women's Rights, shocking statistics revealed 98% of foreign women visitors have experienced sexual harassment while in Egypt and 62% of local Egyptian men admitted to harassing women. To minimize the chances, here are some tips:

- **Dress modestly.** Short sleeves are acceptable, but sleeveless is a no-no. Choose baggy trousers or a flowing ankle-length skirt rather than a knee-high skirt; avoid shorts. Some go the extra mile and put on a headscarf, but I wouldn't recommend it; your features, regardless of where you are coming from, will unveil your true identity, and thus a scarf won't be effective.
- If you are going to one of the city's nightspots, keep a **shawl** in your bag for getting in and out of taxis.
- Put on your sunglasses, and **avoid eye contact.**
- A **ring** on the left hand is precious, and if somebody inquires, say the hubby is relaxing in the room, working out in the gym, or went to fetch some groceries.

Males are not subject to sexual harassment but can fall victim to other creative and cunning scams. Look out for touts trying to get you into a taxi and overcharge you; tellers at the exchange bureau shortchanging you; camel boys who, after you ask them to take a photo with your camera, claim it is theirs and refuse to return it; and tour operators who take you to the so-called "best souvenir shop" in town and try to squeeze an extra penny out of you.

and later the country's intelligentsia; today, however, impressive architecture is all that remains, as the resident community has dramatically changed (for more on this, read *Yacoubian Building;* p. 38). Zamalek, which is actually a Nile island, is a condensed upper-middle-class district that lures foreigners (students, artists, and intellects rather than expats) into long stays in Cairo. It is also Cairo's center for nightlife whether for fine dining or bar-hopping. Islamic and Old Cairo are both monument-infested areas that hold great potential for being world-class open-air museums; however, other than the recently renovated Al Mu'izz le-din Allah Street, monuments and historical buildings are left in disuse with needy communities cancerously encroaching. Most of their residents lack the awareness of how historically important the building next door is, further impeding any effective preservation efforts.

Being in the heart of the action comes with a price. Be prepared for above-average levels of noise, especially in downtown, and for Thursday's midnight traffic jams, especially in Zamalek.

BLOCK C: CAIRO WEST OF THE NILE Block C stretches west of the Nile all the way to the pyramids; it is comprised of the Mohandiseen, Agouza, Dokki, Giza, and Harem districts. As a tourist in Cairo, you trundle this block for either the pyramids or to one of the recommended hangouts. I personally wouldn't recommend basing myself in this block as it is notorious for traffic jams with no particular architecture to behold while roving the bustling streets. Gamea'at el Dwal el Arabia (League of Arab Nations) Street is Mohandiseen's main one and should be avoided at all costs on Thursday nights unless you are fine with spending an hour going from one end to the other.

BLOCK D: MAADI & SUBURBS Cairo's greenest district is the suburb of Maadi. Home to the capital's expat community, it is a wonderful place to take a stroll away from the hustle and bustle of downtown, Zamalek, or Cairo's relentlessly active districts. It can make for a relaxed base during your stay, but you would be consciously trading peace of mind for a daily commute to any of the city's attractions. Suburbia is a new trend in Egypt's upper-middle and elite classes. While still working in Cairo, those with financial might have moved their residence to the suburbs; Cairo's Fifth Settlement, El Rehab, and Sheikh Zayed Town are all examples of the posh gated communities crawling on the desertscapes outside Cairo proper. Other than Maadi, which is well connected via the Metro, the new emerging suburbs can be given a miss unless you have a reliable method of transportation; preferably a car with a driver.

2 GETTING AROUND

Some cities strike you with how well organized they are, others with out-and-out pollution, but when it comes to Cairo it is traffic. It doesn't matter where you are based, it doesn't matter where you are heading, and it doesn't matter what time it is, you are bound to face Cairo's horrendous traffic. As locals we don't aim to avoid it, as it's an embedded character of the place, but rather navigate our way out of the endless crooked lines of cars restlessly honking their horns and safely escape the Formula One wannabes in the drivers' seats who simply cut you off in a blink of an eye.

BY TAXI

Up until 2009, black-and-whites were the order of the day when it came to taxis in Cairo. They are the basic staple of transport for middle-class Egyptians, tourists, and anyone who has to transport anything anywhere. Black-and-whites are quite ubiquitous, and catching one is a 1-minute process; however, paying for one is often 10 minutes of intense haggling, since they rarely put the fare system into use. Like most other businesses in Egypt that don't offer fixed pricing, the fact that you are a foreigner will automatically double the price. If you go for one of those living nightmares (black-and-whites) they mistake for taxis, be sure to bargain quite hard and agree to the price before you step in, sit in the back (especially if you are a single female), and make sure you have the exact amount, as drivers will often claim they are short on change.

Luckily black-and-whites are being phased out and replaced with new all-white taxis with a thin black-and-white strip on the sides and a yellow cap on top. It is a government-backed initiative to eliminate one of the main reasons behind Cairo's traffic and solve, once and for all, the taxi fare mystery. With a flag fall of LE2.50, LE1.25 rate per kilometer (⅔ mile), and LE0.25 for each 70 seconds of waiting, Cairo's new taxi system can be a bit expensive, especially when it comes to short rides; however, taking the hassle

Tips The Survival Guide to Cairene Traffic

- Avoid rush hours (8–10am and 5–8pm) at all costs, especially if you are moving between the city's four main blocks (p. 95). Block A and B are connected through the Six of October Bridge and Al Azhar Tunnel, while Block B and C are connected via a handful of bridges that cross the Nile; these are first-class bottlenecks and can easily chop 1 hour off your life each time you attempt crossing.
- Nothing really gets going on Fridays until the Friday prayer is over, yet most attractions are open. Grab the opportunity, especially if you need to visit a certain place located far from your base (for example, you are based in downtown and want to visit the pyramids).
- If you are left with no other choice but to brave the streets during rush hour, keep a book or your iPod handy.

out of the whole process seems like a very cheap price to pay. If, for whatever reason, the driver doesn't turn on the meter once you step in, get out and hail another one rather than battling with him.

The ambitious Capital Taxi Project was launched in 2006 in a bid to bring Cairo's taxi fleet up to the standards of neighboring Jordan and Syria. Four years down the road and with a handful of shortfalls, the project is far from successful. Though all vehicles are newer models and air-conditioned, with drivers speaking a get-by level of English, the cabs are not that widespread in Cairo and come with quite an expensive fare. Still, they can prove helpful when it comes to long distances, such as an airport transfer. Unlike the new all-whites, these taxis can't be hailed on the street and need to be called in advance (✆ **16516**); buffer in some extra time, as punctuality is a skill they need to work on.

BY BUS

Cairo has a comprehensive and diverse bus system that firmly connects its widely spread districts. Nevertheless, they are usually overcrowded due to demand with respect to their rock-bottom prices. If you opt for one, be prepared to spend a considerable amount of time in transport and at a pretty low level of comfort.

CTA (Cairo Transport Authority) uses big, air-conditioned white buses and offers an acceptable level of comfort; thus it is the most expensive (ticket costs LE2). Sadly its network is far from extensive and its regularity far from frequent.

The **local bus** is the most widely spread among all buses with the most extensive network and cheapest prices (LE0.50–LE1); however, it is crammed full most of the time.

Minibuses were first positioned as a smaller version of buses with places for seated passengers only; hence the relatively higher prices of LE1.50 to LE2. Unfortunately, over time they evolved into a copycat of local buses; avoid them unless you are desperate.

Without **microbuses,** a considerable percentage of Cairenes wouldn't be able to get around. Their network infiltrates about every district in the capital and beyond. They offer a seat for each of their 14 (sometimes squeezed 16) passengers, but are down-right hazardous with reckless drivers. If you are up for an adrenaline rush, wave one down. Fare averages LE1 to LE1.50.

Bus stops are everywhere, but main bus stations are usually located in squares. Local, mini-, and microbuses can all be picked up from any stop (and even hailed anywhere on the street). The most popular ones are Abdel Moneim Riyad (the closest to Tahrir Square), Ramses, Ataba (the closest to Islamic Cairo), and Giza.

BY METRO

Cairo Metro, often dubbed the Underground, is a good option to evade Cairo's traffic on ground level; however, things get jampacked underground at rush hours. Trains run about every 10 to 15 minutes, with relevant efficiency, and transport some 2.2 million passengers a day. Cairo Metro can be described as clean, with reservations, though during the summer months it does become quite malodorous. Women can decide whether to take advantage of the women-only cars, which are the first two in the train (after 6pm, the second car usually becomes general seating); traveling alone, women may find themselves the object of unwanted attention in the mixed cars. On the other hand, unveiled women report increased levels of religious harassment in the women's car, with "modestly" attired Muslim women praying loudly, making comments about their "immodest" fellow passengers, or even overtly proselytizing. The line between a cultural experience and an annoyance is a matter of individual tolerance.

Currently there are two lines up and running, and two more in the making. **Line 1** connects the suburb of Helwan to El Marg by cutting through the heart of Cairo. It is especially helpful if you are based in Maadi (Maadi or Sakanat el Maadi stations) and heading to the Egyptian Museum or Tahrir Square (Sadat station), going to pick up the train from Ramses Train Station (Mubarak station), visiting Coptic Cairo (Mar Girgis station), or going for a stroll in downtown (Urabi, Nasser, or Sadat stations).

Line 2 runs from Shubra to Giza, and you will use this one less frequently than Line 1. Indeed it is quite helpful if you are picking up the train from Giza station or heading to Zamalek (Opera station), though the latter would require a 20-minute walk back to where the action is on 26th of July Street.

Line 3 will have a direct impact on every visiting tourist as it will connect Cairo International Airport to downtown and onward to Mohandiseen. Opening in phases

Road Rules

- Traffic lights are more decorative than functional.
- Lanes are guidelines; please keep them in between the wheels while driving.
- Pedestrians can stop, cars won't.
- Officially, driving is on the right-hand side only. In reality, Egyptians drive on the right, left, and in the opposite direction as well.
- Not wearing a seatbelt or talking on the phone while driving warrants a fine, which can be often paid immediately and at a "discount" if you skip on the receipt.
- The pavement is for pedestrians, but motorbikes and even four-wheel-drives will use it in time of need.
- Hard shoulder . . . what is that?
- Cutting someone off while driving is a norm; shrug it off and you are cool, make a fuss out of it and people will stare at you as if you are coming from Pluto.

Cairo Metro

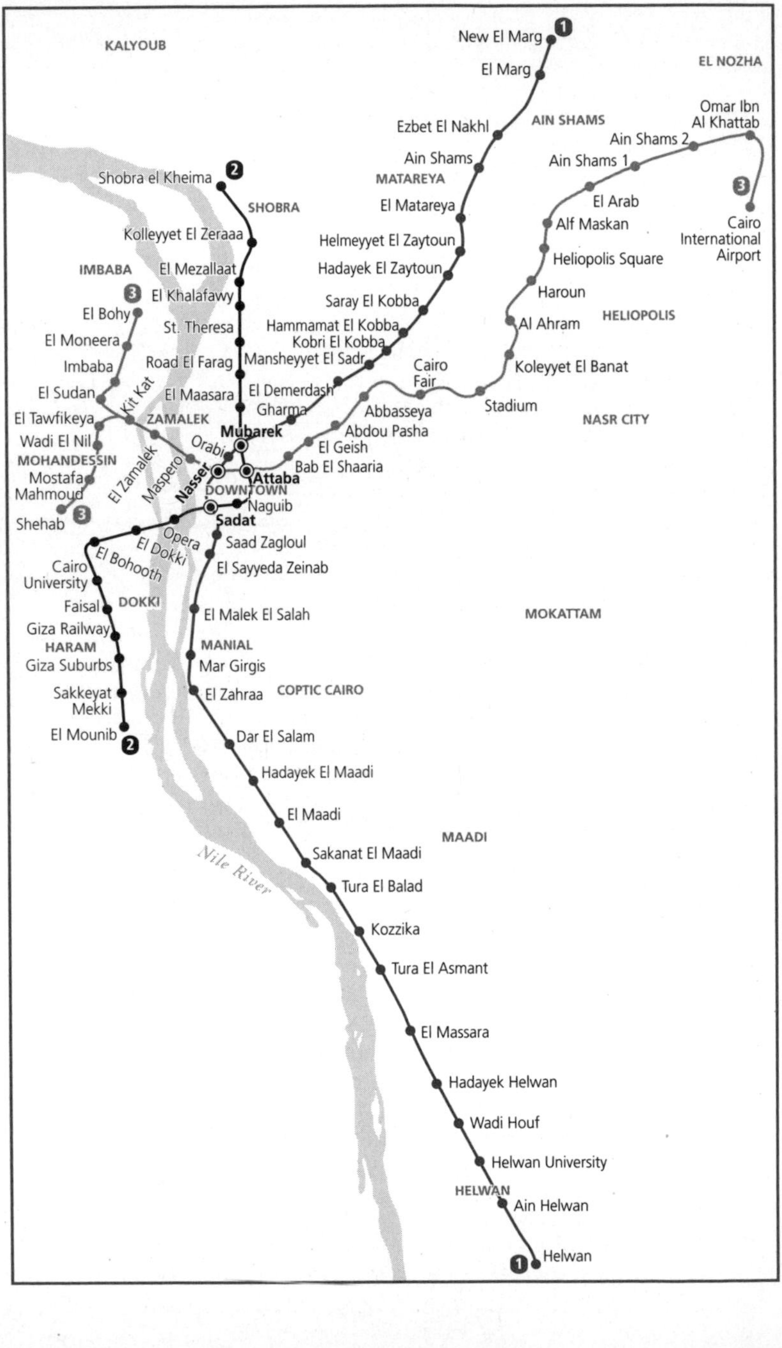
KALYOUB
New El Marg
1
El Marg
EL NOZHA
Ezbet El Nakhl
AIN SHAMS
Omar Ibn Al Khattab
Ain Shams 2
Ain Shams
Ain Shams 1
MATAREYA
Shobra el Kheima
2
SHOBRA
El Matareya
El Arab
3
Alf Maskan
Cairo International Airport
Kolleyyet El Zeraaa
Helmeyyet El Zaytoun
Heliopolis Square
IMBABA
El Mezallaat
Hadayek El Zaytoun
Haroun
3
El Khalafawy
Saray El Kobba
El Bohy
St. Theresa
Hammamat El Kobba
Al Ahram
HELIOPOLIS
El Moneera
Kobri El Kobba
Imbaba
Road El Farag
Mansheyyet El Sadr
Koleyyet El Banat
Cairo Fair
El Sudan
Kit Kat
El Maasara
El Demerdash
Stadium
Gharma
Abbasseya
NASR CITY
El Tawfikeya
ZAMALEK
Mubarek
Abdou Pasha
Wadi El Nil
Orabi
El Geish
MOHANDESSIN
El Zamalek
Maspero
Bab El Shaaria
Mostafa Mahmoud
Nasser
Attaba
DOWNTOWN
Naguib
Shehab
3
Sadat
6
Opera
El Dokki
Saad Zagloul
Cairo University
El Bohooth
El Sayyeda Zeinab
Faisal
DOKKI
El Malek El Salah
MOKATTAM
Giza Railway
HARAM
MANIAL
Giza Suburbs
Mar Girgis
Sakkeyat Mekki
El Zahraa
COPTIC CAIRO
El Mounib
2
Dar El Salam
Hadayek El Maadi
El Maadi
MAADI
Sakanat El Maadi
Nile River
Tura El Balad
Kozzika
Tura El Asmant
El Massara
Hadayek Helwan
Wadi Houf
Helwan University
HELWAN
Ain Helwan
1
Helwan

Tips Limo or a Private Car?

Asking the reception desk at your hotel to rent a car with a driver sounds like a straightforward procedure, and indeed it is. However, many well-reputed hotels in Cairo won't get you a limo from an authorized dealer but rather a private car whose owner is working as a driver or hiring someone to do the job. The cutting-corners attitude is a strong indication of unprofessionalism, and can get you in trouble. Cars with private plates are not formally allowed to be employed for commercial use. You personally won't be incriminated, but your day can easily end up in ruins. Double-check the car's plates and registration before you hop in; plates should be gray and white or yellow and white rather than blue and white, which are for private cars.

(first one scheduled for 2011), Line 3 is expected to be fully operational by 2019; keep your fingers crossed, but don't hold your breath.

Line 4 is the outcome of entrepreneurial thinking and will connect both Six of October City and the Fifth Settlement Suburb to the city center. No timings quoted yet.

Tickets (available from manned station booths; no credit cards) cost LE1, and you will need yours not only to get onto the platform but to work the turnstiles at the other end, so keep the ticket for the duration of the trip. Trains run from about 6am to midnight.

BY CAR

In a nutshell, driving in Cairo is a game of chicken that is not for the fainthearted. Surprisingly, some foreigners enjoy driving in Cairo. "It is like a real-life video game," someone claimed admirably. If you are seriously considering renting a car, there are dozens of car-rental agencies that would rent the smallest car for LE220 per day (100km/62 miles daily allowance and LE1 at minimum for each extra kilometer). Those that can be recommended are **Avis,** 16A Maamal el Sukar St., Garden City (© **02/27947400**), and **CRC Limousine,** 66 Salah Salem St., Heliopolis (© **02/24178769**).

ON FOOT

Cairo is too big to be handled on foot. While it is safe to tread most of its streets during the daytime, and some after dark, it is till undoable to solely depend on your feet as a means of transportation; the distances involved are just too lengthy. However, when it comes to certain districts, you are actually better off walking rather than getting stuck in traffic; this chiefly applies within the downtown or Zamalek districts. A stroll in Maadi is soul soothing for the sheer reason of being surrounded with greenery, while a walk on Art Deco–rich Korba Street in Heliopolis is a must-do for art lovers and architecture enthusiasts.

3 WHAT TO SEE & DO

DOWNTOWN & ZAMALEK

This is where all the action takes place; from spending hours in the Egyptian Museum to paying a short visit to the undiscovered Islamic Ceramics Museum in Zamalek. Make sure one evening is reserved for a dinner on the Nile, sailing in one of Egypt's traditional,

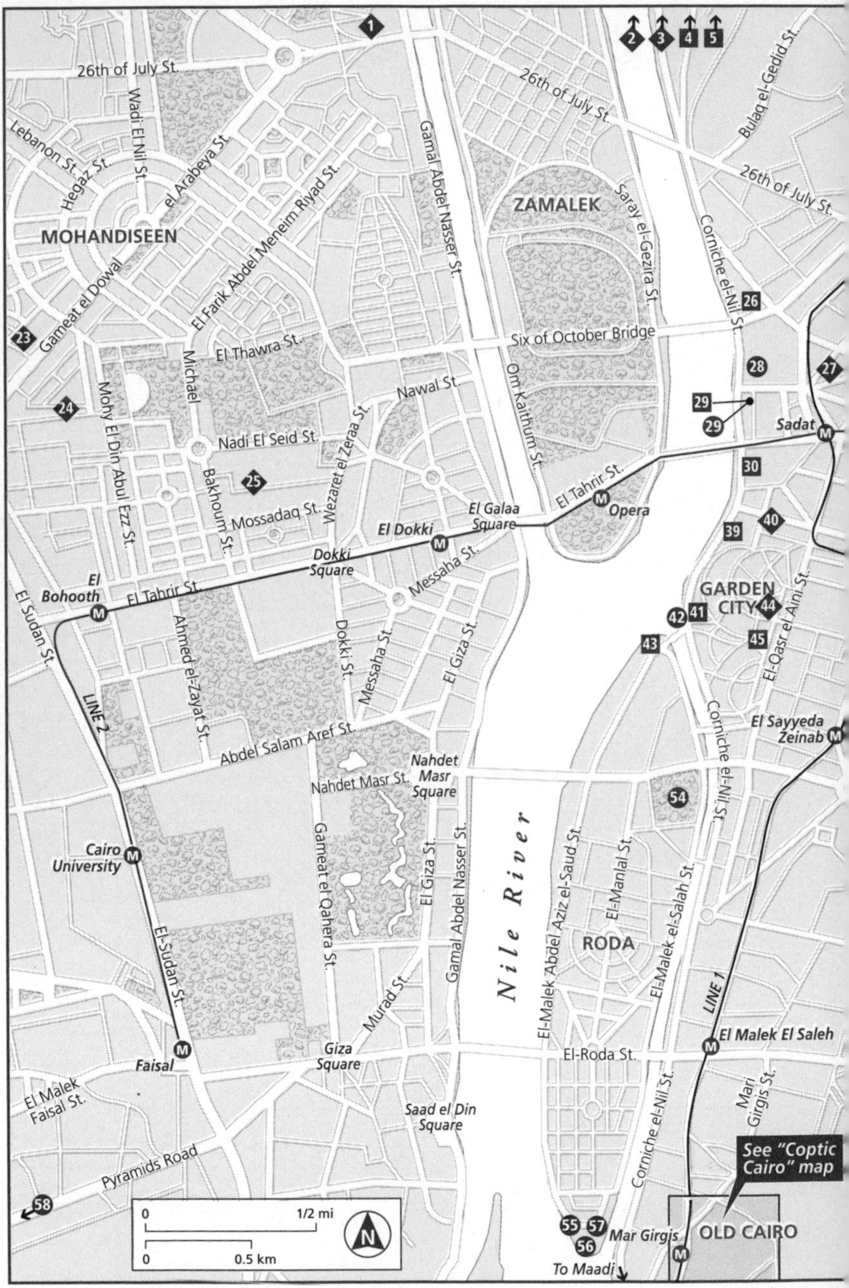
26th of July St.
Wadi El Nil St.
Lebanon St.
Hegaz St.
el Arabeya St.
El Farik Abdel Meneim Riyad St.
MOHANDISEEN
Gameat el Dowal
Gamal Abdel Nasser St.
ZAMALEK
Saray el-Gezira St.
Corniche el-Nil St.
Bulaq el-Gedid St.
El Thawra St.
Six of October Bridge
Michael
Mohy El Din Abul Ezz St.
Nawal St.
Om Kalthum St.
Nadi El Seid St.
Wezaret el Zeraa St.
Bakhoum St.
Mossadaq St.
El Tahrir St.
Opera
Sadat
El Galaa Square
El Dokki
Dokki Square
Messaha St.
El Bohooth
El Sudan St.
GARDEN CITY
El-Qasr el Aini St.
Ahmed el-Zayat St.
Dokki St.
Messaha St.
El Giza St.
LINE 2
El Sayyeda Zeinab
Abdel Salam Aref St.
Nahdet Masr St.
Nahdet Masr Square
Cairo University
Gameat el Qahera St.
Nile River
El-Malek Abdel Aziz el-Saud St.
El-Manial St.
El-Malek el-Salah St.
RODA
El-Sudan St.
Murad St.
LINE 1
El Malek El Saleh
Faisal
Giza Square
El-Roda St.
El Malek Faisal St.
Saad el Din Square
Mari Girgis St.
Pyramids Road
See "Coptic Cairo" map
OLD CAIRO
Mar Girgis
To Maadi
0 1/2 mi
0 0.5 km
N

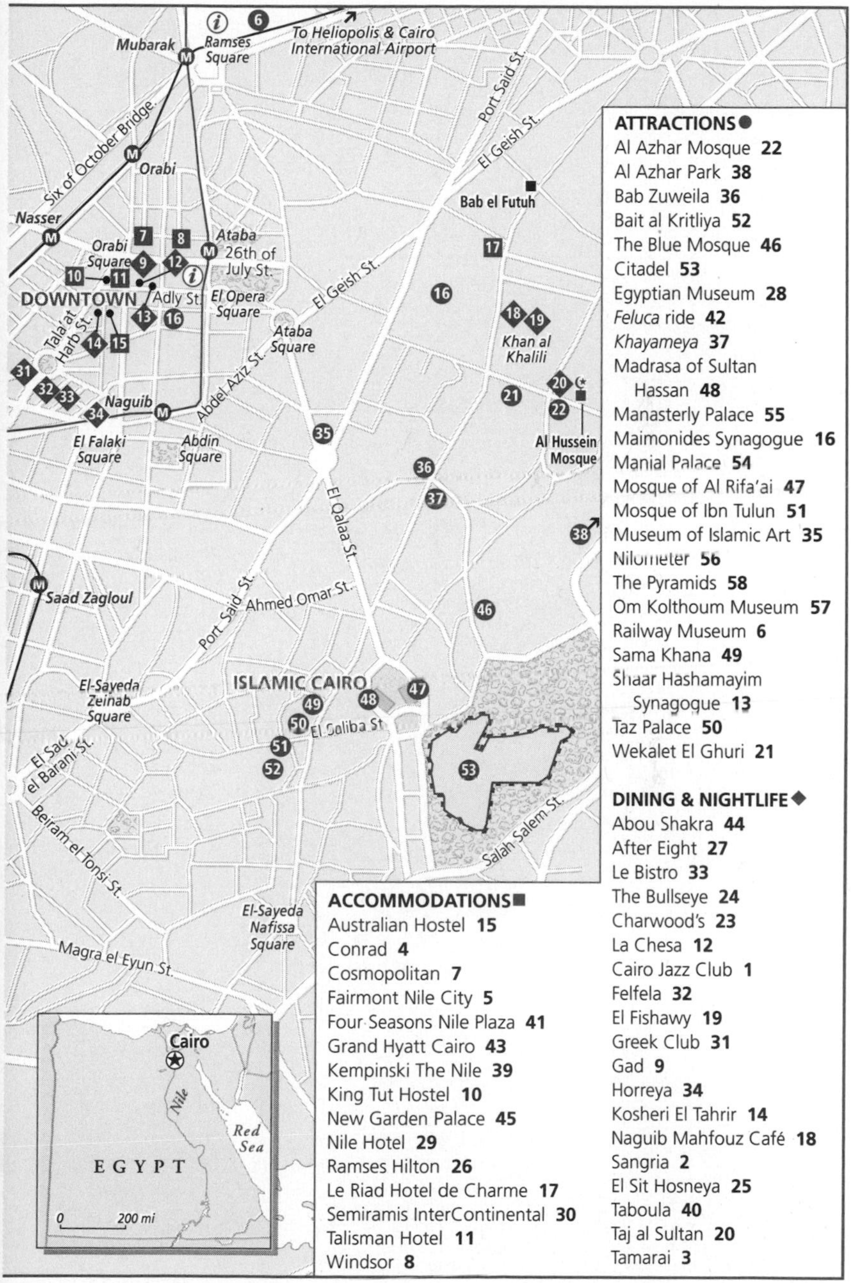

To Heliopolis & Cairo International Airport
Mubarak
Ramses Square
Six of October Bridge
Orabi
Nasser
Orabi Square
Ataba
26th of July St.
DOWNTOWN
Adly St.
El Opera Square
Ataba Square
Tala'at Harb St.
El Geish St.
Port Said St.
Bab el Futuh
Khan al Khalili
Naguib
Abdel Aziz St.
El Falaki Square
Abdin Square
Al Hussein Mosque
El Qalaa St.
Saad Zagloul
Ahmed Omar St.
ISLAMIC CAIRO
El-Sayeda Zeinab Square
El Saliba St.
El Sad el Barani St.
Beiram el Tonsi St.
Salah Salem St.
El-Sayeda Nafissa Square
Magra el Eyun St.
Cairo
Nile
Red Sea
EGYPT
0
200 mi
ATTRACTIONS
Al Azhar Mosque 22
Al Azhar Park 38
Bab Zuweila 36
Bait al Kritliya 52
The Blue Mosque 46
Citadel 53
Egyptian Museum 28
Feluca ride 42
Khayameya 37
Madrasa of Sultan Hassan 48
Manasterly Palace 55
Maimonides Synagogue 16
Manial Palace 54
Mosque of Al Rifa'ai 47
Mosque of Ibn Tulun 51
Museum of Islamic Art 35
Nilometer 56
The Pyramids 58
Om Kolthoum Museum 57
Railway Museum 6
Sama Khana 49
Shaar Hashamayim Synagogue 13
Taz Palace 50
Wekalet El Ghuri 21
DINING & NIGHTLIFE
Abou Shakra 44
After Eight 27
Le Bistro 33
The Bullseye 24
Charwood's 23
La Chesa 12
Cairo Jazz Club 1
Felfela 32
El Fishawy 19
Greek Club 31
Gad 9
Horreya 34
Kosheri El Tahrir 14
Naguib Mahfouz Café 18
Sangria 2
El Sit Hosneya 25
Taboula 40
Taj al Sultan 20
Tamarai 3
ACCOMMODATIONS
Australian Hostel 15
Conrad 4
Cosmopolitan 7
Fairmont Nile City 5
Four Seasons Nile Plaza 41
Grand Hyatt Cairo 43
Kempinski The Nile 39
King Tut Hostel 10
New Garden Palace 45
Nile Hotel 29
Ramses Hilton 26
Le Riad Hotel de Charme 17
Semiramis InterContinental 30
Talisman Hotel 11
Windsor 8

GEM

GEM, or the **Grand Egyptian Museum** is a $550-million mega project equivalent in size to 11 soccer pitches with the capacity to house 150,000 artifacts. Dublin-based Heneghan Peng Architects won the design for this enigmatic new building, which, according to designs, will have a front facade covered with translucent alabaster, allowing it to glow at night. The famous Ramses II statue, which used to stand in front of Ramses Train Station (hence the station's name) has already been moved to the entrance of the new museum. Plans for the inauguration of GEM are set for 2013.

yet clichéd, *felucas.* The central location of downtown and Zamalek offers a wide range of transportation options; the Metro can be a good to avoid traffic, but during rush hours on hot summer days, the new air-conditioned taxis win hands-down.

Cairo Tower The 60-story tower was originally built in the 1960s as a symbol of the will and power of the new republic regime under the helm of ambitious Gamal Abdel Nasser. It was recently renovated and reopened in 2009; the edifice's concrete sheathing on the outside, said to represent the traditional lotus flower, remains unchanged, but high-tech lighting and a VIP restaurant and lounge have been added (the 360-degree revolving restaurant on the 59th floor remains, though). Cairo Tower makes a great photo at night, and during the day you get a spectacular panoramic view of the city from above.

El Burj St., Zamalek. ✆ **02/27365112** or 02/27374206. Fax 02/27383790. www.cairotower.net. Admission LE65. Daily 9am–midnight.

Egyptian Museum ★★ In 1863, Said Pasha, then Egypt's sovereign, ordered the building of the country's first version of the Egyptian Museum (now in its third incarnation), the Bulaq Museum. Unfortunately, it was severely damaged due to a heavy Nile inundation in 1878. Twelve years later, Egypt's national collection of archaeological treasures was moved to a new location in Giza, but the place wasn't spacious enough, and in 1902 they were moved one more time to the neoclassical building on the edge of Tahrir Square that you visit today.

With its collection of more than 120,000 items, the Egyptian Museum is a heavy dose of history that is bound to leave you overwhelmed. Plan at least a half day to briefly cover the two-story condensed museum, though history buffs should plan a full day.

Following a chronological clockwise order, the **ground floor** takes you on an enchanting journey through Ancient Egypt's history. You embark with the Narmer Palette (room no. 43), which stands at the entrance of the building. Ostensibly it is Ancient Egypt's first attempt to document its own history. Discovered in 1897–98, it depicts Narmer wearing the white crown of Upper Egypt on one side and the red crown of Lower Egypt on the other. Narmer is credited for uniting Egypt for the first time. Turning left, you come upon the seated statue of King Zoser (room no. 48), ushering you to the **Old Kingdom** section; the 3rd Dynasty king is credited for building Ancient Egypt's very first pyramid, the Step Pyramid. The Old Kingdom was known as the Age of Pyramids, and it comes as no surprise to have a statue of Khafre (to whom the credit of building the second-largest pyramid is due) inaugurating the collection (room no. 42). The statue depicts the

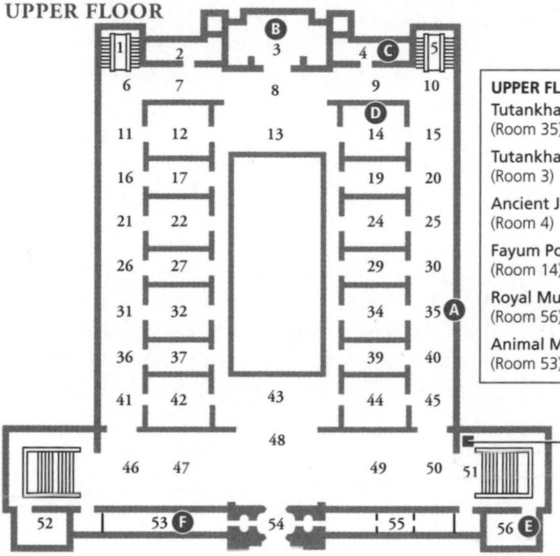

UPPER FLOOR ATTRACTIONS

Tutankhamun's golden throne **A** (Room 35)

Tutankhamun Jewelry Room **B** (Room 3)

Ancient Jewelry Collection **C** (Room 4)

Fayum Portraits **D** (Room 14)

Royal Mummies Exhibit **E** (Room 56)

Animal Mummies Exhibit **F** (Room 53)

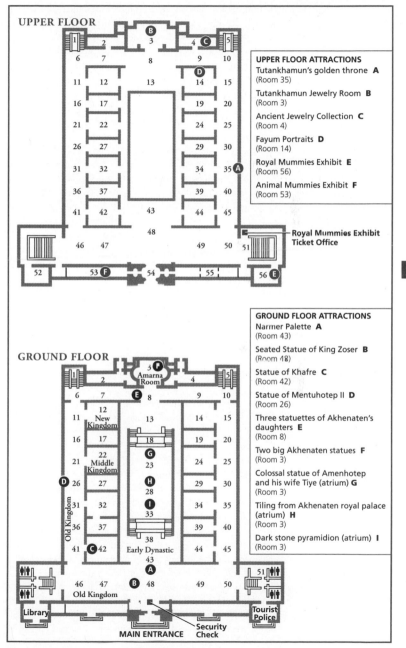

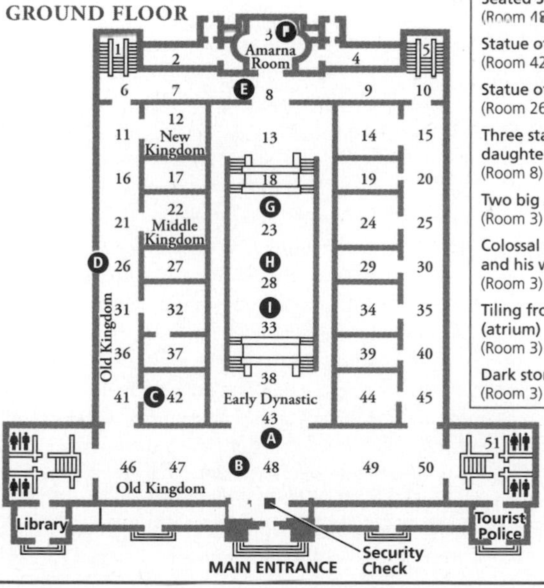

GROUND FLOOR ATTRACTIONS

Narmer Palette **A** (Room 43)

Seated Statue of King Zoser **B** (Room 48)

Statue of Khafre **C** (Room 42)

Statue of Mentuhotep II **D** (Room 26)

Three statuettes of Akhenaten's daughters **E** (Room 8)

Two big Akhenaten statues **F** (Room 3)

Colossal statue of Amenhotep and his wife Tiye (atrium) **G** (Room 3)

Tiling from Akhenaten royal palace (atrium) **H** (Room 3)

Dark stone pyramidion (atrium) **I** (Room 3)

Ancient Egyptian king with a false Royal Beard (note the straps on his cheeks), a royal cobra protecting his forehead, and Horus guarding his shoulders. Mentuhotep II reunited Egypt after the First Intermediate Period and thus established the **Middle Kingdom;** a statue of him (room no. 26) is, deservedly, the main attraction of the Middle Kingdom collection. The unusual statue depicts Mentuhotep II with a darker skin color; a sign of him being deceased. Carrying forward, you come to the exuberantly beautiful and, in my humble opinion, the highlight of the Egyptian Museum—the **Amarna Period.** The Amarna Period is not only characterized by the new religion (monotheistic worship of the sun disk—Aten) and the new capital of Akhetaten (today's Tel el Amarna), it also represents a new revolutionary school of Ancient Egyptian art (p. 35); a deviation from the mainstream where the standardized lines depicting human figures have been replaced with individualized ones. Observe the three statuettes of Akhenaten's daughters (room no. 8) with their tanned skin, probably from worshiping Aten in roofless temples, as well as the two big Akhenaten statues (room no. 3) with the Pharaoh being depicted with a rather horsy face, big thighs, and a prominent breast. Heading back to the main entrance, you go through a second corridor exhibiting a plethora of statues and artifacts that date back to the **New Kingdom.** The atrium in the middle of the ground level features huge relics too big to fit anywhere else in the museum. They include the colossal statue of Amenhotep III and his wife Tiye (this is the same pharaonic couple depicted in the Colossi of Memnon; p. 270), a tiling from Akhenaten royal palace, a dark stone pyramidion (used to cap pyramids' tops), and a number of stone sarcophagi, of which one is exhibited with a mirror that allows you to see the underside of the lid, which is adorned with heavenly depictions of the Goddess of the Sky, Nut.

In contrast to the ground floor's chronological order, the **upper floor** is theme-oriented, dominated by the **Tutankhamun Collection.** Though the boy king died at the age of 18, after ruling for about a decade, he left an astonishingly rich and diverse collection of sarcophagi, shrines, coffins, and even funerary beds and board games. His golden throne (room no. 35) is a marvelous piece of art, living proof of the skillfulness of Egyptian artistry and the lavishness of the Egyptian civilization. The jewel of the Tutankhamun Collection is his mesmerizing 11kg (24 lb.) golden mask, which—along with a collection of golden ornaments, the king's gold-plated middle sarcophagus, and the 110kg (243 lb.) solid-gold innermost sarcophagus—is exhibited here in the Tutankhamun Jewelry Room (room no. 3). When Tutankhamun was buried, three human-shaped sarcophagi were put inside each other and into a rectangular stone one. The outermost of the three is still in the Valley of the Kings (KV 62), where the king's mummy rests in peace. Overshadowed by its neighboring Tutankhamun Collection, the **Ancient Jewelry Collection** features some exquisite items that date back to the Greco-Roman era. Look for the gold hair band with the head of the Medusa and the golden diadem with Serapis in the middle. Another Greco-Roman attraction is the Fayum Portraits (p. 36), a collection of a dozen or so hauntingly beautiful death portraits that were painted on coffins during the first few centuries A.D. And no visit to the Egyptian Museum is complete without a visit to the **Royal Mummies Exhibit.** Standing in front of the well-preserved body of a man who actually lived some 4,000 to 5,000 years ago is both tantalizing and perplexing at the same time. Ramses II's white hair has turned yellow from the use of henna during mummification, while his father Seti I is the best preserved. Exhibited mummies change from time to time, but there are usually 12 of them on display at a time. Kids will like the **Animal Mummies Exhibit;** check out the gigantic 5m (16-ft.) mummified Nile crocodile on display.

For more detailed information, check out *The Illustrated Guide to the Egyptian Museum in Cairo* (AUC Press, 2005), or go for a guided tour. Tour operators all over town arrange guided tours to the Egyptian Museum; however, going for one of the resident guides can be a cheaper option without compromising much on quality. Offering their services in more common European languages, guides hang around next to the ticket office by the main gate. All you need to do is show up and check whose turn it is. Though they are organized when it comes to turns, there is no fixed price and (you will be accustomed by now) you need to bargain. If you end up with $10 for an hour tour or $25 for a 3-hour one, then you have landed yourself a good deal.

Note: Photography is strictly prohibited, and you need to check your camera at the main gate before going in. Using your mobile phone camera can result in a hefty fine.

Tahrir Sq., Downtown. ✆ **02/25782452.** Admission LE60; extra LE100 for the Royal Mummies Exhibit. Daily 9am–7pm.

Feluca Ride ★★★ You shouldn't leave Cairo without taking a sunset or evening cruise on the Nile in one of these traditional lateen-rigged sailboats. The best place to start your cruise is the docks between the Four Seasons and the Hyatt Regency, which are shared by *feluca* owners with two or three boats apiece. There's not much to differentiate them, as they all offer the same traditional affair. Once onboard, more or less anything goes, so feel free to bring a pizza and some beer for a lovely new perspective on dinner in Cairo. The owner of the dock and the boats are from Cairo, but the pilots are usually from Upper Egypt; they will probably appreciate sharing whatever you have onboard, and are usually good for a chat and a whole new perspective on life in the big city.

LE60–LE90 an hour (depending on your negotiation skills and how big the group, and subsequently the boat, is), plus an extra LE10–LE20 to the pilot. No credit cards.

Islamic Ceramics Museum ★ Located a couple of minutes' walk from the Cairo Marriott (p. 131) in a nicely restored palace, the Islamic Ceramics Museum contains a stunning collection of ceramic pots, plates, and bowls from the 9th to the 18th centuries. It is also worth visiting simply for the building, which was originally a small palace for Prince Amr Ibrahim in the 19th century and was seized by the government in 1953. Designed by a Turkish architect, it is a graceful and balanced building, especially in contrast to some of the old colonial piles you'll see if you take the time to stroll around Zamalek or Garden City.

The documentation is uninformative, but most of the pieces in the museum speak for themselves. The atmosphere of the usually half-deserted old palace still makes it a great place to relax after a hectic day in Islamic Cairo.

1 El Marsafy St., Zamalek. ✆ **02/27373298.** Admission LE25. Thurs–Sun 10am–1pm and 5–8:30pm.

Railway Museum (Kids) Cairo is full of dusty little museums tucked away in unlikely spots. This one, founded in 1933, is tacked onto the back of Ramses Train Station and is an absolute must-see for train buffs or for those who love old museums of any sort. The star of the museum's collection is a magnificently opulent 19th-century engine built for Said Pasha, which you can walk into, but the two floors of the museum are stuffed with enough model trains, planes, and bridges to keep your inner (and actual) 12-year-old happy for a couple of hours.

Ramses Train Station. ✆ **02/25763793.** Admission Tues–Thurs and Sat–Sun LE10, Fri LE20; camera LE20. Tues–Sun 8am–2pm.

Giza is all about the pyramids, and visiting them is probably why you got excited about Egypt in the first place. Take a full morning to see this site, peeking into the inside of the Great Pyramid or beholding the Solar Boat, but try to leave before the midday heat sets in, especially in summer. In any case, take plenty of water with you. Taxis remain the most convenient means of transportation to and from the pyramids.

The Pyramids ★★★ Kids The question of how the Ancient Egyptians, without any of the powerful modern building equipment that we've taken for granted for several centuries, managed to build some of the biggest, most enduring, and perfectly engineered structures ever is a toughie, so I encourage you to consult Miroslav Verner's *The Pyramids* (AUC Press, 2002). The truth is that nobody has come up with a watertight answer yet. There are plenty of theories around, and they run the gamut from the truly ridiculous alien-intervention spiels of the "pyramidiot" crowd to some that are eminently reasonable, but in the end they all still fall just short of complete.

Leaving aside the possibility of help from above, the theories fall into two obvious categories: First, that the Ancient Egyptians built ramps up the sides of the pyramids, and second, that they used some kind of lever to lift up the blocks.

Back in the 5th century B.C., the Greek traveler and historian Herodotus recorded the entirely plausible explanation that the blocks had been lifted up one course at a time with "machines made of short pieces of timber." Herodotus was notoriously slack in details (he also wrote that the stone for the pyramids had been brought from Arabia when there was a perfectly good limestone quarry just up the river near Saqqara, and that the number of leeks that the pyramid builders received for their troubles was recorded on the side of the monuments), but in this case he seems to make sense, and many people have followed up with theories about what sort of elaborate machines might have been used for the task.

The problem with the lifting machine theory is that there is very little evidence to actually support it. The Egyptians recorded just about everything else, from harvests to battles to parties, in elaborately detailed wall paintings, but not these "machines made of short pieces of timber." Aside from this, consider on the one hand that some of the individual blocks used in the smallest of the Giza Plateau pyramids, the Pyramid of Menkaure,

Tips Con Artists

The pyramids in Giza have the highest density of con artists and touts of any site in the country. Before you even make it to the gate, you'll be surrounded by eager young men who insist that you will not be allowed in without a guide (don't worry, you will be) or that you need a horse to get around (you don't). Once inside, the offers will keep coming, many of them from uniformed policemen who will offer a variety of favors in return for cash. They may be irritating, but they are not dangerous and can safely be ignored. If you do opt for a horse or camel ride, agree on the price first, and do not pay until you get where you're going—pay upfront, and your horse will "go lame" within a couple of feet, necessitating another steed and another payment. Incidents of theft are also not uncommon; don't hand anyone your camera to get your picture taken—you may find yourself having to buy it back.

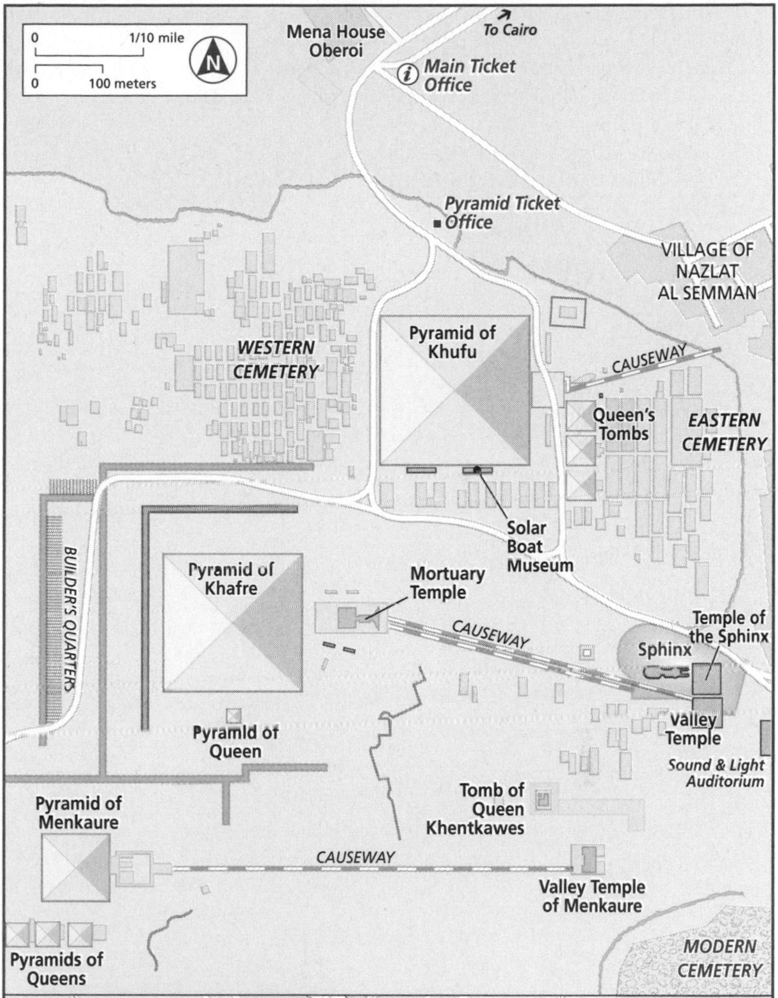
0
1/10 mile
0
100 meters
N
Mena House
Oberoi
To Cairo
Main Ticket
Office
Pyramid Ticket
Office
VILLAGE OF
NAZLAT
AL SEMMAN
WESTERN
CEMETERY
Pyramid of
Khufu
CAUSEWAY
Queen's
Tombs
EASTERN
CEMETERY
Solar
Boat
Museum
BUILDER'S QUARTERS
Pyramid of
Khafre
Mortuary
Temple
CAUSEWAY
Temple of
the Sphinx
Sphinx
Valley
Temple
Sound & Light
Auditorium
Pyramid of
Queen
Tomb of
Queen
Khentkawes
Pyramid of
Menkaure
CAUSEWAY
Valley Temple
of Menkaure
Pyramids of
Queens
MODERN
CEMETERY

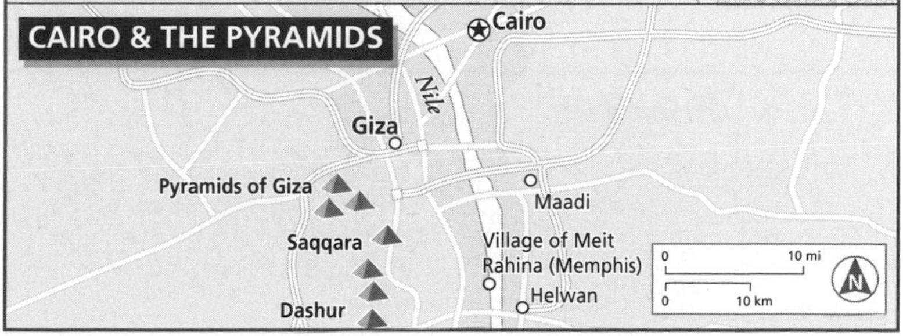
CAIRO & THE PYRAMIDS
Cairo
Nile
Giza
Pyramids of Giza
Maadi
Saqqara
Village of Meit
Rahina (Memphis)
Helwan
Dashur
0
10 mi
0
10 km
N

weighed around 220 tons. A compact car weighs around a ton, so we're talking about 200 cars being shifted in a single go. These would have been quite some timbers.

The other group of theories circles around the idea of ramps. This, too, makes good sense. The Ancient Egyptians were clearly adept at sliding these massive blocks of limestone out of their quarries and down to the Nile, so why not up ramps built onto the side of the pyramid? As each course was added, the ramp would simply have to be made a little higher and a little steeper.

But stand back a little and squint at a pyramid. If you're lucky enough to be in Giza, have a good look at the Pyramid of Khufu. It's 137m (almost 450 ft.) high now, but when it was first built it was 146m (almost 480 ft.). Imagine the size of the ramp needed to get to the top—building it would have been a feat greater than building the pyramid itself. This, of course, isn't an objection in and of itself, but the problem with size is simply that there's no evidence of the material. By one estimate, the ramp would have required more than 4 million cubic meters of material (more than 140 million cubic ft.). A hole that big doesn't just fill up with sand and disappear, and a pile like that doesn't just blow away, yet there is no evidence of either. Another problem plagues the ramp-theorists, however. We know approximately how long the pyramids took to build, and we have a pretty accurate idea (thanks to ultrasound investigations) of how much material they contain. We can therefore calculate how quickly the material would have had to flow up the ramp in order for the whole thing to work out. Many ramps that could have plausibly been built—including some of the ingeniously efficient spiral ramps that would have hugged the outside of the structure—fail this critical test by simply being too narrow to allow the stone to be slid up in sufficient quantities in the time allowed.

At the end of the day, then, we're left not much further ahead than Herodotus. It seems highly possible that both theories contain the essential elements of a complete solution: that the Ancient Egyptians used a combination of machinery made of wooden levers, rollers, and papyrus ropes and inclined ramps to get those blocks of stone to the top of their manmade mountains. Whether the details of how they did it will ever be fully worked out, however, remains an open question.

The pyramids may seem cliché, but there's really no sight like them. For sheer, dominating bulk, the pyramids in Giza have got pretty well everywhere else in the world beat. It used to be that you came upon them slowly, riding on horseback across the green fields that separated the plateau from the city. Nowadays, urban sprawl laps at the very feet of the Sphinx himself, and by the time you see the pyramids, they're right on top of you. It's a moment that you'll never forget.

The **Great Pyramid of Khufu** is the first of the pyramids trio. It is a masonry miracle that used 2.3 million brick blocks, each weighing 2 tons on average. When its construction finally came to a completion, it deservedly claimed the "world's highest structure"

Fun Facts **Off the Mark**

The Pyramid of Khufu in Giza is so precisely laid out that a mere 2cm (1 in.) error in the height of the southeast corner was enough to puzzle Egyptologists. The explanation, it seems, is that when the ancient engineers leveled the site by covering it with water, the prevailing north wind on the plateau was enough to press the water up a little and throw off their calculations.

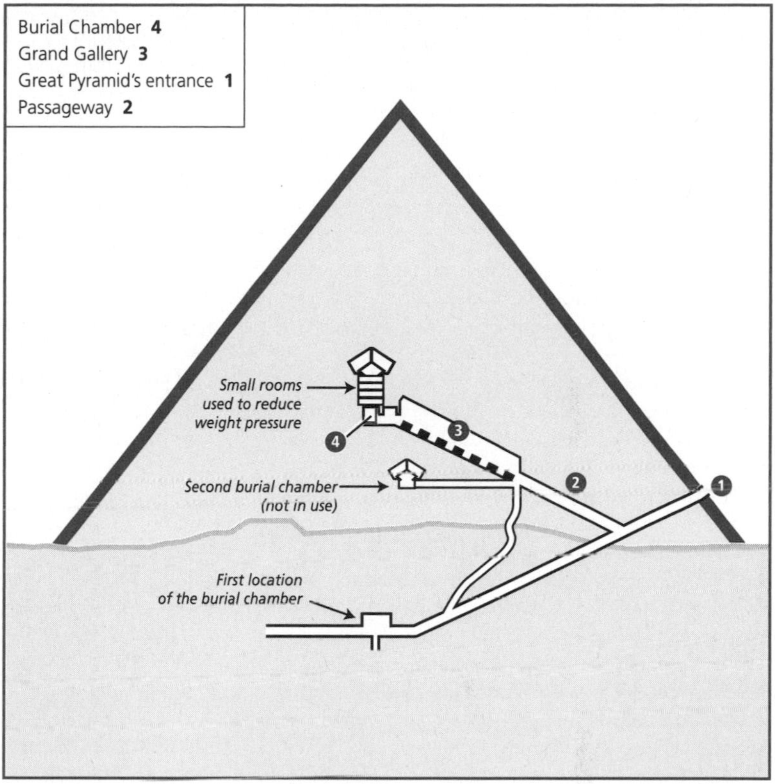

title, which it held for about 4 millenniums until England's Lincoln Cathedral was built. Going inside the pyramid is an enticing adventure; however, if you suffer from the slightest bit of claustrophobia—the passages are narrow and the spaces are tight, and in the heat of the summer stuffed with tourists—the inside of this place is guaranteed to set you off. There is little to see inside the pyramid, but here is what you can expect (numbers below correspond to the map above). The starting point is the pyramid's entrance (1) located on its northern side. From there you descend through a narrow passage, which initially led to the original burial chamber located underneath the pyramid. However, somewhere in time, the plan was modified and another burial chamber was built; this time inside the pyramid. This is why you won't go all the way down through the descending corridor but rather take a right through an equally narrow, though much steeper, passageway (2), this time going up. It will eventually lead you to a 47m-long (154-ft.) and 8m-high (26-ft.) corridor known as the Grand Gallery (3). The Grand Gallery acted as a protection measure against tomb raiders with its sliding granite blocking system. It ends with a small horizontal antechamber that leads to the king's burial chamber (4). Other than a huge red granite sarcophagus missing its lid, the room is practically empty.

Fun Facts The Height of the Matter

The Great Pyramid, as the Pyramid of Khufu is also known, was 146m (479 ft.) high until stripped of its gleaming white casing of limestone. Now it is "only" 137m (449 ft.) high. Napoleon, who actually spent a night alone in its dank depths, is reported to have announced that if it were dismantled and taken back to France, a 2m-high (6½-ft.) wall could be built around the entire country with the stone in this enormous monument.

Around the back of the Great Pyramid of Khufu, on the south side, is the strangely shaped **Solar Boat Museum.** It houses a boat that was disassembled and buried near the pyramid in an airtight sealed pit. When excavators, led by Egyptian archaeologist Kamal el Mallakh in 1954, found the solar boat, it had been carefully stored as 1,224 separate pieces, which had to be fit together in precisely the right fashion before being put on display. The result is a breathtakingly graceful 43m-long (143-ft.) vessel with a high curved 5m (16-ft.) prow, a 7m (23-ft.) stern, and a set of five oars on each side. One solar boat discovery preceded the 1954 one, while another surpassed it. In the 1920s, three boat pits were discovered (content was restricted to rope pieces and fragments of wood), while in 1987 another pit was found; this time no excavation took place as the pit was never opened. Solar boat could be a misnomer, as scholars never fully agreed on its purpose; some believe it was used as a funerary barge bringing the deceased to his final resting place, while others perceive it as more ritualistic, symbolizing the day and night journeys across the sky that the king undertakes in the afterlife in the company of Ra.

The medium-size **Pyramid of Khafre,** 144m (472 ft.) high, is a lot easier to visit than its bigger neighbor—both because it's smaller (not that the corridors are any wider, but they are shorter) and because there are generally fewer people—which is something to consider when you're fighting for tickets. The Pyramid of Khafre still has some of its white limestone casing gracing it. It was designed with a steeper angle and built on a higher ground than the Great Pyramid of Khufu. Both are elements that can easily deceive you into mistaking Khafre's pyramid for Khufu's. Did the son ungratefully do it on purpose? The Pyramid of Khafre still has both its Mortuary Temple and the Valley Temple. The Valley Temple of Khafre is one of the best preserved. A vestibule leads to a 16-pillared hall with 23 self statues (out of which only one survived, currently on display at the Egyptian Museum; p. 104), which were used as part of a funerary ritual known as the Opening of the Moth, which involved touching the king's body parts, each with a different object, so it would function in the afterlife. Afterward, the funeral procession would proceed through the causeway connecting the Valley Temple to the Mortuary Temple and end inside the pyramid.

The **Pyramid of Menkaure,** at 65m (213 ft.) high, is the smallest among the trio. The pyramid is one-tenth the size of its predecessor's, widely blamed on a hurried finishing accommodating Menkaure's sudden death. The position of this pyramid is not geometrically in line with the other two. Knowing how proficient Ancient Egyptian mathematicians were, error is a theory largely dismissed; an interesting theory emerged in the 1990s claiming the terrestrial positions of the three pyramids put them in perfect alignment with the three stars of Orion's Belt: Alnitak, Alnilam, and Mintaka.

It was the Greeks who first came up with the name for the **Sphinx** (strangler) after an imaginary winged creature that had the body of a lion and the face of a beautiful woman. Consequently, there are many sphinxes in Egypt and around the world. The one in Giza, sometimes referred to as the Great Sphinx, is aptly the largest; its body measures a little more than 72m (236 ft.) high. It has a body of a recumbent lion, symbol of power, and the face of a man, often guessed (though recently debated) to be Khafre. The eastward-facing Sphinx greets Ra each morning and is the pyramids' guardian, and stories about it begin as early as Tuthmosis IV. While riding his horse in the desert, the then prince needed to rest and lay in the shade of the Sphinx for a quick nap. In his sleep, he dreamt of the Sphinx asking him to remove the sand that by that time had already surrounded it. As a reward, Tuthmosis IV would find his way to the kingship of Egypt. The ambitious prince hurriedly saw to the removal of the sand, and indeed he was later crowned Pharaoh. When visiting the Sphinx, look for the Dream Stele between the statue's paws; a word of gratitude by Tuthmosis IV. Some parts of the Sphinx went missing; the royal cobra that adorned its head, the Royal Beard, fragments of which are on display in both the British Museum in London and the Egyptian Museum in Cairo, and the Sphinx's nose. Napoleon is rumored to be behind the act of destroying it; however, the Frenchman is innocent, as the guilt falls entirely on a 14th-century fanatic named Muhammad Saim Al Dahr, who was angered by peasants making offerings to the Sphinx in hopes of a good harvest. Al Dahr paid heavily for his vandalism; he was later hanged.

> **Fun Facts** **Hi, My Name Is . . .**
>
> Indeed the Greeks named it Sphinx, but in standard Arabic he is known as Abu Al Hawl, or "Father of Terror."

There is a general ticket for the site in addition to ones for each of the three pyramids and the Solar Boat Museum. The Pyramid of Khufu has a cap of 300 visitors per day, and tickets are sold on the same day; 150 are sold at 8am and the rest at 1pm. At the time of researching this edition, the two smaller pyramids were accepting visitors; however, this is not set in stone. To check for any possible updates, call the Pyramids Tourist Information Office (✆ **02/33838823**), located across from the Mena House Oberoi near the main gate to the plateau.

> **Tips** **Take a Break, Take the Bus**
>
> I am no fan of the organized bus tour, but unless you have someone to drive you out to the pyramids, fight for the tickets, and keep away the touts, it's actually the best way to see the site. The front desk of almost any hotel in town sells the tours, which usually include doorstep service. Thomas Cook has an excellent reputation, but most companies offer the same thing: an air-conditioned bus, tickets, and a guide. About the only thing that you want to look out for when booking your tour is the tacked-on "tour of the papyrus factory" or "visit to the carpet workshop," during which you'll find yourself herded through an overpriced tourist store in Giza and pressured to buy by a "guide" who gets a healthy cut of whatever you spend.

Giza. Admission LE60 for the site; LE100 Pyramid of Khufu; LE35 Pyramid of Khafre; LE35 Pyramid of Menkaure; LE50 Solar Boat Museum. Site daily 8am–4pm; pyramids and museum daily 9am–4pm.

HELIOPOLIS

There is one main "attraction" to visit in Heliopolis—Baron Palace. If you are not staying in the neighborhood, plan your visit on a weekend or on your way to the airport.

Baron Palace If you are arriving at Cairo International Airport and heading to downtown or Zamalek on Salah Salem Street, you are bound to see the palace. No need to keep track of the exact location; its Hindu temple–style architecture will strike you. In an attempt to promote his ambitious New Heliopolis project, Belgium industrialist Baron Empain built himself an extravagant palace, at the time, in the middle of the desert. French architect Alexandre Marcel was responsible for the exotic exteriors, inspired by the mind-boggling Angkor Wat of Cambodia. A Buddha in lotus position, gargoyles, dragons, as well as statues of Hindu gods Krishna and Shiva all adorn the exterior of the palace. Some statues come with a twist; Shiva is carved with four serpent heads instead of the classical four-arm stance. Entrepreneur Empain passed away in 1929, and three successive family generations lived in the palace, but later it was abandoned. Years of neglect took its toll, but in 2005 there was some clean up and the garden was planted. The palace is not open to the public, but if you tip the guard well, you can get a closer look at the exterior.

Salah Salem St., Heliopolis.

ISLAMIC CAIRO

It is difficult to draw a line demarcating Islamic Cairo's boundaries, but it can be roughly described as the area between the Citadel and Ataba Square. It is a seemingly never-ending labyrinth dotted with Islamic monuments, from mosques and palaces to *madrasas* and *sabils*. It is where most of Nobel-laureate Naguib Mahfouz's works took place; read *The Cairo Trilogy* to get a true feel. There is a constant jostling of busy, friendly people packing alleyways lined with stalls selling everything from nightdresses, rope, and fish to pots and pans, buckets, and stools. The easiest way to get here is to hail a taxi.

Al Azhar Mosque The very first prayers held in Al Azhar Mosque date back to A.D. 972. Sixteen years later Al Azhar (The Splendid) was given the status of university. Since then it has grown a reputation for being one of the most prestigious universities for

Just the Facts

The three pyramids in Giza are the oldest and biggest tourist sites ever, and they've been attracting visitors since before Greek historian Herodotus named the biggest of the three as one of the Seven Wonders of the World. The pyramids were built on the western edge of the Nile Valley by 4th Dynasty rulers between about 2589 and 2530 B.C., and given their age, they have survived remarkably well; the most noticeable damage has been the loss of most of the gleaming white limestone casings, which has changed the dimensions of the biggest pyramid, Khufu, giving it a saw-toothed profile when viewed up close. The medium-size pyramid was built for Khafre, the son of Khufu, and the smallest was for Menkaure, who succeeded Khafre.

Sound and Light Show

The keyword here is *cheesy*. This over-the-top light show (✆ **02/33852880** or 02/33847911; www.soundandlight.com.eg; admission LE75), ostensibly narrated by the Sphinx, is historically uninformative and giggle-worthy for the most part. The upside is that you get to be out on the plateau after dark. The downside is that they turn the volume up too high, and the sound system isn't really that great. Unless you are a huge fan of this kind of thing, or have an ironic sense of humor, I would advise saving your sound and light budget for Karnak (p. 271).

There are three to four shows a night, each in a different language. Showtimes in the winter (Oct–Mar) are 6:30, 7:30, 8:30, and 9:30pm. In the summer (Apr–Sept), shows are at 8:30, 9:30, 10:30, and 11:30pm. The logic behind the language schedule has always escaped me, and I would recommend double-checking the information below before trekking out to Giza.

	First Show	Second Show	Third Show	Fourth Show
Sunday	German	French	Russian	English
Monday	English	French	Spanish	No Show
Tuesday	English	Italian	French	No Show
Wednesday	English	French	German	Spanish
Thursday	Japanese	English	French	Arabic
Friday	English	French	Italian	No Show
Saturday	English	Spanish	Italian	No Show

Islamic studies. It took off with teaching traditional theologies but grew to teach a fairly full curriculum of subjects, including medicine, engineering, and agriculture. Today Al Azhar University attracts more than 100,000 students from Egypt and the rest of the world.

Entering Al Azhar Mosque today, you go through Bab Al Mezayenin, one of the mosque's nine gates. Bab Al Mezayenin translates to Barbers' Gate, named after the fact that most students had their hair cut there before starting the academic year. Once you've crossed the central courtyard, or *sahn,* you enter the main prayer area, a huge pillared hall with nine rows of columns; of the 140, 90 are originals. Not to be missed is the genuine inscription around the *mihrab,* the niche to which Muslims direct their prayers, with its Kufic-style calligraphy. Al Azhar is the first monument built by the Fatimids, but the mosque has undergone several restorations and repeated extensions so that it can no longer be related to them, at least not architecturally. Of the original six minarets, five remain. Three were built between the 14th and 15th centuries during the Mamluk sultanate, and two more were added as part of the 18th-century extension led by the influential Ottoman janissary commander Abdel Rahman Katkhuda. Note the difference in their architecture styles.

Today, Al Azhar is a functioning mosque and an active university in religious attire; an ultra-modest dress code (women should cover their arms and men should refrain from wearing shorts) is much appreciated, and if there is no room in your handbag for a headscarf, they are available at the entrance, where you will also leave your shoes with the attendant. There are no official opening hours, but non-Muslims will be gently ushered

Bakshish: The Art of Giving

Everywhere you go in Egypt, you're going to be asked, directly or indirectly, for money, and your life is going to improve immeasurably once you get comfortable with giving a loving handout for people who ask for, or at least expect, it. The guy who carries your bags to the car, the janitor who switches on the lights at the back of the museum, and the old guy at the mosque who takes care of your shoes while you walk around the building—they should all get a LE5 note discreetly slipped into their palms with a smile on your face and a sincere *shokran* (thank you). In English it is called a tip, in Egyptian Arabic it is *bakshish.*

Note: The tip amount you would leave at a burger joint would differ dramatically from that you would leave at a fine-dining restaurant. Likewise, the *bakshish* you hand out should differ from one place to another; the proposed LE5 note is just an example. Though *bakshish* is freely your choice, please consider it if it is indicated next to free admission.

out during prayer times; Fridays are entirely dedicated to prayers. The same set of rules goes for all the functioning mosques in Islamic Cairo.

Al Azhar St. Free admission, *bakshish* expected.

Al Azhar Park Kids The word *park* has slipped overpopulated Cairo's dictionary, but this 30-hectare (74-acre) green patch offers an environmental breather for the heavily polluted megalopolis and an outdoor hangout for its citizens. Built by the Aga Khan Trust for Culture, the park was gifted to Egypt by His Highness the Aga Khan, the reputed imam of the Ismaili Shi'a sect. Members of this sect consider themselves descendant of the Fatimids, whose fourth Caliphate, Al Mu'izz le-din Allah, ordered the building of Cairo. In addition to a couple of not-so-fancy cafes, there is the expensive Alain Le Notre restaurant within the park's premises, as well as a designated kids' area. Al Azhar Park offers superb panoramic scenery of the capital in general, Islamic Cairo in particular, so grab your camera and make it there before sunset.

Salah Salem St. ✆ **02/2510368** or 02/25107378. Fax 02/5121054. www.alazharpark.com. Admission LE7. Daily 9am–10pm.

Bab Zuweila In its heyday, the walled city of Cairo had 60 gates. With its massive 4-ton doors, Bab Zuweila, along with Bab el Nasr and Bab el Futuh, is one of three that remain in good shape. Its door used to be studded with pieces of cloth as well as teeth, offerings for a certain Ottoman sheikh, El Metwalli, whose spirit is believed to live in the doorway; Bab Zuweila is more commonly known as Bawabet El Metwalli. For centuries, thousands of people passed through this gate, but in recent Mamluk and Ottoman times, it was also used as an execution ground (the last heads hung here at the beginning of the 19th century). Over time Cairo grew in size, and 150 years ago they stopped closing the gates at night. With the use of specially designed equipment, the painstaking restoration efforts brought mobility back to the massive Bab Zuweila doors; they were opened and closed for the first time in decades on January 30, 2002. As a by-product to the restoration efforts, a plethora of amulets, talismans, porcelain, nails, and teeth can be seen in the little museum it hosts. The displayed items are nothing special, but the view from the roof can be. If you are not claustrophobic, navigate the narrow staircase of El Moayed Mosque's minaret (located above the gate) for more panoramic views.

Al Mu'izz le-din Allah St. Admission LE15. Daily 9am–5pm.

Bait al Kritliya (Gayer-Anderson Museum) This was the residence of British army officer and doctor R. G. Gayer-Anderson between 1935 and 1942. Gayer-Anderson joined and renovated two adjacent 16th-century buildings (one of them was called Bait al Kritliya, House of the Cretan Woman, as the original owner came from Crete) and collected their present contents, which include contemporary books and art as well as more apropos 16th- and 17th-century furniture and some antique curios, such as a 13th-century sundial. By the time he left, the place was a massive and fascinating warren of restored rooms, courtyards, and balconies stuffed with a museum-ready collection. Before heading back to England, he signed the whole lot over to the Egyptian government, which has been operating the house as a museum ever since.

The two houses are connected through a corridor on the second floor, the same floor that features a number of themed rooms among which is the Damascus Room with its wooden inlaid and gilded walls. Another equally interesting room is the Picture Gallery, where Gayer-Anderson kept his precious collection of paintings. Both the second and third floor exteriors are adorned with finely carved *mashrabeyas* (p. 36). Movie buffs should note that scenes from James Bond's *The Spy Who Loved Me* were filmed inside Bait al Kritliya.

The museum is next to the Ibn Tulun mosque, and it makes sense to visit them both at the same time. It is easy, in fact, to spend a full morning exploring these two buildings and a little bit of the neighborhood nearby. There is excellent shopping to be had at Khan Misr Touloun across the street from the mosque, but there is nowhere to eat.

For a detailed look at the museum, I recommend the excellent Nicholas Warner *Guide to the Gayer-Anderson Museum, Cairo* (Press of the Supreme Council of Antiquities, 2003) and R. G. "John" Gayer-Anderson Pasha's *Legends of the House of the Cretan Woman* (AUC Press, 2001).

4 Ibn Tulun St. ✆ **02/23647822.** Admission LE35. Daily 8am–4pm.

The Blue Mosque This is not Cairo's easiest site to find, partly because it's known by several different names. It is worth the effort, though, especially if you like tiles. The mosque is named for a wall of traditional Turkish tiles that was installed during a mid-17th-century renovation by an Ottoman officer, who brought them in from Istanbul and Damascus. The mosque is also known by the officer's name—Ibrahim Agha Mustahfizan—but the formal name of the place is Mosque of Aqsunqur, who was the original builder back in 1347. There are three tombs in the Blue Mosque, one each for Aqsunqur, Mustahfizan, and Aqsunqur's brother-in-law Sultan Al Ashraf Kuchuk, who sat on the throne for only 5 months after his 6th birthday before being imprisoned in the Citadel and 3 years later strangled to death at his brother's command. Apart from the tiles, the biggest reason to visit the mosque is the *minbar,* from which the Friday sermon is delivered; it is often made of wood, but here it is carved out of marble with an amazing multicolor geometric pattern. The fact that you might be the only tourist in the modest central courtyard is a fact to be cherished in bustling Cairo.

This is not a tour-bus accessible area, but you can reach it within a 10-minute walk. Starting on the northwest side of the Citadel, walk north on Bab al Wazir Street (which runs away from the base of the Citadel) past the first major intersection and another five streets to the right (big and small) before the mosque appears on your right.

Bab al Wazir St. close to the Citadel. Free admission, *bakshish* expected.

The City of the Dead

Cairo's City of the Dead is the world's largest Islamic necropolis, stretching for about 8km (5 miles) from the foot of the Muqattam Hills to the edge of Islamic Cairo. It hosts tens of mausoleums where different people from different periods rest in peace; from Mamluk sultans and reverend Sufis to Ottoman royals and modern Egyptian pashas. In addition, it encompasses several *sabils, tekiyyas* (a place offering accommodation for Sufis), *khanqahs* (a place where Sufis reside and preach their teachings), and mosques. Barkuk Mosque has one of the finest examples of the use of glass in Islamic art, while turban and fez tombstones mark the graves of the Mamluks massacred in the Citadel (below). Genghis Khan's great-great-granddaughter, Khawand Tulbay, is buried close to the modern Egyptian explorer Sir Ahmed Hassanein Pasha. The architectural highlights are numerous and so are the stories behind them.

Unfortunately, the dead are not the only residents of Cairo's City of the Dead; 5% of the capital's population, known as grave squatters, also call this place home, building makeshift houses amidst the graveyard.

Note: Though the City of the Dead is awash with historical Islamic attractions, it is certainly not a classic tourist destination. Venturing into this part of town is not recommended if you are an unaccompanied female traveler, and certainly not after dark. Most attractions don't have a ticket, but have plenty of change for tipping.

Citadel It was Salah al Din who ordered the building of an impenetrable bastion overlooking Cairo. However, what was built is not what you see today; the Citadel was extensively rebuilt and extended during the reign of the Mamluk Sultan Al Nasir Mohamed and the Ottoman sovereign Mohamed Ali that much of its original content has disappeared. Today, the prime attraction of the Citadel is the **Mohamed Ali Mosque.** After the ambitious leader rose to power and eliminated the fierce Mamluk opposition, he razed their palaces inside the Citadel, making way for his formidable mosque. Mohamed Ali Mosque was built between 1828 and 1848 following the Ottoman architecture style, with pencil-shaped minarets and striking similarities to Istanbul's Blue Mosque. The mosque's distinctive style marked a turning point in Egypt's Islamic architecture and art; moving from Mamluk to Ottoman style. Crossing a spacious courtyard, one enters the mosque's main hall characterized by a huge (21m/69 ft. in diameter) central dome flanked by four smaller ones and four half-domes on each corner. The mosque's interior is a single chamber that measures 41 sq. m (441 sq. ft.) with an impressive marble *mihrab* and a gold-decorated *minbar.* It is heavily adorned with impressive ornamental motifs and dozens of low-hanging spherical lamps that add a feeling of mysticism to the sheer grandiosity of the space. Mohamed Ali Mosque is not the only mosque on-site; the Citadel hosts **Al Nasir Mohamed Mosque** and **Suleyman Pasha Mosque.** The former is a prolific Mamluki building distinctively marked with its grand green dome, while the latter is Cairo's very first Ottoman mosque but far less elaborate when compared to Mohamed Ali's.

Within the Citadel you'll also find **Qasr el Gawhara,** a palace-turned-museum built in 1814 and named after one of Mohamed Ali's wives, Qawhara Hanim; it hosts Egypt's then throne as well as a wide collection of gilded furniture. There are three more museums in the vicinity of the Citadel: the **Coach Museum** houses a small but well-preserved collection of ornate coaches used by the royal family and ranking government figures from before 1952; the **Military Museum**'s collection of colonial uniforms and weaponry from the 1970s will certainly interest war buffs; while the **Police Museum** is a shabby, rarely visited place that features political assassination and murder weapons displays.

✆ **02/25121735.** Admission for entire compound LE50. Daily 9am–4pm.

Khan Al Khalili In 1382, a Sunni Mamluk prince by the name of Jarkas Al Khalil obtained a religious diktat denouncing Shiites as non-Muslims; he dug up their Fatimid cemetery and built a marketplace—Khan Al Khalili. Among the disturbed dead was Al Mu'izz le-din Allah, the Fatimid caliph who ordered the building of Cairo.

A *khan* is a place where caravans of traveling merchants could rest and engage in trade. It is often a two- or three-story edifice built around a courtyard. While camels are stabled in the ground floor, traders engage in intense negotiations on the first, and the second is often reserved as housing for merchants. As recently as the early 19th century, Khan Al Khalili was Cairo's main marketplace where, in addition to local goods, Persian carpets, Indian shawls, and even African slaves were traded. However, this is far from what you will see today. Bustling is the key word here, but the dense network of twisting alleys with jampacked stores and stalls is more of a tourist trade. A wide array of exotic souvenirs are up for grabs, including Pharaonic busts and statues, ornamented wooden boxes, alabaster-made lamps, papyrus paintings, camel bone (not ivory) chess pieces, colorful glassware, traditional *shisha* (water pipe), and even spices.

Khan Al Khalili can make for a great night of souvenir shopping, but keep two things in mind. Bargaining is the name of the game; the dealer asks for 100, you offer 50, end up with 75, and everybody walks out happily. Most of the papyrus sold is not real, regardless of how hard the dealer tries to convince you it is; the same goes for black basalt and any other trinket made of a scarce resource. Khan Al Khalili is a densely crowded area, but other than being serially accosted by insistent dealers and the slight risk of pick-pocketing, the whole area is very safe.

Daily mid-morning until late. Cash is king, though some shops accept credit card payments (mainly MC and V).

Khayameya (Tentmakers' Souk) Just across from Bab Zuweila is a short covered souk known in Arabic as Sharia'a Al Khayameya, or "Street of the Tentmakers." This may not sound like much of a shopping opportunity (after all, who wants to pack a tent home?), but the same vibrant embroidery used for centuries to decorate celebratory tents

Fun Facts — Back to School

The *madrasa,* a state religious school, was introduced after the fall of the Fatimids in the 12th century and the return of Sunni government to Egypt under the Ayyubid dynasty. The four bays, or *liwans,* that you see in the courtyard represent the equal hand shown by the government to the four schools of Sunni religious thought named for four early Islamic religious thinkers Malik, Abu Hanifa, Ibn Hanbal, and al Shaf'ai.

Cairo's Jewish Landmarks

Before the 1950s exodus, a considerable population of Egyptian Jews called Cairo home. They left behind a number of historical buildings and sites that constitute part of the city's historical heritage, an aspect that is often neglected and overlooked all together. The Ben Ezra Synagogue is indeed the most famous and frequently visited of all the Jewish sites in Cairo; however, it is not the only one. Located in the heart of downtown, the recently renovated Shaar Hashamayim Synagogue can be visited, but only after obtaining the needed permits, which can be obtained through any reputed tour operator. The Maimonides Synagogue is another landmark, located in the aptly named Haret El Yahood Jews Ally, which is part of Islamic Cairo. Maimonides was a well-known physician who served in the court of Salah al Din, as well as a prominent scholar notable for the three-volume philosophical masterpiece *Guide for the Perplexed.* The decision to renovate his synagogue raised a controversial sandstorm mainly because of its timing; it coincided with Egypt's Culture Minister Farouk Hosny running for head of UNESCO's post.

now finds its way onto everything from quilts to cushions. Much of the work is done in the little shops that line the streets, so you can watch the complicated geometry of the traditional designs slowly taking shape as you decide what to buy. If you have a few weeks, you could place a special order for a particular pattern in colors of your own choosing. Prices are definitely negotiable, but expect to pay LE60 for small pillow covers and up to LE3,500 for elaborately worked bedspreads and wall hangings.

Darb Al Ahmar. Daily mid-morning until late.

Madrasa of Sultan Hassan & the Mosque of Al Rifa'ai These two massive and outwardly similar buildings are located directly below the Citadel and within a few meters of each other, so it's best to consider them as one site. They are monumental examples of Mamluk architecture and engineering and should be high on your list of things to see.

The **Madrasa of Sultan Hassan** is undoubtedly one of Islamic Cairo's most prominent attractions and the Mamluk sultanate's most grandiose monument. Named for Al Nasir Hassan, who sat on the throne between 1347 and 1361 (with a break during his teens), the Madrasa of Sultan Hassan was built in turbulent political times; Sultan Hassan was more of a puppet ruler manipulated by influential Mamluk princes such as Amir Taz (p. 122). Construction began in 1356, but a revolt in 1361 saw the sultan deposed before his *madrasa* was completed. The mausoleum was designed as the sultan's final resting place but doesn't actually hold his body, as it was never found after the revolt.

By that time's standard the *madrasa* was a mega project, plotted on an almost 8,000 sq. m (86,111 sq. ft.) piece of land with four horizon-breaking minarets, planned to be the tallest in Cairo. Ironically, funding was made possible by the bubonic plague that swept through Cairo in 1348, swelling the state treasury with the estates of its victims. The massive building faced some engineering challenges, too. The western minaret collapsed before the whole project was finished, killing hundreds of people. The eastern minaret stayed up for 3 centuries before it collapsed, bringing about the collapse of the building's original wood- and lead-covered dome.

The Madrasa of Sultan Hassan is a lovely place to visit any time of day, particularly in the morning, when the light comes through the mausoleum windows. The entrance is dramatic and rather eerie, with a dark, twisting hallway decorated with stalactites leading to the main building. The main building is composed of four *liwans* (open halls) around a central courtyard following the cruciform *madrasa* plan, and a mausoleum is attached to the western *liwan.* The four Sunni schools each had a *madrasa* in one of the *liwans,* where students and teachers lived and studied. Take time to sit in one of the *liwans* and look up at the incredibly high arches and the lamps hanging from octagonal supports on long chains swinging in the breeze.

Khushyar Hanim, Khedive Ismail's mother, ordered the building of the **Mosque of Al Rifa'ai** 500 years after the neighboring *madrasa.* It was finally completed in 1912 in a neo-Mamluk architectural style characterized by overall symmetry and frontal axiality. It's more straightforward architecturally than the *madrasa* next door; however, the massive enclosed dome makes for a spectacular sense of space. The main point of interest for many here is the tomb of an important Sufi, Sheikh Ali Al Rifa'ai, who is celebrated during an annual *moulid* (local celebration of holy figures). The mosque also contains the tombs of several members of the Egyptian royal family (including Fouad I and Farouk) as well as Mohamed Reza Pahlavi, the last Shah of Iran.

The entrance is at the Citadel side of the enclosure, facing onto the roundabout. Admission LE25 each site. Daily 9am–5pm.

Mosque of Ibn Tulun ★★★ This huge and magnificent mosque and enclosure is almost all that remains of the 9th-century city of Al Qatai, built by the enterprising upstart Ahmad Ibn Tulun. The mosque was subjected to heavy-handed government restoration when a good deal of material was deemed stylistically inappropriate and "cleaned away"; however, it is still one of my favorite places to visit in this city.

Lacking the spectacular interior spaces of Al Rifa'ai or the view of Mohamed Ali, Ibn Tulun's innovative Iraqi-influenced architecture and massive courtyard have a power and space that the others lack. Three characteristics both differentiate this from Cairo's other mosques and illustrate similarities with the Great Mosque of Al Mutawakil in Samarra, Iraq, where Ibn Tulun spent most of his life before being appointed governor of Egypt. First, there is an empty space that surrounds the mosque, insulating it from the busy streets—and noise—outside. Second, the mosque employs plaster decoration in stuccos. And third is the minaret's spiral architecture. The minaret and the roof are usually open; if not, ask the attendant taking care of your shoes, and he will open either for you. The minaret gets quite narrow at places, but the incredible view from above is worth every step.

One of the mosque's key attractions is a 2km (about 1¼ mile) Quranic inscription on sycamore wood that runs around the entire mosque; some of this wood is said to have been salvaged from Noah's ark.

Ibn Tulun St. Free admission, *bakshish* expected.

Museum of Islamic Art Still in the middle of a seemingly endless renovation, the Museum of Islamic Art promises, when it eventually reopens (supposedly this year, though nothing has been confirmed officially), to be an absolute must-see. The square-shouldered 19th-century edifice that houses the museum is impressive in its own right, but the incredibly rich and eclectic collection of Islamic decorative items is the main draw. If you don't have any experience with the history of Islamic art, it's going to be an eye-opener. Responding to the Quranic injunction against representing God with a broad abandonment of figurative art as a whole, artists in Islamic countries developed

Fun Facts A Cross in the Mosque

Finding a cross inside a mosque might be common if you are venturing into Andalusia. In Cairo, it can also be found in the Mosque of Al Rifa'ai. Khedive Ismail and his three wives, one of whom was French, are all buried here. On the French lady's cenotaph lies Gothic arches and cross markings. If they prove difficult to find, ask the guard to point them out for you.

intricate epigraphic and geometric designs that they then applied to everything from stone to glass. The collection includes finely decorated lamps, worked stone fountains and domestic fixtures, and wooden *mashrabeya* screens.

Port Said St. ✆ **02/23901520** or 02/23909930. Closed to public at time of writing.

Sama Khana ★★★ The Mevlevi Sufi fraternity was founded during the 13th century in Konya, Turkey, where the order's guiding spirit and Persian poet, Jalal al Din al Rumi, is buried. Cairo housed one of the most active Mevlevi dervish *sama khanas,* or "listening halls," in the region, until it was abandoned in 1945 after the group dissolved. The two-story structure was completely restored in the 1980s, and its circular dancing hall is marked with 12 Lebanese pinewood columns, symbolizing the 12 Shiite imams. If you can read Arabic, their names are written atop each column. The hall has a dome ceiling, adorned with lovely 18th-century European flair paintings, and a huge sign hanging from the second floor praising Mawlana, an honorary title that was bestowed upon Rumi. The renowned poet and Sufi imam wrote one of the most influential works of both Sufism and Persian literature—the *Masnavi.* Made up of six titles, it poetically illustrates, through 424 stories, man's dilemma in search of God. In addition to a copy of the famous book, which is on display at the small museum that occupies the basement, there are archaeological findings (mainly pottery shreds) retrieved during the restoration of the place, as well as a replica of typical dervish dress. Within the premises of the Cairo *sama khana,* there are also a couple of distinguished tombs that host the remains of pious Sufi sheiks.

El Sioufi St., off Saliba St. (a couple of blocks from Taz Palace). Free admission, *bakshish* expected. Daily 9am–4pm.

Taz Palace ★ If you're curious about how the elite lived in Mamluk Egypt, then head to the Taz Palace. Seif al din Taz was an influential Mamluk prince who built this monumental palace in 1352 in celebration of his marriage to Khawand Zahra, daughter of Sultan Al Nasir Mohamed. The palace is made of two central courtyards and contains all the elements of royal palaces at the time: quarters for men *(salamlik)* and women *(haramlik),* baths *(hammams),* a large seating area *(maqa'ad),* stables, and storerooms. The *maqa'ad* is finely decorated with geometric designs and a large calligraphic bar reciting Quranic verses, and the *hammams'* ceilings are adorned with colored glass. Taz Palace is home to a Mamluk waterwheel, the only one of its kind discovered so far, and there is a permanent exhibition of artifacts excavated during the palace's recent restoration. While the former stables have been turned into exhibition grounds showcasing local art, the palace hosts musical performances, especially on summer nights and during the holy month of Ramadan (for more on the Cairo cultural scene, see p. 148).

17 El Sioufi St., off Saliba St. ✆ **02/25142581.** Free admission. Daily 9am–4pm.

Wekalet El Ghuri This Mamluk commercial building (built in 1504) was once the epicenter of commerce, heaving with all sorts of merchants and buyers. Today it desolately sits in a little corner off Al Azhar Street lamenting the good old days. The same shops that were once used by trading merchants were, until recently, used as a venue for selling traditional artifacts; however, in a bold decision to preserve the place, all the businesses have been relocated to Souk El Fustat (p. 147). Unless you are going for the lovely courtyard or the *tanoura* (below) show, there is no real reason to visit Wekalet El Ghuri. Though the show doesn't start before 8:30pm (Sat and Wed), try to arrive as early as 7:30pm. It is free and available on a first-come, first-served basis. Seats are rather limited and gates will close once all seats have been filled.

Mohamed Abdu St. between Al Azhar Mosque and Al Mu'izz le-din Allah St. Admission LE15. Daily 8am–5pm.

OLD CAIRO

Also known as Coptic Cairo, this is a rich and fascinating area on the site of Fustat, the capital of Egypt until 1169. The area contains a number of religious sites, mostly Christian, several connected by picturesque cobbled streets, and requires at least half a day if you want to see and appreciate them all. Old Cairo is the easiest of Cairo's sites to access; just catch the Metro to the Mar Girgis station.

Amr Ibn Al A'as Mosque Egypt's, and consequently Africa's, oldest mosque is located a stone's throw from the Coptic Museum (the highlight of your visit to Old Cairo). It was built in 642 with a simple rectangular shape and no minarets, which were added in 673. This mosque has undergone major renovations and multiple additions; aside from the several pillars you see at the far left corner of the mosque, nothing remains from its original structure. On Fridays the mosque receives up to 3,000 worshipers; schedule your visit accordingly.

Old Cairo. Free admission.

Ben Ezra Synagogue ★ This simple and graceful little temple behind the Church of St. George is the oldest synagogue in Egypt. Though the site itself has been holy to the Jews as long as they've been in Egypt—it is said to be where Moses was found in the reeds—the structure there today was originally built as the Church of St. Michael the

Devoted to God

Twirl, twirl, until you root yourself out of this world and into an esoteric state of purity; there God can be reached. Sufism can be described as a mystical dimension of Islam, practiced and respected by both Sunni and Shiite sects. Those who practice Sufism are regarded as Sufis, or dervishes. While all dervishes whirl, their outfits differ from one place to the other. In Egypt they are often dressed in white and hold one or two wide and colorful skirtlike pieces of cloth dubbed *tanoura.* As the dervish starts whirling, he manipulates his colorful *tanoura,* making vibrant displays. As he picks up speed, the performer and his *tanoura* become one colorful mass in motion. Whirling was originally a spiritual practice, but today it is a folkloric dance that makes a good night out in Cairo. Many private shows are on offer; the Folkloric Tanoura Troupe is the best in town and periodically performs in Wekalet El Ghuri (above).

Archangel in the 4th century before being closed by the Fatimid caliph Al Hakim and then sold, around the 12th century, to the Egyptian Sephardic community. The building was restored in the 12th century by Abraham Ben Ezra, who was rabbi of Jerusalem, and extensively rebuilt in the 1890s. During the rebuilding process a huge cache of documents was found in a *geniza* (hiding place). More a disposal method than an archive (old scrolls and documents were placed there for fear of discarding something with the word of God written on it), this collection of more than 200,000 pieces of paper includes contracts, receipts, and ordinary correspondence that have allowed researchers to reconstruct daily life in Fustat. Restored again in the 1980s, Ben Ezra is in great condition today and definitely warrants a visit. Photography is not allowed.

Old Cairo. Free admission. Daily 8am–4pm.

Church of St. George One of the most atmospheric churches in Cairo, this Greek Orthodox church owes its peculiar round shape to the north tower of the old Roman fortress of Babylon built on its top. Ascending the long stairway leading to the church, you will come to a great relief of St. George mounting his horse and spearing a dragon. The equestrian saint has more than 20 relics all over Cairo, with the majority depicting him in this dragon-spearing position. The church you visit today is actually a reconstruction of a 7th-century church that almost burned to the ground in 1904. Most of the original church was destroyed in the fire; however, some stained-glass windows miraculously survived along with the Nuptial Hall and its high wooden windows with ivory-made inlays and the remnants of stucco decorations you can still see on the walls and ceiling.

Though the Church of St. George has been Greek Orthodox since the 15th century, it was originally built as a Coptic one and still hosts one of the largest Coptic religious celebrations, Moulid Mari Girgis, which takes place on April 23. Mark your calendar if you are in town.

Note: The round shape of the Church of St. George (Keniset Mari Girgis in Arabic) should help you from straying into the neighboring St. George Monastery and the Convent of St. George. The former is also known as Church of Saints Sergius and Baachus, houses the seat of the Greek Orthodox Patriarchate of Alexandria, and is rarely open for visitors, while the latter is also known as Deir al Banat and hosts a population of nuns and a small chapel. A huge (8m/26 ft.) beautifully carved wooden door opens to a small chains-filled room, where the chain-wrapping ritual, reconstructing St. George's agony at the hands of persecuting Romans, often takes place.

Old Cairo. Free admission.

Coptic Museum ★★★ The Coptic Museum, inaugurated in 1910, its first wing built by Marcus Samaika Pasha, is a well-organized, well-presented, and well-documented museum, and it's a must-see for anyone interested in the history of Egypt. This is also a museum with a mission—the intent behind the layout is to show how Coptic imagery is deeply embedded in all aspects of Egyptian life; following the displays you can see the sun discs of ancient deities morph into iconographic halos and the capitals of Pharaonic columns transform into baptismal basins.

Devote a couple of hours to tour the two-story museum. Start from Room 2 on the ground floor and go counterclockwise, ending up in Room 9. Climb the stairs and tour the upper floor clockwise, from Room 10 to Room 17, then take the connecting corridor to the old wing and continue to Room 26. From there you will exit into the museum's courtyard where some more pieces are on display.

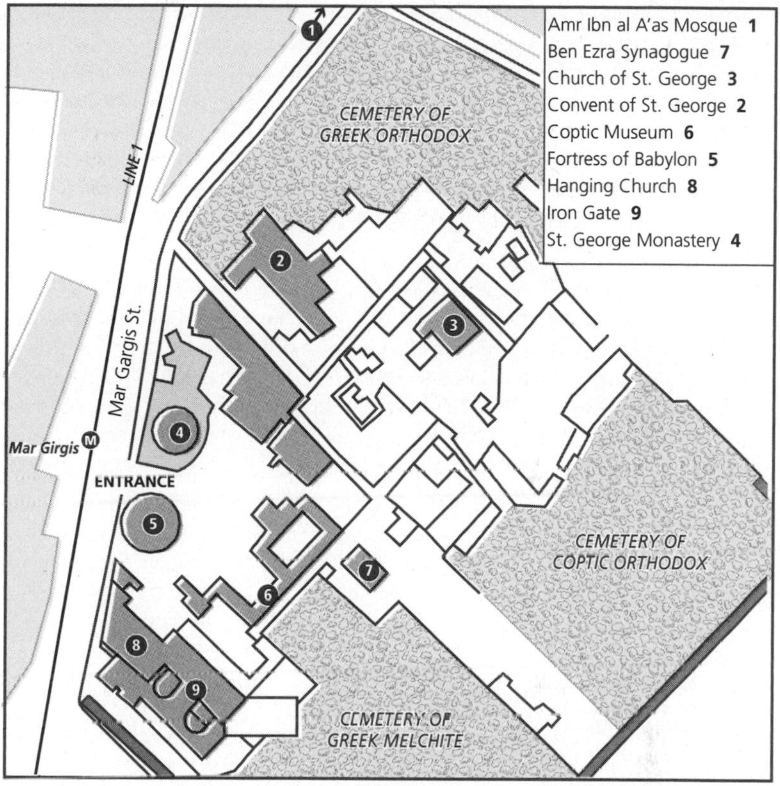

The museum is made up of eight themed rooms, and your tour will start in the **ground floor**'s Room 2, which displays masterpieces of Coptic art. The attention-grabber is a textile depicting a musician and a dancing horse. The textile on display is part of the original one; the missing piece is housed in the Louvre in Paris. Rooms 3 and 4 demonstrate Ancient Egypt's footprint on early Coptic art such as the pharaonic symbol of life, the ankh, transforming into the Coptic handled cross *crux ansata.* Rooms 5 and 6, as well as part of the inner courtyard, exhibit pieces salvaged from the Monastery of St. Jeremiah in Saqqara (p. 155). Room 6 exhibits the "Egyptian Mona Lisa," her haunting eyes following you wherever you go. Rooms 7 to 9 are dedicated to another abandoned monastery, the Monastery of St. Apollo, located in the Western Desert oasis of Bawiti. The main piece depicts three saints, St. Apollo in the middle, and don't miss the painted niche depicting Christ in Ascension and the Twelve Apostles.

The **upper floor** is much larger than the ground one, with 16 rooms displaying Coptic art at its best. Greeting you is a bronze eagle, symbol of the Roman Empire, which originally belonged to the Roman-built Fortress of Babylon. It is speculated to be the Coptic Museum's oldest piece. A comparative wall painting portraying Adam and Eve

before and after the fall from paradise is displayed in Room 11. The painting was discovered in Fayum and dates back to the 11th century. One of the museum's most prized holdings is a manuscript collection of the Nag Hammadi library (popularly known as the Gnostic Gospels). Access to the library is restricted, but several folios, scrolls, and a sublime Book of Psalms dating from the 4th century are on display in Room 15. Stepping into the old wing of the museum doubles the prize; the well-renovated Cairene house is an architectural piece of art in its own right. Rooms 20 to 22 display Coptic art's center of gravity—icons; the majority depict saints and biblical scenes. One particular icon stands out and depicts two local saints, Ahrakas and Oghani, wearing dog's head masks.
Old Cairo, across from Mar Girgis Metro station. ✆ **02/23639742.** Admission LE50. Daily 9am–5pm.

Fortress of Babylon Tradition has it that the Fortress of Babylon was first built by the Persians around the 6th century B.C. before Roman Emperor Trajan (98–117) relocated the massive fortress to its current location. Romans dug a series of canals and interlinked waterways connecting the fortress to the Red Sea. In April 640, and after a 7-month siege, Arab conquerors entered surrendered Babylon passing through the Iron Gate, atop which, today, sits the Hanging Church (below).
Old Cairo. Free admission.

Hanging Church A decade-long restoration finally came to an end in December 2009, bringing much-needed preservation to the 7th-century (or 9th-century, as some historians debate) Hanging Church, named for its location atop the two bastions flanking the fortress Iron Gate. Formally known as the Church of the Virgin, it was originally designed as a basilica with a central barrel-vaulted nave. Its traditional marble pulpit dates back to the 13th century and is supported by 15 pillars, of which 14 represent the Twelve Apostles, St. Mark, and St. Luke, while the front 15th pillar represents Jesus Christ. The collection of more than 100 mesmerizingly beautiful icons includes an 18th-century series documenting the martyrdom of St. George and a much smaller, both in size and count, series illustrating the life of Saint John the Baptist. Both series are the work of the talented Armenian artist Orhan Karabedian. Kids, meanwhile, will be interested in the window that's been cut in the floor to give a view of the water below.

There are a couple of nice stalls at the entrance to the church where you can purchase books, postcards, and reproduction icons.
Old Cairo. Free admission.

RODA ISLAND

Another densely populated Nile island, Roda warrants a visit for its handful of lovely, yet diverse, sites; from an artist-dedicated museum to an Abbasid-built Nilometer. The best mode of transportation is taxi.

Manasterly Palace This lovely mid-19th-century building on the southern tip of Roda Island is now run by the International Center for Music. From October to June, its marvelously ornamented hall features musical performances by world-renowned artists. The overlooking-the-Nile terrace offers splendid views during intervals. The setting alone is worth a visit; however, if you happen to have a free evening, it's worth checking to see what's on. During the day the grounds around the palace offer a nice view downriver and are an excellent place for a picnic lunch between checking out the Nilometer and visiting the Om Kolthoum Museum (see both below). Unless there is a musical event, the palace is not open to visitors.
Roda Island. ✆ **02/33631537.** Fax 02/33631467. www.manasterly.com.

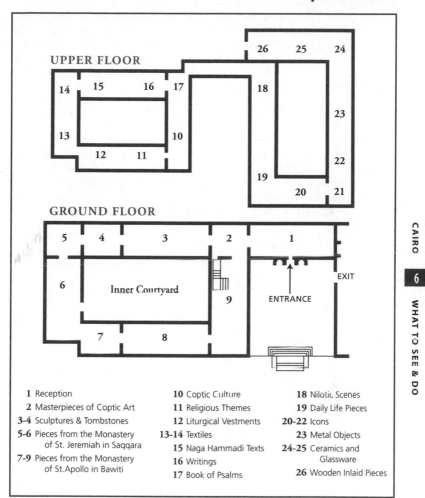

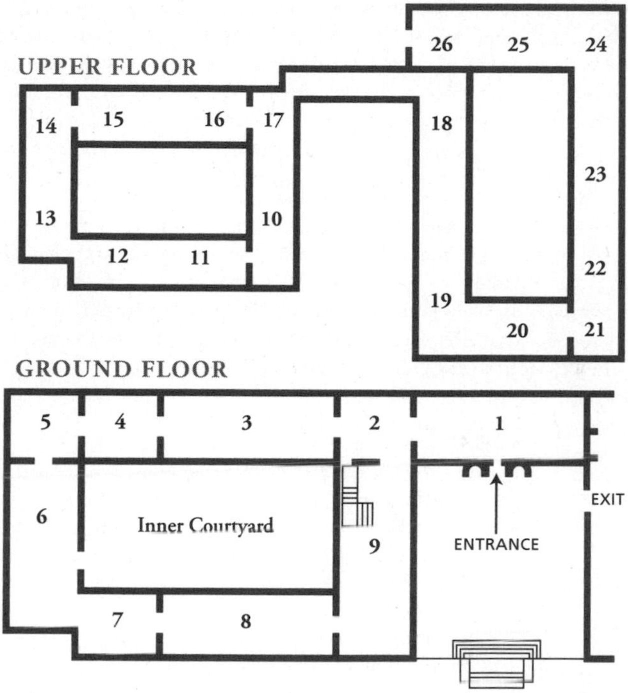

1 Reception
2 Masterpieces of Coptic Art
3-4 Sculptures & Tombstones
5-6 Pieces from the Monastery of St. Jeremiah in Saqqara
7-9 Pieces from the Monastery of St.Apollo in Bawiti
10 Coptic Culture
11 Religious Themes
12 Liturgical Vestments
13-14 Textiles
15 Naga Hammadi Texts
16 Writings
17 Book of Psalms
18 Nilotic Scenes
19 Daily Life Pieces
20-22 Icons
23 Metal Objects
24-25 Ceramics and Glassware
26 Wooden Inlaid Pieces

Manial Palace "This palace was built by Prince Mohamed Ali, son of the late Kedive Tawfik, to revive the Islamic arts and to honor them." This is what the Arabic inscription above the arched entrance reads. Built between 1901 and 1929, Manial Palace is a fusion of different schools of Islamic architecture, primarily Mamluki with Moorish and Ottoman elements. Your visit to this palace starts even before purchasing the ticket; the reception area is lavishly adorned with stained-glass windows, and Iznik tiles and Arabic calligraphy cover the walls. Once you cross the reception area, a path winds through the garden leading to the palace's several sites. The tour starts with a small mosque adorned with Ottoman and Moorish designs, while a clock tower built in the North African minarets style stands next to it. Next in line is the **Hunting Museum,** a 1963 addition that displays King Farouk's hunting trophies next to a comprehensive collection of bugs and butterflies. The palace's original owner (it is now the property of the Egyptian government) loved to travel, collecting pieces from Persian carpets to Mexican cactus. Aside from the cacti trees planted in the garden, the rest of the collection is on display in the palace's 14-room museum.

A few years ago the ceiling of the opulent throne room (a separate building from the palace) collapsed, and the whole palace is currently being restored.

Roda Island. ✆ **02/33687495.** Closed at the time of writing.

Nilometer At the southern tip of Roda Island, between the Manasterly Palace and the Om Kolthoum Museum, this well was used to measure the height of the Nile through the course of its annual inundation. Taxes could be calibrated from knowing the height of water, and the timing of the opening and closing of irrigation and drainage canals around the delta could be determined. Entering at the top, you can walk almost to the bottom by way of a narrow staircase cut into the side. The top is enclosed in an attractive 19th-century conical shaped dome adorned with verses from the Quran written in Kufic calligraphy under its rim. The grounds around the Nilometer are relaxed and pleasant, with, usually, a cool breeze off the water.

Roda Island. Admission LE15. Daily 9am–4pm.

Om Kolthoum Museum An Ottoman-style building hosts this small museum dedicated to the singer Om Kolthoum, who, more than 3 decades after her death, remains a cultural icon and symbol of Egyptian nationalism. Born in 1904, she was the daughter of an imam (a position at a mosque roughly equivalent to a parish priest) in a small rural village in the Delta. During the 1940s, 1950s, and 1960s, she was known throughout the Arab world and held 5- to 6-hour concerts, broadcast on the first Thursday of the month. It is said that when her concerts were aired, Cairo would turn into a ghost city, as people made their way home and to cafes to listen. She died in 1975, but you will still hear her music being played around Cairo. Her death prompted a massive reaction, and it is claimed that millions attended her funeral. The museum plays recordings of her works and reverentially displays ephemera such as her diamond-studded sunglasses and her diplomatic passport.

Roda Island. Admission LE2. Daily 9am–4pm.

4 WHERE TO STAY

Cairo's accommodations seem to lie at extreme ends of the spectrum. You'll either find cheap backpacker places of dubious cleanliness or high-priced, high-rise, tourist-class hotels that are often heavy on glitz and light on actual deliverables. There are a small number of decently priced, clean, basic hotels, and by focusing on a few key areas, you'll find some really good deals.

DOWNTOWN & ZAMALEK

Both districts are centrally located with a good range of different levels of accommodation. However, going inexpensive might come with a considerable amount of noise; downtown and Zamalek are beehives that don't stop buzzing.

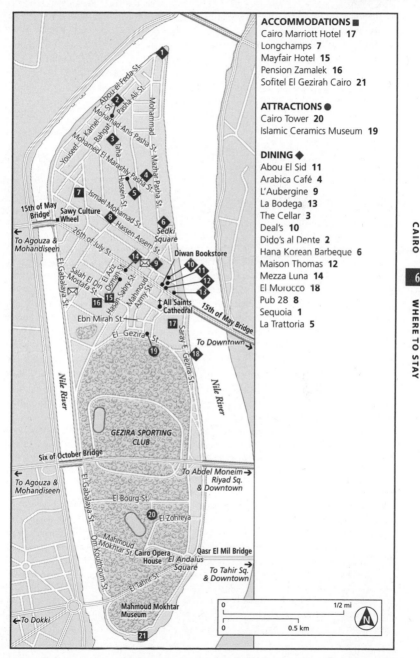

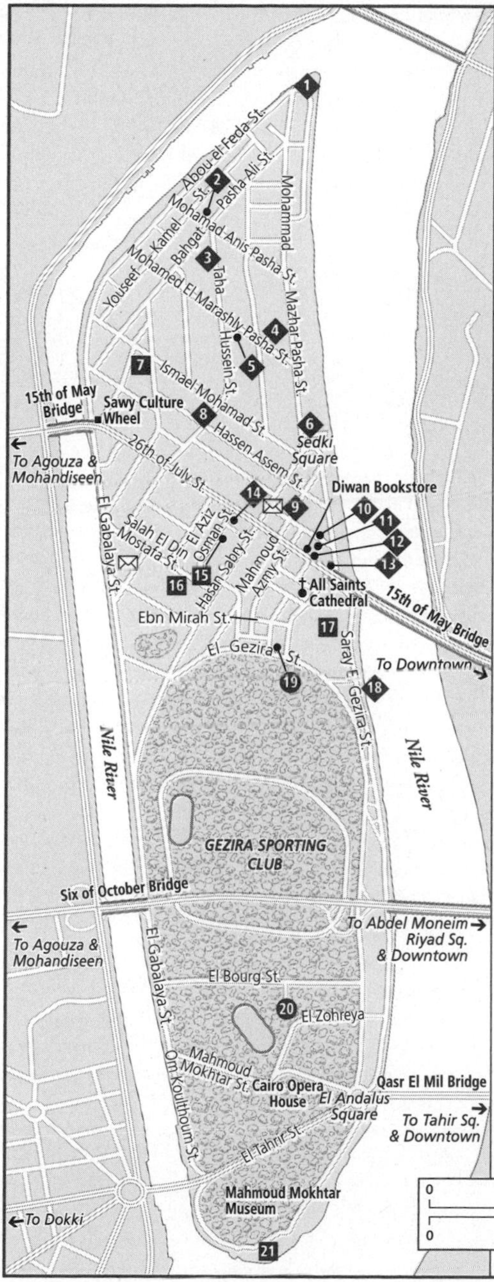

ACCOMMODATIONS ■

Cairo Marriott Hotel **17**
Longchamps **7**
Mayfair Hotel **15**
Pension Zamalek **16**
Sofitel El Gezirah Cairo **21**

ATTRACTIONS ●

Cairo Tower **20**
Islamic Ceramics Museum **19**

DINING ◆

Abou El Sid **11**
Arabica Café **4**
L'Aubergine **9**
La Bodega **13**
The Cellar **3**
Deal's **10**
Dido's al Dente **2**
Hana Korean Barbeque **6**
Maison Thomas **12**
Mezza Luna **14**
El Morocco **18**
Pub 28 **8**
Sequoia **1**
La Trattoria **5**

Very Expensive

Fairmont Nile City ★★ One of the latest additions to Cairo's hotelier scene, Fairmont Nile City opened in January 2010 and has already been dubbed one of the best hotels in town with its panoramic Nile view and professional service. Big windows shower the small yet comfortable standard rooms with natural light, while Fairmont Gold rooms take urban chic to the next level with exclusive pampering comforts such as a dedicated reception, butler service, and access to the Fairmont Gold Lounge. A clear artistic touch differentiates this hotel from its peers with modern paintings and three contemporary statues in the middle of the hotel's lobby. Fairmont Nile City offers fine dining at its best, whether it's California cuisine at Napa Grill or signature Vietnamese-French dishes at Saigon Blue. Lounge at Sky bar with a cocktail and some Lebanese meze, or get a heavy dose of jazz with New Orleans–based bands performing live at O'Bar. The 24th floor is dedicated entirely to the Willow Stream Spa, nominated for the "biggest spa in town" title.

2005B Corniche El Nil. ✆ **02/24619494.** Fax 02/24619595. www.fairmont.com. 566 units, including 82 suites. $400 double. Rate includes buffet breakfast, but subject to 25.44% taxes and service charges. AE, DC, MC, V. **Amenities:** 4 restaurants; 3 bars; babysitting; concierge; health club & spa; 2 pools (including 1 kids'); room service; Wi-Fi. *In room:* A/C, TV, minibar, Wi-Fi (extra charge).

Four Seasons Nile Plaza ★ The Four Seasons might fall short of competitors when it comes to flashy design, but you'd be hard-pressed to find a better-run hotel, even at this price. The Four Seasons sets out to make you feel recognized and special, and it does it very well. This is a hotel that balances the predictability and comfort of a big chain with the up-close-and-personal, tailored service that comes naturally in smaller facilities. Your airport pickup arrives with moist towels and water, and you can begin check-in and even order room service from the car.

Inside, everything is understated and elegant, and the ambience is relaxed and comfortable yet sophisticated. The walls of the second-floor restaurant and bar area are hung with an impressive collection of modern Egyptian art, and there are spectacular flower arrangements everywhere you look. Rooms are large and manage to be homey and elegant at the same time. Like the service, they manage somehow to deliver everything that you need in a relaxed and effortless manner.

1089 Corniche El Nil. ✆ **02/27917000.** Fax 02/27916900. www.fourseasons.com. 365 units, including 60 suites. $490 city-view double; $640 Nile-view double. Rates are on "bed only" basis and subject to 25.44% taxes and service charges. AE, DC, MC, V. **Amenities:** 6 restaurants; 3 bars; concierge; health club & spa; 3 pools (including lap pool); room service. *In room:* A/C, TV, Internet (extra charge), minibar.

Kempinski The Nile ★★★ (Kids) The capital's most recent hotel, set to open in June 2010, molds luxury and elegance in a cast of superior individuality and, put simply, is beautiful. Personal service is taken to the next level here. European-style rooms are decked out in floral wallpaper and French-style furniture, and all come with butler service (your wake-up call is a gentle knock on the door and hand-delivered coffee). At the Blue Restaurant there is no menu; chefs ask what you'd like to eat and more or less anything you desire will be served. If the thought of that much freedom sends your head spinning, head to Floor 10, where you can dine from a contemporary French menu and spend the rest of the night relaxing in its Living Room or rocking all night at the Jazz Club. During the day, the small pool on the rooftop is simply a small pool on the rooftop, but once darkness descends, a glass top covers the pool, and the transparent floor area can be rented out for special romantic occasions, or even transformed into an exclusive lounge with comfy beanbags, *shisha,* drinks, and a big screen where you can watch the game. Kids are welcomed with a special gift and pampered with no-tear shampoo, small bathrobes and slippers, and bed-time milk.

12 Ahmed Rageb St., off Corniche El Nil. ✆ **02/27980000.** Fax 02/27942807. www.kempinski-cairo.com. 191 units, including 54 suites and 1 room for people with special mobility. $450 double. Rate is on "bed only" basis and subject to 25.44% taxes and service charges. AE, DC, MC, V. **Amenities:** 3 restaurants; 3 bars; babysitting; concierge; health club & spa; pool (temperature controlled); room service. *In room:* A/C, TV, movies (complimentary), minibar (non-alcoholic items are refilled daily free of charge), Wi-Fi (free).

Expensive

Cairo Marriott Hotel This former palace was built especially for France's Empress Eugenie, who came to Egypt for the opening of the Suez Canal in 1869. The main building has retained much of its 19th-century charm, but there have been several modern renovations, including two somewhat out of character towers. The Marriott has a limited business center, but its lush gardens and pool are attractive for those looking for a relaxing vacation. The north tower's rooms offer spectacular views of the Nile and the downtown core. Less modern but very comfortable business suites are available in the south tower and feature fold-out desks, high-speed Internet access, and a range of complimentary international newspapers and magazines.

The hotel has several upmarket restaurants, including JW's Steakhouse and the Marriott Terrace. The food at the Terrace is mediocre, but it's a favorite lounging spot for Egypt's TV and movie glitterati and enjoys a steady clientele of those who want to see and be seen.

Overall, this hotel is geared primarily toward an American clientele and manages to balance a relaxed and friendly Egyptian attitude with efficiency.

16 Saray el Gezira St., Zamalek. ✆ **02/27283000.** Fax 02/27283001. www.marriott.com. 1,089 units, including 112 suites. $175 double; $180 Nile-view double. Rates are on "bed only" basis and subject to 25.44% taxes and service charges. AE, MC, V. **Amenities:** 9 restaurants; 3 bars; concierge; gym; pool; room service; Wi-Fi. *In room:* A/C, TV, Internet (extra charge), minibar.

Conrad The Conrad, which looks across the Nile to Zamalek, is at the opposite end of the Corniche from the cluster of the Hyatt, Four Seasons, and InterContinental. With its massive, gleaming lobby and swirl of a staircase, the Conrad works hard to make sure you know you're in a five-star hotel—the only problem is that it could be any five-star hotel. What the place lacks in character, however, is made up for by good service; the rooms are clean and well maintained, and the staff are pleasant and well prepared. The Conrad is very reasonably priced when you consider the competition down the Corniche or across the river in Zamalek.

1191 Corniche El Nil. ✆ **02/25808000.** Fax 02/25808080. www.conradcairo.com. 617 units, including 52 suites. $229 double. Rate includes buffet breakfast, but subject to 25.44% taxes and service charges. MC, V. **Amenities:** 4 restaurants; 2 bars; concierge; health club; 2 pools (1 kids'); room service. *In room:* A/C, TV, Internet (extra charge), minibar.

Grand Hyatt Cairo Overrated Located directly across the water from the new Sofitel El Gezirah and across the road from the Four Seasons Nile Plaza, the Hyatt's massive curved tower is hard to miss. Inside the lobby, huge pillars and a flight of stairs dominate the space; the view of the river is still pretty good, although (unlike the Sofitel) the design keeps you from getting too close to water, which is a pity. The view only gets better from the higher floors, and on the rare day that Cairo has clear air, you can see all the way to the pyramids in Giza. Capitalizing on its location, the hotel has a revolving restaurant that offers stunning views of Cairo.

Corniche El Nil. ✆ **02/23651234.** Fax 02/23621927. www.cairo.grand.hyatt.com. 716 units. $250 double. Rate is on "bed only" basis and subject to 25.44% taxes and service charges. MC, V. **Amenities:** 10 restaurants; 10 bars; fitness center; pool; Wi-Fi. *In room:* Internet, minibar.

Nile Hotel Opened in 1959, this hotel was intended to showcase the new Egypt that then-President Gamal Abdel Nasser was hoping to create. Subsequent bland renovations have reduced the glories somewhat, and maintenance clearly hasn't kept up with problems. However, the Nile Hotel (former Nile Hilton) has a holistic renovation plan in the pipeline since the hotel has recently changed management.

At press time the hotel was still under renovation, and the public areas around the lobby were still somewhat tacky, but the hallways upstairs retain a 1960s feel that is enjoyable. To many, the colors and furniture in the rooms will simply seem dated, but touches such as *mashrabeya* screens and high ceilings echo that earlier time when the likes of Frank Sinatra were guests. The hotel's proximity to the Egyptian Museum means you get the noise from downtown's traffic; go for a Nile-view room on the highest floor.

1113 Corniche El Nil. ✆ **02/25780444.** Fax 02/25780475. www.thenilehotels.com. 369 units, including 29 suites. $215 Nile-view double. Rate includes buffet breakfast, but subject to 25.44% taxes and service charges. AE, DC, MC, V. **Amenities:** 3 restaurants; 4 bars; babysitting; concierge; health club; pool; room service; tennis courts. *In room:* A/C, TV, Internet (extra charge), minibar.

Ramses Hilton The adjective that comes to my mind for the Ramses Hilton has always been *uninviting.* A massive, overhung tower block, it looks like it was designed by the same guy who did the Palazzo Vecchio in Florence—but this time he decided to make something seriously big. The lobby reinforces the notion with a confusing design on several different levels. It only makes sense when you get into the rooms, which are modern and pleasant, if wholly lacking in any particular character.

Stuck between two busy roads with a major bus station on the corner and backing onto a somewhat insalubrious neighborhood, the Ramses Hilton's location isn't great, but it's fairly central and certainly easy to catch a taxi from here. This is a place to stay if you get a really good price or everywhere else is full.

1115 Corniche El Nil. ✆ **02/25777444.** Fax 02/25752942. www1.hilton.com. 755 units. $200 city-view double; $215 Nile-view double. Rates are on "bed only" basis and subject to 25.44% taxes and service charges. AE, DC, MC, V. **Amenities:** 5 restaurants; 3 bars; concierge; gym; pool; room service; tennis courts. *In room:* A/C, TV, Internet (extra charge), minibar.

Semiramis InterContinental Conveniently located on the edge of downtown, the Semiramis is a perfectly fine hotel. Service is friendly, if not as smooth as at the Four Seasons, and facilities are commodious. Substantial differences in the price of rooms at the front of the hotel and the back tell the story of the view: At the front, it's as good a Nile view as you would expect, while at the back, well, it's just not that great. Decor is a little more ostentatious than it should be, a reminder that this hotel—like the Cairo Marriott in Zamalek—does a brisk summer business with tourists from the Gulf, but it remains a staple of diplomats coming to Cairo to work at one of the nearby embassies or at the Arab League just across the street.

Corniche El Nil. ✆ **02/27957171.** Fax 02/27963020. www.ichotelsgroup.com. 708 units. $264 double; $301 Nile-view double. Rates include buffet breakfast, taxes, and service charges. AE, DC, MC, V. **Amenities:** 5 restaurants; bar; concierge; health club; pool; room service. *In room:* A/C, TV, Internet (extra charge), minibar.

Sofitel El Gezirah Cairo ★★ The Sofitel, in a renovated tower at the southern end of Zamalek Island, has real style. Normally, I'm not a fan of Egypt's Accor hotels, finding them overpriced and complacent, but this branch exhibits none of these faults. From the elegant lobby to the chic, earth-tone rooms, the interior decor is innovative and fun. The rooms are a little smaller than the competition's, but for me the experience of being in a well-put-together space outweighs the value of an extra square meter or two. Add to this one of the nicest spas in the city, six restaurants, and a bar within a couple of meters of the river, and you have my recommendation for the nicest of Cairo's five-star hotels.

3 El Thawra Council St., Zamalek. ✆ **02/27373737.** Fax 02/27363640. www.sofitel.com. 433 units. $186 double. Rate includes buffet breakfast, but subject to 25.44% taxes and service charges. AE, DC, MC, V. **Amenities:** 6 restaurants; 2 bars; concierge; health club & spa; pool; room service. *In room:* A/C, TV, Internet (extra charge), minibar.

Moderate

Cosmopolitan *Finds* If you want a glimpse of what Cairo was 50 years ago, the Cosmopolitan's decor and furniture has changed little since then. The lobby is a deeply shadowed place, full of *mashrabeyas* and armchairs, but the upper floors, serviced by a pair of gleaming antique Schindler elevators, are light and spacious. The rooms are not very big (in fact, it's worth checking out more than one because they vary in size), and some of the bathrooms are downright cramped, though they are generally clean and well maintained. Rooms at the front of the hotel have a view across busy 26th of July Street to the Supreme Court or the ruined, collapsing, 1920s Art Deco Theatre Rivoli. The street life (loud and intense) around the hotel is in sharp contrast to the hotel's cool and quiet interior. If you want a reasonably priced refuge in the heart of downtown, the Cosmopolitan offers solid value for money.

21 26th of July St., Downtown. ✆ **02/23923845.** 60 units. $87 double. Rate includes breakfast, taxes, and service charges. MC, V. **Amenities:** 2 restaurants; bar. *In room:* A/C, fridge.

Longchamps ★★★ Nestled in the heart of Zamalek, this quiet midrange hotel has been family-run since 1953. Investment and reenergized management have brought significant improvements over the last couple of years, however, and the Longchamps now shines in its class, putting many significantly more expensive hotels to shame. The surprisingly spacious rooms, and even more spacious executive rooms, have been spruced up with the kind of high-quality fittings that you would expect in a more expensive facility; the restaurant has also been completely renovated. The public areas, which are decorated with photos and furniture collected by the owner's family over the last 5 decades, have a comfortable and homey feel to them. About the only thing that this place doesn't have is a view, but at less than half the price of the cheapest Nile-view rooms in town, this is the only area in which the Longchamps comes up short. It is certainly the best value for money in Zamalek, and possibly in Cairo.

21 Ismail Mohamed St., Zamalek ✆ **02/27352311** or -2. Fax 02/27359644. www.hotellongchamps.com. 22 units. $78 double. Rate includes buffet breakfast, taxes, and service charges. MC, V. **Amenities:** Restaurant; bar; Wi-Fi. *In room:* AC, TV, minifridge.

New Garden Palace Located on a quiet side street of a quiet neighborhood, it's to be expected that this is going to be a quiet hotel. The building has more character from the outside than from inside, and it's very much a budget facility. Rooms are basic and views are limited, but both rooms and public areas, which include a rooftop restaurant/bar, are clean, and staff are friendly and helpful. The immediate neighborhood is pleasant and is an easy 10- to 15-minute walk to the Egyptian Museum; taxis are plentiful and easily available on nearby Kasr El Aini Street for places farther afield.

11 Moderat Al Tahrir St., Downtown. ✆ **02/27964020.** Fax 02/27963630. 55 units. LE350 double. Rate includes buffet breakfast, taxes, and service charges. No credit cards. **Amenities:** Restaurant/bar; Internet. *In room:* A/C, TV, fridge.

Talisman Hotel This one-of-a-kind hotel in the heart of downtown occupies a fully renovated fifth floor of a 70-year-old colonial building. The place is up to modern standards yet still retains the essential character of the building. It still feels like an old house, with long, winding corridors and antique furniture tucked into nooks, and the public areas are furnished with period pieces and wall hangings. Rooms are carefully constructed and have personal touches such as the hand of Fatima door handles and old embroidered bedspreads. The double-glass windows prove priceless, diminishing downtown's noise to bearable levels.

39 Tala'at Harb St., Downtown. ✆ **02/23939431.** Fax 02/23904432. www.talisman-hotel.com. 24 units, including 2 suites. 82€ double. Rate includes breakfast, taxes, and service charges. No credit cards (€ or LE equivalent). **Amenities:** Restaurant; Wi-Fi. *In room:* A/C, TV, minibar.

Windsor This downtown fixture has changed little since it opened in the 1930s. Travel posters from the 1950s adorn the walls, and it still hosts Cairo's, and probably Egypt's, last manually functioning elevator. The building was originally a khedival bathhouse built in 1901 and later served as a British Officers Club during World War II. The heart of the hotel is undoubtedly still the lounge bar on the second floor, with its chairs cut from old barrels and a chandelier of antlers. The vintage reception desk in the lobby, with its original switchboard, however, comes a close second.

Rooms vary considerably, from high ceilinged and spacious to small and quite dank. At the best of times, the whole place is somewhat musty, but if history is your thing, it's going to seem a small price to pay for the sense of time that the hotel conveys.

19 Alfi Bey St., Downtown. ✆ **02/25915277.** Fax 02/25921621. www.windsorcairo.com. 55 units, some without bathtub. $59–$68 double. Rate includes breakfast, taxes, and service charges. AE, DC, MC, V. **Amenities:** Restaurant/bar; room service. *In room:* TV.

Inexpensive

Australian Hostel Freshly painted, relatively spacious, and basic rooms make up this lovely downtown Egyptian hostel. There are no private bathrooms, but rather clean shared ones; however, you may have to line up in the morning. The hostel is plagued by outside noise, and the building's elevator is awkwardly turned off between 1 and 2:30pm and again between 7 and 8pm; thankfully there are only three floors to climb.

23 Abdel Khaliq Tharwat St. (3rd floor), Downtown. ✆ **02/23958892.** www.theaustralianhostel.com. 15 units. LE120 double. Rate includes breakfast, taxes, and service charges. No credit cards. **Amenities:** Internet. *In room:* A/C, no phone, Wi-Fi.

King Tut Hostel *(Finds)* One of Cairo's best-kept budget accommodation secrets, King Tut has basic, clean rooms with spotless, yet small, private bathrooms. The hostel's location on the eighth floor minimizes outside noise despite the windows not being double-glassed. King Tut doesn't serve any alcohol, but there is a liquor store just around the corner. Book 4 nights and get a free one-way transfer to or from the airport.

37 Tala'at Harb St. (8th floor), Downtown. ✆ **02/23917897.** www.kingtuthostel.com. 12 units. LE120 double. Rate includes breakfast, taxes, and service charges. No credit cards. *In room:* A/C, TV, no phone, Wi-Fi.

Mayfair Hotel *(Value)* The Mayfair is a very clean, small hotel located on three floors of a converted residential building in the middle of Zamalek; it's probably the best value for money in Cairo's budget range. The place doesn't have any atmosphere—hallways are narrow and utilitarian, decor is sparse, and furnishings say "budget-hotel" loud and clear—but rooms have high ceilings, comfortable beds, and are far enough from a main road to be relatively quiet. Public areas have better lights and a more spacious feel than other hotels in this price range. Breakfast is served on a balcony overlooking the street.

9 Aziz Osman St., Zamalek. ✆ **02/27357315.** Fax 02/27350424. www.mayfaircairo.com. 40 units. LE220 double. Rate includes breakfast, taxes, and service charges. MC, V. **Amenities:** Wi-Fi. *In room:* TV, fridge.

Pension Zamalek This simple and small hotel in a quiet area of Zamalek used to be my pick for the best budget accommodation in the city, but a recent price hike has made it as expensive as (or even more than) hotels that have a lot more to offer, such as the Mayfair (above) down the street. Value for money aside, I like this place because it feels a little like a pension in France or Portugal—the hallways are wide and a little gloomy, and the owner is usually parked in the small lobby sitting area watching television. With shared bathrooms and clean rooms, Pension Zamalek remains a good, comfortable choice if the Mayfair is booked.

6 Salah El Din St., Zamalek. ✆ **02/27359318** or 012/2110491. Fax 02/27353773. pensionzamalek@msn.com. 20 units. LE225 double. Rate includes breakfast, taxes, and service charges. No credit cards. *In room:* No phone.

GIZA

Some opt for a pyramid view, or at least to be as close as possible. If you wish to join the league, then the below are good options to consider, especially because they also offer good access to Saqqara, Dahshur, and Memphis, which are ideal day trips from Cairo. In addition to the price premium for having the pyramids in sight, there is another price to pay; going to anywhere else in the capital comes with horrendous traffic, there is nothing much to do in the neighborhood, and other than Pharaonic sites and shopping bazaars, you will be restricted to your hotel premises.

Expensive

Mena House Oberoi ★★★ Apart from the fact that it's historically worth a visit in its own right, the Mena House is a good place to stay for those who wish to have the ancient wonder in sight while dining or having a cup of coffee. Originally built as a hunting lodge next to the pyramids for the Khedive Ismail, it was converted to a hotel in the 1890s. Oberoi took it over in the 1970s and distributed a roomful of 19th-century furnishings throughout the present guest rooms.

The hotel's location is not ideal for venturing into Islamic Cairo, but the pyramids of Giza are a stone's throw away. Public areas of the hotel are decorated with dark wood paneling and *mashrabeya,* which evoke a time of more relaxed and elegant tourism. Add to this one of the nicest outdoor pools in the city and one of Cairo's best Indian restaurants, the Mogul Room, and the Mena House makes a pretty good home base for Egypt.

Pyramids Rd. ✆ **02/33773222** or 02/33766644. Fax 02/33775411 or 02/3376/7777. www.oberoimenahouse.com. 523 units. 210€ garden-view double; 230€ pyramid-view double. Rates are on "bed only" basis and subject to 25.44% taxes and service charge. AE, DC, MC, V. **Amenities:** 4 restaurants; 2 bars; concierge; golf course; gym; pool. *In room:* A/C, TV, Internet (extra charge), minibar.

Mövenpick Resort Pyramids This resort is nearly in the shadows of the pyramids (about 2km/1½ miles away). Mövenpick's aesthetic is known for its Swiss restraint, but that's nowhere to be found in this location's lobby, with shiny floors and masses of brass, which give the space a shopping-mall feel. Rooms, however, are large and spread amongst low buildings, decorated in light colors, and open onto a garden.

Alexandria Desert Rd. ✆ **02/33772555.** Fax 02/33775006. www.moevenpick-hotels.com. 240 units. $170 double. Rate includes breakfast, taxes, and service charges. AE, DC, MC, V. **Amenities:** 5 restaurants; 3 bars; concierge; health club & spa; heated pool; room service; 4 tennis courts (floodlit). *In room:* A/C, TV, Internet (extra charge), minibar.

Pyramisa Suites Hotel The quality of the Pyramisa may be below the foreign-run competition, but so are the prices. It wouldn't take much of a discount to make this place a value for money, and it makes up for rough-edged service and bad maintenance by having friendly, helpful staff.

Rooms are large by midrange standards, but not very light due to small windows and a dark color scheme. Because the hotel is located off a main thoroughfare, make sure you get an inward-facing pool-view room, and preferably one on the west side of the building, away from the road. The building seems to ramble on and on, and trying to find your way to the pool, you're likely to pop out beside the bar or the gym and have to retrace your steps to figure out where you went wrong.

60 Giza St. ✆ **02/3337000.** Fax 02/33361936. www.pyramisaegypt.com. 377 units, including 120 suites. $170 double. Rate includes breakfast, taxes, and service charges. AE, DC, MC, V. **Amenities:** 4 restaurants; bar; health club; 2 pools; room service. *In room:* A/C, TV, minifridge, Internet (extra charge).

HELIOPOLIS, AIRPORT & SUBURBS

If you are in town for business that happens to be located in Heliopolis, stay close to where the meetings will be held. If it is a quick in-transit type of visit, then the closer to the airport the better. And if you are seeking relaxation time away from the hustle and bustle of the capital, then the suburbs might be a good option. Other than that, you are better off staying in downtown or Zamalek to avoid losing time stuck in traffic.

Expensive

Dusit Thani LakeView Cairo Following the theme of its location, the Fifth Settlement suburb, Dusit Thani is all about space. It offers the capital's widest hotel room at 52 sq. m (560 sq. ft.). Your expectations of a five-star hotel will be met, yet blandly. The location is a double-edged sword as it offers a unique opportunity for relaxation away from noisy downtown, active Zamalek, or busy Islamic Cairo, yet getting to anywhere in Cairo proper requires a very long drive. Nightlife is virtually nonexistent, but pampering yourself at the spa should make up for it. LakeView is a misnomer unless you want to call a small pond a lake.

El-Tesseen St., Fifth Settlement, New Cairo. ✆ **02/26140000.** Fax 02/26140009. www.dusit.com. 203 units, including 23 suites. $205 double. Rate is on "bed only" basis and subject to 25.44% taxes and service charges. AE, DC, MC, V. **Amenities:** 8 restaurants; 2 bars; concierge; health club & spa; 2 pools (1 heated, 1 kids'); room service. *In room:* A/C, TV, minibar, Wi-Fi (extra charge).

Fairmont Towers ★★ Conveniently located a 5-minute drive from the airport, this hotel takes inspiration from the area's past as a place where locals, more than 5,000 years ago, celebrated the sun, and is modeled after the eye of Horus, said to represent the sun and the sun god, Ra. Fittingly, natural light pours into the glass-fronted hotel, and circles, perhaps representing the sun, take shape in the carpeting and mirrors in the rooms. Rooms face either the atrium (odd numbered rooms and the better choice of the two options) or the pool and garden, and come in two styles, modern or classic. The former are a cool white, accented by pops of purple, while the latter are swathed in rich brown and red, with a peppering of gold and butterscotch. Bathrooms are large and modern, with rain showers and large soaking tubs. The gardenlike atmosphere flows in the streams of water around the lobby and in-house dining options, including **Aqua e Luce,** serving contemporary Italian food with a touch of French influence.

Salah Salem St., Heliopolis. ✆ **02/22696000.** Fax 02/226960300. www.fairmont.com. 247 units. $145 double. Rate is on "bed only" basis and subject to 25.44% taxes and service charges. AE, DC, MC, V. **Amenities:** 3 restaurants; 2 bars; concierge; gym; pool; room service; Wi-Fi. *In room:* A/C, TV, minibar, Wi-Fi (extra charge).

JW Marriott More like a small resort town than a hotel, the JW Marriott has everything from a water park to a golf course. Located a 10-minute drive from the airport, it's a bit out of the way for most attractions. At the end of the day, however, it isn't Cairo's sights that drive this hotel's popularity, but quite the opposite: From the extravagant lobby to the acres of greenery and the artificial beach, the intention is to take you away from the city. The rooms are spacious and lushly decorated, as if compensating for a somewhat generic overall look and feel. All of them look out over either the golf course or the water park. If a pause from the chaos and something absolutely predictable and familiar is what you need, this is a good base for your Cairo visit.

Ring Rd., Mirage City, New Cairo. ✆ **02/24115588.** Fax 02/24112266. www.marriott.com. 357 units, including 79 suites. $230 double. Rate includes buffet breakfast, but subject to 25.44% taxes and service charges. AE, DC, MC, V. **Amenities:** 7 restaurants; 3 bars; concierge; golf course; health club & spa; 2 pools (1 heated); room service. *In room:* A/C, TV, Internet (extra charge), minibar.

Le Méridien Heliopolis Most of the rooms at this hotel, located on Salah Salem Street, get an uninspiring view of the high traffic street. My advice is to try to get a garden- or pool-view room. That said, the gardens and pool offer an excellent, calm ambience for relaxing after a day down at the Khan or trekking through Islamic Cairo. The main advantage that this place has is its proximity to the airport, or if you need to be based in Heliopolis.

51 Salah Salem St., Heliopolis. ✆ **02/22905055.** Fax 02/22918591. www.lemeridienheliopolis.com. 283 units. $155 double. Rate is on "bed only" basis and subject to 25.44% taxes and service charges. AE, DC, MC, V. **Amenities:** 4 restaurants; 3 bars; concierge; health club & spa; pool; room service. *In room:* A/C, TV, Internet (extra charge), minibar.

Le Riad Hotel de Charme ★★ Located in the heart of Islamic Cairo, on the recently renovated Al Mu'izz le-din Allah Street, Le Riad Hotel de Charme offers the opportunity to be based in the middle of bustling Islamic Cairo without sacrificing on luxury or professional service. There are only suites here, and each comes in with its own theme. Cinema's walls are adorned with film billboards; Photographic features a collection of images depicting Egyptian society; Mamluk matches the authenticity of the neighborhood with style; and Calligraphy has an Arabesque bedroom and a quilt embroidered with a famous Egyptian poem, originally sung by Om Kolthoum (p. 128). The

Cairo Going Boutique

Whether high-end five-star chain hotels or basic budget hostels, accommodations in the Egyptian capital are classic. However, Cairo has recently opened up to boutique lodgings, with both Villa Belle Époque and Le Riad Hotel de Charme opening in early 2009.

details, meticulous and in the finest taste, are what bring vibrancy to this boutique hotel; when you return from a long day of sightseeing, instead of a piece of chocolate on your pillow you'll find a poem. Note that this hotel is dry, as alcohol is not allowed anywhere within Islamic Cairo.

114 Al Mu'izz le-din Allah St., Islamic Cairo. ✆ **02/27876074** or -5. Fax 02/27862438. www.leriad-hoteldecharme.com. 17 suites. 240€ junior suite. Rate includes breakfast, taxes, and service charges. MC, V. **Amenities:** Restaurant; concierge; room service; Wi-Fi. *In room:* A/C, TV, Internet, minibar.

Villa Belle Époque ★★ This huge villa-turned-boutique hotel is the place to be if you wish to experience how the life of an Egyptian aristocrat must have been at the turn of the 20th century. Classical furnishing, subtle colors, period chandeliers, and in-room decor with a touch of traditional artistry are all elements that evoke the relaxed rhythm of the good old days. Instead of numbers, rooms are named after Egyptian cities; go for Suez if you are into attics. The hotel's little garden perfectly fits the 5pm tea ambience, while the backyard pool invites a dip to escape the midday heat. The hotel's restaurant offers sophisticated food from around the world; premium priced but superb quality. Only local beer and wine are served.

Villa Belle Époque is located in the green suburb of Maadi, with easy access to Maadi Metro station, which is less than a 5-minute walk away.

Villa 63 Rd. 13, Maadi. ✆ **02/23582991** or 02/23580265. www.villabelleepoque.com. 13 units. 280€ double. Rate includes breakfast, taxes, and service charges. AE, DC, MC, V. **Amenities:** Restaurant; bar; concierge; heated pool; room service; Wi-Fi. *In room:* A/C, TV, Internet, minibar.

5 WHERE TO DINE

With the city's population exceeding the 20-million mark, there are numerous places to eat, from common eateries and fast-food chains to fine-dining and international restaurants. Places categorized as "Very Expensive" or "Expensive" serve alcohol, while others don't unless otherwise indicated. Prices are subject to taxes and service charge unless otherwise indicated.

Note: Due to the standard service and worldwide availability of Burger King, McDonald's, Pizza Hut, KFC, Hardee's, Fuddruckers, Chili's, On the Border, and the like, they are not reviewed as part of this guidebook. However, rest assured you can bump into one anywhere in Cairo, Alexandria, and other tourist cities.

DOWNTOWN & ZAMALEK

Very Expensive

La Trattoria ★ ITALIAN A cool white interior and simple elegance characterize this pricey Italian eatery in the middle of Zamalek. One of a string of good restaurants in Egypt owned by the son of Egyptian movie star Omar Sharif (who can be spotted eating here), Trattoria serves small portions, but the food won't disappoint. Start with spaghetti carbonara (this being one of the very few places in Egypt where you can get safe pork products) and move on to the rich and filling *osso buco.* If you have space left, the ever-changing dessert selection usually includes something for every palate.

13 Marashly St., Zamalek. ✆ **02/27350470.** Reservations recommended. Appetizers LE30–LE40; main courses LE50–LE150. MC, V. Sat–Thurs 1pm–12:30am; Fri 2pm–12:30am.

Expensive

Hana Korean Barbeque ★ (Finds) KOREAN As the name implies, you'll find barbecue here, only you get to make it yourself using small charcoal grills built into the table. Large portions of items such as beef and squid are accompanied by rice or noodles. If self-service isn't your thing, it also has an extensive menu of Korean and Asian food that stretches from Western Chinese standards such as egg fried rice and egg drop soup to more obscure dishes such as shark fin soup (though I'm personally against shark finning). Decor is basic, and service, though slow, is very pleasant and helpful. One nice touch here is the half-dozen or so dishes of assorted kimchi and appetizers that arrive before your food to tide you over until the main course.

21 Aziz Abaza St., Zamalek. ✆ **02/37382972.** Appetizers LE20–LE30; main courses LE40–LE80. No credit cards. Daily noon–9pm.

La Bodega FRENCH Located in a renovated portion of the historic Baehler Mansions, La Bodega is a French restaurant in lounge attire. A combination of high ceilings, huge windows, and muted murals marks the atmosphere of La Bodega, which fits well with the Belle Epoque building in which it is located. The food served misses on quality from time to time; try your luck with Tunisian lamb shank with couscous and vegetables. Though typically half-empty during the day, La Bodega can get quite busy after 7pm, so reservations are a good idea.

157 26th of July St. (next to Cilantro), Zamalek. ✆ **02/27362188** or 02/27350543. Reservations recommended. Appetizers LE30–LE60; main courses LE50–LE110. MC, V. Daily noon–2am.

Taboula ★★★ LEBANESE The warm ambience here is accented by 19th-century furnishings, Middle Eastern decor, a low ceiling, dim lighting, and smudged wall paint. Food is equally pleasurable with *shanklish* (goat cheese salad), *taboula* (Lebanese salad), and Lebanese *fettah* (a mix of bread and rice garnished with yogurt and other toppings). Taboula makes for a good option if you wish to take a break from Egyptian cuisine while remaining in the region, and is also a good opportunity to try the Lebanese tradition *arak*, an unsweetened, distilled, alcoholic aniseed drink. The only downside is the indoor *shisha* smoking.

1 Latin America St., Garden City. ✆ **02/27925261.** www.taboula-eg.com. Reservations recommended. Appetizers LE20–LE30; main courses LE40–LE100. MC, V. Daily noon–1:30am.

Moderate

Abou El Sid ★ EGYPTIAN Abou Sid is simply the best place in Cairo to sample real Egyptian food. The service can be slow and the staff are not that professional, but there's no arguing with either the food or the funky-yet-traditional decor. For appetizers, try *wara ainab* (stuffed vine leaves) or *mombar* (a crunchy, fried cattle intestine stuffed with rice), while for a main dish go for artichoke *tagine* or the delicious Circassian chicken in walnut sauce. End the meal with a traditional dessert such as *om aly* (a raisin-studded variation of bread pudding) or a honey *feteer* (layers of pastry baked pizza-style and drenched in honey). Local beer and wine are served.

157 26th of July St., Zamalek. ✆ **02/27359640.** www.abouelsid.com. Appetizers LE15–LE45; main courses LE40–LE70. MC, V. Daily 1pm–2am.

Abou Shakra EGYPTIAN This is the place for meat-lovers looking to sample real Egyptian fare. If you're hungry, go for the charcoal-grilled kebab and *kofta* plate, which features a full kilo (2¼ pounds) of meat. If you're not quite in full caveman mode, though, go for the grilled pigeon or *ouzi* (grilled lamb). None of the main dishes comes with much on the side, so ask for some grilled vegetables or a rice *tagine.* Portions are big, and the food is heavy; head here when you are starving and equipped with digestive medicines in case of a stomachache.

Note: Abou Shakra has a number of branches in both Cairo and Alexandria. The address listed here is for the main branch.

69 Qasr el A'aini St., Garden City. ✆ **02/25316111** or hotline 19090. Appetizers LE10–LE20; main courses LE35–LE70. MC, V (may differ by branch). Daily noon–1am.

Dido's al Dente Value ITALIAN As every student at the American University's nearby hostel knows, Dido's is the place for moderately priced, filling pasta in an informal setting. Squash into the tiny, usually crowded, main room and watch the cooks whip up your pasta in the open kitchen. The location on a quiet side street is relaxed and pleasant, and the food is filling if not exactly gourmet.

Note: In addition to the main branch listed here, Dido's al Dente has other branches in Cairo.

21 Baghat Ali St., Zamalek. ✆ **02/27359117.** Main courses LE20–LE45. No credit cards. Daily 24 hours.

Felfela Value EGYPTIAN Offering some of the best moderately priced food in downtown, this restaurant has a bit of an eccentric setting; the decor includes water features, a woven-grass roof, live canaries, and a lot of hanging lamps. The food is straight-up Egyptian fare. Start with a side plate of *tahina* and a bowl of lentil soup (served with croutons and lemons), and move on to *dawood basha* (meatball stew) or *kebab hella* (stewed lamb). For a real taste of local food, try a pair of stuffed pigeons or quails, and end the meal with a bowl of sweet, cool *om aly.* Felfela serves local wine and beer, but it also does particularly good lemonade, which may be a better bet on a hot, dry summer day when you have a few hours of sightseeing still ahead.

15 Hoda Sharawi St., Downtown. ✆ **02/23922751** or 02/23922833. Appetizers LE10–LE25; main courses LE30–LE70. MC, V. Daily 8am–1am.

Greek Club INTERNATIONAL More of an expats' hangout than tourists,' the Greek Club is a vestige of 19th century cosmopolitan Cairo with its high-ceilinged, high-windowed rooms that today overlook the bustling traffic of Tahrir Square. Food is not complicated and average in quality. Start with some *saganaki* (fried cheese) and Greek salad, followed by *shish tawook* or deep-fried calamari. Local beer and wine is available, but stay away from the ouzo unless you want to wake up wondering what happened to your head.

28 Mahmoud Bassyouni St., Downtown. ✆ **02/25750822.** Appetizers LE15–LE25; main courses LE30–LE60. No credit cards. Daily 6pm–midnight.

Le Bistro FRENCH An odd little restaurant on the same street as Felfela (above), Le Bistro is easy to miss because it's located well below street level. Blue paint and bright lights give it the feeling that you're in an aquarium looking out, but it's extremely clean and service is very pleasant. Operated by the same management that does catering for the French cultural center, Le Bistro offers a Cairo take on French fare. Try the chicken in red wine sauce with a side of pasta and grilled vegetables, and order the profiteroles for dessert. Though this isn't Paris, it can be a welcome change.

8 Hoda Sharawy St., Downtown ✆ **02/23927694.** Appetizers LE10–LE20; main courses LE30–LE50. No credit cards. Daily 10am–midnight.

Maison Thomas ★★ PIZZA This simple bistro is a delightful breakfast and lunch spot in the city. Dating back to the early 20th century, the Zamalek branch's vintage ambience is offset by tall tables and high chairs. Maison Thomas is reputed for its pizzas, and indeed they are among the best in town, while their sandwiches are equally tasty. For dessert, treat yourself to cherry jam cheesecake.

Note: Other than the main branch listed here, Maison Thomas has other branches in Heliopolis, Maadi, Mohandiseen, and Abu El Tig Marina, El Gouna.

157 26th of July St. ✆ **02/27357057** or 02/27350415. Pizzas LE30–LE55. No credit cards. Daily 24 hours.

Mezza Luna ITALIAN Located on a quiet cul-de-sac off 26th of July Street, this small, bistro-style restaurant has fresh pasta at very reasonable prices. Service can be iffy, but the decor is pleasant and very clean, with Italian pop music in the background. All the dishes come with garlic bread. The only drawback is that you'll have your Italian food without wine.

118 26th of July St., Zamalek. ✆ **02/27352655.** Pasta LE20–LE45. MC, V. Daily 8am–midnight.

Sequoia INTERNATIONAL This open-air, tent-shaped restaurant is where Cairo's trendy lounge on comfortable white cushions, savor finger foods and hand-rolled sushi, and smoke flavored *shisha* all night long. Its location, on the very tip of Zamalek Island, is the main attraction, at least for me, with its incredible panoramic view of the river and the capital. However, the serenity of being a stone's throw away from the Nile is diminished by the young crowd that takes over, especially on weekends, when the level of noise and smoke exponentially increases. The ongoing LE75 minimum charge is hiked up to LE90 Friday through Sunday.

5 Abou el Feda St., Zamalek. ✆ **02/27366359** or 012/7302228. Reservations recommended. Appetizers LE20–LE40; main courses LE40–LE80. MC, V. Daily 10am–2am.

Inexpensive

Gad (Value) EGYPTIAN You can't come to Egypt without tasting *fuul* or *tameya,* and there is no better place than Gad. Mouthwatering sandwiches are made of pita bread freshly baked on the premises and stuffed with different *fuul* variants (p. 42) and freshly fried *tameya.* Menu items include other typical Egyptian sandwiches such as moussaka (doesn't come with minced meat) and *bayd bel basterma* (scrambled eggs with an Egyptian version of pastrami). Gad is a takeaway eatery with a few tables.

Note: In addition to the main branch listed here, Gad has branches all over Cairo and Alexandria.

13 26th of July St., Downtown. ✆ **02/25763583.** Sandwiches LE2–LE10. No credit cards. Daily 7am–3am (may differ by branch).

Kosheri El Tahrir ★★★ (Finds) EGYPTIAN As the name implies, this is a *kosheri*-dedicated eatery. Food for the masses, the typical Cairene dish is an assorted mix of lentils, macaroni, rice, and chickpeas garnished with slices of fried onions and hot tomato sauce on top. Kosheri El Tahrir is centrally located in downtown, making it an ideal place for a quick lunch while touring the locality. Though there is nothing fancy about the seating area (white tables with a cheap-looking plastic flower) I was perplexed when the waiter took my order using a handheld device; my *kosheri* was there in less than a minute. If you are wondering what the greenish bottle next to the hot chili is, it is *da'e,* a vinegar-based sauce with lots of garlic and lemon. Don't miss on it, but keep a mint handy.

19 Tala'at Harb St., Downtown. ✆ **02/21234567.** *Kosheri* LE7–LE10. No credit cards. Daily 11am–11pm.

DOKKI & MOHANDISEEN

The traffic might deter you from Dokki or Mohandiseen, but there are two restaurants that make the journey worthwhile.

Very Expensive

Charwood's ★★ STEAK/PIZZA Though they also serve some of the best pizzas in town, it's the meat that keeps customers coming back for more. All the meals start with an excellent mixed salad topped with a light dressing and fresh bread baked daily on the premises. Try the tournedos, grilled rare, with a side of mustard sauce and a baked potato; cuts come from the best butchers in town. If red meat is not your thing, they also have excellent grilled shrimp. Other than one type of pizza, vegetarians are left choice-less.

53 Gamea'at el Dwal el Arabia St., Mohandiseen. ✆ **02/37490893** or 012/1481344. Pizza LE50–LE70; main courses LE70–LE130. MC, V. Daily noon–midnight.

Moderate

El Sit Hosneya ★★ EGYPTIAN One of the most recent restaurants to open in the capital, El Sit Hosneya is a cheerful, authentic place for a relaxed dinner. Heavily decorated head to toe, from the door handles to the ceiling, the look is more Moroccan that Egyptian, with deep-red low coaches, patterned wall decor, and dangling brass chandeliers. However, the menu is pure Egyptian with a touch of Middle Eastern influence. Start with a couple of appetizers; don't miss on the zucchini with milk and mint. For a main course, go for taro or *molokheya*. Portions are small so you can easily have space for a dessert; sweet pumpkin is the pick of the treats. On Fridays and Saturdays El Sit Hosneya serves a traditional breakfast of *fuul, tameya,* and *feteer.*

47 Michael Bakhoum St., Dokki. ✆ **02/33386007** or -9. Appetizers LE10–LE25; main courses LE30–LE70. MC, V. Sun–Thurs noon–1am; Fri 10am–1am.

HELIOPOLIS

Expensive

Wabisabi JAPANESE This small sushi bar in Heliopolis offers tasty and innovative sushi; try out Tobeko rolls or the restaurant's signature Wabisabi rolls (shrimp tempura with caviar cream and smoked salmon). The interiors are modern but fail to create a unique ambience; there is simply too much light. The staff are friendly and service is both brisk and professional. I wouldn't fight traffic to reach Wabisabi (if you are based on the other side of town), but if you happen to be in the neighborhood, stop in for a couple of rolls.

100 El Marghani St., Heliopolis. ✆ **02/24141045.** Reservations recommended. Sushi LE45–LE200. No credit cards. Daily 10am–2am.

Moderate

Le Chantilly ★★ SWISS Le Chantilly is a lovely place for a couple of beers while having dinner with friends. The Swiss restaurant serves an eclectic set of European dishes, but the traditional cheese fondue is simply the best. If you have a more carnivorous appetite, then the *salad tiede* (chicken liver salad) is a good choice. Decor is simple and the atmosphere is friendly. The indoor dining area is often crowded, while the outdoor one enjoys a pleasant breeze even on hot summer nights.

Note: Le Chantilly has other branches in Cairo; they go under the name of La Chesa in downtown, and Le Chalet and Le Château—both on Nile Street not far from Zamalek.

11 Baghdad St., Korba, Heliopolis. ✆ **02/22907303.** www.swissrest.com. Appetizers LE20–LE50; main courses LE40–LE150. MC, V. Daily 7am–midnight.

Makani Finds INTERNATIONAL My Place, as Makani translates to, is a fusion of hip and modern style with a touch of traditional decor. The cozy deli is adjoined by a tiny sushi bar, so you have a wide selection when it comes to food. This place is a very good option if you are in Heliopolis and want to chill out for a couple of hours before resuming your Cairo tour.

Note: Makani has other branches in Cairo as well as Sharm El Sheikh.

27 Hassan Sadek St. (parallel to El Marghani St.), Heliopolis. ✆ **02/26910310.** Appetizers LE20–LE35; sandwiches LE20–LE30; sushi LE6–LE25 per piece. MC, V. Daily 10am–2am.

ISLAMIC CAIRO

Expensive

Naguib Mahfouz Café EGYPTIAN Hidden in the heart of the Khan Al Khalili shopping district, this Oberoi-run restaurant is the perfect cool-off place for lunch while zigzagging the alleyways of Islamic Cairo. The food is excellent, the air-conditioning is efficient, and the washrooms are spotless. Prices are more on the expensive side, but the Naguib Mahfouz Café delivers the kind of service and food that you would expect from this first-rate hotel chain. Try a sampling of local appetizers such as *tameya,* stuffed grape leaves, and *tahina.* If you're in the mood for something with a little more heft, the kebab is excellent and comes with fresh-baked bread.

5 Sekket el Badistan, Khan Al Khalili. ✆ **02/25903788** or 02/25932262. Reservations recommended. Appetizers LE25–LE40; main courses LE55–LE90. MC, V. Daily 10am–2am.

Taj al Sultan ★ EGYPTIAN/INDIAN Taj al Sultan, a two-floor, upscale restaurant, is new (Aug 2009) to the Islamic Cairo dining scene. The theme is a blend of Middle Eastern and Indian decor, with Arabic paintings, Indian embroidery, and brass-made Hindu gods. Likewise, the menu is a mix of the two cultures. Opting for Egyptian food, start with *shorbet kaware'a* (beef leg soup), a delicious, hard to cook delicacy that locals regard as an aphrodisiac. For the main dish, go for Egyptian *fettah,* which is a big bowl of rice, toasted bread, and chunks of meat with an aromatic tomato and garlic sauce on top; you can also opt for chicken or prawns instead of meat. Overall, the food is good, albeit pricey. Thursday to Saturday nights there is a band playing traditional tunes 8pm to midnight.

1 Al Azhar Sq. (close to Al Hussein Mosque). ✆ **02/27877273.** www.tajalsultan.com. Appetizers LE20–LE40; main courses LE50–LE120. MC, V. Daily 11am–2am.

MAADI

Expensive

Bua Khao ★ THAI This is not only the best Thai restaurant in town, but one of the best places to eat in Cairo. The decor is nothing special, but the food is first-rate. Start with a spicy chicken salad followed by red or green curry or, one of my favorites, the chicken with basil leaves. Menu items change seasonally, but if you're here at the right time of year, I recommend the deep-fried calamari in coconut batter. Try the fried bananas with honey for dessert. Specials vary and are always worth a try.

151 Rd. 9., Maadi. ✆ **02/23580126.** Reservations recommended. Appetizers LE15–LE40; main courses LE50–LE150. MC, V. Daily 6–11pm.

Moderate

Abou el Sid ★ EGYPTIAN This branch of the authentic restaurant comes with much more space than the packed Zamalek branch (p. 139) but with similar decor and an identical menu. The option of an outdoor area makes it a good location for smoking *shisha* or an outdoor meal.

47 Rd. 7, Maadi. ✆ **02/23805050.** www.abouelsid.com. Appetizers LE15–LE45; main courses LE40–LE70. MC, V. Daily 1pm–2am.

Lucille's ★★★ AMERICAN Lucille's serves the best homemade burgers in Egypt and probably beyond; try a Colossus Burger with its double beef patties and twice the amount of cheese. If you are not into burgers but are a big fan of American cuisine, there is a good assortment of Tex-Mex on offer. The American breakfast of bacon (beef, not pork) and eggs served with hash browns and toast is also a good choice. This little restaurant conceals itself on Maadi's most-frequented Road 9.

40 Rd. 9, Maadi. ✆ **02/23781530** or 02/23787975. Reservations not accepted. Burgers LE35–LE45; fajitas and nachos LE50. Prices include taxes and service charge. No credit cards. Daily 8am–midnight.

6 OUTDOOR ACTIVITIES A TO Z

GOLF There are more opportunities than you might expect in and around Cairo to hit the links. Close to the airport, try the **JW Marriott,** Heliopolis (✆ **02/24115588;** www.golf.jwmarriottcairo.com/golf), with its 27-hole, par-72 course, or head to the other side of town for Cairo's most historic golf course attached to **Mena House Oberoi,** Giza (✆ **02/33833222**), which opened in 1889. This 18-hole, par-68 course abuts the Giza plateau where the pyramids are located. Less romantic but more modern is the **Katameya Heights** (✆ **02/27580512;** www.katameyaheights.com) with its 18-hole, par-72 course in the middle of a wealthy housing estate on the southeastern edge of the city. **Amarante Golf City** (✆ **02/46102160** or -2; www.amarantegolfcity.com) offers a challenging 18-hole, par-72 course, while **Dreamland Golf and Tennis Resort** (✆ **02/38553164;** www.dreamlandgolf.com) has a 9-hole, par-36 course with a Pharaonic touch; holes are named after Ancient Egyptian kings.

RIDING There are few better ways to experience the space and atmosphere of the Giza plateau than on horseback, and riding is a popular pastime for visitors and expat residents of Cairo. It used to be that the crowded little village of Nazlet el Samaan, around the feet of the Sphinx in Giza, was the place to go, and there is still a row of stables there. A better place to go is now farther out on the ring road toward Saqqara. Take the Mounib Bridge south of Roda Island, go straight on the highway, and take the Cairo–Alexandria Desert Road exit. Here there will be signs to the **International Equestrian Center** (✆ **02/33820435** or 02/33820435), which is a large stable complex. They have quiet tree-lined driveways and around 100 horses in a series of stables. While they have a number of practice rings for instruction, most of their business is sending riders into the desert, which is just 100m (328 ft.) away. Expect to pay between LE70 and LE100 per hour for a good horse and tack.

7 SHOPPING A TO Z

Depending on what you're looking for, you've either come to the end of the earth or its absolute center. Window shoppers will not go crazy with the latest fashions on display, nor will the prices trigger a shopping spree. However, memorabilia, souvenir, and knick-knack collectors will have a good time shopping in various locations around the city.

BOOKS

In recent years, Cairo's bookshop population has quadrupled. The below are recommended places to go if you are looking for a specific title or want to get a general idea of what there is on offer. They open daily from 9am to 11pm unless otherwise indicated.

Alef The latest addition to bookstores-poor Heliopolis, Alef comes in handy for Arabic book worms; the English collection is very limited. The place has an elaborate Andalusian feel inside with arched corridors and Islamic patterned decoration. Alef had just opened at the time of researching this edition, but I predict a heavy dose of seminars, book discussions, and literary events soon to be unleashed. Opens daily 10am to midnight. 132 El Marghany St., Heliopolis. © **02/24192396.** www.alefbookstores.com.

AUC (American University Cairo) Bookstore AUC Press's (www.aucpress.com) main distribution venue is well stocked with AUC Press titles that tackle different aspects of Egypt, from a comprehensive list of Egyptian, and some Arab, authors in translation to personal memoirs and historical books. AUC Bookstore has a good international travel section, too. When visiting the main branch, enter the AUC campus through the Mohamed Mahmoud entrance (across from McDonald's), and be prepared to leave some form of ID with the security at the gate. The Zamalek Branch (16 Mohamed Thakeb St.; © **02/37397045**) is located in considerably smaller quarters underneath the AUC hostel. Stores are open Saturday to Thursday 9am to 6pm; the Zamalek branch is also open Friday 1 to 6pm. Main campus, American University in Cairo, Tahrir Sq. © **02/27975900** or 02/27975370.

Bookspot If you are looking for secondhand books, this is the only place in Cairo I can wholeheartedly recommend. They also have some brand-new titles for sale, but the selection is limited. The advantage, though, is that Bookspot delivers to anywhere in the world. 71 Rd. 9, Maadi. © **02/23781006.** www.bookspotonline.com.

Diwan Diwan may not have the biggest selection of books in the city (AUC Bookstore's main branch does), but it certainly has one of the best and most diverse. Diwan has a good selection of books in Arabic and English, a much smaller French one, and a symbolic German selection. It carries current nonfiction and a fair range of fiction, light literature, and classics; however, the travel section is a shame. Diwan stocks DVDs of old and new Egyptian movies with English subtitles. In addition to the main Zamalek branch, it has branches in several other locations across the city including Maadi, Heliopolis, and the Cairo Marriott Hotel, in case you don't feel like crossing the street. 159 26th of July St. © **02/27362598.**

Kotob Khan Kotob Khan is a lovely place to spend a morning navigating its shelves or drifting with the flow of one of the recently released novels while having a good cup of coffee. The selection is big and diverse (including a kid's section), especially when it comes to fiction and light reads; however, travel is underrepresented. Kotob Khan is a frequent venue for literature-related workshops and book-signing events, so keep an eye on their website. 3/1 El Lasilky St., Maadi. © **02/25194807.** www.kotobkhan.com.

FOOD & LIQUOR

A good number of hypermarkets dot the capital, from international Carrefour and Spinney's to local Metro and Abou Zikry. And if you don't feel like grabbing a cart and cruising aisles, you can always resort to the little grocery shops on the corner. Dubbed *bak al,* you can pick up an amazing range of items including bottled water, fresh batteries, and basic groceries.

Drinkies This is the retail outlet for the Heineken-owned behemoth Al Ahram Beverage Company (www.alahrambeverages.com), with stores found in almost every Cairene district. It sells all the beers, wines, and hard liquor that are produced in Egypt, including Stella, Saqqara, and Meister beers; Omar Khayyam, Grand Marquis, and Cape Bay wines; and a line of best-avoided hard liquor, which includes the undrinkable Ould Stag whiskey and some headache-inducing vodka. Its drop-off service (minimum order LE50) is pretty efficient and operates year-round. ✆ **19330.** Branches include: 157 26th of July St., Zamalek; 55 Ramsis St., Heliopolis; 29 Mostafa Kamel St., Maadi; and 41 Tala'at Harb St., Downtown.

Sekem Organic Food With poor government regulation and a polluted environment, worries about what kind of chemicals are getting into the food chain are particularly germane in Cairo. Fortunately, Egypt is home to a burgeoning organic food industry, and though most of these products (which are quite expensive by local standards) are produced for export to Europe, enough end up in large local grocery chains (such as Metro). This store stocks a wide range of fruits, biscuits, and juices that can be packed as healthy sightseeing snacks, as well as basic grocery items for those with access to kitchens. 8 Ahmad Sabri St., Zamalek. ✆ **02/27382724.**

HANDICRAFTS, JEWELRY & DECOR

Bedouin handicrafts, antiques, simple silver jewelry, and embroidered cloths are the shopping that you should not miss. Though you can also find some good deals on attractive carpets, they're nothing like what's available in Damascus or Istanbul, so don't have high hopes. Keep in mind that in Cairo haggling is the norm. Most of the places recommended below do offer reasonable fixed prices unless otherwise indicated. In the shops and stalls of Khan Al Khalili or Khayameya, however, there is simply no such thing as a fixed price, and you should expect to be able to take 20% to 25% off the asking price with a little argument. Expect stores to open around 10am and close somewhere between 8 and 10pm.

Al Khatoun Situated in a funky renovated old building behind Al Azhar Mosque, Akhtoun stocks an eclectic variety of furnishings and decor items in original and traditional designs. Cloth wall hangings decorated with calligraphic prints, metalwork lamps and lampshades, fabrics, and prints of old photographs are neatly arranged. There are no antiques here, but the new items are still very nice. Prices are fixed. 3 Mohamed Abdu St., Islamic Cairo. ✆ **02/25147164.**

Azza Fahmy Boutique This is the place to go for elaborate high-end jewelry from Azza Fahmy, one of the first modern Egyptian jewelry designers to get international attention. Her work tends to be big, rich, warm, and studded with semi-precious stones while at the same time recalling traditional Egyptian themes and often using Arabic calligraphy. There are other Azza Fahmy boutiques in town, including the one inside Sofitel El Gezirah Hotel. Very pricey. 15c Dr. Taha Hussein St., Zamalek. ✆ **02/27358354.** www.azzafahmy.com.

Fair Trade Egypt (formerly Egypt Craft Center) This is one of my favorite places to buy gifts in Egypt, because, apart from carrying top-quality handicrafts, the store is attached to a number of nongovernmental organizations (NGOs), which ensures that the profits from selling the goods go to the people who produced them. This is one of the best places in town to buy the now well-known Fayum pottery, and it's also an excellent source for locally woven cloth, scarves, and postcards. Prices are reasonable. 8–27 Yehia Ibrahim St., Zamalek. ✆ **02/27365123.** www.fairtradeegypt.org.

Kasr El Shook Located in the middle of Zamalek, Kasr El Shook is a small but tightly packed silver store that sells everything from card holders to *shisha* pipes. Quality is excellent and prices are, with a little haggling, comparable to Khan El Khalili. The owner is an aficionado of classic Egyptian films, so ask him about the retired actors still living in the neighborhood. 11 Brazil St., Zamalek. ✆ **02/37372111.**

Khan Misr Touloun Located directly across from the front entrance of the Ibn Tulun Mosque, this French-run store is a great spot to shop for a wide variety of handicrafts from around Egypt including glass, cloth, furniture, and an exclusive collection of postcards. The owner tends to leave town during the hottest months, so hours can be a little restricted during July and August. Tulun Bey St., directly across from the Ibn Tulun Mosque. ✆ **02/23652227.**

Nagada This wonderful store brings some of the best handicrafts from around Egypt—including handmade fabrics from Upper Egypt, pottery from the Fayum, jewelry from the oases, and clothing from Cairo—into one spot. Daily 9:30am to 6pm. 13 Refa'a St., Dokki. ✆ **02/37486663.** www.nagada.net.

Nomad Gallery Zamalek's answer to souvenir shopping, Nomad has a diverse array of different items on offer, from traditional silver designs and hand-woven crafts to Bedouin camel-hair carpets and *khayameya* embroidery. Daily 9am to 8pm. 14 Saray Al Gezira, 1st floor. ✆ **02/27361917.** www.nomadgallery.net.

Souk el Fustat This is a great shopping opportunity next to Old Cairo that brings together an excellent selection of the best handicrafts from around the country. It's named for the old city that once occupied the site. Smooth sandstone arches and shaded courtyards make browsing the 40 shops a civil, and even tranquil, experience. Shops offer everything from traditional *khayameya* needlework, handmade lanterns, and furniture to Fayum pottery, soap, and rugs. Prices are more or less fixed, so don't expect to find the kind of cutthroat haggling here that you'll be subject to in Khan Al Khalili, but there should be a little "wiggle room" in the price, especially if you're buying a number of different items. There is also a little cafeteria that's a great place to take a break on a hot day of sightseeing in Old Cairo. Daily 10am to 10pm. About 300m (984 ft.) northward from Mar Girgis Metro station, Old Cairo.

Tips City Stars

Cairo has a number of mediocre malls that you can easily skip. However, **City Stars,** 2 Aly Rashad St., Heliopolis (✆ **02/24800500-53;** fax 02/24800556; www.citystars.com.eg), makes for a good high-end Cairo shopping experience. The mega mall hosts 550 shops that vary from world-leading brands such as Calvin Klein, Levi's, Mango, Zara, Spinney's hypermarket, and Virgin Megastore. There is more than one food court featuring international fast-food chains such as Burger King, McDonald's, Papa John's Pizza, and Wagamama, or take a coffee break at Cilantro, Beano's, Starbucks, or Cinnabon. City Stars hosts a 16-screen cinema complex and an indoor theme park that kids love. There is also a mock Khan El Khalili with a modern look, which I personally find superficial; it lacks the genuine feel and sells machine-made items that are staggeringly overpriced.

Wady Craft Shop A handicraft shop with a mission, Wady supports refugees and people with special needs by showcasing their works. Most of the items sold here have an African or a Christian theme to them. Daily 9:30am to 5pm; Sundays and Fridays 11am to 4pm. 35 Michael Lutfalla St. (inside All Saints Cathedral), Zamalek.

SPORTING GOODS

Sports Mall If you've just decided that you want to head for the Red Sea but arrived in Egypt without your snorkel and fins, or just want to get into the gym at the hotel, the Sports Mall in Mohandiseen can probably come up with everything that you need. Though several sports shops can be found throughout the city, including Adidas and Nike, the Sports Mall is a mega store where you can shop for everything from tennis rackets to snorkels (which, by the way, you can actually rent at most resorts). 80 Shehab St., Mohandiseen. © **02/33026432.**

8 CAIRO AFTER DARK

ARTS & CULTURE

In the 1990s, Cairo's cultural scene was restricted to the **Cairo Opera House** (El Andalus Sq., Zamalek; © **02/27370603;** fax 02/27370599; www.cairoopera.org), with its recitals and classical music performances. Recently, not only did the Opera's scope widen to include traditional musical ensembles as well as contemporary jazz concerts, but Cairo's cultural scene overall has witnessed a boom. Heading the league is the widely acclaimed **Sawy Culture Wheel** (26 of July St., Zamalek; © **02/27368881;** fax 02/27354508; www.culturewheel.com). A complex of cultural activities, it promotes young Egyptian artists showcasing their work through exhibitions, galleries, and concerts. The close-by **Egyptian Center for Culture & Art** (1 Saad Zaghloul St., Downtown; © **02/27920878;** www.egyptmusic.org), better known as Makan, offers a unique opportunity to watch a *zar* ceremony (p. 149). Leading the contemporary art scene, **Townhouse Gallery** (10 Nabrawy St., off Champollion St., Downtown; © **02/25768086;** www.thetownhouse gallery.com) promotes emerging Egyptian contemporary artists. Its events-packed calendar includes exhibitions, film screenings, theatrical acts, experimental musical performances, and public lectures. Following suit is the latest edition to the Egyptian contemporary scene, **Darb 1718** (Kasr El Shama'a St., behind the Hanging Church; © **02/23610511;** www.darb1718.com). **Contemporary Image Collective** (CIC; 20 Safiya Zaghloul St., off Qasr El Aini St., Downtown; © **02/227941686;** www.ciccairo.com) is another independent initiative dedicated to visual arts. CIC offers a wide range of photography-related courses and periodic seminars and symposiums.

Recently, there has been a trend where parts of historical edifices are used as venues for cultural events, mainly musical shows during summer and the holy month of Ramadan (p. 12). Topping the list is **Beit El Harrawi** (Mohamed Abdu St., behind El Hussein Universal Hospital, Islamic Cairo; © **02/25104174**), featuring performances by the Arab Oud House (a regional initiative with the objective of reviving the traditional lute *oud* music, it is spearheaded by Iraqi *oud* guru Nasser Shama). **Wekalet El Ghuri** (Mohamed Abdu St., behind Al Azhar Mosque, Islamic Cairo; © **02/27354234;** ghory@cdf-eg.org) is not to be missed, especially if you are into the twirling *tanoura* dance (p. 123).

Dance of the Jinn

A dim frankincense-filled room is emptied of everything except an altar in the middle, while a group of drummers and participants gather around two main characters: the patient, or rather the possessed, and the *kodia,* the *zar* ritual leader. Eyes half opened with hair loosely tossed and swayed, the patient, often a female, starts dancing to the rhythm of the banging drums as she circles the altar. As the drumming picks up, her movements intensify and she eventually steps into a trance. This is when the orchestrating *kodia* steps in and starts communicating with the possessing *jinn* in an attempt to pacify it. More pagan than religious, *zar* is actually prohibited by Islam. However, being part of the Egyptian culture, especially in Upper Egypt, it is widely accepted and tolerated. Today, *zar* performance in Cairo is more of a folkloric act rather than a true healing cult. Check the Egyptian Center for Culture & Art (Makan, p. 148) for show dates.

BARS & LOUNGES

All of Cairo's high-end hotels, and some moderate ones such as Windsor, will certainly have a bar, but not necessarily a popular one, and you might be left with no one but the bartender to chat with. Outside the hotels' premises, Cairo's nightlife scene is rather limited with a handful of nightspots mostly concentrated in Zamalek and downtown; however, these are the places for bar-hopping, lounging and gossiping, seeing and being seen, and perhaps picking up and getting picked up. All the reviewed venues require reservations and don't apply couples-only or any other restrictive policies unless otherwise indicated. As for prices, a local beer is in the LE2 to LE30 range, while alcoholic cocktails range from LE60 to LE80. Cairo's nightlife comes to an end between 2am and 3am.

After Eight ★ Tucked down an alley in the heart of downtown, After Eight is a stylish live-music venue for a funky, well-heeled set of expats, tourists, and locals. Built into a renovated ground-floor location in an old building, it's not a small venue, but by midnight on a Thursday or Friday night, it's usually packed shoulder to shoulder. Definitely a place for dancing and drinking rather than a quiet beer and an intimate chat, After Eight still manages to maintain an up-market atmosphere. No boisterous late-night tour of Cairo would be complete without stopping by. Couples-only policy applies. 6 Qasr El Nil St., Downtown. ✆ **010/339800.** www.after8cairo.com. Minimum LE50.

The Bullseye There's only one thing that you really need to know about the Bullseye, and it's either going to make the place irresistible or keep you away forever: karaoke, every Wednesday night from about 10pm until late. For the rest of the week the place returns to being a quiet back-street pub with dart boards and reasonably priced beer. 32 Jeddah St., Mohandiseen. ✆ **02/37616888.** Minimum LE75, karaoke night LE100.

Cairo Jazz Club ★★ One of my favorite late-night Cairo hangouts for the sheer reason of its inviting and friendly atmosphere, Cairo Jazz Club is the place to go for live bands playing jazz and fusion rock. Widely known Egyptian band Wust El Balad (p. 41) often performs here. A mix of laid-back yet funky decor characterizes the place, but the food is nothing to brag about. Getting to Cairo Jazz Club can be difficult; the easiest thing is to go online, print their address (written in Arabic and uploaded as a picture), and give it to the taxi driver. 197 26th of July St., Agouza (across the river from Zamalek in the direction of Mohandiseen). ✆ **02/33459939.** www.cairojazzclub.com.

The Cellar This is an affluent dive in the middle of Zamalek that's favored by businessmen and well-heeled locals. Dark and low-ceilinged, the Cellar is a little less lively than its neighboring Pub 28 and a little more expensive. The food's not as good as Pub 28, but I recommend this place on a Thursday night if you're looking for a pub atmosphere and want to be able to hear what your friends are saying. Note that there is usually a minimum charge equivalent to about four beers per person. 22 Dr. Taha Hussein St., Zamalek. ✆ **02/27350652** or 02/27350718. Minimum LE80.

Deal's This is a fun little pub, across the street from Abu Sid. It is frequented by a younger, livelier crowd than you'll find at either Pub 28 or the Cellar, and is the place to watch the football game and meet new friends. The food is good, and you shouldn't ignore this place when considering where to get a reasonably priced lunch or dinner. A chili con carne or a chicken stir-fry with a couple of local Stella beers is as good as comfort food gets. The drawback is inter-table space; already limited, it disappears with the young bargoers on Thursday evenings. 1 Said el Bakry St., Zamalek. ✆ **02/27360502.**

El Morocco This is where Cairo's crème de la crème younger generation spends the night. Things take off as a Moroccan-styled restaurant serving couscous, *tagine,* and *harira* (Morocco's famous soup), but by midnight the quiet elegance is gone as frantic DJs take the lead and party animals swarm the place kicking off an intense night of partying. El Morocco is in a league of its own; prices are higher and a couples-only policy vehemently applied. If your attire doesn't fall into the "dress to impress" category, the bouncers may turn you away. El Morocco opens as a restaurant between 8:30pm and midnight and as a nightclub between midnight and 4am. 9A Saray El Gezira St. (Blue Nile Boat), Zamalek. ✆ **02/27353114.** Minimum LE150.

La Bodega Tucked into the back corner of the bistro side of this popular restaurant, La Bodega—the bar—is subtly lit with experimental music playing in the background. A dark-wood bar with an overkill of stools, hanging drink glasses, solid brass railings, and eerie chalk drawings on the wall wraps up my impression about the place. Cairo's expat community and nouveau riche love the place, but I personally don't. 157 26th of July St., Zamalek. ✆ **02/27362188** or 02/27350543.

L'Aubergine ★ Tucked in the heart of Zamalek, L'Aubergine is one of my all-time favorite chill-out spots in Cairo. Simple furnishings and artistic purple-dominated wall paintings create the feel of a laid-back lounge. The menu for drinks offers the same fare as elsewhere in the city, though they sometimes miss on my favorite, the mojito. The food deserves your undivided attention; the cheese lasagna warrants a recommendation while the vegetarian moussaka is simply the best in town. It is an ideal place for a relaxed dinner and to chitchat while having a couple of beers. If you are more energetic and looking for a hip hangout, finish dinner and go upstairs, where L'Aubergine's bar steams with bar-hoppers and pumped-up speakers. 5 Sayed El Bakry St., off Hassan Sabry St., Zamalek. ✆ **02/27380080.**

Tips Horreya

Horreya, 2 Mazloum St., Downtown (✆ **02/23920397**), is a traditional coffee shop with a twist; it serves local beer at bargain-basement prices. Mingle with backpackers, young artists, and locals going out for a drink.

Shake That Booty

Arabic dance, Middle Eastern dance, belly dancing—all different names for the same thing. The origins of the dance, often performed by a solo female, are debatable, but the Ancient Babylon origin seems to be the most acceptable and widely spread theory (that it originated as a ritual involving the worship of Ancient Babylonian goddess Ishtar). In Egypt, belly dancing was more traditionally rooted into society than one may think. During *moulids,* communal and traditional celebrations that often mark the birth of local sheiks, imams, and sometimes Coptic saints, belly dancers known as *ghawazee* often performed, cheered by the whole community. However, in time belly dancing evolved, and though the artistic side was retained, commercial exploitation stepped in, and it became a prime feature of cabarets and nightclubs. That's when dancers replaced their tight *gallebeya* (a full body garment) with the bra-and-hip-belt costume you typically see today. Since then, the sexual stereotyping of belly dancing emerged, and its acceptance into mass sectors of conservative Egyptian society is less frequent. State-owned television no longer airs belly dancing shows, and official celebrations will often skip on the traditional art. A couple of international belly dancing festivals have recently returned to Egypt, but no proper media attention is given. The shift has caused an influx of foreigners to undertake belly dancing as a career, performing in cabarets and five-star hotels. Cabarets dot Haram Street and are often frequented by nouveau riche Egyptians and well-off Arabs from the Gulf States. These places have a very bad reputation for swindling foreign customers by overcharging. However, many five-star hotels offer belly dancing shows, so check with your receptionist.

Pub 28 When the heat and dust of Cairo begin to get the best of you, Pub 28's cool, dark interior may be just what you need. Though conveniently located in the center of town, this well-established expat watering hole takes you out of the city with its funky faux-candle light fixtures, wood-paneled walls, heavy wood tables, and high chairs. It serves a mix of Western and Egyptian dishes and stocks both local and imported beers and wines. The only downside is its small size. Get here early or reserve ahead, particularly on Thursday and Friday nights, when it can be packed to capacity and too noisy for easy conversation by 8pm. 28 Shagaret el Durr St., Zamalek. ✆ **02/37359200.**

Sangria Built right on the waterline, Sangria enjoys some of the best Nile views in town. The interior is chic with an authentic touch, while outside it is a bit more rustic with a touch of artistry. Regardless of which one you go for, have a drink first at Sangria's open bar, literally a stone's throw from the water's edge. If you have a bunch of friends and are looking for a nice place where you can grab a bite, have a couple of drinks, and enjoy a chat with a lovely view, Sangria is a perfect choice. Corniche El Nil, across from the Conrad Hotel. ✆ **02/25796511.**

Tamarai ★★ Businessmen, corporate hotshots, community celebrities, and Cairo's divas are Tamarai regulars. Stunning interior design by Egypt's rising talent Shahira Fahmy sets the mood with the use of wall partitions, ultra-modern furnishings, and wooden decor. If you are here for the food, then you should try Black Magic (black

Coffee Culture

What the bar or pub is to Western culture, the *ahwa,* or coffee shop (*ahwa* means "coffee" in Egyptian Arabic), is to Cairo. The *ahwa* is a place to relax at the end of the day or late into the night, meet friends, and watch passing strangers. The staples of the *ahwa* are *shisha,* coffee, and tea. *Ahwas* are a ubiquitous presence in Cairo, from the neighborhood dive stuffed into the cranny of an old building to the well-cushioned opulence of a five-star hotel. There are *ahwas* literally everywhere in Cairo, and I highly recommend taking a moment to stop randomly and grab a cup of coffee or a glass of tea. Watch TV, read the newspaper, or find yourself in conversation with whoever in the place speaks a little English. This is the real Cairo.

One of my favorite places is right next door to the popular Downtown Townhouse Art Gallery. This *ahwa* actually features an old car under a tarp that's used to store *shisha* tobacco. Attracting the after-exhibit crowd from the gallery, as well as a full roster of neighborhood locals, this place features a comfortable mix of classes and nationalities. Possibly the most famous *ahwa,* however, is **El Fishawy** in Khan Al Khalili. It's cramped, busy, and incredibly atmospheric, with high ceilings and enormous mirrors on the walls in which you can watch the whole bustling scene of the busy souk from several angles at once. The tea comes in ancient enamel pots, and you'll have a stream of vendors trying to sell you everything from Chinese Rolexes to incense. At night it's particularly attractive, as the alleys between the shuttered stores echo with the words and laughter of the off-work storekeepers.

At the turn of the millennium things took a different turn, and more trendy cafes started competing with the traditional *ahwas.* Some international names, such as Costa Coffee and Starbucks, have a presence; however, the scene is supremely dominated by two rivaling chains, Beano's and Cilantro. They both have the same modern look and provide high-quality coffee drinks with professional service. Menus vary slightly, offering the same staple of American coffee, espresso, latte, and different flavored cappuccinos, mochas, and teas. Prices for a regular-size coffee average LE10 to LE20. Branches are scattered all over the country with some of Cairo's districts hosting more than one branch of the same chain. Opening hours are usually 7am to midnight, though some are open around the clock. Less widespread are a couple of very interesting cafes: **Arabica Café** (20 El Marashly St., Zamalek; ✆ **02/27357982;** sandwiches LE20–LE35; no credit cards; daily 10am–2am) and **Il Pennello Ceramic Café** (2 Omar Ibn Al-Khattab St., Abu Bakr Al-Seddiq Sq., Heliopolis; ✆ **02/2417603;** coffee, snacks, and pottery to paint LE50–LE100; no credit cards; daily 9am–1am). Differentiating themselves from the rest of the scene, the former provides you with table-size paper sheets and a set of crayons, giving your drawing skills a chance to blossom, while the latter provides different sets of ceramic objects for you to paint. Both cafes can be quite entertaining for the young ones.

tagliatelle with shrimp), but if you are here for the drinks, then you are obliged to taste Tamarai's signature cocktail, Jack on Fire (Jack Daniels with a dash of mint syrup and a couple of leaves). This glitzy lounge is pricey; expect a hefty bill. 2005C Corniche El Nil (Nile City Towers), next to Fairmont Nile City. ✆ **02/24619910.** www.tamarai-egypt.com.

9 THE GAY & LESBIAN SCENE

So much has been said about homosexuality in Egypt; some things are true, and others are downright lies. Indeed, the country as a whole is not as gay friendly as, say, the U.S., but gays are not hunted down in city streets, either. It is one of Egypt's biggest taboos and the last subject you would want to open for discussion with locals, especially if they are not open minded.

Cross-gender sexual solicitation is illegal, while same-sex affairs are both illegal and culturally rejected. Gay men are subject to a significant level of officially sanctioned police harassment, detention, and, at times, abuse, while everybody turns a blind eye when it comes to lesbians. Still this doesn't mean same-sex female relations are dealt with overtly; one needs to be discreet about it. Keeping the skeleton in the closet is how Egypt, as a government and a community, continues to deal with homosexuality. The government, every now and then, cracks down on the local gay scene, while a family with a gay or a lesbian member will address it as a scandalous problem, discussed only in closed circles. Local gays and lesbians are pushed to a virtual ghettolike life and a clandestine underground scene extremely difficult to break into. Foreign homosexuals, whether gays or lesbians, are skeptically tolerated, pending that they are here for recreational purposes and don't display affection in public. Still, you will most likely be subjected to harassment in budget hotels and restaurants, so head for higher end places, where they are more concerned with money coming in than to pay any mind to who is sharing your room. Within the capital, civilian pickup places frequently change; Cairo Marriott's Harris Pub has a well established reputation for being gay friendly.

10 DAY TRIPS FROM CAIRO

THE PHARAONIC TRILOGY (DAHSHUR, MEMPHIS & SAQQARA)

The three Ancient Egyptian sites of Dahshur, Memphis, and Saqqara make a perfect day trip out of Cairo. From the Bent Pyramid and Ancient Egypt's very first capital to the Ramses Colossus, the ancient ruins of Saqqara, and the exquisite Imhotep Museum, this is one mega day trip you don't want to miss.

The best way to get to these sites is to hire a car (p. 51), preferably with a driver. If you rent one without, you will need to watch out for the Mariutiya Road, off which all three sites are located. It is not in good condition, with a waterway in the middle, and no safety precautions (that is, no fence between the road and the waterway). From the Ring Road, take the exit reading SAQQARA PYRAMIDS, which will lead you to Mariutiya Road. As you drive southward (in the opposite direction of Giza), the first site is Saqqara, followed by Memphis, and finally Dahshur. The road is poorly signed, particularly when it comes to Memphis. Pay extra attention, as the couple of signs that you do encounter actually read MEIT RAHINA MONUMENTS, which is the name of the village adjacent to the museum.

All three sites are frequently visited and served by well-organized bus tours that are available through the front desks of most tourist-class hotels in the city. If you don't fancy your options there, contact the listed travel agents (p. 51).

Dahshur ★★ If it's possible to have favorite pyramids, then these are mine. Defining exactly why is a little difficult. Compared to the pyramids at Giza, this is not a big tourist site; you are not going to get mobbed by touts as you get out of the car. This is probably a big part of it. The two pyramids here, both of which were built for Sneferu (2613–2598 B.C.), sit a little back from the edge of the valley, and you really get a feel for the desert. The air is clean, hot, and dusty, and the sky goes west forever.

These pyramids came after the relatively crude step, or *mastaba,* pyramid at Saqqara, and before the fully developed Great Pyramid of Giza, which might explain the odd aspect of the **Bent Pyramid:** about halfway up its 105m height (344 ft.), the sides take on a dramatically new angle. The theory is that the builders started at one angle (about 55 degrees) but realized midway that it just wasn't going to work, and made a dramatic alteration (to about 43 degrees). When it came to the **North Pyramid,** the builders used the more conservative 43-degree angle of attack, and made it all the way to the peak without having to make a change. A steep 30m (98-ft.) climb gets you to the entrance of a low-ceilinged 70m (230-ft.) passage that slopes steeply back down into the North Pyramid (if you've got a bad back or suffer from claustrophobia, skip going inside the pyramid). The high-ceilinged chambers in the depths of the structure are worth the scramble, however.

Originally Dahshur hosted 11 pyramids, two belonging to the 4th Dynasty and nine to the 12th Dynasty. In addition to the Bent and the North (also known as Red) Pyramid you might want to peek at the Pyramid of Amenemhet III, dubbed the **Black Pyramid.** Though its outer limestone casting has long collapsed, the mud-brick structure is still hanging on. In 1993, some funerary items were discovered.

Admission LE35. Daily 8am–4pm.

Memphis Constructed on the banks of the river around 3100 B.C., Memphis was one of the world's greatest capitals, where Pharaohs lived in splendid palaces, walked evergreen gardens, and paid homage to pagan deities in grandiose temples. Four thousand years later, the Arab conquest marked Memphis's abandonment, and in time it became a quarry for ready-cut blocks often used as building material (see Islamic Cairo's Bab el Nasr for some visually noticeable engravings). Today, nothing remains but some foundation ruins and a small museum. The open-air Memphis Museum was actually built around an incredibly big 13m (43-ft.) giant limestone statue of Ramses II, known as Ramses Colossus. The rather small collection also includes two smaller statues glorifying the same king and an alabaster Sphinx.

Admission LE35. Daily 8am–4pm.

Saqqara ★★ Due to its proximity to the capital Memphis, Saqqara grew to be an important Ancient Egyptian necropolis featuring Egypt's oldest pyramid—the **Step Pyramid.** More than 4 millenniums ago, King Zoser commissioned his vizier and polymath Imhotep to build a pyramid that would be the king's final resting place. Zoser's Step Pyramid is part of a larger complex that symbolically reenacts the Hed-Sed Festival. The festival, marking the renewal of the king's reign after ruling for 30 years, took place in

Memphis. The entrance corridor opens to a rectangular open court with two letter *B* shaped stones. Representing the four corners of Egypt, the king used to circulate both stones, as part of the recrowning festival, while holding a papyrus. The papyrus represented the gods' will and the circulation around the stones represented a manifestation of the king taking possession of his godly inheritance—Egypt. From the open court an exit leads to the Hed-Sed Court, where shrines dedicated to main Ancient Egyptian deities mark the sidewalk leading to a stone podium. After the king was done with his offerings to the gods, he would be recrowned with both Upper and Lower Egypt's crowns. The Hed-Sed Court exits to an open space where you can contemplate the 60m (197-ft.) high Step Pyramid with its rather enigmatic design; some believe it was out of religious reasons, while some ancient texts mention a stairway to heaven. Continuing farther, there are remnants of two buildings known as the Palace of the North and the Palace of the South. Some graffiti left by Ancient Egyptian tourists who visited this place during the New Kingdom is still visible; look for the one by King Ahmose singing the praise of Zoser. The walk will lead you to an enclosed room, known as the *serdab,* where a seated statue of Zoser stands (the one you see here is a replica, while the original one can be seen in the Egyptian Museum, p. 104). Finally you come to the badly ruined mortuary temple and a corridor leading to Zoser's burial chamber underneath the pyramid. Grave robbers have done a pretty good job, stripping the chamber of everything, even the king's mummy.

In addition to the Step Pyramid, there are two other pyramids you might want to visit. The **Pyramid of Unas,** which dates back to the 5th Dynasty and is attributed with the first appearance of the Pyramid Text carved on its chambers' walls. The Pyramid Text is a religious spell that ensures the king's resurrection and his safe journey through the afterlife, and which later evolved and became the famous papyrus known as the *Book of the Dead.* Unas was succeeded by Teti, who followed his predecessor's footsteps and built the **Pyramid of Teti,** which is just 12m (39 ft.) higher than Unas's. Teti's vizier and son-in-law, Mereruka, is buried next door in the **Mastaba of Mereruka.** Ancient Egyptian kings were buried in pyramids, while noblemen and prominent figures were buried in *mastabas,* a rectangular flat-roofed structure made of mud brick or stone. The Mastaba of Mereruka is among the best examples of this Ancient Egyptian tomb, not only for its impressive size but for its pillared room with Mereruka's statue striding off the niche in which the statue is carved; impressive and indeed dramatic.

The complex also includes the bulls' catacombs known as **Serapeum,** where the Apis bulls were interred. These bulls were considered to be the living manifestation of the god Ptah (who you will also see in wall carvings as a man wearing a tight-fitting cap and grasping an ankh) and were mummified and buried with all due ceremony.

In tribute to Imhotep's pioneering thoughts and achievements, the Supreme Council of Antiquities (SCA) inaugurated, in 2006, the **Imhotep Museum** dedicated to the brilliant polymath in particular and the Saqqara monuments in general. The museum's collection, though limited, is well documented and displayed, with the bronze statuette of Imhotep holding a papyrus roll on his lap being the collection's star. Also on display are monuments retrieved during excavation of the Saqqara site, among which is the well-preserved mummy of King Merenre (6th Dynasty), which was discovered in 1880 by German archaeologists Heinrich and Emile Brugsch. No photography is allowed inside the museum.

The historical importance of Saqqara extends beyond Ancient Egypt and into the Coptic era with the **Monastery of St. Jeremiah,** which was built in 460 but later abandoned

The Camel Market

The Birqash camel market, about an hour's drive from town, is best visited early on Friday morning (try to get there before 9am), which is when the business of buying and selling camels takes place. There is a constant stream of photo opportunities, with men yelling and waving their long *shooma* walking sticks and camels bellowing and jostling for space. Most of the animals here have been herded all the way from Sudan. Though there is less action during the week, a stroll amongst the pens looking at the animals, most bearing elaborate brands identifying their owners, and chatting with dealers is also an atmospheric and interesting experience. Plan on taking half a day to venture out and back, and be sure to take the time to enjoy the view of the countryside along the way. The taxi ride there should cost about LE130 to LE150. There is an LE5 ticket to the market.

in 960. While carvings and wall paintings are now on display in the Coptic Museum (p. 124), what remains of the original Monastery of St. Jeremiah in Saqqara is structural ruins in a very bad state.

English-language guides are available, offering a 1-hour tour of the site at the cost of LE30 per person and a 30-minute tour of the Imhotep Museum for LE10.

Admission LE60 (includes Imhotep Museum); car park LE2. Daily 8am–4pm.

Wadi El Natrun This little depression on the edge of the Nile Delta, about 100km (62 miles) from the city, is, in many ways, the historical seat of Coptic Christianity. There are four thriving monasteries dating from before the Muslim conquest here, so you can get a real taste of Coptic history and its much-appreciated art. The **Monastery of the Romans** (Deir Al Baramus) is the quartet's oldest and plays host to the Church of Virgin Mary, renowned for its exquisite, partially preserved, 13th-century monastic wall paintings. St. Bishoy founded two of Wadi El Natrun's four monasteries: **St. Bishoy Monastery** (Deir Al Anba Bishoy) and the **Monastery of the Syrians** (Deir Al Surian). The former is where his holy body is supposedly preserved, while the latter represents a great opportunity to behold wall paintings and frescoes depicting several biblical scenes. The **Monastery of St. Macarius** (Deir Abu Makar) is the most secluded of the four and the most rewarding to visit. It contains icons portraying saints, among which is one depicting St. Macarius carrying a cross. In addition, there are also a number of relics that belong to different monks and saints.

Wadi El Natrun's importance predates Christianity as it was a source site for natron, a special mineral salt used by Ancient Egyptians as a drying agent during the mummification process. The mineral salt takes the form of deposits that can still be seen today around a water pond locally known by the name El Hamra. Natron adds a reddish color to the pond's water during winter, while summer's strong sun dries the water, leaving swaths of pink mineral salt residue.

Wadi El Natrun is about a 1-hour drive on the Cairo–Alex Desert Road and is best visited with a car. Avoid scheduling your visit during Lent as the monasteries might be closed.

Where to Stay

El Hamra Ecolodge More of a guesthouse than a real ecolodge, this makes for a lovely hideaway from bustling Cairo and an opportunity to relax in rural Egypt. The main building accommodates the restaurant and some rooms, while eight chalets are clustered around a small waterway; with their traditional furnishings and rustic ambience, one of these is where you should be spending the night. Food is very traditional and can be heavy by Western standards. El Hamra is one of those places where you turn off your BlackBerry and remove your laptop's battery before you check in. To get here, take the Cairo–Alex Desert Road to the Masters Rest House (approximately Km 100), make a U-turn (as if you are going back to Cairo), take the first right (signed WADI EL NATRUN), and then follow the signs reading EL HAMRA ECOLODGE.

Wadi El Natrun. ✆ **02/33053081.** 20 units. LE350 double. Rate on full-board basis including taxes and service charges. No credit cards. **Amenities:** Restaurant; pool. *In room:* Fridge, no phone.

FAYUM OASIS

This is the closest of the Western Desert oases and the best option if you don't have time to get out to Bahareya or Siwa. Avoid Fayum City as much as possible—it's dirty and crowded—and preferably stay outside of town at one of the two places listed below. I also recommend picking up a copy of Neil Hewison's *The Fayoum: History and Guide* (AUC Press, revised edition 2009) if you want more information than what is provided below. You can easily do Fayum in a day from Cairo, but a relaxed visit to the area that includes a shopping trip to Tunis and a visit to Wadi Rayan, as well as a bit of lounging, could warrant an overnight stay.

Note: Though there are daily buses connecting Fayum and Cairo, they will take you to Fayum City. Renting a car without a driver, to avoid having to sort out his accommodation, is the best option. From Cairo, Fayum is a little more than an hour drive.

What to See & Do

Pyramid of Hawara Built to the orders of Amenemhet III, to whose credit also goes the Black Pyramid of Dahshur, the Pyramid of Hawara followed the 12th Dynasty's typical construction standards of a mud-brick core and a fine limestone casing. Meeting the same fate as most of the same era pyramids, it eroded over time and today is just a vaguely pyramid-looking mountain. If you are not an Ancient Egyptian enthusiast, or time is not on your side, you can easily give it a miss.

Admission LE35. Daily 8am–4pm.

Pyramid of Lahun Also known as the Pyramid of Senusret II, this, in its heyday, was a complete complex with a queen's pyramid, *mastabas* for the nobles, an entrance, and chapels. However, the mud-brick building material rapidly degraded, and soon the whole site faded to black. In antiquity, tomb robbers stripped the Pyramid of Lahun of all its treasures, with the exception of one cache that miraculously survived. Known as the

Tips **Mouthwash**

If you make it to El Hamra during summer, grab a handful of salt, stir it in a glass of water, and enjoy a 100% natural mouthwash.

Treasure of Lahun, necklaces, bracelets, and rings were discovered from the tomb of Princess Sathathoriunet and are now on exhibit at the Egyptian Museum in Cairo.

Admission LE35. Daily 8am–4pm.

Pyramid of Meidum One of the Fayum pyramid trio, and the best-preserved of the three, this was originally commissioned by King Huni of the 3rd Dynasty to be built as a seven-step pyramid; however, an eighth step was later added. The Pyramid of Meidum was not completed until the reign of Huni's son Sneferu, when it was finished off as a proper pyramid after smoothing the sides. Enduring engineering mistakes, the pyramid, with its relatively acute angle, couldn't bear its own weight, and soon its outer case started to collapse. Some Egyptologists believe that this construction flaw alarmed Sneferu's engineers into changing Dahshur's Bent Pyramid midway through their work. When 15th-century historian Al Maqrizi visited the site, he described it as five-step pyramid. Four centuries later, and during Napoleon's brief occupation of Egypt, it was described as a three-step one, which is what you see today.

Admission LE35. Daily 8am–4pm.

Tunis Pottery The Fayum Oasis has a long tradition of creating pottery, and about 15 years ago, two Swiss potters, Evelyne Porret and Michel Pastore, built the Fayoum Pottery School in the small town of Tunis, above the western end of Lake Qarun, to promote local skills. The center has put Tunis on the map and has spawned an industry. The town's narrow, dusty streets are now alive with more than half a dozen studios, each selling items from plates to sculptures. You could easily spend an afternoon wandering from studio to studio. The two must-see locations are the **Fayoum Pottery School** (**✆ 084/6820405;** daily 9am–8pm) and the studio of **Ahmed Abu Zeid** (ask for directions at the school or anywhere in the village).

Wadi El Rayan ★★ Wadi El Rayan is a depression in the desert to the southeast of Fayum Oasis (*wadi* literally means "valley" in Arabic) that was made a protected area in 1989. In addition to a pair of drainage lakes that attracts a plethora of birds, Wadi El Rayan plays host to the UNESCO World Heritage Site of Wadi El Hitan. Though it is just a 30-minute drive from the Fayum Oasis, the lakes are surrounded on all sides by golden sand dunes and new growth that houses both resident and migratory birds; two bird-watching sites have been established on the southeastern side of the lake.

The protectorate covers around 1,800 sq. km (around 700 sq. miles) with two areas particularly worth visiting in Wadi El Rayan. The **waterfalls** aren't of the Niagara variety, but what makes them worth visiting is the desert setting; they're nestled into the thick reeds between the two lakes and face the beach of the lower. They're a great place for a swim, but there tends to be an audience of young local males. Still, it's a good place to stop for a picnic lunch before moving on.

Wadi El Hitan, or Valley of the Whales, is named for the ancient whale skeletons that were found on the surface of the desert. These spectacular, 40-million-year-old remains are reminders that the entire area was once covered by a giant inland sea. In an attempt to protect the fossils, Wadi El Hitan was declared a World Heritage Site in 2005. The Orientation Center is accessible by car along a rough, unpaved, 34km (21-mile) road. Be prepared to hike from there, however. There is a designated camping area close to the Orientation Center, but you need to be self-sufficient and bring your own food, water, tent, and sleeping bag.

✆ 084/6830535. Admission $3 per person; LE5 per car; LE10 per person for overnight camping. Daily 9am–sunset.

Waterwheels Overrated The water-driven waterwheels (*al sawaei* in Arabic) are still being used in the Fayum Oasis to lift irrigation water into the old canals. They are unique in Egypt (no other area provides the kind of fast-running streams needed to power them) and historically significant (they were introduced by Roman engineers, and the design has not been significantly altered since). Their setting, however, leaves a lot to be desired, and unless you find the wheels themselves to be interesting, you're going to be disappointed.

The most easily accessible and largest of the wheels still in operation are the four in the center of the city. There are seven more, however, on the canal named Bahr Senussi that runs north out of the city. You can follow the canal on foot or by car until the houses become less dense, and you'll come upon the wheels after 10 to 20 minutes (depending how often you get lost). They are big, black, and shiny, and their wood axles make a loud groaning noise as they turn. The setting, which is fairly pastoral, is also unfortunately squalid, and your enjoyment will depend largely on your tolerance for mud and being the center of attention among crowds of curious teenage boys.

Where to Stay

Helnan Auberge Fayoum Originally built in 1937 for King Farouk, the Auberge was run as a hotel by the Oberoi chain before it drifted into the 1980s and 1990s as an increasingly seedy and run-down independent. Recently reopened under the Helnan group, it hasn't exactly been restored to its former glory (Winston Churchill once stayed here), but it's certainly looking a lot better. It's located on the edge of the lake, flanked on either side by beaches, and the view is lovely. Rooms have little character, and while the dining room, with its wood-beamed ceiling, evokes a prewar hunting lodge feeling, you'll have no doubt that you're staying in a chain hotel.

Lake Qarun. ✆ **084/6981200** or -3. www.helnan.com. 70 units. $170 lake-view double; $150 garden-view double. Rates include buffet breakfast, taxes, and service charges. MC, V. **Amenities:** Restaurant, bar; concierge; pool; room service. *In room:* A/C, TV, Internet (extra charge), minibar.

Zad al Musafr Ecolodge This relaxed little place is built among the palm trees in the fields below the town of Tunis. It comes with eight rough-around-the-edges rooms, which are built around a grassy courtyard, while the most comfortable accommodations are the four cottage suites (essentially double rooms with their own bathrooms). These are charming and rustic, tucked into the jasmine of the garden, with reed ceilings and plaster walls. Bedding is good-quality cotton, and the bathrooms are sufficient. The pool is small but perfect for a dip in the warmth of the Fayum afternoon. They also have a number of well-fed and nicely behaved horses. Riding is probably the best way to see the area around Tunis and the lake. The restaurant is, apart from the Helnan, the only place to eat on this side of the Fayum. Grilled meat and chicken are the order of the day.

The lodge is within easy walking distance of the long sandy beach on the edge of Lake Qarun and Tunis. The journey to the latter is a short climb up a bath that runs next to a series of private gardens; you'll find yourself in the back of the village and ready to do a tour of the various potters selling their wares.

Tunis. ✆ **084/6820180** or 010/6395590. 20 units, some with shared bathrooms. LE75 double; LE130 cottage. Rates are on "bed only" basis and subject to 22% taxes and service charges. No credit cards. **Amenities:** Restaurant; pool. *In room:* No phone.

7

Alexandria & the North Coast

A lengthy coastal stretch marks Egypt's northern frontier. The Egyptian Mediterranean coast extends from the commercial city of Port Said, marking the northern end of the Suez Canal, all the way to the shabby border town of Salloum, marking the Egyptian western frontier. Compared to its neighboring Red Sea coast, the Egyptian Mediterranean coast offers a different experience, where sun-and-fun tourism is traded for a more history-oriented one.

The iconic city of Alexandria heads the league with its diverse and multicultural history. It offers a number of different historical attractions that range from the stunning mosaics of the Villa of the Birds and the beautifully crafted Tangara Collection to the eerie Catacombs of Kom El Shoqafa and the subtle-looking Qaitbey Fort. Alexandria is indeed the greatest historical magnet of the region, but certainly it is not the sole one; Rosetta and El Alamein sing history's lullaby but in different tunes. The former was a famous trading port during the Ottoman rule and still hosts some of the finest examples of the period's art and architecture, represented in its famous Ottoman Houses. On the other hand, the latter bore witness to one of World War II's most gruesome yet decisive military encounters—the Battle of El Alamein. The guns came to a halt a long time ago, and today just the solemn Commonwealth, Italian, and German memorials honor the casualties of war.

The Egyptian Mediterranean coast timidly puts on its bathing suit with Marsa Matruh as a promising new relax-by-the-sea destination. It is known today as a good stop for breaking a long haul to the stranded Siwa Oasis, and tourism developers are eyeing its Maldivian white powdered beaches and turquoise blue waters. Recognizing the potential, direct flights now connect the sleepy town of Marsa Matruh to a couple of European cities, raising the question of how long Matruh will remain a sleepy town.

1 ALEXANDRIA

Bearing the name of its founder, Alexander the Great, the country's second-largest city is unquestionably one of the highlights of any trip to Egypt. City planning took off after Alexander's conquest of Egypt in 332 B.C., and in no time Alexandria grew into a world-leading cosmopolitan city, attracting people from farther afield in Egypt as well as Greece and Italy. This multicultural diversity helped shape the identity of the place, evident by taking a walk in the Raml or downtown districts, where the city's Egyptian Art Deco is infused with Greek columns and Italian-inspired architecture. Continue walking to the National Museum of Alexandria where the latest technologies are used to exhibit the city's diverse heritage, from Ancient Egyptian artifacts recovered from the seabed and beautifully crafted Greco-Roman statues to religious Coptic icons and Islamic *mashrabeyas.*

The Great Lighthouse

From the sea, the Egyptian coastline looks like flat land, devoid of hills that could be used as landmarks. One can imagine that before the age of coastal towns and GPS it must have presented navigational challenges. That is, until Ptolemy II built a massive tower on a small island at the entrance to the Alexandria harbor.

One of the fabled Seven Wonders of the World, the Lighthouse of Alexandria was finished around 265 B.C., having been under construction for 15 years. Towering 152m (500 ft.), it was constructed in three sections starting with a square base and ending in a conical peak, which was topped off with a massive statue of Poseidon. Though it didn't acquire its light for another 3 centuries, it would have been visible for miles out to sea, offering pilots a point of reference as they made their way up and down the coast and into the harbor.

Skeptics question the lighthouse's place on the Wonders of the World list (which was compiled in Alexandria), but the tower was undoubtedly ahead of its time. It's still not clear, though, how the light was made to shine (there's a theory that there were oil lamps whose light was shone out to sea by burnished metal reflectors), and there are even indications that it may have been equipped with some kind of telescope.

The lighthouse stood for more than 1,500 years, collapsing after it was heavily damaged by an earthquake in 1303. The island on which it stood is now connected to the shore by a breakwater and hosts the Qaitbey Fort.

Experiencing Alexandria comes with a set of Alexandria only specialties that you won't find anywhere else in Egypt. Start your day with a cup of coffee at the vintage **Brazilian Coffee Store** followed by a local *fuul* and *tameya* breakfast at the always buzzing **Mohamed Ahmed.** The **Bibliotheca Alexandrina**'s avant-garde building is where you should start your sightseeing tour. Alexandria misses on good sunbathing spots; however, its lengthy **Corniche** makes for a great sunset stroll. The **Bahri District** is where Egyptian cuisine is redefined with freshly caught and grilled seafood delicacies; end with a delicious sweet couscous at **El Sheikh Wafik.**

ESSENTIALS

Orientation

Alexandria is a long, narrow city spread out over a 25km (15-mile) strip of coastline, with no part of it more than 5km (3 miles) from the sea. At the western end of the city lies the harbor, where the famous lighthouse once stood; at the eastern end are the Montazah Gardens, once a royal hunting ground and now the site of the Salamlek hotels. The two ends are linked by an enormous road that runs where you would expect the beach to be and cuts the city off from the sea. Known as the Corniche, it is a lovely promenade for a sunset stroll, but other than that there is little to draw you over—the beaches are narrow, rocky, and, in summer, overcrowded.

The most interesting area of the city, which contains almost all the sites worth visiting, is within a 2km (1¼-mile) radius encompassing downtown, Raml, and Bahri. Downtown hosts Misr Train Station (the city's main train station) as well as the historical site of Kom El Dikka. The area is connected by the two busy Safiya Zaghloul and Nabi Daniel streets,

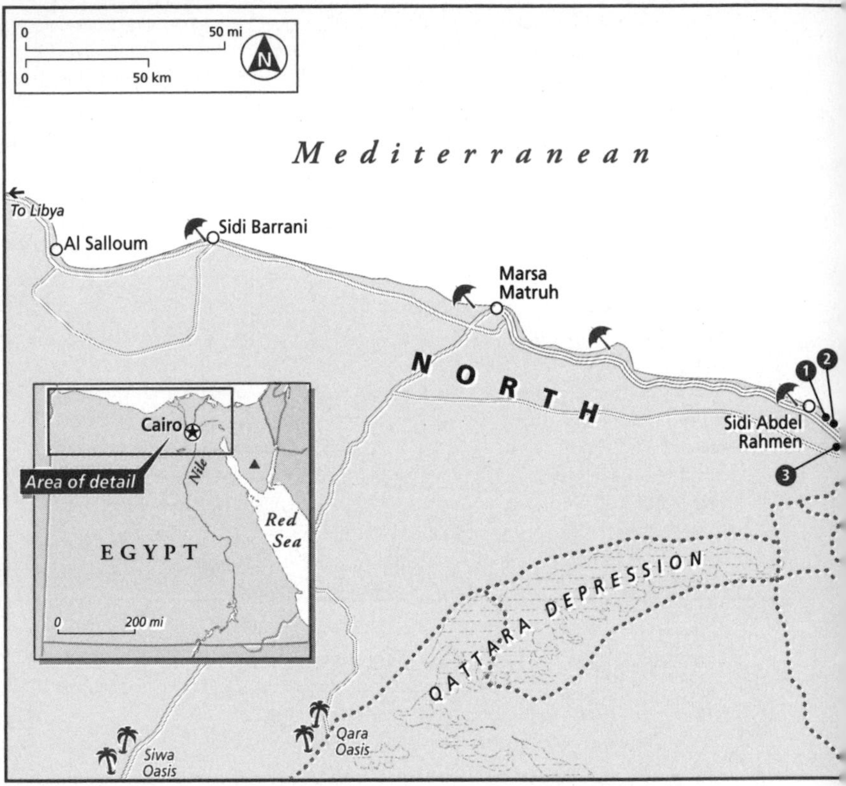

which lead to the more architecturally rich Raml District. Raml (or more properly Mahatet Al Raml, which means "Raml Station" and refers to the station that you might be able to see just over to the left side of the square) represents the cultural amalgamation of Alexandria. It overlooks the Mediterranean and hosts a cluster of adjacent hotels offering some of the best sea views in town. A short stroll eastward will take you to the Bibliotheca Alexandrina, while walking the Corniche westward will eventually lead you to the Qaitbey–Bahri junction. From there, you can go right and head to Qaitbey Fort or left to Bahri District. The former is where Alexandria's famous lighthouse once stood, while the latter offers some of the city's best-kept culinary secrets.

Getting There

BY TRAIN There are three types of trains the run between Cairo (Ramses Train Station) and Alexandria on an hourly basis between 4:45am and 10:30pm. They are named Turbini ("turbine"), Asbani ("Spanish"), and Faransawi ("French"). The first two cut the distance nonstop to about 2½ hours and cost LE50 for first class and LE35 for second. There is not much difference between the two except the latter is marginally more comfortable. As for the Faransawi train, tickets cost LE35 and LE19, respectively. With three

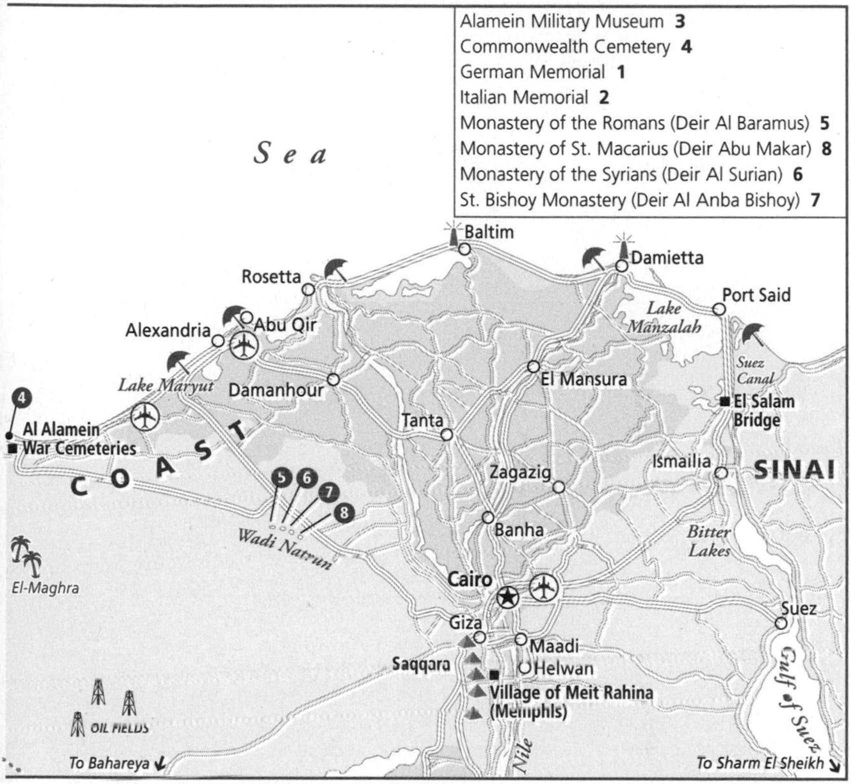

stops, it takes 3½ hours to make it to Alexandria. At the price, there's no point in riding second class, where the seats are narrower and the air-conditioning not so reliable. Your ticket has a car and seat number on it, and if you feel like having someone carry your bags to your seat, an LE3 to LE5 tip should adequately cover this convenience. There is a food and beverage cart on the train, but I wouldn't recommend having dinner aboard.

BY PLANE EgyptAir's internal flights go both to the old, convenient Al Nozha Airport and the newer Borg Al Arab Airport. Prices from Cairo are the same (around LE300) round-trip, but while Al Nozha is a short taxi ride into town, Borg Al Arab is about 30 minutes to an hour away via shuttle or taxi. The downside of Nozha is that the facilities are older and the runway is very short, resulting in some quite abrupt landings.

BY BUS Hourly buses from Cairo to Alexandria leave between 5:30am and 1am from **Turgoman Bus Station** (✆ **02/27735668** or -9), **Almaza Bus Station** (✆ **02/22909017**), or directly from the airport (p. 49). Once out of Cairo it is a 2-hour ride; tickets are LE40 on average. Air-conditioning is often turned to 64°F (18°C), so bring along a sweater. In Alexandria, the bus station has been moved to the Mehram Bey District, which is near

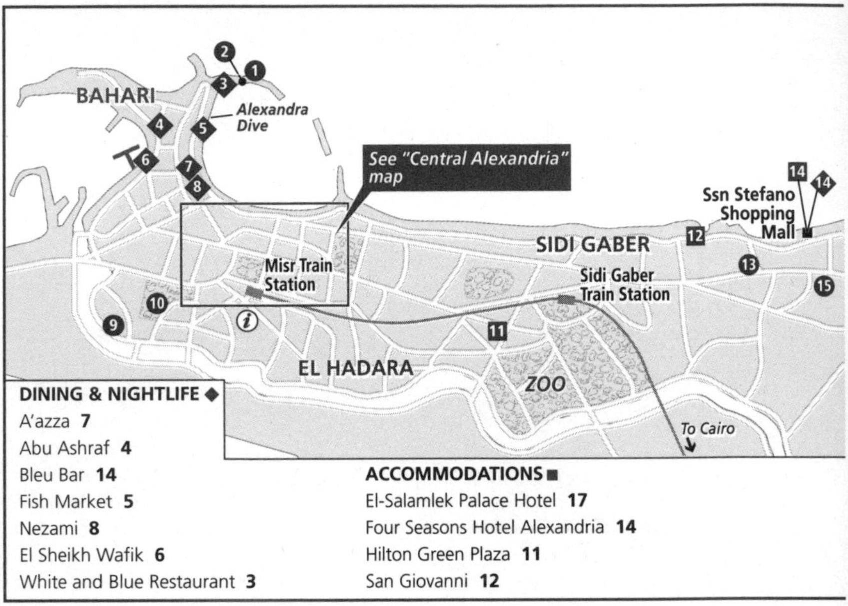

the beginning of the Cairo–Alexandria Desert Road. Expect to pay LE50 for a taxi ride into town (about 30 min.).

BY CAR The 220km (137 miles) Cairo–Alexandria Desert Road (LE4 one-way toll fee) is the main highway that connects the two cities. At the time of researching this edition, the dual-carriage highway was undertaking major expansion work, replacing U-turns with flyovers and adding an extra two lanes each way. Arriving into Alexandria is straightforward, as the Cairo–Alexandria Desert Road feeds directly into the city's main arteries. Head to Misr Train Station or, better, to Saad Zaghloul Square, and ask at the tourist information office for a map. A number of excellent maps can also be purchased at bookstores around the same square.

Getting Around

BY TAXI Other than the color—Alexandria taxis are black and yellow instead of black and white—taxis work the same way here as the old taxis in Cairo, though drivers here tend to be more short-tempered. Set the price before stepping in and negotiate till your last breath. As a general guideline, LE5 to LE10 is good for a short distance, LE15 to LE25 for a 10-minute ride, and no less than LE50 if you are planning to go from one end of the city to the other.

BY TRAM Alexandria has some beautiful old trams rattling up and down its streets. Unfortunately the whole system is extremely run down, slow, and, during rush hours, very crowded. If you're a fan of such things and understand their romance, try a mid-morning trip to Pompey's Pillar or to the east of Raml Station; otherwise you're better off in a taxi.

ATTRACTIONS ●	
Catacombs of Kom El Shoqafa **9**	Montaza Palace Gardens **16**
Mahmoud Said Museum **15**	Pompey's Pillar **10**
Marine Life Museum **2**	Qaitbey Fort **1**
	Royal Jewelry Museum **13**

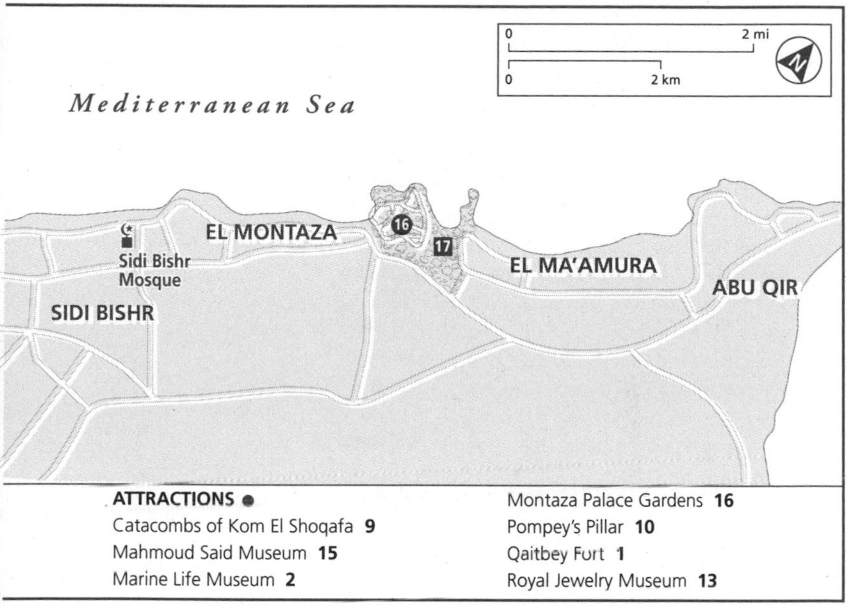

The main hub for tourist purposes is at Raml Station, on the edge of Saad Zaghloul Square. The most useful line is no. 2, which runs east to west. Tickets are LE0.25 and are purchased onboard from the conductor. During busy periods, the front car is reserved for women.

ON FOOT　As long as it's not raining, Alexandria is a fine city for walking. In fact, your feet are probably the best way to navigate the back streets and alleyways around Raml, downtown, or Bahri. I wouldn't recommend trying to make much distance up and down the Corniche, however—the level of traffic and (in the summer) hassle will quickly overwhelm your sense of fun.

BY CAR　Unless you are planning to use the car for day trips out of the city, there is no need to rent one, especially in summer when the city streets are swollen with more than two million vacationing Cairenes, the majority of whom come with their private cars. Renting a small car with a 100km (60 miles) allowance comes with an average price tag

Visa Extension

Just as in Cairo (p. 92), here you take one passport photo along with your passport (original and copy) to the visa extension office, 28 Tala'at Harb St., Max District (between downtown and Bahri), which is open 8am to 1pm. It's a same-day service (if you show up early) that costs LE68 for a 6-month extension.

Dive Right In

When people think of diving in Egypt, they think of the Red Sea, but that might be about to change. The seabed around Alexandria is littered with historical artifacts, monuments, and ruins from not only the Greco-Roman period but the late-18th-century Franco-British conflict over control of Egypt and World War II. Most sites along the coast are shallow, with much to see in less than 10m (33 ft.) of water. However, visibility can be a challenge, so deciding when and where to dive remains much in the hands of the weather report.

Jars, off the Montazah district of Alexandria, offers dozens of jars—Greco-Roman amphorae, to be precise—as well as other artifacts from this extremely busy port site, including anchors and other debris from ships and the remains of some small work boats that were used around the harbor. Depth is around 7 to 10m (23–33 ft.), and the site is an easy swim from the shore.

The remains of the **Pharos lighthouse** are a boat dive but close to the harbor. A big debris field is all that remains now of one of the Seven Wonders of the World—columns, some broken statuary, and a few pieces of hieroglyph-bearing stones lying about on the bottom of the Mediterranean.

The remains of **Napoleon Bonaparte's fleet,** sunk by ships under Rear-Admiral Horatio Nelson in the 1798 Battle of the Nile, lie in about 10 to 14m (33–46 ft.) of water a few kilometers off Aboukir, a small town to the east of Alexandria. Three boats are known, and one, the French flagship *L'Orient,* is intact enough to be an interesting dive.

There is also at least one reasonably intact World War II airplane and a landing craft off Alexandria, though the history, and even nationality, of these remain an open question.

The recently discovered Greco-Roman cities of **Herakleion, Menouthis,** and **Canopus** also lie submerged off Aboukir. Not only are amphorae, millstones, old wells, and other urban artifacts to be found, but around the site of Herakleion lie intact walls, complete temples, and massive statuary.

The shabby looking **Alexandra Dive** (✆ **03/4832045;** www.alexandra-dive.com) seems to be the only dive center in town.

of LE200 per day. **Avis,** in the Hotel Sofitel Cecil Alexandria lobby, Saad Zaghloul Square (✆ **03/4857400**), is a recommended option.

Tourist Information

Alexandria is blessed with one of the most efficient and helpful tourist information offices in Egypt, tucked away at the edge of **Saad Zaghloul Square** in Raml (✆ **03/4851556;** daily 9am–5pm). It may not look too promising, but the ladies know everything they should about the city. Stop at the office in **Al Nozha Airport,** to the left as you are about to exit the main doors (✆ **03/4202021;** daily 9am–5pm), before you head downtown, and anything they can't answer, the main office in Raml probably can. In addition, there's an office at the far end of **Misr Train Station** (✆ **03/4925985;** daily 9am–5pm).

The small bookstore in the **Hotel Sofitel Cecil lobby,** Saad Zaghloul Square (✆ **03/4877173**), has a small but good selection of books about Alexandria as well as some maps. **Al Ahram Bookshop,** 10 Horreya St., Raml (✆ **03/4848563**), has a small collection of English-language books, including some guidebooks and maps; the staff speak no perceptible English, however. **Maarouf Bookshop** is one of Alexandria's very first bookstores and has recently opened a new branch in the **San Stefano Shopping Mall** (✆ **03/4690024;** www.maaroufbookshop.com) dedicated to English-language books; it has a good stock of Egypt-oriented travel titles.

Staying connected in Alexandria is pretty straightforward. You can either go online while lounging in your hotel's lobby (most upmarket hotels provide Internet service for an extra charge), or you can simply go to any of the **Internet** cafes scattered all over the city, especially in Raml District. Expect to pay LE3 an hour.

WHAT TO SEE & DO

Bibliotheca Alexandrina This is a reincarnation of the renowned ancient Ptolemaic Library of Alexandria, which is said to have been the biggest and most comprehensive library of its time. In its heyday, the original library was said to house more than 700,000 scrolls, a figure that, by today's standards, puts it on par with world-leading libraries. The fire during Julius Caesar's conquest of Egypt was the first of a series of disasters that ravaged the Library of Alexandria, bringing it to its demise by the end of the 7th century. In 1974, the idea of resurrecting the ancient library sparked, and in 2002 the Library of Alexandria was finally reborn as the Bibliotheca Alexandrina.

Located on a curve in the main seaside road a couple of kilometers from Saad Zaghloul Square, the sundial-like, tilted roofed, glass-paneled spectacular structure is the work of Norwegian firm Snøhetta. The front slopes gently into a wide pool of water, with obvious reference to the coastline of Egypt. From the street outside, the water is at eye level, while a flying pier structure juts out from the second floor.

Your tour of Bibliotheca Alexandrina begins with the **library** and its 11 cascading levels. It is a commodious piece of art that can accommodate up to 2,000 readers and is stacked with a wide variety of books donated from all over the world. However, censorship is in full swing here, and some subjects in particular are ignored.

The basement hosts the **Antiquities Museum,** which features just fewer than 1,100 artifacts that were found during the excavation of the original library's site as well as other parts of the city. The museum's sundry collection features, among other artifacts, Mamluk glass, Coptic icons, and Ptolemaic gods' statues; the floor mosaic of the sitting dog is

Hymn to the Pagan Martyr

As a notable female mathematician whose lectures in philosophy and astronomy were attended by native Alexandrians, foreigners, and pagans, as well as devoted Christians, Hypatia of Alexandria was a real phenomenon of pagan Egypt, a remarkable character who deserved the utmost respect of men. Her list of accomplished works includes *The Astronomical Canon,* believed to be a possible new edition of Ptolemy's *Handy Tables.* One tragic day during March 415, she was brutally butchered in the name of the cross. The exploitation and politicization of her murder in the Christian versus pagan struggle continued all the way to the early 18th century, with one group portraying her as a witch, while the other regarded her as a victim of religious fanaticism.

 my personal favorite. Following the ancient mosaic *opus vermiculum* technique, it demonstrates skillful artistry by paying attention to the fine details of the dog and how the light is reflecting on it.

Other attractions of the Bibliotheca Alexandrina include the **Manuscript Museum,** with its extensive collection of 1,200 manuscripts and 10,000 rare books, as well as the **Planetarium Center** and its mind-opening science shows and the kid-friendly **History of Science Museum.**

Chatby. ✆ **03/4839999.** www.bibalex.org. Admission LE45 (collective ticket); extra LE20 camera. Sat–Thurs 11am–7pm; Fri 3–7pm.

Catacombs of Kom El Shoqafa ★★★ Kids Perhaps I have a taste for the macabre, but this is one of my favorite Alexandria outings. Part *Lord of the Rings,* part *Indiana Jones,* the catacombs are about 35m (115 ft.) below ground level and reached by a spiral staircase that circles an open central shaft that was once used to lower dead bodies into the tombs below. The story goes that the whole complex was discovered in 1900 when a donkey, working the land above, fell in.

At the bottom of the stairs, you'll find yourself in a funerary complex, with rooms and passages leading off in all directions. It was more formally laid out when it was built in the 2nd century A.D., and many of the interconnecting passages that you see now are the work of grave robbers.

The burial tomb chamber is obvious once you're at the bottom of the stairs; it's through the doorway that's flanked by Anubis and Agathodaemon. Stop for a moment before going in to consider the odd mix of Egyptian, Roman, and Greek symbolism here—it's an excellent illustration of the syncretism of Ptolemaic culture. Anubis is the Egyptian god most closely associated with tombs, and he features prominently on royal tombs in Upper Egypt, where he protected the mummified remains of the occupants. But here, instead of the traditional collar around his neck, Anubis wears the uniform of a Roman legionary. The snake-tailed Agathodaemon, meanwhile, is an expat Greek god associated with good food and plenty, which may or may not be a reference to funeral rites that included feasting in the tombs. The chamber is modeled on a temple, with an antechamber and an inner sanctum. The rest of the catacombs, though less elaborate, are well worth a visit. The **triclinium** is a large room with the benches close to the bottom of the stairs and was the venue where friends and family of the deceased gathered periodically to feast and pay their respects.

The Underwater Museum

It is arguably true; Alexandria has more underwater monuments than inland ones. First-cut excavations of the Bay of Alexandria back in the 1990s revealed thousands of archaeological artifacts that include giant sphinxes, different period statues, and Roman shipwrecks. Some monuments have been lifted and are today on exhibit in Kom El Dikka and the National Museum of Alexandria, or have formed part of a traveling exhibition. More recently, in December 2009, a huge 9-ton granite block thought to be part of an Isis-dedicated temple was raised from the sea. Will all Alexandria's sunken treasures be rescued, or will some be left to decay on the seabed? To answer this question, a UNESCO–endorsed plan is being devised for a one-of-a-kind underwater museum.

The amount of the water in the lower tombs goes up and down, and there are always limits to how far you can explore. Much of what you can access was added well after the original construction, and access was further improved by later raiders in search of treasure. There is an accessible section behind the main tomb where a narrow hallway goes off into a series of little tombs and a wholly separate section known as the **Hall of Caracalla** off to the right (standing with your back to the main stairs).

Tawfikeya St. Admission LE35. Daily 9am–5pm.

The Graeco-Roman Museum ★★ This is a great museum, and with around 40,000 items in its collection, dating back as far as the 3rd century B.C., there's a fair bit to see here. Pieces you must see, for their local relevance, include the giant **Apis bull** from the temple that used to exist around Pompey's Pillar, and the **heads of Serapis.** This uniquely Alexandrian god, Serapis, came into being under Ptolemy Soter, a general under Alexander the Great and the man who took over as ruler when the famous leader died. Looking for a figure that the Egyptian population and their Greek rulers could both worship, Ptolemy anthropomorphized the Egyptian Apis as a bull-necked and heavily bearded Greek god.

The feast for those who like mosaics continues in the museum. There is a splendidly detailed **mosaic portrait of Berenice II,** wife of the 3rd-century ruler Ptolemy III. Also among the must-sees are the **3rd-century-B.C. lanterns** that show the famous lighthouse and a mummified crocodile, **Roman glass and coins,** and a wonderful **stone sarcophagus** that almost everyone thinks is a bathtub on first sight.

Note: At press time, The Graeco-Roman Museum was closed for renovation, with a tentative 2011 inauguration date.

El Mathaf Al Romani St. ✆ **03/4865820** or 03/4876434.

Kom El Dikka ★ Until archaeologists from the University of Warsaw began to excavate this site in the 1960s, it looked like what the name suggests—literally a "hill of rubble." Now, after the removal of more than 10,000 cubic m (340,000 cubic ft.) of earth and the construction of a new building to protect the mosaics, Kom El Dikka is an example of the kind of Roman ruins that likely underlie other sections of modern Alexandria. Though the site is not huge, it comprises a column-lined street leading to a 3rd-century-A.D. theater with 13 intact tiers of seats that accommodated an audience of 600; some archaeologists believe it was originally covered. The prime attraction of Kom El Dikka, often referred to as the Roman Amphitheatre, is not an impressive theater but rather a 2,000-year-old villa. Discovered in 1998, Villa of the Birds features an exceptionally beautiful 110-sq.-m (1,184-sq.-ft.) pavement with different birds' mosaics that include peacock, moorhen, pigeon, and quail depictions. No doubt, it deserves the extra ticket.

Note: For a detailed account of the excavation, *Villa of the Birds: The Excavation and Preservation of the Kom al-Dikka Mosaics* (AUC Press, 2007) can add an insightful, yet a bit technical, perspective.

Ismail Mehanna St. ✆ **03/3902904.** Admission LE20; Villa of the Birds extra LE15. Daily 9am–5pm.

Mahmoud Said Museum A scion of the Egyptian royal family, Mahmoud Said (1897–1964) spent most of his life working as a judge, not a painter. It was only when he retired at the age of 50 that he was able to devote himself to art. By then he had absorbed a good deal of cubism and social realism, and these both came through powerfully in his work. He painted scenes from a range of settings around Egypt, from whirling

A Message to the Caliph

After a relentless 14-month siege, during which no enforcements were sent from Constantinople, Alexandria surrendered on November 8, 641, to the conquering Arabs. The victorious leader Amr Ibn Al A'as sent a message to the Muslim caliph at the time, Omar Ibn Al Khattab. The message read that the Arab army had successfully conquered a city with "4,000 palaces, 4,000 baths, 12,000 dealers in fresh oil, 12,000 gardeners, 40,000 Jews who pay tribute and 400 theaters or places of amusement." If an amphitheater is found today, does that mean that, theoretically speaking, there are still 399 sites waiting to be discovered?

Sufi dancers to prostitutes, in warm, earthy tones. Said was far from a towering artistic talent—his importance lies much more in the way that he used European techniques in rendering Egyptian subjects—but the museum dedicated to him, which is in his columned Italianate villa, is still worth a visit.

6 Mohamed Said Pasha St. ✆ **03/5821688.** Admission LE10. Daily 10am–6pm.

Marine Life Museum I find this kitschy exhibition of stuffed fish and mocked-up sea mammals to be charming and pointless at the same time. One of the great things about it is, of course, that's it's so cheap that if you walk in and decide it's just plain stupid, you can walk away without a worry. Displays include an enormous stuffed sunfish, a fin whale skeleton, and a diorama of a fishing boat from the perspective of the fish.

Near Qaitbey Fort. ✆ **03/4807138.** Admission LE5. Daily 9am–11pm.

Montazah Palace Gardens (Overrated) These gardens used to be the grounds of a royal palace and a hunting lodge built in the late 19th century during the reign of Khedive Abbas Helmy II. Though they are attractively laid out and there's a beach that can be used for a small fee, I'm not sure that the gardens are worth a visit on their own merit. In the summer, they're crowded with local youth, and in the winter they're chilly and bleak. However, they are a lovely setting for the **El-Salamlek Palace Hotel** (p. 172), which is a great place for a quiet lunch or a couple of days' stay. There's an admission to the gardens, which is waived if you're staying at either the Helnan or the Salamlek hotels. Avoid the McDonald's in the garden unless you're truly desperate.

Montazah. Admission LE6. Daily 7am–11pm.

National Museum of Alexandria Occupying a restored Italian-style villa that dates back to 1926, the National Museum of Alexandria exhibits more than 1,800 historical artifacts that portrait the city's history. It is one of Egypt's very few museums that use state-of-the-art technologies when it comes to lighting, audio, and visuals, and it is made up of three stories and a basement. Your tour will kick off at the first floor, dedicated to Greco-Roman artifacts. The highlight of this floor is the Tangara Collection, named after an ancient city in Greece; the selection of small clay-made statuettes sheds some light on the day-to-day life in the Hellenistic empire 2 millenniums back. The same floor also exhibits some statues and artifacts recovered from the Mediterranean's seabed. The second floor features the Coptic and Islamic collection, which includes beautifully painted icons, tombstones adorned with golden crosses, as well as *mashrabeyas* and other Islamic themed artifacts. The ground floor is dedicated to Ancient Egypt, while the basement reconstructs a Valley of the Kings tomb, where a mummy with genuine funerary objects is featured.

Horreya St. Admission LE35. Daily 9am–4:30pm.

Pompey's Pillar Overrated For the casual visitor, this site doesn't offer as much as the spectacular Kom El Dikka or the Catacombs of Kom El Shoqafa. The red granite column for which the site is named is admittedly massive—9m (30 ft.) around and 30m (100 ft.) tall—but had nothing to do with the Roman general Pompey (who was killed here in 48 B.C.), and was erected in A.D. 293 for Diocletian. It used to stand in a large Serapis Temple and is now flanked by a pair of sphinxes from Heliopolis. There are some catacombs underneath that are worth the small fee that you'll need to pay the "guard" for a tour. The rest of the site is an unimpressive and rather bleak hillside.

It's an easy walk from here to the Catacombs of Kom El Shoqafa (p. 168), and it's best to do them as a pair. If you're in a hurry, you can actually get a decent view of the column from the road before continuing on to the catacombs. To walk there, just turn right on leaving, and follow the edge of the dig to the first big street. The entrance to the catacombs will be on your left after about 100m (328 ft.).

Amoud El Sawary St. ✆ **03/9601315.** Admission LE20. Daily 9am–4:30pm.

Qaitbey Fort From almost any place along the Corniche, you can see a short, squat castle perched on the end of the breakwater at the outer rim of the eastern harbor—this is Qaitbey Fort. For fans of military history and kids who like forts, Qaitbey is a great place. Austere and solid inside, you can wander the little rooms and peer across the harbor toward the town through the narrow windows of the upper floors, or check out the massively thick-walled sea side of the fort where they have a few old cannons. There's a small, high-roofed mosque in the center of the fort that you shouldn't miss, more for its simplicity and austerity than any elaborate tile work or architectural flourishes. Unfortunately, Qaitbey lacks any documentation or exhibition of artifacts.

The fort may seem to be in remarkably good condition given its age—it was built between 1477 and 1480 during the reign of the Sultan Qaitbey—but this is due to extensive restoration to repair damage from, among other sources, a British bombardment in 1882.

If you came to Alexandria hoping to see the famous lighthouse (p. 161), this is as close as you're going to get: The fort was built on the site of its foundations about 175 years after it collapsed in an earthquake. Though the lighthouse stood on an island at the entrance to the harbor, the fort lies on a causeway, which was built to provide defense against potential Ottoman attacks, that's accessible by foot. Rubble from the old lighthouse was likely used in the construction of the fort, and there's a theory that the large, red, granite pillars incorporated into the outer defenses came from just this source.

Qaitbey Fort. ✆ **03/4809144.** Admission LE25. Daily 9am–5pm.

Royal Jewelry Museum At press time, the Royal Jewelry Museum was still closed for renovation, though it looked more than ready to accept visitors. From the outside you can see painted glass windows and a lovely garden adorned with a couple of statues.

27 Ahmed Yehia Pasha. ✆ **03/5868348.**

WHERE TO STAY

Alexandria has several stylish high-end hotels and a couple of really good budget ones, but almost nothing in the midrange that I can enthusiastically recommend. Here is the best of the Alexandrian hotelier scene.

Very Expensive

El-Salamlek Palace Hotel ★★ Built in 1892 as a hunting lodge for the then-Khedive Abbas Helmy II, the Salamlek has survived its conversion to a hotel with remarkable grace. The Salamlek is located at the eastern end of the Corniche, which puts it beyond walking distance to most restaurants and sites. On the other hand, you aren't going to be able to avoid taxi rides in Alexandria anyway, so unless you plan to stay up very late, you might as well take advantage of this pleasant location in the middle of the Montazah Gardens and the hotel's direct view of the sea.

The rooms—actually, most of them are suites—have been fitted with somewhat generic modern furnishings, but at least one of them has a beautiful original wood ceiling. Maintenance isn't what it should be, but the view from the front rooms (across the garden to the Mediterranean) is lovely.

One of the best parts of the Salamlek is the room that used to be the khedive's office, which is now the King Farouk dining room. The ceiling and walls are original, as is the fireplace, and there's a door concealed in the back of the room that was first used as a discreet exit for its intended occupant but is now a service entrance. The bar is actually made out of Farouk's secretary's desk, and in the corner there's a lovely old folding pipe table. Unfortunately, quite a few of the royal portraits that now adorn the lobby and other public areas are second-rate reproductions, but the elevators that slide you soundlessly up to the rooms on the second floor are the real thing.

Montazah Gardens. ✆ **03/5473244.** Fax 03/5473585. www.sangiovanni.com. 20 units, including 14 suites. LE1,480 double. Rate includes breakfast, taxes, and service charges. MC, V. **Amenities:** 2 restaurants; bar; airport transfer (extra charge); babysitting; concierge; health club; Internet (extra charge). *In room:* A/C, TV, minibar.

Four Seasons Hotel Alexandria ★ Located as part of the multipurpose San Stefano Grand Plaza mega project (which also includes apartments, offices, a marina, and a shopping mall), this hotel still preserves its trademark charm. Though many guests arrive in a shiny black car, the staff will make you feel like you just stepped out of a limo even if you roll up in a battered taxi with a backpack.

Despite the sweeping and apparently massive facade, the place is actually quite small and has been painstakingly designed to re-create the look and feel of a classic Alex hotel. The rooms have period prints hung on the walls, the wallpaper is striped in shades of sherbet, and the furnishings are highly polished wood. It goes without saying that the difference in the fit and the finish, as well as the overall elegance of execution, between here and the Metropole or Cecil is enormous.

Both the spa and restaurants are what you'd expect from the Four Seasons. The only issue I have with this hotel is the location. Because the building fronts an eight-lane thoroughfare, the sound of the sea outside on the terrace or by the pool is almost drowned out by the din of the traffic. The double-glazing on the windows is excellent, mind you, so as long as you stay inside, it's just fine.

399 Corniche St. ✆ **03/5818000.** www.fourseasons.com. 118 units, including 31 suites. $450 double; $550 sea-view double. Rates include buffet breakfast, but subject to 28% taxes and service charges. AE, DC, MC, V. **Amenities:** 5 restaurants; 3 bars; airport transfer (extra charge); babysitting service; kids' club; concierge; health club & spa; Internet (extra charge); 2 pools (1 kids'); room service. *In room:* A/C, TV, minibar, Wi-Fi (extra charge).

Hotel Sofitel Cecil Alexandria Built in 1928, the Cecil has unfortunately lost much of its old-world charm to a series of renovations, which have stripped away period

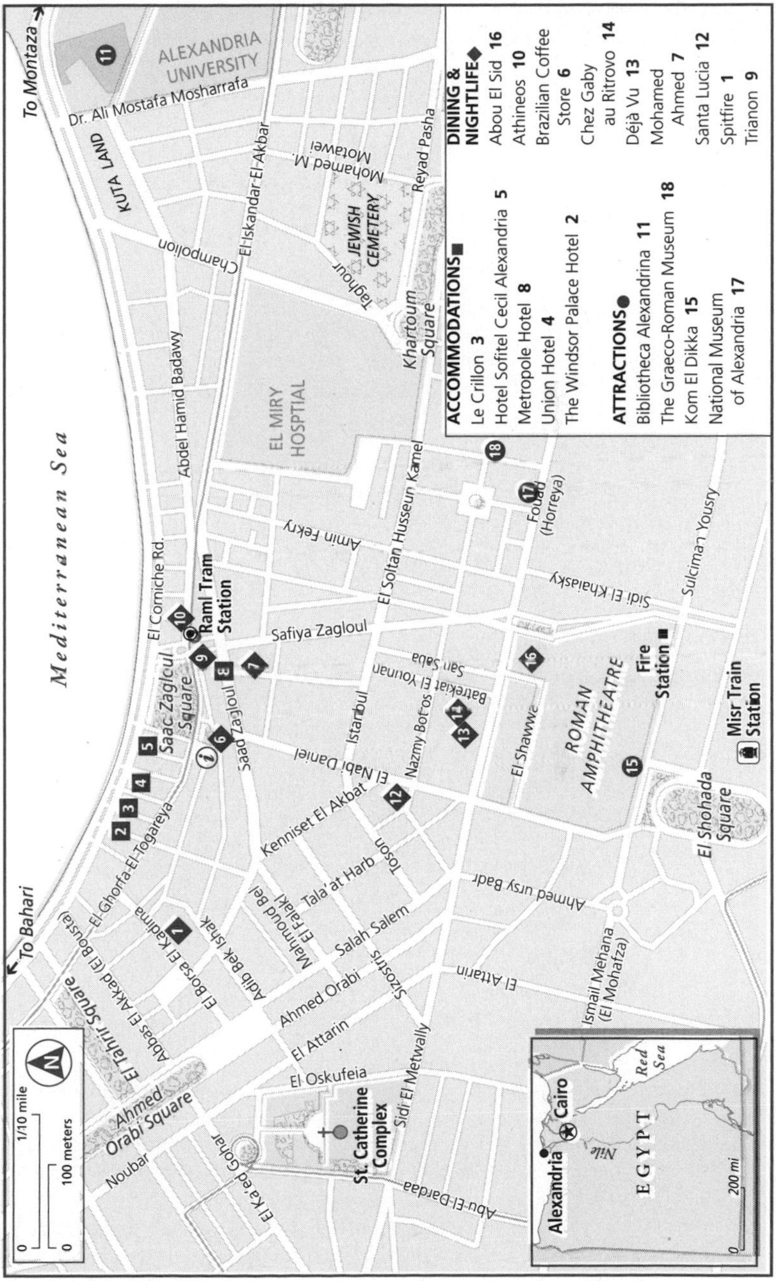
ACCOMMODATIONS
Le Crillon 3
Hotel Sofitel Cecil Alexandria 5
Metropole Hotel 8
Union Hotel 4
The Windsor Palace Hotel 2
ATTRACTIONS
Bibliotheca Alexandrina 11
The Graeco-Roman Museum 18
Kom El Dikka 15
National Museum of Alexandria 17
DINING & NIGHTLIFE
Abou El Sid 16
Athineos 10
Brazilian Coffee Store 6
Chez Gaby au Ritrovo 14
Déjà Vu 13
Mohamed Ahmed 7
Santa Lucia 12
Spitfire 1
Trianon 9
Mediterranean Sea
To Montaza
To Bahari
ALEXANDRIA UNIVERSITY
Dr. Ali Mostafa Mosharrafa
KUTA LAND
Champolion
El-Iskandar-El-Akbar
Mohamed M. Motawei
JEWISH CEMETERY
Taghour
Reyad Pasha
Khartoum Square
EL MIRY HOSPTIAL
Abdel Hamid Badawy
El Corniche Rd.
Amin Fekry
El Soltan Husseun Kamel
Fouad (Horreya)
Sidi El Khaiasky
Suleiman Yousry
Raml Tram Station
Safiya Zagloul
San Saba
Batrekiat El Younan
Saad Zagloul Square
Saad Zagloul
Istanbul
Nazmy Bot-os
El-Shawwe
ROMAN AMPHITHEATRE
Fire Station
Misr Train Station
El Shohada Square
El Nabi Daniel
Kenniset El Akbat
El-Ghorfa-El-Togareya
Toson
Tala'at Harb
Mahmoud Bek El Falaki
Ahmed ursy Badr
Salah Salem
Adib Bek Ishak
El Borsa El Kadima
Abbas El Akkad (El Bousta)
El Tahrir Square
Ahmed Orabi
Sizostris
El Attarin
Ismail Mehana (El Mohafza)
El Oskufeia
Ahmed Orabi Square
Noubar
El Ka'eed Gohar
St. Catherine Complex
Sidi El Metwally
Abu-El-Dardaa
1/10 mile
100 meters
Alexandria
Cairo
Nile
EGYPT
Red Sea
200 mi

fittings and marble and left the rooms with little character. Public areas—the lobby and the Monty bar upstairs—still have original wood paneling, and the elevators and staircase are gleaming originals, too. Located on the corner of Saad Zaghloul Square and facing the sea, the location is hard to beat, with half the rooms having sea views. The rooms, if generic, are large and pleasantly appointed. The atmosphere is a good mix of hustle and bustle, but the staff can be surly and service isn't up to five-star (even Egyptian five-star) standards. The rack rates are ridiculously high, all things considered, and I would only recommend the Cecil if you can get the rooms at a significant discount.

16 Saad Zaghloul Sq. ✆ **03/4877173** or 03/4855655. www.sofitel.com. 86 units. 180€ double; 210€ sea-view double. Rates include breakfast, taxes, and service charges. AE, MC, V. **Amenities:** 3 restaurants; bar; concierge; Internet (extra charge). *In room:* A/C, TV, Internet (extra charge), minibar.

Expensive

Hilton Green Plaza Located away from the crush of people and cars along the seafront, and just a few minutes from Al Nozha Airport, the Green Plaza is a good option if you're just passing through. Surrounded by cinemas, restaurants, cafes, and the very popular and dense Green Plaza Mall, this makes a good base from which to see the monuments, and it's an easy 10-minute taxi ride to where the older restaurants and coffee shops are located.

The lobby and public areas are spacious, modern, and well lit. Rooms are large and pleasant, if somewhat generic, which really sums up the ambience of the whole place quite well.

14th of May Bridge Rd., Smouha. ✆ **03/4209120.** Fax 03/4209140. www1.hilton.com. 650 units. $135 double. Rate includes breakfast, taxes, and service charges. AE, MC, V. **Amenities:** 3 restaurants; bar; babysitting; concierge; health club; Internet (extra charge); pool; room service. *In room:* A/C, TV, Internet (extra charge), minibar.

Metropole Hotel ★ On the other side of Saad Zaghloul Square from the Hotel Sofitel Cecil (p. 172), the Metropole, which dates from 1902, offers much of the same period glamour and atmosphere at less than half the price. The lobby, with its high ceiling and neoclassical friezes, is smaller than the Cecil's and lacks the dark-wood sobriety, but with period lamps and an original lift, it has its own particular, and very Alexandrian, character. The marble reception desk is short, tucked into a corner as you enter beneath a period chandelier, and as you approach it, you half expect to see Agatha Christie sitting in the corner.

Rooms are large and have also suffered from renovations—in this case, the designers have aimed for just a little too much glitz. Huge curtains, gold frill, and Empire-style frippery abound. Fit and finish aren't as good as the Cecil's, but the staff here are friendlier.

52 Saad Zaghloul Sq. ✆ **03/4861467.** 64 units. $119 double; $159 sea-view double. Rates include breakfast, taxes, and service charges. AE, DC, MC, V. **Amenities:** Restaurant; bar; Wi-Fi. *In room:* A/C, TV, minifridge.

San Giovanni This is a nice enough small hotel with some character, a pleasant staff, and a not-so-great location. A few years ago, it had a great location between the road and the sea, but then the road was widened, and the San Giovanni found itself cut off from the sea on one side. It still backs onto a beach, but it's unfortunately not accessible from the hotel. The main drawback of the arrangement is the traffic noise, and if it weren't for the fact that every hotel on the seaside shares the same issue (actually, this place is a little better off than some, in that the surf is loud enough to sometimes to drown out the traffic), I would hesitate to mention the San Giovanni at all. As it stands, it is only worthwhile at a significant discount from the quoted room rates.

There are a restaurant and a cozy bar, both with a view of the beach (though the view of the ocean is partially blocked by a bridge). Rooms vary in size and some are oddly shaped and have bad light (not helped by the dark trim, red carpets, and heavy curtains), so it's worth checking out one or two before making a decision.

205 Corniche. ✆ **03/5467773** or -5. Fax 03/5464408. www.sangiovanni.com. 32 units. $140 sea-view double. Rate includes breakfast, taxes, and service charges. MC, V. **Amenities:** Restaurant; bar; Wi-Fi. *In room:* A/C, TV, minibar.

The Windsor Palace Hotel ★ On the Corniche, a few hundred meters east of Saad Zaghloul Square, the Windsor, with its modestly sized but ostentatious lobby and dining room, used to be a haunt of well-to-do Alexandrians. From the lovingly maintained old elevators and the dining room ceiling, which features a magnificently over-the-top painting, to the gold print wallpaper in the coffee shop, the place has an air of having survived past its time. You could wish for better-chosen carpeting upstairs or more furniture in the lobby (the place feels bare and somewhat empty, though maybe this is to show off the sheer expanse of the marble), but there's no denying that the place has presence. Rooms vary quite a bit but tend to be large and a bit chilly in the winter. Both service and room quality have been patchy in the past, so though things seem to have improved with a recent renovation, check out your room before you commit, and ask to see several if you're not happy.

17 Shohada St. ✆ **03/4808700.** 63 units. $150 double; $160 sea-view double. Rates include breakfast, taxes, and service charges. AE, MC, V. **Amenities:** Restaurant; bar; Wi-Fi (extra charge). *In room:* A/C, TV, minibar.

Inexpensive

Le Crillon (Value) This is probably the most charming of the Corniche pensions, and with a pleasant and efficient staff, it represents excellent value for money in both comfort and location. Simple rooms with high ceilings open onto the harbor with views of the crescent headlands of the harbor and the Qaitbey Fort. Each floor of rooms is built around an apartment-like sitting room. Most of the choice rooms have shared bathrooms (four on each floor, two with large showers). The suites offer little added value, and rooms on the sixth floor should be avoided—they are windowless and reserved for overflow.

5 Adib Ishak St. ✆ **03/4800330.** 28 units. LE150 sea-view double. Rate includes breakfast, taxes, and service charges. No credit cards. *In room:* TV.

Union Hotel Located on the fifth floor of an old building on the seafront, Union Hotel is one of Alexandria's classic budget hotels. "Bare-bones" sums up the facilities, but the place is clean and the staff are friendly and helpful. The lobby and breakfast room areas face the sea and have a great view up and down the coast. The staff may try to describe the rooms, which are down the side of the building and look down quiet side streets, as having a sea view, but this is stretching the truth: You *can* see the sea, but (especially toward the back of the hotel) you have to lean off the balcony and stretch your neck to get more than a thin sliver of blue. Once you hear the traffic noise at the front, mind you, you'll be happy with your room at the back. Breakfast here is as basic as the rooms. The upside of the Union, apart from the price, is the location; just meters from Saad Zaghloul Square, it's an easy walk to several excellent coffee shops and lunch spots, the Graeco-Roman Museum, and shops and services. Taxis are plentiful for farther flung archaeological sites and restaurants.

 164 26th of July St. ✆ **03/4807771** or 03/4807312. 42 units. LE113 double; LE154 sea-view double. Rates include breakfast, taxes, and service charges. No credit cards. *In room:* TV.

WHERE TO EAT

Being an international as well as a domestic tourist destination, Alexandria enjoys a dense culinary scene that varies from fine dining and delicious Greek dishes to common eateries and traditional Egyptian recipes. While some restaurants put you in a nostalgic serene mode as you pass the hours gazing at the endless horizon, traditional restaurants and local eateries' dynamic atmosphere boosts a quantum of positive energy within you.

Expensive

Abu Ashraf ★ SEAFOOD Buried deep in the Bahri district, this is the place to go if you want to experience a filling seafood banquet the Alexandrian way. There is an icebox display at the entrance of what's available for the day, where you get to choose what to you want to eat and how you want it cooked. Though the staff are friendly and helpful, they speak limited English, so ordering is going to be a sign-language process. Dip your finger in some traditional appetizers while your meal is being prepared. Start with a seafood soup (one of the best in town), followed by a heaping dish of grilled shrimp. Though stir-fried Moses fish remains one of my favorites, the calamari *tagine* is not to be missed. For a typical finale to the traditional meal, ask the waiter for a water pipe, and the *shisha* will be served right where you are seated.

28 Safar Basha St., Bahri. ✆ **03/4816597** or 03/4842850. Seafood meal (including salads, appetizers, bread, and main course) LE60–LE150. MC, V. Daily noon–2am.

Fish Market ★ SEAFOOD If you want to experience a good seafood meal with a lovely sea view and a pleasant atmosphere, rather than the traditional down the alley one, then Fish Market is where you should be having dinner. Its location is directly on the water, and the big windows offer a great, unobstructed view over the harbor toward the Qaitbey Fort. Wood floors, white walls, wicker furniture, and grass-shaded lamps give the place a seaside feel, while bread being baked in the traditional oven fills it with a pleasant aroma. Like any self-respecting Alexandrian fish restaurant, it sells fish by the kilo. You choose your meal from an ice-filled table near the door, and then retreat to your table while it's cooked. Go for the *karous* (sea bream) grilled in olive oil and lemon juice accompanied by a pie of grilled vegetables and rice; it is well worth a recommendation.

Corniche (right before you turn left in the direction of Bahri). ✆ **03/4805114** or 03/4805119. Seafood meal (including salads, appetizers, bread, and main course) LE90–LE250. AE, MC, V. Daily noon–1am.

Brazilian Coffee

Just off Saad Zaghloul Square, the **Brazilian Coffee Store,** 44 Saad Zaghloul St. (✆ **03/4865059;** coffee and a pâté LE12; no credit cards; daily 7am–midnight), is a classic Alexandrian coffee shop that has recently been renovated with new fittings and modern colors, yet it still retains much of its original vintage charm. Better yet, it serves the same old coffee, with the beans roasting and grinding on the same old machine, which you can see put to work while the waiter prepares your espresso or cappuccino. There's a seating area upstairs, but I prefer standing downstairs and people-watching.

Sweet Couscous

While you'll easily find sweet couscous throughout the rest of North Africa, here it's a hard-to-find delicacy. **El Sheikh Wafik,** located at the far end of Bahri (✆ **012/3249623**), offers some of the best in the world in two small, characterless indoor halls that are often crammed with people. The entire menu consists of just four things: rice pudding, ice cream, *om aly,* and sweet couscous. Prices range from LE5 to LE10.

Santa Lucia INTERNATIONAL When you're tired of fish (or if you never liked it in the first place), try Santa Lucia. The interior, with its dark-wood paneling, heavy curtains, and a slightly eclectic mix of modern art and Indian handicrafts, makes for a subdued and sophisticated atmosphere. Menu options range from filet Madagascar and shrimp risotto to poached stingray and steak. The tiramisu finishes off the meal nicely, though it's made with neither mascarpone nor raw eggs (for which you should probably be grateful).

40 Safiya Zaghloul St. (off Saad Zaghloul Sq.). ✆ **03/4860770** or 03/4860332. Appetizers LE25–LE50; main courses LE50–LE110. AE, MC, V. Daily 1pm–midnight.

White and Blue Restaurant EGYPTIAN/GREEK Upstairs at the Hellenic Nautical Club, at the end of the breakwater close to the Qaitbey Fort, this place looks a little forbidding from the outside, but push through the doors and head upstairs, and you'll find that it has a great view across the bay. The menu is an odd mix of traditional Egyptian favorites (it has a wonderful, thick lentil soup) and Greek dishes such as moussaka and souvlakia. The meze servings are substantial, and you could easily make a light meal out of one with some soup on the side. Fish is still the number one recommendation.

The atmosphere is lacking (the whole restaurant is one big room with a table of fish on ice near the door) and decorations are sparse, but it's certainly very clean. In summer, the long balcony along the sea side is the perfect place to sit with a cold beer and watch the sunset, taking in the fishing boats and the massive glass slope of the Bibliotheca.

Corniche St. (just before you reach Qaitbey Fort). ✆ **03/4802690.** Seafood meal (including salads, appetizers, bread, and main course) LE80–LE150. No credit cards. Daily noon–11pm.

Moderate

Abou El Sid EGYPTIAN Alexandria's only branch of the Cairo-based Abou El Sid chain restaurant, this place follows the same interior footsteps of its fellow branches (p. 139) but comes with slightly more cheerful colors and a bit of space. The menu is standard.

39 El Horreya St., Raml. ✆ **03/3929609.** www.abouelsid.com. Appetizers LE15–LE45; main courses LE40–LE70. MC, V. Daily noon–1am.

Athineos EGYPTIAN/GREEK I get nostalgic when I think of this place. The main dining room is decorated with crimson walls, a cream frieze depicting cavorting characters from Greek mythology, loads of imitation gold leaf, and the restaurant's original pieces of decor from the 1940s. The menu is an Egyptian-Greek mix, with salad Niçoise alongside fish kebab, moussaka, and baba ghanouj. There's a bar just before the main dining room on the left, but you'll have to flag down a waiter when you need something—a small price to pay to avoid the large groups that pour into this place. The Alexandrian rice with

Take a Break, Have a Gelati

Italy has gelato, Alexandria has *gelati.* This local ice cream, based on a secret homemade recipe and fresh ingredients, comes in a rather limited range of flavors that include chocolate, strawberry, milk (not vanilla), and flavor-rich lemon. It's an Alexandria specialty served at numerous outlets. **A'azza** (Corniche, right before you turn left in the direction of Bahri) is the city's most famous, but **Nezami** (Corniche, a couple of blocks away from A'azza) is unquestionably the best. Expect to pay LE5 per scoop.

seafood, an unlikely combination of calamari and fish with peanuts and raisins, is a bit heavy for summer, but it's a delicious and filling dish.

21 Saad Zaghloul Sq. ✆ **03/4868131.** Appetizers LE20–LE25; main courses LE30–LE50. No credit cards. Daily 8am–midnight.

Chez Gaby au Ritrovo ITALIAN A magnet that attracts Alexandria's beautiful people, Chez Gaby is the place to dine if you want to get a closer look at the city's diversity, from the young intelligentsia to lonesome middle-age diners. Italian in every sense, the place comes in with checker curtains and tablecloths, antique kitchen memorabilia, and Venetian face masks hanging on the walls. The food doesn't divert from the truly Italian theme, with pizza and pasta dominating the menu. My ideal dinner here starts with the oven-baked eggplant with cheese topping followed by penne with calamari and shrimp. If you aren't hungry, the brick bar is a good place to have a couple of beers.

22 El Horreya St., Raml. ✆ **03/4874404** or 03/4846329. Appetizers LE20–LE25; main courses LE30–LE45. No credit cards. Daily 1pm–midnight.

Trianon ★ EUROPEAN Open since 1905, this is easily my favorite light lunch place in Alexandria, with high ceilings and gleaming old paneling. Though it is licensed to serve alcohol, the old bar in the corner seems to be used mostly for blending excellent fresh juices. In recent years, management has modernized the place, adding Wi-Fi and a breakfast menu, without losing any of its original charm.

For lunch, start with the creamy chicken or tomato soup, and then move on to one of the sandwiches; perhaps the thick toasted club, stacked with roast beef, chicken, and cheese, the smoked salmon with capers, or a pizza. Finish with a sampling of the pastries from the picturesque bakery outlet on the opposite side of the building. Service is sedate, and lunch will proceed at a dignified pace.

52 Saad Zaghloul Sq. ✆ **03/4835881.** Sandwiches LE20–LE35. No credit cards. Daily 7am–11pm.

Inexpensive

Mohamed Ahmed ★★ EGYPTIAN Crammed and noisy, Mohamed Ahmed seems like just another Egyptian fast-food eatery, but it's an Alexandrian icon well-known for the super-delicious food and the celebrities who have tried it (look for their autographs in the back of the menu). In addition to the more common *fuul* or *tameya,* Mohamed Ahmed offers two special dishes that you should not miss: *shakshouka,* which is scrambled eggs with tomato, and *fuul eskendrani,* where the famous Egyptian dish gets a good dash of tomato sauce and *tahina* salad. Note that the sign is in Arabic only, so ask around.

17 Shokour St., Raml. ✆ **03/4873576.** Local dishes LE5. No credit cards. Daily 6am–1am.

SHOPPING

When the exodus began after 1952, many foreigners, mainly Greeks, didn't have the money or time to take household goods with them and, as a result, Alexandria became the Egyptian hub for used European furniture. Most of the items left behind were unremarkable, but many were of high quality and quite a few were antiques. The trade in these items has long centered on **Attarin Street,** a disappointingly unromantic street that runs into the back of Ahmed Urabi Square. For antique furniture buffs, as well as those just looking to pick up an old postcard or some knickknacks, an hour or two spent strolling past the windows won't be wasted. Stores range from clean, well-organized emporiums of nicely polished Napoleonic chairs and 19th-century silver services to junk stores with moth-eaten stuffed crocodiles and piles of moldy school books from the 1920s. Take your pick—far better in my opinion to take home a battered piece of the real thing than a shiny factory-produced souvenir. For traveling shopaholics who are into the latest trends rather than antiques, the four-story **San Stefano Shopping Mall** makes for a good half-day shopping venue with more than 180 retail outlets that include some of the world's leading brand names. Check out the 10-screen cinema complex for Egyptian and Hollywood blockbusters.

ALEXANDRIA AFTER DARK

For the country's second-largest city, Alexandria's nightlife scene is shamefully poor. It's a sample platter offering a handful of scenic seaside bars, old traditional taverns, and perhaps a new hip place tucked away in the downtown labyrinth. Venues listed below close between midnight and 2am.

Bleu Bar Moments If you want to break away from typical back-alley Alexandrian bars and wish for something more upscale, romantic, and scenic, then head to Bleu Bar at the Four Seasons Hotel. The bar on the terrace has stunning views of the Mediterranean; there's nothing more romantic than a cocktail around sunset. Open May to November. 399 Corniche St. © **03/5818000.**

Déjà Vu Down a quiet side street and upstairs in an old Alexandrian building, Déjà Vu is a good place to grab a drink or party, but this depends entirely on the crowd, as some nights it's barren. It starts out as a dimly lit spot that's good for a couple of drinks, and as the night progresses, DJ music takes over and turns the place into a hip dance club. Dark-wood furnishings with leather seats and black-and-white photographs mark the interior. It is fairly spacious, and you can choose between high tables in the bar area or a table in the adjoining room. Off Horreya St., Raml. © **03/4878082.**

Spitfire This is a straight-out dive bar with little pretense at anything else. Favored by the crews from visiting cruise ships and expats out for a raucous time, this is the kind of place you want to head when you're tired of drinking from glasses and minding your language. The music is even louder than the patrons, and when the boats are in, it can be extremely crowded. Keep an eye on your wallet, and be prepared for a good time. 7 El Borsa El Adema St. (off Saad Zaghloul St.). © **03/4806503.**

DAY TRIPS

If you are based in Alexandria, then you should consider a 2-day excursion to Cairo, a long weekend in Marsa Matruh, and a day trip to either Rosetta or El Alamein.

El Alamein

Located some 80km (50 miles) west of Alexandria, El Alamein witnessed some of World War II's most grueling encounters between the Allied armies and the Axis forces. Today, nothing remains from the tragedies of war except memorials and a rarely visited museum.

Along the way from Alexandria to El Alamein, there are an increasing number of seaside developments that are largely dedicated to Cairenes spending their summer vacation, or at least a long weekend, away from the blistering heat of the capital.

Getting There

Due to the distance between the sites you would be visiting, having a car proves to be essential (for more information on renting cars in Alexandria, see p. 165). However, if you want to do it the old backpacker way, you can hop in any of the four daily buses heading to Marsa Matruh (ticket LE35) and ask the driver to drop you off at El Alamein. Note, however, that you will probably have to hitchhike from one site to the other.

What to See & Do

Alamein Military Museum This small museum, just up the road from the Commonwealth Cemetery, houses a collection of military equipment and artifacts from both the Allied and the Axis forces. Outside the main building there are field guns and tanks, as well as the remains of a crashed Spitfire. Inside, dioramas, photographs, and mannequins are used to re-create the history of conflict. It's worth 30 minutes to an hour to visit if you have a taste for historical weapons of war.

International Coastal Hwy. (105km/65 miles west of Alexandria). ✆ **046/4100031** or 046/4100021. Admission LE10. Daily 9am–3pm.

Commonwealth Cemetery This is a somber, moving monument to the thousands of Allied troops who lost their lives in El Alamein. As you walk down to the cemetery from the parking lot, the first thing you'll find is El Alamein Memorial. On its walls are panels that commemorate the 8,500 soldiers and 3,000 airmen who died in the Middle East and whose graves are unknown. Passing through the memorial, you come to the cemetery. Rows of white stones set in the sand mark the bodies buried here, and to the southeast there's a large memorial to more than 600 soldiers whose bodies were cremated. There are 7,240 graves in the cemetery, of which 815 are not identified.

The cemetery is well maintained, and its simplicity, as well as the desert setting—the wind whistling through the stones is about the only sound here—underscore both the drama and the tragedy of the battles that were fought here. There are no stairs, but wheelchair access would require some assistance.

International Coastal Hwy. (81km/50 miles west of Alexandria). Daily dawn–dusk.

German Memorial This massive edifice to the Germans who lost their lives in the North African campaign stands between the highway and the sea. It's on the brow of a small hill, from which you can see just how bleak and difficult the territory is. Its octagonal structure and lack of moat or drawbridge are reminiscent of another German military monument, the 13th century Castel del Monte in southeastern Italy. Inside, bodies of 4,500 German troops are interred under black basalt.

International Coastal Hwy. (95km/59 miles west of Alexandria). Daily dawn–dusk.

Italian Memorial Though just 3km (1¾ miles) west of the German Memorial, the Italian Memorial is quite different: Its soaring 46m (150-ft.) white column with sharp, modernist lines stands against the bright blue sky. Inside the echoing interior, casualties from the Italian forces lie in walls of white-faced vaults. There's an altar inside the memorial backed by a large window that faces the sea. It's worth visiting this place when it's empty, simply because voices and footsteps echo loudly through the space.

International Coastal Hwy. (98km/61 miles west of Alexandria). Daily dawn–dusk.

Rosetta

Rosetta (Rashid in Arabic) flourished after the Arab conquest of A.D. 640, which put an end to the Roman administration of Egypt and the dominance of Alexandria over the African Mediterranean coast. Rosetta soon flourished as an important trading port.

Getting There

A car is certainly the easiest way to get into town, have your tour, and leave whenever you feel like it. If you prefer a cheaper way, **West Delta Bus Company** (© **03/3633993**) has four buses that run daily (except Fri) between Alexandria and Rashid. For the LE3 ticket, expect a slow-moving bus.

What to See & Do

The Ottoman Houses Rosetta did particularly well under the Ottoman Turks, and being the easiest Egyptian port to reach from Istanbul, it received a disproportionate benefit from the trade with Turkey. The Ottoman Houses in the Old Port will be the highlight of your short visit, and efforts continue to restore and open some of these houses, of which only 22 remain.

Amasyali House is one of the largest and best preserved, perhaps because the family of the original owner lived there until the early 1920s. One of the first buildings, along with **Killi House,** which has become the Rashid National Museum, to be restored, it also has one of the most impressive exteriors with its decorated colored portico and finely carved *mashrabeyas.* From the inside, the house has some lovely examples of 18th-century wooden *mashrabeya* paneling with mother-of-pearl inlays and various secret rooms and byways that allowed the women of the house to move about unobserved. Look up for the blue-painted ceiling with the finest of decorations. Next door is the **House of Abu Shahin,** which is also known as the **Mill House.** As the name implies, it was used as a mill for grinding flour and rice, and today you can see the wooden mechanics. The whole house has been completely rebuilt, but you can still see the granite pillars with their Greco-Roman capitals in the courtyard. Not far is another marvelous building to visit—**Hammam Azouz.** Public baths, *hammams,* were an important communal facility and a common trait among the different Islamic sultanates. This 19th-century *hammam* is a fine example of Ottoman architecture with marble interiors and wooden decorations.

Old Port. Admission LE25 (collective ticket includes the museum). Daily 9am–4pm.

The Rasheed National Museum On the far side of Gomhoreya Square from the Nile, this new museum is located in the restored 18th-century Killi House. Some of the restoration work was unfortunately heavy-handed, but the collection of local coins and ceramic pieces is interesting. What you're really here for, however, is the building; a four-story one, typical of the tall, brick houses of wealthy Ottoman merchants. There is also a replica of the Rosetta Stone near the entrance.

Gomhoreya Sq. © **045/2921733.** Admission LE25 (collective ticket includes the Ottoman houses). Daily 9am–4pm.

2 MARSA MATRUH

There are two reasons for you to be in Marsa Matruh: You are either on a slow trip to the far and away Siwa, or you are here for the beaches. Marsa Matruh has some of the country's best, with turquoise blue water embracing white-powder sand. Marsa Matruh has recently grabbed tourism developers' attention, and the town's first high-end resort, Jaz Almaza, is already up and running. Direct flights from European cities have kicked off as of summer 2010, and now Marsa Matruh is directly connected to the U.K. Similar to the rest of the cities along the Mediterranean coast, heavy rains are the theme of the short winter season, when Marsa Matruh becomes a ghost town.

ORIENTATION

Matruh (you can drop the official "Marsa" part of the name locally, and will get blank looks if you call the town "Marsa") is situated on a wide bay. The main "downtown" area is concentrated around Alexandria Street, which is the main route from the train and bus stations and from the airport. Alexandria Street meets the Corniche at the eastern end of the bay near the Riviera Palace. The Beau Site is located at the Corniche's western end, while the museum is located at the opposite one.

GETTING THERE

BY PLANE Marsa Matruh slips into a state of hibernation during winter months, leaving flights, whether domestic or international, restricted only to summer. July to October, **EgyptAir** operates a twice weekly flight between Cairo and Marsa Matruh with an average price tag of LE750 for the round-trip. As of summer 2010, **Thomson** (www.thomson.com) has announced its flights to Marsa Matruh directly from London Gatwick and Manchester. From the airport, a taxi into town will set you back about LE30 to LE50; however, I predict a spike once direct flights from Europe start coming in more frequently.

BY BUS All year round, **West Delta Bus Company** connects Marsa Matruh to both Alexandria (LE35) and Cairo (LE45–LE60) with several daily buses, while the more comfy Super Jet runs a summer-only bus (LE65) to the capital. The bus station is on the Matruh–Alexandria Road about 2km (1¼ miles) from the seaside, where there are usually plenty of blue-and-white taxis around (LE10–LE15 will take you almost anywhere in town).

BY TRAIN There is an express train service (seated, air-conditioned) that runs from June to September between Cairo and Marsa Matruh. It costs LE67 and LE34 for first

Warning! Public Beaches

For decades, Marsa Matruh has been one of the most sought after summer destinations for local Egyptians, especially those who can't afford glamorous El Gouna or glitzy Sharm El Sheikh. During the summer school break (July–Sept), Marsa Matruh's public beaches get scores of local beachgoers and are certainly not the best place to work on your tan, especially if you are a woman; you will escape harassment, but you can't hide from the ogling.

and second class, respectively. In Marsa Matruh, the train station is quite close to both the bus one and Alexandria Street; an LE10 to LE15 taxi ride will take you to any of the Corniche-based hotels.

BY CAR From Cairo it is a good 6-hour drive (530km/330 miles), while from Alexandria it is only a 3-hour one (290km/180 miles). Coming from the capital, you first need to take the Cairo–Alexandria Desert Road, and after 110km (68 miles) take the exit marked AL ALAMEIN. From there a byroad will lead you to the International Coastal Road that passes by Marsa Matruh. The International Coastal Road is a dual carriage road in pretty good condition that connects the several Mediterranean cities in Egypt and farther to the Libyan border.

GETTING AROUND

Marsa Matruh is neither tiny nor colossal. Your feet will do just fine for Alexandria Street, but you will need transportation to take you to the town's several beaches and sites. A taxi is the best way to get around; they are plentiful and won't charge you a fortune (LE10–LE15 on average).

TOURIST INFORMATION

Getting online in Marsa Matruh is harder than most places in Egypt. Beau Site Hotel has a good **Internet** connection if you are a guest, otherwise, there are a couple of places scattered around Alexandria Street. Expect to pay LE4 to LE5 per hour.

WHAT TO SEE & DO

Beaches There are a number of lovely beaches to both the east and west of town. The water is a pristine, turquoise blue, and the jagged rocks that tumble to the shore set off the soft white-sand beaches—everywhere you look, you see a postcard here. If you are getting bored of your lovely hotel beach and want to try another one, you can always head to **Rommel's Beach,** just past Rommel's Cave (eastern end of Corniche) and the closest to town. Keep heading west to **Cleopatra's Beach** or **Lover's Beach,** which are around the bay and about a 30-minute drive. At Cleopatra's Beach, you can splash about at a rock pool where Cleopatra and Anthony apparently bathed. Farther west, 25km (16 miles) from town, there's a lovely cove called **Agiba Beach,** which has a long, white-sand beach between high rocky arms. Heading to Agiba or Cleopatra's, you can either check your hotel's travel desk or tour operator for an organized excursion, or rent a taxi for the day (average LE70).

Rommel's Cave ★ If you're a war or history buff, you're not going to want to miss the cave that Rommel used to plan the eastward offensive against the Allied forces that ultimately ground to a halt at El Alamein. Though the military museum that now calls the place home comprises little more than some withering uniforms, including a coat that supposedly belonged to the Desert Fox himself, a clothing chest donated by his son, and some old photos, I think the quick trip outside town or on the way to one of the beaches is worth it for the location and the cave.

About 3km (1¾ miles) west of town. Admission LE10. Daily 9am–3pm.

WHERE TO STAY

The upside of a limited hotelier scene is that it facilitates the decision-making process. If you are in Marsa Matruh for the night and heading to Siwa the next day, then one of the basic hotels by the Corniche will do just fine. If you are here for some lazy days on the beach, then head to Beau Site; for a more memorable beach experience (at a premium), Jaz Almaza is where you should be checking in.

Expensive

Jaz Almaza Beach Resort Located some 38km (43 miles) east of Marsa Matruh, Jaz Almaza is part of a mega tourist project in the making, which is planned to include other five-star hotels and luxury apartments. Staff are attentive and service is professional. Almaza enjoys an amazing beach where you can unwind or engage in one of the many activities the animation team relentlessly organizes. However, aside from the beach, Jaz Almaza is just another high-end accommodation facility with no real soul. Rooms are spacious and dominated by beige and brown, and character is absent throughout the resort. A stone's throw away, there is the similar, yet with a Middle Eastern twist, Jaz Oriental and the recently inaugurated (May 2009) Jaz Crystal. Jaz Almaza was the first among the trio, but there are no real differences between the three.

International Coastal Hwy. (37km/23 miles east of Marsa Matruh). ✆ **046/436000.** Fax 046/436001. 395 units, including 3 suites. 84€ double. Rate includes buffet breakfast, lunch, taxes, and service charges. MC, V. **Amenities:** 3 restaurants; 3 bars; airport transfer (extra charge); concierge; health club; Internet (extra charge); kids' club; 6 pools (including 2 kids'); room service; 2 tennis courts (floodlit). *In room:* A/C, TV, minibar.

Moderate

Arous Al Bahr This beachfront accommodation is more basic than moderate. Rooms are furnished with hard beds and cheap furniture, but they're clean and cheap. Each has a small balcony where breakfast can be served and the sea breeze is nice. Try to get a room at the end of the hallways that run the length of the building—you want to be away from the TV noise (it's in the lobby and probably on all night), and you don't want the teenagers tramping boisterously past your door while you're trying to sleep. McDonald's, Pizza Hut, and Hardee's are nearby.

Corniche St. ✆ **046/4934420.** 50 units. LE300. Rate includes breakfast, taxes, and service charges. No credit cards. *In room:* No phone.

Beau Site This hotel is my favorite in Marsa Matruh. The lobby and restaurant have the look and feel of a low-end Western hotel, with clean white walls and windows that look down on the hotel's beach. Guest rooms are on the upper floors, and most have a view of the sea. Rooms are a bit small, but sufficient, and they come with a relatively small bathroom. Three main advantages to this place are the privacy of its beach, the location (close enough to Marsa Matruh proper yet far enough from Alexandria St. and its nonstop noise), and the food (it's quite tasty, which is something difficult to find elsewhere in town). Beau Site has been undertaking some renovations recently, and at press time, some parts of the hotel were still cordoned off.

Corniche St. ✆ **046/4932066.** Fax 046/4933319. www.beausitehotel.com. 180 units. $122 double. Rack rate includes buffet breakfast, lunch, taxes, and service charges. MC, V. **Amenities:** 2 restaurants; bar; Internet (extra charge). *In room:* A/C, TV, fridge.

Riviera Palace This is the only competition for the Beau Site, and it's just a short walk from the public beach and closer to the shops and restaurants. The decor is a bit cheap and gaudy (stuffed animal tigers), and it has the feel of a place that serves the high-end of the local tourism market during the summer. The basement restaurant and bar are bland but clean. The rooms are large and some of them have small balconies and garden views, so if you have a chance, look at a few before you settle on which one you're going to take. The air-conditioners are in good shape, and the bathrooms are better than anywhere else in town.

Alexandria St. ✆ **046/4933045** or 046/4930472. Fax 046/4930004. 41 units. LE385 double. Rate includes breakfast, lunch, taxes, and service charges. MC, V. **Amenities:** Restaurant; bar. *In room:* A/C, TV, fridge.

WHERE TO EAT

Finding a meal in Marsa Matruh is a culinary adventure, though not necessarily in a good way. There are few options, and choosing is a matter of picking something acceptable rather than heading toward something you really want. All the places listed below are pretty downmarket, and you may want to restrict yourself to eating at the restaurants in Jaz, Beau Site, and Riveria Palace, or at the cluster of fast-food places around the Arous Al Bahr Hotel on the Corniche (which includes Pizza Hut, Hardee's, KFC, and McDonald's).

Hammo Temsah SEAFOOD This is a typical Egyptian fish place, with enthusiastic paintings of fish on the windows, an open grill on the sidewalk, and boisterous staff. Choose your seafood from the wood market-style stalls, and wait while it's cooked to your specifications. Work out the price before you finalize the order—this restaurant is getting a bit of a reputation for hitting tourists with a ridiculous bill once they've finished the meal.

My favorite in these places is always the *bouri singari,* where mullet is opened and cleaned before being grilled. Fish comes with rice on the side, and the usual range of *tahina* and salad-style appetizers are available.

Zaher Galal St., 2 blocks east of Alexandria St. Seafood meal (including salads, appetizers, bread, and main course) LE50–LE150. No credit cards. Daily 11am–2am.

New Alexandria Tourist Restaurant EGYPTIAN Tuck into a pile of grilled *kofta* or kebab, or just go for the standard meal of grilled fish with a pile of rice on the side. The atmosphere is basic tourist-theme: white walls and white ceiling with a cooler for drinks and another for the fish so that you can see what's fresh. They do serve beer, and the staff will happily run down the street to make up for whatever the restaurant lacks.

Alexandria St., directly across the road from Panyotis. Main courses LE30–LE60. No credit cards. Daily noon–11pm.

Panyotis EGYPTIAN This place is small and well established, and its narrow entrance makes it easy to miss. The food is the usual mix of Egyptian standards and local seafood, but the atmosphere is relaxed and jovial, and it serves alcohol. If you can't be in the water, relaxing at a seat near the door with a plate of grilled calamari and a cold beer is about the best way to pass a summer afternoon in Marsa Matruh.

Alexandria St., 1 block south of Riveria Palace Hotel. Main courses LE30–LE50. No credit cards. Daily 8am–11pm.

8 The Sinai Peninsula

For many years, the Sinai Peninsula was the kind of place to which nobody went unless they had to. The Pharaohs sent expeditions to mine turquoise here, and there were a few adventurous types (such as a young Ralph Bagnold, later famous for his exploration of the Western Desert) who set out to see if it could be crossed. But mostly the area was for soldiers (three Egyptian-Israeli military encounters took place here) and the few resident Bedouin who mapped the mountains, valleys, and spectacular coastline of this vast desert and mountainous terrain.

All this changed in the 1980s, when tourism development transformed south Sinai into a tourist-oriented hot spot. Beachgoers and hard-core partygoers take pilgrimages to Sharm El Sheikh, where the warm sun beats down year-round, but for a real pilgrimage, the nearby St. Catherine is a well regarded site for Jews, Christians, and Muslims alike. The burning bush here is supposedly where God spoke to Moses, while Mount Sinai is where he received the Ten Commandments. Whether you are here on a religious pilgrimage, for the historical icons and mosaics of St. Catherine Monastery, or the mountainous trekking, a 1-day excursion to St. Catherine is a must.

Dahab is a world apart from glitzy Sharm El Sheikh. Though its hippie spirit has been downplayed through the years with urban planning and tourism development, the laid-back destination of the peninsula is still a backpackers' favorite. You'll spend lazy days sunbathing with a book in hand or going for lengthy strolls along its promenade, and active travelers will have their pick of adrenaline-pumping activities; this is about the only destination in Egypt offering freediving or rock climbing.

While Dahab is a backpackers' Neverland, Nuweiba is for meditation devotees. It advocates the "back to basics" motto with a coastal stretch dotted with basic, peaceful camps where you can turn off your mobile phone and unwind.

Taba is Sinai's new kid on the block. The secluded destination offers luxury for a selected few, but it is gearing up for a tourism boom.

1 SHARM EL SHEIKH

The glamorous tourism capital of Egypt is in a continuous state of rejuvenation. Twenty-five years ago, Ne'ama Bay was a pristine bay with a couple of ramshackle fishermen's huts. Today, it is a beehive that doesn't cease to buzz. Here you will have dinner, go for *shisha,* do souvenir shopping, have a couple of drinks with friends, and party till dawn breaks. Nabq was once a rarely visited outskirt that today teems with hotels, cafes, restaurants, and shopping malls. It is gearing up for Sinai's "package holiday destination" title. A couple of years back, Hadaba's piazza-like Il Mercato, with its haute couture stores and rustic hangouts, was all the rage, but today the sleek and swanky Soho Square, with its trendy nightclub and ground-breaking ice bar, is the talk of the town. For the inexperienced eye, Sharm El Sheikh appears to be all about lovely beaches and wild parties, but you can just as easily don a wet suit and dive an underwater Eden, get stuck in the sand

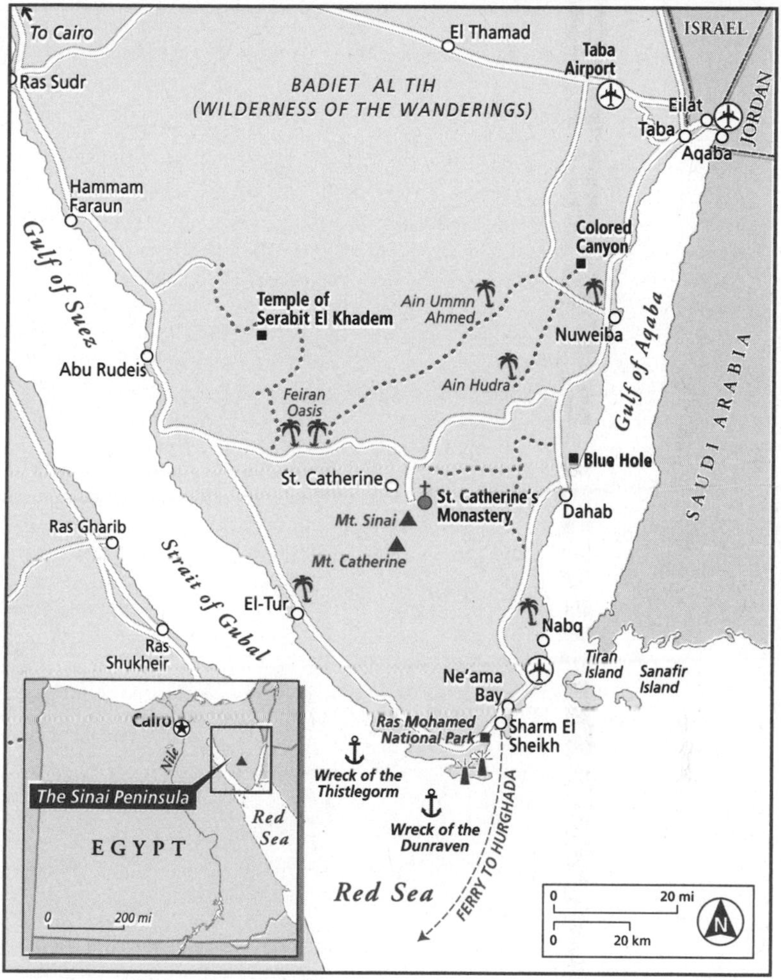

while on a quad safari, or pump up the adrenaline with some world-class go-karting. Whoever you are, whatever your interests, Sharm El Sheikh will leave you breathless.

ORIENTATION

Sharm El Sheikh is divided into four distinct areas that are loosely strung out along the highway like close, but separate, towns. Arriving from the south, with the sea on your right, you come first to the Old Souk (to your left). Then to your right, on a plateau that juts out into the sea, is Hadaba. Another 5 to 6km (3½ miles) up the highway is Ne'ama Bay. The international airport is another 5km (3 miles) or so past Ne'ama Bay, which puts it about halfway to the new, almost exclusively package holiday resort area of Nabq.

Thorns in the Thigh

The beautiful Sinai Peninsula is not heaven on earth; it is marred with chronic issues that lay deep beneath the surface. Tourism is the economy's backbone, but those who reap the benefits are Egyptians from the Nile Valley coming for a better paycheck or an appealing investment opportunity. In both cases, local Bedouins are missing out. Inequality and marginalization fuel feelings of detestation, and though it has never been confirmed who was behind the Dahab and Sharm El Sheikh attacks in 2005 and 2006, strong speculations point at indigenous groups. On one hand, south Sinai flourishes with tourism, while north Sinai regularly makes headline news as the only non-Israeli border crossing between Gaza and the outside world. Tunneling goods and products that range from detergents to weapons is a risky, yet financially rewarding, business for the people of Gaza and north Sinai alike. The Israelis rate it as a matter of national security, while the Egyptians end up caught in the middle. Because of this, El Arish has fallen off the tourism map, while Rafah has become a no-go zone. Illegal immigration is another large issue. Sudan's long civil war, Eritrea's deteriorating economy, and Somalia's continuous anarchy has spilled into Egypt; fleeing refugees risk everything crossing the border to Israel in hopes of a better life. Within the second half of 2009, more than 17 desperate African immigrants were shot dead by Egyptian police; press releases later justified the killings as part of counter people-trafficking operations. In January 2010, Israel announced a new barrier to be constructed along the Egyptian border in a bid to put an end to human trafficking.

OLD SOUK About as close to a "real town" as Sharm El Sheikh gets these days, the Old Souk is a somewhat ramshackle collection of shops and restaurants. Tourist items such as *shishas* (water pipes), snorkels and fins, and T-shirts are significantly cheaper here than in Ne'ama Bay. Behind the Old Souk there's housing for the huge migrant tourism workforce that comes to Sharm El Sheikh from all over the country.

HADABA Originally called Ras Om El Sid, Hadaba is an almost autonomous pocket of residential villas with a handful of high-end hotels and amusement facilities. Along with a water park and two go-kart tracks, there are also a couple of private rocky beaches, one of the best nightclubs in town, and the large pedestrian shopping street known as Il Mercato. Hadaba is also relatively isolated from the goings on down in Ne'ama Bay.

NE'AMA BAY This intense cluster of restaurants, hotels, cafes, and a few bars around the bay is the "downtown core" of Sharm El Sheikh. It's the only part of town where you can get out of your hotel and walk to a restaurant or a bar. For the most part boisterous and crowded, Ne'ama Bay offers a pleasant almost-seaside promenade lined with restaurants where you can cruise for dinner, cafes where you can smoke *shisha,* as well as a couple of bars including Sharm El Sheikh's iconic Camel Bar. Ne'ama Bay also hosts Sharm El Sheikh's nightlife hot spot, Pacha.

NABQ This is a newly developed area north of the airport. Big money has been spent supplying the place with shopping malls and facilities outside the walls of the big, all-inclusive resorts here, but it's quite a ride from Ne'ama Bay, Hadaba, or the Old Souk.

However, the shopping promenade La Strada might be worth checking out if you are a hard-core shopaholic.

Getting There

BY PLANE Sharm El Sheikh International Airport is Egypt's second-busiest airport. There are more than a dozen flights per day out of Cairo, and the cost of the 1-hour flight is around LE600 round-trip. In addition, there are a number of airliners and budget carriers that connect Sharm El Sheikh directly to main European cities.

If you didn't arrange a hotel transfer, there are always taxi drivers waiting for you. The recent blue-and-white models will cost you LE50 to LE60 for a ride into town.

BY CAR You can get to Sharm El Sheikh by car, but it's not worth it unless you enjoy road trips. From the capital, take the Cairo–Suez Road until the sign that reads SINAI; from there take the Ahmed Hamdy Tunnel, which will get you past the Suez Canal. Once on the peninsula, take the well-signed road heading south. It is a single-carriage highway in good condition, better known as El Sharm Road. The total distance from Cairo is about 500km (310 miles) and takes between 5 and 6 hours.

BY BUS Several bus companies connect Sharm El Sheikh to the capital and other Egyptian cities. The well reputed **Go Bus** (**© 19567**) has nine buses a day that head to Cairo, of which two continue farther to Alexandria. Tickets cost LE80 to LE100 for the Cairo bus and LE110 for the Alex bus. In Sharm El Sheikh, buses leave from the Sharm El Sheikh Bus Station, which has recently relocated to the outskirts of the city. However, if you show up 30 minutes before your bus departure time in front of the Go Bus office, conveniently located between Ne'ama Bay and Hadaba, a free minibus will take you to the main bus station. Arriving in Sharm El Sheikh, however, you will have to pick up a taxi into town. In Cairo, the Go Bus station is centrally located at Abdel Moneim Riyad Square, close to Tahrir Square.

East Delta Bus Company (**© 069/3665351**) does not have the most comfy or well serviced buses in the country, but it certainly has one of the most comprehensive networks stretching beyond the capital. In Sharm El Sheikh, they have an exclusive bus station a 5-minute ride from where the Go Bus office is. Eight daily buses head to Dahab (LE20), of which three continue farther to Nuweiba (LE25) and one to Taba (LE30).

Visas

Arriving directly to Sinai from abroad, you have a choice of two visas. One option is the free, 14-day Sinai-only visa, which is good for Sharm El Sheikh, St. Catherine, and the coastal stretch running all the way northeast to Taba. It won't get you anywhere else on the peninsula, though most probably you won't need to. The other option is the regular 30-day visa for all of Egypt that costs $15. Play it safe and pay the $15, as a Sinai-only visa can't be extended or upgraded to the 30-day one. If you decide to stay in Sinai beyond the 14 days, you will literally have to leave the country and come back again.

For a visa extension, requirements and procedure are the same as in Cairo (p. 95). However, your request can't be processed in Sharm El Sheikh, and you have to go to the governorate's administrative capital of El Tur.

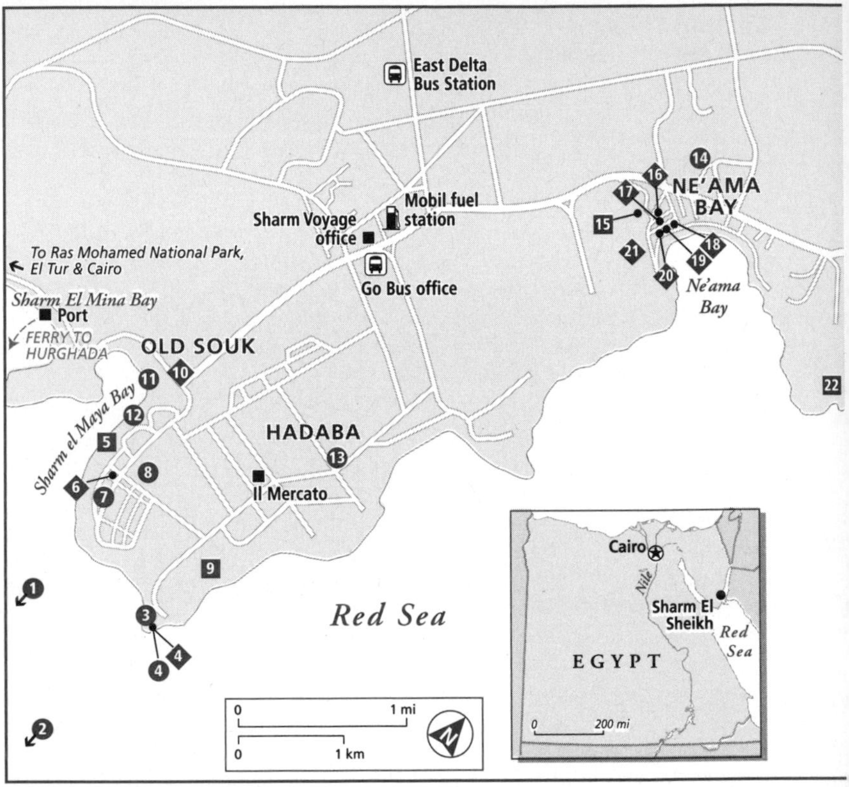

They also have one daily bus that makes the 9-hour ride all the way to Hurghada (LE75). If you have the stamina for long bus journeys, there is another daily bus that heads to Luxor for LE100 and takes between 13 to 14 hours.

BY FERRY The fast ferry makes the 2½-hour sail between Sharm El Sheikh and Hurghada four times a week. From Sharm El Sheikh it departs on Saturday, Tuesday, and Thursday at 5pm and on Monday at 6pm. From Hurghada it departs on Saturday, Tuesday, and Thursday at 9am and on Monday at 4am. It costs LE250/LE150 adults/children. The ferry's agent in Sharm El Sheikh (Sharm Voyage; © **012/8229877**) has their office across the street from the Go Bus office.

Getting Around

BY TAXI Taxis remain a necessity in Sharm El Sheikh, where hotels tend to be a long way from each other and from the nightlife and restaurants of Ne'ama Bay. The fleet here is among the newest and cleanest throughout the country, and if picked up from designated spots (there is one at Ne'ama Bay), the fare is fixed. At press time, the fixed fares were as below:

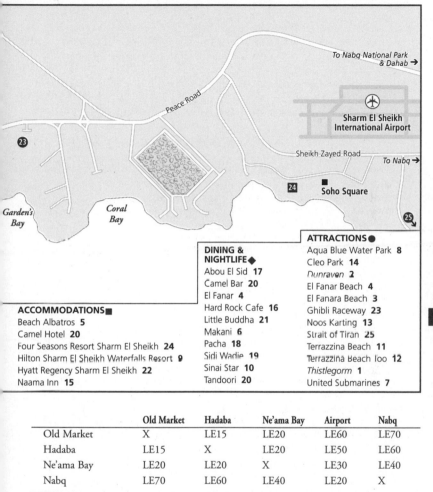

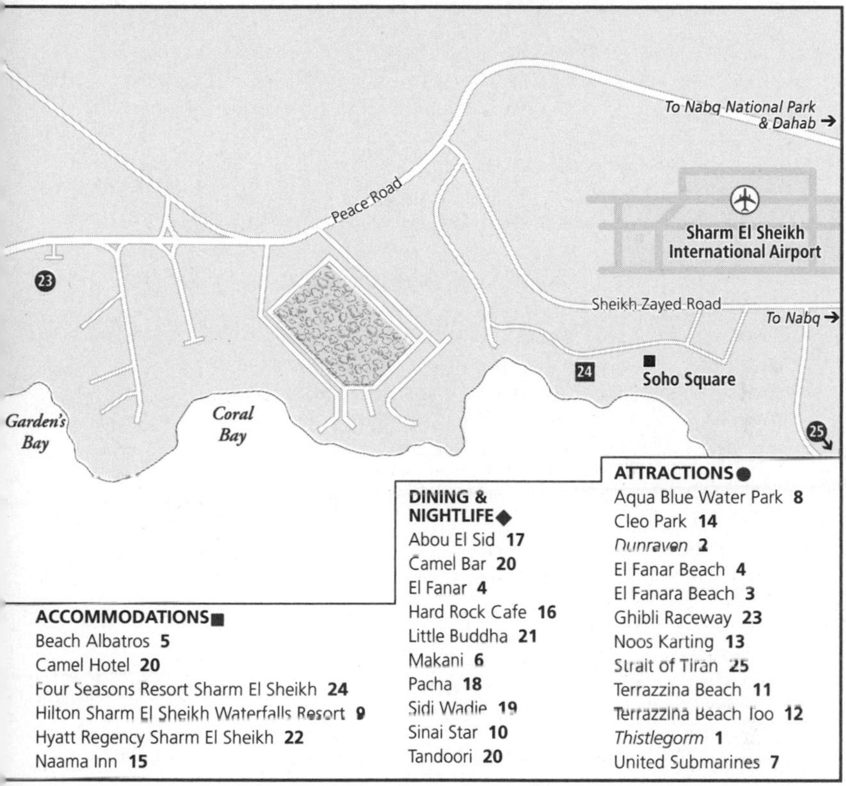

	Old Market	Hadaba	Ne'ama Bay	Airport	Nabq
Old Market	X	LE15	LE20	LE60	LE70
Hadaba	LE15	X	LE20	LE50	LE60
Ne'ama Bay	LE20	LE20	X	LE30	LE40
Nabq	LE70	LE60	LE40	LE20	X

BY CAR If you're going to be running around between the different districts of Sharm El Sheikh, visiting Ras Mohamed National Park, and maybe taking a day trip to Dahab or St. Catherine, you might consider renting a car. With a little bargaining, you should be able to rent something small but reliable for around LE220 per day.

CRC, Plaza Mall, Ne'ama Bay (✆ **069/3601297**), is cheap, but the staff are completely unprofessional and lack a sense of ownership. Rates and conditions are similar to their Hurghada branch (p. 232).

Avis, Morgana Mall, Ne'ama Bay (✆ **069/3602400**), is more expensive, but the cars are generally a little nicer and the staff are flexible and helpful. Rates start around LE220 a day for a compact model (Hyundai Verna) and go all the way to LE600 for a fancy

The Beaches

Sharm El Sheikh is internationally known for its year-round sunshine and beautiful beaches. Though each hotel has its own, a couple of private beaches have recently sprung up. **Terrazzina Beach** is big in Sharm El Sheikh and has recently opened its second branch, Terrazzina Beach Too; both are located at Sharm El Maya Bay (close to the Old Souk area). Terrazzina Beach is small and crammed with beanbags and loungers, and while it misses on music, it enjoys a super panoramic view. Terrazzina Beach Too is where young, beautiful women in tiny bikinis go tanning. There's a weekly (Fri) beach party, but it's good to chill out with a cocktail any day of the week. Entrance to Terrazzina Beach (LE35) and Terrazzina Beach Too (LE50; Fri LE100) includes use of a beach towel (✆ **010/1477577** or 010/9449283).

El Fanar Beach (LE60 includes beach towel and bottle of water) is a lovely tanning spot with a spectacular view of Hadaba's hilly outcrop and the looming lighthouse in the backdrop. However, if you don't like rocky beaches, then head to **El Fanara Beach** (LE20), on the other side of the lighthouse. It's a tiny stretch of sand often jam-packed with sun worshipers.

BMW. All rental rates come with a standard 100km (62 miles) allowance and an incremental per kilometer charge that varies from LE1 to LE2.50.

Tourist Information

Sharm El Sheikh has a tourist information office in the airport that could be helpful. You can also pick up any of the free news and listings magazines you will find on stands while in the airport.

There is an abundance of dedicated **Internet** cafes around town, especially in the Old Souk, where you'll pay LE10 per hour. Speed is adequate and connection is reliable.

WHAT TO SEE & DO

Sharm El Sheikh's attractions range from lounging by the pool, basking in the sun, and plunging in the sea to diving sunken wrecks, going out in the desert, and racing around a go-kart arena—and these are just a small sample of the options.

Aqua Blue Water Park (Kids) This big water park in Hadaba is a great place to spend the day with the kids. There's not much among the 32 slides to hold a teenager's attention, but those 13 and under should be in for all the slippery, speedy fun they can handle. To keep the grownups amused there's a selection of five themed restaurants that range from Mexican to Italian. A long after-lunch float down the lazy river might be just the thing for a hot day in Sharm El Sheikh.

Hadaba. Admission $30 adults, $20 kids 4–12. Daily 10am–sunset.

Cleo Park (Kids) This water park is located up the hill on the inland side of the highway as it runs past Ne'ama Bay. The entry and, indeed, most of the park are gloriously and unashamedly cheesy, with a Pharaonic motif applied willy-nilly to everything from the pylon-style entry to the rides. My favorite is the one where the slide is a gigantic anaconda twisting its way down through the center of a mock pyramid. Managed by Hilton, the place is stuffed with lifeguards who seem attentive and alert, and there is a fast-food restaurant for sugary top-ups when the energy levels start to flag. Like Aqua Blue, there's not much here for adrenalin junkies, but a lot of noisy, good-natured fun for children and parents alike.

Ne'ama Bay. ✆ **069/3604400.** Admission LE200 adults, LE120 kids 4–12. Daily 10am–sunset.

Diving and Snorkeling It's easy to forget in the midst of all the fun-and-sun hoopla that Sharm El Sheikh was—and still is—a diver's paradise. The range of reefs, corals, and undersea life is some of the best in the world. In addition, there are a couple of **wrecks** within easy day-trip reach. Topping the sunken ships' list is the ***Thistlegorm*** (p. 233) with its intact cargo of weaponry. It is closely followed by the *Dunraven* and the *Kingston.* The ***Dunraven*** was an iron sail and steam vessel on its way from Bombay to Liverpool loaded with spices and fabric, which sank in the spring of 1876 after hitting a reef. Now it lies almost upside down offering a breathtaking view of another seafaring disaster. Bound to Aden, the ***Kingston*** went down in pretty much the same fashion as the *Dunraven,* and its heavy cargo of coal keeps the ship almost where it sank. The wreck is in relatively good shape with the stern and the hull partly intact.

The **Strait of Tiran** is a painstakingly difficult to navigate 5km-wide (3-miles) passageway that runs between the Sinai's eastern coast and Tiran Island. Four main sites mark its diving map; namely Gordon, Jackson, Woodhouse, and Thomas. **Gordon Reef** is the biggest reef, offering more than one dive; from the sharks amphitheater, where a school of sharks are often sighted asleep, to the wreck of the *Louilla,* a commercial freighter that went down in 1981 and has partially sunk, leaving parts of the wreck well above sea surface. The **Jackson Reef,** fully covered with soft and hard corals, is a spectacular dive, while **Woodhouse Reef** is a drift dive with strong currents that is certain to put your skills to the test. **Thomas Reef** is the smallest of the Tiran's quartet and is another drift dive that takes you to a 25m-deep (82-ft.) plateau and a farther 35m-deep (115-ft.) canyon.

Ras Mohamed National Park, declared a national park in 1983, offers a number of strikingly different dive sites. Located at the foot of a cliff, **Sharks Observatory,** before the tourism boom, was a point where you could see schools of sharks just by sitting on the cliff above the water's surface. Unfortunately, the large number of divers per day disturbed the sharks, eventually leading them to flee. Today Sharks Observatory is a good dive site where you can see some pelagic fish such as jacks, tunas, and, if you are lucky, a couple of sharks. **Yolanda Reef** gets its name from a vessel that sunk here. Scattered around are the vessel's cargo of bathtubs, toilet seats, and the captain's BMW; the unusual setting makes for great photographs. **Jackfish Alley** is another wonderful dive site in Ras Mohamed where jacks and blue-spotted stingrays are the pick of the day.

Snorkelers should not feel left out, as most of the diving sites here make for good, if not great, snorkeling spots. Tour operators and travel agencies in your hotel's lobby and

Tips Topless Sunbathing

Sharm El Sheikh has the best beaches to work on your tan, and though no one will stop you from sunbathing topless, it is highly discouraged. Despite high-end hotels' liberal attire, deep down Egyptian society is largely traditional, if not outright conservative. Keep your bikini top on out of cultural respect.

(Tips) Taxing the Reef

When booking your diving vacation, probe whether the quoted prices include reef tax or not. It is a government levied fee that usually hovers around 3€ to 5€ per person per day. If you are planning an extended diving holiday, it may add up to a substantial amount.

all over Ne'ama Bay sell Ras Mohamed or Tiran Island as a 1-day boat excursion with an average price tag of LE230 and LE200, respectively. Prices include lunch, drinks, and snorkeling equipment, but not diving equipment.

For first-time divers who want to enroll in courses, Sharm El Sheikh is one of the most expensive places in Egypt, with PADI Open Water costing a staggering 395€. Get your license in neighboring Dahab and come here for the dives.

Ghibli Raceway The track here is huge, and facilities include a grandstand and a full-on pit lane with a row of garages. Though it offers a selection of smaller karts for more casual drivers, Ghibli is really aimed at the high-buck, high-thrill end of the market with a track that can be reconfigured to multiple lengths out to 1.3km (4¼ miles) for international races. "Arrive and drive" customers are limited, however, to about 570m (1,870 ft.). The driver's suit you will be offered, during the briefing prior to racing, adds a Formula One spice to the whole experience.

Airport Rd., Ne'ama Bay. ✆ **069/3603939.** www.ghibliraceway.com. Prices for 10 min., 15 min., and 10 min. + 10 laps packages with 6.5-horsepower and 9-horsepower (fits 2) karts ranges $24–$61. Prices go up after 5pm. Daily 11am–midnight.

Noos Karting With a 620m (2,033-ft.) track and a variety of karts, **Noos Karting** can give the whole family all the speed it needs. While the kids putter about with the little 2.5-horsepower jobs, mom and dad can hit the track with the 6.5-horsepower race karts.

Hadaba. ✆ **069/3662539.** www.nooskarting.com. LE80 for 10 min. in 2.5-horsepower kids' kart; LE120 for 10 min. in 6.5-horsepower race kart. Daily 10am–midnight.

Quad/Dirt Bike Safaris A host of quad safari companies advertise their services in Sharm El Sheikh. Though one of them, **Sinai Safari Adventures** (✆ **019/7276163**), stands head and shoulders above the rest, it's easy enough to explore the competition with a quick browse through the offerings at your hotel's travel desk or with a stroll around Ne'ama Bay. Expect to pay around LE120 per person for single common quads and LE350 per vehicle (fits two) for the less familiar rhino quads or the out-of-a-sci-fi-movie Argocat. The ride takes you along dirt tracks around the outskirts of Sharm El Sheikh for 2 hours.

Submarines (Kids) Making like a fish and swimming about with a snorkel and fins, let alone air tanks and weights, isn't the only way to get close to the corals and sea creatures. In fact, it's probably a lot simpler to get onboard one of **United Submarines'** fleet of "submarines" that takes between 34 and 68 people, with the bigger ones being equipped with toilets. Several trips a day run between 9am and 3pm, each taking about 90 minutes, of which 1 hour is spent underwater.

Hadaba. ✆ **012/7784637** or 010/0059512. www.unitedsubmarines.com. LE270 adults, kids 6–12 half-price, under 6 free. Daily 9am–3pm.

WHERE TO STAY

Very Expensive

Four Seasons Resort Sharm el Sheikh This is probably the best hotel in Sharm El Sheikh. It has that kind of casual perfection that makes the business of pampering guests look as easy as flipping burgers. The setting is lovely. The main building, where the lobby and the main restaurant are, sits at the edge of the plateau, and the rest of the buildings ramble gently down almost to the water. As you descend, either on the stairway or the small funicular railway, the landscape architecture is intimate without blocking the view over the sea. Service is warm, competent, and seamlessly unobtrusive. When you arrive, for example, you're simply shown to your room; the formalities of checking in are handled later. Rooms are big, sheets are high-thread-count Egyptian cotton, and your bathroom is a minispa. The decor manages to be at once traditional and modern, with clean lines, lovely light, and a view of the sea. There is, quite simply, nothing wrong here. On the other hand, there is precious little character either. The formula of quiet perfection that works so well in a densely packed urban setting leaves me a little cold in a resort setting. Though this is a highly recommended place for a long weekend of relaxation or a romantic getaway, it is not the place to bring the kids.

1 Four Seasons Blvd. (behind the airport). ✆ **069/3603555.** Fax 069/3603550. www.fourseasons.com. 136 units, including 27 suites. $650 sea-view double; $550 garden-view double. Rack rates include buffet breakfast, but subject to 25.5% taxes and service charges. AE, DC, MC, V. **Amenities:** 5 restaurants; 3 bars; airport transfer (extra charge); babysitting; concierge; health club & spa; Internet (extra charge); heated pool; room service; 3 tennis courts; dive center. *In room:* A/C, TV, Internet (extra charge), minibar.

The Wild Side of Sharm

Sharm El Sheikh's wild side is not all about hedonist beach parties and glitzy clubbing venues; there are two national parks here, too. **Ras Mohamed National Park** (✆ **069/3660668;** admission $5 adult, $5 car; daily 8am–sunset) is a slender peninsula that extends off the southern end of the Sinai. It's chiefly known for the spectacular diving and snorkeling afforded by the reef here (p. 193). However, Ras Mohamed's natural attractions extend beyond underwater fantasyland. Tens of different bird species call the park home, while others are regular visitors stopping for a respite during the annual lengthy migration between Europe and Africa. Ospreys, kingfishers, herons, and storks are among the long list of bird species you can spot here. The park is also a great camping site, but you need to be 100% self reliant. If you are going to pitch your tent, there is a designated area for camping, which you need to check into before 6pm.

Located on the other end of town in the direction of Dahab is the lesser-visited **Nabq National Park** (✆ **069/36606680;** admission $5 adult, $5 car; daily 8am–sunset). It offers less stunning diving sites, but the virginity of the whole place gives it its own charm. More birds, such as egrets, spoonbills, plovers, and redshanks, can be observed here, especially around the mangrove thickets. During low tide you can easily wade your way through the shallow waters surrounding the mangroves and get surprisingly close to the *Maria Schroeder* wreck. The German vessel still lies half sunk above the water's surface and dominates Nabq's horizon.

Hyatt Regency Sharm El Sheikh (Kids) This is a rare example of a resort with a genuine sense of fun that still manages to maintain very good service on all the serious fronts. Rooms are top-notch, with clean, modern lines and touches of tiles that remind you that you're at the beach. Bathrooms are fairly large in size, and balconies are big enough to lounge *and* dry your towels over the railing at the same time. The food is good, far better than what you get from other hotel outlets; my favorite is the Sala Thai restaurant, but the Beach House Grill isn't half-bad either. The fun part, though, happens in the middle of the resort, where the gardens cascade down to the short beach. There are pools, but there's also a lazy river tucked into the greenery and a small water slide that will keep the younger kids happy.

Ne'ama Bay. ✆ **069/3601234.** Fax 069/3603600. www.sharmelsheikh.regency.hyatt.com. 471 units. $532 double. Rack rate includes buffet breakfast, taxes, and service charges. AE, MC, V. **Amenities:** 5 restaurants; 2 bars; airport transfer (extra charge); babysitting; kids' club; concierge; health club & spa; Internet (extra charge); 3 pools (heated); room service; 4 tennis courts (floodlit); dive center. *In room:* A/C, TV, Internet (extra charge), minibar.

Expensive

Hilton Sharm El Sheikh Waterfalls Resort This is a big resort that sprawls over a large compound above the sea in Hadaba. Because of its size, it can offer something for everyone—the pools, for example, are divided into quiet pools, more boisterous pools, and pools with animation. The beach, which is linked to the main building by one of only two funicular railways in Sharm El Sheikh, is one of the nicest in town, with soft, warm sand enclosed in a small bay with a jetty to get prospective snorkelers out beyond the reef without damaging the coral. The spacious rooms hit just the right balance between beach and hotel, with tiled floors and colorful area rugs; the sea views are simply stunning. The location isn't ideal for getting into Ne'ama Bay, but there is a regular hotel shuttle.

Hadaba. ✆ **069/3663232.** Fax 069/3663228. www1.hilton.com. 401 units. $160 sea-view double; $135 garden-view double. Rack rates include buffet breakfast, taxes, and service charges. AE, MC, V. **Amenities:** 5 restaurants; 8 bars; airport transfer (extra charge); babysitting; concierge; health club; Internet (extra charge); 7 pools (including 2 heated); room service; tennis court (floodlit); dive center. *In room:* A/C, TV, Internet (extra charge), minibar.

Moderate

Beach Albatros One of the oldest hotels in Sharm El Sheikh, the Albatros is located on Hadaba overlooking the broad sandy bay sweep. This is an all-inclusive facility, and even though it's a good one—maintenance has been kept up and the facilities are clean and freshly painted—it has a slightly down-market feel to it. Rooms are comfortable, midrange, and spread out through low buildings that ring the low-key gardens and pool facilities. Though it doesn't make the most of the potential for a spectacular view off the cliff, the ambience is extremely pleasant and relaxed. My favorite part of the place, though, is the elevator that runs down the face of the cliff to the 1.2km (¾-mile) beach.

Hadaba. ✆ **069/3663923.** Fax 069/3663921. 205 units. LE600 double. Rack rate includes buffet breakfast, dinner, taxes, and service charges. AE, MC, V. **Amenities:** 2 restaurants; 2 bars; airport transfer (extra charge); concierge; health club; 4 pools (including 2 kids'); room services; tennis court; Wi-Fi (extra charge). *In room:* A/C, TV, minifridge, Internet (extra charge).

Camel Hotel The Camel is an excellent, midrange hotel in the middle of Ne'ama Bay with one of the best restaurants in town, Pomodora. It's also one of the few places in Sharm El Sheikh where you can really see the history—or maybe that should be prehistory—of the town. Some of the bare stone wall in the lobby is from the original camel station (hence the name of the place) from which the current hotel and dive center developed. Rooms are basic with clean, white-tile floors and comfortable-but-plain beds and bathrooms, and eight of them are handicap accessible. There is no question of a sea view, and the central courtyard is nice, though nothing in comparison to the Hyatt's glorious garden playground. If you want to get out and try the restaurants and bars of Sharm El Sheikh, the location is perfect; from here, all of downtown Ne'ama Bay is accessible by foot. Note that there is a sizable discount available on room rates by booking in advance through the website.

Ne'ama Bay. ✆ **069/3600700.** Fax 069/3600601. www.cameldive.com. 38 units, including 5 rooms for people with special mobility. 56€ double. Rate includes buffet breakfast, taxes, and service charges. MC, V. **Amenities:** 3 restaurants; bar; airport transfer (extra charge); pool; dive center; Wi-Fi (free). *In room:* A/C, TV, minifridge.

Naama Inn This place doesn't look very nice from the outside, but it has been very pleasantly brought up to date inside. Though the rooms don't really keep up with the lobby (a mix of modern and traditional Egyptian furnishings and light fixtures) in terms of style—the furniture is a little older and a little more budget—the beds are comfortable and the place is clean. Rooms vary quite a bit, so look at a few before deciding, or if you booked ahead and are unhappy, ask to see some others. Keep in mind that rooms near the front can get a fair bit of noise from the street, and this noise can go on very late into the night.

Ne'ama Bay. ✆ **069/3600801** or 069/3600805. Fax 069/3600950. www.Naamainn.com. 39 units. $80 double. Rate includes buffet breakfast, dinner, taxes, and service charges. No credit cards. **Amenities:** 2 restaurants; bar; pool; room service; dive center; Wi-Fi. *In room:* A/C, TV, minifridge.

WHERE TO EAT

Sharm El Sheikh is awash with different restaurants, which makes going out for dinner a delightful culinary experience. Head to the Old Souk if you are in the mood for some seafood, Egyptian-style, or to Ne'ama Bay for options ranging from traditional Egyptian and authentic Moroccan to spicy Indian and all-American.

Expensive

Abou El Sid EGYPTIAN Order a few appetizers—*sojok* (little beef sausages cooked the Egyptian way), *tahina,* stuffed vine leaves, baba ghanouj—or just go for the appetizer tray for a broad selection. Main courses are substantial, and both the Circassian chicken (slices of chicken laid on a bed of rice and smothered in a walnut sauce) and the grilled veal chops are worthy recommendations. Decor, like at the Cairo location, includes plush chairs and heavy round tables, traditional lamps hanging from the ceilings, and art prints of Om Kolthoum and other prominent Egyptian cultural figures. If you have any space left over after appetizers and your main course (I highly doubt it), try one of their excellent sweet *feteer* or the *om aly* for dessert.

Above the Hard Rock Cafe, Sultan Al Qaboos St., Ne'ama Bay. ✆ **069/3603910.** Appetizers LE15–LE35; main courses LE35–LE75. MC, V. Daily noon–1am.

Sidi Wadie MOROCCAN This simple Moroccan restaurant is located on the rooftop of the Ne'ama Shopping Mall and overlooks the bustling Ne'ama Bay where you can watch the never-ending stream of people coming and going. The interiors are bland and the Moroccan decor is oddly limited to furniture and utensils. The menu is limited in choices and dishes, and they come in gourmet portions; however, whatever you order retains its original Moroccan tang. *Harira* soup is a classic start that's best followed by the *tagine* Fessi (veal with saffron, cinnamon, and dried prunes).

King of Bahrain St., Ne'ama Bay. ✆ **069/3604358.** Appetizers LE20–LE30; main courses LE90–LE110. MC, V. Daily 1pm–midnight.

Moderate

Hard Rock Cafe INTERNATIONAL Come here if you are in the mood for a greasy American burger washed down with a couple of cold beers. The decor, from the pink Ford Fairlane parked outside the front entrance to the signed guitars and various other pop music "collectibles," and the loud music playing in the foreground set Hard Rock's trademark mood. Start with various Tex-Mex appetizers, followed by the Legendary 10-ounce burger topped with seasoned bacon, cheddar cheese, onion rings, tomato, lettuce, and pickles. Finish off with the hot fudge sundae if you have any space left.

Note: At midnight the place turns into a disco with an LE100 entry ticket and strict couples-only policy. Hard Rock Cafe has two more branches in Egypt (Cairo and Hurghada).

Sultan Qaboos St., Ne'ama Bay. ✆ **069/3602664.** Appetizers LE15–LE25; main courses LE40–LE100. MC, V. Daily 11am–1am.

Makani INTERNATIONAL Tucked away in the back of Hadaba, this is a great place for a quick lunch while you're out exploring the neighborhood. They specialize in fresh-baked pastries and bread, and you can have a fresh fruit juice with a variety of sandwiches while soaking up the early afternoon sun on their little deck. If you have the time and crave sushi, it serves some of the best in town.

Note: In Sharm El Sheikh, Makani has another branch located on the airport road right in front of Ne'ama Bay, open 24 hours. There are also a couple of branches in Cairo (p. 143).

Sheikh Abdullah Shopping Center, Hadaba. ✆ **012/3255897.** www.makani.com.eg. Appetizers LE20–LE35; sandwiches LE20–LE30; sushi LE6–LE25 per piece. Daily 6:30am–2:30am.

Sinai Star SEAFOOD One of Sharm El Sheikh's iconic restaurants, Sinai Star's interior mimics an underwater cave, which I personally find a bit tacky, but the overall ambience is quite dynamic and the place teems with customers, especially around dinner time. Aside from the underwater cave feel, which you can easily avoid if you opt for the outdoor area, the food here is godly. Sinai Star offers hard-core Egyptian seafood dishes with calamari *tagine,* grilled mullet, and oven-baked sea bass topping the menu.

Old Souk. ✆ **069/3660323.** Seafood meal (including salads, appetizers, bread, and main course) LE60–LE80. No credit cards. Daily noon–midnight.

Tandoori ★ INDIAN With no view over the sea, uninspiring decor, and no fancy art on the wall, the inner courtyard of the Camel Dive Club and Hotel isn't going to draw many people in off the street—unless they stop outside for a sniff. Walking in, the smell of roasting spices, that heady mix of cardamom, cinnamon, ginger, cloves, and turmeric that characterizes so much of north Indian cooking, will pick you up and carry you off. Used as a general lounging area and luggage dump during the daylight hours, this space is transformed after dark into one of the best restaurants in Sharm El Sheikh. A subtly spiced *murg malai* chicken kebab with an order of butter *naan* (bread), followed by a syrupy sweet *gulab jamun* (deep-fried milk dumpling) for dessert make for a delightful dinner. Nearly a third of the menu here is vegetarian, which is a rarity in Egypt, and it's all superb.

King of Bahrain St., Ne'ama Bay. ✆ **069/3600700.** Reservations recommended. Appetizers LE15–LE25; main courses LE40–LE100. MC, V. Daily 7–11pm.

SHOPPING

Unlike most of Egypt's tourist-oriented cities, Sharm El Sheikh has more than just bazaar shops—clustered around the Old Souk and Ne'ama Bay—selling the typical *shisha*-to-jewelry fare; there are shopping malls, too. Il Mercato in Hadaba is a lovely place for window shopping, featuring world-leading brand names and a well appreciated Mothercare branch (great if you are traveling with the young ones and forget to pack an item or two). In addition, there are a couple of restaurants and cafes, as well as a rustic bar with dark wooden interiors and high chairs; it can be good for an early evening drink.

The newly developed Nabq has its own shopping promenade, La Strada, which clings to the Italian theme, like Il Mercato, and has a diverse assortment of outlets that vary from fashion and sportswear to fast-food joints; there is also a kids' area.

Ne'ama Bay still ranks first when it comes to shopping in Sharm El Sheikh. Though it misses on international brands, it scores high on more local produce and artistic souvenirs such as colored-sand bottles, hand-woven rugs, and beautiful pieces painted by enthusiastic young Egyptian artists; when in Ne'ama Bay, don't miss out on a quick visit to Ne'ama Bay Mall, especially the underground level.

SHARM EL SHEIKH AFTER DARK

El Fanar The name, which means lighthouse, comes from this club's location at the very far end of Hadaba. During the day it is one of Sharm El Sheikh's best private beaches

Soho Square

A Manneken Pis–like statue is jumping over the fence; another is playing in the garden, while a third is seesawing. **Soho Square** (✆ **010/1609544** or 069/3602752-3; www.soho-sharm.com), Sharm El Sheikh's latest talk of the town, gives an out-of-place first impression, with European period lampposts and Manneken Pis–like statues. But a closer look at the semi-pedestrian promenade (there's a lane for cars) reveals a number of enticing attractions. Chill out, to the literal meaning of the word, at **Ice Bar** (ticket LE150 for 20 min. and a free drink; the –10°C/14°F means the drink has to be vodka), or head to **Oxygen Bar,** where you can try any of its flavored pure oxygen treatments claimed to revitalize your mind (LE25 for 5 min.). If you wish just to sit back and smoke *shisha,* the fountain area in the middle of the promenade has been transformed into an open-air cafe where the fountain has been replaced with a ground-level in-water seating area. **Pangaea Nightclub**'s electric atmosphere draws a super-sexy crowd (doors open at 10:30pm; LE120 gets you two free drinks, women free entry). At press time, **Fashion Lounge** by Fashion TV was in the last stages of preparation, so fashionistas should keep an open eye. However, the space temporarily hosts salsa night twice a week (Mon and Thurs). Doors open at 10pm and admission is free. For a dash of culture, there is **Culturama,** a nine-screen interactive presentation that wraps up the country's history from the Pharaohs to modern day. It has two daily shows; the one in Russian starts at 8pm and the one in English at 9pm. Tickets are LE35.

(p. 192), but as the hour strikes midnight, it transforms into one of the sexiest clubbing venues in town. It is a spectacular place to party, having been cut out of the natural surroundings with views of both the lighthouse and the open sea. The dance floor is right on the edge of the cliff overlooking the sea, as is the separate but similarly cliff-edge bar area. There is also a full-blown Italian restaurant where you can enjoy the stunning view while having dinner. Live performances are off and on, but the Wednesday beach is carved in stone. Tickets cost 25€ and get you one free drink. Club hours midnight to 4am. Hadaba. © **069/3662218.** www.elfanarsharm.com.

Camel Bar Two of my favorite Sharm El Sheikh bars are here. Inside there's your traditional bare-bones dive bar with signed memorabilia on the walls, cheap cold beer behind the bar, and endless bowls of unshelled peanuts on the tables. The place is noisy and friendly, and gets more so as the night progresses. Upstairs on the roof the scene is no less fun or friendly, but the decor is a lot more sophisticated, with soft light from funky little lamps and simple-but-stylish furniture; the place is perfect for a casual night out. Daily 7pm till late. Ne'ama Bay. © **069/3600700.** www.cameldive.com.

Little Buddha Modeled after the Parisian original, this place features an amber-colored bar that glows from inside and a massive Buddha statue on the ground floor that pokes its head up through an opening in the second. Stylishly lit and plushly furnished, there's a restaurant downstairs (around the base of the Buddha) and a bar/nightclub upstairs (at Buddha-eye level) that plays a mix of Asian and progressive house music. It caters to the young tourist and wealthy local market—dress to impress, and get ready to dance till you drop. Tickets cost LE120 and get you one free drink, and a couples-only policy is strictly applied. Club hours 11:30pm to 4am. © **069/3601030.** www.littlebuddha-sharm.com.

Pacha If you have one night to party in Egypt, it has to be at Pacha. Take to the jampacked open-air dance floor and let loose. Mega DJs there are on the decks, and go-go dancers ignite the atmosphere. When things get too hot, jump in the pool to cool off—and party even harder—or head to the foam zone (summer only). For the after-hours set, access to the VIP room and terrace is essential; this is where the hard-core fun is. Single males are denied entry. Tickets include one free drink and cost LE165 if bought before 11:30pm and LE195 afterward. Open 11:30pm till late. Ne'ama Bay. © **069/3600197** or -8 ext 300 or 012/2180873 for VIP area. www.pachasharm.com.

DAY TRIPS FROM SHARM EL SHEIKH

Cairo, Luxor, and St. Catherine are the top day-trip destinations from Sharm El Sheikh. When it comes to Cairo, most travel agencies and tour operators have two options: a crowded bus that costs $50 and involves more than 10 hours on the road round-trip, or (the more comfortable way) flying. With more than a dozen daily flights between Cairo and Sharm El Sheikh, a day trip to Cairo is now an easier option and comes with a $230 price tag. Both bus and air travel prices include lunch, soft drinks, and tickets to the Egyptian Museum and the Pyramids (site ticket only).

Monument-infested Luxor follows Cairo's footsteps but with less flexibility. At press time there were only five weekly direct flights connecting Luxor and Sharm El Sheikh, leaving Sharm El Sheikh at 8am and departing Luxor at 9:25pm. If you wish to do it independently, the flight costs around LE1,100 (around $200) for the round-trip, while most of Sharm El Sheikh's travel agencies will sell the whole excursion for $230. In addition to the flight, the price also includes lunch, soft drinks, and tickets to the Karnak Temple, the Valley of the Kings (site ticket only), and the Mortuary Temple of Hatshepsut.

St. Catherine remains the closest, cheapest, and most demanded 1-day trip out of Sharm El Sheikh. For $30 you get to visit the monastery, check out the museum, and ascend Mount Moses. The price includes lunch, soft drinks, and a ticket to the monastery's museum.

Lastly, some travel agencies list the Colored Canyon and Ras Abu Galum as 1-day excursions for $40 and $45, respectively. There's no need to decide which travel agency or tour operator to book with, as most excursions run on a "shared basis" where agencies form a pool and share the fixed cost (mainly transportation) among themselves.

2 DAHAB

This is the closest you'll get to a true bohemian experience on Egyptian soil, and just a decade or so ago it was; the only restaurant in town was a kiosk on the beach named the Hard Rock Cafe (no relation to the Hard Rock chain), and the nicest hotel for miles had grass walls. Though things have changed in the name of tourism development, Dahab remains a low-key destination that misses on the party scene of neighboring Sharm El Sheikh but scores high on peace of mind and easygoing atmosphere. Here you can easily have a lazy vacation working on your tan, lounging by the sea with a book in hand, or walking up and down its famous promenade in a rewarding culinary pursuit. If you feel like spicing up your vacation, Dahab offers more than the usual bouquet of outdoor and underwater activities; test your body's capabilities with freediving, or conquer desert boulders with Egypt's newest adventure, rock climbing.

ORIENTATION

Dahab is divided into two main parts: new and old. The new part, now referred to as Dahab City, is to the south and is where the high-end hotels are. There is also a large lagoon that offers a range of conditions ideal for beginner and expert wind- and kitesurfers.

The older part of Dahab is a kilometer or so north, connected by both a road and a seaside promenade for pedestrians and bikes. The promenade is divided into three different areas; from south to north they are Mashraba, Masbat, and Assalah. Assalah is the biggest of the three with an additional local market at the back of its seaside walkway. In between Masbat and Assalah there is the famous Fanar Street with Dahab's lighthouse looming on the horizon.

Getting There

BY PLANE Dahab is only 100km (62 miles) northeast of Sharm El Sheikh and is fairly accessible using the well-served Sharm El Sheikh International Airport. Most of Dahab's high-end hotels offer an airport transfer for an extra charge, but you can always get a cab from the airport. Expect to pay no less than LE250 for the one-way taxi ride.

BY CAR Dahab is an easy 20km (12 miles) drive on a dual-carriage road from Sharm El Sheikh, but a newly constructed by-road cuts the distance by a good 10km (6 miles) and leads you directly into town. However, it's a single-carriage road with spine-chilling turns, so I would still use the longer way.

BY BUS **East Delta Bus Company** (**© 069/3641808**) connects Dahab to other south Sinai cities and towns, as well as Cairo and the far-flung Luxor. Running Sinai's eastern coast, daily buses connect Dahab to Sharm El Sheikh (LE20) and Nuweiba (LE11). The short trip from Dahab to either Sharm El Sheikh or Nuweiba takes about an hour. There are four daily buses to Cairo (LE90; 9 hr. one-way from Dahab) and a daily bus to Luxor (LE120; at least 15 hr. one-way).

Getting Around

BY BIKE The long brick walkway along the edge of the water that links all three sections of old Dahab as well as the newer portion of Dahab City is fairly bicycle-friendly (though the pedestrians won't be if you don't ride reasonably), and the traffic through the rest of town is pretty tame as well. The scale is perfect for biking, too. You can get anywhere in town in 15 or 20 minutes, and most places in 5.

Bikes can be rented at various places around town. For an old clunker you'll pay LE30, while for a newer bike the price goes up to LE50. **Desert Divers** (© **069/3640500;** www.desert-divers.com) has some of the best bikes in town.

ON FOOT Most of Dahab, especially if you stay in the older part of town, is walkable. I recommend detouring around the town, in fact, and using the coastal walkway to get to where you're going.

BY TAXI There is no imminent need to use taxis in Dahab; most of the places you'd be interested in going can be reached either biking or on foot. However, if you don't feel like cycling and are heading to Dahab City, for instance, you can hail a taxi for LE5; it is the standard fare for going anywhere in town. Taxis in Dahab are double cabin Toyota Hilux pickups.

BY CAR You certainly won't need a car going around Dahab, but if you are planning to be based here and explore the neighboring destinations, renting one might be wise. **Holiday Car Rental** (© **012/7814113**) has a small fleet for rent with an average price of LE300 per day with a 100km (62 miles) allowance, and LE1 extra charge for each additional kilometer.

Tourist Information

There is no real tourist information center in town that I can recommend, but the Neptune Hotel has a bookstore (9am–11:30pm), right next door to the hotel, well stocked with maps and guide and travel books. Its collection extends beyond titles covering Egypt and its different aspects to fiction and titles of general interest. I was quite surprised to find *Heavy Metal Islam* on sale here.

Internet cafes dot the promenade, especially at the more shopping-oriented back of Mashraba; rates are LE6 per hour.

WHAT TO SEE & DO

Dahab's reputation as a laid-back destination where the most strenuous activity involves reading a book or having a cold beer isn't entirely true. Similar to the rest of the Red Sea destinations, **diving** is the number-one attraction here. Dive the nearby aptly named **Eel Garden,** or go for a drift dive at **Golden Block,** named for the small yellow fish that turn golden in color when light breaks on the water surface. **Caves** offer a different diving experience, with no fish, corals, or wrecks, but the eerie quite can be a draw for some. **Bells,** funnel-like structures that end with an almost vertical tube at 17m (56 ft.) where you have to shoot down straight to 25m (82 ft.), are my favorite dive sites. It's an adrenaline rush that needs at least Advanced Open Water level due to its depth. Bells are part of the many dive sites the **Blue Hole** offers. Located less than a 30-minute drive from Dahab, the Blue Hole is an amazing place to spend the day whether you're interested in diving or snorkeling. Most hotels, travel agencies, as well as dive centers in

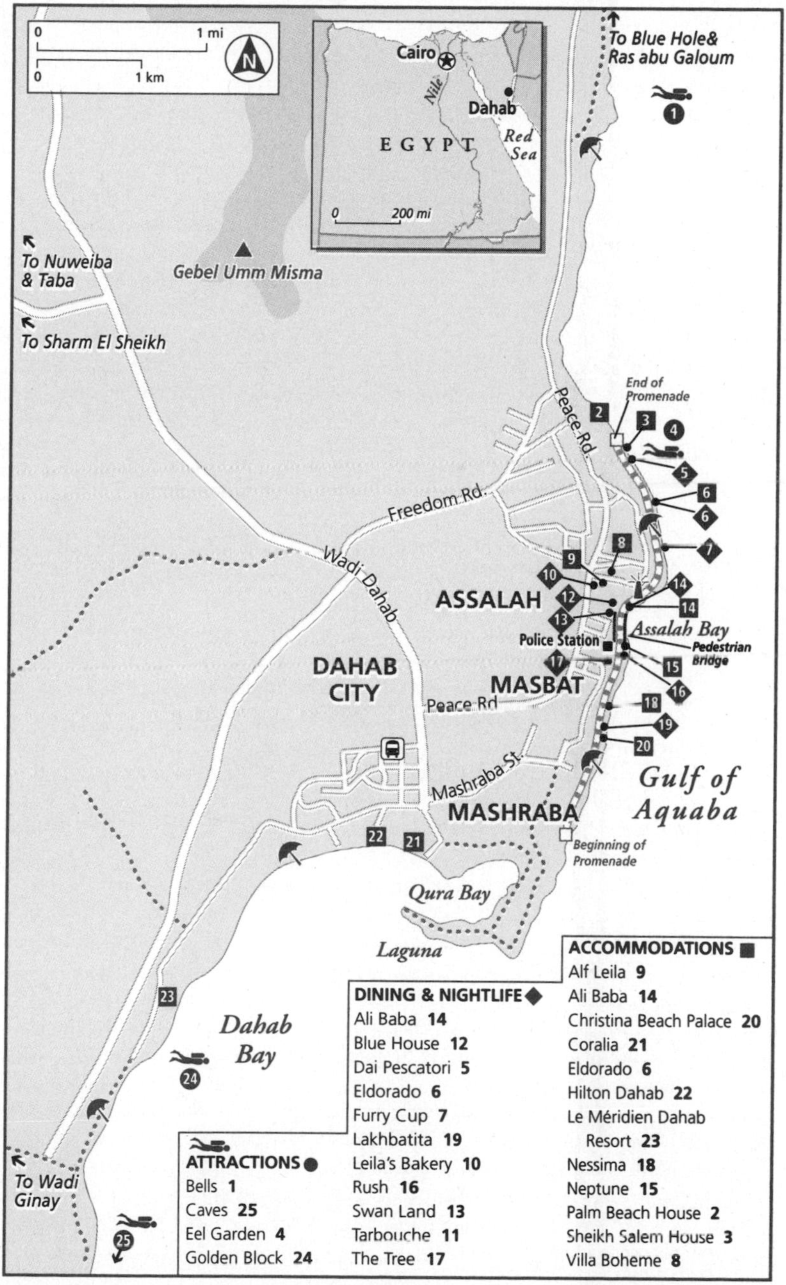

To Blue Hole&
Ras abu Galoum

Cairo

EGYPT

Nile

Dahab

Red
Sea

0 200 mi

To Nuweiba
& Taba

Gebel Umm Misma

To Sharm El Sheikh

End of
Promenade

Peace Rd.

Freedom Rd.

Wadi Dahab

ASSALAH

Police Station

DAHAB
CITY

Peace Rd

MASBAT

Assalah Bay

Pedestrian
Bridge

MASHRABA

Mashraba St.

Beginning of
Promenade

Gulf of
Aquaba

Qura Bay

Laguna

Dahab
Bay

To Wadi
Ginay

ACCOMMODATIONS ■
Alf Leila **9**
Ali Baba **14**
Christina Beach Palace **20**
Coralia **21**
Eldorado **6**
Hilton Dahab **22**
Le Méridien Dahab
 Resort **23**
Nessima **18**
Neptune **15**
Palm Beach House **2**
Sheikh Salem House **3**
Villa Boheme **8**

DINING & NIGHTLIFE ◆
Ali Baba **14**
Blue House **12**
Dai Pescatori **5**
Eldorado **6**
Furry Cup **7**
Lakhbatita **19**
Leila's Bakery **10**
Rush **16**
Swan Land **13**
Tarbouche **11**
The Tree **17**

ATTRACTIONS ●
Bells **1**
Caves **25**
Eel Garden **4**
Golden Block **24**

Coral: Look but Don't Touch

Because of the year-round warmth of the Red Sea's water, coral reefs abound. Everyone who visits the area should experience the richness of life that teems just below the surface of the crystal-clear waters. At first sight, it's easy to imagine that these rocky outcroppings are tough and impervious to human touch, but this is far from the case. Touching the coral or walking on it will break and kill it, leaving behind a dead, gray wall and a hole in a complex ecosystem that can take decades or longer to heal. Most international resorts have opted to do the responsible thing and have built jetties that allow swimmers and divers to get into the water without damaging the coral. Unfortunately, there are many places on the coast—including Dahab—where the government and local entrepreneurs haven't found the foresight to protect this invaluable tourist resource, so it's the responsibility of individual tourists to look beyond the next few days of their holiday and think about the global environment. It's easy enough to do: Find a place where the water is deep enough to swim over the coral, never touch the coral with your hands or your feet, and never throw plastic bags or other refuse into the water.

Dahab can arrange this excursion for you. However, you can easily do it independently by hiring a taxi for the day (LE60) and renting the snorkeling equipment (LE10) from any of the outlets at the Blue Hole or Dahab.

Desert Divers (p. 84) is a dive center with a mission. A joint partnership between a Canadian and a local Bedouin, Desert Divers trains indigenous Bedouins to become dive guides. The model is quite successful, with their entire English-speaking squad made up of local guides. Desert Divers uniquely offers a **camel diving safari,** combining diving with desert trekking (your camel safari reaches a coastal destination, where you dive). The most popular is the 2-day trip to **Ras Abu Galum** (200€ per person, includes four dives and diving equipment), a secluded place surrounded by mountains that offers out-of-this-world diving spots with exotic coral gardens and perhaps an encounter with a peaceful manatee.

If you don't have the zeal for camels or prefer a more comfortable means of transportation, **boat trips** are available to *Thistlegorm* (125€ per person, equipment included), the fabulous diving sites of Ras Mohamed National Park (105€ per person, equipment included), or the breathtaking wall dive and its one-of-a-kind tree coral at Gabr El Bint (85€ per person, equipment included). The serene landscape, both above and under the water, of the nearby Three Pools is an excursion you don't want to miss. It costs LE75 per person including transportation in a four-wheel-drive, lunch, and soft drinks (note that equipment is not included).

Freediving is a challenging sport gaining momentum worldwide, including in Dahab. The Blue Hole offers the ideal freediving conditions: surrounded by mountains and enjoying no prevailing wind or strong currents. Some international freediving competitions take place every now and then in Dahab, so keep an eye out. Courses are available for novices (75€; 1 day), beginners (180€; 3 days), and advanced freedivers (230€; 6 days; AIDA license included).

The lagoon area at Dahab City is famous for its steady wind and stone-free, shallow bay; perfect conditions for **wind-** and **kitesurfing.** There are a couple of windsurfing centers at the high-end hotels nearby (Qura Bay) as well as a couple of kitesurfing ones right here in the lagoon. For equipment rentals (half-/full-day rentals cost 40€/65€), check out **Soul Kiter** (© **016/2495508;** www.soul-kiter.com) or **Happy Kite** (© **019/2244822;** www.happy-kite.com). I wouldn't recommend either for their courses, though; in addition to the language barrier (their Russian and Ukrainian staff don't speak English well), the courses seem a bit brief to me (6 hr. for beginners), with no VDWS license available.

If you've had enough of the sea, opt for a 2-hour desert exploration safari using **quads** (LE180/LE120 per person single/double). There are a couple of outlets around the promenade's bridge that offer the same deal and share the same pool of well-maintained and new quad models. Dahab also enjoys some of the best boulders for **rock climbing.** Desert Divers qualifies local rock-climbing guides and offers beginning (175€; 2 days) and advanced (195€; 2 days) courses. Experienced climbers can take a 1-day excursion to the nearby Wadi Ginay (55€ per person, including full equipment and guide).

WHERE TO STAY

Almost everywhere that's worth staying in Dahab fronts the sea. In the older parts of town, what was once a rough, unlit path along the foreshore has been replaced by an attractive and well-lit brick promenade that stretches the entire 3km (1¾-mile) length of the town. High-end resorts are located at the far southern end of town.

Expensive

Coralia (Kids) The Coralia has everything you need for a great loll-around vacation. The hotel is laid out in a series of buildings spread over a spacious compound that includes tennis courts, a big pool, and a lot of lawn. The beach, which looks out on the lagoon, is an equally great place for paddling and swimming or windsurfing and kiting. I particularly like the big, kid-friendly pool surrounded by comfy wicker furniture for relaxing and keeping an eye on things. The rooms are a mix of fairly standard, comfortable, resort-type offerings and some new, very stylish, rooms that feature bold colors and bolder angles. The super-modern fittings and sleek designs make me think that this is where the Jetsons would vacation if George won the lottery.

Dahab City. © **069/3640301.** Fax 069/3640305. www.accorhotels.com. 139 units. 130€ double. Rack rate includes buffet breakfast, dinner, taxes, and service charges. AE, MC, V. **Amenities:** 3 restaurants; 4 bars; airport transfer (extra charge); kids' club; concierge; health club; Internet (extra charge); pool; room service; tennis court; dive center. *In room:* A/C, TV, minibar.

Hilton Dahab This is a bit of a paint-by-numbers place, but it's none the worse for that. The architecture is generically Mediterranean, with high white walls and domes combined with touches of wood. The center of the compound is a wide lagoon, with a relatively modest pool set into a platform in the middle. Given the length of the beach available a 30-second walk away, however, it seems unlikely that there are too many complaints about the pool. Rooms are spacious and follow the stylistic lead of the rest of the hotel, with white walls, earth-tone curtains, and dark-wood trim. Bathrooms are fitted with the kind of high-end fixtures you expect at this price, and beds, sofas, and chairs are as comfy as they are stylish.

Dahab City. © **069/3640310.** Fax 069/3640424. www1.hilton.com. 163 units. $225 double. Rack rate includes buffet breakfast, taxes, and service charges. AE, MC, V. **Amenities:** 3 restaurants; 3 bars; airport transfer (extra charge); babysitting; kids' club; concierge; health club; pool; room service; tennis court; dive center, windsurfing center; Wi-Fi (extra charge). *In room:* A/C, TV, Internet (extra charge), minibar.

Le Méridien Dahab Resort With the possible exception of the Sofitel Gezirah, this has got to be the sleekest, coolest, best looking big hotel in the country. Starting with the gorgeous, wide open lobby, this is a place that sets out to impress, and it doesn't let up until you've wandered by the series of cascading pools, each level with its own themed loungers; passed through the starkly beautiful garden landscaped with native plants and grasses; and collapsed into a sleek armchair in your bright orange and brown room. From dramatic angles to bold mixtures of textures, this is a hotel where the interior design will give you as much pleasure as the beach. Razzmatazz aside, rooms are spacious and everything from linens to the plasma TVs are the best quality.

Dahab Bay. ✆ **069/3640425.** www.starwoodhotels.com. 182 units. $250 double. Rack rate includes buffet breakfast, taxes, and service charges. AE, DC, MC, V. **Amenities:** 3 restaurants; 2 bars; airport transfer (extra charge); babysitting; kids' club; concierge; health club; Internet (extra charge); 4 pools (including kids' pool); room service; dive center, windsurfing center. *In room:* A/C, TV, Internet (extra charge), minibar.

Moderate

Alf Leila ★★★ Stepping into Alf Leila is like stepping into the ethereal realms of Middle Eastern fairy tales. While Alf Leila's architecture follows that of Moroccan *riads,* built around an open-air courtyard with a water fountain in the middle, rooms' interiors are individually designed and mix authentic Moroccan and Egyptian elements. The whole place, from head to toe, is the outcome of the owner's (a former fashion designer) creativity, so expect bold combinations, eccentric colors, attention-grabbing fixtures, and unusual bathroom designs. A boutique hotel in every sense, Alf Leila is quite a different lodging experience. Alf Leila misses on the sea view, but the beach is only a 3-minute walk. Right next door is the affable Leila's Bakery (p. 209), which serves some of the best baked goods in Egypt, and is where you'll have your breakfast.

Fanar St., Assalah. ✆ **069/3640595** or 017/2271918. Fax 069/3640595. www.alfleila.com. 8 units, including 4 suites. 36€ double. Rate includes breakfast, taxes, and service charges. No credit cards. *In room:* A/C, Wi-Fi (free of charge).

Ali Baba Tucked into the middle of Masbat in the older portion of Dahab, the Ali Baba may be fairly new, but it feels like an old regular. The entrance is down an alley and around the back, and the rooms then run in a line back in the direction of the foreshore walkway, at this point as wide as a two-lane road but pedestrianized. This is probably the most fun part of Dahab, with a host of shops, bars, and restaurants crowded into the immediate neighborhood, and a constant bustle of locals and tourists on their way somewhere (or, more likely, happily nowhere). The best rooms in the hotel are the "superior" rooms closer to the sea-end of the building. These are large and nicely decorated with *mashrabeya* screens and comfortable arabesque furniture. They're worth the difference in price from the standard rooms. For the backpacker on a tight budget, there is a set of smaller, less decorated rooms clustered around a garden farther back from the sea; just ask about Ali Baba Gardens.

Masbat. ✆ **069/3640504.** www.alibabahotel.net. 15 units. LE200 double; LE250 superior double; LE80 Ali Baba Gardens. Rates include breakfast, taxes, and service charges. No credit cards. **Amenities:** 2 restaurants. *In room:* A/C, TV, minifridge.

Christina Beach Palace The Christina is a moderately priced hotel that does a great job of combining laid-back Dahab funkiness with good old-fashioned quality such as soft beds and extreme cleanliness. Laid out in several two-story white buildings, rooms are not very big, but they're exceptionally comfortable. Each one has a decent-size balcony with a sea view, and on the upper floor, ceilings are domed. Down on the other side of the walkway, meanwhile, the lounge area is all Dahab, all the time—the kind of place where time slips away between the late breakfast and the later lunch, and you only have time to squeeze in an hour of snorkeling on the reef before its time for a sunset drink and a stroll up the walkway to see what looks good for dinner.

Mashraba. ✆ **069/3640406** or 069/3640390. www.christinahotels.com. 40 unites. LE323 double. Rate includes breakfast, taxes, and service charges. MC, V. **Amenities:** 2 restaurants; bar; Wi-Fi (free). *In room:* A/C, TV.

Eldorado This very compact, European hotel has the enviable advantage of being laid out around one of Dahab's best Italian restaurants (p. 209). Rooms are frugal and small—white walls and simple wooden furniture—but well proportioned, with comfortable beds and good-quality linens. Rooms vary from the very basic, toilet-down-the-hallway type to somewhat more commodious (but still fairly slimmed-down) doubles with ensuite. The central courtyard is mainly taken up by the restaurant, while on the other side of the walkway there is a beautifully designed graveled seashore area for sitting and watching the sunset or the sunrise.

Assalah. ✆ **069/3641027.** www.eldoradodahab.com. 20 units, 6 with private bathrooms. 50€ double with private bathroom. Rate includes breakfast, taxes, and service charges. MC, V. **Amenities:** Restaurant; bar; Wi-Fi (free). *In room:* A/C.

Nesima (Value) This is one of the first places in Dahab to move away from the purely beach-camp ethos that prevailed in the early 1990s and toward something a little more chic. The two-story buildings are nestled in a well maintained garden, and nice touches such as wooden latticework grills, which made the place the nicest in town when it was built, still stand in good stead today. There's a small-but-elegant pool in a courtyard that opens to the sea, which also means it's open to the public walkway; however, this doesn't detract from the facility. Rooms are not very large, but they're pleasantly designed with Nubian-style brick-domed ceilings and bathrooms that are a class above anything else in this price range. The "superior" rooms open directly onto the pool area, which is very nice, but I'm not sure that it's worth the difference in price. The restaurant is excellent, and the bar is great. This place is value for money.

Mashraba. ✆ **069/3640320.** Fax 069/3640321. www.nesima-resort.com. 51 units. 59€ double. Rate includes breakfast, taxes, and service charges. MC, V. **Amenities:** 2 restaurants; bar; airport transfer (round-trip 60€); pool; dive center; Wi-Fi. *In room:* A/C, TV, minifridge.

Inexpensive

Neptune White and blue make the color scheme for this small and quiet hotel in the middle of Dahab's most famous promenade (located next to the bridge). Rooms lack character, which is expected in this price range, but are clean with spotless bathrooms. At the back there are three wooden rooms that are even more basic, with no amenities, that are offered at a discount; they are a good option if you are on a really tight budget. The hotel has a small portico and a lovely terrace where you can chill out with a drink.

Masbat. ✆ **069/3640568.** Fax 069/3640262. www.neptunedahab.com. 13 units. LE180 double; LE120 wooden room. Rates include breakfast, taxes, and service charges. No credit cards. **Amenities:** Restaurant; bar; airport transfer (extra charge); pool; Wi-Fi (free). *In room:* A/C, TV, minifridge.

Sheikh Salem House (Kids) More of a guesthouse than a hotel, this quiet little place at the northern end of Assalah is one of the best budget options in Dahab, especially if

House for Rent

Renting a house is a new trend in Dahab that's picking up; by the time the next edition of this book is out, I expect the house-renting business to be thriving. For now there are a handful of choices. The boutique-in-style **Villa Boheme** (located off Fanar St.) can easily accommodate six people in its two proper bedrooms and the additional one in the alcove. The house belongs to the owner of Alf Leila (p. 206), so be prepared for out-of-the-box yet simple decorative touches. The house doesn't have a sea view, but the beach is just 3 minutes away. Villa Boheme is rented for 59€ a day.

Following suit, yet with much less artistry and a more beachlike feel, is the aptly named **Palm Beach House.** The two-bedroom beach house has a spacious front yard and a 360-degree view of the sea. It enjoys a secluded location away from the hustle and bustle of the promenade, yet not too far (it's only a 5-minute walk). The daily rental rate is around 75€.

Check out www.dahab-info.com for apartments, houses, and villas for rent in Dahab, and contact Alf Leila owner Eva Hoffman (✆ **010/6935669**) to book any of the above.

you're traveling with kids. Rooms are large, particularly for their price. The decor is nothing fancy, but if you're looking to be away from the party zone and still on the sea, then the location is perfect. There are a range of rooms, from the small and very basic "economy" rooms to the "suites," which are really just large rooms with a niche for a kitchenette (complete except for the stove) that's sufficient to prepare snacks or store leftovers and cold drinks. They can also combine rooms to make apartments, so if you're traveling as a group, it makes sense to contact them by e-mail and plan ahead. All the rooms are different; check the website before booking.

Eel Garden, Assalah. ✆ **069/3641820** or 012/7972361. www.sheikhsalemhouse.com. 16 units. LE200 double. Rate includes breakfast, taxes, and service charges. No credit cards. **Amenities:** Restaurant; airport transfer (round-trip LE420); Wi-Fi. *In room:* A/C, TV, kitchenette (in some).

WHERE TO EAT

Eating in Dahab used to be an adventure, a risky culinary crawl through beachside cafes that all offered the same menu of grilled calamari, *shish tawook,* and fries, and more often than not sent you away with a nasty case of funny-tummy. Nowadays, things have taken a different turn. There are literally dozens of good-standard restaurants along the seaside promenade that offer all sorts of cuisines. Head to Blue House for exotic Thai dishes, to Lakhbatita for the best Italian food in the whole of the Sinai, and look for the Swan Land cart for *kosheri.*

Ali Baba INTERNATIONAL One of the promenade's most famous restaurants, Ali Baba greets its customers with large colorful cushions, traditional vibrant lanterns, and lots of green plants, creating a cheerful dining experience. The place may give the impression of being another typical Egyptian seafood restaurant, courtesy of the fresh seafood display by the entrance, but there is a glass fridge, also by the entrance, where you can choose fresh-from-the-butcher rib, steak, or filet to be cooked on the spot. I recommend a steak with blue cheese sauce or beef stroganoff, but the menu also offers pizzas and pastas.

Masbat. ✆ **069/3642549.** www.alibaba-dahab.com. Appetizers LE20–LE40; main courses LE40–LE100. No credit cards. Daily noon–2am.

Blue House ★★★ THAI Without a doubt, this small family business is the best place in Egypt to savor Thai food. The menu has a long list of Thai dishes, and the homemade sauces and granny's special ingredients add special flavor. I like the papaya salad followed by shrimp Panang curry in thick coconut milk with zucchini, peanuts, and kaffir lemon; the shrimp can be replaced with chicken or meat. Wooden furniture and mostly white, with a touch of blue, painted walls set the easygoing mood of the place, while the open kitchen adds a dynamic effect to the whole experience. Blue House takes up the second floor of a seaside building and enjoys superb views of both the sea and the promenade.

Masbat. ✆ **016/7971416.** Appetizers LE20–LE40; main courses LE35–LE70. No credit cards. Tues–Sun 11:30am–2pm and 6–10:30pm. Closed Feb.

Dai Pescatori ITALIAN Down at the northern end of the seaside walkway in Assalah, Dai Pescatori offers tasty Italian cuisine made of organic ingredients and served in a funky, shaded, water-side dining area. The *risotto a frutti di mare* has a creamy sauce and is full of shrimp and local fish; it goes great with a bottle of white wine. At the end of the walkway here it's very quiet at night, and the only sound is the sea slapping against the rocks and the evening breeze coming through the trees.

Eel Garden, Assalah. ✆ **012/7972361.** www.daipescatori.com. Appetizers LE30–LE50; main courses LE50–LE100. No credit cards. Daily 9am–midnight.

Eldorado ITALIAN Sophisticated European design and the best desserts in Dahab make Eldorado one of my favorite spots for Italian food in town. The roof is grass and the tables are rough wood, but the walls are sleek and made mostly of glass, and the lighting is discreet. The gnocchi is perfectly formed and served in a tomato-and-basil sauce, while the *filetto all'italiana* sees a grilled beef filet well cooked and served with a neat pile of tasty grilled vegetables. Save room for dessert, which includes tiramisu and a stunningly rich *panna cotta* with homemade strawberry or chocolate sauce.

Assalah. ✆ **069/3641027** or 012/7593235. Reservations recommended. Appetizers LE20–LE35; main courses LE50–LE110. MC, V. Wed–Mon 7–11pm.

Lakhbatita ★★ ITALIAN If you like Sam Cooke and the sound of waves; if you think that the sunset makes a nice backdrop for a dining room; and if you like homemade pasta and fresh seafood, Lakhbatita is for you. The interior has funky seating, tiled walls, and braids of garlic hanging from the beams, while outside on the rock breakwater tables are arranged within a high, open-sided structure of large wooden beams with a floor of open-faced rock and lighting that's been carefully thought through. Start with fish carpaccio, followed by ravioli gorgonzola or tagliatelle lobster, and then the delicious milk fish filet cooked in olive oil with a light crusting of rock salt and spices, served with grilled vegetables. For dessert, an exquisite alcohol-free tiramisu finishes off the meal nicely. Lakhbatita doesn't serve alcohol, so have a drink somewhere else prior to dinner.

Mashraba. ✆ **012/8284612.** www.lakhbatita.com. Appetizers LE20–LE40; main courses LE35–LE140. No credit cards. Daily 7–11pm.

Leila's Bakery ★★★ (Finds) BAKERY This is where you should have your breakfast. Though Leila's Bakery offers delicious baguettes and croissants, the real specialties are the

German delights such as the breadlike *laugen* and *brezel,* and the sweet Bavarian *zwetschgen-nudein;* options are mainly cheese or cheese with cold cuts. If you have a sweet tooth, go for a nut or cinnamon roll, and if your sugar craving is still on, finish off with an apple strudel. Leila's Bakery also offers a small assortment of sandwiches; try the signature Ralph baguette with fried turkey and egg with cheese, tomato, lettuce, and mayo. Though they start baking quite early in the morning, by noon most of the shelves are wiped clean.

Fanar St. (next to Alf Leila). ✆ **069/3640594.** Bakery items LE5–LE15. No credit cards. Daily 7am–7pm.

Swan Land EGYPTIAN *Kosheri* is one of Egypt's most popular dishes, a mega mix of lentils, rice, macaroni, and chickpeas with a dash of hot tomato sauce and fried onions for a garnish. Traditionally it was sold from a street cart, but today the *kosheri* cart has almost disappeared and been replaced with proper shops and outlets. In Dahab, Swan Land has revived the tradition, but with a modern flair (*kosheri* is kept in a well-heated and closed container, and plates have been replaced with disposable plastic ones). ***Note:*** If you wish to try Swan Land, it has to be for lunch, as it's only open for 2 hours around lunch time.

No fixed location, but hovers around the bridge area, Masbat. ✆ **016/2282987.** Kosheri LE4. No credit cards. Daily 11:30am–1:30pm.

Tarbouche ★★ Finds FUSION Tarbouche offers dining with more than one twist. The one-man show operates on a preorder basis, so call at least 1 day in advance to place your order; "your order" is just another twist. There is no real menu to choose from, but you'll simply be asked questions such as, "Are you vegetarian? Do you prefer fish, shrimp, lobster, or meat? Do you have any food allergies?" The rest is up to the owner's creativity, but whatever direction it takes (usually Egyptian with a European twist), you are bound to have a memorable dining experience at ground level; there are no chairs here.

Off Fanar St. (call for directions). ✆ **069/3641333** or 010/6577625. Whole meal (includes rice, salads, cooked vegetables, main dish, and dessert) LE75 and up. No credit cards. No set hours; call in advance.

SHOPPING

Dahab's 3km (almost 2-mile) promenade is dotted with souvenir shops that sell the typical Egyptian fare of knickknacks and trinkets, as well as some imported stuff, which varies from African wood masks to Indian-style textiles with heavy embroidery. However, there is one small shop that warrants a mention. **Ahmed El Rassam** (✆ **011/9978278**) is originally from Upper Egypt but has been calling Dahab home for the past 12 years. He uses pigment colors to draw locally inspired scenes on textiles. His work varies considerably from underwater scenes to dancing humans depicted as silhouettes. Prices are fixed and vary from LE20 to LE120 depending on the size of the painting.

DAHAB AFTER DARK

Other than a weekly party, Dahab's nightlife is restricted to bars with view of the open sea.

Furry Cup This oddly named place in Assalah, toward the Eel Garden area at the northern end of the seaside walkway, is one of the nicest places to kick back for a few drinks, have a chat with complete strangers, or just contemplate life. It has high ceilings and a friendly staff, and it's about the only place in town where you can get imported liquor in addition to the local fare. Assalah. ✆ **069/3640411.**

Rush This relatively small open-air place is a restaurant that turns into a nightlife spot three times a week. On Fridays it hosts Dahab's most famous dancing party, Sundays are karaoke night, and Wednesdays you can hear live music. If you opt for any other day of the week, the garden makes for a good dining setup (I recommend the couscous with vegetables). Friday, Sunday, and Wednesday 9pm till late. Masbat. ✆ **069/3641867** or -8.

The Tree Music videos, a couple of open-air pool tables, indoor seating, and the long bar backed up by a wall of liquor bottles create a laid-back and fun ambience here. A weekly (not a fixed day) party turns the atmosphere electric. Daily 8pm till late. Masbat. ✆ **010/6466863.**

DAY TRIPS FROM DAHAB

Dahab might be a more than 9-hour drive from Cairo, but it's less than 5 hours to Petra (via Eilat). For 1-day trips involving border crossings, Petra and Jerusalem dominate the stage. A trip to Petra costs $220 and avoids multiple border crossings by taking the Taba–Aqaba ferry instead of traveling overland via Israel. The expensive day trip might appeal to some, but not to me; 1 day is not enough to see Petra. A 1-day trip to Jerusalem costs $130 but involves having an Israeli stamp on your passport, which automatically translates to a visa refusal when visiting other Middle Eastern countries (though not Egypt). For unfathomable security reasons, both trips are restricted to U.S. and European passport holders only; even Egyptians are not allowed.

For domestic day trips from Dahab, the Colored Canyon (LE200), a narrow canyon in the middle of the desert adorned with naturally colored rock formations, is the most popular. This means, of course, that you'll encounter hordes of other tourists. Luxor and Cairo remain the classic day-trip destinations; the former costs LE2,500 (flying), while the latter costs LE2,000 (flying), LE1,000 (private car, minimum two people), or LE450 (by bus).

If you have the time and an adventurous spirit, a 2-day trip to Serabit El Khadem involves sleeping in the desert in a Bedouin village, where you get to know their culture, traditions, and day-to-day life. A medium-grade trek uphill the next morning takes you to the remains of the only Ancient Egyptian temple outside mainland Egypt. In antiquity, the area was important for mining turquoise, and during the reign of Pharaoh Sesostris I of the Middle Kingdom, a temple was built dedicated to Hathor, the patron goddess of copper and turquoise miners.

King Safari Dahab (✆ **012/4124396;** www.kingsafaridahab.com; daily 9am–11pm) is a well organized and professional local travel agency to use for any of the day trips out of Dahab with the exception of Serabit El Khadem, where I would recommend Desert Divers.

3 ST. CATHERINE'S

St. Catherine's is smack in the middle of the Sinai Peninsula and has an end-of-the-earth feel to it. The town is little more than a single loop of road that passes a few hotels and a couple of stores, and despite the enormous number of tourists and pilgrims who come here, it feels isolated and not particularly welcoming. Just a couple of kilometers outside town, however, is the beautifully preserved 6th-century monastery of St. Catherine, which is said to be built on the site where God spoke to Moses from the burning bush. Just behind the monastery is Mount Sinai, locally known as Jebel Moussa (Mount Moses), where Moses apparently received the Ten Commandments.

The Story of St. Catherine

St. Catherine of Alexandria, according to legend, started out as the daughter of a 4th-century governor of the Mediterranean city. Converted by a monk in an ecstatic, mystical rite, she made a reputation, and a powerful enemy, for herself by converting the wife of Roman Emperor Marcus Aurelius Valerius Maxentius. For her efforts, she was ultimately condemned to a slow death by the breaking wheel (a sort of torture device), but when she was strapped down, the wheel broke (hence St. Catherine's frequent depiction with a broken wheel), and she had to be beheaded instead. Her intact remains were discovered rather mysteriously several centuries later to the south of the monastery on the summit of what is now named Mount St. Catherine (highest peak in Egypt; 2,641m/8,662 ft.). You can climb the mountain and still see the indent where her body was found.

Apart from its religious significance, this area has some of the most spectacular, not to mention bleak and intimidating, topography in the country. For the most part it's arid (hot but dry in the summer and cold in the winter), and the landscape is marked by low jagged mountains that conceal tiny valleys full of greenery. Hiking in this area is tough but certainly rewarding. For those who wish to thoroughly experience the area, or simply want a base for further exploration, there's a lovely ecolodge just outside the town of St. Catherine near the village of Sheikh Awad.

ORIENTATION

Getting There

BY CAR There is a good condition, though single-carriage, road marred with hair-raising turns that connects St. Catherine to the coastal highway and farther to either Sharm El Sheikh (southeast) or Cairo (northwest). Try to avoid being on St. Catherine Road, as it is better known locally, at night; its zigzagging turns prove to be tricky.

BY BUS From **Turgoman Bus Station** (✆ **02/27735668** or -9) in Cairo, there is one daily bus to St. Catherine that leaves at 11am (LE40). In St. Catherine, it stops at the western end of town. At press time, the East Delta bus that connects St. Catherine to Dahab was temporarily suspended. There are no buses between St. Catherine and Sharm El Sheikh.

Getting Around

St. Catherine lacks public transportation in its proper meaning. However, Toyota Hilux pickups fill the void. If you are going somewhere along their route the fee is nominal, but going out of the way comes with a charge, usually a hefty one depending on how far you are going.

Tourist Information

A couple of uninviting **Internet** cafes are spread out across the little mountainous town; they have acceptable speed and charge LE10 an hour. When it comes to ATMs, there aren't any; however, there is a **Banque Misr** beside the gas station that's open Sunday to Thursday 9am to 2pm.

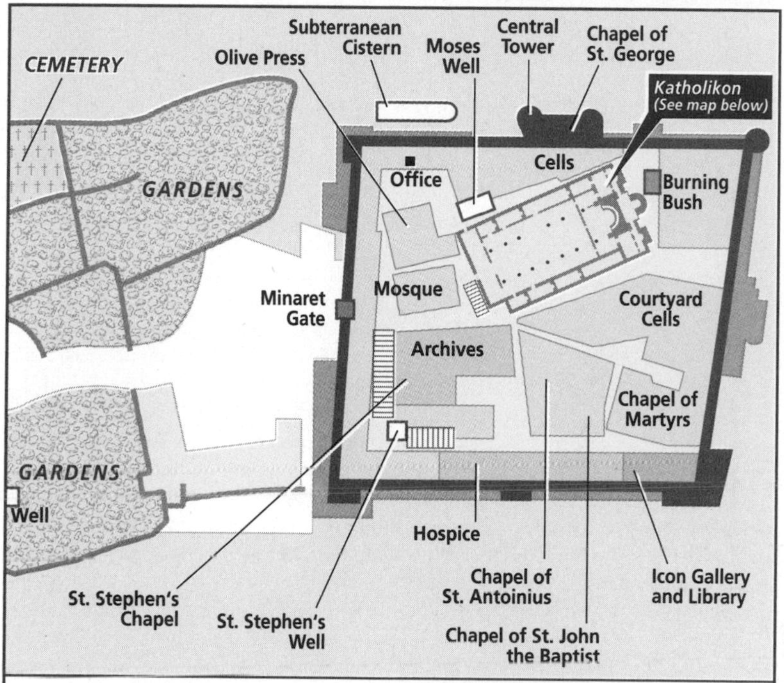

KATHOLIKON

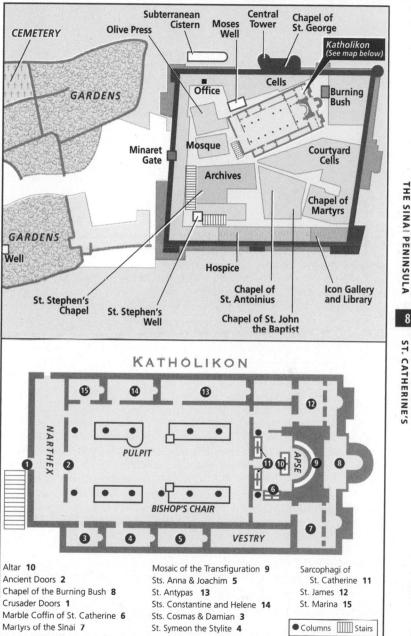

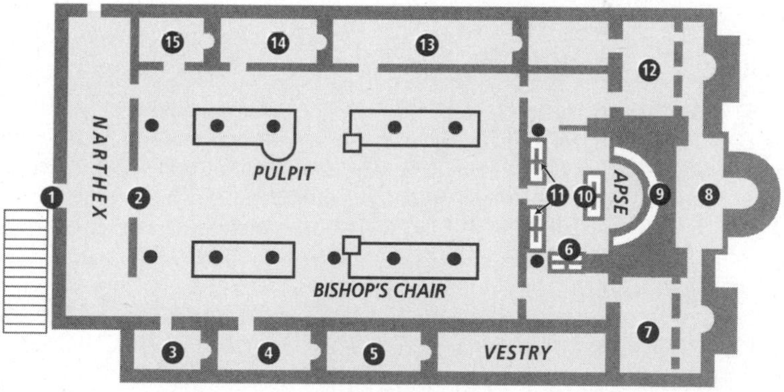

Altar **10**
Ancient Doors **2**
Chapel of the Burning Bush **8**
Crusader Doors **1**
Marble Coffin of St. Catherine **6**
Martyrs of the Sinai **7**
Mosaic of the Transfiguration **9**
Sts. Anna & Joachim **5**
St. Antypas **13**
Sts. Constantine and Helene **14**
Sts. Cosmas & Damian **3**
St. Symeon the Stylite **4**
Sarcophagi of St. Catherine **11**
St. James **12**
St. Marina **15**

● Columns ▥ Stairs

Mount Sinai (Mount Moses) ★ Most people start this walk about 3 or 4 hours before sunrise, timing it to arrive at the summit for the spectacular sunrise over the surrounding mountains. There are two ways up the 2,285m (7,500-ft.) mountain, both fairly easy to find from the base around the monastery. The first, which most people use for the ascent, is—initially, at least—a winding, gently sloped path that starts from behind the monastery. It's quite beautiful to see the thread of lights used by the walkers wending their way up the slope. A little more than about halfway up, at Elijah's Bowl, it turns to stairs (in fact, the last 750 of the Steps of Repentance), and if you're not in good shape, the final part of the climb on the narrow, crowded rock steps can be quite grueling. The other way, which many people use for the descent, is steeper and more direct. Known as the Steps of Repentance, it comprises 3,750 stone steps carved into the side of the mountain. It is sign-posted and easy to find, and from the top it makes for a much quicker descent than going back the way you came up. Reckon on an hour for the descent this way. On the top there was once an old church, possibly dating back to the 4th century, which was rebuilt by Emperor Justinian I. However, it later fell in disuse until 1933, when some of the remaining stone blocks were used to build the Chapel of Holy Trinity, which now marks Mount Sinai summit.

Tips For Divers

Please account for a 24-hour surface interval before you fly or attempt to ascend Mount Sinai.

A flashlight, plenty of water, a snack for the summit, and warm clothing are musts for this climb. Even in the summer, the nights are chilly, and in the winter it's downright cold and possibly snowy when you get to the top. There are a good number of places on the way up to get a hot tea, mind you, and these places often have chocolate bars for sale. Keep in mind that the climb is pretty popular, and that the path as well as the summit itself can get pretty crowded in the hour leading up to dawn.

St. Catherine's Monastery ★ St. Catherine's Monastery, which was built in the 6th century by Byzantine Emperor Justinian I, is one of the oldest continuously functioning Christian monasteries in existence. It is still home to a community of Greek Orthodox monks who guard the compound and its contents, and operate the nearby guesthouse (p. 216). It was built around the Chapel of the Burning Bush, which dates to the 4th century A.D. and was built to the order of St. Helena, mother of Constantine the Great. Tradition holds that the bush growing there today is, in fact, the very same bush from which God spoke to Moses and told him that he was standing on holy ground. The monastery, its location, and the surrounding area hold historical and religious importance to the three Abrahamic religions (Judaism, Christianity, and Islam); in 2002 it was listed as a UNESCO World Heritage site. Visiting the place today, the number-one attraction is the monastery's priceless collection of more than 2,000 **icons** belonging to

Fun Facts In the Thick of It

The walls of St. Catherine's Monastery, which were built in the middle of the 6th century A.D., are 3m (more than 9 ft.) thick in some places.

Ahtiname: The Letter of Protection

A letter, better known as the Ahtiname, from Prophet Muhammad granted protection to the monastery, a pledge that was kept throughout the ages. As a sign of gratitude, a guesthouse inside the monastery was turned into a mosque during the 11th century.

different schools of Coptic and Christian art, with some being produced as early as the 5th century. The rarities among the collection are lovely Byzantine icons that miraculously survived the iconoclastic hysteria that gripped the church in the 8th and 9th centuries. The monastery's **museum** is another attraction for its wide array of perfectly preserved early manuscripts, richly decorated reliquaries, painted icons, and embroidery. Finally, don't miss the **Church of St. Catherine** (more properly known as the Basilica of the Transfiguration), which includes a small sampling of the monastery's rich collection of icons, as well as one of the best-preserved Byzantine mosaics in the world. Adorning the eastern apse of the basilica, they depict various scenes of religious importance, which include the transfiguration, Moses at the burning bush, and Moses receiving the tablets. Both women and men are asked to dress modestly when visiting the monastery.

✆ **069/3470343,** 069/3470677, or 069/3470740. www.sinaimonastery.com. Admission to monastery free; museum LE50. Mon–Thurs and Sat 10am–noon.

Trekking The mountainous topography around St. Catherine makes for spectacular trekking. The country is rugged, however, and it's all too easy to get lost if you set out on your own. Excellent trained local guides are available at **Sheikh Sina Bedouin Treks,** and it would be foolhardy not to take advantage of their services. In addition to short walks to nearby destinations, they have comprehensive trekking programs categorized as Leisure, Adventure, and Specialty. Leisure, as the name implies, is the easiest of the trio, with trekking trips varying from 6 hours to 10 days. The Adventure category is for the more fit. Its most famous trek is Peak-to-Peak-to-Peak, a 5-day trek that takes you from St. Catherine to Al Karm and farther to the scrappy ascent of Gabel El Banat, the summit of Bab El Dunia with its scenic views of the Suez Canal, the natural pools of Galt El Azraq, and a finale atop Mount Sinai. The Specialty category puts your hiking and trekking capabilities to the ultimate test and includes the 14-day Sinai Coast-to-Coast, where you cross from the Gulf of Suez to the Gulf of Aden through some of the most strenuous, rugged, but certainly rewarding, terrains of the peninsula.

St. Catherine. ✆ **011/2551150.** Fax 068/3470880. www.sheikhsina.com. 50€ average per day of trekking.

WHERE TO STAY

El Karm I am a huge fan of this Bedouin-owned-and-operated ecolodge about 25km (15 miles) north of the town. It was developed as part of the St. Catherine's Protectorate, and the buildings were built entirely by traditional methods using beautiful open-stone construction. Facilities are, in some ways, more basic than basic: There is absolutely no electricity, and beds are thin mattresses on stone shelves covered in camel blankets. But it's a very elegant simplicity, and the food, cooked by owner-manager Jamal Atteya, is superb. The last time I was here he had rain-fed local olive oil to sample, and dinner was lake trout baked in the coals of an open fire. There's a dining room with handmade wood furniture, but most of the time you'll end up eating outside under the stars around the cooking fire. El Karm is hard to beat if you want to experience the desert culture, and my recommendation is to use it as a base for hiking the nearby canyons. Jamal and his associates are knowledgeable and considerate guides.

El Karm is up about 5km (3 miles) of track that is impassable without a four-wheel-drive. The best way to get here is to arrange with Jamal to meet in St. Catherine and ride out with, or follow (if you're traveling with your own 4×4), him or someone he recommends. If you're feeling adventurous, go to Sheikh Awad (the little village beside the turnoff to Al Karm), and ask around until you find someone willing to drive you up the road—you'll probably end up in the back of an old pickup truck for around LE50. It is also possible to hike from St. Catherine, but it's lengthy.

✆ **010/1324693** (if there is no answer, leave a message, including contact details; you will eventually get a call back). 12 units. LE120 per person. Rate on full-board basis with taxes and service charges. No credit cards. **Amenities:** Restaurant. *In room:* No phone.

El Wady El Mouqdous A budget hotel with small rooms, El Wady El Mouqdous is a good option if you are just looking for a place to spend the night. There is a pool in the central courtyard that's a great place to relax in the heat of the summer. Views of the low mountains around the town are pleasant, but nothing spectacular.

St. Catherine. ✆ **069/3470225.** 35 units. LE250 double. Rate includes breakfast, taxes, and service charges. MC, V. **Amenities:** Restaurant; pool. *In room:* A/C, TV, minifridge.

Monastery Guest House Nestled up against the monastery, this is the most convenient place to stay in St. Catherine if you're here to climb the mountain and tour the religious facilities. Fittingly, the rooms are almost monastically stark and small. Decor is nonexistent, but the air-conditioning/heating units work well, and the bare-bones bathroom has an ample supply of hot water. Rooms are arranged in a row along a courtyard across from a coffee shop, a small store that sells snacks, and facilities that you will share with busloads of tourists who gather 2 to 4 hours before dawn to prepare for the climb up the mountain. Beside the convenience store is the dining hall, where simple breakfasts and dinners are served to people staying at the guesthouse.

St. Catherine. ✆ **069/3470353.** Fax 069/3470543. 30 units. LE330 double. Rate includes breakfast, dinner, taxes, and service charges. No credit cards. **Amenities:** Restaurant. *In room:* A/C, no phone.

WHERE TO EAT

Eating in St. Catherine is a losing horse you don't want to bet on. Stick to your hotel, or take your chances at any of the small local eateries that you may succeed in finding.

4 NUWEIBA

There are two very distinct sides to Nuweiba. At the southern end is the gritty port area, where you can catch a boat to Aqaba in Jordan. There's not much there, apart from the run-down dock facilities, some small stores, and a couple of hard-bitten fleabag hotels. Between here and the town itself, which is about 10km (6 miles) to the north, there are a number of hotels, many of which have been closed in the last few years or were never quite finished in the first place. The town is nothing special—it functions mainly to sell cheap T-shirts and beer to backpackers. Starting at its northern edge, there is a kilometer or so of beach that has turned into a strip of cheap hotels and camps known as Tarabin. The real deal, however, is the stretch running northeast from Nuweiba to Taba. Dotted with simple camps, it makes for a relaxing, back-to-basics vacation.

ORIENTATION

Getting There

BY PLANE The nearest airport is in Taba, which, at the time of researching this edition, was just opening up for commercial flights with twice weekly flights from Cairo.

BY BUS From Cairo, the same three daily buses that head to Taba continue farther to Nuweiba. Tickets cost LE70 to LE80. From Sharm El Sheikh there are three daily buses making the 170km (105-mile) run. Tickets costs LE25. From the bus station in Nuweiba, you will be able to get a ride into town or to the camps to the northeast. Depending on where your destination is, price may vary considerably.

Getting Around

Transportation is a perennial problem on the Sinai's eastern coast. Staff at any of the hotels listed will be able to put you in contact with a private driver. Negotiate the price hard, and make sure that you nail down the specifics of time, destination, vehicle type, and air-conditioning (important during the summer). You should pay around LE350 to LE400 a day for a late-model, air-conditioned minivan.

WHERE TO STAY

Other than Nakhil Inn and Soft Beach, there are no places in ramshackle Tarabin I would recommend. However, the coastline, running northeast of Nuweiba, is littered with small "camps" that fill in the holes between the half-finished resorts. Most are no more than a dozen woven-grass huts around a central shower and eating facility. The first to open is the iconic Basata, while the best place to stay, at least in my opinion, is Rock Sea. Check out a couple of places before making up your mind; some look quite appealing from the outside but are downright gritty once you step in.

Expensive

Hilton Nuweiba Coral Resort (Kids) The Coral Resort has a lovely location, tucked into a long, sweeping curve of beach beneath a line of jagged granite mountains that catch the light of the setting sun. However, in terms of quality restaurants, bars, and entertainment, it might as well be at the end of the earth. For this reason, almost all of its business is done in all-inclusive packages. Given the alternatives (or lack thereof), it's probably not a bad idea to pay for everything upfront (at a good discount to boot). Rooms are relatively small, though well appointed in a generic, beachfront resort kind of way. The difference between room grades is limited to a few square meters, so think about how much time you're actually going to spend in there before investing. The pools are fun and include quiet areas as well as more raucous kids' areas. The beach, of course, is a lovely great sweep of sand, perfect for sun lounging, early morning jogs, or quiet evening walks to admire the sunset over the mountains.

Nuweiba. ✆ **069/3520320.** Fax 069/3520327. www1.hilton.com. 220 units, including 20 chalets. $170 double; $210 chalet. Rack rates on all-inclusive basis with taxes and service charges. AE, DC, MC, V. **Amenities:** 3 restaurants; 2 bars; airport transfer (extra charge); kids' club; concierge; health club; Internet (extra charge); 2 pools (1 heated, 1 kids'); dive and watersports center. *In room:* A/C, TV, Internet (extra charge), minibar.

Moderate

Nakhil Inn This is a nice, fairly quiet place at the northern end of Tarabin. It has spacious, wood-paneled rooms and a cozy beach area out front. The atmosphere splits the difference nicely between the kind of laid-back attitude and closeness to the water and sand that you get at a camp and the creature comforts of a small hotel. The rooms open directly onto the beach area, which has plenty of seating areas, but is definitely too small for the kind of broad swath of loungers that you get at a real beach resort. The restaurant, with its high ceilings and big windows that look in the direction of the beach, is a very pleasant place to linger over a long breakfast of pancakes and fruit salad.

Tarabin, Nuweiba. ✆ **069/3500879.** Fax 069/35000878. 38 units. LE320 double. Rate includes buffet breakfast, taxes, and service charges. MC, V. **Amenities:** Restaurant. *In room:* TV, no phone.

Nuweiba Village Resort This is a midrange place on the beach a little south of the town itself. The architecture of the main building will make you shudder—it looks like a cut-rate office building in an industrial park—but once you get to the grounds around the nicely sculpted pool, it's all holiday village, with lots of palm trees and sun loungers, and a long, beautiful beach. This is what you're here for, and the facilities are excellent. Rooms are small and have a bit of 1970s feel to them; the decor doesn't really make an effort to rise above generic, but they are spotlessly clean and comfortable. What this place lacks in architectural style it makes up for in beach-lounging value for money (even at the rack rate).

Nuweiba. ✆ **069/3500401-3.** Fax 069/3500407. www.nuweibavillageresort.com. 127 units, including 4 suites. $70 double. Rack rate includes buffet breakfast, dinner, taxes, and service charges. **Amenities:** 2 restaurants; 2 bars; airport transfer (extra charge); Internet (extra charge); 2 pools (1 kids'); room service; 2 tennis courts; dive center. *In room:* A/C, TV, minifridge.

Inexpensive

Basata Nuweiba's very first tourist-oriented accommodation facility, Basata is a simple but sophisticated beach camp run by a German-Egyptian couple. The name Basata, which means "simplicity" in Arabic, is meant to sum up the camp's approach to vacationing. Accommodations are a mix of grass huts spaced out along the sandy beach, newer cement-built spacious chalets you don't want to stay in, and a camping area if you have your own gear. Unlike the uniform, generally constricted, and unpleasant huts at other camps, Basata's are spacious and comfortable, and each is unique. They are, to be sure, simple: grass-mat floors, simple beds, and candles for light (there is no electricity in the huts). Toilets and washing facilities are shared, though bungalows and chalets have their own. You can either cook your own meals (with food you bring in or purchase here) in the common kitchen or reserve a seat for the set meal each evening (LE50–LE60).

25km (16 miles) northeast of Nuweiba. ✆ **069/3500480** or 069/3500481. www.basata.com. 30 units. 40€ beach hut double; 70€ chalet w/up to three occupants. Rates are on "bed only" basis and subject to taxes and service charges. MC, V. **Amenities:** Restaurant. *In room:* No phone.

Rock Sea ★★ Tranquil vibes welcome you to Rock Sea, a personal favorite and one of the most peaceful and least crowded camps along the Nuweiba-Taba coastal stretch. Owned and operated by a lovely German family (who encourage single female travelers with a 10% discount on bungalows), the Rock Sea includes both hut and bungalow accommodations; the latter are more spacious than huts and come with a tiled floor and electricity. The place is favored by simplicity lovers and meditation fans; there is a 50-sq.-m (538-sq.-ft.) white tent, dubbed the Dome, which is ideal for yoga sessions.

Nuweiba–Taba Coastal Rd. ✆ **012/7963199.** www.rocksea.net. 20 units. LE120 hut double; LE150 bungalow double. Rates include breakfast, taxes, and service charges. MC, V. **Amenities:** Restaurant. *In room:* No phone.

Soft Beach This is the best beach camp in Tarabin. Thirty-five small huts are scattered between the side road at the back and the wide, pleasant beach. Dining takes place in an open-sided area, with food coming through a little window from the clean kitchen area. The cabins are not the kind of place you want to spend too much time, but then again, that's not what you're here for. The beach is superb, with (as advertised) very soft sand and a plethora of comfy lounging places.

Tarabin, Nuweiba. ✆ **010/3647586.** www.softbeachcamp.com. 35 units. 20€ double. Rate includes breakfast, dinner, taxes, and service charges. No credit cards. **Amenities:** Restaurant. *In room:* No phone.

WHERE TO EAT

Between Taba and Dahab, there is almost nowhere to eat outside your hotel. The truly desperate, and adventurous, may want to wander up the strip at Tarabin and try their luck with some of the beachside places there.

The Castle Zaman ★ This is a really fun place to spend an evening or even a whole day. Built to resemble the ruins of a crusader castle on a ridge high above the sea, the place incorporates a commodious bar with open beams and rock-faced walls. A balcony along the front lets you enjoy the glorious view while eating dinner or just downing a few cold beers. There's a pool on a slightly lower level that also affords a stunning view out across the sea, and even an underground cellar portion with "treasures" tucked into little niches. Food is excellent, but the portions are enormous—there is no way that anyone with a normal appetite will finish a serving. The slow-cooked lamb comes in a vast, traditional-style, earthenware dish, and the meat and the vegetables, which are cooked together, taste sublime. Keep in mind that you need to order your meal 2 to 3 hours in advance. If you're just stopping by for dinner, make sure that you phone ahead.

25km (16 miles) northeast of Nuweiba. ✆ **018/2140591.** www.castlezaman.com. Dinner (set menu) and use of all facilities 40€. MC, V. Daily midday until the last guest leaves.

5 TABA

Taba proper is nothing more than a small border town with a few shops; however, 17km (a little more than 10 miles) farther south is one of Egypt's hidden gems—Taba Heights. The high-end tourism complex is made up of several five-star resorts that offer top-notch service wrapped in plush style. Though Taba Heights was originally designed to rival El Gouna and Port Ghalib, it doesn't live up to either, and attaining this objective seems far from happening in the near future. Tourism in Taba is still in its infancy, and in a recent attempt to give things a push, EgyptAir has launched a direct flight connecting Taba to Cairo.

ORIENTATION

Getting There

BY PLANE With the newly launched twice weekly flight between Taba and Cairo, Taba has become more accessible. However, it comes with a staggering LE1,000 price tag for the round-trip.

BY CAR From Sharm El Sheikh you can take the coastal road running northeast (the same one leading to Dahab) and follow it all the way till the end. It is a little more than 2 hours, with the first half being an easy drive on a dual-carriage road, while the second requires more attention on a single-carriage road with some cliff-hanging turns; the road literally zigzags between the mountains and the sea. Coming from Cairo or Suez, there is the much easier to drive Nakhil Road, which cuts through the peninsula from the

Ahmed Hamdy Tunnel all the way to Taba, avoiding going to Sharm El Sheikh and Dahab all together.

BY BUS Three buses a day leave Cairo at **Turgoman Bus Station** (✆ **02/27735668** or -9) for Taba. Tickets cost LE70 to LE80.

WHERE TO STAY

Hyatt Regency Taba Heights The ambience here is tranquil, the gardens absorb other guests, and privacy comes easily and naturally because of the way the rooms and the landscape work together. Public areas thankfully lack the garish, over-the-top look of the Cairo Hyatt, and the rooms are designed around clean, modern lines and decorated with soothing earth tones. The Hyatt Regency shares an 18-hole, par-72 golf course with the rest of the Taba Heights hotels.

Taba Heights. ✆ **069/3580234.** Fax 069/3580235. http://taba.regency.hyatt.com. 426 units, including 10 suites. $232 sea-view double. Rate on all-inclusive basis with taxes and service charges. AE, DC, MC, V. **Amenities:** 3 restaurants; 4 bars; airport transfer (extra charge); kids' club; concierge; golf course nearby; health club & spa; 3 pools (including 2 heated); room service; 2 tennis courts; dive center; Wi-Fi (extra charge). *In room:* A/C, TV, Internet (extra charge), minibar.

Sofitel Taba Heights If you're going to stay at a luxurious beachfront resort, you might as well go all out, and the Sofitel certainly fits the bill. The central buildings are constructed in an attractive series of domes and arcades that surround the courtyard, and the pool area is designed to mimic an inlet with stepped "beaches" running down into the five swimming areas. My favorite aspect of this is the walk down to the long, sandy beach; paths lead over islands set in the middle of the swimming areas, so you never feel that you're very far from the water here. Rooms are similarly opulent, with a bold mix of cream walls and dark wood, fabrics with traditional Asian patterns, and *mashrabeya*-style lattice work.

Taba Heights. ✆ **069/3580800.** Fax 069/3580808. www.accorhotels.com. 294 units, including 27 suites. LE750 garden-view double; LE900 sea-view double. Rates on all-inclusive basis with taxes and service charges. AE, DC, MC, V. **Amenities:** 3 restaurants; 3 bars; airport transfer (extra charge); kids' club; concierge; golf course nearby; health club & spa; Internet (extra charge); 5 pools (1 heated, 1 kids'); room service; 2 tennis courts (floodlit); diving and watersports center. *In room:* A/C, TV, Internet (extra charge), minibar.

Taba Heights Marriot Beach Resort This is the most fun of the resorts at Taba Heights. It's built on descending levels in an attempt to give the rooms in the back of the compound a clear view of the sea, and the low, Mediterranean-style buildings are surrounded by theme park–style gardens where lagoon-shaped pools nestle among palm trees. The theme park feel extends to the restaurants, with outlets such as the Grotto Restaurant, which is built in a fake-rock cave. Rooms are fine, lacking in character, but spacious, clean, and comfortable.

Taba Heights. ✆ **069/3580100.** Fax 069/3580109. 394 units, including 22 suites. $130 garden-view double; $130 sea-view double. Rates include buffet breakfast, taxes, and service charges. AE, DC, MC, V. **Amenities:** 4 restaurants; 5 bars; airport transfer (extra charge); kids' club; concierge; golf course nearby; health club & spa; 2 pools (1 kids'); room service; 4 tennis courts (floodlit); dive and watersports center; Wi-Fi (extra charge). *In room:* A/C, TV, Internet (extra charge), minibar.

The Red Sea Coast

The lengthy Egyptian Red Sea coast extends from the Suez Canal all the way south to the Sudanese border. It may mistakenly seem uniform, offering nothing but memorable diving sites and year-round sunbathing. However, it is strikingly diverse, with each town adding a different flavor to your coastal experience. El Gouna is the region's Mr. Perfect, with well-planned streets, commodious villas, sports, and party beaches, and an organized downtown area where you can savor a tasty dinner, have a drink, or go window shopping without a hundred vendors testing your tolerance. Less than a 10-minute drive southward, the picture dramatically changes as you reach Hurghada, with its tarnished reputation for lack of urban planning. Luckily enough, change is on the way with the likes of Hurghada Marina Boulevard. The recently added pedestrian walkway is dotted with chic restaurants, hip bars, and sleek nightspots. The Red Sea party capital offers swanky choices for a hedonist night out (Hed Kandi, Ministry of Sound, or Little Buddha; see p. 237).

Diving is the Red Sea's prime attraction, and though Hurghada's house reefs have been exhausted, tens of other sites up and down the coast still offer great diving opportunities. Just north of Hurghada is the Abu Nahas maritime graveyard with four wrecks in sight. Safaga, farther south, is another wreck-diving favorite with three ferry wrecks close by, including the notorious *Salem Express;* the town is still rough around the edges, though, with only a handful of resorts and no nightlife. El Quseir follows the same unwinding mood, yet with a twist. The old trading and mining port has some history to tell, from the Old Fort to St. Barbara's Church. Between tanning sessions you can visit El Quseir's sites or take a day trip to monuments-awash Luxor. Up next is Port Ghalib, with its ambitious plans for a full-fledged residential town. For now you can still enjoy luxurious accommodation at the over-the-top InterContinental The Palace Hotel while getting pampered from head to toe at the exquisite Six Senses Spa. Marsa Alam wins the region's diving contest hands-down, with the shark-infested underwater paradise dubbed Elphinstone. Marsa Alam takes diving dedication to the next level with dedicated lodges, which vary from the rough-and-basic bungalows of Awlad Baraka to the themed-with-style Oasis Resort. Hamata might be tourism's last frontier, but the tiny fishermen's village offers a great opportunity for divers, adventurers, and adrenaline junkies alike; dive next to whale sharks at Maksur Reef, play with dolphins at Sataya, show off your kitesurfing skills at the lagoon, or test your nomadic spirit with Hamata's specialty, desert sailing.

Whether you're interested in watersports, here for the perfect sun, want to party all night long, or prefer a dash of history with quality relaxation time, the Red Sea seems to have it all—just make sure you have enough vacation time.

1 EL GOUNA

Only 20km (12 miles) north of Hurghada, El Gouna might as well be on another planet. Where Hurghada is the outcome of haphazard building decisions, El Gouna is a role model for urban planning and tourism development. It is the brainchild of one of Egypt's biggest property developers and has gradually taken off as a real community with a sizable residential population. Though it retains the structure of a mega resort compound, it has the atmosphere of a real town and hosts the Red Sea's only international school, as well as a field station that's used as a teaching and research facility for the American University in Cairo. Unlike the typical resorts and resort towns dotting the Red Sea coast, El Gouna has a lively scene where you can stroll Abu El Tig Marina looking for the most romantic restaurant or go on a shopping spree at Tamr Henna. El Gouna also offers a good activities-nightlife balance. While you can go diving, snorkeling, windsurfing, kitesurfing, golfing, go-karting, or even paintballing, there is an equally diverse after-dark scene where you can enjoy live performances, lounge waterside, dance the night away, or just have a couple of beers while shooting some pool.

ESSENTIALS

Orientation

From the moment you turn off the Red Sea Coastal Highway you are in the world of El Gouna, which is enmeshed in a confusing web of streets that curve and weave around the various little islands the town is built on. Every intersection has reasonably clear signposts pointing to the main hotels and the different marinas, however, and there always seems to be a cheerful security guard on hand to point the way. Coming from the main entrance, there are three main zones: First comes the golf area with its villas, club, and Steigenberger Golf Resort. Next is the downtown with its two main areas, Kafr El Gouna and Tamr Henna, which both play host to a wide array of shops, restaurants, and bars, as well as some basic services such as supermarkets, banks, and pharmacies. The third zone is the Abu El Tig Marina, where different shops, cafes, restaurants, and bars are clustered around the boat docks.

Getting There

BY PLANE El Gouna is less than 20km (12 miles) north of Hurghada International Airport, which is served by several domestic flights, as well as international ones. Fare for the 1-hour flight from Cairo is about LE650. A transfer arranged through your hotel is the easiest way to complete the trip, but if you are looking for an alternative, an LE120 taxi ride could be a cheaper option.

BY BUS **Go Bus** (© **19567**) operates six buses a day between El Gouna and Cairo (stops at Abdel Moneim Riyad Square close to Ramses Hilton, not at Turgoman Bus Station) with one continuing farther to Alexandria. Tickets cost LE65 to LE100. Buses originally depart from Hurghada and stop at El Gouna to pick up passengers. If you are on one of those, factor in a 10- to 15-minute delay.

BY CAR From Cairo, El Gouna is a 5-hour drive (430km/267 miles) over the Cairo–Ain Sokhna Road and then the Red Sea Coastal Highway. Most of the road is a dual-carriage road in good shape except for a short zigzagging sector around Zaafrana, where it tends to get much narrower (single carriage) and relatively dangerous due to the sharp turns. At press time, work was underway to widen the Zaafrana road sector.

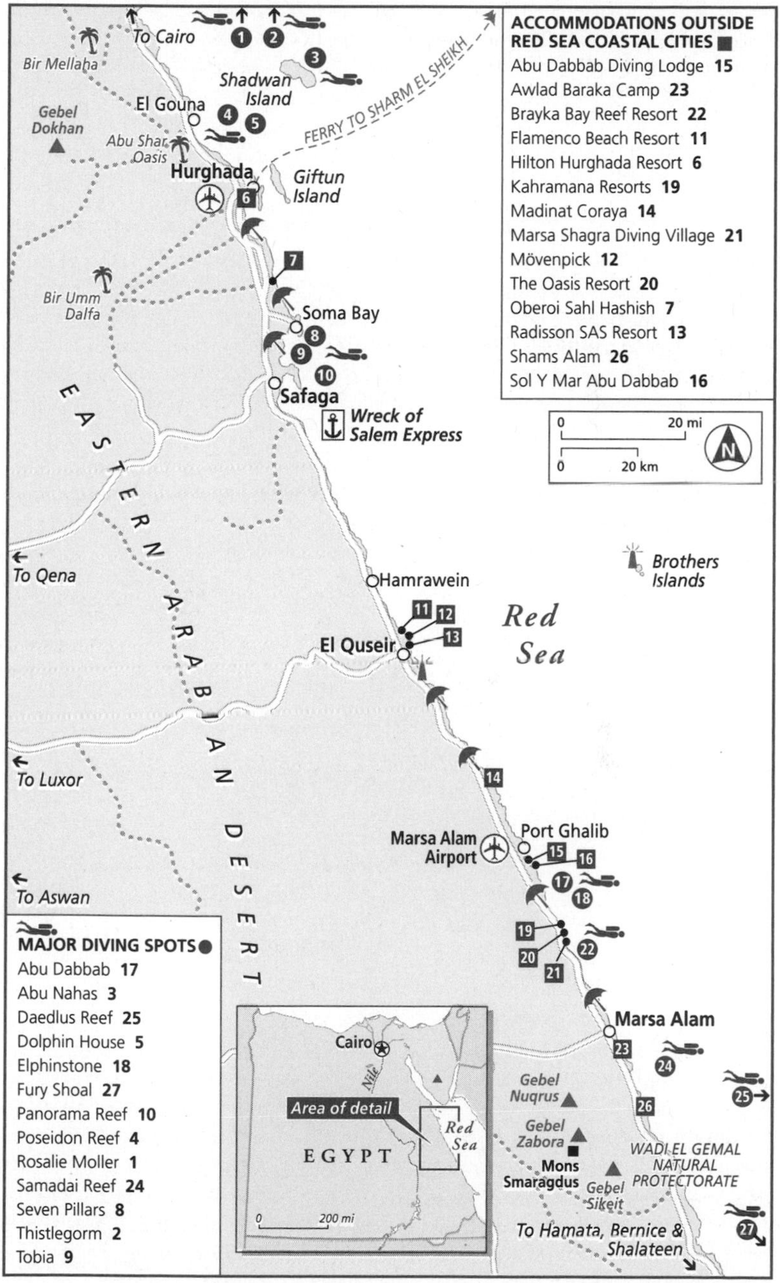
To Cairo
Bir Mellaha
Gebel Dokhan
El Gouna
Shadwan Island
FERRY TO SHARM EL SHEIKH
Abu Shar Oasis
Hurghada
Giftun Island
Bir Umm Dalfa
Soma Bay
Safaga
Wreck of Salem Express
EASTERN ARABIAN DESERT
To Qena
To Luxor
To Aswan
Hamrawein
El Quseir
Red Sea
Brothers Islands
Marsa Alam Airport
Port Ghalib
Marsa Alam
Gebel Nuqrus
Gebel Zabora
Mons Smaragdus
Gebel Sikeit
WADI EL GEMAL NATURAL PROTECTORATE
To Hamata, Bernice & Shalateen
Cairo
Nile
Area of detail
EGYPT
Red Sea
0
200 mi
0
20 mi
0
20 km
N
ACCOMMODATIONS OUTSIDE RED SEA COASTAL CITIES
Abu Dabbab Diving Lodge 15
Awlad Baraka Camp 23
Brayka Bay Reef Resort 22
Flamenco Beach Resort 11
Hilton Hurghada Resort 6
Kahramana Resorts 19
Madinat Coraya 14
Marsa Shagra Diving Village 21
Mövenpick 12
The Oasis Resort 20
Oberoi Sahl Hashish 7
Radisson SAS Resort 13
Shams Alam 26
Sol Y Mar Abu Dabbab 16
MAJOR DIVING SPOTS
Abu Dabbab 17
Abu Nahas 3
Daedlus Reef 25
Dolphin House 5
Elphinstone 18
Fury Shoal 27
Panorama Reef 10
Poseidon Reef 4
Rosalie Moller 1
Samadai Reef 24
Seven Pillars 8
Thistlegorm 2
Tobia 9

Getting Around

BY BUS The cheapest way to hop around El Gouna is by bus; they are decked out with flashy decorations and a rustic look that mimics the Philippines' Jeepneys. Buses run frequently, between 8am and midnight, connecting downtown to Abu El Tig Marina and other areas. It costs LE5 for a daily ticket and LE10 for a weekly one.

BY TOK-TOK *Tok-toks* (motor rickshaw taxis) with vibrant colors (mostly painted in bold yellow) abound. You can flag them down in the street, or you can have them pick you up at your hotel. Regardless of where in El Gouna you are going, the fare is fixed at LE5.

BY SHUTTLE BOAT With all the zigzagging canals and numerous lagoons and water bodies El Gouna is made of, a shuttle boat (operates between 9am–5pm) can be a very good transportation option. The bus ticket gets you on the shuttle boat without having to pay extra.

BY BIKE & MOTORBIKE **El Sahms** (✆ **010/1858596**) has bikes and motorbikes for rent, though they are far from being in mint condition. The rental rates for bikes are LE25 (hourly) and LE80 (daily), while motorbikes are LE100 (hourly) and LE250 (daily).

BY CAR **Limousine El Gouna** (✆ **065/3580061;** www.elgouna-limousine.com) has a wide selection of cars for rent, from the tiny Daewoo Matiz ($25 per day) to the sturdy Toyota Land Cruiser ($140 per day). Though the daily 100km (62 miles) allowance applies across the whole range, the charge for extra kilometers varies from 25¢ to 50¢. Chauffeured service is also available to the airport (LE120 one-way) and Cairo (LE1,650 round-trip). The expensive base prices are still subject to 10% sales tax, so you could be better off renting from Hurghada (p. 232).

TO HURGHADA There is a shuttle bus that makes the run every 15 minutes between 6am and 1am and costs LE5. At El Gouna, it departs from the main bus station close to Tamr Henna; while at Hurghada, it stops at the Go Bus Station in Dahar. Alternatively, you can always call Limousine El Gouna (see above), but be ready to pay LE100 one-way and LE30 for each hour (after the first 30 min.) the driver spends waiting.

Tourist Information

The nice thing about El Gouna is that there's no hassle about information. All hotels and many businesses have a well-designed map with a basic phone directory and a list of services that they hand out for free. There is a central number for El Gouna (✆ **065/3580521** or -3), which you can call and they will direct you to whichever facility or outlet you request.

WHAT TO SEE & DO

Mangroovy Beach has acquired an international reputation for its facilities, beach, and wind. Perfect for **wind-** and **kitesurfing,** the coral- and stone-free lagoon extends for 700m (2,300 ft.), making this an excellent place to learn because you can fall off the board and still stand on the bottom. On the other hand, a little bit out to sea there is a strong, consistent wind and good-size waves to keep experts engaged. Mangroovy Beach's strong reputation has attracted hordes of surfers, and the beach can get very crowded at times; you might want to check the new Buzzha Beach as an alternative. **Kite Boarding Club El Gouna** (✆ **014/2635528** or 012/6610878; www.kiteboarding-club.de) has a station at Buzzha Beach where they keep an ongoing stock of brand-new kitesurfing equipment and offer a variety of courses that range from basic (255€, plus 25€ for license) to instructor (565€). They also have a kite repair facility on-site as well as a pool table, small library, table soccer, and Internet facility to keep you busy during breaks. While Buzzha Beach is dedicated to sports (namely kitesurfing), Mangroovy Beach has a more leisurely side to it with **beach parties** at **Mangroovy Beach Club** (✆ **010/4037238**) Sundays and Wednesdays.

Diving is the Red Sea's biggest attraction and offers reef walls and colorful fish to sunken wrecks and shark schools. El Gouna doesn't fall short with some 40 good diving spots. While Poseidon Reef offers some stunning world-class coral gardens, the nearby Dolphin House is a good opportunity to see bottlenose dolphins. The Red Sea north from El Gouna is renowned for its hard-to-navigate treacherous waters that sent many vessels to their graves. Three close-by wreck sites not to be missed: the *Ulysses,* a slender 19th-century ship that sunk while on journey to Penang, Malaysia; the *Rosalie Moller,* a World War II token that is now densely inhabited by sweepers, lion, and glass fish (due to strong currents, it requires 50 logged dives before putting on your wet suit); and finally Abu Nahas, which offers four wrecks in one (*Kimon M, Christoula K, Carnatic,* and *Giannis D*). **Orca Dive Club** (✆ **012/2480460**) has different programs and trips covering all the wreck sites.

If you are not a big fan of watersports, there are a number of land-based activities to pick and choose from. **Golf** heads the league with an 18-hole par-72 world-class golf course at **El Gouna Golf Club** (✆ **065/3580009**); challenge the wind while hitting the 4th hole and manage the narrow landing zone of the 9th hole, another par-5 signature hole. **Go-karting** (✆ **065/3580521,** ext 32188) is a lot of fun for the family, and though El Gouna doesn't have the biggest track in Egypt or the fastest cars, the little 6.5-horsepower carts are in good shape. Facilities include lap timers so that everyone gets a printout of their time at the end of the race. Open daily from 10am to 10pm. Admission is LE100 for a 10-minute race or LE140 for a 15-minute one. Battleground maniacs will have a good time shooting **paintball** (✆ **016/2532102** or 016/1733255) with the first 100 bullets costing LE150, the second 100 LE60. A less effort-demanding activity is **horseback** or **camel riding** in the desert or by the beach. **Yalla Stables** (✆ **010/1366703**) offers horse and camel rides between 15€ for 30 minutes to 42€ for 2 hours. Ponies and donkeys are also available for 12€ (30 min.) to 35€ (2 hr.). Your kids will love it.

Skipping activities all together, you can opt for a lazy day by the pool with an exotic cocktail or an indulgent **spa** experience at the world-renowned **Angsana Spa** (p. 222), which offers a variety of massages and treatments including the fit-for-queens Nefertiti's Ritual, a 3-hour holistic treatment that includes a relaxing whirlpool session, a wave massage, traditional Lulur treatment (where a mix of turmeric paste and aromatic floral essence is used to exfoliate), and a cooling yogurt splash.

For a little romance, opt for a **Pharaonic raft ride. Beyond the Pyramids** (✆ **018/7770337**) offers a Venetian gondola experience in Ancient Egyptian–styled boats. The 1-hour ride costs LE250 for two people and comes with a bottle of wine and a selection of chocolate.

There is a small **Egyptology Museum** (Tamr Henna) featuring tacky replicas (that you can buy from the bazaars in Hurghada) of some Ancient Egyptian masterpieces; however, the drawings illustrating the Abu Simbel Museum are original and drawn by the renowned Egyptian portrait artist Hussein Bikar. They are splendid to behold and certainly worth 10 minutes of your time and the LE10 ticket. The museum opens from 10am to 2pm and 5 to 9pm. There is an **aquarium** (Kafr El Gouna) that features a couple of fish species, a handful of baby crocodiles, and a mummified shark. It looks quite shabby with small water tanks and cheesy decor, and nothing in comparison to the Marine Life Museum in Alexandria (p. 170). Only if you are bored to death and have 5€ to waste should you head here (daily 10am–10pm).

WHERE TO STAY

Expensive

Mövenpick Resort and Spa El Gouna Mövenpick is a big resort, and it feels like it. The central pool space is vast, with loungers dotted around a series of pools. Rooms are typical of Mövenpick—large and comfortable with clean, sophisticated lines—and here in El Gouna they're decorated in relaxing earth tones with tiled floors and area rugs. The high point of this Mövenpick is the large spa; treat yourself to a massage or a body scrub at the Angsana Spa, which will set you up nicely for a candlelit dinner by the sea or an authentic fine-dining experience at the Thai restaurant Bua Khao. The whole resort is wheelchair friendly.

El Gouna. ✆ **065/3544501.** Fax 065/3545160. www.moevenpick-elgouna.com. 554 units, including 19 suites and 15 rooms for people with special mobility. $250 standard double; $330 deluxe double. Rates include buffet breakfast, taxes, and service charges. AE, DC, MC, V. **Amenities:** 5 restaurants; 4 bars; airport transfer (extra charge); babysitting; kids' club; concierge; golf course nearby; health club & spa; Internet (extra charge); 4 heated pools (including 3 kids'); room service; 2 tennis courts; dive center and snorkeling. *In room:* A/C, TV, Internet (extra charge), minibar.

Sheraton Miramar ★★ The best word for the Miramar is "tranquil." Spread out over nine small islands, the buildings are low and rounded, and ground lighting is used to good effect among the palm trees. The rooms, by contrast, are large and modern, decorated with bold colors and furnished in lushly comfortable style. Windows and verandas offer spectacular views out across the lagoons that surround the hotel on all

The Maritime Graveyard

If you look at any diving map of the Red Sea coast, you will find it marked with numerous shipwreck sites. However, no site can match the notorious Abu Nahas, where you'll find not one—but four—wrecks.

In late 1869, passenger steamer ***Carnatic*** went down with a valuable cargo of spices. The spices were never recovered, though the cut-in-two wreck lies at a shallow 24m (79 ft.) deep. After more than 140 years under water, the *Carnatic* is now encrusted by corals and colonized by moray eels, groupers, and other reef fish.

Lying at a depth of between 4 and 26m (13–85 ft.) is the Greek-registered freighter ***Chrisoula K.*** It went down in 1981 while en route to Saudi Arabia with a cargo of Italian tiles. Though only some of the tiles are still in place, the rudder and the large propeller are mostly intact.

Located more or less at the same depth as the *Chrisoula K* is the ***Giannis D.*** It enjoys good visibility, and it's possible to picture the whole wreck from either end. In addition to the bounty of reef fish you are bound to see, there is a Napoleon fish often spotted here.

Deeper, at 32m (105 ft.), lies the last of the Abu Nahas wrecks quadrant, ***Kimon M.*** The German cargo vessel went down in late 1978 with a huge cargo of lentils. You can venture into the *Kimon M* for a closer look.

sides. My favorite part of the Miramar is the little wooden bridges that connect restaurants and bars and the main building to the beach and dive center.

El Gouna. ✆ **065/3545606.** Fax 065/3545608. www.starwoodhotels.com. 339 units, including 10 suites. 134€ standard double; 159€ sea-view double. Rates include buffet breakfast, taxes, and service charges. AE, MC, V. **Amenities:** 4 restaurants; 5 bars; airport transfer (extra charge); babysitting; concierge; golf course nearby; health club; Internet (extra charge); 5 pools (including 1 heated and 2 kids'); room service; 2 tennis courts; dive center and snorkeling. *In room:* A/C, TV, Internet (extra charge), minibar.

Steigenberger Golf Resort ★ Swinging your golf club with the spectacular view of the Red Sea in sight and majestic desert escapes in the backdrop is any golfer's dream, not to mention you would be playing an 18-hole, par-72 course designed by U.S. PGA tour pro Fred Couples and golf course designer Gene Bates. Away from hole-in-ones and perfect swings, the hotel is quite luxurious with a light summer touch; rooms have white walls with simple decoration. To keep up with your golfing effort, Fairways restaurant is guaranteed to keep you well fed, while Turkish *hammams* will leave you completely relaxed.

El Gouna. ✆ **065/3580140** or -4. Fax 065/3580149. www.steigenberger.com. 268 units, including 19 suites. 100€ double. Rate includes buffet breakfast, taxes, and service charges. AE, MC, V. **Amenities:** 3 restaurants; 4 bars; airport transfer (round-trip 30€); concierge; golf course; health club; Internet; 4 heated pools (including 3 kids'); room service; snorkeling. *In room:* A/C, TV, Internet (extra charge), minibar.

Moderate

Turtle's Inn ★ Value This is a magnificent, cozy, boutique-inspired hotel by the marina that makes you feel right at home. Bold yellow dominates the walls, while vibrant colors take over the furniture and small funky pieces of decor. The service and the staff are at their best, while the inn itself offers panoramic views of the marina and the Red Sea. The location offers easy access to the restaurants and cafes dotting Abu El Tig Marina, as well as the boats for your daily diving excursions. With its lively atmosphere and cheerful look, Turtle's Inn is growing a reputation as a divers' favorite.

Abu El Tig Marina. ✆ **065/3580171.** www.turtles-inn.com. 28 units, including 2 suites. 54€ double. Rate includes buffet breakfast, taxes, and service charges. MC, V. **Amenities:** Restaurant; bar; golf course nearby; pool; dive center. *In room:* A/C, TV, minibar.

WHERE TO EAT

In addition to the restaurants at each hotel, there are a good number of restaurants clustered around Tamr Henna and Abu El Tig Marina. With each being exquisitely good, making a choice of where to have dinner is not an easy one.

Expensive

Bleu Bleu ★ FRENCH This small restaurant has a Parisian feel to it, inspired by its outdoor seating, upscale elegance, and the French dishes it serves. Violet is the theme, from the napkins to the tablecloths to the wall paint. The menu is rather limited, but all the dishes are equally tasty, especially the grilled filet with chutney and mascarpone.

Abu El Tig Marina. ✆ **065/5497021.** Appetizers LE40–LE70; main courses LE70–LE120. MC, V. Daily noon–2am.

Le Deauville FRENCH This restaurant on the waterfront has the look of a small French bistro down pat. With white walls, simple furniture, and a few blue tiles thrown in for a Mediterranean touch, you could be anywhere in the south of France reading the menu off the blackboard. Service is a bit inept, but friendly enough, and the food is good.

Those with an appetite for seafood should try the *crevettes flambées au Pernod* (fresh shrimp expertly sautéed in anise-tinted liqueur). Otherwise, the *carre d'agneau* (rack of lamb) is cooked to perfection and comes with a simple but fresh side of vegetables.

Abu El Tig Marina. ✆ **065/3541132.** Appetizers LE30–LE90; main courses LE90–LE150. MC, V. Daily 1–11pm.

Pier 88 (Moments) INTERNATIONAL This is possibly the most romantic place in El Gouna. The tiny restaurant floats in the marina (anchored at pier 88) and has no more than nine tables crammed around the central kitchen. Seating is upholstered in white, and the glass windbreaker walls are hung with strings of blue lights. The swordfish carpaccio can be an excellent choice for a starter unless you intend to go for the mouthwatering Wagyu beef sirloin (LE250). Pier 88 makes a delicious change from the run of the mill hotel food.

Abu El Tig Marina. ✆ **018/4108820.** Appetizers LE45–LE70; main courses LE80–LE150. MC, V. Daily 7pm–midnight.

Moderate

Athena GREEK Fancy some traditional Greek moussaka or a souvlakia? The latest addition to El Gouna's ever-changing culinary scene, Athena is a traditional Greek tavern that makes an excellent choice for a delightful lunch. Greek extends beyond the theme and the menu into the hospitality; while you go through the menu wondering which dish to have, you will be treated to a shot of ouzo on the house.

Downtown. ✆ **010/6965102** or 010/5283757. Reservations recommended on weekends. Appetizers LE30–LE90; main courses LE65–LE100. MC, V. Daily noon–1am.

La Scala ITALIAN Casual and bustling, La Scala features bare-bones decor and a long, open kitchen where you can watch your food being cooked. Service is brusque and businesslike. Staff don't mess around being too friendly, but they get the food to the table while it's hot. Being the seafood lover I am, I never miss on the flambéed prawns in grappa, and you shouldn't either.

Abu El Tig Marina. ✆ **065/3541145.** Appetizers LE25–LE35; main courses LE55–LE110. MC, V. Daily 6pm–midnight.

Maison Thomas ★★ PIZZA This branch of Cairo's Maison Thomas is one of my favorite pizza places in Egypt. It's a little more rustic than the original, with garlic hanging from the walls, rough wooden tables, and the trademark green hanging lamps. Have a seat in the outdoor area and enjoy the fresh sea breeze while savoring a Quattro Formaggi pizza (a mix of four different cheeses); a medium is enough for one person for lunch.

Abu El Tig Marina. ✆ **065/549702.** Pizza LE30–LE55. MC, V. Daily 9am–11pm.

Saigon ★ VIETNAMESE This is El Gouna's latest addition to the culinary scene and comes with exotic (at least here) Vietnamese cuisine. Outside bamboo sticks and wooden decor dominate, while the inside has a lounge feel to it with velvet couches and glitzy, mirrorlike wall tiling. The food is quite delicious with more than one dish to recommend, including the sweet and sour pork spare ribs or stir-fried calamari with curry and lemon grass.

Abu El Tig Marina. ✆ **010/6762329.** Appetizers LE25–LE55; main courses LE55–LE115. MC, V. Daily 11am–11pm.

EL GOUNA AFTER DARK

As diverse as everything else in El Gouna, the nightlife scene comes in with multiple options and a variety of hangouts to satisfy every taste; from hedonist beach parties at Mangroovy Beach (p. 224) to the trendiest venues at Abu El Tig Marina.

Papas Island Three guys met in a bar and decided to open their own; this is how Papas was born. It started with Papas Bar (p. 238) in Hurghada and has now expanded into neighboring El Gouna with Papas Island. It is the latest craze in town (opened Sept 2009) with its lively atmosphere typical of its elder sister in Hurghada. The place often features live performances that vary from local solo acts to world-renowned trance and rave DJs, as well as professional entertainers and jugglers. Daily 3pm till late. Abu El Tig Marina. ✆ **016/8833554.** www.papasbar.com.

Peanuts Bar This is where party animals dance nonstop from dusk till dawn; the atmosphere is electric and the password is hip. DJ music is the steering wheel but changes attire with the theme of the night; it could be salsa or '70s disco. There is often a ladies night, and once a week there is also a local night when residents enjoy free shots. Daily 10pm till you drop. Abu El Tig Marina. ✆ **012/7991304.**

Studio 52 An energetic atmosphere fills the air with Studio 52's almost-daily live performances. Its vibrant interior and welcoming design add to the formula, and finger food makes for a perfect snack. Daily 4pm till late. Abu El Tig Marina. ✆ **014/4492533** or 065/3580521, ext 77962.

Tambel Irish Pub This small bar has walls overfilled with knickknacks, talismans, souvenirs, and even different currencies' banknotes. The outdoor area has a homey feel to it with red-colored bricks, an attic-shaped decor roof, and small trinkets thrown here and there (and even hung from the trees). There's a TV (though small, you can still watch the game) and a pool table. Daily noon to 3am. Katr El Gouna. ✆ **065/3580521,** ext 32190.

DAY TRIPS FROM EL GOUNA

For day trips, Luxor is the most prominent and most commercially sold destination (for details, see p. 262); however, if you wish to go off the beaten track and explore some of Egypt's least-visited sites, the monasteries of St. Anthony and St. Paul are where you should be heading.

Monasteries of St. Anthony & St. Paul

A 3-hour drive north of Hurghada will take you to two ancient Coptic monasteries named for 3rd-century saints. Visitors are warmly welcomed in both monasteries except during Lent.

The walled compound of the **Monastery of St. Anthony** lies about 45km (28 miles) from the Red Sea Coastal Road, some 270km (168 miles) north of Hurghada. It was built at the foot of the mountain where St. Anthony lived from his youth until he died at the age of 105 in A.D. 356. Having been forbidden to come any closer to his cave, Anthony's followers settled on the site of the present-day buildings and buried him inside its walls in a chapel that is now called the **Church of St. Anthony.** On its walls are some of the most dramatic and important **Coptic murals** in Egypt. They were restored in the 1990s and are well worth a visit. You can also visit St. Anthony's cave, though it is a rather long climb—1,158 stairs. Reckon on about an hour and a good deal of water to drink. The cave is worth a visit both for its original significance and for the scrawled annotations left by visitors over the last millennium and a half.

The **Monastery of St. Paul,** who was Paul the Anchorite, or Paul of Thebes, is about 35km (22 miles) southeast across the desert and mountains from the Monastery of St. Anthony. It was built on or near the site of the cave that St. Paul occupied for about 90 years, living on a half loaf of bread brought to him every day by a crow until he died in about A.D. 345. It is reported that one day St. Anthony made the 2-day hike from his neighboring cave, and when he arrived Paul was expecting him because the crow had brought, instead of the usual half portion of bread, a full loaf. The monastery, which contains the intriguing Church of St. Paul, guesthouses, and an olive press, is an imposing, almost military-looking place, with a high wall around it. There is usually an English-speaking monk in the compound who can show you around.

Both monasteries are located off the Red Sea Coastal Highway with more or less an equal proximity to both Cairo and Hurghada. If you have private transport and are traveling between the two cities, both monasteries certainly deserve a stop. Otherwise, if you are based in either El Gouna or Hurghada, you may end up hiring a car, with or without a driver, as many tour operators have taken this excursion out of their program. **Limousine El Gouna** (✆ **065/3580061**) offers a chauffeured 1-day round-trip to the Monastery of St. Anthony for LE1,200.

2 HURGHADA

The international airport in Hurghada has become the main hub for resort tourism on the northern end of the Red Sea coast. Not only are small towns such as El Quseir and Safaga within easy reach, but a number of world-class resort compounds, such as Soma Bay, Sahl Hashish, and El Gouna, are an easy transfer away.

The city itself, however, is another matter. In fact, when tourism experts get together to discuss development, it's usually only a matter of time before Hurghada comes up as an example of what to avoid. A gold-rush approach to building hotels has left this tourist city an ugly mess. The beaches have been divided between the resorts, and there is almost no public space from which you can see the water. Streets and squares are badly designed and hard to get around, and even if there were somewhere to go, it's all so spread out that you need a taxi for almost anything. In an attempt to make a change, a pedestrian walkway with restaurants, bars, and a small shopping area has been devised. **Hurghada Marina Boulevard** (www.hurghadamarina.com) is a step in the right direction, but could it rival Sharm El Sheikh's Ne'ama Bay? Only time will tell.

ESSENTIALS

Orientation

Dahar, Sakala, and the Villages Road are the city's main districts. Coming from Cairo by bus or by car, you first hit Dahar, a more local downtown with few points of interest to the tourist (mainly the bus station). Following the main road southward, you will come to Sakala, which can be described as a traffic circle with three important streets: one leads to the harbor where you can pick up the ferry to Sharm El Sheikh, another leads to the talk of the town and the place to be (Hurghada Marina Boulevard), while the last one is the long Sheraton Road marked with midrange and budget hotels, shops, restaurants, cafes, and bars. Though Sheraton Road is Hurghada's pulsating heart, things are not the most organized and you will be repeatedly hassled by street vendors or ogling young men. Toward the southern end of Sakala, the Sheraton Road splits into two, with the main one

Warning! The Rumor Mill

You hear it everywhere you go in Egypt, recounted with the same wide-eyed wonderment with which Dick Whittington would have received the news that the streets of London were paved with gold: Foreign women come to Hurghada to meet and have sex with Egyptian men. To working-class men in Egypt, whose relations with the opposite sex are tightly circumscribed by tradition and who may not be able to get married until well into their 30s or even 40s, this is thrilling news, indeed. Whatever the merits of the story, the result is that female tourists in Hurghada, particularly those traveling alone, report a disturbing level of harassment. Keep in mind that what passes for banal conversation in the West may well be seen as an overt come-on when it takes place in the street or in a taxi in Egypt, and that the concept of consent is not as clearly defined in this context as it may be in your mind. Unless you wish to indicate a serious desire to move the relationship to an intimate plane, it is better to sit in the backseat of the taxi and greet the opposite sex with a handshake rather than a hug or kiss on the cheek unless you know and trust the person.

being the Villages Road. It runs parallel to the shoreline and hosts dozens of resorts closely tucked next to one another. Part of the Villages Road is a dedicated shopping area known as the Touristic Walking Promenade, a semi-pedestrian walkway (there is a one-way road for cars but humped with tens of speed breakers) where you can have a drink, grab a bite, or go shopping. The level of harassment here is restricted to persistent sellers.

Getting There

BY PLANE Hurghada International Airport (HRG) is connected to most of the European capitals, major Russian cities, as well as Cairo. Operated by Aéroports de Paris, its facilities are modern but fail to cope with the rapidly growing number of passengers. At press time, jackhammers were carrying out an upgrade. If you are coming directly to Hurghada on an international flight, you will probably have to purchase a visa ($15; not payable in Egyptian pounds) here. There are a number of daily flights connecting Hurghada to the capital with an average price of LE650 for the round-trip. The old 1970s Peugeot wagons that used to be the trademark for an airport taxi are being phased out and replaced with newer models. It is a comfortable ride into town for LE50 or to El Gouna for LE120.

BY FERRY There is a ferry that connects Hurghada to Sharm El Sheikh four times a week. From Hurghada it departs on Saturdays, Tuesdays, and Thursdays at 9am and on Mondays at 4am. From Sharm El Sheikh it departs on Saturdays, Tuesdays, and Thursdays at 5pm and at 6pm on Mondays. It is a 2½-hour sail that costs LE250/LE150 adults/children one-way. Unfortunately, at press time, vehicle transport through the ferry was temporarily suspended. The ferry's agent in Hurghada (Sherif Tours; ✆ **065/3443499**) has its office across the street from the harbor.

BY BUS There are several transport companies whose buses connect Hurghada to other Egyptian cities and towns. To Cairo, **Go Bus** (owned by El Gouna Transport Company; ✆ **19567**) is simply the best, with clean and comfortable buses and, above all, punctual departures. They have 16 daily buses running between Hurghada and Cairo, with two continuing farther to Alexandria. Tickets to Cairo cost LE65 to LE125; to Alexandria LE90. **Super Jet** (✆ **065/3553499**) is a good option for traveling to Luxor. They have one daily bus that leaves Hurghada at 8am and costs LE45. It is important to note, however, that they don't allow more than four non-Egyptian nationals on the bus; book well in advance. **Golden Horse** (✆ **065/3559277**) is the newest transport company connecting Hurghada to the neighboring towns of Safaga, El Quseir, and Marsa Alam. Three daily buses do the southward run costing LE10, LE15, and LE25, respectively. For more information on how to do a 1-day trip to El Quseir, see p. 243.

BY CAR About 455km (282 miles) make up the 5-hour drive to Hurghada from Cairo on the same road that leads to El Gouna (p. 222).

Getting Around

BY TAXI The best option to move around Hurghada is to have a car, but if this is too expensive for your budget, you can always go around by taxi. The orange-and-blue cars are comfortable recent models that can be found on every corner. Set the price before you step in, and expect to pay LE5 to LE50 depending on where in Hurghada you are heading. Expect the fare to at least double if you are heading to either El Gouna or Safaga.

BY BUS Local buses and microbuses can be a good method of transportation to move around the city if you are on a tight budget. Fares range from LE0.50 to LE1.50.

ON FOOT With lengthy promenades and shopping areas, you better gear up for lengthy walks. However, Hurghada is too spread out, and to go from one place to another (from Hurghada Marine Blvd. to the Touristic Walking Promenade, for example), you would certainly need to hail a taxi or microbus.

BY CAR The best way to go around Hurghada and environs is to have your own transport, and renting a car here is pretty straightforward. All you need is your country's driver license, your passport, and a major credit card. There are dozens of car-rental agencies all over the city, but two I find very professional: **CRC** (✆ **065/3463366** or 010/6107387) offers a wide range of Peugeots, from the small and compact 206 ($35 daily rate) to the more spacious 406 ($55 daily rate). The daily rate comes with a free allowance of 120km (75 miles) per day, while each additional kilometer will cost you an incremental 18¢ to 23¢. **Shahd** (✆ **012/7458038**) is another well-reputed car-rental agency. Their fleet is mostly 2009 models that range from the Hyundai Elantra (LE200 daily rate) to the Mitsubishi Pajero (LE750 daily rate). The same 120km (75 miles) allowance applies, but each additional kilometer costs LE1 to LE1.50 depending on how long are you hiring the car and to where you intend to drive.

Tourist Information

The best thing that can be said about the Hurghada **tourist information** office (✆ **065/3446513**) is that it's cool inside, and they usually have a photocopied map they can give you.

Internet has become a given service provided by all hotels and resorts, though it often comes with an extra charge. If you want a cheaper option, you can always head to Hurghada proper (Dahar or Sakala) where Internet cafes abound, but look in the byroads rather than the main streets; they offer more or less the same service and charge LE2 to LE5 per hour.

WHAT TO SEE & DO

Loose environmental controls have meant off-beach snorkeling around Hurghada has been severely degraded in recent years, but if you head to the small islet of **Mahmya** (www.mahmya.com) you will be rewarded with an underwater paradise. Part of Giftun Islands Natural Protectorates, just off the coast of Hurghada, Mahmya is a kid-friendly natural playground where the young ones will enjoy a day out in a semi-wild environment. The island has been equipped with a simple ecotourism facility to accommodate lunch and drinks. Every single tour operator in town has this excursion on offer, but if you want to evade the madding crowds and save some pennies, you can book directly through **Al Alia Company** (✆ **065/3449735** or -6). The 1-day trip costs 55€ per person including transportation, snorkeling equipment rental, and lunch but no drinks, not even water.

Still within the premises of Giftun Natural Protectorate, the main Giftun Island is a large, bleak island surrounded by coral reefs teeming with life. There are at least half a dozen distinct **dive** sites around the rim of the island, and you'll see a huge variety of corals, moray eels, lion fish, lobster, parrotfish, angelfish, and more. If wrecks and maritime disasters fascinate you, then a day excursion to ***Thistlegorm*** is what you should be booking. The British cargo vessel was only a year old when it was sunk by a pair of German planes in late 1941. The explosions blew a huge hole in her superstructure, making the inside of the boat accessible to divers. She lies in about 30m (98 ft.) of water, and a large quantity of cargo—including vintage BSA motorcycles, rifles, and locomotives—is still visible.

If you want to see fish but don't like the idea of joining them in their environment, check out the **Seascope Submarines** (✆ **012/1746550**). They run a couple of trips a day between 9am and 2pm, each taking little less than 2 hours (of which 1 is spent underwater). Tickets are $40 adults and $20 children 6 to 12; under 6 free.

Once nighttime descends, Hurghada unleashes its most hedonistic side with dusk-till-dawn partying at **Hed Kandi** or hard-core clubbing at **Little Buddha.** But if you feel less energetic after a full day of diving and outdoor activities, you can always grab a couple of beers while watching the game at the city's most famous **Papas Bar.**

WHERE TO STAY

Hurghada's once pristine coast has been haphazardly developed into a lengthy stretch of hotels and resorts built one right next to the other. Competition is fierce, but instead of creating an edge and capitalizing on it, the outright majority of accommodation facilities in Hurghada have opted for mass tourism, offering cut-throat prices to international tour operators or offering the whole resort on an exclusive basis to big European vacation clubs. There are a few exceptions, which are reviewed below.

Very Expensive

Oberoi Sahl Hashish ★★★ If you're looking to wipe away the wrinkles and go home feeling a decade younger, you can't do much better than this. From the moment you're picked up at the airport, the Oberoi touches are clear: bits of *mashrabeya* adorn the car, and soft music plays on the stereo. The resort is a spread-out collection of low-domed buildings; one of the things that you're paying for here is a very low guest density. With only 102 suites (no rooms) spread out over the same size compound that other resorts use for many times this number, the grounds and facilities feel half empty even when the resort is fully booked. Standard suites include a small living room and an outdoor dining area, while the superiors enjoy superb bathrooms with a huge bathtub and a shower that's built into a glass wall that opens into a small, jasmine-draped private garden. Grand suites have their own private pool, a luxury you can't find anywhere else in Egypt, and royal ones are just as luxurious and grand, yet far more spacious. Add to this the best horizon pool on the Red Sea coast, a lovely beach with a snorkeling reef at the end of a graceful little jetty, and one of the best spas in Egypt, and you have an unbeatable recipe for relaxation.

Sahl Hashish, Hurghada. ✆ **065/3440777.** Fax 065/3440788. www.oberoihotels.com. 102 suites. 295€ deluxe suite; 420€ superior deluxe suite; 700€ grand suite; 1,220€ royal suite. Rates include buffet breakfast, taxes, and service charges. AE, DC, MC, V. **Amenities:** 3 restaurants; bar; airport transfer (round-trip 60€); health club & spa; pool; room service. *In room:* A/C, TV, minibar.

Steigenberger Al Dau There are two Steigenbergers located across the road from one another. Avoid the overflow facilities (officially the Steigenberger Al Dau Club) that are cut off from the sea by the road—they are not only generic and bland, but sub-par considering the price. The facilities on the sea side of the road, on the other hand, are Steigenberger doing what it does best: a big, standardized hotel with lots of dark wood and chrome, a vast lobby, and friendly, responsive service. Rooms are huge, with big comfortable bathrooms and nice touches such as *mashrabeya* screens. The swimming pool is also vast, as is the sweep of the grounds down to the long beach of golden sand. If you wish to spend some time away from the beach, there is a rather small 9-hole, par-27 golf course where you can practice a couple of swings. To complete your stay, a visit to the Algotherm Red Sea Thalasso & Spa can't be missed; go for the "chill out in Hurghada" treatment with its *hammam* scrub and neck and shoulder massage.

Villages Rd., Hurghada. ✆ **065/3465400.** Fax 065/3465400. www.steigenbergeraldaubeach.com. 372 units. 190€ double. Rate includes buffet breakfast, taxes, and service charges. AE, DC, MC, V. **Amenities:** 4 restaurants; 4 bars; golf course; health club & spa; Internet (extra charge); 2 pools (including kids' pool) and lazy river; room service; dive center and windsurfing center. *In room:* A/C, TV, Internet (extra charge), minibar.

Expensive

Hilton Hurghada Resort This is very much a typical middle-of-the-road Hurghada beach resort. Rooms are big and comfortable, with enough beach-type touches, such as white-tile flooring and big sliding-glass windows that let out to the beach or around the pool. The lobby and buffet restaurants are a bit too noisy and crowded for my taste, especially when you're trying to relax, but the Lagouna restaurant at the end of the garden remains one of my favorite retreats in Hurghada. The beach is a great place to work on your tan, and the public pool areas heat up at night with a show and disco.

Red Sea Coastal Hwy. (10km/6 miles south of Hurghada). ✆ **065/3465036.** Fax 065/3465035. www1.hilton.com. 311 units. $105 garden-view double; $130 sea-view double. Rates include buffet breakfast, taxes, and service charges. AE, DC, MC, V. **Amenities:** 4 restaurants; 5 bars; airport transfer (round-trip $20); babysitting; kids' club; concierge; health club; Internet (extra charge); 3 pools; room service; tennis court; dive center. *In room:* A/C, TV, Internet (extra charge), minibar.

Hurghada Marriott Beach Resort The Hurghada Marriott has a nice location, with its own little beach tucked into a quiet part of Hurghada. Facilities may lack character, but rooms are spacious and comfortable. Public areas are modern and elegant, and the view in most directions cannot be faulted. The small peninsula owned by the hotel offers particularly nice views of the sea and can be used for dining or just lounging about and enjoying the sea air.

El Corniche Rd., Hurghada. ✆ **065/3446950.** Fax 065/3446970. www.marriott.com. 283 units, including 14 suites. $100 double. Rate includes buffet breakfast, taxes, and service charges. AE, DC, MC, V. **Amenities:** 5 restaurants; 4 bars; airport transfer; babysitting; kids' club; concierge; health club; 2 pools (heated and kids'); room service; tennis court; Wi-Fi (extra charge). *In room:* A/C, TV, Internet (extra charge), minibar.

Moderate

Geisum Village ★ More budget than midrange, Geisum Village is a good beach getaway in the north end of Hurghada. Maintenance is a bit iffy in places, with some cracked plaster and peeling paint issues, but facilities on the whole are good enough, and important items—such as air-conditioners—are being kept up to date. Rooms are a bit on the small side, but the view (at least from the rooms closest to the beach) is decent and bathrooms are clean. The beach is short and the sand is a bit rougher and harder packed than you'll find at higher-end places.

El Corniche Rd., Hurghada. ✆ **065/3546692.** Fax 065/3547994. 86 units. LE350 double. Rate includes breakfast, dinner, taxes, and service charge. No credit cards. **Amenities:** Restaurant; 2 bars; pool; dive center. *In room:* A/C, TV.

White Albatros The Albatros, in the middle of Sheraton Road, is probably the best deal for those who are looking for midrange accommodation and are willing to sacrifice staying at a beachfront hotel. Rooms are basic, with second-rate fit and finish, but they are clean, comfortable, and relatively large. The rooftop pool isn't something that you should take too seriously—it's just a little bigger than a whirlpool—and the "sea views" should also be taken with a grain of salt. All around, however, this is a friendly and pleasant place that offers rare value for money.

Sheraton Rd., Sakala, Hurghada. ✆ **065/3442519.** www.walbatros.com. 40 units. LE180 double. Rate includes breakfast, taxes, and service charge. No credit cards. **Amenities:** 2 restaurants; pool; room service. *In room:* A/C, TV, minibar.

Inexpensive

Cinderella Hotel This budget accommodation doesn't pretend to be anything else. The Cinderella offers a bare-bones combination of a bed, bathroom, and some food. The beds are clean, but not the thickest in town, and the decor relies heavily on three-tone (all of them pastel) furniture and linoleum. The place is very clean, though, and staff are warm and friendly.

El Corniche Rd., Hurghada. ✆ **065/3556571.** 36 units. LE150 double. Rate includes breakfast, taxes, and service charge. No credit cards. **Amenities:** Restaurant; bar; Internet. *In room:* A/C, TV, minifridge.

Eiffel Hotel Eiffel Hotel is located close to some busy nightspots, such as Ministry of Sound, but it's quiet enough for sleeping in the morning after. It isn't directly on the beach, but it has beach facilities, as well as a rooftop bar and pool. Rooms are fairly basic but bigger and more comfortable than some of the truly low-end places. The dining room wouldn't be my choice for eating in, and I would think twice about paying for half-board options, but the Café del Mar is just up the street, and beyond that Hurghada Marina Boulevard offers other dining options within easy walking distance.

Sheraton Rd., Sakala. ✆ **065/3444570** or -1. Fax 065/3444572. www.eiffelhotel.org. LE240 double. Rate includes breakfast, dinner, taxes, and service charge. V. **Amenities:** Restaurant; bar; Internet (LE5/hour); 2 pools (Jacuzzi-in-size); room service. *In room:* A/C, TV, minifridge.

WHERE TO EAT

As a tourism-dependent city, Hurghada has a widely diverse culinary scene, from finger food and fine dining to traditional Egyptian cuisine and local fare. Fast food and international chain restaurants are also present; if you feel like KFC, Pizza Hut, McDonald's, or Burger King, they are all clustered next to each other at the southern end of Sheraton Road. Regardless of where you dine, dessert should always be reserved for **Gelateria duo Soli** (Hurghada Marina Blvd.; scoop LE9; daily 10am–midnight), where you can indulge in the ultimate Italian ice-cream experience. Go for licorice if you are into trying new things or the forest berries if you want to play it safe.

Expensive

Bordiehn's ★★★ FUSION Set in an ultra-modern space with artistic touches such as beautiful paintings and a lovely water wall fountain, Bordiehn's is the outcome of German couple Barbara and Thomas Bordiehn's culinary creativity. The menu fuses neo-German and local Egyptian cuisine, with the signature "Local Hero" (a grilled tender camel filet served with chili chocolate sauce and traditional southern German pasta, *knöpfle,* on the side) leading the gastronomical experience; don't forget your camel meat certificate at the end of your meal. The restaurant serves breakfast, lunch, and dinner.

Hurghada Marina Blvd. ✆ **065/3451292.** www.bordiehn.com. Dinner appetizers LE35–LE70; dinner main courses LE95–LE140. MC, V. Daily 9am–2am.

Café del Mar ★ INTERNATIONAL This restaurant sits on the corner of a busy street close to the Ministry of Sound nightclub, but it's far enough away that the party doesn't intrude and close enough that it's just a quick walk down to the beach after a light dinner for a night of dancing. It has a nice selection of sandwiches and salads for lunch, but the place comes alive after dark with just the right balance of conversational hubbub and soft-but-upbeat music. Café del Mar is run by a pair of Swedish chefs who came here for the sun and the nightlife. The steaks and pasta have an excellent reputation, while the thin-but-tasty chocolate cake is the perfect finish.

Mermaid Sq., Sakala. ✆ **010/0716770** or -1. Appetizers LE20–LE45; main courses LE50–LE110. No credit cards. Daily noon–midnight.

El Mina SEAFOOD If you're feeling a little hemmed in by the walls of your resort, tired of eating in "outlets" instead of restaurants, and antsy to see a little bit of the "real" Hurghada, head to El Mina, one of the best known and established of the local eateries. Decorated in traditional Egyptian-fish-restaurant style—which is to say over-the-top marine tableaux on the walls, aquariums, and bright colors—it offers guests a chance to choose their own fish from the ice-packed stand in front of the kitchen and decide how it gets cooked. The only real choice you have to make is between grilled and fried (choose grilled), and everyone knows these words in English.

Sakala Sq. ✆ **065/3556637.** Appetizers LE10–LE25; main courses LE60–LE120. No credit cards. Daily noon–midnight.

Moderate

White Elephant (Value) THAI Pastel painted walls decorated with hanging wooden palettes and traditional Thai statuettes on shelves set the mood for this Thai restaurant. The place offers a good variety of green and red curries, sweet and sour delicacies, and stir-fried Thai dishes; however, the attention grabbers are barbecued duck in red curry and the steamed shrimp in red curry with coconut milk and pineapple. The food is not gourmet, but for the price it is a good bargain. White Elephant has another, much smaller, branch at El Gouna.

Hurghada Marina Blvd. ✆ **010/1025117** or 012/4558940. Appetizers LE15–LE45; main courses LE35–LE120. MC, V. Daily 11am–midnight.

Inexpensive

Abu Kadigah *Finds* EGYPTIAN This iconic eatery has been here ever since Hurghada's early days as a tourism destination. The place has no decor, very basic settings, and looks shabby from the outside—but wait until you taste the food. You will be amazed with the rich flavors; kebab is a good option for meat lovers, while okra is a wise vegetarian choice (just make sure it doesn't contain any minced meat). I first ate here 13 years ago, and the food today tastes just the same—lip-smacking and yummy.

Sakala. ✆ **065/3443768.** Appetizers LE5–LE10; main courses LE10–LE30. No credit cards. Daily noon–10pm.

SHOPPING

There is a shopping opportunity on every corner in Hurghada: at the hotel's lobby, right in front of the resort's main entrance, along the Villages Road with its famous Touristic Walking Promenade, along the bustling Sheraton Road, and most recently at the well-designed Souk Marina (part of Hurghada Marina Blvd.). What is on display doesn't significantly differ from one place to another, and often from one shop to another. The long list includes wooden boxes with inlaid mother-of-pearl, Middle Eastern perfumes, traditional terra-cotta statues, T-shirts with cartoonish prints illustrating sharks eating divers, touristic books, papyrus-made trinkets, alabaster-made pieces of decor, stone statues, and of course pyramids made from whatever material you could think of. For the shopper with taste, two places I find interesting include **Wood U Like,** with two branches at the ends of Sakala Square (one next to the old police station and the other next to Ebead Market). It offers souvenirs with a touch of artistry that are difficult to find elsewhere; the wide selection of lamps and lanterns they have is interesting. **Canvas** is the city's most promising art gallery with abstracts, calligraphy, and locally inspired paintings for sale. Located at the Hurghada Marina Boulevard, Canvas has unusual open hours—5pm to midnight.

HURGHADA AFTER DARK

The upside of being the cheap-package capital of Egypt is that Hurghada has an almost unparalleled party culture. Between European teenagers on term breaks, Russians breaking out of the winter blah, and Brits getting a bit of sun, there's no shortage of tourists who are ready, willing, and able to party all night, night after night. Below are a few of the many alternatives, but improvisation is the name of the game here, and almost every hotel has some kind of disco. Meet up, make friends, and follow the crowd to where the party is happening.

Hed Kandi Beach Bar This is a beachfront lounge bar and dance club with a sophisticated atmosphere and super wow music brought to you from the London-based Hed Kandi label. During the daytime, the place is dedicated to lounging by the pool or suntanning on the private beach. As darkness descends, it turns into the city's nightlife hot spot where partyholics dance till they drop. Hed Kandi's monthly events often include hedonistic pool parties and wild shows where head-turning models and professional clubbers are flown in from Russia. Daily from 9am as a private beach and from 9pm as a club. Men are subject to a strict couples-only policy. Hurghada Marina Blvd. ✆ **016/8833556.** www.hedkandibeachbar.com. Tickets: LE50 for pool lounge (includes towel and a bottle of water); LE80 for the club (includes 1 free drink).

Little Buddha One of Buddha Bar's smaller sisters, Little Buddha follows suit with dangling chandeliers and Far Eastern wooden decor, all centered on the big Buddha statue, creating the trademark Buddha Bar mood. Your night will take off with fine fusion dining; I wholeheartedly recommend the poached lobster tail with avocado and corn salsa, but it may very well break the bank. As Buddha Bar's signature music plays, the lounge-bar turns into the intense, yet smooth, clubbing venue it is known to be. Daily 4pm to 3am. Couples-only policy is strictly applied. Villages Rd., Hurghada. ✆ **065/ 3450120.** www.littlebuddha-hurghada.com. Tickets: LE100 gets you 1 free drink.

Ministry of Sound Head down to the Ministry (of London fame) beach during the day for pub-style food and beach-style lounging, and stay late into the night for an international slate of DJs—which has included Brandon Block, Sonique, Judge Jules, Graham Gold, Miss Kelly Marie—and plenty of dance-party action. Ministry of Sound opens daily from 9am as a private beach and as a club from 10:30pm to 5am. Sakala (close to Hurghada Marina Blvd. and Café del Mar). ✆ **016/8833550.** Tickets: LE80, if bought in advance from Papas Bar or Café del Mar, gives you LE48 value of drinks, but if bought at the door the value goes down to LE36.

Papas Bar Dominated by dark wooden interiors, Papas Bar has a friendly yet cool feel to it. The food is downright delicious and the atmosphere is joyful. Live acts and DJs from the U.K. and the Netherlands exclusively perform here from time to time, but you can always head here for a cold beer on a hot afternoon, lay back and watch the game, or play darts and try out some karaoke. Daily 3pm till late. Hurghada Marina Blvd. ✆ **016/ 8833554.** www.papasbar.com.

Shade Bar One of Hurghada's newest and trendiest bars, Shade Bar comes in with ultra-modern decor and funky colored beanbags where you can sit, chat with friends, and have a couple of drinks. The music is good and the atmosphere is more hip and cozy than sleek and sophisticated. Once a week there is live music. Daily 3pm till late. Hurghada Marina Blvd. ✆ **010/3441813.** www.theshadebar.com.

DAY TRIPS FROM HURGHADA

While Hurghada is hardly an ideal location from which to see the rest of Egypt, it's easy enough to get to Luxor for a day trip. Most hotels offer a roster of possibilities through their travel desks. If they don't, you're never more than a 5-minute walk from a travel agency or a tour operator.

Luxor

The temples and tombs that are around the city of Luxor are also accessible as a day trip from Hurghada, and you'll find many companies that are prepared to sell you a single-day round-trip bus excursion. Tour operators may vary, but the Luxor day trip is quite standard. For 85€ you should get a bus transfer; entrance to Karnak Temple, Valley of the Kings (Tomb of Tutankhamun is an additional ticket), and the Mortuary Temple of Hatshepsut; as well as a lunch box and soft drinks.

El Quseir

This is one of the most interesting places to visit along the Red Sea coast south of Hurghada, but unfortunately it is not on offer by any of the tour operators in the city. To visit El Quseir on a 1-day trip, you can either rent a car (p. 244) or do it the old backpacker way—with public transport. **Golden Horse** (p. 232) has three buses a day that leave Hurghada at 6:30, 7:30, and 9:30am and return at 5, 8, and 10:30pm. It's a 2-hour ride that costs LE15 one-way.

3 SAFAGA

Like Hurghada was 20 years ago, Safaga is a divers' town slowly being won over by the tourism industry. Where roughing it was once the price to be paid for the spectacular diving and snorkeling, it's now possible to eat well, be waited on hand and foot, and sleep on high-quality sheets between dives. Safaga is often perceived as a divers-only destination, but with recent tourism developments, more options, from kitesurfing and catamaran sailing to Thalasso treatments and 18-hole golf courses, are opening up.

ESSENTIALS

Orientation

There's not much to Safaga. Unlike Hurghada to the north or El Quseir to the south, it is bypassed by the highway, but there is still a clearly identifiable road through the middle of the town. The bulk of Safaga is built around the port, which is used mainly for exporting phosphorus, but there is also a brisk ferry business running laborers and pilgrims to and from Saudi Arabia. A little to the north of this is a traffic circle, which features a giant mermaid on a pedestal. It is locally known as Majlis Mahali and features Safaga's most prominent restaurant—Ali Baba. Safaga's northern outskirt is where the resorts are located, and farther north (5km/3 miles) is the upscale resort compound of Soma Bay.

Getting There

BY PLANE About 50km (31 miles) from Hurghada International Airport, Safaga is easily reached by air from Cairo as well as from a variety of European hubs. Arranging for a transfer through your hotel is the easiest way, but not necessarily the cheapest. As an alternative, you can go for a taxi, but don't forget the haggling.

BY BUS Upper Egypt has several daily buses that run between Safaga and Cairo (via Hurghada). The ticket costs LE65. The bus station is located toward the southern end of the town where finding transportation might be a dicey proposition; arrange a pickup with your hotel in advance.

BY CAR The intersections on the main highway are fairly well signposted. If you're headed into town, watch out for the giant mermaid traffic circle—when you see this, you're pretty close. Stopping at Ali Baba's (the town's most famous eatery located 50m/164 ft. or so past the mermaid on the right) for directions should yield useful information. The town is also connected to the Nile Valley via a road that I wouldn't personally recommend due to its poor condition.

Getting Around

A number of companies in Safaga will provide vehicles and drivers to individuals or groups. Some are a little shady, so exercise judgment. Try **Larose Tours** (© **010/3344222**), which maintains a small fleet of vehicles that range in size from compact cars to full-size buses; it can arrange airport transfers and sightseeing trips up and down the coast. The per-day rental rate is LE250 for a car without a driver and LE500 with one.

WHAT TO SEE & DO

While most of the resorts have the "house reef" just offshore, there are literally dozens of spectacular sites for **diving** coral, animal life, or wrecks within a 30- to 90-minute boat ride. Wreck divers, in particular, can feast on Safaga's three big ferries: *Al Kahfain, MS El Arish/El Tor,* and the *Salem Express.* Though all three wreck sites are accessible to divers, please dive the *Salem Express* wreck with respect; after all, this is, in a way, an underwater cemetery. Less tragic dive sites include **Tobia,** also known as the **Coral Garden,** with its spectacular and multifaceted coral reef. At a depth of 5 to 30m (16–98 ft.), you'll see colorful formations as well as moray eels, octopus, stonefish, and, if you're lucky, eagle rays. **Panorama Reef** is a big 400m (1,312 ft.) block of vibrantly colored reef that goes down almost 35m (115 ft.) and offers the possibility not only to see eagle rays and the occasional white-tipped and hammerhead sharks, but also turtles, as they sometimes lurk at the northern end. Just off the Sheraton Soma Bay beach, the eponymous **Seven Pillars** rise up from a depth of between 10 and 12m (33–39 ft.) and are usually surrounded by multicolored flora and fauna. There is a resident Napoleon fish here that is accustomed to humans, as well as puffer, lizard, and lion fish.

If you prefer to remain on the water's surface rather than underneath it, Safaga makes for an excellent **kite-** and **windsurfing** playfield. It has a unique combination of warm water and reliable, strong winds (on average one Beaufort stronger than off Hurghada to the north) that brings an increasing number of watersports addicts. Not only do winds whip up exciting offshore waves, but the relatively sheltered bay means good flat water for beginners. The **watersports center** at Kempinski offers a 30- to 45-minute teaser (5€) where you get a bit of background about either windsurfing or catamaran sailing before trying it out yourself. If you are hooked up you can enroll for a windsurfing ground course that costs 205€ (including the VDWS license) or a catamaran sailing one that costs 230€ that also includes the license. If you wish to have a sailing experience without being in charge of the catamaran, you can go for a 1-hour cruise that costs 30€ per person (minimum two people).

For a taste of life away from the sea, several tour operators arrange safari trips to several desert destinations, including a now-abandoned Bedouin village. But if you don't want to get all dusty after a bumpy ride, then I recommend staying at La Résidence des Cascades, Soma Bay for some chic and challenging golf. The hotel features an 18-hole, par-72 **golf** course designed by South African golf legend Gary Player. The course has stunning views of the desert, the mountains, and the Red Sea, and, of course, a great bar on the 18th hole. Facilities also include a 9-hole "Golf Academy" practice course and a 60-bay driving range.

WHERE TO STAY

There are three areas to stay in Safaga. Safaga proper has a handful of older, diver-oriented hotels. These are basic and relatively cheap, but for the most part lack beach facilities. Just to the north of town there is a line of old resort-style hotels, some of which have been spiffed up a bit in the last few years but are all still a bit musty and overpriced. Finally there is the Soma Bay compound a few kilometers farther north, which is more expensive, a lot nicer, and, given that you can probably get a good package rate through your travel agent, better overall value for your money.

Soma Bay

Very Expensive

Kempinski Soma Bay ★★★ Luxury with style is what Kempinski Soma Bay is all about. The distinct Moorish style, with authentic pieces of decor and themed furniture, is maintained throughout the hotel from the opulent lobby all the way to your deluxe room. Personalized service and tailor-made excursions can be easily catered for, while the romantic dinner by the beach or the in-water lunch is arranged upon request. Sitting on a table right in the sea and having lunch while your feet are immersed in the water is a fantastic experience. The hotel's watersports center offers a great opportunity to explore windsurfing and catamaran sailing, while the Softouch Ayurveda Spa has a wide array of Indian-inspired treatments and therapies; they range from body slimming and anti-dandruff to aphrodisiac and ear cleaning. The hotel intentionally leaves out an animation team, so expect fewer activities but much-appreciated quiet.

Red Sea Coastal Hwy. (5km/3 miles north of Safaga). ✆ **065/3561500.** Fax 065/3561600. www.kempinski-somabay.com. 325 units, including 28 suites and 2 rooms for people with special mobility. 260€ double. Rate includes buffet breakfast, taxes, and service charges. AE, DC, MC, V. **Amenities:** 4 restaurants; 3 bars; airport transfer (round-trip 60€); babysitting; kids' club; concierge; 18-hole golf course nearby; health club & spa; 4 pools (2 heated, 1 kids'); room service; 4 tennis courts (floodlit); sailing center, snorkeling, and windsurfing center; Wi-Fi (extra charge). *In room:* A/C, TV, Internet (extra charge), minibar.

La Résidence des Cascades ★ In the middle of the headland that defines Soma Bay, La Résidence complements the Sheraton, which is just down the road, perfectly; where Sheraton is all about the beach and diving, this place is all about golf. Not only is it surrounded by an 18-hole, par-72 golf course designed by Gary Player, it has bars with names such as Spikes and the Eagles Nest and a subdued, almost serious, feel to it that says, "We're here for a reason." Public areas are marbled and hung with traditional-style lamps, and the large pool is square and purposeful. Touches such as cotton hand towels in public-area toilets give the whole place a high-end feel. Rooms are large and have nice light, and the bathrooms are commodious. Your stay at La Résidence would not be complete without a Thalasso treatment at the opulent Les Thermes Marins. Whether you go for an underwater massage or a seaweed wrap, make sure to finish with a dip in the 750 sq. m (8,073 sq. ft.) toning Aquatonic Pool with 15 different stations, each dedicated to a certain body part.

Red Sea Coastal Hwy. (5km/3 miles north of Safaga). ✆ **065/3542333.** Fax 065/3542933. www.residencedescascades.com. 249 units. 260€ double. Rate includes buffet breakfast, dinner, taxes, and service charges. AE, DC, MC, V. **Amenities:** 3 restaurants; 3 bars; airport transfer (round-trip 60€); babysitting; kids' club; concierge; 18-hole golf course; health club & spa; Internet (extra charge); pool and lazy river; room service; 4 tennis courts (floodlit); snorkeling. *In room:* A/C, TV, Internet (some rooms; extra charge), minibar.

Expensive

Sheraton Soma Bay The Sheraton Soma Bay is at the head of the class when it comes to beach-vacation facilities around Safaga, and it pulls off the role of ostentatious resort with confidence. The massive Pharaonic-themed lobby creates a stunning view across a fountain to the sea, framing the mountains perfectly. The beach and pool areas are designed to combine the sights and sounds of the seaside with just enough shade, and all without losing sight of a bar. The beach, a 8km (½ mile) stretch of shimmering golden sand, is one of the nicest along the Red Sea coast. If this isn't enough for you, there is great reef diving just off the beach and plenty to see for snorkelers, too. The rooms, done up in pastel tones and light wood, are sumptuous, and there are groupings of suites arranged in beachfront bungalows for those who want to splurge a little.

Red Sea Coastal Hwy. (5km/3 miles north of Safaga). ✆ **065/3545845.** Fax 065/3545885. www.sheraton-somabay.com. 310 units, including 35 suites and 2 rooms for people with special mobility. 192€ sea-view double. Rate includes buffet breakfast, dinner, taxes, and service charges. AE, DC, MC, V. **Amenities:** 3 restaurants; 3 bars; airport transfer (extra charge); babysitting; kids' club; concierge; 18-hole golf course nearby; health club; Internet (extra charge); 2 heated pools (1 kids'); 3 tennis courts (floodlit); snorkeling. *In room:* A/C, TV, Internet (extra charge), minibar.

Expensive

Holiday Inn Safaga Palace Though it has been refurbished, the Holiday Inn is still a bit shabby and gloomy, with more of a budget feel than you would expect at this price. But, the pool, with its swim-up bar, is a nice place to spend an afternoon, the rooms are big and comfortable, and the staff are pleasant. For midlevel accommodation during a diving trip or on your way through town, the Holiday Inn will do just fine, but make sure that you get a healthy discount off the rack rate.

North of Majlis Mahali. ✆ **065/3260100.** Fax 065/3260105. www.holidayinn.com. 316 units, including 63 suites. 90€ double. Rate includes buffet breakfast, dinner, taxes, and service charges. AE, DC, MC, V. **Amenities:** 3 restaurants; 4 bars; airport transfer (extra charge); babysitting; kids' club; concierge; health club; Internet (extra charge); 2 heated pools (1 kids'). *In room:* A/C, TV, minibar.

Moderate

Menaville ★ This is the best all-around hotel in Safaga, with a long, well-groomed beach and pleasant well-maintained gardens. Rooms are large and comfortable, though they have a bit more of a budget feel to the furnishings and maintenance than you would expect at this price. The "superior" rooms, which are only an extra 10€, are worth paying for; they are larger, have a nicer view, and have decent balconies. The pool is big and a great place to kick back after a busy day.

North of Majlis Mahali. ✆ **065/3260064** or -7. Fax 065/3260068. www.menaville.com. 301 units. 54€ double. Rate includes buffet breakfast, dinner, taxes, and service charges. MC, V. **Amenities:** 2 restaurants; 4 bars; airport transfer (extra charge); concierge; health club; 2 pools; dive center, kitesurfing center, snorkeling, and windsurfing center. *In room:* A/C, TV, minifridge.

Nemo Dive Club & Hotel This Dutch-run hotel and dive center near the seafront in Safaga is a good, solid, midrange facility. In keeping with the general no-nonsense ambience of the place, the rooms are nothing fancy, but they are clean and comfortable and have good-quality fittings and some nice local touches such as terra-cotta light covers. The bar downstairs is the best place for a drink in Safaga, and staff are friendly and professional. There is a beach across the street, but at the end of the day this is a great place to stay while you're diving, not a resort. Don't confuse the Nemo with its neighbor around the back, the best-avoided Toubia.

Majlis Mahali. ✆ **065/3256777.** www.nemodive.com. 33 units. 54€ double. Rate includes buffet breakfast, dinner, taxes, and service charges. MC, V. **Amenities:** Restaurant; bar; dive center. *In room:* A/C.

Inexpensive

Ali Baba Value Located on a byroad just opposite the Menaville Hotel, Ali Baba is an ideal place if you are planning to spend most of the day diving and want to come home to a clean, quiet place with a hot, filling dinner waiting for you. Rooms are spacious with basic furniture, and it is advisable to go for one on the second floor unless you are fine with trees blocking the view. The general atmosphere is tranquil and relaxing despite the cartoonish drawings of Ali Baba that adorn the lobby and corridors. Taking into consideration the quality of Ali Baba's seafood (there is a branch of the famous restaurant downstairs where you will be served dinner), a half-board accommodation is a good deal.

Opposite to Menaville. ✆ **065/3260600.** www.hotel-alibaba.com. 27 units. 30€ double. Rate includes breakfast, dinner, taxes, and service charges. No credit cards. **Amenities:** Restaurant. *In room:* A/C, minifridge, no phone.

El Yasmin This basic, small hotel is tucked away on a quiet side street in the middle of Safaga. Rooms are modestly sized, with hard beds and basic but spotlessly clean bathroom facilities. Staff are extremely pleasant and helpful. Single rooms are a lot smaller than doubles, so if you're there alone, see if you can negotiate your way into the bigger room at the single price. The rooftop restaurant/bar is a lot of fun for sundown drinks or an early breakfast before heading out to the reef.

Majlis Mahali. ✆ **012/7430638.** Elyassminsafaga@hotmail.com. 15 units. 30€ double. Rate includes breakfast, taxes, and service charges. No credit cards. **Amenities:** Restaurant/bar. *In room:* No phone, A/C, minifridge.

WHERE TO EAT

When it comes to small Egyptian towns that have recently been added to the tourist map, it's expected that most visitors take their meals in their hotels, hence the lack of tourist-targeted restaurants. Safaga is a vital port that serves other business sectors, so a couple of good, but very basic, restaurants can be found.

Ali Baba ★ SEAFOOD You don't need to look for the sign reading ALI BABA; the elaborate, funky entrance will grab your attention. The food is good and can easily beat the best seafood restaurant anywhere in the country. Mexican Calamari, a fajita-like dish with lots of chili and spices, is my personal favorite, though the calamari with basil is equally tasty. The owner is an affable guy who is usually found at one of the tables in either the original branch or the new one in the Ali Baba hotel (p. 242).

Majlis Mahali (50m/64 ft. or so from the square with the giant mermaid). ✆ **065/3250253.** Appetizers LE5–LE20; main courses LE20–LE70. No credit cards. Daily 10am–midnight.

First Cook INTERNATIONAL If you're craving something other than seafood, First Cook is a clean, basic place with an eclectic variety of sandwiches, salads, pizzas, pasta, and even a selection of various garlic breads. The burgers are delicious and the pizza is good (though more Egyptian than Italian).

Majlis Mahali (close to Ali Baba). ✆ **065/3252077.** Sandwiches LE10–LE15; pizza LE15–LE45. No credit cards. Daily noon–midnight.

DAY TRIPS FROM SAFAGA

Luxor is the best day-trip destination out of Safaga. Tour operators offer an 85€ (minimum 10 people) bus excursion. However, if you are looking for something more upscale and less commercial, Soma Bay's hotels can arrange the daily excursion with a private car for 200€ for the first person, 100€ for each additional person (maximum three people), which also includes lunch, soft drinks, and entrance to Karnak Temple, Mortuary Temple of Hatshepsut, and Valley of the Kings (the Tomb of Tutankhamun is extra).

4 EL QUSEIR

The Red Sea might be all about diving, but El Quseir adds a bit of history. For centuries, the small town on the Red Sea coast was one of the most important ports in Egypt. Pharaohs sent a maritime expedition from this little port town to the land of Punt to collect precious cargoes of gold, ebony, and myrrh. Later, after the Arab invasion, it became a vital stop on the pilgrimage route to Mecca as well as a thriving commercial hub for the trade to India and the Persian Gulf; by the 10th century it reached its zenith. Soon after, things started deteriorating and the opening of the Suez Canal in 1869 rendered a shift in maritime trade routes; El Quseir slipped into oblivion. In the early 20th century the phosphorus mining industry, set up by an Italian company, brought back some of the El Quseir glory days. But the Italians left in the 1960s, and the deep-water port in Safaga to the north displaced El Quseir's relatively small facilities. All that was left behind were a couple of uniquely styled houses and a beautiful church.

Today, El Quseir is a growing tourist destination that, contrary to the rest of the Red Sea tourism hot spots, is more famous for quality relaxation time than diving. Chill out at the lovely Hassan Fathy–styled Mövenpick, and if you feel a need for some action, head to El Quseir's famous fort for a historical 1-hour adventure with its old mining carts, a watchtower, and iron cannons with a subtle posture ostensibly safeguarding the Red Sea coast.

ESSENTIALS

Orientation

There are two streets through El Quseir—the main road, which runs past the old fort in the middle of town, and a loop that goes down to the waterfront. Between the two is the town, a pleasant jumble of run-down old buildings, a few small stores, and the old Italian company premises with the few remaining distinctively styled buildings and the recently renovated St. Barbara's Church. Resorts take the town's outskirts.

Getting There

BY PLANE El Quseir is more or less equidistant between the Marsa Alam and Hurghada airports. The greater frequency of flights into Hurghada means that coming from the north is cheaper and easier. All the hotels here can arrange a transfer from either airport. You can still arrange your transport independently by negotiating prices with the taxi drivers you will find at both airports; however, the small price difference doesn't justify the bargaining hassle.

BY BUS Upper Egypt has six daily buses that connect El Quseir to Cairo for LE70 to LE80. The buses are not in the best condition, and I would recommend picking up one of **Golden Horse**'s (✆ **012/7770469**) three buses that head to Hurghada (LE15) and continue farther to Cairo (LE80). From the bus station you can easily catch a taxi to your hotel.

BY CAR Driving 85km (53 miles) south of Safaga will bring you to El Quseir. The dual carriage road sector of the Red Sea Coastal Highway ends 50km (31 miles) north of El Quseir; the rest of the road all the way down to the Sudanese border is single carriage. If you are coming from the Nile Valley, there is a good-condition road connecting El Quseir to the small town of Qus, from which Luxor is less than a 30-minute drive.

Fun Facts **Shorty!**

It is said that El Quseir acquired its name from the Arabic word *qasiir,* meaning "short," as the shortest distance between the Red Sea and the Nile Valley touches the coast at El Quseir.

Getting Around

Local transportation options are limited in El Quseir. However, most hotels offer daily excursions to El Quseir proper or have a shuttle bus should you wish to visit the town independently. Alternatively, and if you want to do some exercise, you can use your hotel's mountain bike, if available, as a means of transportation; however, check the prevailing wind before you leave. A tailwind on the way into town can make for a long, hard pedal back home at the end of the day.

Tourist Information

There are a couple of **Internet** options scattered around the city. They more or less offer the same service, with the same young kids playing games or chatting teenagers making up the crowd; they charge LE3 to LE5 per hour.

WHAT TO SEE & DO

El Quseir Fort ★ Shortly after the invasion of Egypt was completed in the 16th century, Ottoman conqueror Selim I ordered the building of El Quseir's fort to defend the key harbor on the Red Sea coast from marauding Portuguese traders who were attempting to force entry to the lucrative trade in timber, pepper, and silk with India and China. During the French interlude, Napoleon's forces briefly occupied the strategic fort in May 1799 before the British fleet showered it with a heavy bombardment 4 months later. The salvo caused considerable damage, but the fort was largely restored during the reign of Mohamed Ali, as he used it as a base for fighting Wahhabis in the Hejaz (modern day Saudi Arabia). During the 18th century the fort fell into disrepair until a 21st-century holistic restoration project brought it back to life.

The entrance is on the main street through a narrow tunnel, where you're sure to find unofficial guides offering their services. If you have read *Quseir: An Ottoman and Napoleonic Fortress on the Red Sea Coast of Egypt* (AUC Press, 2007), then cordially refuse their service; if not, then expect to pay an LE20 to LE30 tip, depending on how well-informed the guide is. The surviving structure of the fort isn't elaborate, but a look at the displays of Bedouin cultural artifacts in the northern bastion and the trade goods in the west is worth 15 or 20 minutes. Climb the watchtower in the middle for a moderately good view of the surrounding town while the kids climb in and out of the old phosphate carts that are parked on a piece of old narrow-gauge railway line. Don't miss the pearl fishing boat or the old cannons. Combine your visit to the fort with a visit to the nearby marketplace, where you can shop for spices, incense, trinkets, and souvenirs.

Admission LE15. Daily 9am 5pm.

St. Barbara's Church St. Barbara's Church was first built in 1920 by the Italian Phosphate Company. At the time, it was a Catholic church whose builders considered it a guardian of the phosphate mines. By 1964, the church changed hands and became Orthodox before it was finally integrated in 1995 as Virgin St. Mary & St. Barbara's Church. After the Italian company left El Quseir, the church fell into disuse and was completely rebuilt in 2008. Though the beautiful ceiling and wall paintings are replicas of the original ones, there are a couple of genuine Italian icons that date back to 1932. Don't forget to check out the church's glass-painted windows, which are a fine example of Italian artistry.

There are no open hours or admission fees, but the guard is more than happy to show you around. He vehemently refuses any tips but directs you to the church donation box if you feel so inclined. St. Barbara's Church is a religious building more than a tourist attraction; female visitors are asked to dress modestly, but if you show up in shorts and a sleeveless shirt, there are long robes available.

Inside the Italian Phosphate Company deserted premises. Free admission.

WHERE TO STAY

Unlike Hurghada farther north, with its never-ending shoulder-to-shoulder resorts taking up the entire coast, El Quseir is blessed with a few resorts on the town's outskirts. In addition, there is also a good basic hotel right in the heart of town.

Very Expensive

Radisson SAS Resort The closest to El Quseir proper, Radisson does a good job of standardized service and amenities with some local touches. Still, it is working on a one-size-fits-all template, which doesn't quite fit with amiable El Quseir. That said, staff are friendly and professional, and the beach and jetty provide excellent swimming and diving. I particularly like the spa, which features Ayurvedic massage in Indian-themed treatment rooms. Accommodations come in three different themes that attempt to give an essence of the place.

Red Sea Coastal Hwy. (3km/2 miles north of El Quseir). ✆ **065/3350260.** www.radissonblu.com. 250 units. $150 garden-view double; $170 sea-view double. Rates include buffet breakfast, taxes, and service charges. AE, MC, V. **Amenities:** 4 restaurants; 2 bars; airport transfer (extra charge); babysitting; quad rental; kids' club; concierge; health club & spa; Internet; 2 heated pools; room service; dive center, snorkeling. *In room:* A/C, TV, minibar, Wi-Fi (extra charge).

Expensive

Flamenco Beach Resort The Flamenco is almost next door to the Mövenpick and has more of a beach-vacation resort tone. If you're looking for an active and fun-filled weekend, this should be your choice. The tall white buildings embrace the main pool, and there is a wide marble lobby. Rooms are spacious but a bit generic, with uninspiring but adequate bathroom facilities. The gardens around the hotel are lush, however, and there are plenty of activities to keep you busy when you don't feel like lolling on the beach. Diving and snorkeling on the spectacular reef is accommodated by a 150m (492 ft.) jetty, which means you don't even need to get wet to go feed the multicolored fish that bob and weave about the coral.

Red Sea Coastal Hwy. (7km/4 miles north of El Quseir). ✆ **065/3350200-9.** Fax 065/3350211. www.flamencohotels.com. 320 units, including 22 suites. 86€ double. Rack rate includes buffet breakfast, dinner, taxes, and service charges. AE, MC, V. **Amenities:** 4 restaurants; 4 bars; airport transfer (extra charge); babysitting; kids' club; concierge; health club; Internet; 5 pools (1 heated, 1 kids'); room service; tennis court (floodlit); dive center, snorkeling. *In room:* A/C, TV, Internet, minifridge.

Mövenpick ★★★ Kids This great hotel, on the northern edge of El Quseir, is situated on a little bay that was used in the Roman era as a port; my favorite aspect of the resort is the way it spills down almost to the edge of the water. Rooms are spread out through a series of single-story sandstone buildings that are built around 12 courtyards and are designed to blend with the shape and color of the coastline with their dome shapes, taupe colors, and stone texture. Inside they are commodious with traditional touches.

The bay provides a 700m (½-mile) beach that curves away to the Subex Dive Center (p. 86) and has a relaxingly low sun-shade quotient; no need to feel packed onto the sand like a bunch of beached sardines. The bay also accommodates diving and snorkeling off the nearby reef directly from the beach. The Top of the Rocks bar is built just above the spray line, and at night, with the lights turned low, it has to be one of the most romantic spots on the entire coast.

Red Sea Coastal Hwy. (6km/4 miles north of El Quseir). ✆ **065/3332100.** Fax 065/3332129. www.moevenpick-quseir.com. 250 units, including 3 suites. $88 garden-view double; $127 sea-view double. Rates include buffet breakfast, taxes, and service charges. AE, DC, MC, V. **Amenities:** 5 restaurants; 2 bars; airport transfer (extra charge); babysitting; quad and mountain-bike rental; kids' club; concierge; health club; Internet (extra charge); 2 pools (1 heated); room service; tennis court; dive center, snorkeling. *In room:* A/C, TV, Internet (extra charge), minibar.

Inexpensive

Hotel Al Quseir *(Value)* Located in a restored historic stone building on the waterfront in the middle of El Quseir, this hotel is best described as boutique on a budget. The fabric of the building is all there—restored, clean, and ready, with high ceilings and wooden floors—and it's tough not to stand at the bottom of the stairwell and look at the simple wooden staircase and rock facing of the walls and think, "What if some light fixtures were sourced out of an old villa and the money were spent to bring in some antique furnishings?" The bathrooms are fine—better than you would expect at the price—but they are shared. What could be a fantastic breakfast nook upstairs, surrounded by old *mashrabeya* screens and looking through a tree and out over the Red Sea, is apologetically presented by staff who don't seem to appreciate how close this place is to a being a diamond in the rough.

Port Said St., El Quseir. ✆ **065/3332301.** 6 units. LE180 double (bathroom across the hall). Rate includes breakfast, taxes, and service charges. No credit cards. **Amenities:** Restaurant. *In room:* No phone.

WHERE TO EAT

Unfortunately finding a decent meal in El Quseir is not that easy; get ready for an adventurous pursuit not for the fainthearted.

Marianne SEAFOOD This is the best place to eat in El Quseir, located on the seafront of the town, with a good assortment of freshly caught fish, calamari, and shrimp; the grilled calamari is a perfect choice. The setting is neat, but certainly not fancy, and you get to choose from the shaded porch or the other side of the street on the beach.

Port Said St. ✆ **010/9468198** or 065/3334386. Main courses LE30–LE110. No credit cards. Daily 11am–10pm.

Said Alam *(Finds)* EGYPTIAN There is no real restaurant, not even an eatery, to look for, but rather a cloth-made sign in Arabic that directs your attention to a congregation of tables and chairs scattered on one section of the pavement. This is the Said Alam, El Quseir's most famous *fuul* joint. The place doesn't serve anything except *fuul*, and it's still being prepared the same way Said's father, and before him his grandfather, used to. I can't put my finger on what makes his *fuul* so special, probably some secret ingredient in the family-honored recipe, but without a doubt it is the best *fuul* throughout the country.

The unnamed street that runs parallel to the fort. *Fuul* LE3–LE5. No credit cards. Daily sunrise–sunset.

DAY TRIPS FROM EL QUSEIR

Luxor (p. 262) is the most common day trip from El Quseir; for around 80€ (minimum 10 people) you get to see Karnak Temple, Valley of the Kings (Tomb of Tutankhamun is an additional ticket), and the Mortuary Temple of Hatshepsut. Price includes lunch and soft drinks.

5 PORT GHALIB

In contrast to the Red Sea's urban centers, with the exception of El Gouna, Port Ghalib is not a tiny fishing village turned buzzing resort town—it's a plain desert that's currently turning into a full-fledged city. The ambitious Kuwaiti-financed mega project encompasses four international hotels, a Red Sea Champs-Elysées, a massive golf estate, a cutting-edge convention center, and residential areas for summer vacationers and year-round residents. State-of-the-art infrastructure comes hand in hand with all the luxurious facilities and high standard of living; from water desalination and sewage treatment plants to a whole district cooling system that covers the project's 750 hectares (1,850 acres).

While phase one has been successfully completed, the project still has a long way to go; however, for a visiting tourist there are no needs left unsatisfied. Enjoy the posh hotelier experience at InterContinental The Palace, or get pampered at the world-leading Six Senses Spa. Don't forget your Open Water diving course; after all, this is the Red Sea.

ESSENTIALS

Orientation

Getting your bearings is straightforward; the marina area is the focal point. The pedestrian promenade is gradually filling up with cafes, restaurants, hangouts, and a modern version of the Cairene Khan El Khalili. Farther down the bay is the beach. This is where the hotels are, with the exception of the Marina Lodge, which is located on the other side of the bay.

Getting There

BY PLANE Located midway between El Quseir and Marsa Alam, Port Ghalib is actually closer to Marsa Alam International Airport (p. 251; about 5 min. away) than either of the two. Your hotel will automatically arrange the airport transfer once your reservation is confirmed.

BY BOAT Sailing your private boat across the Red Sea, you can always use Port Ghalib International Marina as a port of entry into Egypt. Visa processing is available at no additional cost to the usual $15. And if you are short on cash, credit card (Visa or MasterCard) payments are accepted. The privately owned harbor provides some maintenance as well as refueling and berthing services. For an average 6m- to 14m-long (20–46 ft.) vessel, the monthly berthing tariff is around $24 per meter. The harbor is still in its first stages, with an annual number of arriving tourists, mostly Europeans with their private boats, averaging 400. The duty-free shop is still under construction.

BY BUS The two daily buses that connect Shalateen to Cairo pass by Port Ghalib. You can ask the driver to drop you off at the main entrance, but expect to pay the full LE100 fare.

BY CAR The main gate to Port Ghalib is difficult to miss when you're driving the Red Sea Coastal Highway; it's 70km (43 miles) south of El Quseir. Port Ghalib is also reachable directly from the Nile Valley by driving the Marsa Alam–Edfu road.

Getting Around

Everything within the premises of the hotels and the marina area is within walking distance, but if you don't feel like exerting any effort, you can always ask the concierge to arrange a golf cart for you; Marina Lodge is the only exception due to its location on the other side of the marina. A free water taxi service operates from 8am to 1pm, breaks for an hour, and resumes from 2 to 11pm. Alternatively, a shuttle bus can be arranged.

Tourist Information

In addition to two **ATMs** in the lobbies of InterContinental The Palace and Crowne Plaza Sahara Sands/Oasis, there is also a **CIB branch** at the marina. It's open Sunday to Thursday from 9:30am to 5pm.

Fun Facts A Legend Behind the Name

This is a local Romeo and Juliet story. Envision poor spice merchant Ghalib turning every stone to fetch his lover's dowry. Conspiracy steps in, and rival suitor Salim banishes Ghalib to a forsaken bay, where sirens call and a fleet of Ancient Egyptian ghost ships sail the water. Determined and persistent, Ghalib's hard work sees the barren bay prospering into a trading port. This is when the villain prepares a mighty fleet to crush Port Ghalib. As he approaches, the Ancient Egyptian ghost ships appear in the horizon. Terrified Salim hastily retreats, and Ghalib gets the happily-ever-after ending with his lover Budour. A real myth or a product of some marketing guru, I will leave this one up to you.

WHAT TO SEE & DO

Diving still tops the chart, but Ghalib shares the same diving spot with neighboring Marsa Alam (p. 250). There is nothing special on offer other than an overnight to *Thistlegorm;* Emperor Divers (p. 86) has a diving center at the Marina Lodge, and they are about the only diving center in the region that offers such a trip. With *Giannis D* and *Carnatic* included in the Abu Nahas five-dive trip, it is a wreck-diving crash course you don't want to miss. For more on northern Red Sea dive sites, see p. 225.

If you are longing for some body and mind relaxation, there is no better choice than the Six Senses Spa. The spa recently opened its first branch in Egypt with an array of treatments from Thai massage and hot stone therapy to foot acupressure and detoxification in the colonic room.

And when night descends and you don't feel like following your hotel's entertainment program, head for the marina area. Grab a cold beer at T.G.I. Friday's or tasty dumplings at Fusion Restaurant; dance the night away at the Budour's; or simply have a stroll (perhaps the best option after a heavy dinner). Most restaurants in Port Ghalib are franchises of Cairo-based chains and include KFC, Pizza Hut, Hardee's, and Fish Market; find reviews for them in chapter 6.

WHERE TO STAY

Three hotels represent Port Ghalib's current hospitality scene. Each is equally beautiful and yet characteristically distinctive, so deciding which one to go for can be tricky.

Very Expensive

InterContinental The Palace ★★ The Palace should have been named the Arabian Castle. While the passage to the lobby involves crossing a water canal using a medieval castle bridge, rooms come with Arabesque-flavored furniture and Islamic decorative motifs. Luxury is the name of the game, and if you want to experience the height of opulence, go for the Emir Suite. Be forewarned: Breaking the bank is highly probable. Don't miss the Look Out Bar, with its holistic 360-degree view of the whole resort—don't worry, having a look comes free of charge.

Red Sea Coastal Hwy. (70km/43 miles north of Marsa Alam). ✆ **016/6691777.** Fax 065/3360025. www.portghalib.com. 309 units, including 14 suites. $350 garden-view double; $370 lagoon-view double; $390 sea-view double. Rates include buffet breakfast, taxes, and service charges. AE, DC, MC, V. **Amenities:** 4 restaurants; 1 bar; airport transfer (extra charge); mountain-bike and quad rental; kids' club; concierge;

 health club & spa; 2 pools (1 heated, 1 kids'); room service; 3 tennis courts (2 floodlit); water-skiing, kayaking, and snorkeling. *In room:* A/C, TV, Internet (extra charge), minibar.

Expensive

Crowne Plaza Sahara Sands & Crowne Plaza Sahara Oasis ★ Kids These two hotels share more in common than just the lobby, beach, restaurants, and bars. They are technically one big resort with two main differences: the sea view and room style. The Oasis has a lagoon view, while the Sands enjoys the much more spectacular sea view. At the Sands, Nubian-inspired architecture—with white painted walls, built-in shelves, and smoothly curved corners—meets rustic Arabian decorations wrapped in warm Mediterranean colors. The Oasis, on the other hand, follows the same pattern yet in a more subtle way, with greens and browns dominating the scene. Shamlula's Fast Food Court may sound awkward for a seaside resort, but it gives kids a chance to play freely and parents can enjoy a worry-free lunch; there is no fancy glassware to break here.

Red Sea Coastal Hwy. (70km/43 miles north of Marsa Alam). ✆ **065/3360000.** Fax 065/3360025. www.portghalib.com. 639 units, including 12 suites. $210 garden-view double; $230 lagoon-view double; $250 sea-view double. Rates include buffet breakfast and dinner, taxes, and service charges. AE, DC, MC, V. **Amenities:** 3 restaurants; 2 bars; airport transfer (extra charge); mountain-bike and quad rental; kids' club; concierge; health club & spa; 4 pools (1 heated, 1 kids,' 1 lazy); room service; 3 tennis courts (2 floodlit); snorkeling, water-skiing, and kayaking. *In room:* A/C, TV, Internet (extra charge), minibar.

Marina Lodge ★ This is "the" place for divers. Here you can literally jump from your breakfast table right into your boat and off for a day of underwater activities. And, one of Marina Lodge's three pools is 3m (10 ft.) deep and accommodates Open Water introductory pool dives. The hotel has a more artistic touch to it than its peers, with an overall Nubian architecture style infused with funky blue and orange colors and simple room furnishings. If the desert people had built their Nubia by the sea, it would have certainly been the Marina Lodge. Note that while the resort overlooks the marina, the location is a double-edged sword: It's missing its own beach, so you need to take a shuttle bus or a water taxi to have a dip in the sea.

Red Sea Coastal Hwy. (70km/43 miles north of Marsa Alam). ✆ **065/3700222.** Fax 065/3700221. www.portghalib.com. 203 units, including 6 suites. $150 double. Rate includes buffet breakfast, lunch, dinner, taxes, and service charges. AE, MC, V. **Amenities:** 2 restaurants; 2 bars; airport transfer (extra charge); mountain-bike and quad rental; kids' club; concierge; health club & spa; 3 pools; room service; 3 tennis courts (2 floodlit); water-skiing, kayaking, and snorkeling. *In room:* A/C, TV, minibar, Wi-Fi (extra charge).

6 MARSA ALAM

Marsa Alam is the place to escape bustling Sharm El Sheikh and chaotic Hurghada. Dive with hammerheads in the underwater Eden dubbed Elphinstone, search for the elusive dugong in Abu Dabab, head for an up-close experience with playful dolphins at Samadai Reef, or follow the desert trails leading to the Emerald Mountain. Diving Marsa Alam is simply unparalleled, but if you are more into relaxing, you have made it to the right place. There are 365 days of sunshine here, so enjoy your favorite cocktail while working on the perfect tan. Scoring high on watersports has its downfall on nightlife; outside your hotel premises, it is virtually nonexistent.

Hotels and resorts are located on the coastal stretch running north and south of Marsa Alam proper. This leaves the shabby old town with nothing more than a couple of streets and a few grocery shops, so you can certainly give it a miss.

ESSENTIALS

Getting There

BY PLANE Marsa Alam International Airport (RMF) serves international destinations in Europe as well as the Middle East; charter flights ply the runway on a daily basis. Locally, EgyptAir flies from Cairo to Marsa Alam five times a week. The 1-hour flight costs LE1,200 for a round-trip ticket. There are two ATMs in the arrival hall and a couple of fast-food joints in the international departure one. However, waiters frequently check out the local departure hall collecting to-go orders. Contrary to the welcome committee of taxi drivers you would expect in front of any Egyptian airport, Marsa Alam offers a different scenario. Limousine drivers holding yellow taxi signs will politely wait for you to approach them rather than jumping on your back. As the airport is located a good 65km (40 miles) north of Marsa Alam proper, fares considerably vary from LE75 to LE200 depending on your resort's location.

BY BUS From **Turgoman Bus Station** (✆ **02/27735668** or -9) in Cairo, two daily buses depart at 1:30 and 11pm heading to Shalateen via Marsa Alam. The ticket costs LE100, and the journey can easily top 9 hours; breaking it up in Hurghada is recommended. From Hurghada, you can pick up one of **Golden Horse**'s (✆ **065/3559277**) three daily buses heading to Marsa Alam. It is a little less than a 3-hour bus ride that costs LE25. In Marsa Alam, the Golden Horse ticket office number is ✆ **012/7771396.**

BY CAR Marsa Alam is reachable from Cairo by driving the Red Sea Coastal Highway; however, be forewarned that it's an 800km (500-mile) drive that takes 9 hours on average. From Aswan or Luxor, it is a much shorter ride via the Marsa Alam–Edfu road.

Getting Around

If your curiosity is piqued and you want to check out Marsa Alam, all you need to worry about is the transfer from your hotel. Marsa Alam proper is small enough to be toured on foot.

WHAT TO SEE & DO

While diving is the number-one attraction throughout the Red Sea, in Marsa Alam it is one of many water activities and excursions you can experience.

Samadai Reef's horseshoe reef has an inner lagoon that's home to a pod of spinner dolphins. The reef is a natural protectorate with on-site rangers. Two lines define the lagoon: the first is where boats are allowed to moor, the second a no-go area where the dolphins breed; between the two lines is where swimmers are allowed. Watching the cheerful dolphins in an open-air aquarium is one thing, but swimming with them in the wild is a completely different thing. Most dive centers in Marsa Alam organize this 1-day trip for an average of 65€ per person (minimum six people), which includes the 15€ protectorate entry fee, lunch, and soft drinks; divers should add 44€ per person to the two-dive cost. For more information, see the chapter "Active Vacation Planner" (p. 81).

Looking at the south Red Sea coast from an underwater perspective, it looks like a staircase of reef-covered plateaus that finally lead to the shore; reefless bays are an infrequent occurrence. One of the few, and in my opinion the best, is Abu Dabab. The perfect turquoise water is irresistible, and to add to the charm, Abu Dabab is home to the elusive dugong. Often associated with sirens' legends, this shy-looking marine mammal is more timid than anything else. Worldwide, dugong are falling victim to human intrusion; the population is rapidly dwindling. As a local protective measure, no mooring is allowed within the premises of Abu Dabab bay, and I request that you refrain from touching the one dugong individual present at the bay. Unfortunately, with the number of daily tourists who search for it, disturbance is a fact of life. This is not a divers-only excursion, as the dugong is often seen at shallow depths. Abu Dabab is sold as a 1-day trip for 25€, which also covers transport. If, by any chance, you managed your own transport, the entrance fee to the beach is 10€.

If the Red Sea is a divers' mecca, no pilgrimage is complete without a visit to Elphinstone. Elphinstone looks like a table mountain rising from the abyss, with two mind-boggling sections to dive. The northern one will certainly put your diving skills to the test, and it is also home to a collection of sharks (white-tip, oceanic white-tip, and grey reef). The southern section is much easier to dive, with an underwater world painted in Technicolor bloom. Head for an early-morning or late-afternoon dive if you wish to encounter exotic-looking hammerhead sharks.

For desert lovers in Marsa Alam, **Fustat Wadi El Gemal** (**© 012/1001109;** www.wadielgemal.com) offers camel-riding tours. The breakfast or sunset ride takes you through the vegetated valleys of Wadi El Gemal Natural Protectorate; if you're lucky you may encounter one of the last remaining dorcas gazelles (p. 255). Empowered by local staff, the ecofriendly company also offers a gourmet dinner infusing nomadic flavors with Middle Eastern and European cuisine. Enjoy savoring camel meat casserole on ground level. Dinner is often followed by a folkloric show.

To visit nearby El Quseir, **Madinat Coraya** (below) offers a shuttle bus service. Running once a day, it departs the hotel complex at 4pm and leaves El Quseir 3 hours later. With the low cost of 10€, spaces can fill up, so call in advance to check availability.

WHERE TO STAY

This is the land of "all inclusive," and by that I don't only mean buffet breakfast, lunch, and dinner, but also water and local spirits, particularly beer and wine. You can drink as much as you want with no extras hitting your bill. Most hotels and resorts opt for mass tourism; groups are the norm, while individual travelers are a rarity. Having said that, the misguiding "rack rate" is the order of the day; nonetheless, some facility management were collaborative enough to provide me with the "real rate" (for more on rack versus real rate, see p. 55). Pay extra attention to the respective rates after each forthcoming hotel review. Hotels below are listed in order from north to south.

Expensive

Madinat Coraya A 1,200-unit resort, the overly dense Madinat Coraya is made up of five hotels. While Solaya, Samaya, and Lamaya could be easily grouped as one due to their common lack of character, Coraya and Dar El Madina get a brush. Coraya's outer

Fun Facts The Tomb of the Pharaoh

At the end of Elphinstone's southern section, there is 6m (20-ft.) tunnel-like archway. At its eastern entrance lies a big rock formation that resembles a coffin. Known as the Sarcophagus, could it be a Pharaoh's tomb (as the legend assumes), or is it just the nitrogen narcosis effect? Diving this part of Elphinstone is not for rookies; the archway's entrance is at a depth of 50m (164 ft.), while its exit is at 65m (213 ft.).

architecture has an Andalusian touch to it, but its rooms are stripped bare of any style, while Dar El Madina misses on the sea view but scores on character. With a relatively small piazza of traditional Middle Eastern cafes and souvenir shops, the piazza pulsates with life once the dinner plates are removed. Rooms at Dar El Madina are elegantly furnished with espresso-brown furniture and simple Arabic motifs hanging on the walls. The latest addition to the complex is Aqua Coraya (reservations © **065/3750015**), a small water park that operates daily from 10am to noon and 2 to 6pm. Vacationers at Madinat Coraya are welcomed free of charge, while outside guests pay 10€ for a full-day ticket and 5€ for a half-day.

> **Tips** **Elphinstone**
>
> Diving Elphinstone is largely sold as a full-day excursion where you can do two boat dives. However, if you are short on time, check out **Orca Dive Club Abu Dabab** (p. 86). They do one-dive trips to Elphinstone. It is a 15-minute speedboat ride, and the whole excursion costs 39€ (minimum four people).

Red Sea Coastal Hwy. (75km/47 miles north of Marsa Alam). © **02/38542020** in Cairo. Fax 02/38542029 in Cairo. www.jaz.travel. 1,244 units, including 11 suites and 3 rooms for people with special mobility. 160€ double; 180€ sea-view double. Rack rates on "all inclusive" basis with taxes and service charges. AE, MC, V. **Amenities:** 8 restaurants; 15 bars; airport transfer (extra charge); mountain-bike and quad rental; kids' club; concierge; health club; Internet (extra charge); 17 pools (7 heated, 5 kids'); room service; 8 tennis courts (floodlit); dive center, snorkeling. *In room:* A/C, TV, minibar.

Sol Y Mar Abu Dabab Other than the stunning location and the beach, this is just another not-that-fancy hotel with nothing in mind except how big the next group is. Occupying the southern part of the exquisite Abu Dabab bay, this hotel enjoys a really long sandy beach (almost a mile). Have a sunset stroll, a plunge in the sea, or engage in one of the many sun and fun activities on offer. Rooms are typical and restaurants follow suit.

Red Sea Coastal Hwy. (30km/19 miles north of Marsa Alam). © **010/0096001** or -4. Fax 010/0096005. www.jaz.travel. 256 units, including 2 suites. 105€ double; 160€ sea-view double. Rack rates on "all inclusive" basis with taxes and service charges. AE, DC, MC, V. **Amenities:** 2 restaurants; 3 bars; airport transfer (extra charge); quad rental; kids' club; concierge; health club; 17 pools (7 heated, 5 kids'); room service; 1 tennis court; dive center, snorkeling. *In room:* A/C, TV, Internet (extra charge), minibar.

Kahramana Resorts ★★ This resort complex is made up of three equally beautiful hotels; Kahramana, Calimera Habiba, and Kahramana Garden. Egyptian rural architecture dominates, but elements from the local seaside environment, such as stone walls and dome-shaped buildings, are also integrated. Room clusters with different degrees of brown and smudged paint are scattered in swaths of greenery. Wooden doors and balconies come in just perfect, with spacious, well-furnished, and simply decorated rooms. If you are looking for a stunning sea view with quietness in mind, then go for Kahramana. Energetic beachgoers and activities addicts will have loads of fun at the hip and friendly Calimera Habiba. With no sea in sight, Kahramana Garden is reserved for the ultimate silence seekers. A free, regular shuttle bus service takes Kahramana guests to Abu Dabab bay.

Red Sea Coastal Hwy. (22km/14 miles north of Marsa Alam). © **065/3380008** or -9, or 012/7458801. Fax 065/3380010 or 012/7458799. www.balbaagroup.com. 556 units, including 8 suites and 6 rooms for people with special mobility. 130€ double (Kahramana); 120€ double (Calimera Habiba); 100€ double (Kahramana Garden). Rates on "all inclusive" basis with taxes and service charges. AE, DC, MC, V. **Amenities:** 6 restaurants; 9 bars (including 1 pub); airport transfer (extra charge); quad rental; kids' club; concierge;

Mons Smaragdus

Cleopatra. The unmatched Pharaohs' celebrity gained her fame with a tragic love affair and a romantic suicide. Did you know she had an irresistible passion for emeralds? The eccentric queen didn't only dispatch high-level ambassadors with giant emeralds on which her portrait was engraved, she went on and announced all of Egypt's mines as her own personal property! Prior to A.D. 1492 and the discovery of the New World with its high-grade emerald, only one site throughout the Roman Empire yielded the precious gem—Mons Smaragdus, the Emerald Mountain.

The mighty 180-sq.-km (70-sq.-mile) Mons Smaragdus encompassed nine equally buzzing mining communities, the best preserved among which is Sikeit. To avoid seasonal floods that periodically hit the area, Sikeit was built on hillsides rather than valley beds. The town's several hundred edifices are mostly in ruins today, except its temples. The larger of the two temples is a rock-cut, three-chamber temple with a small columnar hall. Though a 4.5m (15-ft.) inscription once adorned its front entrance, only a few letters now remain. The smaller temple, on the other hand, has more decorative motifs and Greek inscriptions still visible. One reads, "And to our Lady Isis of Senskete [Sikeit] . . . and to Apollo, and to all the other gods enshrined with them."

Visiting Sikeit can be a good option for a desert-oriented excursion. **Wadi El Gemal Safari** (✆ **012/1027161**) arranges this half-day trip for 45€ (minimum six people). Price includes lunch, soft drinks, and needed permits.

health club; Internet (extra charge); 8 pools (2 heated, 3 kids'); room service; 6 tennis courts (floodlit); dive center, snorkeling. *In room:* A/C, TV, minibar.

The Oasis Resort ★★ If I am heading to the Red Sea for a diving vacation, I undoubtedly choose the Oasis. The resort is located on a hilly beach, and room clusters are scattered at different altitudes, allowing all of them a blissful sea view. Perfectly blending in with the surrounding environment, rooms' exteriors are painted in taupe and adapt a distinctive traditional architecture. The interiors are meticulously decorated with elements that build each room's identity; one is Arabic-styled while another is Indian-inspired. Enjoying a drink in the wood-covered balcony on a summer night, you can easily forget what modern life stands for. Stay there for too long, however, and you can fall victim to the peacefulness addiction. As with other diver-dedicated lodges along this part of the coast, nightlife is nonexistent. At the Oasis, the reef plateau takes over the shallow water; you need to walk over the jetty instead of jumping right into the sea.

Red Sea Coastal Hwy. (20km/13 miles north of Marsa Alam). ✆ **010/5052855.** www.oasis-marsalam.com. 50 units. 102€ double. Rate includes buffet breakfast, dinner, taxes, and service charges. MC, V. **Amenities:** 1 restaurant; 2 bars; airport transfer (round-trip 25€ Marsa Alam, 140€ Hurghada); pool; dive center, snorkeling. *In room:* A/C, minibar.

Marsa Shagra Diving Village This is one of the oldest lodging facilities in Marsa Alam, and its tent-based accommodation section is a token to the heyday of pioneer divers. With a panoramic view of the coast, accommodation options include chalets, huts, as well as royal tents. If you want to enjoy the simple life without really roughing it, then go for a chalet; they are quite comfy, and the ones with air-conditioning are great

Tips The Last of the Dorcas

This is Egypt, not wildlife-rich Kenya; spotting an animal takes more than a bush walk or a game drive. One of the very few locations in Egypt that still offers a probability for observing wildlife is **Wadi El Gemal Natural Protectorate.** Located 50km (31 miles) south of Marsa Alam, it plays host to the last Egyptian herd of dorcas gazelles. The elegantly beautiful creatures that once roved the Egyptian deserts in the hundreds have been reduced to a handful of fleeing individuals. If you want to join a league of lucky few dorcas gazelle–sighters (myself included), rent a camel and hire a local guide. Fustat Wadi El Gemal (p. 252) can be very helpful, as they manage the logistics for you; this is not a standard service so is subject to availability.

for hot summer nights. If you are here for diving, with accommodation a second priority, then go for a royal tent. Handmade beds using local wooden materials can be a little less comfortable than your average bed. Versus normal tents, which are also available, a royal one is more spacious and equipped with a fan and a fridge. Huts are basically a smaller-size chalet with less in-room amenities; air-conditioning and private bathroom are not available.

Red Sea Coastal Hwy. (20km/13 miles north of Marsa Alam). ✆ **065/3380021** or -6. Fax 065/3380027. www.redsea-divingsafari.com. 126 units, including 61 chalets, 25 huts, 10 royal tents, and 30 tents. 120€ chalet with A/C double; 100€ chalet double; 80€ hut double; 80€ royal tent double; 70€ tent double. Rack rates on full-board basis with taxes and service charges. MC, V. **Amenities:** Restaurant; bar (serves beer only); airport transfer (round-trip 40€ Marsa Alam, 80€ Hurghada, 160€ Luxor); quad rental; Internet (extra charge); dive center, snorkeling. *In room:* A/C (in some chalets), minifridge (chalets and royal tents), no phone.

Brayka Bay Reef Resort There's no better location than Brayka Bay. The part reef part reefless bay accommodates both snorkelers and swimmers (most hotels have only one or the other). Privacy has been taken into consideration, sun beds don't cram the beach, and a few planted palm trees give a more local flavor as well as providing natural shade. The resort is popular with European package vacationers, and rooms lack identity but have an acceptable level of comfort. The fresh lick of paint adds a cheerful touch.

Red Sea Coastal Hwy. (18km/11 miles north of Marsa Alam). ✆ **065/3380065** or -9. Fax 065/3380070. www.braykabay.net. 460 units, including 15 suites. 140€ double; 150€ sea-view double. Rack rates on "all inclusive" basis with taxes and service charges. MC, V. **Amenities:** 3 restaurants; 3 bars; airport transfer (extra charge); quad rental; kids' club; concierge; health club; Internet (extra charge); 2 pools (1 heated, 1 kids'); room service; 2 tennis courts; dive center, snorkeling. *In room:* A/C, TV, Internet (extra charge), minibar.

Moderate

Abu Dabab Diving Lodge ★ Colonial flavored wooden bungalows make up this cozy lodge. While rooms with triangular-shaped ceilings and simple furnishings win hands-down, the lodge misses on bigger resorts' luxuries (the tiny pool, for example). However, it doesn't compromise on professional service. Located right across the highway from Abu Dabab beach, don't let the not-right-by-the-sea location get to you; it's less than a 3-minute walk. Plus, after a full day of nothing but diving, it is a couple of beers in the bar and off to bed. For in-house guests, entering Abu Dabab beach comes free of charge. As the name might imply, it is a diver-dedicated lodging facility.

Red Sea Coastal Hwy. (30km/19 miles north of Marsa Alam). ✆ **010/2339271.** Fax 010/2330151. www.balbaagroup.com. 60 units. 64€ double. Rate on "all inclusive" basis with taxes and service charges. AE, DC, MC, V. **Amenities:** 2 restaurants; 2 bars; airport transfer (extra charge); Internet (extra charge); pool; dive center, snorkeling. *In room:* A/C, TV, minifridge.

Shams Alam The two main reasons I recommend Shams Alam are quietness and pricing. Striking a fine balance, this resort is remotely located some 50km (31 miles) south of Marsa Alam proper (from the airport that's a little more than an hour drive). With such a remote location, any possibility of noise is diminished by default. Designed following Nubian dome-intense architecture, the resort attempts to color the barren desert surrounding with a lush green. For the price tag on the rooms, it can be a good option if you are on a tight vacation budget. There is a mini shopping center right across the highway.

Red Sea Coastal Hwy. (50km/31 miles south of Marsa Alam). ✆ **012/2444931** or -2. Fax 012/2401425. www.shamshotels.com. 160 units, including 2 rooms for people with special mobility. 62€ double. Rate on "all inclusive" basis with taxes and service charges. MC, V. **Amenities:** 2 restaurants; 5 bars; airport transfer (extra charge); quad rental; health club; Internet (extra charge); pool (part is kids'); dive center, snorkeling, and windsurfing center. *In room:* A/C, TV, minibar (in some).

Inexpensive

Awlad Baraka Camp "Back to basics" is the undisclosed motto here. Dedicated to the hard-core underwater junkies, the camp revolves around diving and the food to sustain the effort. Thank you, Lord, accommodation is on a full-board basis. Options range from hut to bungalow. The former is small in size, and at times crammed, while the latter is more spacious and has its own bathroom. TV, hot water, and bathtub are luxuries that we don't speak of here. The camp is located on the other side of the old highway, but the opposite beach can be used (note that it's a shared facility with other camps and dive centers); the location is not an inconvenience as the old highway is in disuse.

Red Sea Coastal Hwy. (14km/9 miles south of Marsa Alam). ✆ **010/6460408.** Fax 065/3442394. www.aquariusredsea.com. 30 units, including 19 huts and 11 bungalows with bathroom (shower only). 52€ hut double; 76€ bungalow double. Rack rates on full-board basis. AE, DC, MC, V. **Amenities:** Restaurant; 2 bars; airport transfer (extra charge); dive center, snorkeling. *In room:* No phone.

DAY TRIPS FROM MARSA ALAM

At first, Marsa Alam may seem stranded and cutoff, but history-rich Luxor, dreamy Aswan, and African Shalateen are all just a short drive away.

Luxor & Aswan

Adding a dose of history to your summer beach vacation can be a great idea. A newly inaugurated 220km (138 miles) road connects Marsa Alam to the Nile Valley at Edfu. From there it is a little more than an hour drive to either Luxor or Aswan, meaning you can easily spend a day in each city visiting the major sites. ***Note:*** There are no direct flights available.

Most tour operators sell a 1-day trip to Luxor for around 100€ (minimum 10 people). In addition to lunch and soft drinks, price includes entry fees to Karnak Temple, Valley of the Kings (but not Tomb of Tutankhamun), as well as the Mortuary Temple of Hatshepsut. For more on Luxor attractions, see chapter 10.

Aswan follows suit when it comes to pricing. Included in the price are the entry fees to Isis Temple Complex/Philae, the Unfinished Obelisk, and the High Dam. For more on Aswan attractions, see chapter 10.

Shalateen

Here you can close your eyes and smell Africa; this is Egypt as African as it can get. Wander in the Camel Market where thousands of Sudanese camels take center stage. And if you feel like taking photos, just ask the herders (they may look uptight, but after breaking the ice with a couple of a sign-language moves, you will discover some of the friendliest people on this planet). For shopaholics, Shalateen offers real African handmade trinkets; cash is king (plastic has no place here).

Shalateen is home to Bishari, part of the much larger Beja Tribe. As one tribesman puts it, "A Bishari would rather starve to death than to go without his *jabena* (coffee)." Mixed with ginger, the beans are roasted and grinded fresh before being served in small cups. *Jabena* is more than just a drink; with coffee gatherings several times a day, it constitutes a form of social bonding. If you get invited to a coffee gathering, make sure not to stop at an even number of servings; it is considered a bad omen.

Day trips to Shalateen cost 65€ (minimum six people). Price includes lunch, soft drinks, and needed permits.

7 HAMATA

This is tourism's last frontier; the ultimate Egyptian outdoors destination. Grab your binoculars and get ready for a world-class bird-watching experience. Wade your way through mangrove thickets, or set sail on a wild dolphin encounter in the Sataya Reef. Have you checked your pressure regulator? Diving fanatics need to keep their equipment handy; a minute not spent underwater is time well wasted. And if diving is not your thing, harness the power of nature as you go windsurfing. Up for trying new things? Check out the latest craze in town—kitesurfing; the adrenaline rush is simply addictive. Looking for some soul-cleansing relaxation time? Book the Ras Honkorab excursion, which offers mind-boggling snorkeling; the crystal-clear turquoise water meeting white-powdered sand will leave you completely hypnotized. In my opinion, Ras Honkorab is where Hollywood blockbuster *The Beach* should have been filmed.

ESSENTIALS

Orientation

Hamata is a tiny fishing village, and I do mean tiny, as there are some 20 houses in the whole community. In addition, there are the newly built marina, the kitesurfing village, and less than five resorts with a couple of them still under construction.

Tips Vultures at Bay

Camels endure a journey of great distance and hardship, and it comes as no surprise that some don't make it. If you are a hard-core bird-watcher with an irresistible urge to see an Egyptian vulture or lappet-faced vulture at close range, then head to the dumpsite next to the marketplace, where herders dispose of their fallen camels. Both bird species are scavengers, and where carcasses can be found, so can they. Be warned that a strong, unpleasant odor fills the air.

Getting There

BY PLANE Serving the southern Red Sea area, Marsa Alam International Airport is the closest to Hamata. By default, Hamata's few resorts, or your tour operator, will arrange the airport transfer. If you wish to arrange your own transfer, you can always negotiate the rate with limousine drivers at the airport. Be prepared for no less than LE500.

BY BUS There are two daily buses that run from Cairo all the way to Shalateen, passing Hamata on the way. They leave **Turgoman Bus Station** (© **02/27735668** or -9) at 1:30 and 11pm. Tickets cost LE100.

BY CAR Driving the Red Sea Coastal Highway, you will reach Hamata some 100km (62 miles) south of Marsa Alam. If you are coming from Cairo, you will get used to the scenery; desert to your right, sea to your left, and that's it. Don't forget to refuel your car at Marsa Alam; except for the one in Shalateen (farther south), there are no stations southward.

Getting Around

There is no public transportation. If you don't have your own transport, and don't fancy a jog, you can either ask your hotel to get a limousine for you or you can simply hitchhike. Hamata might sound like the end of the world, but it's a safe place to be.

WHAT TO SEE & DO

An immense reef system, **Fury Shoal** starts off Hamata and runs southeast in the direction of Bernice. Housing some of the Red Sea's best diving spots, Maksur Reef is the

Warning! Shark Feeding

Sharks are remarkable agile creatures, but don't forget they are ferocious predators, and diving shark-infested waters is stepping into their home turf. Play by their rules, not yours.

Golden rule: No snorkeling, no free diving. Imagine this. You are a floating body on the water surface with light coming from above you. For the curious shark below, you are a silhouette rather than an identifiable creature. This is a recipe for disaster; the shark is intrigued to find out if you are dinner potential.

Silver rule: No feeding, baiting, or chumming. There is no such thing as a guaranteed shark sighting, even if the diving spot is well known for sharks. For one reason or another, sharks may decide to wander elsewhere. The irresponsible among us, when frustrated by not spotting the animal, place a scented trail mashed with blood in the water (chumming). Some even go a step further and throw raw chicken. I recall one diving instructor telling me about divers going underwater with chicken drumsticks to feed the sharks. Such a disturbance to sharks' eating habits may produce a conditioned behavior, associating boats, or even divers, with food. This time it is chicken; next time it could be you.

In the past 10 years, only two fatalities have been recorded in Egyptian waters. The most recent occurred on June 1, 2009, at St. John's Reef. According to an eyewitness, Frenchwoman Katrina Tipio free dove to get a zoomed-in photograph of an oceanic white-tip. On her way back to the surface, the shark pursued and bit her leg. Suffering severe hemorrhaging, she died soon after being pulled out of the water. For detailed tracking of global shark incidents, check www.sharkattackfile.net.

ultimate jewel of the Fury Shoal crown. While soft, hard, and fan corals adorn Maksur Reef, manta and eagle rays, hammerhead and grey sharks, tunas, and barracudas are among the regular reef dwellers and visitors. Dive Maksur Reef late May through early August, and if you are lucky you may encounter a whale shark. Other Fury Shoal dive spots that leave you bedazzled are Claudio Reef and Abu Galawa Kebir. Get lost in the easy-to-dive cave system of the former or wreck dive the latter for a glimpse of *Tienstin,* a Chinese tugboat that went down on October 26, 1943. This is one of the most attractive coral-encrusted wrecks in the whole of the Red Sea. For more on Hamata's diving centers, see the chapter "Active Vacation Planner" (p. 81).

Sataya offers a combination of **diving** as well as **swimming with dolphins.** This 4km-long (3-mile) reef engulfs a large lagoon that plays host to several pods of spinner and bottlenose dolphins. Treasure hunters should clean up their goggles pretty well; being en route and in proximity to the ancient trading port of Bernice (p. 261), Roman amphorae and other ship relics can still be found. Including lunch and soft drinks, a day trip to Sataya costs 55€ for snorkelers (minimum six people); two dives cost an additional 44€. Start this trip as early as possible; reaching Sataya takes a good 2 hours.

Kitesurfers rove the world in search of the perfect lagoon, and Hamata just happens to offer one. Three kilometers (2 miles) long and 2km (1 mile) wide, this knee-deep lagoon enjoys favorable wind conditions year round. Kite-Village (p. 91) has lots on offer from equipment rental and storage to basic courses and private tuition. A 3-day basic course costs 260€ and an additional 35€ for the must-have VDWS license. The tide gets pretty low during July and August but picks up again in September.

You can also take to the winds deep into Hamata's hinterland with **desert sailing,** where three-wheel metal carts are equipped with mast and sail. Catching the wind, they glide effortlessly on the desert's flat terrain. Red Sea Desert Adventures (p. 90) offers a 2-hour thrilling desert sailing excursion for 50€ (minimum four people). Price includes transfer to and from the desert.

I am a nature lover, and could easily spend the day photographing mangrove thickets and watching birds. Harboring a plethora of bird species among its mangrove-dotted shoreline, Hamata is an undisclosed **bird-watching** haven, from the endemic Red Sea white-eyed gull and the hunter-at-dusk sooty falcon to the bizarre-looking spoonbill and black-winged stilt with its thin, pinky legs. Topping the list is my all time favorite—osprey. This majestic-looking piscivore is indeed a beauty to behold. At press time, there were no organized bird-watching tours; you need to put on your hard boots, grab your ornithology equipment, and do it the old-fashioned way—independently.

WHERE TO STAY

This is the far south, and tourism is still in its infancy. The four reviewed accommodation facilities are about all that Hamata currently offers.

Expensive

Hotel Lahami Bay ★★★ This is the place to be when it comes to vacationing in Hamata. Clusters of Mediterranean-inspired villas make up this intimate resort. Each villa contains four rooms that range between standard, superior, and sea view. Other than space and a complimentary bottle of red wine, there is not much difference between the first two. Skip both and go for a sea view; opening your eyes in the morning to such a wide-angle sea view is soul enriching. All rooms are elegantly furnished, meeting five-star hotel expectations. The beach is fragmented into three sections: a reef shore for snorkeling and two reefless small bays, one for windsurfing and the other for swimmers. This is

Far & Away

Diving doesn't stop at Hamata. Farther north, south, and east are four more diving hot spots. Stranded in the middle of the Red Sea, Brothers Islands, St. John's Reef, Daedalus Reef, and Zabargad Island are not to be missed. Because of their remote locations, they can be visited only as part of a liveaboard sea safari rather than a day trip. See the chapter "Active Vacation Planner" (p. 81) for more information.

Marked with a Victorian-style stone lighthouse, the **Brothers Islands** are two solitary islands in the middle of the open sea. Representing the tip of colossal reef pillars, they are awash with vibrant soft and hard corals as well as reef and pelagic fish. In addition, Big Brother Island hosts the coral-covered *Aida II* and the *Numidia* wrecks, with the latter being famous for its coral-encrusted railway engine wheels.

Located just 26km (16 miles) north of the Sudanese border, **St. John's Reef** is the southernmost tourist diving spot. It's an immense reef system that offers a complete diving bouquet, from stunning wall dives and atmospheric caves to gigantic shoals of barracuda, tuna, batfish, snappers . . . you name it. This is a shark zone, so abide by safety precautions and measures. See "Shark Feeding" (p. 258) for more details.

Mined in antiquity for its precious olivine, **Zabargad Island** was formerly known as Topazos. In time, mining exhausted the island's natural resources, man left, and birds stepped in. The island's virgin beaches are also known for being an important green turtle breeding site. Nicknamed "The Graveyard," Zabargad Island hosts three shipwrecks within its vicinity: the British steamship *Maidan,* Russian spy vessel *Khanka,* and a Swiss-run liveaboard that sank in 1981.

Located a good 83km (52 miles) off Marsa Alam, **Daedalus Reef** is Egypt's farthest reef from the coast, located eastward in the direction of Saudi Arabia. An almost circular reef rising from a 1,000m (3,280-ft.) depth, it is guarded with a lighthouse, strong currents, and a restless patrolling squad of sharks. Dive Daedalus October through January for the thresher shark season, or May to July for the biggest congregations of scalloped hammerheads; heads up, hammerhead schools can easily reach the hundreds.

about the only resort with a windsurfing center in the southern Red Sea area. The friendly and helpful staff easily score top marks.

Red Sea Coastal Hwy. (115km/72 miles south of Marsa Alam). ✆ **012/3173344.** Fax 012/3168410. www.lahamibay.com. 220 units, including 2 for people with special mobility. 176€ double; 196€ sea-view double. Rates include buffet breakfast, dinner, taxes, and service charges. AE, MC, V. **Amenities:** 3 restaurants; 4 bars; airport transfer (round-trip 90€ Marsa Alam, 130€ Hurghada); kids' club; concierge; heated pool (part is kids'); room service; 2 tennis courts (floodlit); dive center, snorkeling, and windsurfing center. *In room:* A/C, TV, Internet (extra charge), minibar.

Wadi Lahmi Diving Village This is owned and operated by the Red Sea Diving Safari, the owners and operators of Marsa Alam's Marsa Shagra Diving Village (p. 254). Wadi Lahmi Diving Village comes as a copycat of its northern neighbor, with a very quiet ambience. There are no huts available, leaving accommodation options restricted to chalets, tents, and royal tents.

Red Sea Coastal Hwy. (110km/68 miles south of Marsa Alam). ✆ **065/3380021** or -6 in Marsa Alam. Fax 065/3380027 in Marsa Alam. www.redsea-divingsafari.com. 70 units, including 15 chalets, 5 royal tents, and 50 tents. 100€ chalet double; 80€ royal tent double; 70€ tent double. Rack rates on full-board basis with taxes and service charges. MC, V. **Amenities:** Restaurant; bar (serves beer only); airport transfer (round-trip 60€ Marsa Alam, 110€ Hurghada, 190€ Luxor); quad rental; Internet (extra charge); dive center, snorkeling. *In room:* Minifridge (chalets and royal tents), no phone.

Moderate

Wadi Lahmi Azur The newest addition to Hamata's rather limited hotelier scene, Wadi Lahmi Azur is technically a "work in progress" with some construction still going on. The real merit here is the price; a soft opening often translates to a discounted rate. All rooms enjoy a sea view and come with the average four-star type of furniture; however, you'll find plastic chairs on the balcony.

Red Sea Coastal Hwy. (112km/70 miles south of Marsa Alam). ✆ **016/5514920.** Fax 016/5510600. www.azuregypt.com. 120 units. 74€ double. Rates on "all inclusive" basis with taxes and service charges. MC, V. **Amenities:** Restaurant; 4 bars; airport transfer (extra charge); kids' club; concierge; Internet (extra charge); heated pool (part is kids'); room service; dive center, snorkeling. *In room:* A/C, TV, minibar.

Zabargad Dive Resort There are two main reasons to vote for Zabargad Dive Resort: first, for hosting one of the Red Sea's well-reputed diving centers, Orca Dive Club (p. 87); second, for pricing. Other than that it is a sheepish-looking hotel with very basic rooms, seldom decorated. Staff are indeed friendly but they can take ages to see to your requests.

Red Sea Coastal Hwy. (103km/64 miles south of Marsa Alam). ✆ **012/2367010.** Fax 010/0852345. www.zabargad.net. 80 units. 70€ double. Rate includes buffet breakfast and dinner, taxes, and service charges. MC, V. **Amenities:** 2 restaurants; 2 bars; airport transfer (extra charge); quad rental; pool; room service; dive center, snorkeling. *In room:* A/C, minibar.

8 BERNICE

The Ptolemies were in need of elephants. By the 3rd century B.C., war in the Near East was reaching its zenith, and their restless foes, the Seleucids, were blocking the trade route to India. An alternative solution was thought of—Africa. Moving elephant supplies to Ethiopia and environs, King Ptolemy II built a new harbor on the Red Sea coast. He named it after his mother—Berenike. It was the perfect spot, with the protruding peninsula of Ras Banas acting as a natural shield against the mighty northern wind. In addition, being located this far south avoided navigating the treacherous reef-dense waters with its roving pirates farther north.

After Romans gained control of Egypt, they exploited the Red Sea ports as trading outposts. Soon enough, Berenike flourished into a trading emporium. The Romans took it a step further, diversifying the range of traded goods as well as the overseas trading partners. Recent excavations in Berenike revealed some stunning artifacts: Spanish pottery, Indian basketry, and Sri Lankan beads. Though the trading port of Berenike reached its height by the 4th century A.D., it was rather unfathomably abandoned by the 6th century A.D.

Today, ruins of the once bustling port are in a pretty bad shape, and for anyone other than an archaeology devotee, it would be of no interest. The excavation site lies 15km (9 miles) away from the village of Bernice. This part of the Red Sea coast is still virgin; sparsely inhabited, its pristine sceneries are guaranteed to put you in a dreamy mood. Will it be developed for tourism proposes? Rumor has it that plans are in the pipeline, especially with a large military airport already up and running.

10

Upper Egypt

This is where the mighty Ancient Egyptian civilization flourished, on the banks of the great river Nile, and on its East Bank is where they built one of the greatest capitals in the history of mankind—Thebes (now known as Luxor)—where they excelled in architecture and built what by that time's standards surpasses today's skyscrapers and horizon-breaking towers. They built dedicated temples with colossal hypostyle halls, kilometers-long avenues flanked with identical handmade sphinx statues, and extravagant tombs for their Pharaohs to dwell in in the afterlife. Luxor is the focal point of your trip to Egypt and the one place in the country where monuments literally dot the city.

Farther down the river comes Aswan, a sleepy town on the banks that has always been overshadowed by its more enigmatic neighbor up north. And though it retains its share of monuments, its culture is what makes it click. Aswan's frontierlike location allowed frequent interaction with the intriguing Nubia farther south, but by the 1970s things took a different turn as Egypt's ambitious Aswan High Dam was about to be turned on. With the cheap electricity came a hefty price for the Nubians—resettlement. As the water rose behind the subtle walls of the dam, their homeland sunk to oblivion. Now they have been largely moved to Aswan and environs, bringing their unique culture and time-honored traditions with them. Walk their village on Elephantine Island, or head to the well executed Nubian Museum for a closer look.

Upper Egypt's charms don't stop there. The lake behind the dam is for nature lovers and history buffs; have your binoculars handy for sightings of birds and crocodiles while cruising to Abu Simbel, where Ancient Egypt's notorious Pharaoh Ramses II deified himself. If you're up for a real treat, cruise the Nile as 19th century aristocrats once did, aboard a slow sailing *dahabeeya,* with its period enamels.

1 LUXOR

This was the capital when Ancient Egypt was a dominating world power. And though the flourishing civilization has long been eclipsed, its temples and necropolis bear witness to the grandeur of a bygone age. With a long list of perplexing historical sites, the monument-congested Thebes, Luxor today, was declared a UNESCO World Heritage site in 1979. The Karnak Temple is a micro version of Luxor, with its dozen or so temples dotting the Great Temple of Amun and the mammoth-size columns of its hypostyle hall. Luxor Temple might be less dense than its neighbor at the end of the street, but it certainly has its own charm (a mosque, built on the foundation of an older church, right in the middle, and Sphinxes Avenue, which is illuminated at night; head to the rooftop of any overlooking temple for a memorable photo).

Ancient Egyptians rigorously regarded death and the afterlife, and in their quest for immortality they all built tombs; from the over-decorated royal ones in the Valley of the Kings to the much simpler workmen tombs in the necropolis of Deir El Medina. About a thousand tombs have been discovered on Luxor's West Bank over the years, but the most impressive, by far, is the Tomb of Tutankhamun.

ESSENTIALS

Getting There

BY PLANE With a dozen daily flights out of Cairo, flying is the best way to get to Luxor. Fares are about LE650 for the 1-hour flight; though more expensive than the train, they're still fairly reasonable. Many national airliners, as well as budget liners and charter flight operators, connect Luxor directly to major capitals and cities in the region, Europe, and even Japan. The airport is a 15- to 20-minute ride from town, but taxis are plentiful. The easiest solution is to book a transfer through your hotel or travel agency, but check on the price. A taxi ride into town will set you back LE50.

BY TRAIN If you have time, or you want to save some cash, the train is a fine way to get to Luxor. **Abela Egypt** (✆/fax **02/25749474;** www.sleepingtrains.com) has three daily sleeper trains connecting Cairo to Luxor and Aswan. Train no. 84 departs from Giza Train Station at 8pm, while train no. 82 departs from the same train station 30 minutes later. Train no. 86 departs from Ramses Train Station at 9:10pm and stops at Giza Train Station 20 minutes later. All come with sleeping cabins that cost $80/$120 for a single/double; however, train no. 84 has an additional cart with first-class seats. A regular seat costs LE165 and can be a cheaper option if you can do with the inconvenience.

To book your ticket, the best way is to show up in person a couple of days in advance, but if time in not on your side, you can fax Abela Egypt, who are reported to respond promptly with a reference number. Take a copy of the fax along with your passport, and head to their office at either Giza Train Station or Ramses Train Station 24 hours prior to your train departure, pay (in either U.S. dollars or euros for the cabins, local currency for the seats), and collect your ticket. In Luxor, the train station is conveniently located downtown, and taxis are readily available to take you wherever you want to go. Expect to pay LE20 to LE30 if your destination is on the East Bank, but double that if you are heading to the West Bank.

BY BOAT The river route from Cairo to Luxor has been closed for several years and doesn't look set to open any time soon. It's a good idea to factor the cruise boats that shuttle between Luxor and Aswan, or Aswan and Abu Simbel (see "Cruising the Nile," p. 282), into your transport plans. Cruises last from 3 days to a week and run frequently between the two cities. The northbound and southbound cruises are mirror images of each other, so take advantage of whichever one suits your priorities.

BY BUS **Upper Egypt Bus Company** (✆ **095/2323218**) operates six daily buses to Hurghada for LE30 to LE35 and one daily bus each to Cairo (LE100), Sharm El Sheikh (LE120), and Dahab (LE130). I personally keep them as the very last resort when looking for transportation options due to their scruffy, uncomfortable, and freezing cold fleet of buses. **Super Jet** (✆ **095/2367732**) makes a better option, though with a lesser number of destinations served and fewer buses; they only have one daily bus to Cairo (LE130) and another to Hurghada (LE45). Buses currently leave from the bus station located next to the train station; however, there are strong rumors about the bus station moving from its very convenient downtown location to a new facility north of town and closer to the airport, so keep that in mind.

BY CAR It's a hideous 700km (435-mile) drive from Cairo to Luxor on a single-carriage road that's notorious for its daily fatal crashes; you are better off on the train. If you are coming from the Red Sea coast, there is a less-frequented tarmac road, also a single carriage, which cuts through the Eastern Desert connecting the coastal town of El Quseir to the Nile Valley at Qus, and farther to Luxor. The total trip takes about 4 to 5 hours.

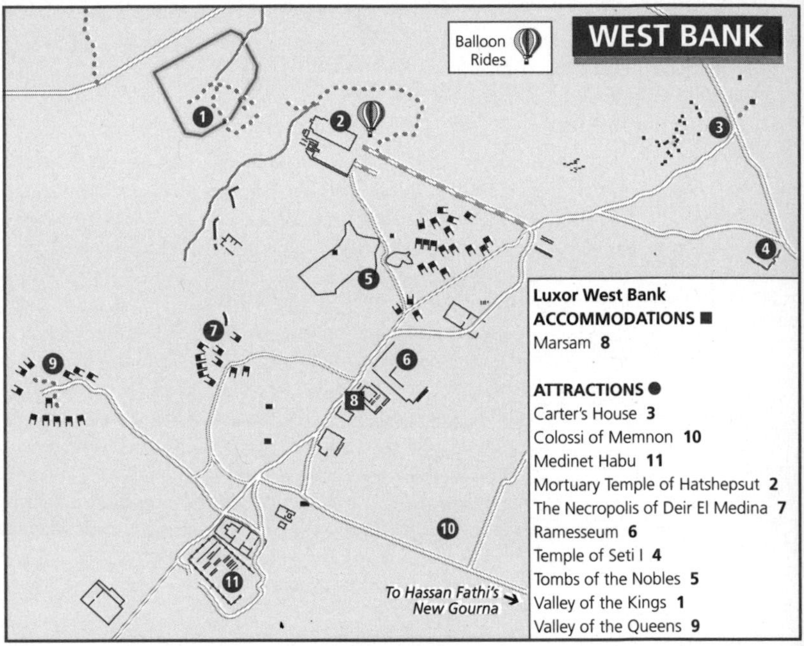
WEST BANK
Balloon Rides
To Hassan Fathi's New Gourna
Luxor West Bank
ACCOMMODATIONS ■
Marsam 8
ATTRACTIONS ●
Carter's House 3
Colossi of Memnon 10
Medinet Habu 11
Mortuary Temple of Hatshepsut 2
The Necropolis of Deir El Medina 7
Ramesseum 6
Temple of Seti I 4
Tombs of the Nobles 5
Valley of the Kings 1
Valley of the Queens 9

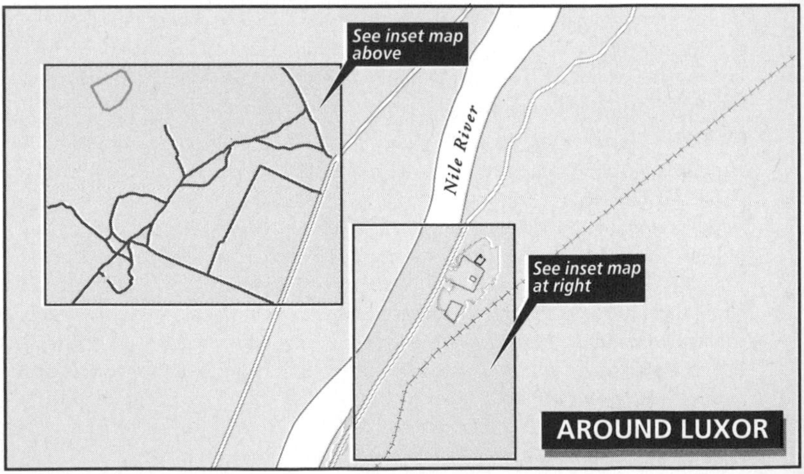
See inset map above
Nile River
See inset map at right
AROUND LUXOR

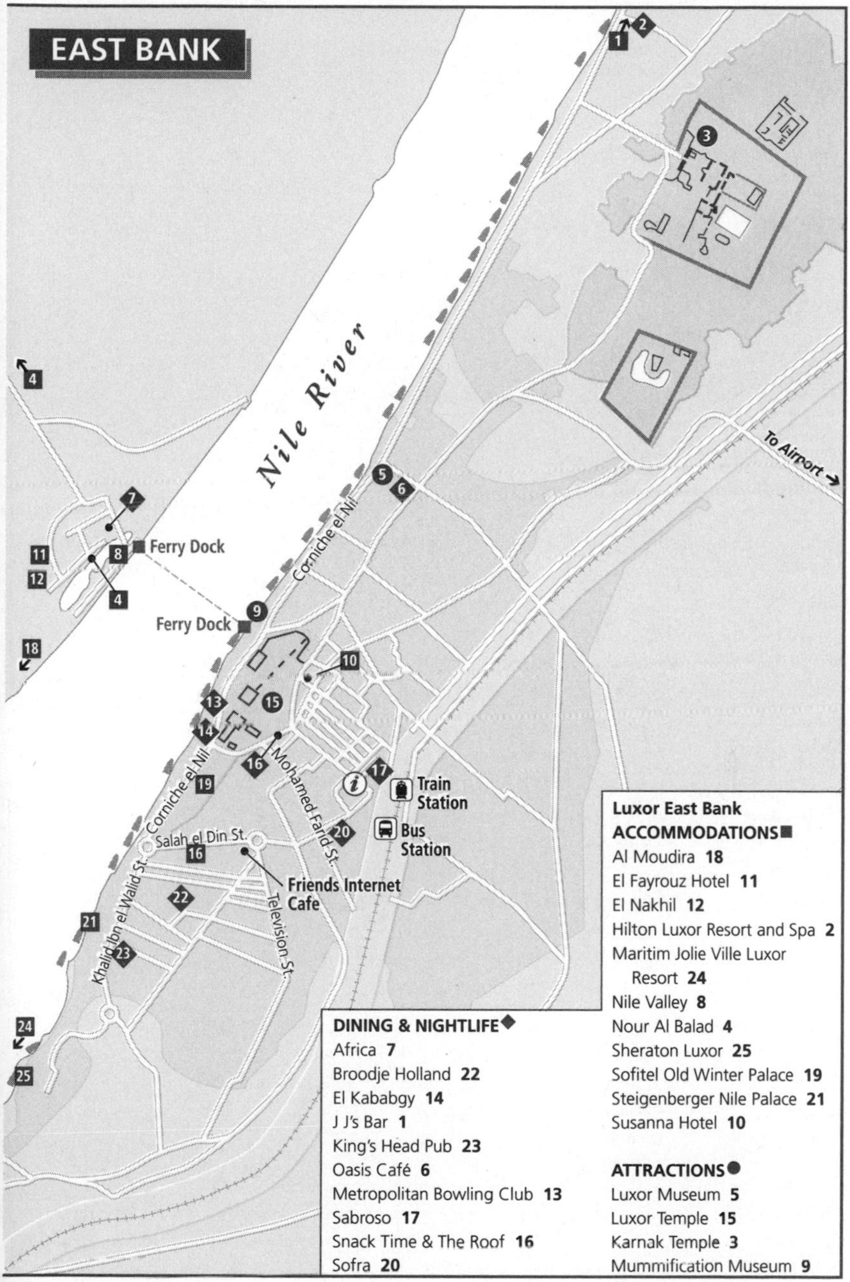

EAST BANK

Nile River

To Airport →

Ferry Dock
Ferry Dock

Friends Internet Cafe

Train Station

Bus Station

Salah el Din St.
Corniche el Nil
Mohamed Farid St.
Television St.
Khalid Ibn el-Walid St.

Luxor East Bank
ACCOMMODATIONS■
Al Moudira **18**
El Fayrouz Hotel **11**
El Nakhil **12**
Hilton Luxor Resort and Spa **2**
Maritim Jolie Ville Luxor
 Resort **24**
Nile Valley **8**
Nour Al Balad **4**
Sheraton Luxor **25**
Sofitel Old Winter Palace **19**
Steigenberger Nile Palace **21**
Susanna Hotel **10**

ATTRACTIONS●
Luxor Museum **5**
Luxor Temple **15**
Karnak Temple **3**
Mummification Museum **9**

DINING & NIGHTLIFE◆
Africa **7**
Broodje Holland **22**
El Kababgy **14**
J J's Bar **1**
King's Head Pub **23**
Oasis Café **6**
Metropolitan Bowling Club **13**
Sabroso **17**
Snack Time & The Roof **16**
Sofra **20**

Getting Around

BY CAR Staying on the East Bank, there is no practical need to rent a car, as most places of interest are a short taxi ride away. The need for a car comes up once you start planning for the West Bank, where sites are scattered across a fairly large area. **Erous Tours** (✆ **010/1555048**) has some recent Toyota Corolla models for LE350 daily, which come with a 100km (62 miles) allowance. For each additional kilometer, expect to pay LE3.50. It is important to note that Erous Tours demands an LE1,000 to LE2,000 cash deposit, so pass by the ATM first. A good alternative is to rent a chauffeured car from the West Bank. Anwer Seleam (✆ **012/3327582**) is an excellent driver who won't rush you to finish your sightseeing or charge you more if you go on for an extra hour. For a full-day tour of the West Bank the charge is LE200, while the daily rate spikes to LE600 to LE800 if you wish to visit farther afield destinations such as Aswan or Hurghada.

BY TAXI The blue-and-white cabs of Luxor tend to expect ludicrous fares, at least compared to anywhere else in Egypt. Negotiate firmly for the fare before getting in. It's going to cost you LE10 to LE20 for little jaunts up and down Corniche El Nil Street and no less than LE40 to LE50 if you intend to use the taxi for crossing to the other bank. The main reason why taxi fares double once the West Bank is mentioned is the location of the bridge, which is a good 10-minute drive outside town.

BY BIKE Bicycles are a great way to get around Luxor, especially on the West Bank, where the traffic is more tame. There are several rental outlets on both banks, such as the one in front of Luxor Temple on the East Bank and the one next to Africa Restaurant on the West Bank. The average rate is LE20 per day.

ON FOOT It's possible to walk around Luxor, but it's not very pleasant. Along the Corniche, the hassle from touts is some of the worst in Egypt, and as you get away from the river, the view becomes unappealing and the traffic gets worse. The only walkable areas are the immediate vicinity of Luxor Temple and the souk, and between the ferry landing and the hotels on the West Bank.

BY CALÈCHE I'm no fan of carriages that cruise the streets of Luxor drawn by underfed horses, drivers aggressively touting their services to all and sundry. Prices depend very much on your bargaining skills and the state of the market, but expect to pay LE50 to LE80 per hour. *Calèches* can also be used for short rides costing LE5 to LE10.

BY FERRY The ferry is the easiest way to get from one bank to the other. Though recently renovated, it is still basic in many ways, and takes around 15 minutes to fill up and less than 5 to cross. Tickets are LE1 and the dock, on the East Bank, is next to the Mummification Museum. If you are in a hurry, there are plenty of speedboats around that will charge LE5 to LE10 for the one-way crossing.

BY MINIBUS Plying Corniche El Nil and Khalid Ibn El Walid streets, minibuses can be a good, cheap means of transportation to get into the busy area around Luxor Temple from either the far northern part of the city around the Hilton Hotel or the southern one around the Steigenberger Hotel. The ride costs LE0.50.

Orientation

The administrative, religious, and living areas of Thebes were all built on the East Bank under the rising sun, with its symbolic associations with life and rebirth. The great necropolises of the Valley of the Kings, Tombs of the Nobles, and the Valley of the Queens, along with the associated mortuary temples, are located on the West Bank, the land of the setting sun, associated with death. Modern Luxor has developed in much the same fashion, with the main hotels, offices, and restaurants all on the East Bank, where the main streets Corniche El Nil and Khalid Ibn El Walid running the length of the city. The most important point of reference is Luxor Temple, which marks the city's downtown with both the souk and the train station to the back of it.

The West Bank is less commercially developed, a lot quieter, and a little less densely populated by annoying touts. Here, attractions outnumber tourist facilities, which are limited to a handful of hotels and eateries.

Tourist Information

Luxor's **tourist information office** (✆ **095/2373294;** daily 8:30am–8pm) is located right in front of the train station and is the best such office in Egypt. Staff speak very good English and French and are quite knowledgeable about Luxor as well as the rest of the country. If you are interested in buying a couple of books about Luxor or Egypt, or a map of the city, Gaddis & Co. (www.gaddis-and-co.co.uk; daily 9am–10pm) is the best option available. Despite its shabby look (it probably hasn't been renovated since the place opened in 1907), the store is well stocked with many Egypt titles.

Internet is easily available with plenty of joints dotting the city. The going rate is about LE10 per hour.

There are tens of tour operators and travel agencies all around Luxor. If you prefer an organized tour rather than doing it independently, I would recommend going for one of the international names such as **Thomas Cook** (El Sawy Building Khaled Ibn El Walid St.; ✆ **095/2372620;** www.thomascookegypt.com; daily 8am–8pm), as it insures the quality of the service you are getting and eliminates any corner cutting.

HOT-AIR BALLOONING The idea of floating over the West Bank as the sun rises over Medinet Habu, the Tombs of the Nobles, and the Colossi of Memnon has caught on with a vengeance. There are now dozens of companies vying for your business. The four below have been in business for several years, employ certified pilots, and carry insurance. That said, services vary little. They will all pick you up at your hotel very early (around 5am) and take you via boat (if you are staying on the East Bank) to the other side of the river, and you're in the air a little after sunrise. Flights last 35 minutes to an hour and go where the wind blows. Exactly which monuments you'll float over depends on the wind, but you're likely to get fantastic views of the Mortuary Temple of Hatshepsut, the Ramesseum, and the Temple of Seti I. The village of El Gourna, with its surrounding patchwork of green fields, will be spread out below, and you'll get a great view of the Nile as well.

During winter (the high season), the per person price within a group averages LE600 to LE800 including insurance.

- If you book through a hotel or a tour operator, you may well find yourself flying with **Sinbad,** which is well established and heavily promoted. 37 Abdel Hamed Al Omda St.; ✆ **095/2272960** or 095/2270437; fax 095/2276344; www.sindbadballoons.com.
- **Viking Air** is one of Luxor's most famous and well reputed hot-air ballooning companies. In the early morning you will often see their trademark yellow balloons with a big "Viking Air" written on it dotting the sky. Ahmed Urabi Street; ✆ **095/2277212;** www.vikingballoonsegypt.com.
- **Skycruise** is another good option. 110 Khalid Ibn El Walid St. (close to the Luxor Sheraton); ✆ **095/2270408** or 095/2276515; skycruise@skycruise-eg.com.
- A little more expensive than the others, **Hod Hod Soliman** has been in the business since it started, and once you've been featured on CNN, you can afford to charge a little more. Omar Ali Street (on the second floor close to the Golden Palace hotel); ✆ **095/2270116** or 012/2151312; hodhodoffice@yahoo.co.uk.

WHAT TO SEE & DO

Luxor is the world's largest open-air museum and offers a feast of Ancient Egyptian history.

East Bank

Karnak Temple ★★★ Karnak Temple is simply jaw dropping and should not be missed under any circumstances. The mega complex is made up of the Great Temple of Amun and a number of much smaller temples dedicated to various Ancient Egyptian gods. Over a vast period of 1,300 years, every Pharaoh seeking personal glorification or wanting to please the gods added a temple, a hall, or at least a shrine. Venturing into the historical labyrinth of Karnak Temple, from the main entrance on the western side, the general rule is that the farther you go into the complex, the older the surroundings become.

You'll enter through the massive **First Pylon** that, though unfinished, still stands 43m (41 ft.) high, and into the **Great Temple of Amun.** The grand temple is widely famous for its awe-inspiring **Hypostyle Hall,** where 134 papyrus-like columns rise around you like the trees of a giant forest, dwarfing anything of human scale. They measure 15m (49 ft.) in height, except for the 12 columns right in the center, which measure about 21m (69 ft.). This spectacular hall was planned by Amenhotep III but was actually built by Seti I, with Ramses II adding relief work and decoration. In ancient times, the Hypostyle Hall was roofed, and its columns and walls were brightly painted. The Great Temple of Amun also encompasses 10 pylons and a **Sacred Lake** where Amun's priests were believed to bathe twice a day as a purification ritual. The **Tenth Pylon** leads to the ram-headed **Sphinxes Avenue,** which in turn leads to the **Precinct of Mut,** a badly ruined temple that was originally built by Amenhotep III. It is believed that the Pharaoh, devoted to the worship of Mut and her northern counterpart Sekhmet, placed some 700 statues of Sekhmet, representing each morning and evening of the year, where offerings were presented twice a day.

North of the First Pylon, and within the premises of the Great Temple of Amun, is the **Open Air Museum.** Three main chapels highlight your visit: the **White Chapel of Sesostris I** and its well-preserved Middle Kingdom reliefs; the aptly named **Red Chapel of Hatshepsut,** which was recently reconstructed in 2000; and the **Alabaster Chapel of Amenhotep I** with its beautiful collection of statues. The Open Air Museum certainly deserves the extra ticket.

To cover the massive Karnak Temple in greater detail, I recommend hiring a guide. An English-speaking guides costs LE150 for a 2-hour tour.

Corniche El Nil. ✆ **095/2380270.** Admission LE65 (additional LE35 for the open-air museum). Daily 6am–4:30pm.

I Believe I Can Fly

For a different experience of Luxor, **Lont Group** (✆ **02/26906596** or -7; www.lonttravel.com) offers a 30-minute flight in a small Cessna plane. It costs $100 to $120 per person (insurance included) with a minimum of two people.

Luxor Museum ★★★ Though a lot smaller than the Egyptian Museum in Cairo, the Luxor Museum is a lot better put together and is worth at least an hour or two. It's hard to pick highlights from its stunning collection, but you should see the 2.5m-tall (8-ft.) quartzite **statue of Amenhotep III,** which is part of the 26-statue collection found at Luxor Temple in 1989. Better known as the **Luxor Cache,** the collection includes a statue of Horemoheb offering pots to Atum (another holy member of the Ancient Egyptian

Look, Don't Touch

It's the sad truth of mass tourism that our presence can damage the monuments that we come to admire. Despite massive investment in protecting sites, perspiration and even exhaled breath (average hourly exhalation rate per person can amount to 2 cups of watery moisture) damage the delicate paintings in tombs; the lights thrown up around temples all too often heat and damage the ancient stone; and the exhaust from tour buses and cruise ships forms chemical compounds that destroy delicate relief carvings.

Fortunately, there is an easy and cheap way that we can reduce our impact on these irreplaceable artifacts—simply don't touch.

pantheon). Other key highlights include the **mummy of Ahmose I** as well as the **Wall of Akhenaten.** The wall is made up of small blocks known as *talatat* (which simply means "threes" in Arabic) that were used by Amenhotep IV at Karnak Temple before he changed his name to Akhenaten and moved the capital away from Thebes (now Luxor) to Tel El Amarna (near Minya). After his death, they were reduced to rubble, but they've been painstakingly pieced back together to form a tableaux that shows the Pharaoh and his wife. Also, don't miss the pieces retrieved from Tutankhamun's tomb, which include three beautifully preserved chariots, some model boats, footwear, and a bow and arrows. Corniche El Nil. ✆ **095/2380269.** Admission LE80. Daily 9am–3pm and 4–9pm.

Luxor Temple ★ Luxor Temple was originally built by Amenhotep III in the 14th century B.C. and was followed by a sizable expansion during the reign of Ramses II. Entering the temple from the tourists' main gate, you will first come to the **Sphinxes Avenue** on your right. In its heyday, this long road lined with dozens of identical sphinxes stretched all the way to the Karnak Temple 3km (2 miles) downriver. To your left stands the temple's **First Pylon,** flanked by two seated statues of Ramses II as well as one giant obelisk. Originally there were two obelisks, but one was gifted to France in 1829 by the Albanian-in-origin sovereign at the time, Mohamed Ali. Today it stands at the Place de la Concorde Square in Paris. The First Pylon hosts one of Luxor Temple's key attractions: a magnificent relief depicting Ramses II killing the Hittites at the Battle of Kadesh. Walking into the **Peristyle Courtyard of Ramses II,** you will come to the striking **Mosque of Abu El Haggag,** which dates back to the 13th century and was actually built on the ruins of a church. When both the church and the mosque were built, Luxor Temple was still buried (excavations unearthed it as recently as the 19th century). One peculiar aspect of the recently renovated mosque is its northern minaret; it dates back to the 11th century and is one of the very few Fatimid monuments surviving today. Note the apparent difference in architecture when compared to the rest of Egypt's minarets. Ramses II's courtyard ends with a 100m (328-ft.) colonnade lined with seven pairs of papyrus-like columns that stand 19m (62 ft.) high. The **Colonnade** opens up to the **Great Sun Court of Amenhotep III** and the **Hypostyle Hall** at its rear. Though it is a great architectural achievement in its own right, the 32-column hall is not as striking as the spectacular Hypostyle Hall at Karnak Temple. Luxor Temple saw several additions through the ages, among which are the **Chapel of Serapis** added by the Roman Emperor Hadrian and the **Barque Shrine** of Alexander the Great at the very end of the temple. Corniche El Nil. ✆ **095/2381994** or 095/2372408. Admission LE50. Daily 6am–8:30pm.

Two Festivals, One Boat

If you're in Luxor during the month before Ramadan, you may be lucky enough to catch the *moulid* of Sheikh Abu El Haggag, a local festivity that commemorates the pious sheikh's birth and life. It lasts 2 days and draws participants from all over Egypt parading the streets with raucous music, and model boats that are held above the fray on poles. The festival is reflective of the scenes depicted on the walls of the Colonnade at Luxor Temple, which show the ancient festival of Opet with the priests of Karnak carrying the boats of Amun, Mut, and Khonsu to the temple to mark the annual flood of the Nile. There are certainly no religious ties; it is just a personal observation.

Mummification Museum Kids This museum is one of Egypt's more modern. The display is excellent, but the collection is not comprehensive, especially if you've already been to the Luxor Museum. Head here if you are an avid fan of Ancient Egypt or have kids with you. Displays include mummified animals as well as the mummy of Maserharti (a 21st dynasty priest), along with the tools of the trade—scrapers, scoopers, and hooks used to remove the internal organs and brains of the corpses.

Corniche El Nil. ✆ **095/2387320.** Admission LE50. Daily 9am–2pm and 4–9pm.

West Bank

You can easily arrange to do any, or all, of the sites on the West Bank with either private transport or an organized bus tour, but to finish all sites, you will definitely need more than 1 day. It is just as easy to pay LE1 to cross the Nile on the public ferry that departs from the dock next to the Mummification Museum, but once on the other side you will need to negotiate your itinerary and the price with one of the many taxis that wait there.

Tickets to all of the West Bank sites are bought from the central ticket office close to the mountain village of El Gourna, some 200m (656 ft.) south of the Colossi of Memnon. The only exceptions are the Valley of the Kings and Mortuary Temple of Hatshepsut.

Carter's House Opened in November 2009, this is Luxor's latest attraction. It was archaeologist Howard Carter's residence during his time in Luxor in the early 20th century. The renovated house features some old photographs, vintage furniture, and memorabilia; I personally like the small fan and the goliath camera. The house is not huge, but the restoration has been done professionally. The dark room is particularly interesting.

Free admission. Daily 6am–4pm.

Colossi of Memnon These two statues of Amenhotep III are all that remain of a massive compound this Pharaoh built to house his mortuary temple. According to archaeologists, the site would have been bigger than Karnak, making it the biggest such complex in all of Thebes. Built on the actual flood plain of the Nile, however, it washed away, and all that remains now are these 18m-high (59-ft.) twin statues. From about the middle of the 1st century B.C. until the early 3rd century A.D., when a crack in it was fixed by the Roman Emperor Septimius Severus, the northern statue of the pair used to make a low wailing noise each morning. The Greek explanation associated the statue with the Homeric character Memnon and the noise with him singing a greeting to his mother Eos, the Goddess of Dawn.

Admission free. No opening hours.

Karnak Sound & Light Show

Gloriously over the top, the sound and light show at **Karnak** (© **095/2386000;** fax 095/2380100; www.soundandlight.com.eg) is some of the best entertainment in Egypt. The 1-hour, heavily voiced-over show takes you through some of the history of the site and moves from the courtyard, through the Hypostyle Hall (which is absolutely magnificently lit), and then to the sacred lake. Even if you don't like the loud music, it's worth it for the walk through the temple at night. Make sure that you edge to the front of the crowd in the hall so that you get a good seat on the bleachers that are set up at the sacred lake. Admission is LE100. Winter shows are at 6:30, 7:45, and 9pm; summer shows at 8, 9:15, and 10:30pm. If you have missed your preferred language, or prefer narration to be in Russian or Polish, go for the most convenient timing and ask for a DVD audio device that translates the show into nine different languages.

	1st show	2nd show	3rd show
Saturday	French	English	X
Sunday	German	English	Italian
Monday	English	French	Spanish
Tuesday	Japanese	English	X
Wednesday	German	English	French
Thursday	English	French	Arabic
Friday	English	French	X

Medinet Habu Often passed over by tours and guidebooks, Medinet Habu is a great place for an afternoon visit. The complex seems to have been started by Hatshepsut in the 15th century B.C., when she built a small temple dedicated to Amun, but it was vastly expanded about 3 centuries later by Ramses III when he added a mortuary temple. Over the millennia it was used for various purposes: once the village of Djeme was built within the walls (hence the *medinet,* or "town" in Arabic, in the site's modern name), and for a while one of the temple's courts was used as a Christian church.

The temple complex of Medinet Habu greets its visitors with a rather gory illustration on the **First Pylon** portraying Ramses III killing his enemies and subjugating their lands, but the images become more religious as you progress inside. The columns of the **Inner Hypostyle Hall** have unfortunately been reduced to stumps, but the temple's vestibule and sanctuary farther in are worth a wander through. Medinet Habu is littered with depictions, reliefs, and inscriptions; have a thorough look and try to see the depiction of two soldiers engaged in a karate-like drill or perhaps 19th-century graffiti left by some early European visitor. Medinet Habu has a lot in common with the Ramesseum; likewise, other than a couple of ceilings that still cling to their original colors, the whole site is barren.

Admission LE30. Daily 6am–4pm.

Anubis

Long a favorite of the manufacturers of repro fake-basalt statuettes, Anubis is represented as a slender dog with tall pointed ears. You'll see him quite often at the entrance to a tomb, from where he guards the bodies of the interred from the depredations of the jackals he resembles. His color, black, is said to represent not only the color of decayed flesh (and, thus, death) but also the black, fertile earth of the Nile Valley (and, thus, life). It was Anubis who wrapped the body of the murdered Osiris and facilitated his resurrection, hence Anubis's association with mummification. He had many titles, among them Khentimentiu, which meant "first among Westerners" and referred to his dominance over the necropolis of the West Bank.

Mortuary Temple of Hatshepsut ★ The grandiose Mortuary Temple of Hatshepsut is set against rugged, 300m-high (984-ft.) limestone cliffs; the result is a dramatic photograph of an ancient grandeur. Built during the reign of Hatshepsut, with the functionality of a mortuary temple, the temple follows a different architectural style than others of that time. At one time the temple had its own avenue of sphinxes and a massive garden planted with various exotic trees, but it witnessed all types of persecution, inflicted first by angry Tuthmosis III, who eliminated any reference to his stepmother, and later by Akhenaten as he eradicated the name of Amun. Early Christians followed suit and defaced pagan statues and turned the whole temple into a monastery (hence the more common name of El Deir El Bahari, the Western Monastery).

Approaching the temple, you'll see that it rises in **three massive terraces;** the middle one will be the highlight of your visit. The northern colonnade, to your right, has reliefs that depict Hatshepsut's birth and eventually leads to the **Chapel of Anubis** with its 12 fluted columns and amazingly preserved colors. The main relief inside the chapel depicts Tuthmosis III and his stepmother, Hatshepsut, in front of a congregation of Ancient Egyptian gods; Hatshepsut's depiction is, as mentioned above, disfigured. The southern colonnade, to your left, is better known as the **Punt Colonnade,** where wall paintings and depictions detail Hatshepsut's five-ship maritime expedition to the Land of Punt. The reliefs portray Punties with their distinguished African features; Chief of Punt Parahu and his wife Queen Ity; and exotic gifts that included baboons, leopards, ivory, and (Hatshepsut's favorite) a myrrh tree, whose incense was used in the temple's ceremonial rituals. At the end of the colonnade lies the **Chapel of Hathor** with its two chambers pillared with Hathor-headed columns; both rooms host various reliefs including a colorful depiction of a massive naval parade.

The visitor center has a silicon model of the site, a couple of computers if you want to know more and don't have a guide, and a screen often showing a documentary about Hatshepsut. It is a short walk from here to the temple itself; if you don't feel like walking, there is an electric train.

Admission LE30, extra LE2 electric train. Daily 6am–4pm.

The Necropolis of Deir El Medina ★★ Deir El Medina is a fascinating site for anyone interested in how the Ancient Egyptians actually lived. It's close to the Valley of the Queens and incorporates a small Ptolemaic-era temple and the remains of a small walled village that housed the workers who built the temples and tombs of the West Bank. The village, which contained around 70 small houses, is still defined enough that you can make out streets and the walls of individual buildings. The name of the area comes from the small 3rd-century-B.C. temple to Hathor on the site, which was taken over by early Coptic priests and named Monastery of the Town, or Deir El Medina.

Next to the village there is a 361-tomb necropolis, which acted as the final resting place for the men who worked in the Valley of the Kings. Perhaps the most famous, and indeed the most fascinating, is the tomb of **Sennedjem,** a tomb builder in the 13th century B.C. The tomb was discovered intact by an Italian expedition in 1886, and much of its original content is now on display in the Museo Egizio in Turin. The wall paintings are well preserved and include an unusual depiction of Sennedjem and his wife, Lyneferti, playing a board game. The **Tomb of Peshedu** is decorated with two depictions of Anubis, as a jackal sitting on a pedestal and a self portrait of Peshedu by a palm tree near water. The tomb of **Inherkhau** is decorated with pictures of its owner from his quotidian life; judging by the pictures, Inherkhau was not only bald, at least for part of his life, but an enthusiastic harp player.

Admission LE30. Daily 6am–4pm.

Ramesseum The mortuary temple of Ramses II is not in the best condition and may actually be best viewed from a hot-air balloon in the early morning. The one feature of the temple, in addition to its size, that makes it worth a visit is the 18m-high (59-ft.) statue of Ramses II, nicknamed Ozymandias Colossus and the inspiration for 19th-century poet Percy Bysshe Shelley's poem (below). The original entrance would have been to the left as you walk through the modern entrance, between two massive pylons

My Name Is Ozymandias

Even among Pharaohs, whose careers were devoted to building monuments to themselves, Ramses II, whose name comes through Greek transliterations as Ozymandias, seems to have been a bit of an egocentric. He left Egypt littered with massive tributes to his greatness, including the enormous Ramesseum on the West Bank of the Nile at Thebes, where he also had an 18m (57-ft.) statue of himself erected. It was this statue that inspired Percy Bysshe Shelley to write a beautifully metered poem that, more than 2 centuries later, still has remarkable resonance in Egypt.

I met a traveler from an antique land
Who said: Two vast and trunkless legs of stone
Stand in the desert . . . Near them, on the sand,
Half sunk, a shattered visage lays, whose frown,
And wrinkled lip, and sneer of cold command,
Tell that its sculptor well those passions read,
Which yet survive, stamped on these life-less things,
The hand that mocked them, and the heart that fed:
And on the pedestal these words appear:
"My name is Ozymandias, king of kings:
Look upon my works, ye Mighty, and despair!"
Nothing beside remains. Round the decay
Of that colossal wreck, boundless and bare
The lone and level sands stretch far away.

that are worth checking out for their depictions of Ramses II's military triumphs. To the right, more than half the original columns of the hypostyle hall are still erect and, if you follow on beyond, there is a smaller hall with a portion of the original celestial decorations on the roof that are still visible.

Admission LE30. Daily 6am–4pm.

Temple of Seti I One of the New Kingdom's great Pharaohs, Seti I is credited for successful military campaigns abroad and huge construction projects at home. He cut himself one of the finest Valley of the Kings tombs, was credited for the building of Karnak Temple's colossal hypostyle hall, and attempted to build an equally turgid mortuary temple. Unfortunately, time was not on his side, and the Temple of Seti I was completed by his son Ramses II. It has sadly decayed over time due to weather and the fact that locals used it as a quarry through the 18th century. The walls of the ruined hypostyle hall have some excellent relief carvings showing both Ramses II and Seti I with the gods. There is a small chapel at the south of the temple, which is dedicated to Ramses I, Seti I's father, whose short term in the royal court left him with no monuments to call his own.

Admission LE30. Daily 6am–4pm.

Valley of the Kings ★★★ The Palace of Truth is what the Ancient Egyptians decided to call their most elaborate and mesmerizing royal necropolis. New Kingdom Pharaohs competed in designing their final resting places with the most skilled craftsmen and tomb builders. The result is a collection of superbly crafted and finely decorated tombs where no two are alike. Until recently there were only 62, but a 2006 discovery revealed a 63rd. The numbering follows the chronological order of their discovery with the Tomb of Ramses VII heading the league; it was discovered in the Ptolemaic Period. These magnificent treasures have suffered greatly; first at the hands of tomb raiders during antiquity and more recently at the hands of you and me—tourists. The amount of moisture each one of us exhales into the poorly ventilated tombs causes irrecoverable damage to the paintings and pigments. In response to the ongoing disaster, dehumidifiers have been installed, and a rotation program has been adopted, leaving about a dozen tombs open at any given time. The tombs reviewed below are the ones open at press time, but if open, you should also check out KV7 (Ramses II), 17 (Seti I), and 57 (Horemoheb).

Similar to the Mortuary Temple of Hatshepsut, the visitor center here comes with the same silicon model of the site, computers, and the screen showing a documentary (this time about Howard Carter discovering the Tomb of Tutankhamun). Here you can also

Art That Failed

Hassan Fathy was a pioneering Egyptian artist and architect who wanted to revive traditional architectural style by employing modern techniques. His most ambitious project was the innovative New Gourna, where he built a whole rural village using traditional building materials and followed the local architectural style. The result is a beautiful village that somehow failed to win locals' admiration. Most of the original buildings are gone, except his house and the village's mosque. You can include a 5-minute stop during your tour of the West Bank; just tell the driver to take you to Hassan Fathy.

buy your ticket; **note that this allows you to visit three tombs of your choice excluding those of Tutankhamun and Ramses VI.** If you wish to see more, you can buy more than one three-tomb ticket. Tickets for both the Tomb of Tutankhamun and the Tomb of Ramses VI can be bought from the ticket office at the valley's entrance. It is a 10-minute walk uphill to the well-signed valley where the tombs are, so it is wise to conserve energy, as you will need it later negotiating the numerous stairs that take you down to the tombs. Photography is not allowed, and the rule is strongly enforced; breaking the rule comes with a hefty LE1,000 fine, not to mention the considerable damage done to the paintings.

Tomb of Ramses VII (KV1) is the closest tomb to the valley's entrance. It was hastily finished after Ramses VII's sudden death. It lacks elaborate depictions but contains well-preserved wall inscriptions and passages from several funerary texts such as the Book of Caverns and the Book of Earth. Graffiti from earlier Ptolemaic and Roman visitors is still visible today.

Tomb of Ramses IV (KV2) is another unfinished tomb with a last-minute modification: The pillared hall was turned into a burial chamber. Today the tomb is empty except for a large granite sarcophagus, said to be the largest in the valley. Similar to many tombs, the ceiling is adorned with stars and a depiction of Nut, Goddess of the Sky; however, unique to this tomb are the inscriptions from the funerary text, the Book of Nut. During the early days of Christianity, the tomb acted as a shelter for fleeing Coptic hermits, so look for the religious graffiti they left behind.

Tomb of Ramses IX (KV6) is one of the most visited tombs of the Valley of the Kings for its significantly preserved passages from ancient texts such as the Book of the Day and the Book of the Night, as well as wall paintings and depictions showing different funerary rites including the Opening of the Mouth Ritual, which involved holding the strapped mummy in an upright position while priests in leopard skin and Anubis masks touch the deceased's mouth, eyes, and ears with a special wand in order to rejuvenate the senses.

Tomb of Ramses VI (KV9) is a double-bill tomb with both Ramses V and Ramses VI originally buried inside. Considered one of the valley's largest tombs, its walls are awash with beautiful scenes from several funerary texts, especially the set of depictions from the Book of the Earth detailing the sun's journey into the night and how the forces of darkness attempt to stop the sun god from reaching dawn. The ceiling doesn't fall short on decoration, and is adorned with astronomical depictions and texts. This tomb certainly deserves the extra ticket.

Tomb of Ramses III (KV11) measures 125m (410 ft.) in length, making it one of the longest in the valley. In addition to the usual funerary scenes and ancient texts' passages, there are two beautiful nonreligious scenes. One depicts a display of foreign tributes that include Aegean pottery, and the other portrays two blind men playing the harp, hence the nickname of Tomb of the Harpers.

Fun Facts How Many Ramses Were There?

There were 11 Ramses, though a few sources put the number at 12. Together they formed an era known by Egyptologists as the Ramesside Period.

Tomb of Tawosret (KV14) originally belonged to Queen Tawosret, wife of Seti II, who—after her husband's successor, Siptah, died—grabbed the throne for herself. Though she stayed in power for only a couple of years, she modified her husband's tomb by adding depictions of herself as a king. Her angry successor, Sethnakht, moved her burials and expanded the tomb by adding a second burial chamber for himself. Tawosret's portraits had been reworked to reflect the tomb's new owner, Sethnakht.

Tomb of Seti II (KV15) is where Seti II's body ended up after the angry Sethnakht moved it from KV14. It is a rather small tomb that was hastily finished. Nut, Goddess of the Sky, adorns the star-dotted ceiling, while passages from several funerary texts such as the Litany of Ra, the Book of Amduat, and the Book of the Gates decorate the walls.

Tomb of Montuhirkopshef (KV19) belongs to a prince rather than a Pharaoh. Montuhirkopshef, or "The Arm of Montu is Strong," as his name means, was one of Ramses IX's sons. Beautiful wall paintings portray the young prince presenting offerings to a handful of Ancient Egyptian deities, including Osiris, Ptah, Thoth, and Khonsu.

Tomb of Tuthmosis IV (KV43) was discovered by Howard Carter in 1903, 19 years before he discovered Tuthmosis IV's great-grandson's, Tutankhamun's, tomb. The tomb is fairly large and deep, with two long flights of stairs leading to the burial chamber. Depictions follow the footsteps of neighboring tombs as far as theme is concerned and are still in a pretty good state. One particular depiction I admire is that of Tuthmosis IV receiving an ankh (key of life) from Hathor. There is also interesting graffiti that dates back to 1315 B.C. affirming the checking and restoration of the tomb in the reign of Horemoheb.

Tomb of Siptah (KV47) was discovered just 2 years after the Tomb of Tuthmosis IV. Other than a few decorations, which adorn the doorway and the entrance corridor, the rest of the tomb is plain.

Tomb of Tutankhamun (KV62) is the jewel in the Valley of the Kings' crown. The small tomb is a must-see. When it was discovered in 1922, its four chambers were filled to their roofs with all types of regalia and funerary items, from statues and jars to musical instruments and board games. Most of the original contents are in the Egyptian Museum in Cairo, and a handful are in the Luxor Museum. Both Tutankhamun's outer stone sarcophagus and mummy are in his tomb. The tomb paintings are finely executed and exceptionally preserved; they mainly depict him before the gods and his funeral

Guarding the Dead

Grave robbing was around even before the collapse of the Ancient Egyptian civilization. In an attempt to save their Pharaohs' mummies, priests moved them to safer grounds. In 1898, a French mission excavating the Tomb of Amenhotep II, one of the Valley of the Kings' deepest and most difficult to access, was surprised when they came across a cache of 13 mummies including that of Amenhotep II lying peacefully in his sarcophagus with a wreath of flowers still tied around his neck. The other, more stunning, cache was discovered 17 years earlier at an Ancient Egyptian communal cemetery, south of the Mortuary Temple of Hatshepsut. It contained 40 mummies including that of Seti I (Ramses II's father), which is now part of the Royal Mummies Exhibit at the Egyptian Museum in Cairo.

procession. There is an entire wall dedicated to 12 depictions of squatting apes, which represent the 12 hours of the night as per the oldest Ancient Egyptian funerary text, the Book of Amduat.

At press time the famous Tomb of Ramses II (KV2), Tomb of Seti I (KV17), and Tomb of Horemoheb (KV57) were closed for restoration.

Admission LE80 (3 tombs); Tomb of Tutankhamun extra LE100, Tomb of Ramses VI extra LE50; electric train extra LE4. Daily 6am–4pm; Tomb of Tutankhamun daily 6am–1pm and 2–4pm.

Valley of the Queens ★★ Effectively down the road and up the next valley from Valley of the Kings, the Valley of the Queens tends to be a little less crowded but is no less interesting. It's slightly misleadingly named, for although there are a number of 18th-, 19th-, and 20th-dynasty queens buried here (previous to this, queens tended to be buried with their husbands), there are also other royal family members as well as some high officials.

At press time only two tombs out of the 88 were officially open: the **Tomb of Khaemwaset** (QV44) and the **Tomb of Titi** (QV52). Discovered in 1903, the Tomb of Khaemwaset belongs to another son of Ramses III. The tomb is noted for its well-preserved wall paintings depicting various scenes, including Khaemwaset and his father in front of Anubis and Ra. The Tomb of Titi's wall paintings are not in great condition, but you can still make out some scenes and depictions such as those of a winged Maat and the queen in a religious posture in front of Ptah, the God of Creation and Artisans.

The **Tomb of Nefertari** (QV66) is the crown jewel of the Valley of the Queens, and is both the largest and the most elaborately decorated, with walls covered in stunning paintings commissioned by Ramses II to honor his favorite wife (he had four others). Though a special permit will open the door for a few minutes, second-hand accounts put the costs at a staggering $5,000 for a group of 10 visitors.

Admission LE35. Daily 6am–4pm.

Tombs of the Nobles

Between the Valley of the Queens and the Valley of the Kings lies another necropolis, this one used by high officials and the wealthy from the 6th to the Ptolemaic dynasties. Because the Tombs of the Nobles is not as intensely developed a tourist site as the Valley of the Kings, it is less crowded and also a little harder to access. Signage is poor, and it would be a good idea to have a flashlight with you. At press time only 14 of about 415 tombs were open for tourists. They are divided into six groups, each with a separate ticket, and open daily from 6am to 4pm.

The Living Goddesses

Only two Ancient Egyptian queens were worshiped as living goddesses: Queen Nefertari (Ramses II's favorite wife), who had a small temple at Abu Simbel dedicated to the cult of her deity, and Queen Tiye (wife of Amenhotep III and mother of the controversial Akhenaten), who was worshiped as the goddess Hathor-Tefnut. Queen Tiye is depicted as a small statue standing by her husband's knee in the Colossi of Memnon.

Khonsu & Benia The resting place of the holy man Khonsu preserves much of its original paintings detailing the Festival of Montu that took place in the town of Armant located some 20km (12 miles) south of Luxor. Unlike the common stars and Nut ceiling depiction, this one is decorated with images of flying ducks.

Chief Treasurer Benia, who lived during the reign of Tuthmosis III, has his tomb right behind Khonsu's. It is more colorful than its neighbor, with vivid depictions of the deceased worshiping and making offers to the gods. The niche at the rear depicts Benia and his parents, all with disfigured faces.

Admission LE15.

Roy & Shuroy Both located in the area known as Dra'a Abu El Naga, located toward the far northern end of the necropolis, these are the only two tombs, out of an original 114, to escape with little damage to their wall paintings. The royal scribe **Roy** made himself a well-painted tomb with beautiful funerary depictions, while the **Tomb of Shuroy**'s ceiling is elegantly decorated with geometric patterns and its wall paintings include a depiction of the deceased and his wife presenting offerings to the gods.

Admission LE15.

Nakht & Menna If you're going to see one set of tombs in the Tombs of the Nobles, this is the pair to see. **Nakht** was a high official in the court of Tuthmosis IV, and during his lifetime held the posts of astronomer, keeper of the king's vineyards, and chief of the granaries. **Menna,** on the other hand, was an agriculture inspector. In addition to the more common funeral rites, judgment, and the afterlife depictions you find in most of the Ancient Egyptian tombs, these tombs both have depictions portraying daily life, from fishing and fowling to cultivation and husbandry. I particularly like the finely executed wheat harvest depiction in the Tomb of Menna, while in the Tomb of Nakht there is a well-preserved wall painting of the very famous three lady musicians.

Admission LE25.

Neferonpet, Nefersekheru & Dhutmosi The **Tomb of Neferonpet** is probably the most interesting of the three for its depiction of its owner, who was a treasury official, weighing gold. If you're in here, the **Tomb of Nefersekheru** is also worth a visit with its ceiling painted in a geometrical design. **Dhutmosi**'s final resting place is not in good shape these days, however.

Admission LE25.

Ramose, Userhet & Khaemet The **Tomb of Ramose** remains unfinished because its owner, who began his career under Amenhotep III, ended it under Akhenaten, the ruler who moved the capital from Thebes to Armana, disrupting not only public religious and administrative functions, but the private arrangements of his functionaries as well. This tomb is highly significant because both its style and content bridge the two periods, with the western wall showing some of the earliest depictions of Akhenaten worshiping the new god. The relief work is also exceptionally fine.

Userhet was a royal scribe and tutor in the reign of Amenhotep II. His tomb has fine depictions of winemaking, gazelle hunting, and hair cutting on the walls, while the heavy damage done to the scene of the funeral feast was done by early Coptic hermits. **Khaemet** was also a royal scribe, though he served the subsequent Pharaoh, Amenhotep III. His tomb's wall paintings include depictions of funerary nature and religious devotion as well as those of daily life in rural Egypt. Though attention has been given to meticulous details such as wig curls, which also applies to the Tomb of Ramose, the depictions are devoid of any color.

Admission LE25.

Rekhmire & Sennofer **Rekhmire** was a governor under Tuthmosis III and Amenhotep II, and came from a long line of governors. Depictions are in very good condition and follow the usual funerary theme. However, there is an unusual one depicting different tributes paid to Ancient Egypt by various foreign countries (incense trees and baboons from Punt, giraffes and ivory from Nubia, chariots and horses from Syria, and pots and vases from Crete). It sheds some light on the foreign politics of Ancient Egypt with its neighbors. **Sennofer** was an agricultural official and mayor of Thebes during Amenhotep II's reign. Depictions in his tomb are also in very good condition with the highlight of the collection being the grape and vine ones.

Admission LE25.

South of Luxor

Three main temples lie en route from Luxor to Aswan. Most Nile cruises stop on the way to visit them, but if you are not boarding one, you can always reach the temples overland. I would strongly recommend hiring a chauffeured car for the day (LE600) to take you from Luxor to Aswan and visit the three below temples on the way.

> **Tips** **Feluca Ride**
>
> If possible, you should save your *feluca* ride for Aswan, where the Nile is much wider, views are more scenic, and bird-watching is at its best. However, if you are not heading south, or feel compelled to go for a ride in Luxor and enjoy a view of the monuments from a different angle, there are plenty of sailboats lining both banks. How much you pay is a function of your bargaining skills; LE60 per hour plus an extra LE10 to LE20 to the pilot is a good deal.

Temple of Horus at Edfu ★★★ If I could see only one temple in Egypt, I would, without hesitation, choose this one. Because it was one of the last big temples to be built (it was started under Ptolemy III in about 237 B.C. and finished under Ptolemy XII about 140 years later) and was built well above the Nile and escaped flood damage, it's one of the best preserved. The temple is actually a reconstruction of an older building on the same site, and was part of the Ptolemaic project to solidify their dynastic hold on Upper Egypt by identifying themselves with the Pharaohs. Not only is the design a copy of the old temple, so are the inscriptions on the walls.

The temple was actually buried, like Luxor Temple, under the village when it was discovered by French Egyptologist Auguste Mariette in 1863. It took almost 40 years to clear it out entirely. A massive 36m-high (118-ft.) **First Pylon** welcomes you to the Temple of Horus. Similar to many other first pylons, this one depicts the propaganda relief with the mighty Pharaoh grabbing enemies, pleading for mercy, by their hair and about to chop off their heads. It opens to the temple's first court, where, on the opposite side, lies the entrance to the Outer Hypostyle Hall. Both this entrance and the main one are adorned with a pair of giant granite statues of Horus as a falcon. The 12-column Outer Hypostyle Hall leads to a roofed, 12-column Inner Hypostyle Hall, then to the Offering Hall, and lastly the Sanctuary. It follows, more or less, the standard Ancient Egyptian temple structure, despite this one being Ptolemaic. The key highlight of the temple is the **Passage of Victory,** a narrow corridor that goes around three sides of the temple between its walls and the enclosure's outer ones. Reliefs depict the triumph of Horus over Set, where the latter is portrayed as a small hippo often speared by Horus. At the height of the sanctimonious struggle, the temple priests are portrayed consuming a hippo, a metaphor for Set's defeat. There is also an amazing relief depicting the crowned Pharaoh accompanied by two ladies, Nekhbet (patron of Upper Egypt) and Wadjet (patron of Lower Egypt).

Edfu, about 110km (68 miles) south of Luxor. Admission LE50. Daily 7am–4pm.

Temple of Khnum at Esna ★ Located 54km (33 miles) south of Luxor, right in the middle of the small town of Esna, is the temple dedicated to the Nile God and protector of its source, Khnum. The building of the Greco-Roman Temple of Khnum took off during the reign of Ptolemy IV but was completed during the Roman Period. Approaching the temple from The Nile Street, you will go through a narrow alley bustling with shops before you arrive at a huge pit where the temple lies at a much lower level than the surrounding ground. Much of what remains today is the temple's 24-column hypostyle hall with its finely crafted columns' capitals; they vary in designs featuring papyrus and palm heads (Ancient Egyptian influence) as well as grapes (Roman influence). Reliefs are in very good condition and depict, in addition to the usual ceremonial temple rituals, scenes such as the triumphant Pharaoh slashing his enemies, the amused Pharaoh fishing in the company of the gods, and the gods being presented generous offerings.

Admission LE15. Daily 7am–4pm.

Temple of Kom Ombo Like its neighboring structure at Edfu, this is a Ptolemaic construction but has an unusual symmetrically twinned architecture in which the whole temple is mirrored around its central axis. Even from the First Pylon, there are twin entrances, followed by a twinned court, a twinned 10-column hypostyle hall, a twinned offering hall, and finally a twinned sanctuary. The temple is co-dedicated to two gods, Haroeris (an elder form of Horus who was the Solar War God) and Sobek (the Crocodile God of Fertility), which might be an explanation for the architectural symmetry. Real crocodiles, it's said, used to bask here, and there is even a small pool where the younger ones were taken care of and raised; mummified crocodiles were interred in crypts beneath the building. The highlight of your visit to the Temple of Kom Ombo is certainly the twinned **Sanctuary,** with its well-preserved reliefs that depict Ptolemy XII in various religious ceremonies as well as being crowned with the dual crown of Upper and Lower Egypt.

Apart from being the center of exalted rituals, it was also a place of healing, where ordinary people came to have their ailments tended to. If you look closely, you may still be able to find their graffiti scratched into the inside of the remains of the outer wall of the complex.

The unprepossessing town of Kom Ombo, which is about 4km (2½ miles) from the temple, is about 40km (25 miles) from Aswan to the south and 175km (110 miles) from Luxor to the north.

Admission LE30. Daily 7am–4pm.

North of Luxor

Temple of Hathor at Dendera Located on the western bank of the Nile about 60km (37 miles) north of Luxor, the Temple of Hathor at Dendera is a magnificently preserved temple you can't afford to miss. Built over the ruins of a much older one, the temple you see today was started during the 30th Dynasty but finished during the Roman Period, with most of the work carried out during the Ptolemaic one. The temple's entrance leads to a 24-column **Outer Hypostyle Hall,** which takes you to a smaller **Inner Hypostyle Hall** with six Hathor-headed stone columns. Some of the capitals were vandalized by intolerant Christians during the country's shift to Christianity; however, they still possess much of their faded charm. The **Hall of Offering** and **Sanctuary** are the nuclei of the temple where celebrating the New Year, coinciding with the annual inundation of the Nile, was marked by presenting offerings to Hathor before carrying his statue up to the roof. Reliefs of the holy procession are recorded on the western staircase.

The roof is actually the highlight of your visit, with its **Shrine of Osiris,** which hosts a plaster cast of the famous **Zodiac of Dendera** (see box, "Catch a Thief," below) on its ceiling. The disc is unique not only because it's the first-known representation of the stars in the form of the zodiac in Egypt, but also because it shows a very detailed arrangement of the night sky that allowed for precise dating of the temple's construction. Apart from its archaeological importance, it's also quietly beautiful and shows some particularly Egyptian twists (Virgo is represented by a figure that is probably Isis, and Cancer's crab replaced by a scarab).

Dendera is a popular day trip from Luxor with lots of transportation options. The best two are either by hiring a taxi (LE400–LE600) or taking a day cruise. The boats usually leave at 6am and return at 6pm. The round-trip should cost no less than LE400. Some Nile cruises include visiting this temple as part of their standard itineraries.

Admission LE35. Daily 6am–4pm.

WHERE TO STAY

Luxor enjoys a wide range of accommodation options, from the pampering spa suites at the Hilton to the basic rooms in El Fayrouz Hotel.

Very Expensive

Hilton Luxor Resort and Spa A 2008 renovation gave Luxor Hilton a fresh, head-turning look. The hotel's focus on wellness is seen in everything from the use of pastels to the slow-dripping fountains scattered throughout the property to the calorie indicator next to each buffet dish. Room interiors follow suit with locally inspired decorative motifs and period furniture designs. Guests have free access to the thermal area of the spa; spa suite guests have their own private healing room.

East Bank. ✆ **095/2399999.** Fax 095/2399928. www1.hilton.com. 236 units, including 10 suites and 2 rooms for people with special mobility. $360 garden-view double; $390 Nile-view double. Rack rates include buffet breakfast, taxes, and service charges. AE, DC, MC, V. **Amenities:** 3 restaurants; 5 bars; airport transfer (extra charge); babysitting and kids' club; concierge; health club and spa; 2 heated pools; room service; Wi-Fi (extra charge). *In room:* A/C, TV, minibar, Wi-Fi (extra charge).

Sofitel Old Winter Palace Overrated Dating back to the 19th century, the Sofitel Old Winter Palace has some real atmosphere despite a number of soulless renovations. The corridors are wide enough to drive a horse and carriage down, and the high ceilings and period furniture contribute to making this hotel something different in Luxor. The

Catch a Thief

The Zodiac of Dendera was first observed by Napoleon's savants at the end of the 19th century, and the massive map of the stars became the object of competition between the French and British in Egypt over the following 2 decades. It was ultimately nabbed by French antiquities dealer Sebastien-Louis Saulnier, who imported a master stonemason from France who used specially made tools, as well as a quantity of gunpowder, to remove the disc of stone, about 2.5m (8 ft.) in diameter and almost a meter (more than 3 ft.) thick, from the roof of the Shrine of Osiris at the Temple of Hathor at Dendera. After being paid the at-the-time exorbitant sum of 150,000 francs for the piece, Saulnier handed it over to the French state, and today it is on display at the Louvre in Paris.

Cruising the Nile

Sailing the Nile is a romantic dream that's as magical as you imagine it to be. Though the mighty river is indeed navigational, at least in Egypt, only two routes are open for tourism. The more demanded of the two is the classic Nile cruise that takes you from Luxor to Aswan, or vice versa, and varies from 4 to 7 days depending on what type of cruiser you choose. The menu has a few different options; the big, three-story cruisers are perfect if you want your own pool, gym, and perhaps a dancing hall, while the much smaller, 19th-century *dahabeeyas* offer more classic luxury that harks to the days of Agatha Christie's *Murder on the Nile.* Note, however, that the latter aren't recommended for those with kids due to the lack of space.

There are dozens of big cruisers lined next to each other at the docks along Luxor's Corniche El Nil; most of them offer the same thing at more or less the same price and with the same level of service. However, Oberoi's luxury cruiser, ***Zahra*** (© **02/33773222;** www.oberoihotels.com; 1,160€ per week all-inclusive double), stands out. It's a real treat that takes a full, leisurely week, giving you time to take advantage of the comprehensive onboard spa facilities. With only 27 suites, it's wise to book as far ahead as possible. As for slow-sailing *dahabeeyas,* **Belle Epoque Travel** (© **02/25169649;** www.dahabiya.com; 3,500€ per week all-inclusive double) runs six ultra chic and classy eight-cabin *dahabeeyas* with period pieces, antique fixtures, and handmade furniture. Each of the six boats come with its own theme; **El Bey** (a Turkish title that referred to high-ranking men during the Ottoman period) has rooms in honor of prominent Egyptian figures (Ahmed Zewail, Naguib Mahfouz, and Mohamed El Baradei), while the entire boat, from the wooden deck to the posh cabins and the chic dining room, are themed around royal aristocracy.

The other sailing route along the Nile is from Aswan southward to Abu Simbel along Lake Nasser. In contrast to the northern route, which revolves chiefly around historical sightseeing (see "South of Luxor," p. 279), this cruise's route has more free time to enjoy the surrounding nature, sunbathe, or watch the sunset with a gin and tonic in hand. In addition to the grand finale at the Temple of Abu Simbel, there are a couple of temples' ruins you will see on the way (see "The Last of the Nubian Temples," p. 299). **Belle Epoque Travel** (© **02/25169649;** www.eugenie.com.eg; 1,500€ all-inclusive double for 4-day cruise) operates the *M/S Eugenie* and *M/S Kasr Ibrim.* The two cruisers might be less luxurious than the company's *dahabeeyas,* but they are just as charming with their elegant interiors and the warm hospitality of their crews.

gardens are neatly kept and extensive, and they're especially pleasant in the cool of the evening. This hotel is also more wheelchair accessible than most and has wheelchair-equipped rooms. Prices are too high for the sometimes lax service and unremarkable food, but you're paying for the past at the Sofitel Old Winter Palace and not the present. I recommend dipping into its charms for an expensive tea or drink in the garden and staying somewhere else.

Corniche El Nil. ✆ **095/2380425.** Fax 095/2374087. www.sofitel.com. 92 units, including 6 suites. 310€ garden-view double; 375€ Nile-view double. Rack rates include buffet breakfast, taxes, and service charges. AE, DC, MC, V. **Amenities:** 4 restaurants; 3 bars; airport transfer (extra charge); concierge; health club; pool; room service; Wi-Fi (extra charge). *In room:* A/C, TV, Internet (extra charge), minibar.

Expensive

Al Moudira ★★★ This marvelous, one-of-a-kind boutique hotel on the quiet West Bank of the Nile is easily the best hotel in Luxor and certainly one of the 10 best in Egypt. Its traditional-style buildings are spread gracefully over extensive grounds, with domes, arches, and fountains fitting together in relaxing harmony. The construction has incorporated beautiful period pieces, including old doors, *mashrabeya* screens, and stone basins, and each room is an individual creation decorated with paintings, carpets, and tiles. I love the carefully designed gardens, where jasmine hangs gracefully over the walled courtyards and palms whisper in the desert breeze, but fans of bowling green–style lawns may be disappointed. The hotel is located far from the hubbub and tourist hassles of the East Bank, but transport is easily arranged, and 30 minutes should be enough to put you back into the land of bright lights, loud music, and crowds. My advice on this one is if you can afford it, bite the bullet and go for it.

West Bank. ✆ **095/2551440.** Fax 095/2551484. www.moudira.com. 54 units. 220€ double. Rate includes buffet breakfast, taxes, and service charges. AE, MC, V. **Amenities:** Restaurant; 2 bars; airport transfer (extra charge); babysitting; health club; pool, Wi-Fi. *In room:* A/C, TV, minibar.

Maritim Jolie Ville Luxor Resort Kids If you're traveling with children, the Jolie Ville is *the* place to stay in Luxor. Located on an island 15 minutes by taxi south of the town, the hotel has a range of features to keep the kids occupied while you relax in the nicest Nile-side horizon pool in Luxor or trek through the Valley of the Queens. The Maritim has pleasant rooms distributed in a series of shady bungalows surrounding the main building and connected to it with covered walkways. Each room has a small seating area out front, but Nile views are in the minority and fill up first, so book well in advance if this is a priority. Kid-friendly features include an all-day kids' club with activities such as pottery painting and donkey races, a small zoo (some farm animals, but it does have monkeys and a crocodile), and a lifeguard at the pool.

Kings Island. ✆ **095/2374855.** Fax 095/2374936. www.jolieville-hotels.com. 326 units. $245 garden-view double; $265 Nile-view double. Rack rates include buffet breakfast, taxes, and service charges. AE, MC, V. **Amenities:** 2 restaurants; 2 bars; airport transfer (extra charge); babysitting and kids' club; concierge; health club; Internet (extra charge); 2 pools; room service; 4 tennis courts. *In room:* A/C, TV, minibar, Wi-Fi (extra charge).

Sheraton Luxor One of the nicest features of the Sheraton Luxor is its location—most of its competition either backs onto a busy road or looks over it, but the Sheraton is surrounded by gardens and fronts the Nile. The result is a quiet and very relaxing atmosphere. The architecture, which is supposed to mirror a cruise ship, isn't going to win any awards (frankly, it looks like it was built out of LEGO blocks), and though the fit and finish of the rooms aren't quite up to the Steigenberger standard, they're acceptable on the whole. The other thing that the Sheraton does well—and this goes for most of its facilities in Egypt—is the friendly, relaxed service it offers.

Khalid Ibn El Walid St. ✆ **095/2274544.** www.sheraton.com/luxor. 290 units. $160 garden-view double; $180 Nile-view double. Rack rates include buffet breakfast, taxes, and service charges. AE, MC, V. **Amenities:** 3 restaurants; 2 bars; airport transfer (extra charge); babysitting; concierge; health club; 2 pools (heated, including kids' pool); room service; 2 tennis courts; Wi-Fi (extra charge). *In room:* A/C, TV, minibar, Wi-Fi (extra charge).

Steigenberger Nile Palace This may be the quintessential cookie-cutter hotel, but it does it well. Rooms are spic and span, the food is inoffensive, and the view from the pool and barbecue area is one of the best in Luxor. Standard (as opposed to Nile-view) rooms look down onto the enclosed central courtyard of the hotel, which is used at night for entertainment, so watch out for noise. The only facility that really lets the hotel down is the gym, which, while sufficient, is smaller and more basic than it should be.

Khalid Ibn El Walid St. ✆ **095/2366999.** Fax 095/2365666. www.luxor.steigenberger.com. 304 units, including 19 suites. 92€ double; 122€ Nile-view double. Rack rates include buffet breakfast, taxes, and service charges. AE, MC, V. **Amenities:** 4 restaurants; 2 bars; airport transfer (extra charge); concierge; health club; 2 pools (1 kids); room service; tennis court; Wi-Fi. *In room:* TV, Internet (some units, extra charge), minibar.

Moderate

El Nakhil Tucked away in the heart of the rural West Bank, this is a little hotel that really punches above its weight. At the same price as several cheaper places, it offers substantially more than its competition. Rooms are spacious and feature nice local touches such as traditional *mashrabeya* screens and domed ceilings in some. This is also the only hotel that I know of on the West Bank that's wheelchair accessible, with ramps from the street and to the ground-floor rooms. One room is wheelchair-equipped. They can also provide appropriate van transport from the airport.

Gezirat Al Baraat, West Bank. ✆ **095/2313922.** Fax 095/2314670. www.el-nakhil.com. 20 units, including for people with special mobility. 35€ double. Rate includes breakfast, taxes, and service charges. No credit cards. **Amenities:** Restaurant; airport transfer (extra charge); Internet. *In room:* A/C, TV (in some), no phone (in some).

Nile Valley Kids It's not the greatest midrange hotel in Luxor, but the Nile Valley is probably the most kid-friendly place on the West Bank. The rooms are basic, clean doubles and triples with windows placed too high for good light, but most look down on the swimming pool. There is a kids' pool, too, and the restaurant is fun, moderately priced, and has good food. There is one room with a kitchenette, and though it's pitched by the hotel as a family room, take note that it's simply a triple with three single beds.

West Bank. ✆ **095/2311477.** www.nilevalley.nl. 18 units. LE238 double. Rate includes breakfast, taxes, and service charges. No credit cards. **Amenities:** Restaurant; bar; pool. *In room:* TV, minifridge.

Nour Al Balad Nour Al Balad is trying, with some success, to be a budget Al Moudira. Behind an unprepossessing facade lies a traditional-style building with high ceilings, arched doorways, and straw-thatched ceilings. Nour Al Balad is located on the edge of the desert and doesn't have air-conditioning, so avoid it during the summer months (try mid- to late Oct, when the weather cools).

Two big rooms at the front of the hotel have an unobstructed sunset view of the rocky cliffs that edge the Nile Valley, and those at the back overlook green fields and a small village. These front rooms will seem overpriced to those who aren't taken with the charm of the large, airy rooms with a four-poster bed, desert view, and colorfully tiled bathroom. Other rooms are better value for money, and since they vary in size and view as well as price, you would be wise to check out everything that's available before making a decision. It's possible to hike to many of the antiquities, including Valley of the Kings, in a couple of hours from the front door.

West Bank. ✆ **095/2311430.** 14 units. LE250 double. Rate includes breakfast, taxes, and service charges. No credit cards. **Amenities:** Restaurant. *In room:* Fan, no phone.

Susanna Hotel ★★ This is a good midrange option in proximity to about everywhere you would want to go, from the souk and the West Bank ferry to the train station and Sofra Restaurant. Susanna Hotel minimizes transportation costs, which can easily add up if you are going to use taxis. Rooms are clean and come in three different price categories depending on what they overlook. Go for the highest priced ones, as they offer spectacular views of Luxor Temple, especially at night.

52 Karnak Temple St. ✆ **095/2369915.** Fax 095/2369904. susannahotel_luxor@hotmail.com. 45 units. $30–$40 double. Rates include breakfast, taxes, and service charges. No credit cards. **Amenities:** Restaurant; bar; pool. *In room:* A/C, TV, minifridge, Wi-Fi (extra charge).

Budget

El Fayrouz Hotel ★★ At the low end of the moderate price range, the Fayrouz is very accommodating and stacks up well against other locations costing substantially more. The building is new, and rooms are large and clean. There is a large, quiet garden restaurant with good shade. The other big plus of the Fayrouz is that it's located in an almost entirely hassle-free location on the West Bank. The road outside is unpaved and serves as a playground for children from the surrounding homes; the atmosphere is almost that of a tranquil village. Rooms come with either a street or garden view; I would certainly go for the greener of the two.

Gezira Al Bairat, West Bank. ✆ **095/2312709.** www.elfayrouz.com. 23 units. LE130 street-view double; LE160 garden-view double. Rates include breakfast, taxes, and service charges. No credit cards. **Amenities:** Restaurant; Internet (extra charge). *In room:* A/C (in some), no phone.

Marsam ★ One of the West Bank's oldest hotels, Marsam was, and probably still is, quite famous among backpackers and archaeologists on excavation missions. A large, traditional two-story house turned hotel, Marsam greets you with the warmth of home (the friendly Australian resident manager will welcome you in person). Some rooms are very spacious, while others are stuffed with up to three beds; however, all are neat and clean, and come with very basic furniture. Marsam means "the drawing place" in Arabic, and the hotel frequently hosts art exhibitions.

West Bank. ✆ **095/2372403.** 30 units. LE160 double. Rate includes breakfast, taxes, and service charges. No credit cards. **Amenities:** Restaurant; Wi-Fi. *In room:* No phone.

WHERE TO EAT

Luxor's culinary scene covers a wide range of options, from authentic traditional to a fast-food joint with a "wow" view.

Africa EGYPTIAN This small rooftop restaurant has lovely views of the Nile and the East Bank. The decor is a tacky mix of pieces that vary from local rural wall sketches to a dusty Spanish guitar, but the homemade Egyptian dishes they serve make the place worth going to. For lunch and dinner, it's a set menu that includes rice, a vegetable stew (usually potatoes), some *tahina* salad, a chicken or meat entree, and seasonal fruit for dessert. The place also has a strong breakfast of *fuul, tameya,* cheese, and eggs; you'll have enough energy to monument-hop all day.

West Bank. ✆ **095/2311488.** Breakfast LE15; lunch/dinner LE45. No credit cards. Daily 8am–midnight.

Broodje Holland ★ Finds INTERNATIONAL This is a tiny restaurant with only four tables and an open kitchen where you will see the owner, chef, and waiter prepare your food. The place is homey, while the menu is a bizarre mix of Dutch, English,

 Egyptian, and even Indonesian dishes. The chef's favorite is the Indonesian Nasi Satay, where baked rice is cooked with dried shrimp powder, chili, and beef or chicken. The dining experience is different from anywhere else in Luxor and worth the hop to the outskirts where it is located.

Al Roda Al Sharifa St., off Khalid Ibn El Walid St. Appetizers LE20–LE30; main courses LE35–LE50. No credit cards. Daily 10am–10pm.

El Kababgy EGYPTIAN This is a great place for lunch, especially if you're staying on one of the cruise boats that dock below Luxor Temple. Located below the Corniche, and between it and the Nile, the restaurant is quiet and more or less hassle-free. Better yet, it looks over a small *feluca* dock, so your view is unobstructed by the massive boats that blight much of the waterfront here. The outside seating has the best view and is protected from the sun by an awning; inside the atmosphere is pleasant with tiled floors, dark wood trim, and paintings of local scenes. The menu is an unremarkable mix of grilled chicken and pizza, but the grilled fish is excellent. They serve local beers and sunset cocktails, but if sundowners are what you're after, try the Cocktail Sunset Bar a couple of hundred meters to the north.

Corniche El Nil. ✆ **010/2666620.** Appetizers LE20–LE30; main courses LE40–LE95. No credit cards. Daily 10am–1am.

Oasis Café INTERNATIONAL This is a great little place for sandwiches, coffee, and dessert. Located in a renovated old building with loads of character, high ceilings, and a unique collection of local art on the walls, it's a rare example of a place with a sense of history that offers modern service and excellent food. It makes for a great meet-up place to have a chat with friends, but it misses big time on the view with an indoor seating area overlooking another city street.

Dr. Labib Habashi St. ✆ **095/2372914.** Appetizers LE15–LE35; main courses LE40–LE55. No credit cards. Daily 10am–10pm.

Sabroso FAST FOOD Sabroso is a typical fast-food joint with no edge, but you can opt for a quick bite, a cup of coffee, or to check your e-mail (if you have your laptop; Wi-Fi is free) if you arrive early for your departing train; it's opposite Luxor Train Station.

Opposite to the train station. ✆ **095/2388000.** Sandwiches LE10–LE25. No credit cards. Daily 9am–2am.

Snack Time & The Roof FAST FOOD/EGYPTIAN As the name hints, this is a good place to grab a quick bite after you're done with Luxor Temple but before resuming your city tour. Snack Time serves an eclectic fast-food menu, while the Roof strictly serves Egyptian dishes. The building's rooftop offers lovely views of Luxor Temple and the Nile, especially around sunset. Both Snack Time and the Roof have free Wi-Fi.

In front of the Mosque of Abu el Haggag, Luxor Temple. ✆ **095/2375405.** Snack Time: sandwiches LE10–LE25. The Roof: appetizers LE10–LE25; main courses LE25–LE40. No credit cards. Snack Time daily 8:30am–2am. The Roof daily 12:30pm–2am.

Sofra ★★★ EGYPTIAN Sofra not only has the best Egyptian food in Luxor, but one of the nicest settings as well. The restaurant is located on a crowded and dusty back road off Al Manshiya Street, close to the train station, and features *mashrabeya* screens, traditional lanterns hanging from the ceiling, and lovely period floor tiling. There's an air-conditioned, slightly more formal area downstairs and a relaxed rooftop area that features low round tables, old chests, and little colored domes. Start your meal with plates of the best hummus, baba ghanouj, and *tahina* in Upper Egypt, and probably the whole country, or the signature Kebdet Sofra (veal liver flambéed with onion, lemon, garlic, and lots of herbs). Kamonia, veal stewed in spicy tomato sauce with onion and cumin, is a winning main course. The menu features enough variety to keep you busy for quite a few nights and it includes a couple of seafood and vegetarian dishes such as Sayadeyet Gambary (oven-baked shrimp in coriander, parsley, and tomato) and eggplant casserole.

90 Mohamed Farid St. ✆ **095/2359752.** www.sofra.com.eg. Appetizers LE10–LE25; main courses LE25–LE60. No credit cards. Daily 11am–11pm.

SHOPPING

Unless you are looking for a T-shirt with your name written in hieroglyphs, a stuffed toy camel, or a bag of overpriced saffron, the Luxor shopping scene is going to be a bit of a letdown. However, if you are, then you're in for a treat—the heavily touristy **souk** behind Luxor Temple is bursting with stalls full of repro figurines, cheap water pipes, and souvenir shirts and hats. **Habiba** (Sidi Mahmoud St., next to Susanna Hotel; ✆ **095/2357305**) is one of the few places in Luxor where fixed prices really stick. It offers uniquely designed T-shirts and a wide range of handmade embroidery and textiles you won't come across elsewhere in Luxor. **Nile Shopping Center,** on Corniche El Nil next to El Kababgy, has better-looking handicrafts and a specialized textile shop that sells some excellent *khayameya* (p. 119) pieces if you've missed buying in Cairo. **Akhmim Fabric Store** (Corniche El Nil, closer to Karnak Temple; ✆ **018/3829677**) stocks a small but tasteful range of high-quality cloth from Akhmim, a Nile Valley town close to Sohag.

LUXOR AFTER DARK

There is no shortage of drinking places in Luxor, where every midrange and high-end hotel has at least one place to hoist a cold one. However, partygoers are left stranded in Luxor's classic nightlife scene.

J J's Bar This is a good option if you're stuck in this part of town (Luxor's northern end) and looking for a good place to have a couple of drinks without breaking the bank (the Hilton is right next door if you wish to break it). There's nothing spectacular about the interior, but the place gets a kick with live performances several nights a week. If you miss the crowds, a chitchat with the English couple who owns and operates the place can be a good option. Closed Wednesday. Off Hilton St. ✆ **016/4263878.** www.jjsbarkarnak.com.

King's Head Pub Finding a real pub in this part of the world is rare, but King's Head gets it right. The brainchild of a local entrepreneur, the pub is decorated with a mix of Princess Diana memorabilia and odds and ends from around Egypt. The effect is homey, a little down-market, and a bit odd, but all in the right proportions. Oh, and the food's not bad either. Open daily 11am to midnight. Khalid Ibn El Walid St. ✆ **095/2380489.**

Metropolitan Bowling Club The name of this place does not mislead; the Metropolitan has the only bowling lanes in Luxor. Located on the banks of the Nile, just next door to El Kababgy (which supplies food here as needed), this place is outfitted with dark wood and plush furnishings, and the bar serves local and imported liquor and has a small espresso machine. The flip side of the place is a small disco with a large plasma-screen TV, so you'll have something to do while you wait for a lane (there are only two) to open up. Open daily 11am to 2am. Corniche El Nil. ✆ **095/2386543.**

2 ASWAN

After an intense dose of history and historical sites in Luxor, laidback Aswan comes as an appreciated break with the right amount of sightseeing. Start with the amazing Nubian Museum to get a full background of the place, its people, and their culture, followed by a visit to the impressive Temple Complex of Philae. Island-hopping is one of my favorite activities in Aswan; head to Kitchner's Island for its one-of-a-kind botanical garden or to Elephantine for a close-up peek into the daily life of resettled Nubians, and finish with lunch at El Dokka restaurant. The Tombs of the Nobles will whet your appetite for outdoor excursions, but a trek to the Monastery of St. Simeon will certainly leave you full. The Nile here is ocean-wide with a vibrant blue color and frequent appearance of grayish boulders rising from the river's bed; ideal for a picturesque *feluca* ride.

Aswan is located at the strategically vital chokepoint of the first cataracts on the Nile. It has the feel of being somehow at the limit of Egypt—the place where Egypt ends and Africa begins. It also makes for a perfect base if you are up for some off-the-beaten-track type of adventures into Lake Nasser, or a more timid lake cruise to watch Abu Simbel's famous solstice. Twice a year, the sun shines on the face of a congregation of Ancient Egyptian gods seated deep into the rock-cut temple, which is worth planning your trip around.

ESSENTIALS

Getting There

BY PLANE Unless you're particularly fond of train travel, or you are on a tight budget that makes time less important than money, flying is the best way to get to Aswan. There are upwards of 10 flights a day out of Cairo, and the 75-minute flight costs about LE800. The surprisingly pleasant and modern airport is outside town. If you haven't arranged a transfer with your hotel beforehand, negotiate the 25km (15-mile) ride with one of the waiting taxis. You may be able to do better, but I would expect to pay upwards of LE60.

BY TRAIN The train is the most pleasant way to arrive in Aswan, which is only about 3 hours from Luxor via train. Coming from Cairo, the sleeper is the same price as for Luxor, and departure times are the same as well (p. 263); however, arrival is 3 hours later. From Aswan, the **Abela sleeper trains** (© **097/2302124;** www.sleepingtrains.com) depart at 5, 6:30, and 8:30pm. Only train no. 85, which departs at 6:30pm, has the option of first-class seats (LE165). From Luxor to Aswan, you can always pick up the train originally coming from Cairo and pay LE40 to LE70 for the ticket; however, the train often arrives late, so expect delays. As with any train travel in Egypt, take a warm sweater (even in the summer); the air-conditioning is always set to arctic. In Aswan, the train station is at the edge of the souk, and there are several hotels within an easy walk as well as plenty of taxis.

BY BOAT Aswan is the southern terminal for the numerous cruise boats that shuttle between here and Luxor, or here and Abu Simbel. For more information on Nile cruise options, see p. 282.

BY BUS Buses might not be the best option (trains are) when it comes to traveling between Aswan and Luxor or Cairo, but they are a good option when it comes to Abu Simbel and Hurghada. Each is served with two buses a day and tickets cost LE25 (Abu Simbel) and LE50 (Hurghada). In Aswan, the bus station is around 4km (2½ miles) from

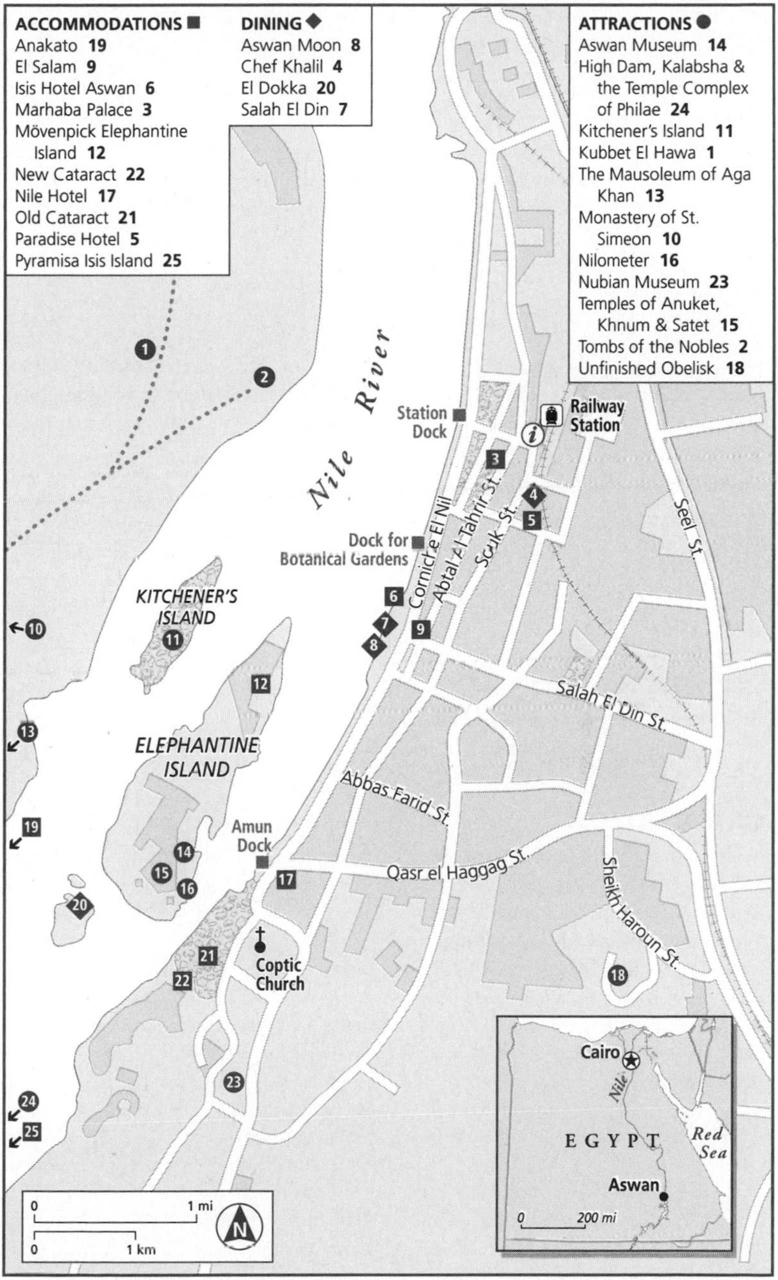

ACCOMMODATIONS ■
Anakato **19**
El Salam **9**
Isis Hotel Aswan **6**
Marhaba Palace **3**
Mövenpick Elephantine Island **12**
New Cataract **22**
Nile Hotel **17**
Old Cataract **21**
Paradise Hotel **5**
Pyramisa Isis Island **25**

DINING ◆
Aswan Moon **8**
Chef Khalil **4**
El Dokka **20**
Salah El Din **7**

ATTRACTIONS ●
Aswan Museum **14**
High Dam, Kalabsha & the Temple Complex of Philae **24**
Kitchener's Island **11**
Kubbet El Hawa **1**
The Mausoleum of Aga Khan **13**
Monastery of St. Simeon **10**
Nilometer **16**
Nubian Museum **23**
Temples of Anuket, Khnum & Satet **15**
Tombs of the Nobles **2**
Unfinished Obelisk **18**

Nile River

Station Dock

Railway Station

Dock for Botanical Gardens

Corniche El Nil

Abtal el-Tahrir St.

Seel St.

Scuk St.

Salah El Din St.

KITCHENER'S ISLAND

ELEPHANTINE ISLAND

Abbas Farid St.

Amun Dock

Qasr el Haggag St.

Sheikh Haroun St.

Coptic Church

N

0 1 mi
0 1 km

EGYPT
Cairo
Nile
Red Sea
Aswan

0 200 mi

UPPER EGYPT

10

ASWAN

the middle of town. There are plenty of taxis around the station to negotiate your trip into town, which should cost you about LE30.

BY CAR Hypothetically speaking, you can get to Aswan by car; however, it is not the most practical option unless you are fine with driving about 1,000km (620 miles) from Cairo on a single-carriage road notorious for its daily accidents.

Getting Around

BY TAXI Aswan is stuffed with taxis, usually old Peugeot station wagons that are guaranteed to wallow gently over the creased and pitted tarmac. Prices are on par with Luxor, which is to say higher than Cairo, but drivers are a lot mellower when it comes to negotiation. Expect to pay LE20 to LE30 for longer distances within town and LE5 to LE10 for shorter distances.

BY MINIBUS They run from one end of Corniche El Nil Street to the other, as well as to the bus station. Fares are LE0.50 on average.

BY BIKE Biking is a great away to get around Aswan. There are rental places scattered about—look for clusters of bikes near a kiosk—but around the train station, heading up toward the souk, is a good place to start. Expect to pay LE20 to LE40 per day for the use of a rattling, squeaking, single-speed with bad brakes.

ON FOOT If the weather is reasonably cool, Aswan is eminently walkable.

BY FERRY Since some of the attractions are located on the West Bank and the city of Aswan is located on the East Bank, you are bound to use the ferry. Along Corniche El Nil Street there are three different ferry docks: Station Dock, Marsa El Mahta, from where you'll pick up the ferry heading to the Tombs of the Nobles and Kubbet El Hawa; Dock for the Botanical Garden, Marsa El Nabatat, where the ferry goes to Kitchener's Island and the Botanical Garden; and lastly Amun Dock, Marsa Amun, where you get the ferry heading to Elephantine Island. Tickets for any of the three ferries cost LE1. Alternatively, you can always rent a speed boat if you don't wish to wait for the ferry to fill up. The fare just to cross to the other side averages LE10 to LE20. It is significantly higher than in Luxor, as the Nile in Aswan, characterized by rocks and boulders, is much more difficult to navigate.

ORIENTATION

Aswan is pretty simple to get around. There are just three main streets, and they run parallel to the Nile on its eastern bank. Corniche El Nil, as the name suggests, runs along the water. Abtal Al Tahrir Street, a mixed shopping and residential street, is the first street inland, and then there's Souk Street, which is where the shopping is. The famous Old Cataract Hotel could be considered the southern end of the town, while the bus station is almost at its northern end.

The West Bank is scarcely inhabited, but hosts a couple of sites you might be interested in visiting, namely the Valley of the Nobles, Monastery of St. Simeon, and the Mausoleum of Aga Khan. A couple of Nile islands, Elephantine and Kitchener's, also pose as enticing attractions. Getting to the sites by boat is nearly half the fun.

Around 5km (3½ miles) south of the city lies the original Aswan Dam, now more than 100 years old, and another 7km (4½ miles) south is the famous Aswan High Dam, built in the late 1960s. Between the two dams lies the little island of Agilkia, site of the transplanted temples of Philae. Almost 300km (186 miles) farther south lies the famous Temple of Ramses II, lifted out of the Nile Valley and repositioned at Abu Simbel on the edge of Lake Nasser.

Tourist Information

The **tourist information office** (© **097/2312811**) is immediately to your right as you emerge from the train station in the direction of the Nile. It's open daily 8:30am to 2pm and 6 to 8pm, while on Fridays it opens midmorning (after the Fri prayers). The man in charge speaks very good English and can be of some help. However, if you are looking for something more informative than tourist brochures (the tourist information office will hand you a couple), then head to **Nubia Tourist Book Center** (Souk St.; © **011/4119777**; open 9am–midnight). It stocks a comprehensive selection of books covering Egypt in general and its Pharaonic history in specific. The collection comes mainly in English, though French, Italian, and German titles are also available. The bookstore has maps of Aswan and Egypt, as well as DVDs and postcards. Nubia Tourist Book Center has two more branches at the Unfinished Obelisk site and at the Dock for the Botanical Garden.

Places for **Internet** are around every corner, especially in side streets off Souk Street. Signs are mostly in Arabic, so ask around. Expect to pay LE10 an hour.

WHAT TO SEE & DO

Aswan is often mistaken to be Luxor on a smaller scale, but this perception is deceiving. While Luxor is the epicenter of Ancient Egyptian heritage, Aswan takes a different turn with a more diverse bouquet of attractions; see the Monastery of St. Simeon via camelback, or grab your binoculars for Aswan's diverse bird-watching scene.

Elephantine Island One of the largest Nile islands, Elephantine hosts a 3,000-strong Nubian community that resettled here after the flooding of their hometowns as a result of the High Dam. Today, you can visit their village to get a glimpse of their life amidst the sprawling zigzag alleys, colorful walls and doors, and distinctive Nubian architecture. Elephantine also plays host to a number of historical sites.

Located on the northern end of the island, **Aswan Museum** opened in 1912, but has lost much of the good stuff in its collection to the new Nubian Museum (p. 293), and the few mummies and sculptures that are left are unremarkable. The building that houses the collection, which belonged to the architect of the Aswan Dam, Sir William Willcocks,

Come Low Water

Coming in from the airport, or heading out to Abu Simbel, you will cross the Nile on a 2.5km (1½-mile) dam made of local granite. This is the original Aswan Dam, built by the British between 1898 and 1902. The house belonging to the lead engineer on the project is now the Aswan Museum, located on the southern end of Elephantine Island. The dam is an impressive feat of engineering when you consider that it was built more than a century ago and is still being used. Water flow through the dam was controlled by 180 sluice gates, which were raised and lowered with a crane that slid back and forth as needed.

It was originally built 30m (100 ft.) high, but it was raised twice after it became apparent that this was not enough, and ended up 42m (138 ft.) high at the outbreak of World War II. It almost overflowed during the 1946 inundation, but instead of a third phase of expansion, it was decided to build a second dam upstream.

is worth a few minutes for its architecture, while the new annex contains some interesting items dug up on the island itself.

At the back of the Aswan Museum's garden lie the two badly ruined temples of Khnum and Anuket, as well as the recently reconstructed Temple of Satet. The **Temple of Khnum** is believed to have been built by Hatshepsut and dedicated to Khnum, the Nile God who was the guardian of the Nile source, and often depicted with the body of a man and the head of a ram. His cult was concentrated around Aswan and Esna, where a temple, also dedicated to him, is in a much better state and can be visited today (p. 280). The **Temple of Anuket,** who was Khnum's daughter, is in complete ruins, while the **Temple of Satet,** Khnum's wife, has been recently reconstructed and has a couple of reliefs that could be of interest.

The Nile was an important element in the life of Ancient Egyptians, and its inundation was a crucial one; it directly impacted agriculture as well as taxes. Many Nilometers were constructed to measure the flood, among which is the Ptolemaic **Nilometer,** the more interesting of two such devices for measuring the level of the Nile on the island. If you have a flashlight with you, descend the stairs from the Aswan Museum; otherwise, check it out from the boat on the way back. From there you can see the inscribed cartouches of Tuthmosis III and Amenhotep III.

Elephantine Island. ✆ **097/2313628.** Admission LE30 (includes museum, Nilometer, and all three temples; the Nubian Village is free). Daily 9am–4pm.

Kitchener's Island This small island, between Elephantine Island and the West Bank, was turned into a botanical garden by Lord Horatio Kitchener in the late 19th century. It is well worth a visit if you're in need of a quiet stroll along palm-lined walkways or have a zeal for botany; however, it's best avoided on Fridays when it can become quite noisy and crowded. The second dock along Corniche El Nil Street, dubbed the Dock for Botanical Garden, takes you from Aswan to Kitchener's Island.

Admission LE10. Daily 8am–4pm.

Kubbet El Hawa A brief scramble above the Tombs of the Nobles is the small tomb of a local sheikh, Sidi Ali. The structure itself is nothing to write home about, but the view from the edge of the desert back over Aswan is worth the climb.

West Bank.

Outdoors in Aswan

The Nile in Aswan is different from anywhere else farther north; here it is marked with big gray boulders that add a touch of dynamic beauty to the scenic view. A *feluca* ride, especially around sunset, is a serene way to admire and appreciate the natural beauty of the place. If you're into bird-watching, it's better to go for one of the speed boats, which enables you to cover more distance in less time. Ask the pilot to go to Saluga and Ghazal, two river islands that are awash with birds. They were declared a natural protectorate in 1986 and offer an opportunity to watch a long list of birds that includes cormorants, herons, moorhens, gallinules, and ibises. Make sure your camera batteries are fully charged. Expect to pay LE60, plus an extra LE10 to LE20 for the pilot, for a 1-hour *feluca* ride, while a 1- to 1½-hour tour of Saluga and Ghazal costs LE80 to LE120.

The Mausoleum of Aga Khan From any high point in Aswan, you can see what looks like a single isolated Fatimid tomb high up on the opposite bank. This, in fact, is the final resting place of the 48th leader of the Ismailis, Muhamed Shah Aga Khan III, and his French wife, Begum Aga Khan. He predeceased her by a considerable margin, dying in 1957. She kept a lonely vigil, placing a red rose on his sarcophagus every day until her death in 2000. Though it's a long walk up and the mausoleum itself was still closed to visitors at press time, the view from the top is stunning.

West Bank.

Monastery of St. Simeon About a kilometer (½ mile) into the desert from the boat dock on the West Bank, the ruins of the Monastery of St. Simeon remain 8 centuries after it was heavily damaged by Salah El Din's troops back in 1173. What you see here, in fact, are the remains of a 10th-century rebuilding of a 7th-century monastery that was dedicated to St. Hadra, Bishop of Aswan. At the height of its power, this fortress-monastery (it was surrounded by a 10m/33-ft.-high wall) housed 300 monks and had guest accommodations for up to 100. Inside the basilica there are fading frescoes that can still be seen, while on the second floor you can visit the old cells with their rock-hard sleeping benches.

The walk up to the monastery from the dock takes about 30 minutes. On the other hand, you can usually hire a camel and guide at the boat dock; your bargaining skills should get you within the LE40 to LE70 range.

West Bank. Admission LE20. Daily 8am–4pm.

Nubian Museum ★★★ This is a modern interpretation of the word "museum" and an utter contrast to the Egyptian Museum in Cairo. The large complex on the hill near the old granite quarries houses an enormous number of the artifacts that were saved from being inundated after the High Dam was finished in 1971. The exhibits are arranged chronologically, starting with prehistoric rock carvings and simple hand tools, and running through the successive dynasties of Egyptian domination, the arrival of the Ptolemies and the Romans, and finally the Islamic period, before coming to an abrupt halt with the construction of the dam. The "modern Nubia" section is particularly poignant, with a lovely display of gold and silver jewelry that underscores the cultural sophistication of the land that has vanished. The statues and artifacts that date from the Ancient Egyptian era are peculiarly different from the same period artifacts found anywhere else in Egypt; note the individuality of the statues and their different physique.

It's worth visiting the Nubian Museum before doing anything else in the area, simply to give context to everything that you see. Reckon on spending an hour here.

El Fanadek St. ✆ **097/2319222.** www.numibia.net. Admission LE50. Daily 9am–9pm

Tombs of the Nobles Looking across the river from Aswan, just over to the right of the massive tower of the Mövenpick Elephantine Island, you should be able to make out little black specks in the face of the golden-brown cliff. These are the Tombs of the Nobles, the final resting place of the officials who ran Aswan and controlled the lucrative trade with Nubia and Sudan. In terms of execution and quality, the experts will tell you that these are inferior to those found to the north (they pale in comparison to the royal tombs of the Valley of the Kings). I think, however, that the setting adds a certain something here and that, after a trek up the steep slippery path from the boat dock, these tombs, not to mention the view back eastward to the land of the living, are a pretty rewarding experience.

Most of the tombs remain closed, and many have sanded up inside or collapsed altogether. Of the open tombs, the most interesting is probably **Sirenput II.** The owner was a governor under the 12th-dynasty Pharaoh Amenemhet II. It's worth making your way to the burial chamber at the back of the tomb for illustrations of Sirenput with his family. The next tomb along is also a good one. The owner, named **Harkhuf,** was another governor who led several trading expeditions to the south and brought back what he described as a "dancing pygmy" to the delight of the Pharaoh. A letter from the Pharaoh is transcribed on the wall exhorting Harkhuf to hurry to the royal court with the pygmy, but to take care of him on his way and surround him with trusty men so that he wouldn't fall into the Nile or tumble from his hammock in the night. If the New Kingdom **Tomb of Kakemkew** is open, it's worth a look as well. It was discovered by Howard Carter about 20 years before the opening of Tutankhamun's considerably more illustrious tomb at the Valley of the Kings, which made him famous, and there are notable illustrations of funerary rites and mourning family that adorn the walls. For a different wall painting than the usual funerary nature, head to the 6th dynasty **Tomb of Mekhu and Sibni** for its depiction of a fishing scene.

West Bank. Admission LE30. Daily 9am–4pm.

Unfinished Obelisk This 42m (138-ft.) slab of granite partially cut from the rock of an ancient quarry was probably destined to become the biggest column in Karnak. Masons discovered a flaw in the stone, however, and the project was abandoned, leaving the obelisk-to-be still attached on one side. Maybe the most impressive aspect of it is that its makers were fully prepared to cut loose this massive rock (it would have weighed in at more than 1,100 tons), drag it down to the water, and barge it several hundred kilometers down the river with nothing more than some levers, ropes, and a whole lot of manpower.

Admission LE30. Daily 9am–4pm.

South of Aswan

Until the 1970s, there was a whole region between Aswan and Sudan. With the completion of the High Dam in 1971, however, and the subsequent flooding of the river valley, Nubia was inundated and submerged beneath more than 5,000 sq. km. (almost 2,000 sq. miles) of water that was named Lake Nasser. (Actually, only the Egyptian portion of

Come High Water

Completed in 1971 with the help of the erstwhile Soviet Union, the High Dam was a nationalist dream for then-President Gamal Abdel Nasser, who died the previous year. The generating capacity of the massive dam doubled Egypt's supply of electricity, and its control of the floodwaters increased the cultivatable land by almost one-third. On the other hand, downsides have been significant. The dam cut off the flow of nutrient-rich silt that came with the annual floods, forcing farmers to turn to chemical replacements that have had their toll on the ecosystem. The heavier price was actually paid by the Nubians, an ethnic group whose homeland was flooded by Lake Nasser (created as a result of the dam). In both Egypt and Sudan, more than 100,000 Nubians were forced to resettle; around half of them are living today in Kom Ombo, north of Aswan.

the lake is named Lake Nasser. The Sudanese, with a fine sense of irony, named the portion that spilled southward over the border Lake Nubia.) Now there are just three major sites south of Aswan that you can still visit in a half-day trip.

High Dam Overrated The High Dam may be a popular tourist destination, but most visitors seem to come back wondering why they bothered. The views are interesting, if you're fascinated by dams, but not spectacular. There is a truly garish monument to Soviet-Egyptian friendship set in a small park at the western end of the dam. The permissibility of photography on the dam is a bit questionable. The theory seems to be that point-and-shoots are fine, but that big lenses and video are not. I would recommend combining the High Dam with the Temple of Philae. The best way to get here is by taxi. About 15km (9 miles) south of Aswan. Admission LE20. Daily 8am–5pm.

Kalabsha ★★ An island south of the High Dam, Kalabsha hosts three saved monuments that were transplanted from other locations. The highlight of your visit is the **Temple of Mandulis,** more commonly known as the Temple of Kalabsha. Work on this temple took off during the Ptolemaic Period but was not finished before the reign of Roman Emperor Augustus (30 B.C. to A.D. 14). It is dedicated to the Nubian God of Fertility, Marul (Mandulis in Greek), and follows the same architectural standards of the time with striking similarities to the Temple of Horus at Edfu. Considered to be Nubia's biggest free-standing temple, the Temple of Mandulis was transplanted from its original location, some 35km (22 miles) to the south, known as Bab Al Kalabsha (hence the name) in 1970. The rescue operation was financed by Germany (West Germany at the time) and involved cutting down the temple to more than 13,000 pieces.

To the northeast of the Temple of Mandulis lies another Ancient Egyptian temple known today as **Beit El Wali** (House of the Holy Man). Built by Ramses II, it is a pre-Ptolemaic temple that was dedicated to Amun and a handful of local deities. The highlight of this temple is the narrow court's reliefs depicting the Pharaoh's military superiority over Nubians and Ethiopians (on the southern wall to your left), as well as Libyans and Asiatics (on the northern wall to your right).

Another rescued monument is the **Kiosk of Qertassi,** a single-room kiosk that was originally on a site about 10km (6¼ miles) north of Bab Al Kalabsha. Decorations are few, though there is a relief depicting Nubia paying a hefty tribute of gold, ivory, leopard skins, and ostrich feathers. There are two Hathor-headed columns that you can't miss.

The small **Temple of Gerf Hussein** was built during the reign of Ramses II and dedicated to a number of Ancient Egyptian gods, among which is Ptah the God of Creation and Artisans. The temple got its name from the Nubian village where it was originally located (Gerf Hussein).

The Gifted Temples

In an act of gratitude for their support during the UNESCO-led Save the Monuments of Nubia Campaign, the Egyptian government gifted four small temples to other countries' governments. Temple of Debod now tops the Mountain Park in Madrid, Spain, while the Temple of Taffeh is now on display in Rijks Museum in Leiden, Holland. The Temple of Lessya is exhibited in the Museo Egizio in Turin, Italy, and, finally, the Temple of Dandour is now part of the Metropolitan Museum in New York.

To get to Kalabsha Island you need to first rent a taxi from Aswan and then pick up a boat from the Crocodile Island Dock between the dam and the Soviet-Egyptian friendship monument. For the round-trip, expect to pay LE100 for the taxi and LE50 for the boat.

Admission LE35. Daily 9am–4pm.

Temple Complex of Philae ★★ Now trapped between the British-built Aswan Dam and the High Dam 6km (3¾ miles) upstream, the stunning Ptolemaic monuments on Philae Island were already being flooded regularly well before they were moved in the 1970s to a site on nearby Agilkia Island, 20m (66 ft.) higher than their original location. They are a must-see for visitors to Upper Egypt.

The **Temple of Isis** is the largest structure on the island, covering about a quarter of the available space. The boat dock is by the Hall of Nectambo, the oldest part of the whole complex, and you pass a colonnade (a Roman addition to the temple) on your way to enter through the Gate of Ptolemy II. I particularly like the forecourt of this temple, with its densely worked columns and scenes of offering incised into the massive pylon that separates it from the hypostyle hall inside. Once inside, you will find crosses inscribed on almost every column, as well as a small Christian alter on the side. In 540, a diktat by Roman Emperor Justinian I ordered the official closure of the temple and turned it into a church. It was the final blow dealt to the worship of Isis and marked the end of paganism in Egypt.

In addition to the **Temple of Augustus** at the northern side of the island, there is the unfinished **Temple of Hathor** on the eastern one. The former opens to the **Gate of Diocletian** with a panoramic view of the Nile and its boulders in the background, while the latter is noted for the reliefs of musical entertainment that include Bes, the dwarf God of Childbirth, playing a harp.

The **Kiosk of Trajan** is another key attraction of the Philae complex. Nicknamed the Pharaoh's Bed, this massive structure on the riverbank is illustrated with scenes of the Emperor Trajan making offerings to the Ancient Egyptian deities of Isis, Osiris, and Horus. Perhaps it is the most famous among the site's various monuments due to its different architecture and the fact that Victorian artists repeatedly painted it.

The best way to get to Philae Island is by hiring a taxi from Aswan for about LE100. Once you reach the docks you need to hire a boat; it is a fixed LE32 fare for the round-trip.

Admission LE50. Daily 9am–5pm; summer 7am–4pm.

WHERE TO STAY

Finding a place to stay in Aswan that doesn't lack style is a pursuit made more difficult with the temporary closure of both the Old and New Cataract (closed for renovation until 2011). Your options are limited to a handful of midrange hotels, a couple of high-end ones, and one authentic Nubian-style boutique hotel on the West Bank.

Very Expensive

Mövenpick Elephantine Island Overrated Locations don't get much better than this: The Mövenpick has the northern end of Elephantine Island, in the middle of the Nile, all to itself. However, the 2007 renovation brought a massive 14-story cement tower, with huge windows and sleek modern attire, that shutters the picturesque view of Aswan. Standard rooms are large, well appointed, and comfortable, while the pool area, which features a bar, kitchen, and barbecue, is commodious.

Sound & Light Show at Philae

The show at Philae is perhaps a little more muted than its Karnak counterpart, but it follows the same formula: music, lights, and a voice-over that runs you through the history of the temples. Even if you're not a particular fan of sound-and-light shows, this one's worth it for the experience of being out on the river at night and seeing the temples lit up. There are three shows a night, starting at 6:30, 7:45, and 9pm, with an admission fee of LE75. If you are big group, it is recommended to call in advance (✆ **097/2317867** or 097/2302037).

	1st show	2nd show	3rd show
Saturday	English	Arabic	X
Sunday	German	French	English
Monday	English	French	X
Tuesday	French	English	X
Wednesday	French	English	X
Thursday	French	Spanish	English
Friday	English	French	Italian

Elephantine Island. ✆ **097/2303455.** Fax 097/2303485. www.moevenpick-aswan.com. 226 units, including 38 suites. $270 double. Rack rate includes buffet breakfast, taxes, and service charges. AE, DC, MC, V. **Amenities:** 3 restaurants; 2 bars; airport transfer (extra charge); concierge; health club; Internet (extra charge); pool; room service. *In room:* TV, Internet (extra charge), minibar.

Expensive

Anakato ★★ The aptly named Anakato ("our home" in Nubian) is made up of two traditional houses. The boutique hotel is distinctively different from any other lodging facility in Egypt, with its authentic architecture and genuine identity. Artistic Nubian style is the dominating factor, with the use of domes and arches, vibrant colors, and extensive wall paintings. The attention given to the smallest of details retains the place's character throughout the whole premises and your room, which come with individual designs and some variations in furniture; check out a couple before making up your mind. Anakato's location on the West Bank makes it a great hideaway from the city lights, while the free shuttle boat into town (operates 9am–5pm) keeps you connected. The small ecolodge-like facility offers a bouquet of different excursions and activities that include a visit to a Nubian village and sandboarding. Anakato doesn't serve alcohol, but you are welcome to bring your own.

Ghareb Suhail. ✆ **097/3451744.** Fax 097/3451745. www.anakato.com. 11 units. 100€ double. Rate includes breakfast, dinner, taxes, and service charges. No credit cards. **Amenities:** Restaurant; Wi-Fi (extra charge). *In room:* A/C, minifridge, no phone.

Pyramisa Isis Island This big pile of 1970s-style buildings occupies its own island just above the first cataract. Complete with tennis and squash courts, swimming pools, a waterfall, a health club, and its very own farm, the over-the-top architecture and generally cheesy feel to the whole complex may give you the feeling that it was designed by the villain of a James Bond movie. Rooms are spacious, but the color scheme—a combination of light maroon carpets with green walls and red trim in one wing—leaves a bit to

Solstice of the God

The Temple of Abu Simbel (admission LE90; daily 9am–4pm) is one of Ancient Egypt's most widely pictured monuments, with its four colossal (20m/65 ft.) statues of Ramses II guarding the entrance. The monuments-frantic Pharaoh carved this temple into the rock of the Nile Valley between 1274 and 1244 B.C., with the intention of using it as a venue for his deification. Inside, the temple goes about 60m (200 ft.) back into the rock, passing eight smaller statues of Ramses II and some stunning reliefs proclaiming his military superiority on the way, and finally leading to the Sanctuary. This is where Ramses II is sculptured as a god, in a seated position, and in the company of three important Ancient Egyptian gods: Amun of Thebes, Ptah of Memphis, and Ra of Heliopolis. Self-glorifying Ramses II didn't stop at that; the whole facility is designed and oriented so that every February 22 and October 22, the first light of the rising sun shines through the door all the way back to the Sanctuary, illuminating his face. Before the temple was raised up from its original location, this happened 2 days earlier, thus marking the Pharaoh's birthday and coronation day.

There is actually a second temple in Abu Simbel, also built by Ramses II, but dedicated to the cult of his wife, Nefertari. The temple is situated a little to the north of its more famous counterpart, and about half the size. It is interesting, however, that, in this case, a wife is shown the same size as her husband.

Abu Simbel will take a full day out of your schedule if you go by car, 2 if you opt for public transport. If you are running on a tight schedule, consider the flight from Aswan. Though it's expensive (around LE1,000 for the round-trip), it gets you there in 45 minutes instead of 3 hours. If you are here for the night, there is a sound and light show at the Temple of Abu Simbel (✆ **097/3400326;** www.soundandlight.com.eg; admission LE75; schedule changes constantly, so call in advance).

be desired. It's a fun place to stay if the price is right, with the main drawback being the food, which is really bad.

Pyramisa Island, Luxor. ✆ **097/2317400.** Fax 097/2317405. www.pyramisaegypt.com. 447 units. 147€ double. Rack rate includes buffet breakfast, taxes, and service charges. AE, MC, V. **Amenities:** 6 restaurants; 2 bars; airport transfer (extra charge); concierge; health club; Internet (extra charge); 2 pools; room service; 4 tennis courts. *In room:* A/C, TV, minibar.

Moderate

Isis Hotel Aswan ★ Located between the road and the river, the Isis is probably the best moderately priced option in town. The hotel is close to the Nile with a low-profile, one-story layout that puts the restaurant and 20 of the rooms directly on the water. The rooms are not particularly large, and the garden-view units can feel like rabbit hutches; both pool- and Nile-view rooms are very acceptable. A word of caution: There is at least one pool-view room at the end of the row that has a view of nothing but the registration desk, so be sure to ask whether your room really has a view of the pool.

Corniche El Nil. ✆ **097/2315100.** Fax 097/2315500. 102 units. $120 double. Rack rate includes buffet breakfast, taxes, and service charges. V. **Amenities:** 2 restaurants; bar; airport transfer (extra charge); concierge; Internet (extra charge); pool; room service. *In room:* A/C, TV, minifridge.

The Last of the Nubian Temples

The remoteness of Lake Nasser and the inhospitality of the terrain that surrounds it means that even though its temples were saved from being submerged under the rising waters of Lake Nasser, they are still on the very bottom of Egypt's most-visited sites. If you are going to book any of the Lake Nasser cruises (p. 282) or have opted for a fishing trip down the lake (p. 301), here are the sites you will be visiting.

Wadi El Sebou'a (admission LE35; daily 9am–4pm), Valley of the Lions in Arabic, is probably the most famous after the Temple of Abu Simbel. Its name likely derives from the avenue of sphinxes that lead to the **Temple of Ramses II,** one of the three temples it hosts. As with the Temple of Abu Simbel, the Temple of Ramses II at Wadi El Sebou'a was also dedicated to Amun, Ra, Ptah, and the deified Ramses II. In proximity lies another temple, the **Temple of Dakka,** dedicated to Thoth, the God of Wisdom. The building of this temple started in the reign of the Nubian King Arkamani, but was not finished before the reign of Roman Emperor Augustus. The temple is noted for the relief depicting the Nubian king presenting an offering to Thoth. The smallest of the temple trio is the **Temple of Meharraga.** The unfinished temple was dedicated to both Ancient Egyptian Isis and the Ptolemaic Alexandrian Serapis. Other than the small hypostyle hall, nothing much remains of it.

Qasr Ibrim (free admission) is the only Nubian monument still in its original site. It was once a garrison town that hosted six temples, of which one was built by the 25th Dynasty Kushite Pharaoh Taharka and was dedicated to Isis. And even 2 centuries after Egypt adopted Christianity, paganism was still flourishing here. But when it finally converted, it flourished to become one of Lower Nubia's most important Christian centers, and the last to accept Islam when it fell to Ottoman troops in the 16th century. The ruins you see today are all that remain of a sandstone cathedral built over the Temple of Isis.

Amada (admission LE35; daily 9am–4pm) is the last of the Nubian sites, and it encompasses two temples and a tomb. The **Temple of Amada** was built during the 18th Dynasty period and was dedicated to the ancient gods Amun and Ra. It has some of the most well-preserved reliefs among the Nubian temples, with one stele depicting Amenhotep II's military campaign into Levant, and another depicting a failed Libyan attempt to invade Egypt. The other temple on site is the **Temple of Derr.** Also built by Ramses II, this temple's reliefs mainly depict the Pharaoh's campaign into Nubia. The **Tomb of Pennut,** belonging to the viceroy of Nubia during Ramses IV reign, is the only Nubian tomb that was discovered and salvaged.

Marhaba Palace Located less than a 5-minute walk from the train station, Marhaba Palace has one of the most gloriously tasteless facades (an odd sort of neo-Pharaonic pastiche) in town. Once you're inside, though, everything follows suit for a fairly bland, midrange hotel. Rooms vary in size and design, so look at a few before deciding, if possible. If not, try to avoid paying for a "side Nile view," as these really stretch the point of what constitutes a view. The health club is basic and quite small, and the pool area is cozy. Staff are well trained and very pleasant. With a bit of a discount from the rack rates listed, it can be a good bet for a comfortable, midrange place if you turn a blind eye on the interiors. Marhaba Palace is an alcohol-free hotel.

Corniche El Nil. ✆ **097/23301024.** www.marhaba-aswan.com. 78 units. $136 double. Rack rate includes buffet breakfast, taxes, and service charges. MC, V. **Amenities:** Restaurant; babysitting; health club (small); Internet (extra charge); pool. *In room:* A/C, TV, minibar.

Nile Hotel ★ This is probably one of the best values for money in Aswan. Rooms are basic but fairly large and very clean. Furnishings are modern and thoroughly innocuous. The rooms in the front of the building have a great view of the Nile, albeit across the wide and busy street. What really separates this place from the pack, apart from nice, new rooms at a decent price, is the staff, who are more friendly and helpful than those in more upmarket establishments.

15 Corniche El Nil. ✆ **097/2314222** or 097/2332600. www.nilehotel-aswan.com. 30 units. $60 double. Rate includes buffet breakfast, taxes, and service charges. No credit cards. **Amenities:** Restaurant; bar; Wi-Fi. *In room:* A/C, TV, minifridge.

Paradise Hotel Located a stone's throw away from both the train station and Corniche El Nil Street, Paradise Hotel is a small three-star hotel right in the heart of Aswan's souk. It overlooks the busy street, so opt for a higher floor unless you are fine with the nonstop market noise. Both the exteriors and the lobby give a strong sense of character, but that doesn't continue to the rooms, which are clean but not spacious, and lack balconies and bathtubs.

Souk St. ✆ **097/2329690.** Fax 097/2329691. www.paradisehotel-aswan.com. 62 units. LE160 double. Rate includes breakfast, taxes, and service charges. No credit cards. **Amenities:** Restaurant. *In room:* A/C, TV, minifridge.

Inexpensive

El Salam This is one of Aswan's few good budget accommodations. El Salam's rooms are very basic but clean, and all of them are air-conditioned. My favorite feature is the view—granted, it comes with significant road noise (even on the fourth or fifth floor)—and from the Nile-facing rooms you can see up and down the river for a long way. Oddly, these rooms with the premium view are also the ones that have the bathroom-down-the-hall option. Go figure.

101 Corniche El Nil. ✆ **097/2302651.** 70 units. LE90 Nile-view double. Rate includes breakfast, taxes, and service charges. No credit cards. **Amenities:** Restaurant. *In room:* A/C, no phone.

WHERE TO EAT

"Where to eat?" is a perplexing question when it comes to Aswan, especially if you're not in the mood for fish. Hotel restaurants serve food that ranges from disappointing to overpriced, while the string of floating Nile-side restaurants along Corniche El Nil Street are a hit and miss affair. After a couple of days spent in an unsuccessful culinary pursuit, I, with great disappointment, resorted to the only McDonald's in town (next to the Dock for the Botanical Garden).

Aswan Moon EGYPTIAN The Aswan Moon is the best of the floating Nile-side places and is just a couple of doors upstream from Isis Hotel. Walk down through the landside building and sit on the float. The furniture is wicker and comfortable, the clientele is a mellow mixture of foreign and local, and most of the time the only soundtrack is the gentle gurgling of water underneath. Though the menu is a trove of malapropisms ("buck with orange" and "veal bane"), the fish is excellent—lightly battered and not overcooked—and the service is pleasant and efficient.

Corniche El Nil. ✆ **097/2316108.** Appetizers LE10–LE15; main courses LE25–LE40. No credit cards. Daily 11am–11pm.

Chef Khalil SEAFOOD This little fish restaurant in the depths of the souk has a little more polish than the rest. The decor is a bit surreal, with a small water feature and a line of dolphins and turtles cavorting about the room, but the food is good. Either go to the back of the seating area to pick your own fish out of the cabinet or ask what's fresh. Much of the stock comes from the Mediterranean, but the tilapia, which is local, is great grilled and served with a side of rice. Service is both better and more businesslike than you're likely to find elsewhere in Aswan.

Souk St., close to the train station end. ✆ **097/2310142.** Seafood meal (including salads, appetizers, bread, and main course) LE35–LE70. No credit cards. Daily noon–midnight.

El Dokka ★ EGYPTIAN This is probably the best place to eat out in Aswan, if not for the food then certainly for the boat trip and the scenic views. Located on an island right in the middle of the river, a free boat ride will take you from El Dokka's private dock to the island restaurant. The Nubian atmosphere is strengthened with locally inspired decorative motifs, and the use of basketry, stone, and wood. The menu, on the other hand, is more Egyptian than anything else. Full meals come with an assortment of salads as starters, followed by a couple of cooked vegetable dishes and a bowl of rice, and finally a main course of meat, chicken, pigeon, or fish. Portions are huge.

Finding El Dokka's private dock on Corniche El Nil Street can be tricky; look for the red Coca-Cola sign close to Amun Dock. In between the two, there is a small staircase that leads to the dock.

Eissa Island. ✆ **097/9108000** or 012/2162379. Full meal (including salads, appetizers, bread, cooked vegetables, rice, and main course) LE50–LE70. No credit cards. Daily 11am–11pm.

Salah El Din EGYPTIAN A copycat of Aswan Moon (above) with only two exceptions: the food is downright bad, and it serves alcohol. If you are coming here for the

Wild . . . Wild . . . South

Lake Nasser is Egypt wildlife's last frontier. The sparsely populated lake is home to the country's largest Nile crocodile population as well as being an important habitat for resident and migratory birds alike; come here at the right time of the year, and you will be overwhelmed with the variety of bird species found. From colorful Egyptian geese and exotic flamingos to beautiful pelicans and graceful cranes, the list is lengthy and diverse. The wild side of Lake Nasser is certainly not restricted to birdlife and monster-size crocs. Venturing into Wadi El Allaqi, one of the lake's widest valleys, holds a strong probability of spotting gazelles, foxes, and, if you're lucky, jackals.

Commercially, Lake Nasser is promoted as an outdoor destination for fishing with two main operators dominating the stage: **African Angler** (✆ **097/2309748;** www.african-angler.co.uk) and **Lake Nasser Adventure** (✆ **097/2323636;** www.lakenasseradventure.com). While the former is more focused on fishing, the latter has some interesting cruises mixing historical sightseeing with outdoor activities.

view, the good service, and to have a drink right by the water, you will enjoy your time; just have dinner somewhere else.

Corniche El Nil. Appetizers LE10–LE15; main courses LE25–LE40. No credit cards. Daily 11am–11pm.

SHOPPING

Though it has been drastically spiffed up in recent years, the **souk** in Aswan remains one of my favorites in all of Egypt. It is strung out along Souk Street, but excursions up the innumerable alleys and side streets are always rewarded with a new sight, sound, or shopping opportunity. You'll find the usual range of T-shirts, bottles of colored sand layered into pictures of camels, Pharaonic statues, and cheesy mini pyramids, but the Aswan souk is actually a good opportunity to pick up a few things. I particularly enjoy the wooden sculptures, which are usually reproductions of Pharaonic artifacts and are relatively rare to find farther north. If you search carefully among the mass-produced trinkets, you can also find some distinctively Nubian silver at the jewelry stalls. Visit the **Nubian Museum** (p. 293) first to get an idea of what you're after.

11

The Western Desert

If you think all deserts look the same, think again. Every oasis, and sometimes location, in the Western Desert has its own spirit, identity, and trademark.

Up north is the Berber oasis of Siwa, with its distinctive *kersheef* (mud and salt mix) buildings, ethnically distinct people, and time-honored culture. Siwa grabbed conquerors' attention ever since its Oracle started blessing, or denouncing, world leaders. Cambyses wanted it destroyed, while Alexander the Great sought its blessing. The Oracle might be in ruins today, but a couple of Ancient Egyptian tombs can give your desert trip a historical flavor. You can't be in Siwa and miss out on the oasis's number-one outdoor activity—sandboarding. Hosting some of the best dunes in the Great Sahara, Siwa accommodates the rookies as well as the pros. And during the hot summer season, the lovely oasis makes for a great detoxification destination with its hot summer sand baths.

Bahareya is actually the closest real oasis to the capital, and it's a great desert trip, especially if you are short on time. Before you catch the next 4×4 out of Bahareya, make sure to visit the museum for a glance of the stunningly beautiful Golden Mummies, and make a quick visit to the Ancient Egyptian tombs.

The picturesque desertscape is what the road to Farafra is all about. In addition to the Black Desert and the glimmering Crystal Mountain, the White Desert is the key attraction here; the alien-like terrain is a moon surface covered with eccentric-looking naturally shaped chalk formations. Farafra is a small oasis that's the perfect place to relax and recharge after a camping trip in the White Desert and before heading to the next oasis, Dakhla.

The largest of all of the Western Desert's five main oases, Dakhla embraces its visitors with its diverse history: from the Roman necropolis of Muzwaka and the Ancient Egyptian temple of Deir El Hagar to the small collection of rock art at the edge of the oasis and the ancient Islamic town of Qasr. With its zigzagging alleyways, shoulder-to-shoulder buildings, and peculiar architecture, Qasr is guaranteed to take you back in time. One of Dakhla's trademark experiences is a midnight plunge in one of its hot springs.

If you are looking for the majestic sight of an ancient desert necropolis, there is none better than the Bagawat Necropolis. The distinctively designed necropolis hosts more than 260 tombs and a couple of chapels; look for the Chapel of the Exodus and the Chapel of Peace amid one of the world's oldest cities of the dead. The road south of Kharga is marked with a couple of rarely visited historical sites; have a respite at the Roman fortresses of Qasr El Ghueta or Qasr El Zayyan before continuing your trip south to the Temple of Dush. Once upon a time, the now stranded Ancient Egyptian temple is believed to have been covered in gold, which is no longer there, but it's still quite a sight with the open desert in the background. If you are looking for off-the-beaten-track attractions, it doesn't get better than in El Gilf El Kebir, the gigantic plateau that rises in the middle of the desert like a massive iceberg in the Arctic. Before civilization, it was heaven on earth for hunter-gatherers, and they left us a priceless heritage of beautiful rock art.

1 SIWA

Tucked away in Egypt's westernmost corner, Siwa lies closer to Libya and the Maghreb than to any of its fellow Egyptian urban centers or even oases. But the proximity is not all about distance; it extends to culture as well. Siwans are ethnically Berber and prefer their mother tongue to Arabic, retain their own set of customs and traditions, and use tribal politics to govern their affairs. Up to this day, they cling fiercely to their identity and feel overtly proud of being Siwans. Architecture follows the same traditional Siwan techniques, employing local *kersheef* to create some of the most artistic looking buildings you can imagine. When compared to the rest of Egypt, this far and away place is distinct in every aspect.

Siwa gained its first mention in the book of history with its famous Oracle, but more recently, Siwa was the last of all the Western Desert oases to fall under Egyptian control. It retained its independence all the way until 1819, when Mohamed Ali's powerful artillery brought the shrewd oasis to its knees. Nowadays, Siwa has made a less dramatic comeback from the edge of oblivion, positioning itself as one of Egypt's hottest destinations. During the winter season, it is favored for its warm weather and outdoor desert activities; go sandboarding or take a plunge in any of the natural springs. If you are here during the summer time, Siwa's famous sand baths will completely rejuvenate and detoxify you.

ESSENTIALS

Getting There

BY PLANE Rumors of an on-site airport in Siwa have been around for a long time, but they are nothing more than that. Marsa Matruh remains the closest airport to the oasis, located some 300km (186 miles) to the north. With the increase in direct flights connecting Marsa Matruh to Europe, tourism in Siwa is sure to rise.

BY CAR From the capital, it is a lengthy 9-hour drive, first to Marsa Matruh and then on a single-carriage low-density road, to Siwa. Arriving at the oasis itself is straightforward, as there is only one main road that leads into the main village of Shali.

BY BUS There are six buses a day that connect Siwa to Marsa Matruh, with only one of them continuing farther to the capital. Tickets to Marsa Matruh cost LE15; to Cairo LE60. If you prefer to break the journey with a stop in Alexandria for a day or two, there are four daily buses from Siwa that make the 600km (372-mile) run for LE35. All buses are operated by the **West Delta Bus Company** (✆ **046/4602495**) and come and go from the one and only bus station located a 5-minute walk from Siwa's main souk.

Getting Around

ON FOOT The area around Siwa's main souk can be easily covered on foot. Hotels, shopping, and dining, as well as the bus station, ATM, and tourist information facilities are all within a 5- or 10-minute stroll of each other.

BY BIKE To see Siwa's attractions beyond Shali, you need more than just your feet. Bikes are a fitting method of transport and can be rented for LE20 per day. Several rental shops are found around the main souk, with one right in front of Abdu Restaurant and another next to Albabenshal Hotel.

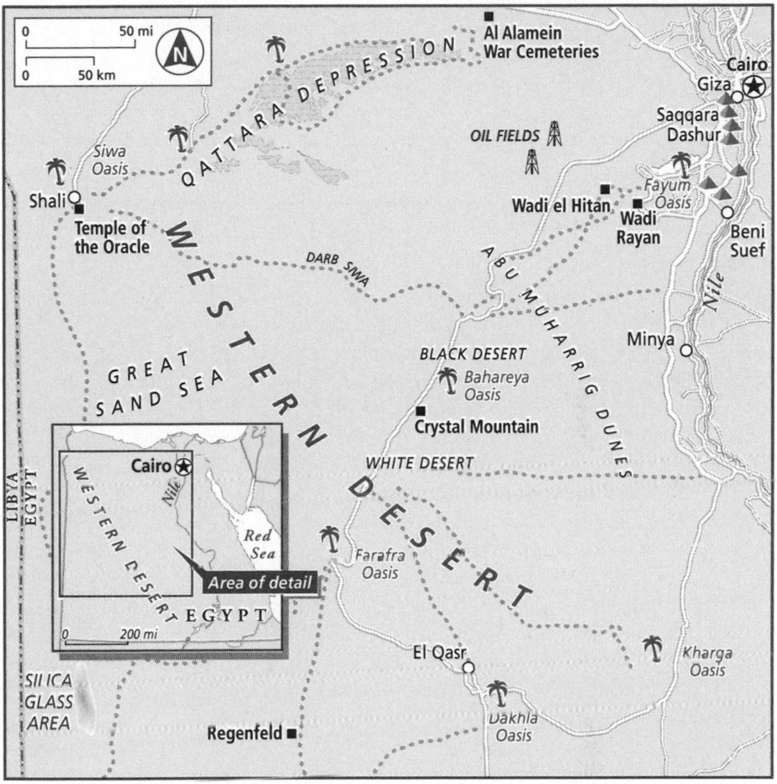

BY "TAXI" Everywhere in Siwa you'll find boys with brightly painted donkey carts—these are the local taxis. Other than being a little hard on the backside, they're a great (if not especially speedy) way to get around. Negotiate your fare before setting out, and expect to pay LE5 to LE10 for a short ride, LE50 for a half-day service, and LE80 to LE100 for a full-day sites tour.

BY 4×4 You can see most of the oasis proper with a bike or a donkey cart, but for anything beyond the limits of the settlement, you'll need to hire a 4×4 vehicle with a qualified driver. Expect to pay around LE600 to LE900 a day depending on the car's condition.

A 4×4 also offers a good alternative to the bus when time comes to get out of town and move on. Instead of going north from Siwa by bus to Matruh and Alexandria, you can simply head southeast to the oasis of Bahareya. The state of the 420km (260-mile) road ranges from passable to nonexistent, however, and you need a 4WD vehicle and an experienced driver. The one-way rate per vehicle is LE1,500 to LE1,700 for the 5-hour drive (which can be split between three people), and you need a permit from security, which the driver easily manages.

Tips Before Night Descends . . .

Devised for your own safety, or so it is claimed, tourists are not allowed on any of the Western Desert tarmac roads between 6pm and 6am. Make sure you reach your next destination before sunset, or simply get off the road and take a shortcut through the desert, which is recommended only if you are well-equipped and have an excellent guide/driver; off-roading after dark requires a different set of skills.

Orientation

The main souk area is where all the action takes place: It is where the bus will drop you; where you will be staying unless you opt for Adrére Amellal, Shali Resort, or Taziry; where you go out for dinner followed by souvenir shopping; and where the haunting ruins of Shali look upon you from their hilly position. Other than the souk, the rest of the tourist attractions are well signed and close by. A 20-minute walk to the north of the souk will take you to Gebel Al Mawta; a southwestern tour, by bike or local taxi, will take you to the Temple of the Oracle, the Temple of Amun, and Cleopatra's Bath.

The **tourist information office** (**✆ 046/4601338**) is just across from the bus station in a traditional-style building. Friendly, helpful, and English-speaking staff can supply updated bus schedule information and a serviceable map of the oasis. Hours are daily 9am to 2pm and 5 to 8pm, but note that evening hours are iffy—the rule is that if you see the lights on, someone's there. My advice is to go between 10am and 1pm.

There are a couple of **Internet** cafes around the souk area (one is next to Abdu restaurant) with rates around LE10 per hour. There is only one **ATM** in town; you can find it outside the Banque du Caire building close to the bus station. The bank is open Sunday to Thursday 9am to 2pm.

WHAT TO SEE & DO

The landscape around Siwa is some of the most spectacular on Earth. The oasis sits on the very edge of the Great Sand Sea, and the area is literally littered with fossilized remnants of prehistoric life. There are several ruins to visit, and a number of hot springs and minioases where you can soak yourself under the stars.

Abu Shruf Spring ★ Of Siwa's many natural springs, this one is a personal favorite. Least visited, especially when compared to the more famous Cleopatra's Bath, it is quite likely that you will have Abu Shruf Spring all to yourself. It is an oval-shape natural pool with walled edges. The rocks in the bottom, along with the small fish swimming around, give you the feeling of being in a natural aquarium. There is a tarmac road that goes all the way to Abu Shruf Spring, but it is a bit of a ride to hire a "local taxi." If you don't have a car, it's best to combine Abu Shruf with a half- or full-day excursion to Bir Wahed.

Bir Wahed and Shiatah If you wish to get a feel for the desert without having to spend a couple of days camping outdoors, a half-day trip to Bir Wahed does the trick. Well Number 1, as the name translates, has two natural springs (one hot, one cold) where you can go for a dip. A full-day trip to Bir Wahed gives you enough time to either check out Abu Shruf Spring or go sandboarding (p. 308). If you are new to the sport, stick to Bir Wahed and its friendlier dunes, but if you are playing in the professional division, then Shiatah's colossal dunes are where you should be boarding. The half-day trip costs

ATTRACTIONS ●
Abu Shruf Spring **18**
Bir Wahed **17**
Cleopatra's Bath **16**
Fatnas Island **8**
Gebel Al Mawta **3**
Shali **9**
Siwan House
 Museum **4**
Temple of Amun (Temple
 of Umm Ubayda) **14**
Temple of the Oracle **7**

ACCOMMODATIONS ■
Adrére Amellal **1**
Albabenshal Hotel **11**
Kilany **5**
Palm Trees Hotel **12**
Shali Lodqe **13**
Shali Resort **19**
Siwa Safari Paradise
 Hotel **6**
Taziry **2**

DINING ◆
Abdu **10**
Albabenshal Hotel **11**
Kenooz **13**
Tanta Wa **15**

THE WESTERN DESERT

11

SIWA

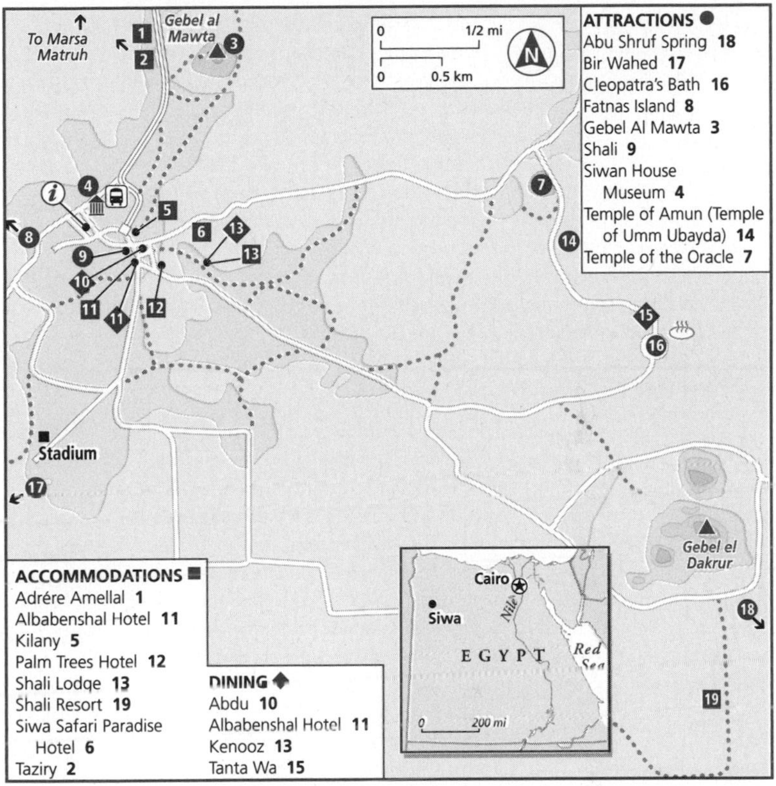

LE550 per vehicle plus LE80 per person, but expect the vehicle cost to hike up to LE950 for a full day.

Cleopatra's Bath Whether or not it was ever visited by the eponymous queen, the spring will be something of a disappointment to a modern visitor hoping for romance. Enclosed in a circular wall, the rather small pool is uninviting with its dark pool bed. There's a nearby restaurant with good pizza and excellent fruit juice, however, and the location deep in the palms makes this a pleasant stop on a tour around the oasis.

Fatnas Island This is a palm-treed island in Siwa Lake with a spring for bathing amongst the trees. It makes for a great picnic, but my preference is to come here in the late afternoon, drink tea, and watch the spectacular colors of the sunset; just make sure your camera batteries are fully charged.

Gebel Al Mawta ★ You'll see this easily accessible low mountain if you look to the east of the road as you come into town. It's about 1.5km (a little less than a mile) from the market square. The name literally translates to Mountain of the Dead, and this refers to the various tombs cut into the side of the rock. Over the centuries, the tombs have been used as a refuge during invasions or storms. The original tombs' contents have been removed

Tribal Politics

The population of Siwa is divided into tribes *(qabila)*, with the broadest division between Easterners and Westerners. The Eastern families were the original builders of the Shali-fortified town, and the Westerners arrived later (local history has them as a mixed group of Berbers and Arabs who were brought in after the town was built). The Eastern tribe divided into three tribes, one of which (the Adadsa) then further subdivided into another three. The Western Tribe subdivided once, into three. Each of these tribes is headed by a hereditary leader (the Sheikh Al Qabila) who is responsible for meting out justice, maintaining the peace, and negotiating on behalf of the tribe. He maintains land ownership records and adjudicates conflicts through meetings known as *meiyad*. In modern times, the Sheikh Al Qabila has also become the intermediary between state institutions and the people of his tribe.

and most of the decorations stripped away; however, four main tombs still hold onto their fading glory. Dating back to Ancient Egypt's 26th dynasty, the **Tomb of Niperpathot** is probably the oldest among Gebel Al Mawta's quartet. It belongs to a holy man who held a high rank in the local Osiris worship hierarchy. In the burial chamber, some inscriptions and paintings, mainly depicting Osiris, are still visible. Another tomb with Osiris depictions is the **Tomb of the Crocodile.** The anonymity of its owner, as well as the fact that a mummified crocodile was found inside, are the reasons behind the naming. The **Tomb of Mesu-Isis** is an unfinished tomb with the entrance being the most attractive part. Above the doorway it is decorated with 21 relatively well-preserved paintings of blue and red cobras, each adorned with a sun disk, while on the sides there are two paintings depicting Isis and Osiris. The **Tomb of Si-Amun** is the finest of the Siwan necropolises. It dates back to the 3rd century B.C. and belongs to a wealthy Greek man named Si-Amun. The tomb walls are awash with paintings depicting the owner worshiping several Ancient Egyptian deities, as well as scenes from the afterlife. The ceiling is the best preserved part of the tomb and is adorned with stars and a representation of Nut, the Goddess of the Sky. Admission LE25. Daily 9am–5pm.

Sandboarding ★★ With some of the best sand dunes in Egypt, and perhaps the whole of Africa, sandboarding in Siwa is a must. Nearly every local tour operator, hotel, and even bazaar shop in town can rent you a board for LE40 to LE50. However, if you are looking for a real deal on a half-day excursion, **Somewhere Different** (**© 016/5840018;** www.somewheredifferent.com) seems to be among the best in town when it comes to organizing and guiding. If you're a beginner, guides will make sure the dunes they choose match your experience level, but if you're familiar with the sport, Somewhere Different can take you to some hair-raising dunes that will unquestionably put your sandboarding skills to the test.

Shali Thanks to the written records kept in Siwa since the 7th century A.D., we know that the old fortress town was founded in about 1203 by the residents of the nearby town of Aghurmi (near to the Temple of Amun). Built on a hill, the town originally had only a single gate—Bab Enshal (for which Albabenshal Hotel is named)—with a second gate added about a century later. In the evening, many of the town's sheep and farm animals were brought in through the gates before they were locked for the night. As the town developed within the confines of its walls, the limited amount of space meant that buildings grew upward and the streets became narrow and dark. By the 19th century, there were more than a dozen entrances to Shali, and its residents had seen a number of determined attempts to invade the town. It was subjugated to central rule in 1819 by Mohamed Ali, whose forces were able to take the town after a 3-hour battle, despite the residents flooding its approaches by diverting irrigation water.

Shali was finally abandoned, not because of a military conquest but because of rain. The whole town was built of *kersheef,* as well as blocks of rock salt. In 1926, a particularly severe storm occurred, and the destruction was such that most residents opted to abandon their homes and start fresh nearby.

These days, having suffered through a few more rains and decades of neglect, the town is in ruins but well worth an hour of exploration. You can wander about freely on your own, but it's not a bad idea to have a guide—even just one of the donkey-taxi kids who hang around the market square—as some of the paths are treacherous. The view from the top is spectacular.

Siwan House Museum Located in the middle of a park, this small two-story museum sheds some light on the traditional life in the oasis. It exhibits a wide range of items from day-to-day tools to various Berber outfits; the wedding one is eye-catching with its heavy embroidery. Many of the items on display, such as the traditional wood bowls and the jewelry, are the same as those still in use today.

Admission LE5. Sat–Thurs 10am–2pm.

Temple of Amun (Temple of Umm Ubayda) A pleasant 5-minute bike ride past the Temple of the Oracle up a quiet, palm-lined road takes you to the 30th Dynasty Temple of Amun. Today it's nothing more than a pile of rocks, though it actually stood fully intact until the beginning of the 19th century. The final blow was struck in 1896, apparently, by the Ottoman governor who used explosives to remove some rocks he wanted to incorporate into a stairway in his house. Walls and columns lie on their sides in a clearing by the road. With no apparent guard or office nearby, visitors are free to clamber about and examine the hieroglyphs at their leisure.

Temple of the Oracle Another Amun-dedicated temple, Temple of the Oracle was once the main reason for coming to Siwa, but its remains now stand alone on a small hill. Built by the 26th Dynasty King Amasis, the temple constitutes some of the earliest evidence that the Ancient Egyptians controlled the oasis (then called *Sekhet-imit,* Place of the Palm Trees). The Oracle was an important and influential source of information to the Greeks, who consulted it and sought its blessings, but its significance declined under the Romans, who perceived the desert oasis of Siwa as a place of banishment. Today, there is nothing much left, except for some faded inscriptions on the wall. At the entrance, a mosque following the local Siwan style was added to the premises at one time and remains in relatively good shape.

For Treasure Hunters

According to ancient local records, King Khuraybish, the last king of Siwa, buried his treasures somewhere in the village of Aghurmi.

A 10- to 15-minute ride from the middle of town, this site makes an excellent short bike excursion. Because it is situated on a small hill among the ruins of the abandoned town of Aghurmi, the view from the top gives you a good sense of where you are. Though the temple has been poorly restored, it's still worth a 30-minute visit.

Admission LE25. Daily 9am–5pm.

The Lost Army of Cambyses

According to Herodotus, after Persian Emperor Cambyses, son of Cyrus the Great, conquered Egypt in 525 B.C., the priests of the Temple of Amun refused to bless his claim to Egypt. Blinded by anger, he ordered a 50,000-man force to march to the desolate oasis and destroy the Oracle. After Cambyses's army left Kharga Oasis (one of the Western Desert's other oases), it vanished without a trace. Some blame it on a catastrophic sandstorm while others dismiss the whole story as a myth.

WHERE TO STAY

Siwa doesn't have any cookie-cutter five-stars—yet. Hotels in downtown (this remains a one-square town) and around the bus station tend to be down-market and not great, with two exceptions: the Shali Lodge and the Albabenshal. Development outside the town aims at a higher-end market and looks to deliver a natural, Siwan experience. I suspect that there isn't a single panel of double glazing among them, and the nearest business center is at least 3 hours' drive from here; the more you pay, it seems, the more stripped down this experience becomes. Expect good (in some cases excellent) food, rough-edged but efficient service, and loads of atmosphere from these places, but minibars, satellite TV, and air-conditioning are simply not on the menu. If you're just getting off the bus and looking for somewhere to stay, avoid the first couple of hotels that you come to, and head straight to Kilany or the Palm Trees Hotel.

Very Expensive

Adrére Amellal ★★★ Less is once again more, it seems, and at this stunning ecolodge, less is also a lot more expensive. It may not make sense at first—not only does this place have no TV, no phone, and no Internet, it doesn't even have electricity: You'll eat, drink, and read by the light of candles or oil lamps and be heated by hot coals in open braziers. Stay a while, however, and things will begin to drop into place.

The design, which is intended to blend the manmade seamlessly into the natural, is simply gorgeous. Nestled between the base of Gebel Gafa (Gafa Mountain) and the stunningly beautiful Lake Siwa, the buildings, made largely from traditional *kersheef,* are low and gracefully rounded. Exploring inside is an adventure of caves and oddly curved rooms, each one appointed in high-quality cotton cushions and furnished with painstakingly fashioned handmade wood tables and chairs. Modern fittings are kept to a minimum. My favorite items, though, are those carved out of solid blocks of local salt. These range from heavyset benches in the rooms to translucent blocks built into the walls, which let in sunshine during the day and light up from outside with the glow of lamps and candles at night. There is even a whole bar carved out of salt.

Eating is done in a number of different rooms throughout the lodge, some laid out as formal dining rooms, some carved into niches in the cliff walls and furnished with cushions and pillows. The bar facilities are similarly distributed. Each guest room is unique, but most are very large and have high (5m/16 ft. in some cases) ceilings. Bed linens and towels are extremely high quality, and the bathrooms are lovely, with natural fittings, deep bathtubs, and rock-salt benches.

Cairo office, 18 El Mansour Mohamed St., Zamalek. ✆ **02/27367879.** Fax 02/27355489. www.adrere amellal.net. 41 units. $370 double. Rate is on all-inclusive basis that includes buffet breakfast, lunch, dinner, day trips into the desert, taxes, and service charge. AE, MC, V. **Amenities:** Restaurant; bar; pool. *In room:* No phone.

Expensive

Taziry Built on a low escarpment over Siwa Lake, Taziry also looks at the back of Gebel Gafa. Like its neighbor, Adrére Amellal, it bills itself as an ecolodge and eschews the use of electricity in favor of candles and oil lamps. Though it doesn't take the concept quite as far (there are some modern conveniences, including a generator), it does pursue the same concept of getting away from the loud noises and bright lights. There is a lovely spring-fed pool, and the whole place is built around a nicely laid out single-story restaurant and lounge building.

The rooms, which are separate from the main buildings, are pleasant and cool, with stone floors, palm-leaf ceilings, and Bedouin carpets. There is no air-conditioning, but windows have been carefully sited to provide cross-flow ventilation and cooling. Each room has a veranda that looks out over the mountain and the lake, which are about .8km (½ mile) away across the road and the desert. I recommend the second-floor rooms—they have the best view.

Cairo office, 1 Abdallah Al Kateb St., Dokki. ✆ **012/3408492.** 30 units. $225 double. Rate is on full-board basis with taxes and service charges. MC, V. **Amenities:** Restaurant; pool. *In room:* No phone.

Moderate

Albabenshal Hotel ★★ (Finds) Taking its name from the original gate that led into the fortress town of Shali in the 13th century, this is a wonderful hotel built in the traditional style. The whole building blends with its surroundings, giving guests a boutique version of the Siwan experience. Like the Shali Lodge, rooms at Albabenshal don't have air-conditioning but are kept cool in the summer by high ceilings, small windows, fans, and good ventilation. Touches such as exposed palm-tree beams and light covers carved from local rock-salt accent the traditional feel, while at the same time you're pampered with quality cotton towels and bed covers. The restaurant is one of the best gastronomical experiences in Siwa. In this price range, this and the Shali Lodge, which operates on the same basis, offer very good value for money if you're looking for a real Siwan experience.

Souk. ✆ **046/4601499.** Fax 046/4602266. Cairo office, 18 El Mansour Mohamed St. ✆ 02/27367879. Fax 02/27355489. 14 units. LE340 double. Rate includes breakfast, taxes, and service charge. No credit cards. **Amenities:** Restaurant. *In room:* TV.

The Healing Sands

For most travelers, summer might not be the best time of the year to visit Siwa, but for those seeking remedy in its sand, summer might just be the best season. **Siwan sand baths** provide a natural detoxification well reputed for enhancing blood circulation and healing rheumatic ailments. Lasting between 3 to 7 days, your treatment retreat revolves around sand baths, where you are buried up to your neck in a specially dug hole in the sand, followed by a natural sauna session in a tightly pitched tent. By the afternoon, you are ready for a lengthy shower followed by a good meal. Sherif El Senossi (✆ **010/3661905**) offers some of the best sand baths in town. Between July and September, it costs LE80 to LE100 per day including accommodation and therapy.

Somewhere Different

A former British paparazzi photographer decided to quit the rat race and give life a complete makeover. He founded **Somewhere Different** (✆ **016/5840018;** www.somewheredifferent.com), a sort of unregistered local tour operator. In Siwa he has a jewelry shop, a sandboarding business, and a lovely house for rent. Located in the middle of Shali, the house follows the traditional architecture style and has simple but creative furnishings; I particularly like the kid's palm-tree bed. The four-bedroom house is quiet, spacious, and can easily accommodate up to nine people. For LE1,000 a day, you get full use of the house plus cleaning and taxi service.

Shali Lodge This lovely little hotel, built in a style that matches the architectural curves in the old city, is situated down a quiet unpaved road that winds through palm trees. A 3-minute walk from the tourist-dense souk area, here you feel alone in the oasis, with a palm grove all to yourself. The walls are rough, sandy plaster, and the lighting is subdued at night. Arched doorways, terra-cotta light shades, and simple but elegant furniture hand-carved with traditional motifs really make this place special. The rooms are large and follow the style of the rest of the hotel, with rounded shapes and handmade furnishings; they also have fans. For eating, choose between seating on the roof amidst the top of the palm trees, with a view across the grove, or downstairs on low cushions next to the fireplace. Staff are friendly and well trained, and the food is excellent.

El Seboukha St. (right behind the souk). ✆ **046/4601699** or 046/4601395. Fax 046/4601799. Cairo office, 18 El Mansour Mohamed St., Zamalek. ✆ 02/27367879. Fax 02/27355489. www.siwa.com. 20 units. LE340 double. Rate includes breakfast, taxes, and service charge. No credit cards. **Amenities:** 2 restaurants; pool. *In room:* TV.

Shali Resort Though it doesn't make the most of its great location between the golden sand of the desert and the dark green palm of the oasis, the Shali Resort (not to be confused with the Shali Lodge) offers a spacious layout and a pleasant garden with a pool and a canal running through the middle. Buildings are small and in traditional style to blend with the landscape. The sound of running water and the view of the dunes from the garden create a delicious ambience.

Rooms are basic but spacious, with only a few local touches such as handmade glass light covers and Bedouin rugs. I'm not thrilled by the cement floor, but at least it's neatly painted. Don't bother with the suites, as the extra room they offer is wasted on a cramped and badly lit sitting area. The downside of the location is that you'll need some kind of vehicle to get into town to visit the museum, use the Internet, or eat at the restaurants there (the Shali Resort has its own very adequate restaurant). A rented bicycle will get you there in about 20 minutes, but isn't very practical, especially in the heat of the summer or after dark. A car can be easily arranged through the hotel staff.

Gebel El Dakrur. ✆ **046/9210064.** www.siwashaliresort.com. 77 units. LE360 double. Rate includes breakfast, dinner, taxes, and service charge. MC, V. **Amenities:** Restaurant; pool. *In room:* A/C, TV.

Siwa Safari Paradise Hotel This hotel is a comfortable, if slightly ramshackle, place about 5 minutes' walk from the souk, giving the place a relaxed and quiet atmosphere. The rooms are distributed throughout a cluster of small buildings surrounded by the garden, and the bathrooms are more modern than elsewhere around town. The furnishings are also fairly modern, and the domed ceilings of some rooms add charm. The hotel lacks the ambience of Shali Lodge or Albabenshal, but on the other hand offers a range of modern accouterments that they lack. The pool is a big plus after a hot day in the desert.

Souk. ✆ **046/4601290** or 046/4601590. 90 units, 70 with A/C. 45€ double; 65€ double with A/C. MC, V. **Amenities:** Restaurant; pool. *In room:* A/C (in some), TV, minifridge.

Inexpensive

Kilany Value This is a decent, clean, budget hotel that's at the low end of this price range, and is the best place in town unless you're looking for something super-cheap and super-basic. Several rooms have a view of the old town, which is spectacularly lit up after dusk, and the hustle and bustle on the street below is fun to watch. Bathrooms are very basic, with no shower stall, leaving you to mop the floor afterward, and mattresses are thin. A rooftop restaurant affords a good view of downtown and the old city. Look at a few different rooms before deciding which one you're going to take, and try to get as far from the entrance lobby and office as you can; between the phone, the TV, and the socializing, it can get a little noisy down there.

Souk. ✆ **046/4601052** or 0122274355. 14 units. LE70 double. No credit cards. **Amenities:** Restaurant. *In room:* No phone.

Palm Trees Hotel Very much a budget place, the Palm Trees is just outside the main square, making it convenient to the town center with its unique Siwan atmosphere, shops, and businesses. A "chalet" around the garden is a better bet than a room in the main building. The prime advantage of this place is its walled garden where fellow backpackers come together for a chitchat.

Souk. ✆ **046/4601703** or 012/1046652. 25 units. LE75 chalet; LE50 double. No credit cards. **Amenities:** Restaurant. *In room:* No phone.

WHERE TO EAT

Abdu Value INTERNATIONAL This is one of Siwa's most famous restaurants and is favored by locals and tourists alike. The street side of the restaurant is open, giving you a view of donkey taxis and dusty 4×4s piled with food and supplies. The menu is an eclectic mix of Western and Egyptian, and though there's pasta, I'd stick with items such as pizza and grilled chicken. The beef shish kebab is excellent, with a tasty and fresh side of french fries, and comes with *tahina,* fresh-cut cucumber, and Siwa olives.

Souk. Appetizers LE6–LE15; main courses LE20–LE35. No credit cards. Daily 8am–10pm.

Albabenshal Hotel ★★ FUSION The restaurant on the roof of this hotel is literally built into ruins on a hill above Siwa's old town and looks over the town's main square and the ruins, which are lit up spectacularly at night. Local specialties get a European twist, thanks to the French chef who was brought on to develop the menu and train the cooks. Dishes include a tasty mixed salad with crispy croutons, *shorbat maghrebi* (a vegetable soup with little pieces of beef in it), and lamb *moza* (shank of lamb, braised and served with couscous and a side of vegetables in a light tomato-based sauce). Dessert includes *konafa* pastry with date sauce. I also highly recommend this place for breakfast, which, in addition to excellent a la carte options such as the date crepes, features a set menu of an omelet, *fuul,* local bread, Siwa olives, and some of the best marmalades I've ever had; don't miss the sycamore or olive ones.

Souk. ✆ **046/4601499.** Appetizers LE7–LE15; main courses LE20–LE40. No credit cards. Daily 8am–10pm.

Siwa Jewelry

The styles and patterns of Siwan jewelry owe more to the Berber heritage of the Siwan people than anything you'll find in the far-off Nile Valley. Though beautiful and decorative, jewelry also served a number of social roles. Jewelry, in the days of bartering and in the absence of any kind of savings banks, served as a family's capital investment scheme, and a large proportion of savings could be literally hung around the necks of daughters and wives. Original work is scarce these days, but modern, locally made jewelry is just as nice, and buying it instead of the antiques ensures the dwindling heritage of Siwa stays where it belongs—in the hands of Siwans.

Visiting the stores and stalls of Siwa, you're sure to find a large selection of *aswira,* or bracelets. The narrow bands have a bird motif, the design that's most closely associated with the area, and are usually worn in pairs by the women of the oasis. The elaborate headdresses of Siwa are also highly characteristic of the area. If you're lucky, you may spot a woman with an ornate headband across her forehead. This is a *lugaya* and is originally a Libyan style of ornament. The large, and quite heavy, crescent-shaped earrings that are hung with chains and bells are called *tilakin,* and if they look a bit much for your earlobes, don't worry: They are, in fact, hung from a strap that fits across the head.

The most interesting piece of jewelry in Siwa is a pair of pieces that are usually worn together as a necklace by single women of marriageable age. The first piece is a hoop of silver, called *aghrou,* worn around the neck like the chain of a necklace. Tapered, it has a loop at the thicker end that's secured by nine windings of wire. The thinner end of the hoop has a hook, which fits into the loop and secures it around the woman's neck. It's said that the hook and loop represent the male and female reproductive organs, and the nine windings of the wire refer to the 9 months of pregnancy. A medallion, decorated with a variety of motifs, is hung from the *aghrou.* When the woman wearing the *aghrou* gets engaged, part of her marriage ceremony involves handing this piece of jewelry to the next woman in her family to be married.

Kenooz ★★ FUSION At Kenooz, located inside the Shali Lodge, you can choose to eat on the roof with the stars above you or in a cozy location downstairs that's equipped with low tables, cushion seating, and a fireplace.

Like the architecture, the food is a sophisticated version of traditional local fare twisted to suit European tastes. Try the free-range chicken in a thick, rich sauce (made from local organic olives) with a big pile of rice on the side, or the lamb kebab with french fries. They also offer vegetarian dishes, which is almost unheard of in the rest of the country; try out *rommanya* (oven-baked lentils with eggplant and a dash of herbs and pomegranate syrup). All meals come with fresh, warm bread, and the food is served on traditional clay plates. For dessert, the date crepe is a tried and tested recommendation.

El Seboukha St. ✆ **046/4601299.** Appetizers LE7–LE15; main courses LE20–LE40. No credit cards. Daily 8am–10pm.

Tanta Wa INTERNATIONAL This basic restaurant is located in the palm trees next to Cleopatra's Bath. Seating is on cushions with your back to a palm log, and the structure is more reminiscent of a beach hut than a real restaurant. Both the pizzas and the sandwiches are good, and the fresh fruit juice is some of the best around.

Cleopatra's Bath. Appetizers LE6–LE15; main courses LE20–LE40. No credit cards. Daily 8am–10pm.

SHOPPING

Siwa has long been Egypt's best source for traditional jewelry. Worn by local women on festive occasions, the simple silver designs have increasingly been attracting international attention. The oasis is also the source of beautiful, simple clay pots and tableware in unusual shapes, locally woven rugs, and embroidery. Unfortunately, much of the original household production has been bought up by unscrupulous collectors, and though an effort is now being made to keep these precious cultural artifacts in Siwa for the museum, you may still find them for sale. You can play a direct part in preserving a unique and special culture by leaving these in Siwa and taking away only newly produced pieces, which are just as genuine and beautiful.

The **souk,** the main and only square in Siwa, is the place to go for shopping. The square is rung with small stores offering local weaving and embroidery and simple jewelry. Browse and haggle are the rules.

Next to the Albabenshal Hotel, which you can see at one end of the square, is the **Albabenshal Concept Store,** open daily 8am to 5pm, offering a range of unexpected but delicious local food products. A bottle of date syrup or a jar of olive marmalade makes a great local gift.

2 BAHAREYA

From Cairo, Bahareya is the closest real desert oasis. The main town of Bawiti (which is what most people mean when they talk about Bahareya) is an excellent base for trips into the Western Desert. But hang around for a couple of days, and you'll see that Bahareya has a couple of local attractions for you to savor. The Golden Mummies heads the list. The mummies were discovered by archaeologists in 1993 after a donkey fell in a hole. Dubbed the Valley of the Golden Mummies, it has already yielded more than 100 mummies and is thought to contain as many as 10,000 more. The site of the necropolis hasn't yet been developed as a tourist site, but a few of the mummies are on display at the museum in Bawiti. During the Ptolemaic and subsequent Roman periods (around 2,000 years ago), the oasis was a rich and fertile agricultural center and may have had a population of up to half a million people. Some became very rich and decided to build themselves lavish tombs. To see how elite Ancient Egyptians cared about death and the life after it, head to the tombs of Zed-Amunerankh and Banentiu, belonging to a local wealthy businessman and his son. For outgoing nature lovers, Bahareya offers excellent opportunities; plunge in the natural hot or cold springs, hike the close-by Gabel El Ingleez, El Dest, or El Maghrafa, or perhaps go on a safari to the Black and White deserts.

ESSENTIALS

Getting There

BY BUS From **Turgoman Bus Station** (© **02/27735668** or -9) in Cairo, there is one daily bus that departs for Bahareya and two others for Farafra, stopping in Bahareya along the way. Tickets will set you back LE40, but the buses running this route are not the best in the country; be ready for an uncomfortable 5-hour bus ride. In Bahareya, the "bus station" is a kiosk in the middle of the town.

BY CAR If you are up for it, the drive from Cairo is a 375km-long (232-miles) stretch that cuts right through the Western Desert. Other than desert scenery, there is practically nothing. Your car needs to be in mint condition, and you must carry enough food, water, and perhaps fuel. There is one fuel station midway, but sometimes it runs out of petrol. From Cairo, the single-carriage road that leads to Bahareya, and consequently Farafra, Dakhla, and Kharga, is an offshoot of Cairo–Fayum Road; head to Midan El Remaya in Haram, follow the signs reading CAIRO–FAYUM ROAD, and then take the right that reads SIX OF OCTOBER CITY/WAHHAT ROAD. Some of the lodging facilities reviewed below can arrange a pick-up from Cairo; it comes with a hefty price but may be worth checking, especially if you're in a group.

Getting Around

ON FOOT There are no taxis in Bawiti, but for the most part it's small enough to get around on foot when you are not in your guide's vehicle. For running between the different villages of the oasis, you will certainly need more than just your feet.

BY CAR If you don't already have a guide and a 4×4 booked, ask at your hotel—there are plenty of both around. Expect to pay about LE350 to LE450 for the day inside the oasis. It's better to include nearby sites (in other villages than the one you would be based in) as part of your bigger tour of the desert to cut costs.

Orientation

Bahareya is made up of a number of smaller villages, with Bawiti being the largest and the most visited by tourists. There is really only one main street in Bawiti, and it runs through a central square. The post office, tourist information office, bank, and bus station are all very close to this square. The village sprawls outward, becoming older, lower, and more ramshackle in all directions until it peters out into the desert. None of the hotels, services, and shops listed here is more than a 15-minute walk from the main square.

The **tourism office** (✆ **02/38473039**) is located on the main square. If you're coming down from the bus stop, it's the office on your left inside the large, gray government building. In addition to supplying you with colorful pamphlets, the man in charge can be quite helpful answering your oasis-related questions, as well as finding a hotel if you haven't already booked one. The office is open Sunday to Thursday 8:30am to 2pm; closed April to November.

There are a couple of places where you can access the **Internet,** not far from the main square; LE10 is the going price.

There is a **National Bank for Development,** just past the main square on the right. It's open Sunday to Thursday 9am to 2pm. It doesn't have an ATM, and its services are limited to exchanging currency.

WHAT TO SEE & DO

The desert is what brought you to this far and forgotten land, and most visitors coming to Bahareya will be here at the beginning or the end of a desert safari. Below are the main sites within the oasis and around it.

Black Desert ★ Fifty kilometers (31 miles) south of Bahareya on the road heading to Farafra, the desert begins to look dirty, like there is a dusting of black muck across the

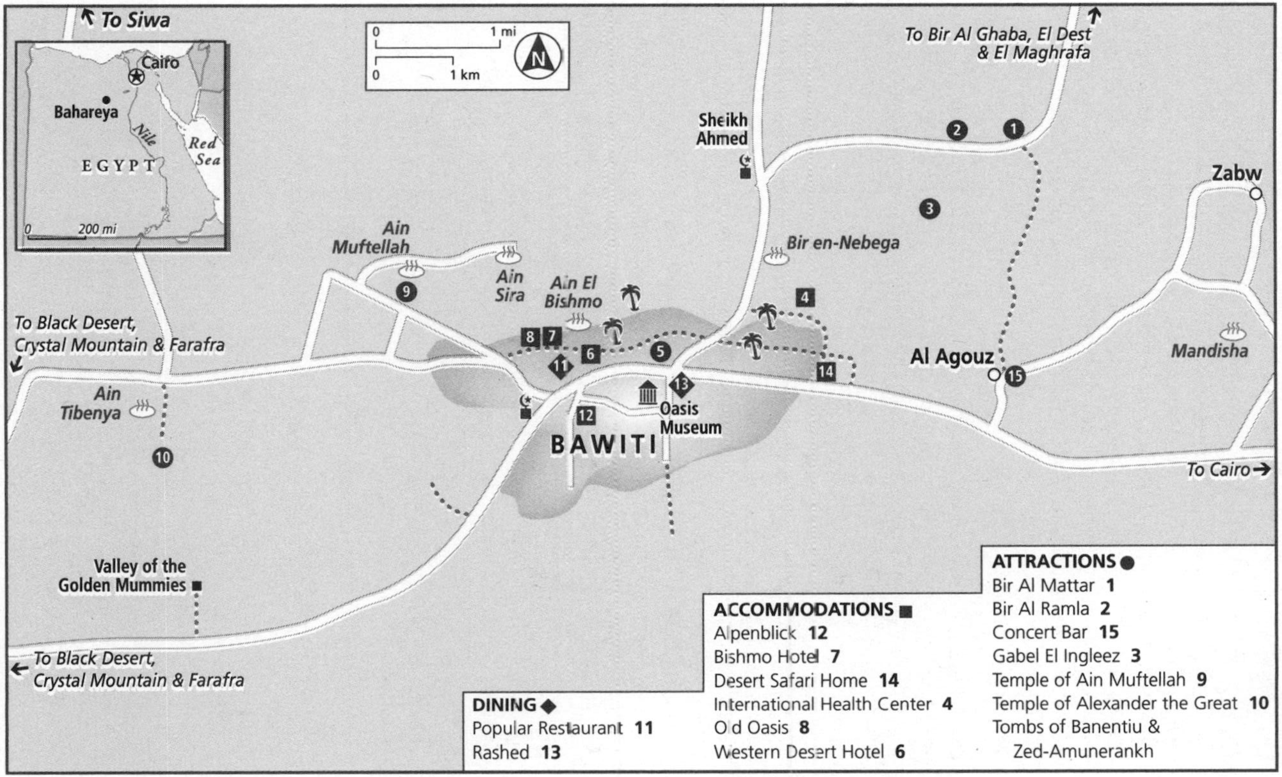
To Siwa
Cairo
Bahareya
Nile
Red Sea
EGYPT
0 200 mi
0 1 mi
0 1 km
N
To Bir Al Ghaba, El Dest & El Maghrafa
Sheikh Ahmed
Zabw
Bir en-Nebega
Ain Muftellah
Ain Sira
Ain El Bishmo
To Black Desert, Crystal Mountain & Farafra
Al Agouz
Mandisha
Ain Tibenya
Oasis Museum
BAWITI
To Cairo
Valley of the Golden Mummies
To Black Desert, Crystal Mountain & Farafra
ATTRACTIONS
Bir Al Mattar 1
Bir Al Ramla 2
Concert Bar 15
Gabel El Ingleez 3
Temple of Ain Muftellah 9
Temple of Alexander the Great 10
Tombs of Banentiu & Zed-Amunerankh
ACCOMMODATIONS
Alpenblick 12
Bishmo Hotel 7
Desert Safari Home 14
International Health Center 4
Old Oasis 8
Western Desert Hotel 6
DINING
Popular Restaurant 11
Rashed 13

hitherto pristine sand—this is the Black Desert. The most interesting feature of the area, aside from its color, may be the large conical hills that rise straight up like rounded pyramids. The hike to the top of one of these is tough, but the view from even halfway up can be an ample reward. The Black Desert is an utter contrast to the aptly named White Desert (p. 324), not far off.

Concert Bar When you've had enough of dead rulers and their tombs, head out to the village of El Agouz, about 5km (3 miles) from Bawiti. Here, recording artist Abdel Sadek El Badramany, who plays the *sensemeya* (a five-stringed lute), has created a place where you can settle by the fire and get a taste of Bedouin culture and music. If you don't have a guide to take you out there, head down to the Popular Restaurant (p. 321) and ask. Someone will be happy to take you out and bring you back for about LE50.

Admission LE30. Nightly around 9 or 10pm.

Crystal Mountain Known locally as Gabel El Crystal, this is actually more of an enormous hunk made up of quartz crystal rather than anything close to a real mountain. The hunk has a hole through the middle, while small pieces of crystal litter the vicinity. It is one of Farafra's most famous attractions and is an essential stop on your way to the White Desert.

Hiking & Trekking Bahareya offers a couple of good hiking and trekking sites that make good half- or full-day trips.

Gabel El Ingleez was used during World War I by the British to keep a lookout for marauding Senussi tribesmen coming from Libya. You can easily get to the top and check out the view and the ruins of the British outpost.

El Dest reminds me of South Africa's Table Mountain, yet on a much smaller scale. It is one of the hiking locations a stone's throw away from Bahareya.

El Maghrafa is another close-by location that needs no less than half a day to attempt. It acquired its name from its conical shape that resembles an upside-down ladle.

Springs Desert hot springs are rough-and-ready things, so don't expect changing facilities, wooden decking, and a swim-up bar. Sometimes the pool is just a natural depression, but most of the time it's actually a cement tank designed to collect water. There are a number of hot springs around Bahareya, and choosing the right one is a bit like Goldilocks choosing her porridge—Bir Al Ramla (Sand Spring) is too hot (113°F/45°C), while Bir Al Mattar (Rain Spring) is too cold (unless it's a really hot day).

Off to the Desert

Bahareya's relative proximity to the capital has given it an edge; being used as a base for longer hauls deep into the desert. On offer is a long list of destinations and a never-ending combination of tailor-made trips. Price-wise, the cost for a 2-day (1-night) trip out in the desert varies from LE200 to LE400 depending on how many people are in the group (minimum two). Prices include transportation in a 4×4, dinner, water, and camping gear (tents but not sleeping bags). The most classic trip is the 2-day Night at the White Desert (p. 324) excursion, which passes by the Black Desert (p. 316) and Crystal Mountain (p. 318) on the way. Longer desert trips go as far as the Libyan and Sudanese borders to the secluded and stranded El Gilf El Kebir (p. 339)

Bir Al Ghaba, at least for me, is just right. Unlike several others, it's also a bit off the beaten track; about 15km (10 miles) northeast of Bawiti. El Bishmo, next to the hotel of the same name, has some of the best views of the oasis, but the water is not where you should be taking a plunge.

26th Dynasty & Greco-Roman Sites

Before you head out to see any of the 26th Dynasty and Greco-Roman sites, stop by the kiosk by the museum to buy a ticket for all five sites (Tomb of Zed-Amunerankh, Tomb of Banentiu, Temple of Ain Muftellah, Temple of Alexander the Great, and the Golden Mummies). Hours are 8am until 4pm; a 1-day ticket costs LE35.

Golden Mummies ★★ In 1996, a Roman period necropolis was discovered just 6km (4 miles) south of Bawiti and not far from the Temple of Alexander. It uncovered multi-chamber family tombs where rows of marvelously decorated coffins were lined one next to the other. Since some of the mummies have gold-painted face masks, the discovery became known to the world as the Valley of the Golden Mummies. Not all the mummies shimmer in gold; some have vibrantly painted cartonnage coffins, while some have subtle pottery ones. The coffins chiefly belong to the Roman population of the oasis. Unlike Ancient Egyptians, the Romans missed on the ancient mummification secrets, and the mummies' bodies inside did not last like those in earlier burials. Ten spectacular golden sarcophagi are now on display at the oasis museum (off the main road in the middle of Bawiti).

Temple of Ain El Muftellah The temple is actually made up of four chapels that date back to the 26th Dynasty before being significantly expanded during both the Ptolemaic and Roman periods. The temple was discovered in 1901, and it got its name from the nearby El Muftellah water spring, a little to the west of Bawiti. The chapels don't conform to the classic temple designs that were followed in Thebes and throughout the country at the time, but they do cling to the Ancient Egyptian style when it comes to reliefs, some of which are quite beautiful. One of the chapels seems to have been entirely dedicated to Bes, the dwarf God of Musicians and Dancers.

Temple of Alexander the Great This temple, built outside the town but quite close to an old pass through which travelers from Siwa had to descend to get into Bahareya, presents a bit of a puzzle. When it was excavated by the well-known Egyptian architect and archaeologist Ahmed Fakry in the late 1930s, it was found to have Alexander the Great's effigy and cartouche inscribed in the wall. Both have since unfortunately been erased, literally sandblasted away by the wind, but the question remains of why, if the Macedonian never came farther south than Siwa, his image was engraved here. Though the temple is relatively large, it is in ruins, with only a handful of withering engravings left to see.

Tomb of Banentiu ★★ This tomb belongs to a powerful businessman who decided to build himself a lavish, by nobility standards, tomb next to his father Zed-Amunerankh (below). A depiction of ancient deities Horus and Thoth guard the entrance that leads to a relatively large square-pillared hall with three side chambers. Wall paintings in earth tones depict an array of Ancient Egyptian gods and religious scenes. Of particular interest is the panel depicting the journey of the moon god Khonsu (you'll see it to the right of the entrance to the main burial chamber); Khonsu is seated in the middle of the panel between the horns of the crescent moon. Worship of the moon god was particularly important in the oases, where the sun could be harsh, and both work and travel were often easier and safer at night. The four chains made of ankhs descending from the moon in this panel represent life.

Tomb of Zed-Amunerankh ★ It's assumed that the original inhabitant of this tomb was a wealthy 26th Dynasty businessman, perhaps a trader in the wine for which the oasis was once famous. It was one of four tombs excavated by Ahmed Fakhry back in 1938; but the tomb had been robbed a long time before then. It is large, by the oases's tomb standards, and comes with unusual round pillars. Reliefs are in a relatively good state and depict the customary religious and funerary scenes. Reaching the tomb via an iron ladder down a deep shaft adds an Indiana Jones feel to the experience.

WHERE TO STAY

I recommend staying at one of the hotels on the edge of town to take advantage of the space and the quiet there. All the hotels that I've listed will pick you up at the bus station if you let them know in advance when you're coming in.

Alpenblick Alpenblick has rooms on two levels facing a central garden. The single rooms are small enough to make you feel claustrophobic, and certainly too small for the price, but the doubles are standard budget-size rooms. There is a coffee shop on the roof, and all the rooms have air-conditioning. The place is very clean, and the staff are friendly and helpful. However, it doesn't offer the same value for money as some of the other places in town.

Bawiti. ✆ **02/38472184** or 010/2266599. alpenblick_hotel_oases@hotmail.com. 25 units. LE220 double. Rate includes breakfast, taxes, and service charges. No credit cards. **Amenities:** Restaurant. *In room:* A/C, no phone.

Bishmo Hotel If the Old Oasis (below) is full, try the Bishmo, which is right next door. I prefer the Old Oasis because it has a garden and pool, and the view across the desert isn't blocked. The Bishmo rooms are clean, however, with palm ceilings, stone walls, and scattered Bedu wall hangings. The best rooms are nos. 303 and 305—this is fairly well known, however, so you have to book well ahead to get them.

Bawiti. ✆ **02/38473500.** el_bishmo@hotmail.com. 18 units. LE220 double. Rate includes breakfast and taxes. No credit cards. **Amenities:** Restaurant. *In room:* No phone.

Desert Safari Home (Value) This great little budget place, tucked away from the center of town, is owned and run by Badri Khozam, who has been working as a guide in the area for more than 20 years (p. 88). The rooms are distributed around a central garden overflowing with jasmine and are fairly standard for the price range. They're not very big, but they're comfortable and very clean. Perhaps, most important, if you're ending a safari here, the showers are supplied with plenty of hot water. The little restaurant is basic, with a menu that tends heavily toward meat, rice, and okra. Staff are accommodating and helpful, and there's a motor rickshaw that they can use to run you around town if you need.

Bawiti. ✆ **02/38471321** or 012/7313908. desertsafarihome@hotmail.com. 27 units, 12 with A/C. LE75 double; LE120 double with A/C. Rates include breakfast, taxes, and service charges. No credit cards. **Amenities:** Restaurant; Internet (extra charge). *In room:* A/C (in some), no phone.

International Health Center ★★ Run by a German-Japanese couple, this hotel is locally known as "Peter's Hotel," after its owner. Nestled into the foot of the Black Mountain about a kilometer (½ mile) from the middle of town, the main building incorporates a large hot spring–fed soaking pool, with the rooms spread out in low, bungalow-style buildings around the gardens. The decor around the hotel is more evocative of a

European spa (indicative, perhaps, of their market) than the Bedouin culture of the desert, and the wooden-floored rooms are spotlessly clean and fairly spacious. The restaurant has its own building with a thatched roof. Unless you're looking for something a lot more toward the budget end of the scale, the IHC offers good value for money and is a great place to base yourself for desert adventures.

Another good reason to stay at the IHC is that they can offer a one-stop shop for almost any conceivable safari need through their White Desert Tours company (p. 88). Staff speak excellent English.

Bawiti. ✆ **02/38473014,** 012/3212179, or 012/7369493. Fax 02/38472322. www.whitedeserttours.com. 45 units. LE336 double. Rate includes breakfast, dinner, taxes, and service charges. No credit cards. **Amenities:** Restaurant; bar; gym; Internet (extra charge); hot spring. *In room:* TV, minifridge.

Old Oasis ★ Situated behind the main town of Bahareya, the Old Oasis literally sits on the edge of the desert. Though it doesn't make the best use of the location (the view of the desert is partially blocked by a fence), there's a pleasant garden, and the whole place is very quiet and tranquil. The pool in the garden is a great place for a refreshing dip after a hot, dusty day of desert touring. Rooms are basic and vary quite a bit. The nicest are the newest, many of which have domed ceilings and local touches, but on balance I would request one of the older rooms that face the garden (and, thus, out to the desert as well). If possible, though, have a look at a few rooms before making a final decision. The restaurant, with its rock walls and palm ceiling, has some atmosphere. There is usually someone there who speaks English.

Bawiti. ✆ **02/28473028,** 02/28472177, or 012/2324425. Fax 02/8471855. 36 units, 24 with A/C. LE120 double; LE160 double with A/C. Rates include breakfast, taxes, and service charges. No credit cards. **Amenities:** Restaurant; pool. *In room:* A/C (in some), TV, no phone.

Western Desert Hotel Smack in the middle of town, across from the Popular Restaurant, this is an attempt at a modern budget hotel. It doesn't have a garden, and the seating area on the roof of the building is a poor substitute, but the rooms, though basic, are clean. The Western Desert's advantage is its central location—it's literally around the corner from the bus station and the tourist information office. On the other hand, there's really nothing else in the town and no reason to be staying in the middle of it. Unless you're transiting here and need an easy place to spend the night, you're better off somewhere farther away with more character.

Bawiti. ✆ **02/38471600** or 012/4336015. www.westerndeserthotel.com. 54 units. 40€ double. Rate includes breakfast, taxes, and service charges. No credit cards. **Amenities:** Restaurant. *In room:* A/C, TV, minifridge, no phone.

WHERE TO EAT

There are no restaurants in Bahareya that I can actually recommend. When you get tired of the food at your hotel, try the International Health Center (assuming that you're not already staying there). The two below are strictly eat-at-your-own-risk affairs. Unlike Siwa, which is virtually dry, beer is available in Bahareya.

Popular Restaurant EGYPTIAN This place has been here forever and has become the social center of gravity for the town. Hang out at Bayoumi's (as it's known locally) for long enough, and you'll see everybody in town. On the other hand, the food is bad and overpriced, and the toilet is unpleasant. Come here for a cup of tea or a couple of beers.

Bawiti. Main courses LE25–LE50. No credit cards. Daily 9am–midnight.

Rashed EGYPTIAN This basic restaurant, on your left after you pass the second gas station when coming into town, serves local food. It's perhaps a little better than Popular (above), but there's not much to differentiate the two except the social life.

Bawiti. Main courses LE20–LE30. Daily 11am–midnight.

SHOPPING

In a short row of little shops across from Popular Restaurant, the **Oases Bookstore** makes the most of a very limited stock, which includes Cassandra Vivien's essential, if hard to follow, *Guide to the Western Desert,* Ahmed Fakry's books on the western oases, and Sir Ahmed Hassanein Pacha's tales of turn-of-the-20th century exploration. They also carry maps, a few souvenirs, and T-shirts.

The **Girls Work Shop** sells local handicrafts made by the women of Bahareya. Wares include simple embroidery, some jewelry, and wool caps and scarves. Not only are prices very reasonable, and fixed, but the money goes directly to the women who make the products. The store is in the corner of a schoolyard a couple of hundred meters from the main square. Don't be discouraged if the front door seems to be locked; just walk 20m (66 ft.) down the wall to your left, enter the yard through the gate, and go into the store from the back. Hours of operation are approximate, but they're usually 10am to 1pm and 4 to 8pm.

Ganoub is an attractively arranged place that sells handmade baskets and camel-wool blankets, as well as locally made scarves, embroidery, and pottery. It's just off the main square near the bank, and is open daily 9:30am to 1pm and 4 to 8pm.

3 FARAFRA

Farafra is the smallest, yet one of the most prepossessing, of the main Western Desert oases. At first glance, the place doesn't seem like much more than a cluster of buildings on the side of the highway—a place to stop for gas, perhaps, and that's about it. Stick around for a while, though, and you'll find that the town has a very distinct character. A lot less touristy than Bahareya, and not so richly endowed with tombs and monuments, it nonetheless boasts a couple of lovely natural springs, a local artist house chock-full with paintings and artistic installations, and the world's most spectacular desert—the White Desert.

ORIENTATION

Getting There

BY BUS Two daily buses serve Farafra connecting the small oasis to the bustling capital. In Cairo, they arrive and depart from **Turgoman Bus Station** (✆ **02/27735668** or -9), while in Farafra the bus station is on the side of the road in the middle of town. Tickets cost LE65. The two buses stop at Bahareya on the way to Farafra and sometimes continue to Dakhla farther south.

BY CAR Farafra is about 200km (124 miles) south of Bahareya. It's a 2-hour drive on a single-carriage road with very little traffic that travels through some of the most beautiful desert scenes; you pass the beautiful trio of the Black Desert (p. 316), the White Desert (p. 324), and Crystal Mountain (p. 318) on the way. There is no service station on the Bahareya–Farafra sector of the road.

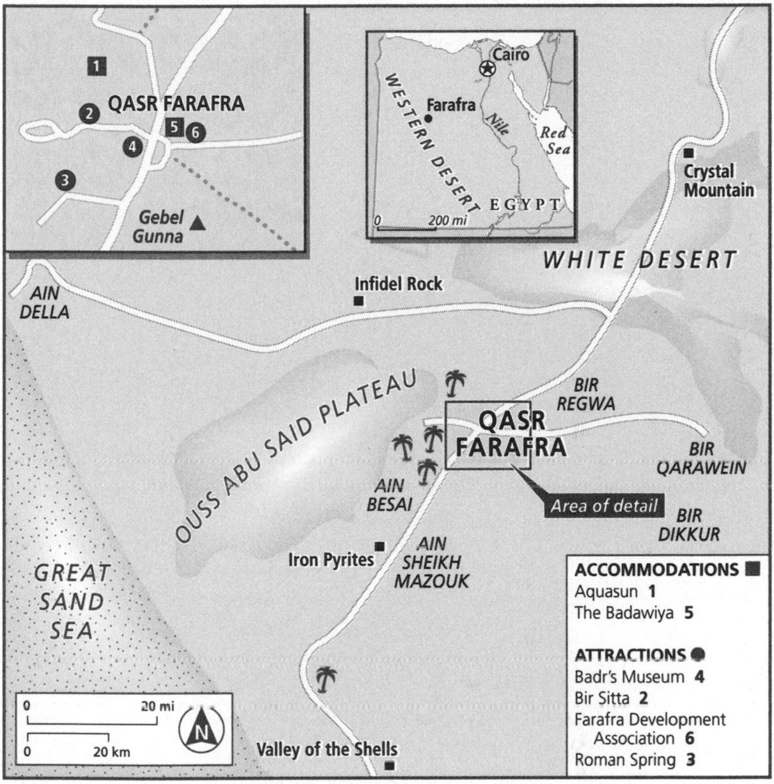

Getting Around

BY CAR Since the places you would visit are largely distanced from each other rather than clustered in one place, the only way to get around the oasis is to hire a local car and driver by the hour or day. Ask at your hotel—there are plenty of both around. Expect to pay about LE350 to LE450 for the day.

WHAT TO SEE & DO

In all honesty, there's very little to see in Farafra proper; the real fun is out there, in the desert.

Badr's Museum This is the creation of local painter Badr Abdel Moghny, who started by doing paintings of village scenes around town in a distinct, grippingly earthy, and detailed style. With success he branched out to off-the-wall sculpture and more commercially oriented techniques for his paintings. The museum is a constantly expanding building, with rooms and courtyards being added all the time to accommodate the fruits of Badr's latest artistic endeavors, and is worth a visit if only to liven up your day with something completely different.

✆ **092/7510091.** Admission varies. Daily late morning to some time in the evening.

Qasr & Gardens Most of the desert oases in Egypt and across the border in North Africa share the same conceptual structure, where a *qasr* (where the people built mud brick houses to live in) is built and surrounded by gardens, which were the fields they cultivated. Farafra is no different from the rest of the oases, though the remains of its *qasr* are not in the best shape. The gardens, or *ganayen,* are a delight for an afternoon stroll.

Springs Similar to its neighboring Bahareya oasis up north, Farafra enjoys a couple of natural water springs. The **Roman Spring** is touted as the last Roman spring in Egypt still in use. Tucked into the gardens behind the town itself, it's in need of a cleanup before it qualifies for much more than a 2-minute glance on your way somewhere else. On the far end of the spectrum is **Bir Sitta.** Well Number 6, as the name translates, is a cement water tank that is clean enough to jump in. One end of this utilitarian construction is an oblong tank big enough to accommodate 8 to 10 people in the steaming hot water, while the other end, where the water comes roaring in from the well head, is about the size of a Jacuzzi. A long, hot soak here under the stars at the end of a day out in the desert is heaven.

White Desert ★★★ This is a surreal part of the Western Desert that begins around 50km (30 miles) north of Farafra and runs all the way to the edge of the oasis. At first, looking out the window, you think it's some kind of mirage. The ridges of the rocks seem to have a frost on them. Then you'll see a snowdrift, and pretty soon you're in a winter wonderland. In fact, what you're seeing is a combination of chalk and limestone. The effect is extraordinary, not only because of its unnervingly accurate impression of snow, but because the uneven hardness of the rocks has caused them to form massive, dramatically carved outcroppings known as inselbergs. Kids will delight in coming up with shape associations (look for the mushroom, the chicken, and the rabbit), and photographers will fill up their memory cards trying to capture the brilliant hues of the setting sun reflecting off the inselbergs's shiny surfaces. Waking up amongst them is one of the highlights of any camping trip into the desert.

WHERE TO STAY

Taking into consideration the small size of Farafra, there are a surprising number of hotels here, but only two I can recommend. If you arrive in town and the below are full (which would be surprising), try Al Waha, over by Badr's Museum.

Aquasun This is a rather generic place out on the edge of Farafra. It does make an effort with wicker furniture and small, terra-cotta light covers in the rooms, but in the end it's comfortable but lacking in character. The central courtyard is nice, however, and the pool, while a little small, is definitely the kind you want to be in on a hot desert afternoon. The other nice feature of the Aquasun is the hot spring 50m (164 ft.) from the back step—just a walk down the slope to a hot soak under the stars.

Farafra. ✆ **0128139372** or 0101882808. 22 units. 50€ double. Rate includes breakfast, taxes, and service charge. V. **Amenities:** Restaurant; pool; hot spring. *In room:* A/C, no phone.

The Badawiya ★★ This is a great, comfortable hotel conveniently located at the northern entrance of Farafra (you can tell the bus driver, and the bus will stop a 1-min. walk from the front gate). The whole facility is only one story high, and the architecture of arches and domes blends into the desert background. Every room or chalet opens into a courtyard, and there is a village feel to the place that I find very comfortable. The food is not thrilling—the set menu is hearty and all right—but nobody comes to Farafra for the gourmet experience. The rooms are comfortable but sparse, with clean plaster walls;

local wood and terra-cotta touches abound. I recommend splurging on one of the chalets with living rooms and fireplaces in the new section. The hotel also has a pool.

Farafra. ✆ **092/7510060.** Fax 092/7510400. 33 units. 35€ double; 50€ double chalet. V. **Amenities:** Restaurant; pool. *In room:* A/C, no phone.

SHOPPING

Farafra Development Association The name's not exactly exciting, but this is a great shopping opportunity if you want to pick up quality local handicrafts at excellent prices. Even if you're just passing through the oasis on your way to Dakhla or to Bahareya, it's worth pulling off to check out the wares being produced by the women of the village. The association is actually retraining local women in traditional crafts, so the slit-weave carpets, camel-hair scarves, and embroidered *gallebeyas* are not only handmade, but made to patterns that have been handed down over the centuries from generation to generation. Prices are fixed and reasonable. Daily 8am to 1pm. ✆ **092/7510060.**

4 DAKHLA

If you're coming from the north, the road into Dakhla is where you really begin to feel that you could see the end of the Earth with a good pair of binoculars. The road is a thin band of black that stretches out ahead of the car, snaking between shimmering mirages, while over to the right the massive, sinuous dunes of the Great Sand Sea appear and disappear on the horizon. Just outside town, you come to a place where the dunes seem to threaten the road itself, riding up the power poles until they're half-buried and sending fingers of sand across the tarmac.

Yet, like most places that seem to be in the middle of nowhere, Dakhla is very much the middle of where it is. It was an important town in the Pharaonic period and up through the Roman and Islamic periods, and each successive era has left its monuments. Kellis, or Asmant El Kharab as it is called today, was a thriving community during the Roman period. Nothing but ruins remain today, but you can still see the community's aqueduct and church. Balat and Qasr were other urban centers that flourished through the subsequent Islamic periods, from the Ayyubid to the Ottoman rule. Though abandoned, both are in pretty good shape, and their zigzagging alleyways offer a beautiful surprise around every corner, from the House of Abu Nafir to the town's mosque with its 21m-high (69-ft.) minaret looming in the horizon. For a dash of Ancient Egyptian history, go to Deir El Hagar, where ruins of a 1st-century Roman-built temple remains, or head to the village of Bashendi, where the Tomb of Kitinos lies next to that of a local sheikh, Pasha Hindi. Speaking of tombs, the best in Dakhla are Muzwaka, a Roman necropolis that hosts two of the most beautiful tombs in the Western Desert. The finale for your Dakhla visit is unquestionably its rock-art site located about 8km (5 miles) south of the oasis. It's not as stunning as the ones you can see in El Gilf El Kebir, but they shed light on a period of time that precedes civilization and properly recorded history. Can you imagine that those simple engraved lines forming a camel or a giraffe have stood the test of time for more than 5,000 years?

ESSENTIALS

Getting There

BY BUS Two daily buses connect Dakhla to Cairo. Tickets cost LE65. In Dakhla, the main bus station (more of a stop actually) is in Mut, but if you ask the driver, he will drop you off anywhere you want. There are two roads leading to Dakhla; one is a continuation of the Oases Road that passes through Bahareya and Farafra, while the other is through the Nile Valley and Assiut. Check which route your bus is taking in case you are heading first to Bahareya or Farafra. Both routes take about 10 hours to Dakhla.

BY CAR Coming from the capital via the Oases Road, Dakhla is about 220km (136 miles) south of Farafra. It is an extension of the same single-carriage road with little traffic that leads to Bahareya and Farafra. Alternatively, there is another route that runs west of the Nile Valley until Assiut and then ventures off through the desert all the way to Dakhla. It is 50km (31 miles) shorter than the Oases Road, but the road until Assiut is heavily trafficked with trucks and often witnesses tragic accidents.

BY PLANE The nearest airport is in Kharga, which used to be served by a weekly EgyptAir flight. When the service will resume is a matter of speculation.

Getting Around

BY BIKE There are a couple of places to rent bikes in Mut. The Abu Mohamed restaurant has a few that they rent out for LE30 a day, and so does the **Garden Hotel** (© **092/7821577**). Unless you want to cycle around to pick up bus tickets or see the Ethnographic Museum, you'll be wasting your time and energy. It makes far more sense to save your cycling for Qasr, where the Desert Lodge will rent full-on Euro-spec 18-speed bikes for LE120; the maintenance has been a bit dicey, but the bikes are fine. The museum is 10 minutes by bike from the lodge, and you can also tour the old town of Qasr (just watch your head on the long, hanging arches).

BY CAR The only way to get around the oasis is to hire a local car or minibus and driver by the hour or day. Ask at your hotel—there are plenty of cars around. Expect to pay about LE350 to LE450 to rent a 4×4 for the day.

BY MINIBUS If you are on a budget or don't wish to rent a car, minibuses are always a good and much cheaper option. A good network of minibuses connects the different villages together. After sunset, service begins to slow down and gradually stops. Fares average LE1.50

Orientation

Dakhla, with more than a dozen small villages strung out over 80km (50 miles), each with its distinct patch of green, feels more like a series of oases than one big one. To the northeast and north (the valley curves like a banana) looms the escarpment that actually defines the edge of the desert, giving you a dramatic point of reference on how deep below the level of its surroundings the oasis lies. To the south there are great rolling dunes of golden sand. At some points the patches of green disappear completely, with the desert cutting across the depression, but then around the next corner in the road you find a thin green field that widens into a whole farm and then a well-shaded village.

Mut (pronounced Moot), the main town, is located in the middle of the oasis and is where you'll find most of the tourist facilities. While Mut can be described as charmless, Qasr El Dakhla (often shortened as Qasr) is simply out of this world. It's located about 20km (12 miles) northwest of Mut and almost at the end of the oasis. Between the two there are a number of smaller settlements such as Dohous and Budkhuli. East of Mut, the green thins out and is lost completely for several miles before reappearing around the ancient town of Balat.

The major sights are spread the length of the oasis starting in the northwest with Deir El Hagar and ending somewhere out near the eastern town of Bashendi or a little beyond

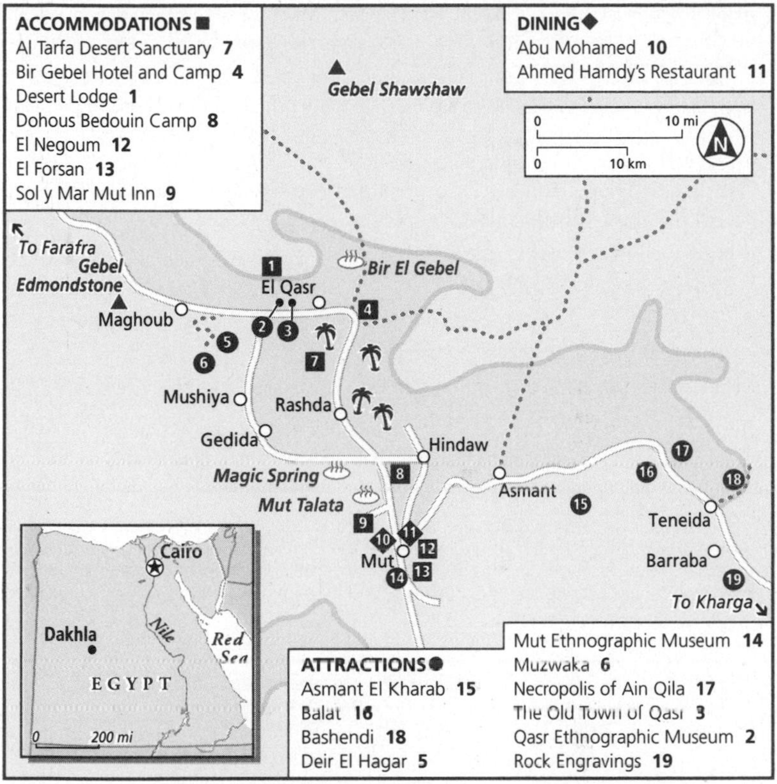

(depending on whether you consider the rock paintings near the highway a major sight). You could probably do the oasis in a day, but I recommend taking at least two.

The **tourist information office** (✆ **092/7821686**) is on your left as you enter Mut coming from the north. If you arrive at the first roundabout without seeing it, you've gone too far. The office is open daily 9am to 2pm and 6 to 8pm.

Going online is not an issue, even in the desert oasis of Dakhla. A couple of **Internet** cafes are scattered around, mainly in Mut. Service is not that bad, and costs LE5 to LE10.

There are no ATMs, but there is a **Banque Misr** (daily 8am–2pm, closed Fri and Sat), just off Horreya Square, where you can change foreign currency (mainly dollars, euros, and sterling).

WHAT TO SEE & DO

Asmant El Kharab ★ East of the modern town of Asmant lies Ruined Asmant, or Asmant El Kharab, which is the site of a major Roman city by the name of Kellis that began to emerge from the sand in the last few years. Visible ruins include a Roman aqueduct and an amazingly well-preserved 4th-century church. A wealth of documents—ranging from business documents to private correspondence to religious tracts—found at the site indicate that it was inhabited at least from the 1st century B.C. to the 5th century A.D., and reveal information about everyday life in the Roman era. Interestingly, they also indicate the presence of many Manichaeans. Manichaeism was officially frowned upon by the Romans, and the tracts found at Asmant Al Kharab pose some puzzling questions about why it was apparently tolerated here and who the tracts were intended for.

Free admission, *bakshish* expected.

Fun Facts Ancient Houses

The discovery of 200 round, Neolithic huts (in the same part of the oasis where rock paintings are still seen today) suggests that Dakhla may have been the site of the first major settlement in Egypt 7,000 years ago.

Balat ★★ This is a little town on a hill about 30km (19 miles) east of Mut. Like the old town in Qasr, at the other end of the oasis, Balat has been abandoned relatively recently, with its younger generations moving to more modern dwellings that now ring the ancient site. Where the Ottoman houses of Qasr rise as much as five stories above the streets, Balat's are considerably more modest, and everything is low and rounded. Doors are ovoid, and sit in bowl-like sills. Many of the narrow streets are covered to protect residents from sun and sand, but also supposedly as a defensive measure to stop cavalry from penetrating the town; door heights are too short for a mounted man to get in. Though it was a vibrant community even 100 years ago, only a handful of residents remain in Balat, and it's slowly disappearing. The mosque in the center of the town, though obviously in a state of collapse, is still occasionally used.

Free admission, *bakshish* expected.

Bashendi At the eastern end of the oasis, the little town of Bashendi is, like most of the towns in the oasis, built on the site of a much more ancient town. For me, the town is worth a look for the unusual design of the houses, many of which have a covered front porch supported by square pillars. The design is said to be based on ancient Pharaonic patterns.

The tombs are at the back of the village. The domed one belongs to a medieval sheikh named Pasha Hindi (from which the name of the village is contracted), but Roman elements are still visible in the construction of the dome. The adjacent tomb, known as the Tomb of Kitinos, is from the 2nd century A.D. and was more recently used as a billet for Senussi soldiers during World War I. There are six chambers inside, and the walls are decorated to show the original owner of the tomb meeting his makers.

Admission LE20. Daily 9am–5pm.

Deir El Hagar ★★ This sandstone temple to the Egyptian gods Amun, Mut, Khonsu, and Seth was actually built by the Roman Emperor Nero (A.D. 54–67) and finished a few decades later by Domitian (A.D. 81–96). What makes it a real must-see for me is that it's covered with graffiti from the who's-who of early desert explorers. Names to be found include Sir Archibald Edmondstone, the first European to get to Dakhla (in 1819), and Bernadino Drovetti (the French diplomat who accompanied Mohamed Ali's army to Siwa). The temple itself is small but elegant and follows the customary Ancient Egyptian temple building style. The Sanctuary, more specifically its ceiling, is the prime attraction of your visit with its astronomically themed decorations depicting Osiris in the center of the Orion Constellation, while other holy deities represent other elements of the universe (Geb representing Earth, for example). The temple was restored not long ago, and the reliefs are in good shape (much better than the rest of the Western Desert's Ancient Egyptian sites).

Admission LE20. Daily 9am–5pm.

Hot Springs Soaking at night in one of the many hot springs in the oasis is a popular local pastime, and as soon as you try it, you'll see why: The stars shine, the breeze whispers, and the mineral-rich hot water undoes the knots and bows put there by the day's bumps. Mind you, most of these facilities are little more than irrigation tanks designed to catch well water and distribute it efficiently. Don't get your hopes up for a cabana and a cold drink (unless you bring it yourself), and be prepared to appreciate the rough-edged aesthetic for what it is. Your guide will whisk you off to his favorite spot. In general, desert springs have a bit of an obscure dark water color, yet that is nothing to worry about: It's constantly running through the pool, and that's just the color it comes out of the aquifer.

Mut Ethnographic Museum On a sleepy side street on the western side of Mut, this museum doesn't look like much from the outside, but the inside is modeled on a traditional mud-walled house and is filled with domestic and agricultural artifacts from around the oasis. Exhibits include a collection of old handmade clothing, a mortar and pestle for salt, and an ancient goat-skin churn.

Admission LE20. Hours are not consistent, though noon–2pm is a good time to catch it open.

Muzwaka ★★ A necropolis that dates back to the Roman period, Muzwaka (The Decorated One) acquired its name from two beautifully decorated tombs. The first is a single-chamber tomb that belongs to a man by the name of Petubastis. Wall paintings in vibrant colors depict its owner and the usual religious and funerary scenes typical to Ancient Egyptian tombs. The second one belongs to Padiosir Petosiris; it has two chambers with depictions of its owner, ancient deities, and the placing of the heart on the Scales of Justice during the Judging of the Heart. The ceiling has a beautiful painting of a zodiac along with depictions of birds and animals. No bodies were found in these two tombs, but several of the necropolis's 300 tombs contain mummified bodies and a few inscriptions on the walls.

Closed for restoration at press time.

Necropolis of Ain Qila Just across the road from Balat, there's a site containing several ancient mastaba tombs, one of which—the 6th Dynasty tomb of a local governor—is open to visitors. The tombs are nothing to look at, but they're historically significant, demonstrating the wealth and importance of the oasis more than 3,000 years ago.

Admission LE20. Daily 9am–5pm.

The Old Town of Qasr ★★★ This is not only Dakhla's prime attraction, it is the most beautiful site to visit in the Western Desert. Just behind the more modern town of Qasr, Old Town is a labyrinth of twisting and turning alleyways that dates back to the Ayyubid period. It flourished during the Ottoman rule when four- and even five-story buildings started to rise. A downward spiral followed, and soon the whole town was completely abandoned. I recommend hiring a guide since you can easily get lost in the town's zigzagging narrow streets. It is not dangerous, even if you get lost, but I don't think you want to miss out on the best of the buildings, which include the town's 12th-century mosque with its 21m-high (69-ft.) minaret; the mausoleum of a local sheikh named Nasr

Al Din; the ancient olive press; and the restored Beit Abu Nafir. At its zenith, the doors to Qasr's houses were mostly adorned with acacia wood lintels bearing fine carvings of verses from the Quran. Today, 37 of them remain, and each bears the signature of the craftsman who made it; the oldest, and one of the most beautiful, is the one adorning Beit Ibrahim, which dates as far back as 1518. The last time I visited Qasr, a couple of workshops were functioning; they still follow the same old handicraft techniques.

Free admission, *bakshish* expected.

Qasr Ethnographic Museum ★ This museum is located in an old mud-brick building on the edge of the ruins of the old town of Qasr, and the exhibits ramble through a series of rooms to the back of the building. Some of them are a bit cheesy, such as the mocked-up traditional oven, but there's quite a lot here that can give you insight to life in the oasis. My particular favorites are the land-tenure deeds. You don't have to be able to follow the complex swirl of the handwritten Arabic script to see how sophisticated the system of land usage is in the oasis, and, taken together with the toothed sluice board exhibit in the Ethnographic Museum in Mut, they begin to give a context for the complex interweaving of irrigation channels that you'll see on any excursion into the countryside.

Admission LE10. Daily 9am–5pm.

Rock Engravings The village of Teneida marks the end of the oasis, but if you head out about 8km (5 miles) farther, to the first bend in the road, on the southern side you'll find a group of rocks adorned with some rock engravings. They depict, in very basic style, a giraffe, camel, and, perhaps, antelope. No exact date is determined, though it is widely believed to be prehistoric.

WHERE TO STAY

Very Expensive

Al Tarfa Desert Sanctuary ★★★ One of the top places to stay in the country, Al Tarfa Desert Sanctuary blends the posh elegance of European flair, present in the classical period furnishings, with the authenticity and ruggedness of the surrounding environment and Bedouin style, evident in the wide use of beige, the ceilings made of palm tree trunks, and the arches that mark its architecture. Al Tarfa redefines the luxury desert tourism concept with a pampering spa, the only one in the Western Desert. There are no rooms here, only individually styled suites, out of which two enjoy small private pools. Al Tarfa delivers with style and has deservedly gained itself a prestigious position among the world's tops hideaways. In 2010, it won Best Adventure in the *Tatler* Travel Awards.

Ain Al Dome, Al Mansoora. ✆ **092/9105007** or -9. Fax 092/9105006. www.altarfa.travel. 20 units. 484€ junior suite. Rate is on all-inclusive basis that includes buffet breakfast, lunch, dinner, excursions within the oasis, spa usage, taxes, and service charge. MC, V. **Amenities:** Restaurant; bar; pool. *In room:* A/C, minibar.

Expensive

Desert Lodge ★★ Perched on a plateau overlooking the village of Qasr, the Desert Lodge has become a favorite for European tour groups. Built mostly of local materials, it re-creates the look and feel of the old town of Qasr, which is spread out below, while maintaining modern standards of comfort. The rooms are large, comfortable, and clean, and the water is solar heated. Doors and window blinds are handmade locally, and the walls are decorated by the same hand-lettered calligraphy that you'll encounter in the old town. The hot spring has a stunning mountain view, and I particularly recommend a dip

Of Waterless Seas and Precious Green Stones

Occupying a large expanse of the Great Sahara west of Egypt's main oases and into Libya, the Great Sand Sea is infested with dunes that range from simple crescent-shaped mounds to gargantuan whalebacks. There are dunes as far as the eye can see. No one realized how immense the Great Sand Sea was before 1874, when German explorer Gerhard Rohlfs embarked on a desert-crossing journey from Dakhla oasis in Egypt to Kufra oasis in Libya. When he left Dakhla in his seven-camel caravan, he had no idea he was heading straight into a labyrinth of dunes. He was soon trapped with supplies quickly running out. By the time he made the decision to return, he didn't have enough water. Lucky for him, in an unusual twist of fate, it rained. The site where it did is marked and better known as Regenfeld (rain field). Rohlfs might have scratched the surface of how immense the Great Sand Sea is, but there was still a major discovery to be made—silica glass. The natural formation is unique to this part of the world and scientists remain puzzled about how it was formed. The most plausible theory points at a meteorite that crashed in the area. The light gray to pale green glass comes with a wide clarity range; from cloudy to fully transparent. It can weigh from a few grams to the largest chunk recording 27kg (60 lb.). Unfortunately, the irresponsible among us felt free to deal with silica glass as some kind of a desert souvenir; if you make it to the Great Sand Sea, keep the taking to pictures.

at sunset, when the fading light of day washes the face of the escarpment in a warm, orange glow. This place may not fit everyone's budget, but it's certainly one of the nicest places in the oasis.

Qasr. ✆ **02/26905240** Cairo office. Fax 02/26905250 Cairo Office. www.desertlodge.net. 32 units. 120€ double. Rack rate includes buffet breakfast, dinner, taxes, and service charge. AE, MC, V. **Amenities:** Restaurant; bar; bike rental; hot spring. *In room:* Fan.

Sol y Mar Mut Inn This hotel was developed in three parts: The first part, which has 10 rooms, is built around the swimming pool–like hot spring. The second part is 50m (164 ft.) down the road and has five rooms (only one of which has its own bathroom). The third part is made up of a half-dozen small huts in a garden behind the second part. You want to be around the hot spring, which is pleasant though small, as the other rooms are only for the desperate. As a walk-in, you'll be charged the same for any of these, and prices are far too high for any of them except perhaps the two big air-conditioned rooms by the hot spring. Check it out (there's a large sign on the road), but unless you get a good deal, you're better off at the Desert Lodge or the Al Tarfa Desert Sanctuary.

Mut-Qasr Rd. ✆ **092/7929751.** Fax 092/7927983. 21 units. $92 double. Rack rate includes buffet breakfast, dinner, taxes, and service charge. No credit cards. **Amenities:** 2 restaurants; Internet (extra charge); hot spring. *In room:* A/C, TV, minifridge.

Moderate

Dohous Bedouin Camp Perched on the edge of the oasis about halfway between Qasr and Mut, the Dohous camp (named for the nearest small village) has grown over the years. If you want to experience tourist accommodations as they were 10 years ago, you can stay in their original cluster of huts, though I don't recommend this. Better are the new ones built into the ridge below the building that houses the breakfast restaurant.

The domed rooms are dark, tackily decorated, and very basic, but they're fairly clean and relatively cool, even in the heat of the summer. There's also a new section, two stories high, with more standard rooms that have ceilings of woven palm fronds that let in some breeze. The beds have mosquito nets and the rooms have a fan. If you've been a week in the desert, this place is going to be fine, but if you're on a Sheraton-based tour, try the Desert Lodge or perhaps Al Tarfa Desert Sanctuary. Proprietor Abdel Hamid (p. 89) also maintains a small fleet of 4×4s and a herd of 35 camels for desert expeditions.

Dohous village, 5km (3 miles) north of Mut. ✆ **092/7850480** or 010/6221359. www.dakhlabedouins.com. 36 units. LE120 double. Rate includes breakfast, taxes, and service charge. No credit cards. **Amenities:** Restaurant. *In room:* A/C, no phone.

El Negoum ★ Possibly the friendliest hotel in the New Valley, the Negoum (which means "stars"), off the main street behind the tourist information office in Mut, has long been favored by archaeologists working in the oasis. From the outside, it looks like just another low-rise cement block, but inside, the lobby's decorated like an Egyptian living room, with mirrors, photos, and a long line of chairs. The rooms are very clean and spacious, and some of them have very good light. The restaurant is a little soulless, but functional. The staff are exceptionally welcoming.

Mut. ✆ **092/7820014.** Fax 092/7823084. 47 units, 35 with A/C. LE110 double. Rate includes breakfast, taxes, and service charge. No credit cards. **Amenities:** Restaurant. *In room:* A/C (in some), TV.

Inexpensive

Bir Gebel Hotel and Camp (Value) This is a simple little hotel close to the bottom of the escarpment and next door to the hot spring after which it's named. Most of the very basic rooms are arranged in pairs that share a bathroom and a small common area between them, but there are four rooms with their own bathroom facilities. The restaurant is indoors, but the outside eating area around the barbecue pit is a lot nicer. The food is good, though only a little less basic than the rooms, and the kitchen area is clean. Staff are very pleasant—you'll probably end up chatting and playing dominoes with them.

Qasr. ✆ **012/1068227.** Fax 092/7727122. elgabalcamp@hotmail.com. 12 units. LE120 double. Rate includes breakfast, taxes, and service charge. No credit cards. **Amenities:** Restaurant. *In room:* No phone.

El Forsan The Forsan is in an older, quiet part of town and backs onto a rather scraggy little garden where you can sit and have food from the restaurant. Rooms are a bit too small for the number of beds that they have in them, and the feeling of being cramped is made worse by the bad light, but they're clean. Staff are less casual and more polite than is usual in Egyptian budget hotels, but also more helpful.

Forsan St., Mut. ✆ **092/7821343.** Fax 092/7821347. elforsan1@yahoo.com. 30 units. LE110 double. Rate includes breakfast, taxes, and service charge. No credit cards. **Amenities:** Restaurant. *In room:* No phone.

WHERE TO EAT

Eating well is a bit of a problem in Dakhla, and I've found it's best to stick to the hotels. The food at the Desert Lodge in Qasr is an unexciting set menu of soup, meat, vegetables, and dessert, but the meal is substantial and the service is very pleasant. A few kilometers south, the Bir Gebel Hotel and Camp can supply a tastier, but rough around the edges, meal of meat, rice, and a traditional dessert of *agwa,* a sticky, sweet mash of dates and olive oil that can serve as a meal in itself. In the central town of Mut, the Negoum serves passable food, and the restaurant at the Forsan is also decent. If you want a real treat, then head to Al Tarfa Desert Sanctuary, but your wallet should be well prepared for the financial disaster about to hit. There are also several small local restaurants in Mut. The cleanest are two on the main road into town from the north and across from the tourist information office; both are explicitly aimed at the tourist market.

Abu Mohamed EGYPTIAN Just down the street from Ahmed Hamdy's (below), Abu Mohamed serves up great plates of vegetable stew and rice, as well as the usual grilled chicken and meat fare. There's not much to distinguish this place from Ahmed Hamdy's except for the overpriced Internet service and some so-so desserts.

Main courses LE20–LE40. Daily 10am–10pm.

Ahmed Hamdy's Restaurant EGYPTIAN Much like Abu Mohamed, Ahmed Hamdy has a small, tree-shaded seating area out front with basic food and beer. Don't expect anything more elaborate than *shish tawook* here, but dishes are substantial enough to keep you going and tasty enough to fill in the gaps.

Main courses LE20–LE40. Daily 10am–10pm.

SHOPPING

There are a few shops around Mut, but they don't do much beyond the Khan Al Khalili–style reproductions of Pharaonic carvings and cheap T-shirts. In Qasr, however, there's a small store with local handicrafts located just inside the entrance to the Ethnographic Museum. The prices aren't bad, and considering the options, you could do a lot worse than to acquire your Dakhla souvenirs here.

Some years ago, a few local women set up a stall selling local woven goods near the entrance to the old town of Qasr. Though a bit ad hoc, it's still there. Asking prices tend to be outrageous, but can be brought down to merely high with a bit of bargaining. All things considered, you're still only paying LE35 to LE65 for genuine local goods, and the money's going directly into some low-income households.

At the other end of the oasis, the women around the tomb of Pasha Hindi in Bashendi have been selling local jewelry to visitors for several years, and on my most recent visit their wares included some locally made clothes and a neat handmade wooden lock that you can see not only in the Ethnographic Museum in Mut, but in use around the orchards and pens of the oasis.

Enjoy a Late-Night Dip in a Hot Spring

The whole length of Dakhla is dotted with hot springs. Almost any time a well is drilled for irrigation, the water comes out hot and mineral-rich from aquifers as much as 1km (2/3 mile) below the desert. Wherever it gushes from the pipe, a large pool inevitably forms. Generally, these days a cement tank is built, with a sluice system to control the flow of the water into the irrigation channels.

The experience of bathing in one of these, particularly at night, can be unforgettable. With no bright city lights to interfere with the view and only infrequent clouds, the stars shine exceptionally bright.

Etiquette demands that you wait your turn if the spring is occupied, and they frequently are. It is not recommended for single women to bathe alone. Also, keep in mind that the minerals in the water may stain whatever they get on; consider it a free souvenir of a night to remember.

5 KHARGA

The last on the trail of the Western Desert's most visited oases, Kharga warrants a visit for desert lovers and travelers in transit alike. It has been a place of exile and banishment, where Bishop Nestorius of Constantinople and other reverent men suffered greatly during the early days of Christianity; no wonder the oasis's prime attraction is a vast Christian necropolis. The Bagawat Necropolis marks the horizon with its trademark dome-shaped roofs, while the chapels of Exodus and Peace are a must for anyone with the slightest interest in art and how it illustrates religion. Even before honorable bishops arrived, Kharga was well known to the Ancient Egyptians, and today the beautiful Temple of Hibis, along with what remains of the once busy settlement of Al Nadura, bears witness to how Ancient Egyptian civilization flourished even out in the desert. Kharga played the role of the far and away desert post during the successive Islamic periods and up to the Ottoman rule. The delightful-to-visit Kharga Museum exhibits some of what the ancestors left behind.

ESSENTIALS

Getting There

BY PLANE EgyptAir used to serve El Kharga with one weekly flight; however, at press time, the flight in question was suspended.

BY BUS Two daily buses connect Kharga to Cairo with a ticket price of LE60. In Cairo, buses depart from **Turgoman Bus Station** (✆ **02/27735668** or -9), while in Kharga they arrive at the **oasis bus station** (✆ **092/7934587**) in the old town, from where a taxi will set you back LE10.

BY CAR Two roads lead to Kharga from the capital. One is the Oases Road (via Bahareya, Farafra, and Dakhla) and is more of a smooth drive on a less trafficked single-carriage road; however, the total distance will cross the 1,000km (620 miles) mark. Alternatively, you can take the much shorter Nile Valley Road till Assiut, from where another road ventures off to Kharga. Total distance is about 600km (372 miles), but the Nile Valley Road is often plied with trucks, the majority of which are in desperate need of an overhaul; drive very cautiously.

Getting Around

BY TAXI In contrast to the rest of the Western Desert oases, here you can easily wave a taxi. The green-and-white taxis are abundant with much lower prices than in Cairo. Depend on sign language.

Orientation

The main road in Kharga is the north–south Gamal Abdel Nasser Street. At the northern end is Nasser Square, and at the southern end is Saha Square. The museum, tourist information office, EgyptAir office, and banks are all along this street. The Kharga Oasis Hotel and the Pioneers Hotel are just beyond Nasser Square. The old town lies to the east of its axis.

Tourist information (✆ **092/7921206**) is run out of a shabby office just off Nasser Square. It opens, officially, from 8am until 2pm and then again between 3 and 8pm. It is more show than substance, so unless you're here for a couple of colorful glossy pamphlets, you can easily give it a miss.

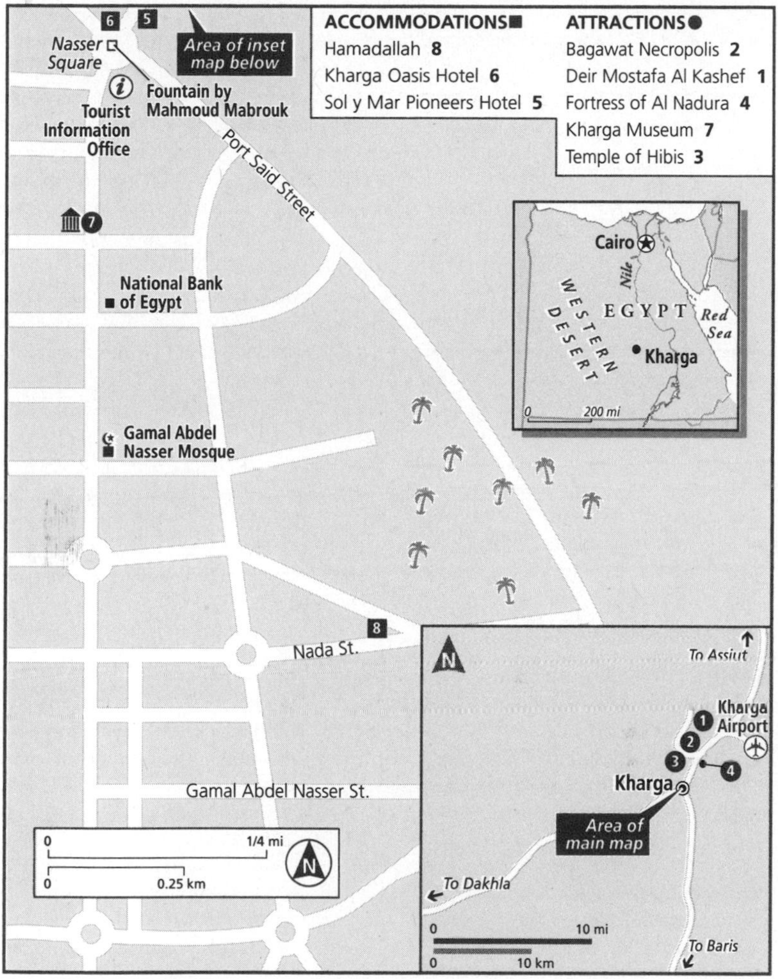

There are two **banks** that can change money in Kharga. The National Bank of Egypt is right across from the museum on Gamal Abdel Nasser Street, and there's a Banque du Caire on the next traffic circle south. They're both open 8:30am to 2pm.

A couple of **Internet** places can be found, though you would need to ask around as most signs are in Arabic. Expect to pay LE5 to LE10 for the hour.

WHAT TO SEE & DO

Bagawat Necropolis ★★ Built over an Ancient Egyptian graveyard, Bagawat started grabbing Christian attention at the time of Nestorius's exile to the oasis. By the time it grew into a full-fledged city of the dead, it had intersecting streets lined with more than 260 mausoleums, which range from one room to family size and share faux columns and their distinctive mud-brick dome-roof architectural trademark. The highlight of your visit is the two chapels. The **Chapel of the Exodus** is the older of the two, dating back to the 4th century. It gets its name from the scenes of Moses and his followers on their journey out of Egypt. Other scenes are also Old Testament and portray Noah's Ark, Daniel in the lion's den, the suffering of Job, and Jonah and the whale. The **Chapel of Peace** has brighter wall paintings depicting biblical figures in their allegorical settings. There are a couple of other chapels where you can see one or two wall paintings (in need of restoration), of which one depicts the Sacrifice of Abraham.

Fun Facts **Traffic Stopper**

The fountain in the middle of the Nasser Square traffic circle was completed in 3 days by local sculptor Mahmoud Mabrouk. The buxom woman represents Egypt, leading her people into the modern world.

A bit like the old city of Qasr in Dakhla, Bagawat is one of those sites where it's probably worth accepting the attention of one of the "guides" who'll approach you. For a modest tip, they will ensure that you get to see the nooks and crannies of this large site that you would otherwise miss.

Admission LE35. Daily 8am–5pm.

Deir Mostafa Al Kashef On the cliffs north of Bagawat Necropolis looms the ruins of an old building named for the Mamluk governor Mostafa Al Kashef. It is very much a ruin, but the remains of a 5th-century church can still be identified inside it, and there are some inscriptions there that are fast being eroded.

Free admission, *bakshish* expected.

Fortress of Al Nadura Between the town and the Bagawat cemetery lies the remains of the settlement of Al Nadura. It hosts two 2nd-century temples that are in ruins, with nothing much to see except the main temple's southern wall and some fading hieroglyphs. However, the climb will reward you with a panoramic view of the whole Kharga oasis. Used as a fortress by Ottoman troops, Al Nadura also hosts the remains of a Christian church.

Free admission, *bakshish* expected.

Kharga Museum ★ Built following neo-Christian architecture, probably inspired by the distinctive designs of Bagawat Necropolis, the three-story Kharga Museum warrants a serious visit. The first floor has a collection of prehistoric tools, with the Greco-Roman hand tools the most interesting. It also features a couple of Ancient Egyptian funerary items, as well as parts salvaged from a 6th Dynasty Pharaonic tomb. The second floor is dedicated to Coptic and Islamic arts. The items on display include 4th-century embroidered fabrics, a small selection of lovely 18th-century tiles, and a peculiar collection of 19th-century tableware from the Manial Palace in Cairo (p. 127).

Admission LE30. Daily 9am–5pm.

Temple of Hibis ★ This well-preserved 26th Dynasty temple was almost completely buried under farmland until it was discovered and excavated by a team from the Metropolitan Museum of Art in 1909. At press time it was still undergoing restoration, but a friendly smile and a modest tip were sufficient to gain enough access. The temple actually sits in the middle of a much bigger site but is by far the most interesting location to visit. Stop to examine the Roman gate as you approach the temple—the inscriptions there

Darb Al Arba'ain

Kharga was once a major stop on one of the most important major trade routes between Egypt and Sudan. Today, the highway south of the city follows almost exactly the same route of what was known as Darb Al Arba'ain, or the Forty-Day Road. For more than 700 years, this was the conduit of the untold wealth in ostrich feathers, gold, ivory, and slaves that Sudan sent to Egypt in return for weapons, cloth, and metal goods.

Nowadays the old route is abandoned, and though the name is still in use, it actually refers to quite a different route: a camel-trading track that starts in Omdurman, across the river from Khartoum, and makes its way to Daraw, near Aswan in Upper Egypt. The new route sticks close to the Nile and, being a little shorter and easier than the old one, only takes about 30 days.

Back in the heyday of the big trading caravan, staying so close to the Nile would have invited attack and robbery, and so the route looped far out into the relative safety of the open desert. The Sudanese town of Dongola, on the Nile between the third and fourth cataracts, was the major southern terminal back then, and the caravans, which were made up of more than 10,000 camels, bore due north across some of the most arid and inhospitable territory on Earth. After a pause in Kharga, they would angle northeast, reentering the Nile Valley around Assiut, where the riches could be unloaded and sold to merchants from Cairo.

have proven to be a fruitful source of information on the oasis during the 1st century A.D. Just past that is a gate decorated by Darius I. It is an extremely rare example of work done for the Persian king in Egypt. A line of sphinxes then ushers you into a colonnade and ultimately to the sanctuary. As you look around, watch for the signed graffiti left behind by 19th-century explorers such as Drovetti, Houghton, and Rohlfs.

Officially closed, but a friendly smile and a modest tip to the guard will get you in. Daily dawn–dusk.

WHERE TO STAY

Hamadallah Only stay here if the Kharga Oasis is full (which I can't imagine happening). The building is a crumbling cement block, and inside is dark and, at least during my visit, echoingly empty. That said, the staff are very pleasant, the rooms are fairly clean, and the air-conditioners work well. Bathrooms were clean enough, but maintenance doesn't seem to be as good as at the Kharga. Peeling paint and crumbling plaster are not hard to spot.

Just off Nada St. ✆ **092/7920638.** 32 units. LE90 double. Rate includes breakfast, taxes, and service charge. No credit cards. **Amenities:** Restaurant. *In room:* A/C, TV.

Kharga Oasis Hotel Unprepossessing from the outside, with its run-down courtyard, the Kharga improves a little inside, with high ceilings and good light. The rooms are spacious, clean, and comfortable for the price, which is low. The garden in the back is cleaner than the one in front, and is pleasant enough to look at from your balcony. The staff are friendly and helpful. The dining room is joyless and the food is bad; skip dinner and eat up the street at the Pioneer.

Nasser Sq. ✆ **092/7924940.** Fax 092/7921500. 36 units. 40€ double. Rate includes breakfast, dinner, taxes, and service charge. No credit cards. **Amenities:** Restaurant; bar (closed at the time of writing). *In room:* TV, no phone.

Sol y Mar Pioneers Hotel ★ By all means, this is the best place to stay in town (though whether it represents value for the money is another question). Rooms are generic but clean and comfortable. If you can get one at the back, the view across a palm-lined field to the desert is very nice. There is a pleasant if unimaginative coffee shop, bar, and restaurant setup, and the central garden is clean. A cold beer by the pool could be the ticket after a few days in the hot, dusty desert, but on the other hand, LE70 will get you into the pool as an outside guest if you want to save some money by staying down the street at the Kharga Oasis.

If you're having problems finding the place, it's locally known as *Al Row-wad.*

Gamal Abdel Nasser St. ✆ **092/7929751** or 092/7929753. Fax 092/7927983. 102 units. 108€ double. Rack rate includes buffet breakfast, dinner, taxes, and service charge. AE, MC, V. **Amenities:** 2 restaurants; bar; Internet (extra charge); pool. *In room:* TV, minibar.

WHERE TO EAT

There is the usual concentration of kebab and *fuul* places in the old town, particularly around the service station, but I recommend eating at your hotel. The restaurant at the Pioneer, serving a mix of generic European dishes and Egyptian food, is as good as it gets in Kharga. The *shish tawook* is edible, but the desserts are surprisingly fresh and tasty.

DAY TRIPS FROM KHARGA

If you have your own car, a day trip to **Baris** is an easy excursion that doesn't require any off-roading or guides. It's located 90km (56 miles) south of Kharga and can be easily reached following the Oases Road. Once upon a time it was an important trading outpost, being on the Darb Al Arba'ain caravan route, but today it is a small sleepy oasis. For whatever the reason it was named after the French capital, Paris (Egyptian Arabic pronounces the *p* letter as *b*). Baris grabbed some attention during the 1960s when Egyptian pioneer artist Hassan Fathy embarked on his artistic New Baris project. Much like the New Gourna project (p. 274), New Baris is a settlement model that infuses traditional building materials and modern building techniques. Unfortunately, the project came to a halt when the Six Day War broke out in 1967. New Baris was never resumed, and today a couple of abandoned buildings can be visited.

Continuing 13km (8 miles) farther south, you will come to one of Ancient Egypt's most secluded temples, the **Temple of Dush** (admission LE20, daily 9am–5pm). The sandstone temple was built during the rule of Roman Emperor Domitian and enlarged twice; once during Trajan's rule and again during Hadrian's. It was dedicated to the worship of Isis and Serapis and is believed to have once been covered, at least partially, in gold. Of course, that is long gone now; still, the view of the Ancient Egyptian temple with the vast open desert in the background makes for a priceless photograph.

On the way to Baris and the Temple of Dush, you will come across three sites that may interest you. **Qasr El Ghueta** (admission LE20; daily 9am–5pm) is an ancient Roman fortress that dominates the desert horizon with its subtle posture. The fortress hosts the remains of a 25th Dynasty temple that was enlarged during the rule of Darius I. Similar is **Qasr El Zayyan** (admission LE20; daily 9am–5pm), another fortress hosting another temple. The third site is a small defense structure locally known as **Tabiet El Ingleez,** as it was built by the British after driving out the Mahdi forces that briefly occupied the tiny oasis of Maks Qibli during the Mahdi uprising in neighboring Sudan.

6 EL GILF EL KEBIR

It appears out of nowhere. After hours of driving through an open desert, a massive 300m-high (980-ft.) wall blocks your vision, the gigantic plateau equivalent to the size of Switzerland. Welcome to El Gilf El Kebir. The Black Escarpment, as named by the Egyptian explorer Prince Kamal El din Hussein, might appear barren and desolate, but a few millenniums back it thrived with life; green fields, zigzagging rivers, bountiful lakes, and a bounty of game. It was heaven for early hunter-gatherers who called the place home. Predating civilization, they left us no colossal buildings or heavily decorated temples, but rather mesmerizing rock art. If you have a zeal for priceless heritage, book a tour of El Gilf El Kebir; it has the largest concentration of rock art sites in Egypt. The very first was discovered by the Hungarian aristocrat Count Almásy, who until the award-winning Canadian novel *The English Patient* wove a completely different story about the man, was known as a daring, even reckless, explorer of the Western Desert. It was 1933 when he came across the Swimmers Cave, which acquired its eccentric name from the rock art it hosts; it depicts a man swimming. Following suit was the British archaeologist W. B. K. Shaw, who in 1935 discovered Shaw's Cave with its excellent-condition cattle depictions. The last on the list dates as recently as 2002, when ex-military Egyptian colonel Ahmed El Mestekawy discovered the largest of all of El Gilf El Kebir's rock art sites—El Mestekawy Cave. When I first laid eyes on it, I was literally breathless for more than a minute; it is indescribable. Dozens of paintings and engravings shed light on how hunter-gatherers' lives must have been. They depict hunting scenes, dancing, and perhaps religious ceremonies, and various game that includes giraffe, ibex, and gazelle. It doesn't miss an inch on the element of mystery, with a couple of alien-in-nature engravings and a repeated figure of a headless animal; perhaps it is the mythical water creature ancients believed to have rain-bringing powers. Another question mark is the pairs of hand palms stamped all over El Mestekawy Cave. The two palms of the pairs often vary in shape, indicating the possibility of belonging to two different human beings; could it be the hunter-gatherers' marriage certificate? Rock paintings in the Swimmers Cave are in desperate need of preservation, with a real effort beyond just declaring the whole area a national park (which hasn't even taken place yet). The rare depictions of swimmers in the middle of the desert have gravely suffered from camera flashes and even worse: people spraying water so they could get a more vibrant photograph. The coloring material and fragile nature of the sandstone on which the paintings are depicted can't sustain such vandalism. Save the desert swimmers before it's too late.

During World War II, El Gilf El Kebir held strategic military importance as the Allied forces feared the Italians, occupying nearby Kufra oasis, which is actually closer to El Gilf El Kebir than Dakhla is, would stage a surprise attack on the Nile Valley crossing the desert via El Gilf El Kebir. Touring the plateau today, fuel cans, car parts, and even a whole car wreck are war tokens that you can still see. In addition, there is a memorial dedicated to the Egyptian explorer Prince Kamal El din Hussein, who discovered the plateau. It is adorned with a marble tablet with an Arabic text that reads, "In the memory of His Royal Highness Prince Kamal El din Hussein, the great explorer of the Libyan Desert. This monument was erected by some who appreciate his great efforts."

Dramatic scenery of dried lakes, eccentric desert formations, and a subtle wall-like plateau that stands in the middle of nowhere are some of the photographs you'll take away from touring El Gilf El Kebir. Because this is one of Egypt's most remote corners,

Zarzora: The Atlantis of the Desert

Before he discovered the Swimmers Cave, Count Ladislaus Edouard de Almásy flew over the whole area in 1920 and spotted a lush green vegetated valley. As the news flew, an old myth was instantly revived—Zarzora. The first record of the wealthy city in the middle of the desert goes back to the 15th century, when an Arabic script titled *The Book of Pearls* mentioned the mythical Zarzora. It drew on the romanticism of lost Atlantis and intrigued the curiosity of historical scholars and treasure hunters alike. The description reads: "You will find palms and vines and flowing wells. Follow the valley until you meet another valley opening to the west between two hills. In it you will find a road. Follow it. It will lead you to the City of Zarzora. You will find its gate closed. It is a white city, like a dove. By the gate you will find a bird sculpture. Stretch up your hand to its beak and take from it a key. Open the gate with it and enter the city. You will find much wealth and the king and queen in their place sleeping the sleep of enchantment. Do not go near them. Take the treasure and that is all."

choose your tour operator carefully, as the slightest mistake in fuel or supplies calculation can put your life at risk. The one company I recommend is **Zarzora Expeditions** (✆ **010/1188221;** www.zarzora.com). They have several 2-week expeditions running between October and April that cost around 1,500€ on an all-inclusive basis.

Note: In 2008, the Darfur instability in neighboring Sudan spilled over, and 11 European tourists were kidnapped. They were later released unharmed, though it was never officially confirmed if a ransom was paid or not. It resulted in a temporarily halt on tours to El Gilf El Kebir, which has now been lifted.

Fast Facts

1 FAST FACTS: EGYPT

AREA CODES Egypt's country code is +2. Its local area codes are Cairo, Giza, and Bahareya: 02; Alexandria: 03; Marsa Matruh and Siwa: 046; Hurghada and the Red Sea: 065; Sharm El Sheik and south Sinai: 069; Fayum: 084; Farafra, Dakhla, and Kharga: 092; Luxor: 095; and Aswan: 097.

BUSINESS HOURS All banks are open Sunday to Thursday from 9am to 2pm, though a few non-government-owned banks (such as some branches of NSGB and HSBC) are open till 5pm. On Saturdays, fewer branches are open; check with the banks' call centers (NSGB ✆ **19700;** HSBC ✆ **19007**). In resort cities such as Hurghada and Sharm El Sheikh, banks are generally open from 9am to 2pm and in the evening from 5 to 7pm. Stores generally open between 9 or 10am and stay open until between 9 and 10pm. Small grocery stores are open the longest hours, and you can expect to find milk or a pack of cigarettes easily at midnight.

DRINKING LAWS By law, serving or selling alcohol is not allowed to anyone under 18, and the bartender has the right to ask for your ID or passport if he doubts your age. Some nightspots will have a bouncer denying you entry if you are below the minimum age (though this is not regularly enforced). Drinking and driving is a felony according to Egyptian law, but it is largely overlooked. Driving while intoxicated is completely at your own risk. Alcohol consumption in public is not tolerated, especially from a cultural standpoint; please resort to the bar or the privacy of your hotel room.

DRIVING RULES See "Getting There & Getting Around," p. 49.

ELECTRICITY Electrical current is 220 volts in Egypt. Plugs are European-style, with two prongs. Adapters are readily available for three-pronged or two-pronged North American plugs

EMBASSIES & CONSULATES The U.S. Embassy is located at 8 Kamal El Din Salah St., Garden City, Cairo (✆ **02/27973300;** http://cairo.usembassy.gov). In Alexandria, the American Center Alexandria (ACA) is located at 3 Pharaana St. (✆ **03/4861009**). The Canadian Embassy is located at 26 Kamel El Shenawy, Garden City, Cairo (✆ **02/27918700;** cairo@dfait-maeci.gc.ca), while the Australian one is on the 11th floor of the World Trade Center, Corniche El Nil, Boulac, Cairo (✆ **02/25740444;** cairo.austremb@dfat.gov.au). The U.K. Embassy is located at 7 Ahmed Ragab St., Garden City, Cairo (✆ **02/27916000;** http://ukinegypt.fco.gov.uk). The U.K. has a Consulate General in Alexandria (3 Mina St., Kafr Abdou; ✆ **03/5467001** or -2; Information.alexandria@fco.gov.uk) and four honorary consulates in Sharm El Sheikh (✆ **010/1695074;** Dawn.Bacon-HonCon@fconet.fco.gov.uk), Luxor (✆ **010/5000119;** Ehab.Gaddis-HonCon@fconet.fco.gov.uk),

Hurghada (✆ **010/1695029;** Brian.John Evans-HonCon@fconet.fco.gov.uk), and Suez (✆ **012/2101343;** Dr.Samir-Hon Con@fconet.fco.gov.uk).

EMERGENCIES For the police, dial ✆ **122;** fire, **180;** or ambulance, **123.**

GASOLINE (PETROL) Egypt is one of the cheapest countries in the world when it comes to petrol prices: diesel is at LE1.10 a liter (LE4.16 a gallon), while 90 octane petrol is at LE1.75 a liter (LE6.62 a gallon), and 92 octane is at LE1.85 a liter (LE7 a gallon).

HOLIDAYS Holidays in Egypt can be split into fixed and moveable; the former follows the Gregorian calendar, while the latter follows the lunar Islamic one (with the exception of Sham El Nessim, p. 42), and hence falls back 11 days each year against the Gregorian calendar. All holidays render a closure of banks and government and civil offices, but restaurants, stores, or sites and attractions remain open. The only exceptions are Eid El Fitr and Eid El Adha, when the whole country comes to a standstill. For more information on holidays, see "When to Go," p. 45.

HOSPITALS In Alexandria: Egyptian British Hospital, Bahaa el Dien Gatwary St., Smouha (✆ 03/4274777); German Hospital, 56 Abdel Salam Aref St., Saba Pasha (✆ 03/5841806). In Cairo: Al Salam Hospital, 3 Syria St., Mohandiseen (✆ 02/33030502 reception, or 02/33034780-1 emergency and ambulance); Al Shorouk Hospital, 5 Bahr el Ghazal St., Mohandiseen (✆ 02/33044901 reception, 02/33459941 emergency); Cleopatra Hospital, 39 Cleopatra St., Heliopolis (✆ 02/24143931); Dar Al Fouad, Six of October City (✆ 02/38356030 reception, 02/35777300 emergency and ambulance); Nile Badrawi Hospital, Corniche el Nil, Maadi (✆ 02/25240022 reception, or 02/25240212 emergency and ambulance). For medical helicopter service (with a doctor and nurse), call ✆ 02/24184531 or 02/24184537 24 hours. In El Gouna: El Gouna Hospital (✆ 065/3580012). In Hurghada: Nile Hospital, Airport Road (✆ 065/355 0974). In Sharm El Sheikh: Sharm Specialized Hospital, Peace Road, El Noor District (✆ 069/3661745).

INTERNET ACCESS Internet access, through small cafes and shops, can be easily found in the capital as well as the stranded oasis of Siwa. But don't expect anything fancy, speed or connectivity wise, when you are paying LE2 to LE10 an hour. Most, if not all, high-end hotels and resorts offer Internet access (some Wi-Fi) at an extra cost.

LANGUAGE If you are in a tourist-oriented city or town, such as Luxor, you won't have any problem communicating in English, and often German or Italian (mainly in Hurghada and Sharm El Sheikh). However, throughout the rest of the country, Cairo included, you will probably resort to sign language, especially if you are dealing with an older person. Most of the younger generation speaks some sort of English. See chapter 13 for some useful Arabic terms and phrases.

LEGAL AID Tourists who find themselves in legal entanglements should immediately contact the consular department of their embassy in Cairo for advice and aid. Contacts are provided earlier in this chapter.

MAIL Egyptian post offices are not swift, but they are a reliable way of sending postcards and letters home. A card will cost LE2 to destinations in the U.S., Canada, Australia, and the U.K., while envelopes of 50 grams or less will cost LE4.5 to LE6.5 depending on the destination. For fast, trackable delivery service, you can always use **FedEx** (✆ **02/2687888;** http://fedex.com/eg) or **DHL** (✆ **16345;** www.dhlegypt.com).

NEWSPAPERS & MAGAZINES For newspapers, ***Al Ahram Weekly*** (http://weekly.ahram.org.eg) is Egypt's leading English-language newspaper. It comes out every Thursday and once a month features an informative four-page travel supplement. As the name might imply, it is another Al Ahram publication, the same state-owned publishing house that produces the country's leading Arabic-language daily *Al Ahram. Al Ahram Weekly* reflects the government perspective on matters and rarely strays off its message. Following suit is ***The Egyptian Gazette*** (www.algomhuria.net.eg/gazette), though it lacks any real content and can easily be given a miss. ***The Daily News*** (www.egyptdailynews.com) is the closest thing to an independent English-language newspaper in Egypt and is the best bet for local news coverage. The *News* comes bundled with the *International Herald Tribune*. ***Al Masry Al Youm*** (www.almasry-alyoum.com) is an emerging independent newspaper that's a fierce critic of the government, and at press time, printed only in Arabic; their English-language site, however, deserves a look. As for magazines, ***Egypt Today*** (www.egypttoday.com) has long dominated the scene, but it's fallen short on delivering the quality work it was once known for. The same goes for its more focused sister publication ***Business Today.*** For a good light read on heritage, ***Turath*** is a recommended option, though it only comes out on a quarterly basis. More frequent are the monthly ***Enigma*** (fashion and lifestyle; www.enigma-mag.com), ***Alter Ego*** (eccentric but enticing lifestyle), and ***Community Times*** (bits and pieces from here and there; www.communitytimesmagazine.com). English-language newspapers and magazine are widely available at bookstores, department stores, and big newsstands in tourist-oriented districts and cities.

POLICE The police emergency number is ✆ **122.**

SMOKING Egyptians smoke everywhere, though the trend of banning smoking indoors at places such as malls and banks is becoming more common. Still, most civil workers light up where they work.

TAXES Tourist services are subject to 12% service charges and 10% taxes, adding up to a number that varies between 22% and 25.44%, depending on how the calculation is applied.

TIME Egypt is GMT+2, which means GMT+3 when daylight saving time (DST) is in effect. DST comes into effect during late April and ends during late August.

TIPPING The general rule for tipping in Egypt is simple: When in doubt, tip. Tip drivers (except for taxi drivers, whom you pay by the ride), waiters, bellhops, and guides. Tip anyone who performs a service for you (shows you to your seat on a train or opens an extra door at the museum), and tip those who haven't done anything directly but ask for it anyway (often the case with street sweepers). How much depends on circumstances and service—a bellhop in a $400-per-night hotel who gives good services should be slipped LE30 or more, while waiters should receive a percentage of the bill that reflects the quality of the service. Being provided extra access at monuments or museums is worth LE10 at least. Bathroom attendants are well served with LE2 to LE5, as are street sweepers and anyone else looking for a handout.

TOILETS The best bet for toilets in Egypt is to head for the nearest tourist-class hotel. If there's nothing in sight, the next best option is a Western-style fast-food operation or a cafe. Public toilets, if you manage to find any, are downright dire.

VISA INFORMATION According to the Egyptian Ministry of Foreign Affairs, all foreigners except for nationals of Afghanistan, Armenia, Azerbaijan, Bangladesh, Bosnia & Herzegovina, Chechnya, Croatia, Georgia, India, Indonesia, Iraq, Iran,

Israel, Kazakhstan, Kyrgyzstan, Lebanon, Macau, Macedonia, Malaysia, Moldavia, Montenegro, Pakistan, Palestine, Philippines, Russia, Serbia, Sri Lanka, Tajikistan, Thailand, Turkmenistan, Ukraine, Uzbekistan, and all African countries are granted a 30-day single-entry tourist visa on arrival. It costs $15 (payable only in foreign currency) and can be bought from most of Egypt's major entry points (it excludes arriving at Aswan by ferry from Sudan). A 24-hour transit visa can be granted after disclosing the appropriate documents. To obtain a visa prior to your arrival, you need to check with the Egyptian diplomatic representation in your country. For a 14-day Sinai Only visa, see p. 189; for visa extension, see p. 95 and p. 165.

WATER Tap water in Egypt is not generally suitable for drinking, but it is often used for cooking or preparing hot drinks. Bottled water costs LE1.50 to LE2.50 depending on the size.

2 AIRLINE, HOTEL & CAR RENTAL WEBSITES

MAJOR AIRLINES

Air France
www.airfrance.com

Alitalia
www.alitalia.com

BMI
www.flybmi.com

British Airways
www.british-airways.com

Delta Air Lines
www.delta.com

EgyptAir
www.egyptair.com

Emirates Airlines
www.emirates.com

Iberia Airlines
www.iberia.com

KLM
www.klm.com

LOT Polish Airlines
www.lot.com

Lufthansa
www.lufthansa.com

Olympic Airlines
www.olympicairlines.com

Royal Jordanian
www.rj.com

Swiss Air
www.swiss.com

Turkish Airlines
www.thy.com

United Airlines
www.united.com

BUDGET AIRLINES

Aegean Airlines
www.aegeanair.com

Air Arabia
www.airarabia.com

Air Berlin
www.airberlin.com

Condor
www9.condor.com

easyJet
www.easyjet.com

Fly Dubai
www.flydubai.com

Iberworld
www.iberworld.com

Ted (part of United Airlines)
www.flyted.com

Thomas Cook
www.flythomascook.com

Thomson
www.thomson.co.uk

Transavia
www.transavia.com

MAJOR HOTEL & MOTEL CHAINS

Crowne Plaza Hotels
www.ichotelsgroup.com/crowneplaza

Four Seasons
www.fourseasons.com

Hilton Hotels
www.hilton.com

Holiday Inn
www.holidayinn.com

Hyatt
www.hyatt.com

InterContinental Hotels & Resorts
www.ichotelsgroup.com

Marriott
www.marriott.com

Radisson Hotels & Resorts
www.radisson.com

Renaissance
www.renaissancehotels.com

Residence Inn by Marriott
www.marriott.com/residenceinn

Sheraton Hotels & Resorts
www.starwoodhotels.com/sheraton

Westin Hotels & Resorts
www.starwoodhotels.com/westin

CAR RENTAL AGENCIES

Auto Europe
www.autoeurope.com

Avis
www.avis.com

Budget
www.budget.com

Hertz
www.hertz.com

Kemwel (KHA)
www.kemwel.com

13 Useful Terms & Phrases

The official, and most widely spoken, language in Egypt is Arabic, though many people, especially if they work in the tourist industry, speak enough English to get by. The social rewards of learning even just a few Arabic words, however, are enormous, and you'll find yourself embraced (literally quite a lot of the time) for your efforts.

Arabic as a language comes in a number of versions. In addition to the very classical Arabic of the Quran, which is more or less restricted to the holy book and not much in use today, there is transnational Modern Standard Arabic (MSA), which is the language used for official documents, newspapers, and so on. In addition, there is the colloquial Arabic, better known as *'ameya,* which comes in dozens of versions that vary from one Arab state to the other; Tunisian Arabic, Lebanese Arabic, Sudanese Arabic, and, of course, Egyptian Arabic. Though they all share the same 28-letter alphabet and the same grammar rules, vocabulary can just as easily differ as overlap; pronunciation is one of the key differences. Take the letter "jeem," for example. In MSA and much of the Arabic dialects, it is often pronounced as a *j* in jar, while in Egyptian Arabic it is pronounced as "geem," as in garden. Not all Egyptians speak the same dialect; pronunciation differs from one region to the other, and from one socioeconomic group to the other. A resident of Upper Egypt will pronounce the MSA letter "qaf" (a sort of heavy *k*) as g, while residents of Cairo will replace it with a glottal stop.

The Hamza

Hamza is a phonetic mark often preceded with a vowel and pronounced like a glottal stop. It can come as a', e', or u'.

Arabic is a very rich language, yet on the level of colloquial versions and dialects, things can get quite confusing. The below pronunciation guide compares MSA, Egyptian Arabic (the most common Cairene version), and the closest corresponding English pronunciation. ***Note:*** The dash between the different letters of the same word indicates a very short pause.

Pronunciation of the Arabic Alphabet

MSA Letter	MSA (English translation)	Egyptian Arabic	English
Alef	a in *ard* (land)	a in *ard*	a in land
Beh	b in *bab* (door)	b in *bab*	b in bat
Teh	t in *tareekh* (history)	t in *tareekh*	t in tab
Theh	th in *thalathah* (3)	th in *talatah*	th in theft/t in taxi
Jeem	j in *jamal* (beauty)	g in *gamal*	j in jar/g in garden
Hhah	h in *hadara* (civilization)	h in *hadara*	unvoiced h that comes out as a puff of air
Khah	kh in *khawf* (fear)	kh in *khawf*	ch in loch
Dal	d in *dar* (house)	d in *dar*	d in dad
Thal	th in *thaleck* (that)	z in *zaleck*	th in that/z in zap

MSA Letter	MSA (English translation)	Egyptian Arabic	English
Reh	r in Ramadan	r in Ramadan	r in ran
Zein	z in *zaman* (long before)	z in *zaman*	z in zap
Seen	s in *salam* (peace)	s in *salam*	s in Sam
Sheen	sh in *shagar* (trees)	sh in *shagar*	sh in shadow
Ssadd	ss in *ssefr* (0)	s in *sefr*	heavy a as in s sudden/slightly lighter s
Ddadd	dd in *ddameer* (conscience)	d in *ddameer*	heavy d as in dark
Ttah	tt in *ttarab* (music)	t in *tarab*	heavy t as in tear/slightly lighter t
Zzah	zz in *zzarf* (envelope)	z in *zarf*	heavy z/slightly lighter z
'Aein	a in *alam* (flag)	'a in *'alam*	a short, hard, but strangled a
Ghein	gh in *ghadeer* (spring water)	gh in *ghadeer*	gh in Ghana
Feh	f in *fahd* (leopard)	f in *fahd*	f in fan
Qaf	q in *qamar* (moon)	a' in *'a-mar*	heavy q as in Qatar/a glottal stop
Kaf	k in *kalam* (words)	k in *kalam*	k in karma
Lam	l in *lahhma* (meat)	l in *lahhma*	l in land
Meem	m in *momken* (please)	m in *momken*	m in more
Noon	n in *nas* (people) n in *nas*	n in Nasa	
Heh	h in *helal* (crescent)	h in *helal*	h in hail
Waw	w in *washm* (tattoo)	w in *washm*	w in Washington
Yeih	y in *yasmeen* (jasmine)	y in *yasmeen*	y in yard

1 BASIC VOCABULARY

ENGLISH-EGYPTIAN ARABIC PHRASES

A lot of social interaction takes the form of standard greeting and response patterns. Just saying a casual hello takes a lot longer, culturally, in Egypt than it does in the West. You'll find that Egyptians will appreciate your taking the time to say hello properly. This not only means saying hello, but inquiring after everyone's health and well-being.

ENGLISH	ARABIC
Yes	**Aywa** (more casual)/**na'am** (more respectful)
No	**La'**
Thank you	**Shokran**
You're welcome	**'Afwan**
No, thanks	**La', shokran**
Sorry	**Assef/Assfa** (M/F)
Go away	**Emshi**
God willing	**In-sha'-Allah**

ENGLISH	ARABIC
Hello	**Es-salam 'alaykom**
Response	**Wa 'alaykom mes-salam**
Good morning	**Sabahh el kheir**
Response	the same or **Sabahh el noor** (more common)/ **Sabahh el fol** (more friendly)
Good evening	**Massa' el kheir**
Response	the same or **Massa' el noor** (more common)/ **Massa' el fol** (more friendly)
Welcome	**Ahhlan wa sahhlan** (often shortened to Ahlan)
Response	**Ahh-lan beek/beeki** (M/F)
Greetings	**Marhaba**
Response	**Marhaba**
How are you?	**Izayak/Izayeik?** (M/F)
Response	**Quayess/Quayeissah** (good; M/F)
Praise God	**Al hamdo-lel-Allah** (praise God)
Great	**Tammam** or **zay el fol** (great; very casual)
What's new?	**Akhbarak eh?/Akhbarik eh?** (M/F)
What's your name?	**Esmak eah?/Esmik eah?** (M/F)
What's his name?/What's it called?	**Esmo eah?**
My name is	**Esmee** [your name]
No problem	**Mesh moshkela**
Where are you from?	**Enta menein/Enti menein?** (M/F)
I'm from	**Ana min** [country]
It's a pleasure to have met you	**Forsa sae'ada**
Response	**Ana asa'ad**
Goodbye	**Salam**
Foreigner	**Khwaga**
Okay	**Mashi**

What Goes Around . . .

European languages, particularly Spanish, and Arabic have a huge number of cognates. Many words that begin with "al" or "el," for example, come from Arabic (alcohol, alchemy, algebra, almanac, elixir). The word "hazard" was picked up and brought back by crusaders who learned to say *"haza!"* for luck as they threw their dice. Crusaders also brought back a variety of essential words for luxuries, including sugar (from *sukr*), sherbet (from *shorba*), and gauze (which came from Gaza). My favorites include admiral, which comes from either *emir al bahhr* (commander of the sea) or *emir al rahl* (commander of transport); floozy, which came back with the British soldiers who frequently came across Egyptian women offering their favors in return for *fellous,* or money; and serendipity, which comes from *serendip,* the name Arab traders gave to Sri Lanka.

Hieroglyphs: An Ancient Mystery

When Napoleon invaded Egypt in 1798, he arrived as well prepared to deal with a foreign culture as any invader ever had been. Apart from his soldiers and planners, he brought along 167 experts on just about everything that Europe had expertise in at that point: There were linguists, mathematicians, astronomers, surveyors, doctors, Arabists—the list could go on. One thing they found, however, stumped them entirely: the strange picture-script known as hieroglyphs, found all over the tombs and ancient temples.

The French experts weren't the first to try to figure out the language. For at least 2 centuries, Europeans had been scratching their heads over the code, and though some progress had been made—by the time of the invasion, a German named Carsten Niebuhr was correctly postulating that the signs had alphabetic value and that the Coptic language might be the key to unlocking their meaning—the end was nowhere in sight. A major part of the problem was that nobody had used the signs for a long time. Hieroglyphs had gradually slipped out of use during the Roman era, and the last inscription known to use them was at the Temple of Isis at Philae (p. 296) in A.D. 394, so there was nobody around to help.

In the end, the break came with the discovery of the Rosetta Stone, a large slab of black stone on which the same text was repeated in three different scripts, including hieroglyphs, by French soldiers refurbishing a fort in the coastal town of El Rashid. Its final decipherment is now generally credited to a French prodigy named Jean-François Champollion, who realized, by cross-referencing the Greek text and hieroglyphs of the Rosetta Stone, that each ancient symbol must have a dual meaning—both a sound and thing. On September 14, 1822, he managed to decipher the name Ramses in a cartouche, whereupon he is supposed to have yelled, "I've got it!," and fainted.

For a guide to hieroglyphs, see the inside front cover of this book.

NUMBERS

0 **sefr**
1 **wahid**
2 **etneain**
3 **talata**
4 **arba'a**
5 **khamsa**
6 **settah**
7 **sab'a**
8 **tamanyya**
9 **tes'ah**
10 **'ashrah**
11 **hhedasher**
12 **etnasher**
13 **talattasher**
14 **arba'atasher**
15 **khamstasher**
16 **settasher**
17 **sab'atasher**
18 **tamantasher**
19 **tes'atasher**
20 **'eshreen**
30 **talateen**
40 **arbe'aeen**
50 **khamseen**
60 **setteen**
70 **sab'aeen**

80	**tamaneen**	200	**metean**
90	**tes'aeen**	1,000	**alf**
100	**meyah**	2,000	**alfean**

DAYS OF THE WEEK, PERIODS OF TIME

The week starts on Sunday, and the weekend is Friday and Saturday. You'll notice if you compare the names of the days to the numbers (above) that they are simply numbered sequentially. Days of the week are usually preceded by the word *youm,* meaning "day."

Sunday	**youm el hhad**
Monday	**youm el etneain**
Tuesday	**youm el talaat**
Wednesday	**youm el arba'a**
Thursday	**youm el khamees**
Friday	**youm el gom'ah**
Saturday	**youm es-sabt**
Day/days	**youm/ayam**
Week/weeks	**esbu'a/asabee'a**
Month/months	**shahr/shehour**
Today	**en-naharda**
Yesterday	**embarehh**
Tomorrow	**bokrah**
Now	**hhalen/dilwa'-ti**
Later	**ba'adein**

STATEMENTS OF FACT

Ana mesh fahem/Ana mesh fahma (M/F)	I don't understand
Ana 'ayyan/Ana 'ayyana	I'm sick
Ana ta'aban/Ana ta'abana	I'm tired
Ana 'agebni dah	I like that
Enta 'agebni (if you are addressing a male)/**Enti 'agbani** (if you are addressing a female)	I like you
Ana baheb	I love you
Dah mesh 'agebni	I don't like that
Ana 'andi hasasiya...	I am allergic...
mel mekassarat	to nuts
mel benseleen	to penicillin
mel asbereen	to aspirin

ASKING QUESTIONS

eh?	what?
meen?	who?
emta?	when?
fein?	where?
ezzay?	how?
law samahhet/law samahhti (M/F)	excuse me
ana 'ayez/'ayzza dah	I want this

ana 'ayez/'ayzza (M/F)	I want/would like…
asht-teri	to buy
arohh el hhammam	to go to the toilet
arohh el haram	to go to the pyramids
arohh el m'abed	to go to the temple
arohh el kenissah	to go to the church
arohh el masged	to go to the mosque
a-koll	to eat
ashrab	to drink
anaam	to go to sleep
Ana badawer…	I'm looking for . . .
'al Four Seasons	the Four Seasons Hotel
taxi or **taks**	a taxi
Ya'ani eh?	What does that mean?
El corniche menein?	How do I get to the Corniche?
El sa'a kam?	What time is it?
El sa'a [number]	It is [number]

INSULTS

It is always good to know a few insults, if not to use them, then at least to know if you are being called one. All the words listed here are derogatory in Egypt, and I personally don't advise using any of them.

Note: Being gay, especially when it comes to males, is something Egyptian society doesn't accept; hence, several insults rotate around homosexuality.

'arss	pimp
ibn/bent el metnaka or ibn/ bent el sharmuta	son of a bitch (M/F)
Hhaneekak/Hhaneekik	I will screw you
humar	donkey
kalb	dog
khawal	homosexual, feminine, weak (used in a broader sense versus **'aglah**)
kos omak	son of a bitch
ghabee/ghabeiyah	idiot
sharmuta	prostitute (used in reference to females only)
sha'-t	an easy woman

Fun Facts Hindu in Origin

The numbers we use today were, and to a certain extent still are, commonly used in North Africa. They were once called Western Arabic numerals before being introduced to Europe by Arab traders during the Middle Ages. The Arabic numerals we know today were once called Eastern Arabic numerals, and they are more common to Egypt and the Middle East. Both the Western and Eastern Arabic numerals evolved from the Hindu-Arabic numeral system that originated in India sometime during the 9th century A.D.

The Two Most Important Egyptian Arabic Words

There are two Egyptian Arabic words you should memorize. *Ma'alesh* is a word of excuse that explains the lame state of productivity chronic to Egyptian society. It is used when you are late, skipping the queue, cheating on your partner, missing dinner, cutting someone off, not finishing your work on time, or simply asking the person who is blocking your way to step aside. The other word is *basha.* The 21st-century jargon was originally used as an honorary title for aristocrats and nobles during the Turkish rule. Today, it is the most used title and will be bestowed upon you for being well dressed, not looking poor, or for no particular reason. You are not the only *basha* in town; indeed the shopkeeper will call you *basha,* but his own assistants will also call him *basha,* and in turn the little barefooted boy begging in the street will also call the shopkeeper's assistant *basha,* and perhaps some lower caste street boy will call the little street boy *basha.*

2 MENU TERMS

Basic Terms

iftar breakfast
hesab check/bill
'asha dinner
ghadah lunch
kefaya enough
kaman more

DISHES

fettah a mix of bread and rice garnished with yogurt and other toppings
feteer layers of pastry baked pizza-style and stuffed with meat and cheese or drenched in honey
fuul a stew of fava beans; Egypt's most popular dish
kosheri an assorted mix of lentils, macaroni, rice, and chickpeas garnished with slices of fried onions and hot tomato sauce on top
mahshi comes in number of variants; the most famous is *wara ainab* (below), but the outer wrapping of this stuffed vegetable dish can be made with cabbage, zucchini, bell pepper, or even tomato
molokheya a gluey, green souplike sauce made from Jew's mallow; traditionally served with roasted rabbit
moussaka oven-baked eggplant with bell pepper, tomato, and often minced meat; very similar to the Greek and Turkish versions but misses on the cheese topping
shakshouka the Alexandrian way of making scrambled eggs by adding a dash of tomato
tagine an oven-baked stew of vegetables; often comes with meat or chicken
tameya fava beans mashed and deep-fried in balls; very similar to falafel
wara ainab vine leaves stuffed with a combination of rice, onion, and (often but not always) minced meat

ACCOMPANIMENTS

zebda butter
gebna cheese
homous chickpea paste
'aesh flatbread
  'aesh shami white
  'aesh baladi whole wheat
baba ghanouj eggplant puree
patates french fries
zabadi yogurt
tahina sesame seed paste

FRUITS & VEGETABLES

tufahh apple
mesh-mesh apricot
mooz banana
balahh or **tamr** date
betengan eggplant
fuul fave beans
teen fig
lamoon lemon
bortua' -n orange
khoakh peach
ananaas pineapple
romman pomegranate
farawla strawberry
battekh watermelon

MEAT

ferakh chicken
bayd egg
samak fish
hot dog or **sawsees** hot dog
lahhma meat
kebab grilled meat on a skewer
kofta ground meat shaped around a skewer
shish tawook chunks of chicken
sojok sausage

DRINKS

yansoon anise drink
bira beer
kharoub carob
kerfa bel laben cinnamon with milk
ahwa torkey coffee (Turkish)
  ziyada sweet coffee
  mazbut medium-sweet coffee
  sada coffee with no sugar
karkade hibiscus
'aseer juice
erk sous licorice
laban milk
Cola, Fanta, or **Pepsi** soft drink
tamr hindi tamarind
shai tea
  shai fetla w/tea bag
  shai kosheri w/tea leaves
  shai bi-na'ana'a mint tea
maiya water
  maiya ma'adaneya bottled water
nebeet wine
  nebeet ahhmar red wine
  nebeet abiyad white wine

3 MINI DIALOGUES

In the Taxi

Before You Step In

You: **Ana rayehh/rayehha el Zamalek** (M/F; I am going to Zamalek)
Taxi Driver: **Etfadel/Etfadeli** (M/F) (Please, get in)
You: **Ana adfe'a 'ashrah genah** (I will pay 10 pounds)

Taxi Driver: **La', ya khwaga, mayenfa'ash** (Sorry, foreigner, that doesn't work). **Khalihom 'eshreen** (Make it 20).
You: **La', dah keteer** (No, that's a lot). **Ana adfe'a khamstasher bas** (I will only pay 15).
Taxi Driver: **Mashi** (Okay)

As He Approaches Zamalek

Taxi Driver: **Fein fel Zamalek ya khwaga?** (Where in Zamalek?)
You: **'And maktabet Diwan** (Next to Diwan bookstore)
Taxi Driver: **Elli 'al yemen henak dih?** (The one on the right over there?)
You: **La', elli 'al shemal** (No, the one to the left)
Taxi Driver: **Henah?** (Here?)
You: **La', ouddam shwayah** (No, a bit farther away). **Henah** (Yes, here).

A Few Other Useful Words

'ala ganb on the side
arabeya car
banzen gas/petrol
el nasiah el gayah the next corner
fellous money
foa' up or above
khosh go
mataar airport
mathhaf museum
Men fadlak shaghel el 'adad Please put the meter on
seffara embassy
  seffaret Amrika American embassy
  saffaret Canada Canadian embassy
  seffaret Engeltera British embassy
tawali straight
wara behind

At the Train Station

In Front of the Ticket Office

You: **Sabahh el kheir** (Good morning)
The man in charge: **Sabahh el noor** (Good morning)
You: **Lessah fi tazaker l-atr eskendria?** (Are there any train tickets left for Alexandria?)
The man in charge: **Aywa, 'ayez/'ayzza atr kam?** (M/F; Yes, which train do you want to book?)
You: **Awel atr el sa'a kam?** (What time does the next train leave?)
The man in charge: **Kamman nos sa'a** (In half an hour)
You: **Mashi, 'ayez/'ayzza tazkara wahhdah** (M/F; Okay, I want one ticket)
The man in charge: **Oula walla tanyah?** (First or second class?)
You: **Momken oula** (First, please)
The man in charge: **Tes'ah wa talateen genah** (39 pounds)
You: **Etfadel** (Here you go)
The man in charge: **Wa a'-di el tazkarah** (And here is the ticket)

You: **Shokran** (Thank you)
The man in charge: **'Afwan** (You're welcome)

A Few Other Useful Words

atr el noam sleeper train
mahata station
mahatet el otobees bus station
raseef dock
raseef nemra khamsa dock no. 5

At the Hotel Reception

You: **Sabahh el kheir** (Good morning)
Receptionist: **Sabbah el noor ya fandem** (Good morning sir/madam)
You: **'Andek/'andik ghurfah/oudah fadya?** (Do you have a room?)
Receptionist: **Single walla double?** (Single or double?)
You: **Single, men fadlek** (Single, please)
Receptionist: **Mawgood ya fandem** (Yes sir/madam, there is)
You: **El ghurfah/oudah bel takeef walla fi marwahha** (Does it come with an A/C or a fan?)
Receptionist: **Bel takeef wa hhammam dakheli kaman** (With A/C and ensuite as well)
You: **Bekam fel lelah?** (How much does it cost a night?)
Receptionist: **Kam lelah?** (How many nights?)
You: **Lelah wahhda** (1 night)
Receptionist: **Meet genah bel fetar wel dariba** (100 pounds with breakfast and taxes)
You: **Momken ashoef el ghurfah/oudah?** (Can I see the room?)
Receptionist: **Etfadel/etfadeli** (M/F; This way please)

Later That Evening

You: **Massa' el kheir** (Good evening)
Receptionist: **Massa' el noor ya fandem** (Good evening sir/madam)
You: **Ana 'ayez/'ayzza a'-ger 'agala, te'araf menein?** (M/F; I want to rent a bike, do you know from where?)
Receptionist: **Fi wahhed fi akher el share'a** (There is one at the end of the street)
You: **'And el banzeena?** (Close to the gas station?)
Receptionist: **La', 'and el mostashfa** (No, close to the hospital). **Emshi tawali, ba'ad el sayidalaya shemal** (Go straight, it will be to your left after you come to the pharmacy).

A Few Other Useful Words

'agala bike
bab door
balacona balcony
fundu' hotel
kebeer big
sereer bed
shebak window
soghyer small
tareekh date

. . . Comes Around

For centuries Europeans absorbed Arabic into their languages, but the flow now goes the other way. *Televizeon, otobees,* and *batatis* (potato) are all fairly obvious. My favorites are *feren-geh* (which you don't hear in Egypt, mind you), a now archaic word referring to the Franks, which came to refer generically to foreigners. Another good one is something you'll hear every day on the streets of Zamalek. It is the cry of the junk and used clothing dealer as he pushes his cart along, announcing his wares: *"Roba becchia! Roba becchia!"* (from Italian, meaning "old clothes").

At the Fast Food Joint

You: **Wahed fuul wa wahid tameya law samahhet/i?** (One *fuul* and one *tameya,* please)
The man in charge: **Besalta?** (With salad?)
You: **Mengher** (Without)
The man in charge: **'Ayez/'Ayzza torshi?** (Do you want pickles?)
You: **Aywa** (Yes)
The man in charge: **Hena walla take away?** (Here or take away?)
You: **Hena** (Here)
The man in charge: **Talata genah** (3 pounds)
You: **Etfadel** (Here you go)
The man in charge: **Shokran** (Thank you)
You: **'Afwan** (You're welcome)

At the Shop

You: **Massa' el kheir** (Good evening)
Shopkeeper: **Massa' el noor** (Good evening)
You: **Dah yadawy?** (Is it handmade?)
Shopkeeper: **La', makanah** (No, machine-made)
You: **Bekam** (How much is it?)
Shopkeeper: **Metean genah** (200 pounds)
You: **Yaah, dah ghaly geddan** (Oh! That's very expensive)
Shopkeeper: **Enta 'ayez/'ayzza tedfa'a/i kam?** (M/F; How much are you willing to pay?)
You: **Ma'ayeesh ghear meyah** (I only have 100)
Shopkeeper: **Dah oulayel a'-wi** (that's too little). **Khaliha meya wa khamseen** (make it 150).
You: **Meya wa 'eshreen akhri** (120 is my final offer)
Shopkeeper: **Mashi ya basha** (Okay, *basha*)

A Few Other Useful Words

aslee original
bardi papyrus
haga thing
rekhees cheap
segada carpet
ta'-lead not original
temsal statue
wala haga nothing

INDEX

See also Accommodations and Restaurant indexes, below.

General Index

Accommodations

Restaurants

NOTES

NOTES

NOTES

NOTES